REFERENCE ONLY

90 0247174 1

THE CONFLICT OF LAWS

WITHDRAWN
FROM
UNIVERSITY OF PLYMOUTH
LIBRARY SERVICES

D1354581

LONGMAN LAW

GENERAL EDITORS

PROFESSOR I. H. DENNIS, *University College London*
PROFESSOR R. W. RIDEOUT, *University College London*
PROFESSOR J. A. USHER, *University of Exeter*

PUBLISHED TITLES
PETER STONE, *Conflict of laws*

PETER STONE

THE
CONFLICT
OF LAWS

LONGMAN
LONDON AND NEW YORK

Longman Group Limited,
Longman House, Burnt Mill,
Harlow, Essex CM20 2JE, England
and Associated Companies throughout the world

Published in the United States of America
by Longman Publishing, New York

© Longman Group Limited 1995

All rights reserved; no part of this publication may be
reproduced, stored in a retrieval system, or transmitted
in any form or by any means, electronic, mechanical,
photocopying, recording, or otherwise without either the
prior written permission of the Publishers or a licence
permitting restricted copying in the United Kingdom issued
by the Copyright Licensing Agency Ltd.,
90 Tottenham Court Road, London W1P 9HE

First published 1995

ISBN 0 582 083818 CSD
ISBN 0 582 08380X PPR

British Library Cataloguing-in-Publication Data
A catalogue record for this book is
available from the British Library

Library of Congress Cataloging-in-Publication Data
Stone, Peter, 1947–
Conflict of laws / Peter Stone.
p.   cm. — (Longman law)
Includes bibliographical references and index.
ISBN 0–582–08381–8 (cased). — ISBN 0–582–08380–X (paper)
1. Conflict of laws. I. Title. II. Series.
K7040.S78 1995
340.9–dc20
94–20221
CIP

Set by 3 in Linotron 202 Plantin 10/12
Produced by Longman Singapore Publishers (Pte) Ltd
Printed in Singapore

UNIVERSITY OF PLYMOUTH

Item No. 900 247174 1

Date 21 DEC 1995 B

Class No. REF.340.9 STO

Contl. No. 0 582 08 38 18

LIBRARY SERVICES

REFERENCE ONLY

CONTENTS

PREFACE

Work on this book was completed on 1 September 1994 and attempts to state the law as at that date.

I am grateful to all my colleagues in the Law Department at the University of Essex for providing an environment conducive to academic endeavour. I am especially grateful to Professor Janet Dine (now head of the Department) for help in reading this work in draft, and suggesting many valuable improvements. Responsibility for the opinions (and errors) herein remains, of course, exclusively my own.

I am also grateful to the editors of the series (especially Professor John Usher, of the University of Essex), and to the Longman staff involved for their help in bringing the work to completion.

I dedicate the volume to my friends in the NACSA support group.

Peter Stone
Colchester
30 September 1994

TABLE OF CASES

TABLE OF STATUTES

TABLE OF STATUTORY INSTRUMENTS

TABLE OF TREATIES

xl

LATIN PHRASES

executor de son tort:	a person who, by unauthorised interference with a deceased person's estate, incurs the liabilities of a personal representative
in casu:	in the instant case
in limine:	at the outset, without the need to consider other aspects
lex causae:	the law which governs the relevant substantive rights and obligations, relationship or issue
lex fori:	the law of the country whose court is seised of and is in the course of determining the relevant matter
lex loci:	abbreviation for lex loci -actus, -celebrationis, -delicti, or -solutionis; as indicated by the context
lex loci actus:	the law of the country where the relevant act was done
lex loci celebrationis:	the law of the country where the relevant marriage was celebrated
lex loci delicti:	the law of the country where the relevant tort occurred
lex loci solutionis:	the law of the country where the relevant contract or contractual obligation was or should have been performed
lex patriae:	the law of the country of which the relevant person was a national
lex situs:	the law of the country where the relevant property was situated
renvoi:	a reference of an issue by the conflict rules of the foreign law to which the forum's conflict rules first refer the issue, to the law of the forum or the law of a third country (see Chapter 16)
situs:	the location of the relevant property

I

INTRODUCTION

The conflict of laws

Private law problems arising from factual situations which are connected with
more than one country are commonplace in the modern world. Individuals or
families move from one country to another for a variety of purposes (for
example, economic, social, familial, educational, or touristic), and for a variety
of contemplated or actual durations. Companies based in one country establish
branches or subsidiaries in other countries. Much international commerce is
carried out by way of dealings between parties based in different countries, and
investments are often made by individuals or companies in assets located in a
country other than that in which the investor is based. With a view to achieving
to some extent a satisfactory resolution to the private law problems to which
such 'multi-country' factual situations give rise, developed legal systems have
adopted special rules (known as conflict rules), and these rules form the legal
area known in England indifferently as both 'the conflict of laws' and 'private
international law'.[1]

This sphere of law comprises the rules ('conflict rules') contained in the law of
a country ('the forum country', whose courts are seised) which regulate three
kinds of problem which may arise, in connection with relationships governed by
private law, where the factual situation is in some way connected with a country
other than the forum country (it involves 'a foreign element'). In principle,
conflict rules may relate to any area of private law (such as marriage, divorce,
contract, tort, transfer of property inter vivos, or succession on death). For
conflict purposes, 'country' normally refers to a territory having a distinct legal
and judicial system (such as England and Wales; Scotland; New York; California; Ontario; British Columbia; Victoria; or Queensland), rather than to a state

---

[1] Terminology varies elsewhere. In France, *droit international privé* is wider than the English
concept, in that it also covers the rules on acquisition or loss of French nationality, and on
restrictions on the activities in which foreigners may engage in France; while *conflit de lois* is
confined to choice of law (to the exclusion of direct jurisdiction and foreign judgments). In the
United States, 'conflict of laws' usually implies a focus on cases involving sister-states within the
United States, while 'private international law' implies reference to cases where the foreign
element is external to the United States.

having international personality (such as the United Kingdom; the United States; Canada; or Australia).

The foreign element may arise from a connection of a person involved (such as the foreign domicile, habitual or other residence, or nationality of an individual, or the foreign location of the place of incorporation, the headquarters or a branch of a company); or of acts or events involved (for example, that the contract involved was concluded or performed abroad, or contained a clause choosing a foreign law or court; or that the accident giving rise to a tort claim occurred abroad); or of property involved (such as the foreign location of land whose title is at issue).

In the modern world, every country having a developed legal system has its own set of conflict rules, which form part of its private law. They differ from one country to another in the same way as other rules of private law, and have no greater connection with public international law than have any other rules of a country's private law. In this book we examine the conflict rules which currently form part of English law.

Like any other rules of a country's private law, its conflict rules may of course be harmonised with those of other countries by means of international treaties; or, in the case of member states of the European Union, by means of acts of Community institutions. Such harmonisation, both at general-international level (in particular, through the conventions negotiated at the Hague Conference on Private International Law) and at Community level, has had an increasingly important impact on the English conflict rules in the last three decades. Another important recent trend, arising from the work of the Law Commissions, has been the increasing revision or codification of English conflict rules by statute, so as to alter or replace earlier common law rules.

The three kinds of problem dealt with by conflict rules relate respectively to direct judicial jurisdiction; choice of law; and the recognition and enforcement of foreign judgments. More fully:

(1) Rules on direct judicial jurisdiction define the circumstances in which the courts of the forum country are competent, and should be willing, to entertain proceedings in respect of disputes which have some connection with another country.

(2) Rules on choice of law select from the connected countries the one whose law is to supply the substantive rules which are to be applied by the forum in determining the merits of the dispute.

(3) Rules on the recognition and enforcement of foreign judgments define the circumstances in which a judgment of a foreign court is to be given some, and if so what, effect in the forum country.

The structure of conflict rules

Most conflict rules specify a connecting factor and a type of proceeding or issue. Thus current English rules on direct jurisdiction include the following:

(1) The English courts are competent to entertain an action seeking damages for a breach of an ordinary contract if the defendant is, at the commencement of the action, domiciled (in the sense of substantially resident) in England, or if the contractual obligation on which the action is based should have been performed in England.

(2) The English courts are competent to grant a divorce if at least one of the spouses was domiciled (in the sense of origin or permanent residence) in England at the institution of the proceedings, or if at least one of them had been habitually resident in England for a year up to such institution.

(3) The English courts in general lack jurisdiction to entertain proceedings whose principal subject-matter is a dispute as to title to land which is situated abroad.

Choice of law rules typically refer a specified type of issue to a law with which, or the law of a country with which, a specified connection exists. Thus for example, the following general rules are part of the current English conflict system:

(1) Rights and obligations under a contract are governed by the law expressly or impliedly chosen by the parties, or, in the absence of party choice, by the law of the country with which the contract is most closely connected.

(2) Liability in tort exists to the extent that it is recognised both by English internal law and by the law of the country in which the acts and events giving rise to the liability occurred.

(3) The formal validity of a marriage is governed by the law of the country in which the marriage ceremony was performed.

(4) A person's capacity to marry is governed by the law of his or her domicile at the time of the marriage.

(5) Title to land is governed by the law of the country in which the land in question is situated.

(6) The beneficial succession to the movable property of a person who has died intestate is governed by the law of his last domicile.

Again, rules on the recognition or enforcement of foreign judgments often require that a specified connection should have existed with the country of the original court. Thus under current English rules:

(1) A judgment awarding damages for a breach of contract or a tort, given by a court of a country outside the European Union, will not be recognised or enforced in England unless the party to the foreign action against whom the judgment is now invoked was resident in the country in which the judgment was given at the institution of the action there, or he submitted by agreement or appearance to the jurisdiction of the courts of that country.

(2) A divorce granted by a court of a country outside the United Kingdom will not be recognised in England unless, at the institution of the foreign divorce

proceedings, one of the spouses was domiciled or habitually resident in, or was a national of, the country in which the divorce was granted.

Rationale

Why have conflict rules at all?

The need for rules on direct jurisdiction is fairly obvious. No country could sensibly wish to claim universal jurisdiction for its courts. Such a claim would either waste the time of its courts in making ineffective decisions on matters of no concern to it, or would reflect a political policy of world conquest.

The need in some cases to apply foreign law, or to recognise and enforce foreign judgments, is less immediately obvious. The grounds for doing so can perhaps be summarised in positive terms by saying that, in modern world conditions, where states claim equality of status and there is no world-wide imperial power to which all other authorities grant even apparent homage,[2] conflict rules are the only way in which a minimum of order in international private law relationships can be achieved, so as to offer some degree of justice, certainty and convenience to the private parties involved, and some prospect of furthering the various policies which underlie ordinary rules of private law (such as the generally admitted purpose of contract law, to add legal support to reasonable expectations of parties to agreements).

From a more negative viewpoint, one may consider the consequences of a state choosing to require its courts always to apply its own internal rules, regardless of all foreign elements, and to deny recognition to any foreign judgment. Among the consequences would be distortion of the intended obligations under contracts entered into in reliance on foreign law; the imposition of tort liability for conduct which the defendant was required by the law of the place where he acted to perform; the invalidation of marriages celebrated abroad on account of non-compliance with formalities specified by the lex fori, but impossible to comply with outside its territory; the abduction of children across borders with impunity; and automatic changes in the ownership of goods when they crossed a border. Moreover these consequences would arise in a haphazard way, and not in furtherance of any policy underlying the internal rules of the lex fori.

These considerations explain the almost universal acceptance of conflict rules on the three types of conflict issue. They do not, of course, dictate the detailed content of the most beneficial conflict rules, and in fact there is much divergence between the conflict rules adopted by various countries. Such divergences are in themselves inimical to achievement of the purposes of conflict rules, and it is noteworthy that within the European Community it has been found necessary, despite the existence of numerous general-international treaties endeavouring to harmonise conflict rules in various areas, to negotiate at Community level a number of measures designed to achieve such harmonisation.

---

[2] It is noteworthy that conflict rules first emerged, in anything like their current form, towards the end of the Middle Ages.

Choice of law: rules or influential factors?

In the English and most other conflict systems, choice of law is dealt with by means of fairly definite rules, which refer a type of issue to a law identified by means of a connecting factor, and pay limited attention to the content of the substantive rules in conflict. Gravely oppressive results are avoided by the availability of the public policy proviso, which enables a court to refuse to apply a foreign substantive rule (otherwise applicable under the forum's choice of law rules) if its content outrages the forum's judicial conscience.

Particularly in the last few decades, this traditional model has been challenged in the United States, where numerous other approaches to choice of law have been advocated or applied.[3] Particularly noteworthy is the American Law Institute's *Restatement, Second, Conflict of Laws*[4] which typically refers an issue to the law of the country which has 'the most significant relationship' with the specific problem arising in the instant case, ascertained in the light of a list of factors specified in s 6(2). These choice-influencing considerations are:

(a) the needs of the interstate and international systems,
(b) the relevant policies of the forum,
(c) the relevant policies of other interested states and the relative interests of those states in the determination of the particular issue,
(d) the protection of justified expectations,
(e) the basic policies underlying the particular field of law,
(f) certainty, predictability and uniformity of result, and
(g) ease in the determination and application of the law to be applied.[5]

To the present writer, two comments on this approach seem called for. First, the factors listed do indeed excellently summarise the matters which should be taken into account by a legislator or court *when devising or modifying a choice of law rule*. Secondly, their use on a case-by-case basis, *instead of rules*, amounts to a formula for chaos; and that is what the American conflicts revolution has in fact achieved.[6]

Amidst the chaotic practice which has developed in the United States, there shines like an intellectual beacon the contribution of Brainerd Currie, in ident-

---

[3] The breakthrough decision was *Babcock v Jackson* [1963] 2 Lloyd's Rep 286, New York CA. See Chapter 13, below.

[4] (1971); Reporter: Willis Reese. Other influential writers in the American conflicts revolution include Brainerd Currie, *Selected Essays on the Conflict of Laws* (1963); Cavers, *The Choice of Law Process* (1965), and (1977) 26 ICLQ 703; and Robert Leflar, *American Conflicts Law* (3rd ed, 1977).

[5] A similar approach has been advocated by Robert Leflar, except that he adds a preference for the substantive rule which, in the opinion of the court seised, accords best with the needs of substantive justice. To treat a serious matter frivolously, it is suggested that this addition has the seductiveness of Cleopatra, but in the end puts Caligula in the driver's seat.

[6] Cavers (see note 4 above) has endeavoured to use the opportunity arising from the discrediting in the United States of traditional conflicts methodology to devise new and much narrower choice of law rules, which explicitly take substantial account of the content of the conflicting substantive rules. Unfortunately the specific rules which he has proposed seem to the present writer to have little merit.

ifying the concept of interest (or functional) analysis. This involves identifying the substantive policies underlying a substantive rule, and excluding the application of the rule if such application would not further the achievement of those policies to any substantial extent. While Currie's advocacy that this concept should serve as a replacement for all choice of law rules, and on its own as an almost complete solution of choice of law problems, seems a clearly excessive claim, it is suggested that Currie's concept offers an essential corrective to the excessive rigidities which can be possessed by choice of law rules of the traditional type. Thus, as will be argued in Chapter 13 below, it is only by invoking Currie's ideas that a sound exception can be devised to the traditional choice of law rules applicable to torts.

Pleading and proof of foreign law

Where, under an English conflict rule, foreign law is in principle applicable to an issue which arises in English litigation, the content of the relevant foreign rule must be pleaded and proved by the party who relies on it. Otherwise the English court simply applies the English internal rule on the point – not by virtue of some presumption that the foreign rule is the same as the English rule, but simply on the basis that English internal law remains applicable, even where an English conflict rule points in principle to a foreign law, unless the content of the relevant foreign rule (or, more accurately, the manner in which it differs from the corresponding English rule) is properly pleaded and proved by the party who relies thereon.[7] As Vanderbilt CJ (of New Jersey) once put it, in a contractual action where the plaintiff had failed to plead or prove the relevant rules of French law, the proper law of the contract, and the defendant had argued that the action should therefore be dismissed:

> instead of indulging in any presumption as to the [foreign] law, the courts ... merely apply the law of the forum as the only law before the court[,] on the assumption that by failing to prove the foreign law the parties acquiesce in having their controversy determined by reference to the law of the forum, be it statutory or common law.[8]

He added that this rule 'may be universally applied regardless of the nature of the controversy'. Less neatly, but to similar effect, in *Bumper Development Corp v Metropolitan Police Commissioner*[9] Purchas LJ emphasised that [i]n the absence of any evidence to the contrary, [foreign law] is to be assumed to be the same as English law'.

---

[7] See Dicey & Morris, at p 238. A minor and rarely used exception to the need for pleading, as well as proof, of foreign law exists under the British Law Ascertainment Act 1859, which enables the English court to state a case for the opinion of a court of a Commonwealth country; see *Topham v Portland* (1863) 1 De GJ&S 517. See also the Council of Europe Convention on Information on Foreign Law (1968), Cmnd 4229.

[8] *Leary v Gledhill*, 84 A2d 725 (1951). Cf *Walton v Arabian American Oil Co* 233 F2d 541 (1956), where a tort action between Americans in respect of a traffic accident in Saudi Arabia was dismissed because the plaintiff had failed to plead or prove the content of the lex loci delicti.

[9] [1991] 4 All ER 638, [1991] 1 WLR 1362.

It is often said, rather unhelpfully, that for English purposes foreign law is treated as fact. If all that is meant is that the content of a foreign law must be pleaded and proved by the party who relies on it, and that the English courts have much less freedom to develop or manipulate foreign rules than English rules, the assertion is innocuous. If more is meant, the assertion becomes misleading, and it seems better to consider the content of foreign law as material which is sui generis.[10] For an English appellate court will be considerably more willing to interfere with a decision of a lower court on a point of foreign law than on a question of simple fact, dependent solely on the credibility of eyewitnesses (for example, as to which of two cars was stationary when the other ran into it).[11] Moreover an English court will resolve a conflict in expert evidence as to the content of foreign law by applying its own legal expertise to the foreign materials referred to by the experts and will be prepared, in the light of such materials, to decide a point which is unsettled in the relevant foreign country;[12] though it will not conduct its own investigations into other foreign legal materials than those referred to by the expert witnesses.[13] Of course the English courts have to decide what foreign law is, or will probably be held in the foreign country to be, and not what they themselves would prefer it to be; whereas their power to determine English law enables them, within the limits of precedent and respect for legislative authority, to decide that it is what they consider it ought to be.

Foreign law is usually proved by the evidence of an expert witness. By s 4(1) of the Civil Evidence Act 1972, in civil proceedings a person who is suitably qualified to do so on account of his knowledge or experience is competent to give expert evidence as to foreign law, even if he has not acted and is not entitled to act as a legal practitioner in the foreign country in question. The expert witness will usually be either a legal practitioner from the foreign country, or an English academic lawyer who has specialised in the relevant foreign law.

An alternative method of proving foreign law is offered by s 4(2)–(5) of the 1972 Act, which applies where a question of foreign law has been determined by or on appeal from the English High Court or Crown Court, or by the Judicial Committee of the Privy Council on appeal from a court outside the United Kingdom, and the decision is reported or recorded in citable form; that is, in a written report, transcript or other document such that it could be cited in English proceedings as an authority on a question of English law. The said

---

[10] It should be remembered that it is necessary to plead a point of *English* law, if there would otherwise be a danger that the other party would be taken by surprise; and that, although an English court takes judicial notice of English law, counsel is expected to draw the attention of the court to authorities on which he relies, and it is improper for the court to decide on the basis of authorities discovered by its own research, without first giving counsel an opportunity to comment on them.

[11] See *Parkasho v Singh* [1968] P 233; *Dalmia Dairy Industries v National Bank of Pakistan* [1978] 2 Lloyd's Rep 223; and *Bumper Development Corp v Metropolitan Police Commissioner* [1991] 4 All ER 638, [1991] 1 WLR 1362.

[12] See *Re Duke of Wellington* [1947] Ch 506.

[13] See *Bumper Development Corp v Metropolitan Police Commissioner* [1991] 4 All ER 638, [1991] 1 WLR 1362.

finding or decision on the question of foreign law is then admissible in evidence in subsequent English civil proceedings for the purpose of proving the foreign law, and, in the absence of a conflicting finding or decision by a similar English court, is rebuttably presumed to be correct.

A further exception to the need for expert evidence arises from the Evidence (Colonial Statutes) Act 1907, which enables English courts to take judicial notice of the text of statutes of Commonwealth countries.

Since the need for proof (as distinct from pleading) of foreign law arises from the English court's ignorance of, and limited power to interpret, such law, the requirement does not apply to the House of Lords, in relation to the law of another part of the United Kingdom. The House, sitting on appeal from any part of the United Kingdom, takes judicial notice of the law of all such parts.[14]

In general the current rules on pleading and proof of foreign law seem satisfactory. However it is suggested that it would be an improvement if the English courts were given a discretion, in certain cases where foreign law had been properly pleaded, to permit counsel to cite in argument foreign legislation, case-law and other authorities, without the need for an expert witness, in the same way as English authorities are cited. Such a discretion seems desirable where the foreign law is that of a common law country whose official language is English, and the court has reasonable confidence in its ability accurately to ascertain the foreign law in this way.

---

[14] See *De Thoren v Attorney-General* (1876) 1 App Cas 686; *Cooper v Cooper* (1888) 13 App Cas 88; and *MacShannon v Rockware Glass* [1978] AC 795.

2

PERSONAL CONNECTIONS OF INDIVIDUALS

INTRODUCTION

As explained in Chapter 1, conflict rules use connecting factors to determine the existence of jurisdiction on the part of forum or foreign courts, and to ascertain the laws applicable to substantive issues. In the spheres of family law and succession to movable property on death, it is the connections of the persons involved (rather than the location of the places where acts or events involved occurred or property involved is or was situated) which are dominant. Thus these areas may be said to be governed largely by personal (rather than territorial) laws.

Until about 50 years ago, under the English conflict system the overwhelmingly dominant connection of an individual for these purposes was his domicile. Today, however, partly as a result of social and demographic changes and partly under the influence of international conventions (particularly those negotiated at the Hague Conference on Private International Law), the English system has come to give approximately equal importance to an individual's domicile and to his habitual residence, and also to pay some attention to his nationality.[1] Thus current English rules include the following:

(1) A person's capacity to marry is in general governed by the law of his or her domicile at the time of the marriage.

(2) A spouse may petition the English courts for a decree of divorce, judicial separation, or annulment of marriage, or a declaration of marital status, if at the date of the petition either the petitioning or the respondent spouse is domiciled in England, or if either has been habitually resident in England for the preceding year. Similarly English jurisdiction to make declarations of filial or adoptive status can be founded either on the English domicile of the applicant child at the date of the application, or on his English habitual residence for the preceding year.

(3) Conversely, a divorce granted by a foreign court may be recognised in

---

[1] Outside the spheres of family law and succession, it is habitual residence, and not domicile, which is relevant to choice of law in respect of contract or tort. Habitual residence, along with nationality, is also relevant to the international or internal character of an arbitration agreement.

England if either of the spouses was domiciled in, or habitually resident in, or a national of, the country where the divorce was granted, at the institution of the divorce proceedings there.

(4) The habitual residence (and not the domicile) of the child in question is important in relation to the return of an abducted child,[2] and to English jurisdiction to determine child custody otherwise than ancillarily in matrimonial proceedings. On the other hand, English jurisdiction to make an adoption order remains based largely on the British domicile of the proposed adoptive parent, or where the application is by a married couple, of either of them.

(5) The administrative system of child (and in reality mother) maintenance introduced by the Child Support Act 1991 applies only where the child, the carer (if an individual) and the absent parent are all habitually resident in the United Kingdom.[3]

(6) On the death of the owner, the beneficial succession to his movable property is governed mainly by the law of his domicile at death. However a will is valid in respect of formalities if it complies with the formal requirements specified in the law of the testator's domicile, or in that of his habitual residence, or in that of his nationality, existing (in any of these cases) either at the date of the execution of the will or at the testator's death; or indeed with those specified in the law of the place of its execution. Moreover an English domicile of the owner at his death is essential to enable orders to be made against his estate under the Inheritance (Provision for Family and Dependants) Act 1975.

In this chapter we shall examine the traditional English concept of domicile, which continues to apply in the spheres of family law and succession on death. Another, totally different, concept, also using the name 'domicile', has been introduced by the Civil Jurisdiction and Judgments Acts 1982 and 1991, which implement the European Community and associated Conventions on civil jurisdiction and judgments (1968–89). The new statutory concept is operative for the purposes of those Conventions and of related British legislation. Such purposes include judicial jurisdiction over actions in contract or tort; but not family law (other than maintenance) or succession on death. It is examined in the context of civil jurisdiction in Chapter 8 below.

In the current chapter, unless otherwise explicitly indicated, references to domicile are to the traditional English concept. As well as the traditional concept of domicile, the concept of habitual residence is also examined here, and their similarities and differences are identified.

Changes in the traditional concept of domicile were proposed by the Law Commission (along with the Scottish Law Commission) in its Report No 168

---

[2] Most of the numerous recent cases involving consideration of habitual residence (whether of adults or children) are cases of child abduction.

[3] See s 44; and text to Chapter 4, and note 96, below.

(1987).[4] These have not been implemented, but will be mentioned where relevant. They are not intended to operate retroactively so as to affect a person's domicile at a time before the entry into force of the implementing legislation; but for the purpose of determining a person's domicile at a time after the commencement date, it is proposed that the new rules should be treated as having always been in effect.[5]

Unlike nationality, which is by its nature a connection with a state having international personality, domicile and habitual residence are (like most connecting factors used in the English conflict of laws) connections with a law district: that is, a territory, which may comprise the whole or only part of a state, but which has its own separate legal and judicial system, at least for the purpose in question.[6] Throughout this chapter, unless otherwise indicated, 'country' must be understood in this sense. A unitary state (such as France) is also a law district, but federal or composite states (such as the United Kingdom, the United States, Canada, or Australia) comprise several law districts (such as England and Wales, Scotland, New York, California, Ontario, Quebec, New South Wales, or Queensland), each of which has its own laws and courts for some or all of the purposes for which domicile and habitual residence are relevant.

In general, and in accordance with the general rule that connecting factors are construed in accordance with the lex fori, an English court determines a person's domicile exclusively in accordance with the English concept, and it is immaterial that some foreign law with which the case has some connection has different rules on domicile and these would lead to a different result.[7] By way of exception, foreign conceptions of domicile may be relevant under s 46 of the Family Law Act 1986 for the purpose of divorce recognition, or for various purposes in the application of the doctrine of renvoi.[8] Similarly an English court determines a person's habitual residence in accordance with the English rules thereon.

On the other hand, to the limited extent that nationality is used in English conflict rules, the question of whether a person is a national of a given country will in general be referred to the law of that country. But, like other choice of law rules leading to the application of foreign law, this general rule gives way to a stringent English public policy, and the latter could in some circumstances

---

[4] *Law of Domicile*, Law Com 168, Scot Law Com 107, Cm 200 (1987). See also the earlier Working Paper 88 (1985).

[5] See Part X of the Report, recommendations (19)–(21).

[6] See *Bell v Kennedy* (1868) LR 1 Sc & Div 307, and *Attorney-General for Alberta v Cook* [1926] AC 444.

[7] See *Re Martin* [1900] P 211 at 227, per Lindley MR; and *Re Annesley* [1926] Ch 692, where a woman of English origin was held to have acquired a French domicile by permanent residence there, despite the non-recognition of such a domicile by French law on account of her failure to obtain the governmental authorisation then required for such acquisition.

[8] See *Re Annesley* [1926] Ch 692. On the doctrine of renvoi, see Chapter 16.

cause recognition here to be denied to oppressive foreign legislation depriving a person of the foreign nationality, for example on racial or religious grounds.[9]

DOMICILE

The peculiar character of the English concept of domicile

The English concept of domicile differs fundamentally from the concept of that name used in Continental European countries and the United States, and indeed everywhere other than the United Kingdom and countries which, while under British rule, received, and have retained, the English concept. Elsewhere domicile has a meaning similar to the English concept of habitual residence. Thus, for example, under American law, according to the American Law Institute's *Restatement, Second, Conflict of Laws*,[10] a person acquires a domicile in a country by making his home there for the time being. In contrast the English rules refer to a permanent home, and require a firm intention to live until one's death in the relevant country.

Rather than resembling habitual residence, or more generally accepted concepts of domicile, the English concept of domicile, as developed since the middle of the 19th century, in substance amounts to nationality in disguise. The judicial decisions on which the current English concept is founded were taken at a time when other European countries were by legislation substituting nationality for domicile as the test of the personal law, and reflected the same recognition that Europe was then a continent of emigration, and the same desire to treat expatriates who left Europe to make their fortune elsewhere as still belonging to the country of origin. At the same time the United States, as a country of immigration, continued to use domicile, in a normal sense, with a view to assimilating immigrants.

In the United Kingdom, the existence of three law districts[11] within the principal national territory, as well as the existence of British colonies and other dependent territories, meant that the adoption of a nationality test would have been inadequate to solve conflict problems, unless supplemented by rules for connecting a British subject with a particular territory within the Empire. So the courts responded by retaining a domicile test, but revising the meaning of domicile so as to place great, or even overwhelming, emphasis on the person's origin.

---

[9] See *Oppenheimer v Cattermole* [1976] AC 249, where the House of Lords avoided deciding whether English law would have recognised, as such, Nazi legislation depriving Jews of German nationality, since the House of Lords felt able to apply the subsequent law of the Federal Republic, which made decisive the subsequent conduct of the person affected.

[10] (1971); see ss 11–20.

[11] That is: England and Wales; Scotland; and, in the second half of the 19th century, when the current law of domicile was being created, Ireland, or, now, Northern Ireland.

Despite some early confusion,[12] it was established in *Udny v Udny*[13] that domicile and nationality are distinct concepts, and that a person may change his domicile between different states without changing his nationality.[14] Conversely, a person may change his nationality without changing his domicile.[15]

Nonetheless by emphasising a person's origin, the English concept of domicile resembles a nationality test in that it seeks primarily to reflect the person's own perception of his identity.[16] Such a rationale seems most important in cases where the choice is between countries whose laws on the relevant matters reflect greatly differing cultures; for example, between England or France (on the one hand) and Saudi Arabia or Pakistan (on the other). The English concept of domicile seems to reflect the view that, in matters of family law and succession, it is more important to ensure that an Englishman who goes to an Oriental country remains governed by English law than that an Oriental immigrant to this country becomes subject to English law. In other words, to the extent that domicile is decisive, a policy of cultural respect prevails over a policy of assimilation. On the other hand, the increased use of habitual residence in the last half century reflects the opposite policy.

It is arguable that the policy underlying the current English law on domicile would be more conveniently furthered by moving to a system based on nationality, which would also facilitate harmonisation within the European Union in this sphere. Such a change would, however, require subsidiary rules for the purpose of identifying the part of the national territory (the three territories comprising the United Kingdom, along with the various Channel Islands and the Isle of Man) to which a British citizen belongs. Possible solutions to this will be considered in Chapter 16, in the context of the doctrine of renvoi, under which even at present this problem can arise.

Overview

Under the English concept, there are three types of domicile: domicile of origin, which is acquired at birth; domicile of dependence, which may be acquired during childhood; and domicile of choice, which may be acquired during adulthood. At any given moment in his life, an individual has a domicile, and has only one domicile (at least for the same purpose). If he has no other domicile, his

---

[12] See *Moorhouse v Lord* (1863) 10 HL Cas 272.

[13] (1869) LR 1 Sc & Div 441.

[14] See also *Boldrini v Boldrini* [1932] P 9.

[15] See *Wahl v Attorney-General* (1932) 147 LT 382, and *Re Fuld's Estate* [1968] P 675.

[16] Admittedly the grant or denial of nationality is an act by a state reflecting its political values and purposes. But it is submitted that in normal circumstances such a grant accords with the person's own perception of his identity, and that conflict rules which use nationality as the relevant connecting factor are rationally explicable by reference to an implied purpose of respecting such perceptions.

domicile of origin is operative. While a domicile of dependence or choice sub-sists, it displaces for the time being any prior domicile.

At his birth a person acquires as his domicile of origin the then existing domicile of one of his parents. Subsequently during his childhood, a person's domicile follows that of a person with whom he has his home; if his domicile changes in this way, the domicile so acquired is a domicile of dependence.

On or after reaching adulthood, a person may acquire a domicile of choice in a country by settling there permanently or making it his permanent home. A combination of presence in the country and a firm intention to reside perma-nently there is required, and this intention is very difficult to establish.

An adult may abandon a domicile other than his domicile of origin by leaving or remaining absent from the country in question with the intention of not returning there, or of returning there only temporarily. If such abandonment occurs without the simultaneous acquisition of a domicile of choice elsewhere, his domicile of origin revives.

In any event an existing domicile is rebuttably presumed to continue, and the burden of proving a change of domicile is on the party so asserting.

The rule that a person can only have one domicile at a given moment is probably subject to qualification in connection with federal or composite states, where some matters to which domicile is relevant are governed by a law which is operative throughout the state, while other such matters are governed by the separate laws of the territories comprising the state. Thus in Australia and Canada divorce is now governed by federal law,[17] while succession to movables remains governed by the laws of the constituent territories. Hence it is probable that a person may now be domiciled (in the English sense) in Australia or Canada for purposes of divorce, but in New South Wales or Ontario for purposes of succession. Moreover, if a person of English origin were to emigrate to Australia or Canada, and to become resident in New South Wales or Ontario with the intention of settling permanently in Australia or Canada, but without such an intention in relation to New South Wales or Ontario, he would probably acquire an Australian or Canadian domicile for divorce purposes, but remain domiciled in England for purposes of succession.[18] The Law Commissions, in their *Report on the Law of Domicile* (1987),[19] have recommended the enactment of a special rule that an adult who is present in a federal or composite state with the intention of settling in that state for an indefinite period, but who would not otherwise be domiciled in any country within that state, should be domiciled in the country within that state with which he is for the time being most closely connected.[20]

---

[17] See the (Australian) Family Law Act 1975, and the (Canadian) Divorce Act 1968. In the United States, however, divorce is still governed by 'provincial' law.

[18] See *Lloyd v Lloyd* [1962] VR 70.

[19] Law Com 168, Scot Law Com 107, Cm 200 (1987). See also the earlier Working Paper No 88 (1985).

[20] See Part X, recommendation (18).

Domicile of origin

At his birth, a person acquires as his domicile of origin the domicile then possessed by one of his parents. If the person is a marital child at his birth,[21] and his father is then living, the relevant parent is his father.[22] This is probably so even where both his parents are then living, but they are living apart and have different domiciles, for s 4 of the Domicile and Matrimonial Proceedings Act 1973 is probably concerned only with domicile of dependency as distinct from domicile of origin.[23]

If the person is a non-marital child at his birth, the relevant parent is his mother.[24] Probably the same applies in the case of a marital child whose father had died before the child's birth.[25]

If the identity or domicile of the relevant parent is unknown, the country in which the child was born, or is first known to have been present, is treated as his domicile of origin.[26]

A person's domicile of origin is fixed at his birth, and cannot be changed by anything which happens subsequently. His domicile may change during childhood so as to follow that of a person with whom he has his home, but any domicile so acquired is merely a domicile of dependency, which the person may abandon on or after attaining adulthood, even without acquiring a domicile of choice, with the result that the domicile of origin revives to fill the gap. Moreover, the domicile of origin has a strongly adhesive quality, so that the type of change of domicile which is most difficult to establish is the acquisition by an adult of a domicile of choice, so as to displace his domicile of origin, while the type of change least difficult to establish is the abandonment by an adult of a

---

[21] That is, within the meaning of s 1 of the Family Law Reform Act 1987. Strictly, it may be more correct to speak of a person who is legitimate at birth, since s 1 of the 1987 Act does not actually affect the determination of a person's domicile of origin, the question being governed by the common law, and not by the wording or interpretation of an enactment or instrument. Whatever terminology is preferred, the reference is to a person:

(a) whose parents were married to each other at his birth, at his conception or at any time during the pregnancy (see 1987 Act, s 1(2) and (4)); or
(b) who qualifies as legitimate at birth by virtue of a putative marriage, under s 1 of the Legitimacy Act 1976 (see 1987 Act, s 1(3)(a)); or
(c) who qualifies as legitimate at birth under the law of his father's foreign domicile at that date (see 1987 Act, s 1(3)(d), and Chapter 5 below).

But only the situation at the person's birth is relevant, so in the case of a person born as a non-marital child, but subsequently legitimated, for example by the subsequent marriage of his parents, his domicile of origin is taken immutably from his mother's domicile at his birth, despite the fact that he counts as a marital child under s 1(3)(b) of the 1987 Act. Similarly adoption does not affect the person's domicile of origin, despite s 1(3)(c).

[22] See *Udny v Udny* (1869) LR 1 Sc & Div 441 at 457, per Lord Westbury.
[23] Accord: Dicey & Morris, at pp 124–5. Dicey leaves open the situation where the parents divorce during the pregnancy, but it is submitted that there is neither authority nor any other justification for making an exception in that case.
[24] See *Udny v Udny* (1869) LR 1 Sc & Div 441 at 457, and *Re Grove* (1888) 40 ChD 216 at 238.
[25] See Dicey & Morris, Rule 9(1)(b).
[26] See *Re McKenzie* (1951) 51 SRNSW 293, and Dicey & Morris, Rule 9(1)(c).

domicile acquired dependently during childhood, so as to revive his domicile of origin.[27]

Probably the immutability of the domicile of origin applies even in the case of adoption, which merely affects the child's domicile of dependence for the remainder of his childhood, and not his domicile of origin.[28]

The Law Commissions, in their 1987 Report,[29] have recommended the abolition of the concept of domicile of origin. A person's domicile at birth would be determined in the same way as at any other time during his childhood, and the domicile at birth would have no specially adhesive quality, and no capacity to revive.[30]

Domicile of choice: acquisition

An adult acquires a domicile of choice in a country (other than that of his domicile of origin, and that of an existing domicile of choice or an existing domicile acquired dependently during childhood) by settling permanently there: more precisely, by residing in a country with the firm intention of residing there permanently, of making his permanent home there. The two requirements, residence and intention of permanent residence, must be fulfilled at the same moment. The effect of the acquisition of a domicile of choice is to displace during its continuance the person's domicile of origin, and to destroy permanently any intervening domicile (whether a domicile of choice or a domicile acquired dependently during childhood).

As will be explained more fully below,[31] for purposes of domicile 'adult' now refers (subject to transitional rules) to a person (whether male or female, and single or married) who has attained the age of 16 or has validly married below that age, and 'child' to a person who is under 16 and has not validly married.[32]

A person's domicile may change during his childhood by reason of a change in the domicile or identity of the person depended on, so that on attaining adulthood he may hold a domicile acquired dependently in a country other than his domicile of origin. In most cases, however, a person's domicile continues unchanged from his birth until he attains adulthood, and it seems appropriate now to focus primarily on the situation where the question arising concerns the

---

[27] See *Henderson v Henderson* [1967] P 77.

[28] See the Adoption Act 1976, s 39(1) and (5), by which an adopted child is treated as if he had been born as a child of the marriage of the adoptive couple, or as if he had been born in wedlock to the single adopter, from 1976 or the date of the adoption, whichever is later. Cf Dicey & Morris, at p 125, where it is suggested that these provisions retroactively alter the status at the time of birth and thus the domicile of origin.

[29] See note 4 above, Part X, recommendations (3), (8), (10) and (13).

[30] See further under 'Merits', p 27 below.

[31] See under 'Domicile of dependence', p 33 below.

[32] If an adult is suffering from severe mental disorder, he may be factually unable to form the kind of intention necessary to acquire or abandon a domicile of choice, and will therefore retain his existing domicile, but this seems to be an application of the normal rules rather than a special exception; see Dicey & Morris, Rule 16.

acquisition during adulthood of a domicile of choice so as to displace a domicile of origin which has continued undisplaced hitherto.

Residence

For present purposes 'residence' refers merely to actual physical presence in person in the country for at least a moment at which the requisite intention of making one's permanent home there exists. One cannot acquire a domicile of choice by intention alone, and it is not enough to set out for the country; one must actually arrive. But if the requisite intention exists, momentary residence suffices and a domicile may be acquired immediately on arrival in a country. It is not necessary to purchase or lease a dwelling there, though such acts are relevant as evidence of intention. One must, however, be present in person, and a domicile cannot be acquired through the residence of an agent, as where a wife and the children move to a country to establish the family home there but the husband remains in the country of the former home to wind up his business there.[33]

However a domicile of choice within the United Kingdom cannot be acquired by means of residence which is illegal under British immigration law.[34] It is unclear whether the same applies to residence in a foreign country which is illegal under its law.

Intention of permanent residence

For a person to acquire a domicile of choice in a country, his residence there must be accompanied by a firm intention of residing there permanently, of making his permanent home there.[35] The intention must be to reside there permanently, and not merely indefinitely; subject to minor qualifications, what is required is a firm decision to spend the rest of one's life there.[36] On the other hand it is in general immaterial whether the person wishes to adopt the law of the country as his personal law.[37]

The establishment of a domicile of choice is difficult and rather uncommon.

---

[33] See *Bell v Kennedy* (1868) LR 1 Sc & Div 307 at 319, 320, and 323–5; *Udny v Udny* (1869) LR 1 Sc & Div 441 at 449 and 454. Cf Dicey & Morris, at pp 126–7, and *IRC v Duchess of Portland* [1982] Ch 314, requiring 'presence as an inhabitant', a concept rightly found unhelpful by Hoffman J in *Plummer v IRC* [1988] 1 All ER 97, [1988] 1 WLR 292.

[34] See *Puttick v Attorney-General* [1980] Fam 1, and *Smith v Smith* [1962] 3 SA 930.

[35] The leading decisions are: *Bell v Kennedy* (1868) LR 1 Sc & Div 307; *Udny v Udny* (1869) LR 1 Sc & Div 441; *Winans v Attorney-General* [1904] AC 287; *Ramsay v Liverpool Royal Infirmary* [1930] AC 588; and *IRC v Bullock* [1976] 3 All ER 353.

[36] See especially *IRC v Bullock* [1976] 3 All ER 353.

[37] See *Douglas v Douglas* (1871) LR 12 Eq 617 at 643–5; *Re Fuld* [1968] P 675 at 683; *IRC v Bullock* [1976] 3 All ER 353 at 357; *Re Steer* (1858) 157 ER 606; *Re Annesley* [1926] Ch 692; and *Re Liddell-Grainger* [1936] 3 All ER 173.

This is partly because the burden of proving the requisite intention lies on the party alleging such acquisition; partly because of the wide-ranging character of the evidence which may be invoked, which leads to a likelihood that the various pieces of evidence will point in different directions, and therefore lead the court to find against the party who shoulders the burden of proof; and partly because the domicile of origin has a peculiarly adhesive quality, so that it is particularly difficult to establish a domicile of choice where the existing domicile, to be displaced, is the domicile of origin. But it is mainly because of the nature of the intention which must be shown: an intention to stay in the country for the rest of one's life, whatever may happen, apart only from contemplated contingencies which are so ill-defined or unlikely that an intention to return or move on on their occurrence can be ignored as wholly unreal. Essentially, it is like trying to prove that someone who has cut off his thumb while apparently trying to peel an apple injured himself deliberately; an explanation so unlikely that a court will seldom be persuaded that such was the reality.

On the other hand, the concept leaves the courts considerable room for manoeuvre, and it is evident that they are sometimes willing to manipulate their findings in order to fix the person's domicile in the country whose jurisdiction or law appears to offer the most acceptable solution to the particular problem in hand; especially where the alternative solution is clearly unacceptable.

The difficulty of establishing a domicile of choice appears clearly from the leading cases. The decision in *Bell v Kennedy*[38] is essentially that there must be a firm intention to settle permanently in a particular law district. Thus in the 1830s a wealthy cultivator with a Jamaican domicile of origin, being displeased by the abolition of slavery, sold his estate and left Jamaica for Great Britain, intending never to return. He leased a house in Scotland for a year, and looked for a suitable estate in Scotland or England to purchase. During that year his wife died in childbirth. The House held that at her death he was still domiciled in Jamaica, for he had not made a firm decision to reside permanently in Scotland rather than England until the following year, when he purchased a Scottish estate.

It is clear that mere length of residence will not in itself permit the inference of the requisite intention. Thus in *Udny v Udny*[39] the House were divided as to whether a man of Scottish origin who had lived in a leased house in London for 32 years had during that period acquired an English domicile. He had lived in England largely because of his interest in horse-racing, and had retained estates in Scotland, in whose management he had taken an interest, and had made visits to Scotland. Eventually he left England for France to escape his creditors, and finally returned to Scotland, where he lived for his last seven years. Lord Chelmsford, denying the acquisition of an English domicile, found that the man had always hoped, if not expected, that a change in his fortunes might eventually enable him to assume his proper position as a Scottish landowner. Lord

---

[38] (1868) LR 1 Sc & Div 307.
[39] (1869) LR 1 Sc & Div 441.

Westbury would have reached the opposite conclusion, in favour of the acqui-sition of an English domicile, but the House were able to agree that the man had abandoned any English domicile, and revived his Scottish domicile of origin, when he left England for France.

Similarly in *Winans v Attorney-General*[40] the House held by a majority that a man of American origin who had spent all or part of the last 38 years of his life in England, and the remaining parts of those years elsewhere in Europe, had not acquired an English domicile. He had initially come to England from Russia for reasons of health, and had lived in England in furnished houses and hotels. He was an eccentric, his main interests being the development of spindle-shaped ships and of a property owned by his family in Maryland to service such ships. Lord Macnaghten found that the man had to the last an expectation or hope of returning to America and seeing his schemes carried out, while Lord Halsbury reached the same conclusion by reference to the burden of proof.

Again, in *Ramsay v Liverpool Infirmary*[41] the House unanimously held that a man of Scottish origin and idle habits, who had followed other members of his family from Glasgow to Liverpool, and lived in Liverpool for the last 36 years of his life, had not acquired an English domicile, despite the fact that he had refused to return to Glasgow for his mother's funeral, had refused at the age of 69 to join his sole surviving sister in Glasgow, and had arranged to be buried in Liverpool. The decision emphasised the colourless character of the residence, and relied on a dictum in *Winans* that the requisite intention is not to be inferred from a disinclination to move increasing with increasing years.

In reality, this decision reflects the determination of the House to uphold the formal validity of the man's will in favour of charities, which complied with Scottish but not English requirements, against an attack by somewhat distant relatives. It offers an example of adherence to the domicile of origin, in the teeth of the evidence, in order to reach a law whose content was regarded as more suitable.

More recently, in *IRC v Bullock*[42] the Court of Appeal held that a man of Canadian origin who had lived in England for nearly 40 years and married an Englishwoman had not acquired an English domicile, since he had come to England for reasons of employment, he would have returned to Canada on retirement but for his wife's reluctance to live there, and he still intended to return there if he outlived her.

The decision in *Bullock* rejects the test of indefinite (as opposed to permanent) residence, though this formulation is still supported by Dicey & Morris.[43] As Buckley LJ explained, a person who resides in a country with the intention of staying so long as a particular employment of uncertain duration continues, but no longer, would intend to reside indefinitely, but would not acquire a domicile.

[40] [1904] AC 287.
[41] [1930] AC 588.
[42] [1976] 3 All ER 353.
[43] See Rule 10.

One must intend to make one's home in the country until the end of one's days, unless something happens to make one change one's mind.

The decision in *Bullock* has also clarified the minor exceptions to the requirement of a definitive intention which had been recognised obiter in such cases as *Re Fuld*,[44] *Qureshi v Qureshi*[45] and *Buswell v IRC*.[46] One such qualification is that an expressed intention of returning or moving on will be disregarded if the event contemplated is so vague in concept as to make the intention unreal. For example, where the person says that he will return or move on if he makes his fortune, a condition said in *Doucet v Geoghegan*[47] to be analogous to an expectation of reaching the horizon; or when he gets fed up. Similarly in *Re Furse*[48] a man of American origin, who had lived in England for many years and was entirely happy here, was held to have acquired an English domicile of choice despite his intention, expressed to his son, of reluctantly returning to America if he ceased to be able to live an active life on his English farm, an intention discounted by Fox J as altogether indefinite, almost infinitely adjustable to meet his own wishes, and ultimately lacking in reality to the man himself.

The second such qualification is that an intention to return or move on will be disregarded if it is contingent on an event which is so unlikely to occur that it cannot be regarded as a real determination to return or move on the event occurring, but only as an unreal hope or aspiration. Examples would be an intention in 1960 of returning to the Ukraine if it ever became an independent state,[49] or of returning if one wins at least £100,000 on the football pools.[50]

But beyond these exceptions, *Bullock* establishes that any actual intention in some event to return or move on will prevent the acquisition of a domicile of choice. For example, on outliving one's similarly-aged spouse, as in *Bullock* itself;[51] on attaining the age of 60; on retiring from employment; on gaining a particular professional qualification, such as FRCS.[52] A fortiori the intention to reside permanently must not be conditional on such events as that the person and her lover should both obtain divorces from their respective spouses and then marry each other.[53]

On the other hand, an intention to reside permanently may be unconsciously formed, in the sense that the person need not be aware of having made such a decision, if the court is satisfied that such a decision would be made if circumstances requiring a decision arose.[54]

---

[44] [1968] P 675 at 682–6.
[45] [1972] Fam 173.
[46] [1974] 2 All ER 520.
[47] (1878) 9 ChD 441.
[48] [1980] 3 All ER 838.
[49] See *Pletinka v Pletinka* (1965) 109 SJ 72.
[50] Cf a dictum in *Re Fuld*.
[51] *Bullock* effectively overrules *Anderson v Laneuville* (1854) 14 ER 320.
[52] As in *Qureshi v Qureshi* [1972] Fam 173.
[53] As in *Cramer v Cramer* [1987] 1 FLR 116, [1986] Fam Law 333.
[54] See *Winans v Attorney-General* [1904] AC 287, and *Gulbenkian v Gulbenkian* [1937] 4 All ER 618, which also disregarded the remote possibility that the man would be compelled to change his residence by a parental threat of disinheritance.

In general it is immaterial whether or not the person wishes to adopt the law of the alleged domicile of choice as his personal law.[55] But there are two exceptions in which the person's wishes as to his personal law may be taken explicitly into account: where he has two permanent homes, and neither is clearly the principal home;[56] and where the permanent residence is dictated by necessity, such as overwhelming health reasons.[57] Normally a person who intentionally and permanently divides his time between two countries will have a domicile of choice in the one in which he has his principal residence.[58]

In their 1987 Report,[59] the Law Commissions recommended legislation specifying that a person who has attained the age of 16 should acquire a new domicile by presence in the country in question with the intention of settling there for an indefinite period, and that the requisite intention should be determined without reference to any presumption. In substance they do not intend any major change in the existing law on these points. An earlier inclination in Law Commission Working Paper No 88 (1985), to propose that habitual residence for seven years should give rise to a rebuttable presumption of the requisite intention, was abandoned after consultation.

Domicile of choice: abandonment

It was established in *Udny v Udny*[60] that an adult who has acquired a domicile of choice may abandon it by leaving or remaining absent from the country in question, with the intention of not returning there, or returning only for a temporary purpose. If one domicile of choice is abandoned without another being acquired, the domicile of origin revives to fill the gap.

In *Udny v Udny* itself, a man of Scottish origin had resided in England for 32 years, but then, to escape his creditors, had left England for France, where he stayed for nine years, and finally returned to Scotland for his last eight years. The House held that if he had acquired an English domicile, he had abandoned it when he left England with the intention of not returning permanently, and his Scottish domicile of origin had then revived.

To abandon a domicile of choice, intention alone is not sufficient. One must leave or remain absent from the country, as well as deciding not to return there. Thus in *Re Raffenel*[61] a widow of English origin had acquired a French domi-

---

[55] See *Douglas v Douglas* (1871) LR 12 Eq 617 at 643–5; *Re Fuld* [1968] P 675 at 683; *IRC v Bullock* [1976] 3 All ER 353 at 357; *Re Steer* (1858) 157 ER 606; *Re Annesley* [1926] Ch 692; and *Re Liddell-Grainger* [1936] 3 All ER 173 – the three last-mentioned cases holding that a domicile of choice had been acquired, despite a contrary declaration in the person's will.

[56] See *Huntly v Gaskell* [1906] AC 56.

[57] See *Re James* (1908) 98 LT 438.

[58] See *Udny v Udny* (1869) LR 1 Sc & Div 441, per Lord Westbury, and *Plummer v IRC* [1988] 1 All ER 97, [1988] 1 WLR 292.

[59] See note 4 above.

[60] (1869) LR 1 Sc & Div 441.

[61] (1863) 164 ER 1190.

cile by marriage and lived in France with her husband. After his death she attempted to return by boat to England, but was taken ill and had to disembark before the boat left Calais harbour. She died a few months later without having sufficiently recovered to make the journey. It was held that she died domiciled in France, since she had never left France and abandonment could not be achieved by intention alone.

As well as leaving or remaining absent from the country, the person must form a firm and unequivocal intention of not returning there, or returning only for a temporary purpose. Thus in *Re Lloyd Evans*[62] an elderly man of English origin who had acquired a Belgian domicile reluctantly left Belgium in 1940 to avoid the German occupation, and returned to England, where he died in 1944. Wynn-Parry J held that he had retained his Belgian domicile, for it was not established that he had made a firm decision not to return permanently to Belgium after the war. Certainly he had no intention of staying in England any longer than necessary, and had expressed different views to different people as to his intentions after the war was over, sometimes speaking of settling in Australia, which he had visited earlier, and sometimes of returning to Belgium. Probably he was often in two minds, and thus an unequivocal intention was not established.

Some confusion has arisen from dicta of Megarry J in *Re Flynn*,[63] which were also endorsed by Simon P in *Qureshi v Qureshi*.[64] Megarry J rightly recognised that an intention of returning may wither away, without a conscious decision; but in such a case the court must be satisfied that the person would have declared such a decision if the occasion had arisen. On the other hand, his suggestion that a person who goes on a world tour with a view to making up his mind whether to return to the domicile of choice or to settle elsewhere would abandon his domicile of choice is unjustifiable, for a state of conscious indecision is the antithesis of a firm and unequivocal intention, and the suggestion conflicts with both *Udny v Udny*[65] and *Re Lloyd Evans*.[66] The even less satisfactory decision of Nourse J in *IRC v Duchess of Portland*,[67] to the effect that a domicile of choice continues despite departure from the country if the person intends to return there for the purpose of temporary residence, can be confidently rejected, as conflicting with all other authority.

The doctrine of abandonment and revival is not accepted in the United States,[68] and the Law Commissions have recommended that it be abolished in the United Kingdom, so that an adult's domicile of choice would continue until he acquired another domicile of choice.[69]

---

[62] [1947] Ch 695.
[63] [1968] 1 WLR 103.
[64] [1972] Fam 173.
[65] (1869) LR 1 Sc & Div 441.
[66] See note 62 above; and Cheshire & North, at pp 156–7.
[67] [1982] Ch 314.
[68] See *Re Jones' Estate* 182 NW 227 (1921).
[69] See Report No 168 (1987), note 4 above, Part X, recommendation (13).

Proof of change of domicile

Burden and standard of proof

An existing domicile, whether of origin, choice or dependence, is rebuttably presumed to continue, and the burden of proof rests on the party who asserts a change of domicile.

The type of change most difficult to establish is the displacement of a domicile of origin, continuing in adulthood, by the acquisition of a domicile of choice. Thus it has been said that in this type of case the requisite intention must be proved 'with perfect clearness and satisfaction',[70] or 'clearly and unequivocally',[71] or (more recently) by clear evidence going beyond a mere balance of probabilities.[72] In *Winans v Attorney-General*[73] Lord Macnaghten added that a domicile of origin differs from a domicile of choice in having a more enduring character, a stronger hold, and being less easily shaken off, though in *Re Lloyd Evans*[74] Wynn-Parry J insisted that even for abandonment of a domicile of choice, so as to revive the domicile of origin, an unequivocal intention and act must be shown. In *Henderson v Henderson*[75] Simon P explained that abandonment after attaining adulthood of a domicile acquired dependently in childhood is the type of change least onerous of proof. More recently, however, it has become accepted that, even to displace the domicile of origin, the civil standard of proof on a balance of probabilities is sufficient, though a change of domicile is a serious matter not to be lightly inferred from slight indications or casual words.[76]

In their 1987 Report,[77] the Law Commissions have recommended legislation specifying that the normal civil standard of proof on a balance of probabilities should apply in all disputes about domicile, and no higher or different quality of intention should be required when the existing domicile is the domicile acquired at birth.

As regards evidence of intention, it has often been emphasised that every act, word, circumstance or project in a person's life is relevant, and that trivial acts may be more indicative than acts of greater importance to the person himself.[78] In *Bell v Kennedy*[79] Lord Colonsay lamented (with quiet irony?) the need to

---

[70] Per Lord Westbury in *Bell v Kennedy*, note 38 above, and Lord Macnaghten in *Winans v Attorney-General*, note 40 above. Does this mean: 'beyond a shadow of a doubt'?

[71] Per Lord Chelmsford in *Moorhouse v Lord*, note 12 above.

[72] Per Simon P in *Henderson v Henderson* [1967] P 77.

[73] See note 40 above.

[74] [1947] Ch 695.

[75] [1967] P 77.

[76] See per Megarry J in *Re Flynn* [1968] 1 WLR 103; per Scarman J in *Re Fuld* [1968] P 675; per Russell LJ for the Court of Appeal in *Steiner v IRC* (1973) 49 TC 13; and per Russell and Orr LJJ in *Buswell v IRC* [1974] 1 WLR 1631.

[77] See note 4 above.

[78] See *Drevon v Drevon* (1864) 34 LJCh 129 at 133, *Hodgson v De Beauchesne* (1858) 12 MooPCC 285; *Hoskins v Matthews* (1856) 25 LJCh 689; *Winans v Attorney-General*, note 40 above; and *Re Flynn* [1968] 1 WLR 103 at 107.

[79] See note 38 above.

determine the intention of persons who either had died without leaving any clear record of their intentions, or were alive and interested and, perhaps unconsciously, tended to give their previous feelings a tone suggested by their present inclinations. More recently it has been recognised that too much detail may stultify.[80]

The oral evidence of the person in question as to his past or present intentions is admissible, but if he is an interested party such evidence will be viewed with considerable reserve.[81] The person's extra-curial declarations of intention are also admissible, but are regarded as the lowest species of evidence, and need to be supported by consistent conduct.[82] Even uncontradicted declarations in casual conversations cannot be allowed to outweigh all the person's acts and documents.[83] Nonetheless, declarations made by the person at a time when his domicile was not in issue and in circumstances where he had no interest in lying were considered of great importance in *Qureshi v Qureshi*.[84] Declarations made in applications for naturalisation are of some, but not of dominant, importance.[85] Statements in the person's will, or in income tax forms, are of little weight.[86]

Evidential factors

MOTIVE

A person's motive for going to or leaving a country is relevant evidence for or against an intention of permanent residence, and unattractive motives are not penalised. Thus one may change one's domicile in order to institute or avoid matrimonial proceedings,[87] to avoid one's creditors,[88] to obtain greater testamentary freedom,[89] or to avoid taxation and obtain a better climate for one's performing chimpanzees.[90] If a person moves permanently to a country for reasons of health, he will acquire a domicile there, unless the medical reasons were utterly compelling, in which case he will not acquire a domicile unless he wishes to adopt the law of the country as his personal law.[91]

---

[80] See *Re Flynn*, note 78 above, and *Qureshi v Qureshi*, note 64 above.

[81] See *Bell v Kennedy*, note 38 above, at 313; *Gulbenkian v Gulbenkian*, note 54 above; and *Qureshi v Qureshi*, note 64 above, at 339.

[82] See *Hodgson v De Beauchesne*, note 78 above, at 935, and *Ross v Ross* [1930] AC 1 at 6–7, per Lord Buckmaster.

[83] See *Doucet v Geoghegan* (1878) 9 ChD 441.

[84] See note 64 above.

[85] See *Wahl v Attorney-General* (1932) 147 LT 382, and *Steiner v IRC* (1973) 49 TC 13.

[86] See *Re Steer* (1858) 28 LJEx 22, *Re Liddell-Grainger's WT* [1936] 3 All ER 173, *Re Annesley* [1926] Ch 692, and *Buswell v IRC* [1974] 1 WLR 1631.

[87] See *Firebrace v Firebrace* (1878) 4 PD 63 at 66; *Drexel v Drexel* [1916] 1 Ch 251; and *Wood v Wood* [1957] P 255. Cf *White v White* [1950] 4 DLR 474, [1952] 1 DLR 133.

[88] See *Udny v Udny* (1869) LR 1 Sc & Div 441.

[89] See *Haldane v Eckford* (1869) LR 8 Eq 631.

[90] See *Wood v Wood*, note 87 above.

[91] See per Turner LJ in *Hoskins v Matthews* (1856) 44 ER 294; per Lords Cranworth and Kingsdown in *Moorhouse v Lord* (1863) 10 HL Cas 272; per Lord Halsbury in *Winans v Attorney-General*, note 40 at 288–9; and *Re James* (1908) 98 LT 438.

MEMBERS OF THE ARMED FORCES

Normally a member of the armed forces will retain the domicile which he had on entering the service,[92] but it is possible for him to acquire a domicile of choice in a country where he is stationed, or where he goes on leave, if he decides to live there permanently, except insofar as his duties otherwise require.[93]

CHANGE OF (OR FAILURE TO CHANGE) NATIONALITY

A change of nationality is an important indication of intention to establish permanent residence, but is not conclusive. Thus in *Wahl v Attorney-General*[94] a German who acquired British nationality was held to have retained his German domicile, since he had not severed a single tie with Germany, and in *Re Fuld*[95] a German Jew was held to have retained his German domicile despite acquiring Canadian nationality while living there during the Second World War; afterwards he returned to Europe and lived 'between England and Germany'. On the other hand in *Re Flynn*,[96] in holding that the actor, Erroll Flynn, whose origin was Australian, had acquired a Californian domicile by August 1942, Megarry J relied in part on his acquisition of American nationality. Similarly in *Qureshi v Qureshi*[97] Simon P held that a Moslem of Indian origin had acquired a domicile of choice in Pakistan during a short residence there, during which he acquired its nationality, before coming to England with a view to obtaining a medical qualification. Again in *Steiner v IRC*[98] a Jew of Czech origin, who had acquired a German domicile of choice in the inter-war period, and then came to England in 1939 and made his principal home here thereafter, acquiring British nationality in 1947, was held to have acquired an English domicile in the early 1950s. In *IRC v Bullock*[99] the man's failure to acquire British citizenship was a factor in the decision that he retained his Canadian domicile.

PRECARIOUSNESS

While, as we have seen, a domicile in the United Kingdom cannot be obtained by residence which is illegal under British immigration law,[100] the fact that a person's residence in a country is precarious, in the sense that he is there by virtue of permission granted by its authorities and is subject to their powers of deportation, does not prevent him from acquiring a domicile there if, despite such precariousness, he forms the intention of living there permanently unless

---

[92] See *Cruickshanks v Cruickshanks* [1957] 1 WLR 564.
[93] See *Donaldson v Donaldson* [1949] P 363, and *Stone v Stone* [1958] 1 WLR 1287.
[94] (1932) 147 LT 382.
[95] [1968] P 675.
[96] [1968] 1 WLR 103.
[97] [1972] Fam 173.
[98] (1973) 49 TC 13.
[99] [1976] 1 WLR 1178.
[100] See text to note 34 above.

prevented by the authorities; and this is so even if the permission to reside was granted subject to conditions as to the purpose of the residence, such as study or training, or to a fixed time-limit.[101] Moreover, a person who has acquired an English domicile does not lose it merely because a criminal court has, on his conviction for an offence, recommended that he be deported, and the Home Office intends to deport him as soon as practicable.[102] Nor does a person lose a domicile in a country if he is actually deported therefrom, if he intends to return and may legally do so.[103]

POLITICAL REFUGEES

In cases involving political refugees, the courts use the usual terminology of intention to reside permanently, and often hold, where it leads to no injustice in the instant case, that a refugee has retained a domicile in the country from which he fled.[104] But where adherence to a refugee's domicile of origin would lead to a denial of justice, for example (under earlier tests of English divorce jurisdiction) by making it realistically impossible for a person whose marriage has broken down to petition for divorce anywhere, the courts will somehow manage to establish a domicile of choice in the country where the refugee has become resident.

Thus in *May v May*,[105] a German Jew had been admitted to England in 1939 as a trainee on condition that he would emigrate on completion of his training, and had also obtained a visa which would enable him eventually to emigrate to the United States. In holding that the man had acquired an English domicile by January 1942, when he filed an English divorce petition, Pilcher J emphasised his determination never to return to Germany in any circumstances, and found that during 1941 the idea of proceeding to the United States had faded from his mind and he had come to regard England as his home.[106] Tested against the normal approach to the acquisition of a domicile of choice, such reasoning is

---

[101] See *Boldrini v Boldrini* [1932] P 9; *May v May* [1943] 2 All ER 146; and *Szechter v Szechter* [1971] P 286.

[102] See *Cruh v Cruh* [1945] 2 All ER 545.

[103] See *Thiele v Thiele* (1920) 150 LTJ 387, which involved a German prisoner of war, repatriated after the First World War.

[104] See *De Bonneval v De Bonneval* (1838) 163 ER 296, *Re Lloyd Evans* [1947] Ch 695, *Re Fuld* [1968] P 675, and *Steiner v IRC* (1973) 49 TC 13. See also *Re Martin* [1900] P 211, where the Court of Appeal held that a French professor who had come to England to avoid prosecution for an offence, but had returned to France 22 years later, after any prosecution for the offence had become time-barred, had meanwhile acquired an English domicile, since he could not initially have intended to return without any means of livelihood, and his eventual return was due to reasons of health and matrimonial difficulties, and was made possible by the fortune unexpectedly acquired from a laundry business established in England by his wife.

[105] [1943] 2 All ER 146.

[106] See also *Pletinka v Pletinka* (1965) 109 SJ 72, where a man of Ukrainian origin, who had come to England after the Second World War, and was petitioning for an English divorce in 1965, was held to have acquired an English domicile despite his admitted wish to return to the Ukraine if it ever became an independent state.

unconvincing. But it accords with the policy subsequently adopted by art 12 of the United Nations Convention of 28 July 1951 relating to the Status of Refugees,[107] that in no circumstances should the personal status of a political refugee be referred to the law or jurisdiction of the persecuting state, and to avoid such a result conflict rules referring to nationality or domicile in the English sense should be amended so as to refer instead to domicile in a more normal sense or to habitual residence, or even, as a last resort, to actual presence, however transitory.

CULTURAL AFFINITIES

Major cultural differences between the countries of a person's origin (or former permanent home) and his subsequent residence militate against his forming the requisite intention to settle permanently in the latter country. Thus in *Qureshi v Qureshi*[108] Simon P took such considerations into account in holding that a Moslem of Indian origin, who had first moved permanently to Pakistan and then came to England with a view to obtaining a medical qualification, remained domiciled in Pakistan. Conversely in *Schwebel v Ungar*[109] Canadian courts readily concluded that a Jew of Hungarian origin had acquired an Israeli domicile immediately on arrival there in 1948.

Merits

The Law Commission proposals to abolish the concept of the domicile of origin, its peculiarly adhesive quality, and the doctrine of revival, are more radical than is immediately apparent, despite their ultimate abandonment of the suggestion that habitual residence for seven years should give rise to a rebuttable presumption of intention to reside indefinitely.

---

[107] The United Kingdom is a party to this Convention, but has not enacted legislation specifically implementing art 12.

    Article 12 provides:

    (1) The personal status of a refugee shall be governed by the law of the country of his domicile or, if he has no domicile, by the law of the country of his residence.

    (2) Rights previously acquired by a refugee and dependent on personal status, more particularly rights attaching to marriage, shall be respected by a Contracting State, provided that the right in question is one which would have been recognised by the law of that State had he not become a refugee.

    The Convention defines a refugee as a person who, owing to well-founded fear of being persecuted for reasons of race, religion, nationality, membership of a particular social group or political opinion, is outside the country of his nationality and is unable or, owing to such fear, is unwilling to avail himself of the protection of that country; or who, not having a nationality and being outside the country of his former habitual residence is unable or, owing to such fear, is unwilling to return to it.

[108] [1972] Fam 173.

[109] (1963) 42 DLR 622 and (1964) 48 DLR 644.

The emphasis on the domicile of origin has been at the heart of the English tradition for over a century, and it is submitted that this emphasis accurately reflects a legitimate, if not always clearly stated, policy of respecting a person's own sense of identity. In general a person's domicile of origin *is* the country to which he instinctively regards himself as belonging; and where this is not so, the existing rules will usually permit a wise court to discover a domicile of choice.

Of course the doctrine of revival has some artificiality, but the proposed substitution of a rule whereby a domicile of choice continues despite resolute abandonment would be worse. Revival copes satisfactorily with many cases: for example where a family of English origin emigrate to Australia, meaning to settle permanently, but are eventually disappointed with economic or social conditions there, and move to the United States, intending to stay for a few years only, and without any definite view of their long-term future, other than that they will not return to Australia.

The doctrine of revival is least satisfactory where the person has resolutely abandoned both the country of origin and that of any domicile of choice which he has had, in the sense that he will not (unless compelled) return to any such country in any circumstances. It might be best in such cases to substitute habitual residence for domicile; and if the person does not even have an habitual residence, to accept that he is effectively stateless. In that event, he would lack any personal law of his own, but issues normally governed by his personal law could easily be solved using other types of connection. For example, his capacity to marry could be referred to the law of the domicile of the other spouse (or if they both lack any personal law, to the law of the place of celebration); the essential validity of his will as to movables could be referred to the law of the place of its execution; and on his intestacy each movable asset could devolve according to the law of its own location.

The main deficiency in the present law in the current area would seem to lie not in the results reached, which are usually acceptable, but in the invitation to investigate in a lengthy and expensive trial everything the person has ever said or done, with the result that conflicting indications of intention become apparent, and the ultimate result is that the court finds that the domicile of origin has not been displaced. For this reason there is much to be said for the United Kingdom joining most of the other EC countries by substituting nationality for domicile as the principal personal connection for conflict purposes. It is surely not beyond the wit of mankind to devise suitable subsidiary rules to allocate a British citizen to one of the parts of the United Kingdom, and to deal with cases of multiple nationality or statelessness.

HABITUAL RESIDENCE

Like domicile, habitual residence is a connection with a law district, rather than a state as such. Unlike domicile, however, a person may have no habitual residence at a given time, and the possibility cannot be ruled out that for some purposes a person may have several habitual residences at the same time.[110]

Like a domicile of choice, an adult acquires an habitual residence by a combination of residence and intention, but the requisite intention for habitual residence is weaker. Its precise nature is, however, not yet clear. An intention to stay for the rest of one's life is not necessary, but some limited degree of settled, even if temporary, purpose is essential, and it may be that long-term residence must be intended.

In relation to habitual residence there is no concept corresponding to a domicile of origin. A child acquires at birth an habitual residence of dependency, on the same principles as his habitual residence during his childhood, and the first habitual residence has no propensity to revive in adulthood. Rather, if an adult abandons one habitual residence without acquiring another, he is for the time being without any habitual residence. There is, however, a presumption in favour of the continuance of an habitual residence, once acquired.

In general a child shares, by way of dependency, the habitual residence (or lack of any habitual residence) of one or more parents or other persons who have custodial rights over the child. But where custodial rights are shared, the child's habitual residence can only be changed with the consent of all the persons who have custodial rights over him.

Habitual residence: acquisition

It is now clear that, like a domicile of choice, the acquisition of an habitual residence by an adult[111] requires a combination of residence and intention, but that in relation to habitual residence both these elements differ in important respects from those necessary for the acquisition of a domicile of choice.

As regards actual residence, the decision of the House of Lords in Re J[112] has established that, unlike a domicile of choice, an adult cannot acquire an habitual

---

[110] Most of the recent cases on habitual residence (of both adults and children) have arisen under the Hague Convention on the Civil Aspects of International Child Abduction (signed on 25 October 1980), which is implemented in the United Kingdom by Part I of the Child Abduction and Custody Act 1985. The decision of the Court of Appeal in Re A [1988] 1 FLR 365 suggests that a child can only have one habitual residence at a given moment, at least for the purposes of that Convention. The decision dealt with a perhaps unusual situation: both parents had custodial rights; under an agreement or court order the child was living with them alternately for equal periods at their habitual residences in different countries; and one of those countries was the country in which the whole family had been habitually resident before the parents parted. In such a situation it was held that the child remained habitually resident in the country where the whole family had been habitually resident; even during the period when he was living with the parent habitually resident in another country. Further support for the view that a child cannot have more than one habitual residence at a time can be drawn from s 41 of the Family Law Act 1986, under which, for the purpose of British jurisdiction to make custody orders, a child retains his habitual residence in a part of the United Kingdom for a year after a wrongful removal elsewhere. The decision of Ewbank J in Z v Z [1992] 2 FLR 291 perhaps suggests that an adult cannot have more than one habitual residence at the same time for matrimonial purposes.

[111] Probably for purposes of habitual residence, 'adult' refers to a person aged at least 16; see 'Habitual residence of children', p 37 below.

[112] [1990] 2 AC 562.

residence immediately on arrival in a country. The residence must endure for an 'appreciable' period of time before it becomes habitual. However the decisions in *V v B*[113] and *Re F*[114] indicate that a period of one or two months can be regarded as appreciable. A fortiori a period of three or four years is clearly sufficient, as the Court of Appeal recognised in *Re C*.[115] Thus the lower courts have recognised that the adoption by the House in *Re J* of a requirement of an 'appreciable' period of actual residence amounts to a false step, and that its effect should be minimised so far as possible.

In addition to an appreciable period of residence, the acquisition of an habitual residence by an adult requires an element of intention, but in *Shah v Barnet London Borough Council*[116] the House of Lords (per Lord Scarman) emphasised that the intention necessary for habitual residence must not be confused with that required for domicile. Lord Scarman explained that habitual residence does not require an intention to reside permanently or indefinitely. Rather, it refers to an abode in a particular country which the person has adopted voluntarily and for settled purposes as part of the regular order of his life for the time being, whether of short or long duration; to a regular, habitual mode of life in a particular country, whose continuance has persisted despite temporary absences, and which has been adopted voluntarily and for a settled purpose. The residence must be voluntarily adopted, in the sense of not resulting from overwhelming compulsion (for example, by reason of kidnapping or imprisonment), and there must be some degree of settled purpose. But the duration of the purpose may be limited, and purposes relating to education, employment, health or family will suffice. No deep examination of the person's state of mind is required.

Lord Scarman also emphasised that habitual residence may exist although the person's presence in the country is precarious, in that under the nationality and immigration law of the country he has neither a right of abode there nor permission to stay indefinitely, but merely permission to stay for a limited period and for limited purposes, such as education. However one whose presence is actually illegal or prohibited under the immigration law of the country cannot assert that he is habitually resident there. On these points concerning precariousness and legality, the position is similar in respect of habitual residence and of domicile. Lord Scarman's approach was followed by Bush J in *Kapur v Kapur*,[117] so as to enable an Indian husband, studying at the English Bar, to petition for an English divorce on the basis of his English habitual residence for the relevant year.

[113] [1991] 1 FLR 266.
[114] [1992] 1 FLR 548.
[115] 6 December 1991.
[116] [1983] 2 AC 309. The case involved a requirement of three years' ordinary residence in the United Kingdom as a condition for the award of a local authority grant to a student in higher education. However, despite the public law nature of the dispute, the House of Lords explained and applied what they regarded as the normal concept of ordinary or habitual residence, terms which they regarded as synonymous.
[117] [1984] FLR 920; specifically disapproving the confusion between habitual residence and domicile of Lane J in *Cruse v Chittum* [1974] 2 All ER 940.

Subsequently, however, the intention required for the acquisition by an adult of an habitual residence seems to have been considerably strengthened, and brought closer to that required for the acquisition of a domicile of choice, by the decision of the House in *Re J*,[118] where Lord Brandon spoke of a settled intention to take up long-term residence in a country.

Evidently the precise nature of the requisite intention awaits further clarification. Even under Lord Scarman's view, there must be some limit to the shortness of the intended duration which can be considered consistent with a settled purpose – presumably a visit to relatives, intended to last for about six months, would not suffice. Conversely, Lord Brandon's requirement of a settled intention of long-term residence must be something less than the intention to stay till death, which is a feature of domicile; presumably an intention to stay for several years for reasons of employment would suffice. In any event, in view of the elasticity of the concepts of settled purpose or long-term residence, it seems likely that, as in the case of domicile, other factors, such as the extent to which social and legal traditions of the country in question reflect values with which the person in question would identify, are likely to be taken into account, at least subliminally.[119]

In any event, as the Court of Appeal recognised in *Re R (No 1)*,[120] the burden of establishing a change of habitual residence is on the party who so asserts. In that case the mother of a non-marital child who had emigrated with the child to Canada was held to have remained habitually resident in England, with the result that the child remained subject to English custody jurisdiction, since the mother had not in her evidence adequately answered the obvious implication from her letter to the father, that in moving to Canada she was playing games with a view to extorting a better financial settlement from him.

Habitual residence: abandonment

In respect of abandonment a clear difference between domicile and habitual residence emerges from the decision of the House of Lords in *Re J*,[121] which has settled that in some circumstances a person (whether an adult or a child) will have no habitual residence. Lord Brandon explained that an adult ceases to be habitually resident in a country if he leaves it with a settled intention not to return to it, but to take up long-term residence in another country. But he cannot become habitually resident in a country immediately on arrival there; an appreciable period of time, as well as a settled intention, is necessary. Moreover where a very young child is in the sole lawful custody of his mother, his habitual residence follows hers.

In that case a child, aged two, of unmarried parents of English origin had been living with both parents in Western Australia when the mother secretly

---

[118] See note 112 above.
[119] See text to notes 108 and 109 above. See also *Re S*, 17 December 1992, CA.
[120] [1992] 2 FLR 481.
[121] [1990] 2 AC 562.

left, with the child, for England, with the settled intention not to return to Australia but to make a long-term home for herself and the child in England. Less than a month afterwards the father obtained from a Western Australian court an order giving him sole guardianship and custody of the child. Under the law of Western Australia, the mother of a non-marital child was entitled to custody and guardianship in the absence of a court order.

The House ruled that there had been no wrongful removal or retention, within the meaning of art 3 of the Hague Convention on child abduction, since, at the time when the mother took the child to England, the father had no custody rights under Western Australian law; and by the time the father obtained a custody order from the Western Australian court, the mother and, therefore, the child had ceased to be habitually resident in Western Australia.

It is worth emphasising that this decision entails that, if the father, instead of obtaining an Australian court order and then applying for the child's return under the Hague Convention on child abduction, had simply dashed to England, kidnapped the child and taken him back to Australia, before the mother and the child had lived in England for an 'appreciable' period of time, that removal also would not have been wrongful under the Convention; nor, indeed, if the child had been kidnapped and removed by a complete stranger. So it may be inferred that, since the absence of any habitual residence is possible for the purpose of the Hague Convention on child abduction, the context where it is capable of doing the most harm, it must also be possible for all other purposes for which habitual residence may be relevant.

Other cases indicate, however, that the courts will go to some lengths to avoid a finding that a person has no habitual residence. Thus in $V v B$[122] the parents (a man of English origin and a woman of New Zealand origin) of a non-marital child had met in New Zealand and lived together there for two years, before moving to England, where they stayed for a year. Then they went, with the child, to New South Wales, where they stayed with the mother's aunt for about two months up to the crucial date, when the father snatched the child and brought him to England. Under the law of New South Wales, despite the absence of a marriage, both parents had custodial rights. Brown P held that a sufficient degree of continuity of residence had been established by the parents with the child for them to be regarded as habitually resident in New South Wales immediately before the removal.

Similarly in $Re F$[123] a married couple (the husband of English and the wife of Australian origin) who, after a period of habitual residence in England, went with their baby to Australia, were held to have become habitually resident there by the time, less than three months after their arrival, that the husband secretly removed the child to England. The Court of Appeal, per Butler-Sloss LJ, found that the family had intended to emigrate from the United Kingdom and settle in Australia, and explained that, with such a settled intention, a month could be an

[122] [1991] I FLR 266.
[123] [1992] I FLR 548.

appreciable period of time. Moreover by the time of the removal the child had been resident in Australia for the substantial period of nearly three months.

Butler-Sloss LJ explicitly recognised the importance for the successful operation of the Hague Convention on child abduction that, where possible, a child should have an habitual residence. Otherwise he or she could not be protected under the Convention from abduction by a parent from the country where he or she was last residing. Thus the court should not strain to find a lack of habitual residence where on a broad canvas the child had settled in a particular country.

Moreover, in *Re E*[124] the Court of Appeal ruled that (as in the case of domicile) there is a presumption in favour of the continuance of an existing habitual residence, and that the burden of proving a change of habitual residence lies on the party so asserting. Thus to establish the abandonment by an adult of his habitual residence, it is not enough to show that he has left the country in question. It must also be shown that he has formed a settled intention not to return, and it is not enough for the person to have suspended the decision of his future until the resolution of a contingency, such as the conclusion of proceedings concerning the custody of a child.

DEPENDENCE AND CHILDREN

Domicile of dependence

Where a person is dependent as to domicile, his domicile follows that of another person depended on. Today, subject to transitional provisions, it is children, in the sense of persons who are under the age of 16 and have not validly married, who constitute dependent persons for this purpose. A child's domicile now depends on that of a person with whom he has a home. At common law a married woman's domicile depended rigidly on that of her husband, but such dependency was abolished, as from the beginning of 1974, by s 1 of the Domicile and Matrimonial Proceedings Act 1973. Under s 1, if a woman was alive and married at the end of 1973, she then became independent as to domicile, with the same results as in any other case in which a dependency terminates, so that she could, then or subsequently, acquire a domicile of choice or revive her domicile of origin by an appropriate combination of residence and intention.[125] It is perhaps regrettable that Parliament failed to respect actual family unity in a non-discriminatory way by specifying that while a married couple are living together and are habitually resident in the country in which one of them is domiciled, the other should also be treated as domiciled in that country and not elsewhere.

[124] [1993] Fam Law 15, [1992] 1 FCR 541.
[125] Cf *IRC v Duchess of Portland* [1982] Ch 314, where Nourse J suggested that in this case abandonment of the domicile acquired dependently is more difficult to establish than in other cases where dependency comes to an end. It is difficult to see any justification for this suggestion, either in principle or in the wording of the 1973 Act.

In view of transitional provisions, a person counts as a child, dependent as to domicile: as regards times before 1970 (to which the common law rule on infancy applied), while he was under the age of 21; as regards times after 1969 and before 1974 (to which the rule on minority, laid down by s 1 of the Family Law Reform Act 1969 applies), while he was under the age of 18; and as regards times after 1973 (which are governed by s 3 of the Domicile and Matrimonial Proceedings Act 1973), while he is under the age of 16 and has not validly married. It must, however, be borne in mind that a person who is under 16 and is domiciled in England lacks capacity to marry,[126] so that any purported marriage of his will be void, and he will continue to have a domicile of dependence as a child. Moreover where a female validly married under 21 before 1970, or under 18 before 1974, her domicile became dependent on her husband's, instead of that of a parent or similar person with whom she had a home. A person under 21 but over 18 at the beginning of 1970, or under 18 but over 16 or married at the beginning of 1974, became independent at the beginning of 1970 or 1974 respectively.

As we have seen,[127] a person acquires at birth as his domicile of origin:

(1) the then existing domicile of his father, if the person is at his birth a marital child and his father is living; or
(2) in any other case, the then existing domicile of his mother; or
(3) if the identity or domicile of the relevant parent is unknown, the place where he was born or found.

A person's domicile of origin cannot change, but it can be displaced during his childhood (that is, from the moment immediately after his birth to the moment immediately before he attains adulthood) by a domicile of dependency elsewhere, taken from that of a person with whom he has a home. The identity of the person depended on must be determined in accordance with somewhat scanty and ill-reasoned common law decisions, as modified by s 4 of the Domicile and Matrimonial Proceedings Act 1973, an ill-drafted provision apparently written in misunderstanding of the common law. Nonetheless it is clear that in general a child's domicile of dependence is taken from that of a person with whom he has a home,[128] and it is submitted with some confidence that the following more detailed rules emerge from the authorities:

(1) A marital child[129] who has a home with his father takes the father's

---

[126] See Chapter 3 below.

[127] See 'Domicile of origin', pp 15–16 above.

[128] It seems that for purposes of domicile (unlike habitual residence, as to which see 'Habitual residence of children', pp 37–42 below): court orders as to custodial rights (other than adoption orders) are not in themselves decisive, but merely offer some indication as to where the child has a home.

[129] As defined by s 1 of the Family Law Reform Act 1987, and thus including:

  (a) a legitimated child, who from legitimation is treated as a marital child of his biological parents (see the Legitimacy Act 1976, ss 2 and 3; and Dicey & Morris, Rule 15(2)); and
  (b) an adopted child, who from adoption is treated as a marital child of his adoptive parent(s) (see the Adoption Act 1976, s 39; cf Dicey & Morris, Rules 9(2) and 15(5)).

domicile, even if he also has the same or another home with his mother and she has a different domicile.[130]

(2) Otherwise a child who has a home with his mother takes her domicile.[131]

(3) If a child at one time had a domicile by dependence on his mother by having a home with her and not having a home with his father at a time when both parents were living but they were living apart, then his domicile continues to depend on the mother's even if he ceases to have a home with her or she dies, unless he subsequently has a home with his father.[132]

(4) Otherwise a child takes as his domicile that of some other person (often a relative) with whom he has a home;[133] or if there is no such person (as in the case of an orphan who is living on his own), he retains his last previous domicile.[134]

If a person's domicile changes during his childhood, the new domicile is merely a domicile of dependency. The domicile acquired at birth remains the domicile of origin, which may be revived in adulthood if some other domicile is abandoned. If on attaining adulthood the person has a domicile of dependence different from his domicile of origin, he may abandon his last domicile of dependence in the same way as a domicile of choice, and thus revive his domicile of origin, and this type of change in domicile is the easiest type to establish.[135]

Dependency may terminate in various ways: by a child attaining adulthood; or, in the case of a married woman, by widowhood or divorce before 1974, or the chiming of midnight commencing 1974. In all these cases,[136] the following rules apply:

(1) If the last domicile of dependency is in the same country as the domicile of origin, then on and after independence that domicile is presumed to continue, as an undisplaced domicile of origin. But this presumption is rebuttable, and the said domicile may be displaced, at or after independence, by a domicile of choice, acquired by a combination of residence and intention to settle permanently in the new country. If at independence the requisite residence and

---

[130] See *D'Etchegoyen v D'Etchegoyen* (1888) 13 PD 132; *Re Macreight* (1885) 30 ChD 165; and s 4(1) of the Domicile and Matrimonial Proceedings Act 1973.

[131] See *Potinger v Wightman* (1817) 36 ER 26; *Udny v Udny* (1869) LR 1 Sc & Div 441; *Re Grove* (1888) 40 ChD 216; *Hope v Hope* [1968] NI 1; s 4(1), (2) and (4) of the 1973 Act; and Dicey & Morris, Rule 15(3). An adopted child will count as a child of the adoptive parent(s) for the purpose of determining his domicile of dependence as at times after the adoption, but not as at earlier times; see the Adoption Act 1976, s 39; cf Dicey & Morris, Rules 9(2) and 15(5).

[132] See ss 4(1)–(3) of the 1973 Act, which in this situation has the unfortunate effect, probably arising from a misunderstanding by the draftsman as to the common law framework, of preventing the child's domicile from following that of a grandparent or other relative with whom he now has a home.

[133] See *Re Beaumont* [1893] 3 Ch 490, where, after the father's death, the mother moved from Scotland to England but left a marital daughter to live with her aunt in Scotland.

[134] See Dicey & Morris, Rule 15(4).

[135] See *Henderson v Henderson* [1965] P 77.

[136] A dictum in *IRC v Duchess of Portland* [1982] Ch 314 suggests that a dependent domicile held by a married woman at the end of 1973 is more adhesive than other domiciles acquired dependently. There seems no justification for this distinction, either in principle or in the wording of the 1973 Act.

intention exist, a domicile of choice is acquired immediately, and an intention formed during dependence may be assumed to have continued up to independence in the absence of evidence to the contrary.[137]

(2) If the last domicile of dependency is in a different country from the domicile of origin, then at and after independence the last domicile of dependency is presumed to continue, as a domicile of choice acquired dependently. Thus it will continue as long as the person remains resident in the country of dependence;[138] and it will also continue despite his absence from that country, until he firmly decides not to return there at all, or to return there only temporarily.[139] But again the presumption is rebuttable, and the domicile acquired dependently may be destroyed, at or after independence, not only by the acquisition of a domicile of choice in a third country through residence there with the intention of settling permanently; but also by abandonment, so as to revive the domicile of origin, through absence from the country of dependence with a firm intention of not returning there, or returning only temporarily.[140]

Law Commission proposals

Changes in the rules on the determination of the domicile of children (as well as adults) have been proposed by the Law Commissions in their 1987 Report.[141] Under these proposals the concept of 'domicile of origin' would be abolished. A person's domicile at birth would be determined in the same way as at any other time during his childhood, and the domicile acquired at birth would have no specially adhesive quality, and no capacity to revive. An adult who had acquired a domicile of choice would retain it until he acquired another domicile of choice elsewhere. 'Child' would simply refer to any person under the age of 16, including one who had married or even become a parent. A child would be domiciled in the country with which he was for the time being most closely connected. Where the child's parents were domiciled in the same country and he had his home with either or both of them, it would be rebuttably presumed that he was most closely connected with that country. Where the child's parents were not domiciled in the same country and he had his home with one of them, but not with the other, it would be rebuttably presumed that he was most closely connected with the country in which the parent with whom he had his home was domiciled.

---

[137] See *Re Scullard* [1957] Ch 107, where (before 1974) a married woman of English origin and dependence who had left her husband and settled in Guernsey was held to have acquired a Guernsey domicile of choice on his death.

[138] As in *Re Raffenel* (1863) 164 ER 1190, and *Re Wallach* [1950] 1 All ER 199.

[139] See *Re Macreight* (1885) 30 ChD 165, where a serving soldier retained his last domicile acquired dependently; and *Henderson v Henderson* [1967] P 77.

[140] See *Harrison v Harrison* [1953] 1 WLR 865, where (before 1970) a man of English origin who had acquired a dependent domicile in South Australia during childhood was, on attaining 21, temporarily resident in England with the intention of making his permanent home in New Zealand, and it was held that his English domicile of origin then revived.

[141] Law Com 168, Scot Law Com 107, Cm 200 (1987).

Fortunately Parliament has shown no eagerness to implement these proposals. The rebuttability and incompleteness of the envisaged presumptions seem calculated to maximise uncertainty. The proposed insistence on eliminating the relevance of legitimacy no doubt reflects a trend in the Law Commission's approach to English family law, but one, it is submitted, which is wholly regrettable.

Habitual residence of children

As we have seen, there is no concept of an habitual residence of origin, but a child has an habitual residence of dependence. Although the point cannot be considered beyond doubt, it seems probable that, for purposes of habitual residence, a person counts as a child, and thus remains dependent, until attaining the age of 16, but counts as an adult, able to choose his own habitual residence, thereafter. Such a rule is supported not only by the analogy of domicile, but also by s 41 of the Family Law Act 1986, which in certain circumstances and for certain purposes preserves, despite wrongful removal or departure, the habitual residence of a child under 16, and by the fact that the Hague Convention on child abduction (by art 4) ceases to apply when the child attains the age of 16. Moreover it is noteworthy that (by art 13) the Convention deals with the reluctance of an older child to be returned, not in terms of his habitual residence, but by giving a discretion to a court to refuse to order the return of the child if it finds that he objects to being returned and has attained an age and degree of maturity at which it is appropriate to take account of his views. It is also supported by dicta of Lord Denning MR in *Re PG*,[142] and by the well-established reluctance of the English courts to enforce a custody order against the wishes of a minor who has attained 16, which is now reinforced by s 9(6) and (7) of the Children Act 1989.[143]

The only statutory provision which attempts to define the habitual residence of a child is s 41 of the Family Law Act 1986. This applies where a child, under the age of 16 and habitually resident in a part of the United Kingdom, becomes habitually resident elsewhere in consequence of his being removed from or retained outside, or himself leaving or remaining outside, the part of the United Kingdom in which he was previously habitually resident, without the agreement of every person having, under the law of the part of the United Kingdom in which he was previously habitually resident, the right to determine where he is to reside, or in contravention of an order made by a court in any part of the United Kingdom. In such a case the child is treated for the purposes of Part I of the 1986 Act (which regulates the jurisdiction of the English, Scottish, and

---

[142] [1965] 1 Ch 568 at 585.
[143] These provisions prohibit the English courts, unless satisfied that the circumstances of the case are exceptional, from making a residence, contact, prohibited steps or specific issue order (ie any order affecting custody in a generic sense) with respect to a child who has reached the age of 16, or which is to have effect for a period which will end after the child has reached that age.

Northern Irish courts to make custody orders) as continuing to be habitually resident in the part of the United Kingdom in which he was previously habitually resident, for one year from the removal, retention, departure or absence. But this continuance ceases earlier if he attains the age of 16, or he becomes habitually resident elsewhere with the agreement of the persons having, under the law of the relevant part of the United Kingdom, the right to determine where he is to reside, and without contravention of an order made by a court in any part of the United Kingdom.

It is submitted that this elaborate enactment should be regarded as a limited declaration of a general principle, inherent in the concept of the habitual residence of a child, and therefore applicable for purposes other than the British custody jurisdiction, and even where the initial habitual residence is outside the United Kingdom. The principle, which overrides other rules on habitual residence, is that the habitual residence of a child cannot be changed by anything done, by the child himself or any other person (other than a court making a custody order), if it is done in contravention of custodial rights then existing under the law of the country where the child was previously and would otherwise have remained habitually resident.

Most of the recent decisions on the habitual residence of a child have been given in cases under the Hague Convention of 25 October 1980 on the Civil Aspects of International Child Abduction, which is implemented in the United Kingdom by Part I of the Child Abduction and Custody Act 1985, and included as Sched 1 to the Act. The Convention is designed to secure the almost automatic return of a child who has been wrongfully removed from the contracting state in which he was habitually resident, at least if the application for his return is made within a year of the abduction.[144]

The Convention, by arts 3 and 4, defines a wrongful removal or retention of a child as one which infringes rights of custody which are attributed to a person, an institution or any other body, either jointly or alone, under the law of the contracting state in which the child was habitually resident immediately before the removal or retention, and which at the time of removal or retention were actually exercised, either jointly or alone, or would have been so exercised but for the removal or retention. 'Rights of custody' are defined by art 5 as including rights relating to the care of the child's person, and, in particular, the right to determine the child's place of residence; and contrasted with 'rights of access', which include the right to take a child for a limited period of time to a place other than the child's habitual residence.[145] Article 3 also specifies that rights of custody may arise, in particular, by operation of law, or by reason of a judicial or administrative decision, or by reason of an agreement having legal effect. Moreover the Court of Appeal has held in *B v B*[146] that a foreign court seised of a

---

[144] See arts 3, 12, 13 and 16 of the Convention.

[145] The concepts of 'rights of custody' and 'rights of access', used in the Convention, appear to correspond closely to rights conferred by, respectively, a residence order and a contact order, within the meaning of s 8 of the Children Act 1989.

[146] [1993] Fam 32.

custody dispute itself constitutes a person, institution or other body having rights of custody, within the meaning of the Convention. Similarly in *Re R (No 2)*[147] Brown P held that, where English wardship proceedings based on the child's habitual residence in England at their commencement were pending, a non-marital child remained habitually resident in England despite the facts that she was actually resident with her mother in Canada, that her mother had meanwhile formed an intention to settle there, and had obtained a Canadian interim custody order, including an injunction restraining the father from removing the child from Canada. Thus the father's removal of the child to England in breach of the Canadian injunction was not wrongful, within the meaning of the Convention.

Especially in the context of the Convention, it is not surprising that the courts have held that a child's habitual residence follows that of a person (usually a parent) who has, and is exercising or would but for wrongful interference be exercising, rights of custody in respect of the child. In this there may be a certain circularity, since (under the Convention at least) it is the law of the child's habitual residence which determines what person or persons have custodial rights in respect of the child. Thus the situation could conceivably arise where a child is living with both parents (simultaneously or for alternating periods), but the parents are habitually resident in different countries, and each of the parents has sole rights of custody under the law of his or her respective habitual residence. No doubt a suitable knife can be found to cut such Gordian knots if they arise. Of more practical importance is the likelihood that the relevant law will have different rules as to custodial rights according to whether or not the parents of the child are or have been married to each other. Thus under English law, in the absence of a court order, both parents have custodial rights in respect of a marital child (within the meaning of s 1 of the Family Law Reform Act 1987), but only the mother has custodial rights over a non-marital child.

On the basis of a case-law which has developed rapidly in recent years, a number of situations can be distinguished. The most normal case was envisaged by Lord Denning MR in *Re PG*:[148] that of a marital child whose parents are living together and are both habitually resident at the matrimonial home, and who is also himself based at the matrimonial home. In such a case the child also is habitually resident at the family home, even while he is away, for example at boarding school. Similarly in *Re F*[149] Butler-Sloss LJ no doubt envisaged such cases in saying: 'While parents live together the child is habitually resident with both parents.'[150]

Presumably if in otherwise similar circumstances a matrimonial home were

---

[147] [1993] 1 FLR 249.
[148] [1965] 1 Ch 568 at 585.
[149] [1992] 1 FLR 548, CA.
[150] See also *Re K*, 24 June 1991, CA, where a husband of Greek nationality and a wife of British citizenship but Cypriot connections settled in Greece with the child, on a supposedly permanent basis, and lived largely there for about two years until the marriage broke down.

established for purposes so temporary that neither parent became habitually resident in that country, and both parents remained habitually resident in the country where the family had previously lived and the parents intended to return, the child would share the habitual residence retained by both parents. However a not very dissimilar situation arose in *Re B*,[151] where a married couple (a man of Scottish and a woman of German origin) and their child had been habitually resident together in Scotland for several years, but, marital difficulties having arisen, the couple moved with the child to Germany with the limited common purpose of achieving a reconciliation and reaching agreement as to their future. After a few months in Germany, they came to England for a short holiday. Waite J's decision that they had a sufficiently settled purpose to acquire an habitual residence in Germany seems almost preposterous. The right view would seem to be that the parents had jointly abandoned their habitual residence in Scotland, but only the wife (if anyone) had acquired an habitual residence in Germany, and she could not unilaterally impose an habitual residence on the child.

If a child in respect of whom both parents have custodial rights (usually a marital child) is living with one of them, with the consent of the other, for a not insubstantial period, the child shares the habitual residence of the parent with whom he is living. For this purpose, a school year was regarded as a substantial period in *Re S*,[152] which involved a marital child aged 12 whose parents had divorced. The Court of Appeal ruled in effect that where both parents have custodial rights and the child is living with one of the parents in the country of that parent's habitual residence under an agreement between the parents for an agreed period comprising a school year, as distinct from being there for a passing visit, the child has the same habitual residence as the parent with whom he is so living. But other decisions show that, where both parents have custodial rights, the child's habitual residence will not be changed where one parent consents to the child going elsewhere to or with the other parent for a limited and insufficiently substantial period, such as a visit for three or four months to the other parent's home[153] or country of origin,[154] or a holiday of a few weeks or months to see grandparents.[155]

If both parents have custodial rights, and under an agreement or court order the child lives with them alternately for equal periods at their habitual residences in different countries, the child is habitually resident in whichever of those countries the whole family was habitually resident in before the parents parted.[156]

In the case of a child over whom both parents have custodial rights, his habitual residence cannot be changed by kidnapping him and taking him from

[151] 21 August 1992.
[152] [1991] 2 FLR 1.
[153] See per Lord Denning MR in *Re PG* [1965] 1 Ch 568.
[154] See *Re A* [1991] 2 FLR 241, CA.
[155] See *Evans v Evans* [1989] 1 FLR 135, CA.
[156] See *Re A* [1988] 1 FLR 365, CA.

his home, even if one of his parents is the kidnapper. Even more generally, the habitual residence of such a child cannot be changed by one parent without the consent of the other.[157] It is submitted that this principle is supported rather than contradicted by the remarks of Butler-Sloss LJ in *Re F*[158] that, when the parents separate, the child's habitual residence may change and will in due course follow that of the principal carer with whom he resides, but that the change of habitual residence of a child would require either a court order, or an agreement between the parents, or at least that one parent should take no step to prevent the other parent from changing the child's home for a sufficient period to amount to acquiescence.

If only one of the parents has custodial rights (most typically, the mother of a non-marital child), and the child is living with that parent, his habitual residence will follow that parent's, even if the parents are living together and the child is living with both of them. Thus in *Re J*,[159] which involved a non-marital child aged two, the House ruled (inter alia) that in the case of a very young child who is in the actual, and sole lawful, custody of the mother, his habitual residence follows hers. Similarly if, as in *Re G*,[160] the court of the habitual residence (in casu, Ontario) of a marital child gives custody to the mother and permits her to take the child permanently to another country (in casu, England), and she does so, the child will become habitually resident in the latter country. On the other hand, if, as in *Re N*,[161] upon an order by the court of the child's habitual residence transferring custodial rights from the mother to the father, made while the mother and child are temporarily visiting another country, the mother decides not to return, the child will remain habitually resident in the original country.

If, as in *Re M*,[162] the person with sole custodial rights, such as the mother of a non-marital child, permits the child to live for a substantial period, such as a year, with other relatives, such as the child's paternal grandparents, at their habitual residence in a country other than that in which the mother is herself habitually resident, the child will become habitually resident at his new home. But if the child then returns to the mother for a short holiday, and during this she decides not to return him, he will immediately lose his habitual residence with the grandparents and also (according to the better view, adopted by Hoffmann LJ) regain an habitual residence in the mother's country. Presumably the same result would be reached if the mother, instead of waiting for the child to visit her, had written to the grandparents, demanding his immediate return.

Cases may arise where no-one has custodial rights, for example on the death of the mother of a non-marital child. In the context of wardship (rather than the

---

[157] See per Lord Denning MR in *Re PG* [1965] 1 Ch 568. See also *Re F* [1991] Fam 25, CA.
[158] [1992] 1 FLR 548.
[159] [1990] 2 AC 562.
[160] [1993] 1 WLR 824.
[161] 3 December 1992, CA.
[162] [1993] 1 FLR 495.

Hague Convention), the question was raised, but not resolved, in *Re G*,[163] where Balcombe J decided only procedural issues. The safest solution would be to apply the presumption of continuance, in favour of the habitual residence existing before this situation arose.

[163] Unreported, 21 May 1991.

3

MARRIAGE

In the English conflict system, the factors which may have the effect of invalidating a marriage are classified under three headings: formalities, which are in general governed by the law of the place of celebration; the capacity of a spouse, and the validity of his or her consent to enter into the marriage, which are in general governed by the law of the domicile of the spouse in question; and the possible invalidating effect of non-consummation of the marriage, which is probably governed by the lex fori. Additional conflict problems arise in relation to polygamous marriages, celebrated abroad in accordance with foreign law, since polygamy is an institution unknown to English internal law.

VALIDITY[1]

Formal validity

The general rule is that the formal validity of a marriage is governed by the lex loci celebrationis, the law of the country where the marriage ceremony took place. Thus in *Berthiaume v Dastous*[2] a marriage celebrated in religious form in France between Quebec domiciliaries was held invalid by the Privy Council (on appeal from Quebec) because French law (unlike Quebec law) required a civil ceremony. Conversely in *Apt v Apt*[3] the Court of Appeal held valid a proxy marriage celebrated in Argentina between a man domiciled there and a woman domiciled in England, since Argentinian law (unlike English law) permitted a spouse to be represented at his or her marriage ceremony by a proxy. The woman had appointed her proxy by a power of attorney which she had executed

---

[1] In its Report No 165 (1987) on *Choice of Law Rules in Marriage*, the Law Commission declined to recommend a comprehensive restatement in statutory form of the choice of law rules relating to marriage, and proposed only some minor amendments to legislation on the formalities of marriages celebrated abroad before British consuls or army chaplains. These amendments have been implemented by the Foreign Marriage (Amendment) Act 1988, which entered into force on 12 April 1990.

[2] [1930] AC 79.

[3] [1948] P 83.

in England, but it was the place of the ceremony, rather than that of the appointment of the proxy, which was decisive.

The formal validity of a marriage covers such questions as the need for a civil or a religious ceremony;[4] the need for certain words to be used in the ceremony;[5] the possibility for a spouse to be represented at the ceremony by a proxy;[6] and the need for certain steps to be taken prior to the ceremony, such as the publication of banns,[7] or subsequent to it, such as registration of the marriage.[8] It has also been extended, by a well-established but unprincipled line of decisions,[9] to cover requirements that a spouse should obtain parental consent to his or her marriage, even where the law of the spouse's domicile considers that its requirement of parental consent affects the spouse's capacity.

The reference of formal validity to the lex loci celebrationis must probably be understood as an alternative reference to the internal law of that country, and to any other law referred to by its conflict rules, whichever is more favourable to validity.[10] In any event a retroactive change in the lex loci, validating an earlier marriage, will be respected in England, unless one of the spouses has remarried in the intervening period before the retroactive validation takes effect.[11]

There are no exceptions to the positive aspect of the rule: a marriage complying with the formal requirements of the lex loci is always valid as regards formalities. But there are a number of exceptions to its negative aspect, which in certain circumstances enable a marriage, celebrated abroad without complying with the formal requirements of the lex loci, to be upheld by reference to special rules of the lex fori. These exceptions concern British military marriages; British consular marriages; situations where insuperable difficulties prevented compliance with the lex loci; and marriages connected with a foreign army of occupation.

British military marriages

Legislation dating from 1823 establishes the formal validity in the United Kingdom of what may be referred to as British military marriages, despite non-compliance with the formal requirements of the law of the country of celebration. The current enactment comprises s 22 of the Foreign Marriage Act

[4] See *Berthiaume v Dastous* [1930] AC 79; and *Gray v Formosa* [1963] P 259, which involved the former Maltese requirement of a religious ceremony.
[5] See *Taczanowska v Taczanowski* [1957] P 301.
[6] See *Apt v Apt* [1948] P 83.
[7] See *Hooper v Hooper* [1959] 1 WLR 1021.
[8] See *Taczanowska v Taczanowski* [1957] P 301.
[9] See *Simonin v Mallac* (1860) 164 ER 917, *Ogden v Ogden* [1908] P 46, *Bliersbach v MacEwan* 1959 SC 43, and *Lodge v Lodge* (1963) 107 SJ 437.
[10] See dicta of Karminski J and Hodson LJ in *Taczanowska v Taczanowski* [1957] P 301. Cf *Hooper v Hooper* [1959] 1 WLR 1021, a decision which seems to refer exclusively to the conflict rules of the lex loci, but in any event would seem to misapply the English law, referred to by the Iraqi lex loci, by ignoring a restriction on the requirement of banns, imposed by the Marriage Act 1949, to marriages celebrated in England.
[11] See *Starkowski v Attorney-General* [1954] AC 155.

1892, as substituted by s 2 of the Foreign Marriage Act 1947 and amended by s 6 of the Foreign Marriage (Amendment) Act 1988,[12] taken with SI 1964/1000, 1965/137 and 1990/599.

The current legislation establishes the formal validity of marriages celebrated outside the Commonwealth with the authorisation of the commanding officer of United Kingdom military forces serving in the country of celebration. The marriage must be celebrated by a chaplain serving with such forces, or by some other person authorised by such commanding officer; and at least one of the spouses must be (in broad terms) a member of such forces, or a civilian connected with such forces, or a family member of such a person residing with him.[13] Provision is also made for the recognition of Australian or New Zealand military marriages.

British consular marriages

Other provisions of the Foreign Marriage Act 1892, as amended by the Foreign Marriage (Amendment) Act 1988,[14] together with SI 1970/1539 and SI 1990/598, establish the formal validity in the United Kingdom of what may be referred to as a British consular marriage, despite non-compliance with the formal requirements of the law of the country of celebration. Such a marriage is one celebrated outside the United Kingdom by or before a marriage officer appointed by a Secretary of State (usually a British consul), at his official house, and in English internal form.[15] At least one of the spouses must be a 'United Kingdom national', defined as: a British citizen, a British Dependent Territories citizen, a British Overseas citizen, a British National (Overseas), a British subject, or a British protected person, under the British Nationality Act 1981.

It is at the British government's discretion whether to appoint a marriage officer for a territory, and at present a marriage officer, before proceeding with a ceremony, must be satisfied that the government of the country of celebration will not object to the ceremony, that there are insufficient facilities for the marriage under the local law, and that the marriage will be recognised in the countries in which each of the spouses is domiciled.

A marriage purporting to be celebrated under the 1892 Act will be valid if the actual ceremony complies with the Act, despite non-compliance with various statutory preliminaries and despite non-registration;[16] and, if celebrated and registered at the official house of a British ambassador or consul, despite his non-appointment or restricted authority as a marriage officer.[17]

---

[12] Implementing minor recommendations made in Law Commission Report No 165 (1987), on *Choice of Law Rules in Marriage*.

[13] For the detailed definition of qualifying persons, see SI 1964/1000, art 2, as substituted by SI 1990/599, art 2.

[14] Implementing minor recommendations in Law Commission Report No 165 (1987), on *Choice of Law Rules in Marriage*.

[15] English requirements as to parental consent apply, except in the case of a person domiciled in Scotland.

[16] See *Corbett v Corbett* [1968] P 482.

[17] See s 13.

Foreign consular marriages are not recognised as such. Their validity depends on the lex loci celebrationis.[18]

Common law marriages

Despite common parlance, for present purposes 'common law marriage' is not a euphemism for unmarried cohabitation, but refers to a marriage ceremony whose formal validity falls to be determined, by an English court, by reference to the requirements of English common law, modified in the light of conditions existing in the country of celebration.

Where applicable, the common law requires some form of ceremony at which the spouses are present, and in which they exchange before a witness declarations that they now marry each other. In *R v Millis*[19] the House of Lords ruled that, subject to an exception for Jewish marriages, a common law marriage could only be contracted in England or Ireland in the presence of an episcopally ordained priest (such as an Anglican, Roman Catholic, or Greek Orthodox priest; but not a Presbyterian or Methodist minister). But it has not been possible to contract a valid common law marriage in England since the Marriage Act 1753, and this will remain impossible in the absence of enemy occupation, natural or man-made disaster, total breakdown of order (at least in a locality), or contrary enactment. So we proceed on the (possibly optimistic) assumption that a valid common law marriage ceremony must take place abroad.

There are three types of unusual situation in which a valid common law marriage (for English purposes) may be entered into abroad; and the case-law establishing such unusual circumstances also recognises that the same circumstances make the requirement of an episcopally ordained priest, as envisaged in *Millis*, unsuitable and therefore inapplicable, so as to leave as the only applicable formalities the presence of both spouses and a witness, and their declarations of intention immediately to marry each other.[20]

The first situation where a valid common law marriage is possible is where the applicable lex loci comprises or includes the English common law. Such was the case in New South Wales in the early 19th century;[21] for marriages in China between British subjects in 1938;[22] and for marriages in Singapore in 1937 between persons of different religion.[23]

The second situation where a marriage may be validly celebrated in accordance with the common law is where there is insuperable difficulty in complying with the requirements of the lex loci. This exception can be traced to *Ruding v*

---

[18] See *Radwan v Radwan (No 2)* [1973] Fam 35.
[19] (1844) 8 ER 844.
[20] See *Catterall v Catterall* (1847) 163 ER 1142, *Wolfenden v Wolfenden* [1946] P 61, *Penhas v Eng* [1953] AC 304, and *Preston v Preston* [1963] P 411. Cf *Taczanowska v Taczanowski* [1957] P 301.
[21] See *Catterall v Catterall*, note 20 above.
[22] See *Wolfenden v Wolfenden*, note 20 above.
[23] See *Penhas v Eng*, note 20 above, which involved a marriage between a Jewish man and a Chinese woman.

Smith,[24] which involved a marriage between British subjects in the Cape, which had recently surrendered to British forces. But the common law applies in cases of insuperable difficulty even if the parties have no connection with England, the United Kingdom or even the Commonwealth.[25]

The third exception, permitting a valid common law marriage, applies where at least one of the spouses is a member of a foreign army of occupation, or of a civilian governmental organisation connected with a foreign army of occupation. This exception was invented by the Court of Appeal in *Taczanowska v Taczanowski,*[26] and developed in *Merker v Merker,*[27] *Kochanski v Kochanska,*[28] and *Preston v Preston;*[29] a striking piece of judicial legislation exemplifying the confidence of the English judiciary and the adaptive strength of English law in that era. These cases arose from the chaotic conditions prevailing in enemy territory under allied occupation in the months surrounding the end of the Second World War. Thousands of marriages were then celebrated in allied-occupied Germany or Italy, between persons from Poland or other Eastern European countries, in Roman Catholic or Jewish form, and not in accordance with the lex loci; since German law required a civil ceremony, and Italian law, while accepting a religious ceremony, required some additional formalities.

Some of these couples subsequently emigrated to England or Australia, and the validity of such marriages came before English and Australian courts. In Australia some marriages were upheld on the ground that compliance with the local formalities was impossible;[30] but in other Australian cases, where there had been no insuperable difficulty in complying with the local law, the marriages were held invalid.[31] In none of the English cases was insuperable difficulty established, but in *Taczanowska v Taczanowski*[32] the Court of Appeal invented a new basis for upholding such marriages in accordance with the common law.

Taczanowska involved a Roman Catholic ceremony in Italy in July 1946. It was conducted between a Polish army officer and a Polish civilian refugee before a Polish army chaplain. The marriage was upheld by the Court of Appeal on the ground that it was entered into in an occupied country by a member of the occupying forces. Similarly in *Merker v Merker*[33] Simon P upheld, as a marriage

---

[24] (1821) 161 ER 774.
[25] See *Savenis v Savenis* [1950] SASR 309, 25 ALJ 72, approved by the English Court of Appeal in *Taczanowska.* Cf *Fokas v Fokas* [1952] SASR 152, and *Maksymec v Maksymec* (1956) 30 ALJ 95.
[26] [1957] P 301.
[27] [1963] P 283.
[28] [1958] P 147.
[29] [1963] P 411.
[30] See *Savenis v Savenis* [1950] SASR 309, which involved a Roman Catholic marriage between Lithuanians in Germany in November 1945, no civil registrars being available as they had fled the Russian advance; and *Maksymec v Maksymec* (1956) 30 ALJ 95. The decision in *Savenis v Savenis* was approved by the English Court of Appeal in *Taczanowska v Taczanowski* [1957] P 301.
[31] See *Fokas v Fokas* [1952] SASR 152, and *Milder v Milder* [1959] VR 95.
[32] [1957] P 301.
[33] [1963] P 283.

within the lines of a foreign army of occupation, a Roman Catholic ceremony conducted in Germany in April 1946, between Poles who were both serving in the Polish forces forming part of the allied army of occupation, before a Polish army chaplain in the garrison chapel.

Again in *Preston v Preston*[34] the Court of Appeal upheld a Roman Catholic marriage celebrated in June 1945 in a camp (the Nordheim camp) in the Western zone of Germany. The husband had served in the Polish Home Army and taken part in the Polish uprising and had never been demobilised. After the uprising he had moved west to escape the Russian advance, and eventually reached the Nordheim camp. On the evidence before the Court of Appeal, this was found not to be simply a displaced persons' camp, but a military camp established and organised by the allied armed forces for the collection of Polish soldiers with a view to organising them under military command and training them and eventually incorporating them into ordinary service units for the purpose of consolidating conquest. The marriage was celebrated in the camp before the camp chaplain, who held Polish military rank. Ormerod LJ explained that the rule in *Taczanowska* applied to persons in a foreign country as part of the organisation commonly set up when there is hostile occupation; and Russell LJ was of the opinion that it applied to all members of a group of allied soldiers organised under military command for the military purposes of the allies, one of whom is in actual control of the territory in which the group is situated.

Earlier in *Kochanski v Kochanska*[35] Sachs J had upheld a marriage celebrated by persons living in the same camp a week later than the *Preston* marriage, but (on different evidence) he had not recognised the military character of the Nordheim camp, and had viewed it simply as a displaced persons' camp. In *Kochanski* a local church had been used for the ceremony, but again the camp chaplain had presided. Emphasising that the Poles in the camp were living as a separate community based on the principle of having nothing to do with the Germans, and showing full perception of the breakdown of civilisation in Europe which has characterised the 20th century, Sachs J followed *Taczanowska* and construed it as extending to an organised community in an unusual position.

This decision has subsequently met with some adverse judicial comment. In *Merker v Merker*[36] Simon P took the view that *Kochanski* should be confined to persons in a strictly analogous position to a foreign army of occupation, such as members of an organised body of escaped prisoners of war; and in *Preston v Preston*[37] Russell LJ considered that *Kochanski* went too far and that *Taczanowska* should not be extended beyond the military context. But Ormerod LJ was much more cautious, indicating only that *Taczanowska* would *not necessarily* extend to inmates of a civilian displaced persons' camp. It is submitted that the criticism of *Kochanski* by the Court of Appeal in *Preston* is too guarded (as

[34] [1963] P 411.
[35] [1958] P 147.
[36] [1963] P 283.
[37] [1963] P 411.

well as obiter) to amount to its overruling; and that *Kochanski* stands as authority for extending the benefit of common law marriages, where chaotic conditions exist, to members of any distinguishable group which is in an unusual position, such as to make it clearly unreasonable to insist on their compliance with the lex loci. Thus the benefit of the rule should extend, for example, to civilian relief workers in Bosnia or Somalia in 1994, even though their function is to assist, and not to isolate themselves from, the local population.

Capacity and consent

The dual domicile doctrine

As a general rule, a person's capacity to marry, and the validity of his or her consent to a marriage, are governed by the law of his or her domicile at the time of the marriage. In other words, the husband's capacity and consent are governed by the law of his domicile, and the wife's capacity and consent are governed by the law of her domicile. The law of the place of celebration, as such, is irrelevant to such issues.[38] This general rule, which is often known as the dual domicile doctrine, is well supported by judicial decisions,[39] statutory provisions,[40] and academic opinion;[41] and Cheshire's arguments against the dual domicile doctrine and in favour of the law of the intended matrimonial residence have been abandoned by his editors.[42] Probably the dual domicile doctrine is to be understood as involving renvoi: in other words, as referring a person's capacity to marry to whatever law the courts of his or her domicile would apply, rather than to the internal law of the domicile.[43] Like all English choice of law rules, the dual domicile doctrine is subject to a proviso in favour of stringent English public policy, and this will exclude the application of foreign rules whose content is repugnant to the English judicial conscience.[44]

---

[38] See *Re Swan* (1871) 2 VR (IE & M) 47, and *Reed v Reed* [1969] 6 DLR(2d) 617; cf *Breen v Breen* [1964] P 144. It is submitted that dicta in *Pugh v Pugh* [1951] P 482, indicating that it is otherwise for marriages celebrated in England, are inadequate to establish such an anomaly. Cf Dicey & Morris, Rule 70, Exception 2, which tentatively recognises such an exception.

[39] See (among others) *Mette v Mette* (1859) 164 ER 792; *Brook v Brook* (1861) 11 ER 703; *Sottemayor v De Barros (No 1)* (1877) 3 PD 1; *Re De Wilton* [1900] 2 Ch 481; *Re Bozzelli's Settlement* [1902] 1 Ch 751; *Re Paine* [1940] Ch 46; *Pugh v Pugh* [1951] P 482; and *Szechter v Szechter* [1971] P 286.

[40] See the Marriage (Enabling) Act 1960, s 1, and the Matrimonial Causes Act 1973, s 11(d).

[41] See Dicey & Morris, Rules 70 and 71.

[42] See 12th ed (1992), at pp 587–95. However an isolated decision, *Radwan v Radwan (No 2)* [1973] Fam 35, has held that capacity for polygamy as such is governed by the law of the intended matrimonial residence; see 'Capacity for polygamy', pp 58–60 below.

[43] See *R v Brentwood Registrar ex parte Arias* [1968] 2 QB 956, and *Padolecchia v Padolecchia* [1968] P 314. Admittedly these cases are no longer authoritative on the incidental question of divorce recognition with which they were concerned, but they probably stand as authority for using renvoi in connection with ordinary questions of capacity to marry, for example by reference to consanguinity or lack of age. Such use of renvoi would be justifiable on the ground that the reference to the law of a person's domicile to determine his or her capacity to marry is based on desires to respect the policy of the most interested country, and to avoid conflict with decisions which would be given by its courts. On renvoi generally, see Chapter 16 below.

[44] See *Cheni v Cheni* [1965] P 85.

In terms of merit, the dual domicile doctrine respects the policy of the country which is considered to have most interest in regulating a person's capacity and protecting him or her from engaging in or suffering from ill-considered or involuntary actions, and also offers a substantial degree of certainty. On the other hand, it leans strongly towards invalidation, and there would be some advantage in the introduction of an exception which would uphold a marriage as regards capacity where the parties were capable under the law of a country in which one of them was domiciled at its celebration, and the other became domiciled within a short period (say, six months) after the ceremony.

Prohibited relationships

The largest number of cases on capacity are concerned with the prohibited degrees of consanguinity (blood relationship) or affinity (relationship through a prior marriage), which prevent a marriage between persons so related. Current English law permits, for example, a marriage between first cousins or between a man and his former wife's sister, but prohibits a marriage between uncle and niece, or between a man and his former wife's mother or daughter. It is interesting, though unimportant in principle, that many of the conflict cases involve relationships of affinity which English law then prohibited but has subsequently come to permit.

In accordance with the general rule, a marriage celebrated abroad between English domiciliaries is invalid if they are related within the degrees prohibited under English law, even if such a marriage is permitted by the lex loci.[45] Similarly a marriage celebrated in England between persons domiciled in the same foreign country is invalid if their relationship prohibits marriage under the law of their domicile, though not under English internal law.[46] Conversely a marriage abroad between persons domiciled in the same foreign country is valid in this respect if their relationship is acceptable under the law of their domicile, even if it would prohibit marriage under English internal law;[47] and a foreign rule permitting marriage between uncle and niece is not so offensive to the English judicial conscience to be excluded from recognition under the public policy proviso.[48] Presumably, however, a foreign rule which permitted a man to marry his sister or daughter would be rejected on that basis.[49]

Moreover a marriage celebrated abroad between an English domiciliary and a foreign domiciliary is invalid if their relationship prohibits marriage under English law, even if such a marriage is acceptable to the law of the other spouse's

---

[45] As in *Brook v Brook* (1861) 11 ER 703, and *Re De Wilton* [1900] 2 Ch 481.

[46] As in *Sottemayor v De Barros (No 1)* (1877) 3 PD 1.

[47] As in *Re Bozzelli's Settlement* [1902] 1 Ch 751, and *Cheni v Cheni* [1965] P 85.

[48] *Cheni v Cheni* [1965] P 85.

[49] Similarly foreign incapacities based on race or religion are likely to be rejected on grounds of English public policy. See *Sottomayor v De Barros (No 2)* (1879) 5 PD 94, and *Chetti v Chetti* [1909] P 67. Cf *Corbett v Corbett* [1957] 1 All ER 621.

domicile and the place of celebration, and whether the English domiciliary is the husband[50] or the wife.[51] On the other hand, a marriage abroad between English domiciliaries is valid in this respect if their relationship is acceptable under English law, even if their relationship falls among those prohibited by the law of the place of celebration.[52]

In the case of the degrees of affinity which are made acceptable in English internal law by the Marriage (Enabling) Act 1960,[53] the Act adopts the dual domicile doctrine by specifying that it applies wherever the marriage is celebrated, but does not validate a marriage if at its celebration either spouse is domiciled in a country outside Great Britain, under whose law there cannot be a valid marriage between the parties.

Lack of age

Incapacity may also arise from lack of age. Under English law a marriage of a person under the age of 16 is void, and in *Pugh v Pugh*[54] Pearce J applied this English rule so as to invalidate a marriage celebrated in Austria between a domiciled Englishman and a girl who was domiciled in Hungary and aged 15. The best explanation of this decision seems to be that it interprets the English rule against the marriage of persons under the age of 16 as not only incapacitating an English domiciliary under that age from marrying, but as also incapacitating an English adult from marrying a person under that age, even if the latter is domiciled abroad. In other words, just as English law prevents an adult Englishman from marrying his niece, it also prevents him from marrying a person whom it regards as a child.

On this basis the decision does not affect age requirements imposed by foreign law: whether the French rule that a man cannot marry under the age of 18 prevents a French lady aged 80 from marrying an Englishman aged 17 will depend on the French interpretation of its rule, unaffected by the decision in *Pugh v Pugh*. But even on this limited interpretation, and after full acceptance that the English age requirement reflects a reasonable policy of preventing marriages which, on account of immaturity, are unlikely to succeed, the decision in *Pugh v Pugh* seems unnecessarily rigid. It gives too little weight to the policy of validation in conflict cases, especially where the invalidating rule draws a definite line which is necessarily arbitrary. A person does suddenly move from idiocy to perfect wisdom as the clock strikes midnight on his or her sixteenth birthday.

Public policy would no doubt be invoked against a marriage of a very young

---

[50] As in *Mette v Mette* (1859) 164 ER 792.
[51] As in *Re Paine* [1940] Ch 46.
[52] As in *Re Swan* (1871) 2 VR (IE & M) 47, and *Reed v Reed* [1969] 6 DLR(2d) 617.
[53] This permits a marriage after 1960 between a man and the sister, aunt or niece of his deceased or divorced wife, or the former wife of his deceased or divorced brother, uncle or nephew.
[54] [1951] P 482.

child. However in *Mohamed v Knott*[55] a marriage celebrated in Nigeria between Nigerian domiciliaries was upheld even though the wife was aged 13.

Validity of consent

The dual domicile doctrine extends to the validity of a spouse's consent to the marriage, in terms of factors such as duress or mistake.[56] Thus each spouse must validly consent under the law of his or her own domicile respectively. But, despite a dictum by Sir Jocelyn Simon P in the leading case of *Szechter v Szechter*,[57] it is generally accepted that, where the spouses have different domiciles, there is no need that each should validly consent under the law of the other's domicile as well as his or her own domicile.[58] The validity of the consent of a spouse must be distinguished from the possible need for the consent of a spouse's parent, which has long been treated as a formality, and submitted to the lex loci celebrationis.[59]

Stringent English public policy is, of course, an exception to all choice of law rules, insofar as they would lead to the application of foreign law. Thus it seems likely that a stringent English public policy would override a foreign law which would validate a marriage entered into under what English internal law would regard as duress.[60] Moreover such policy may have a validating effect, as in *Vervaeke v Smith*,[61] where the House of Lords held that public policy requires the application (regardless of any contrary rule of the foreign law normally applicable) of the English rule that a 'sham' marriage is nonetheless valid, where the marriage was celebrated in the United Kingdom between a British citizen and a foreign national, for the sole purpose of enabling the foreigner to acquire British citizenship and thus to reside in the United Kingdom free from immigration control.

A forum orientated exception

A forum orientated exception to the dual domicile rule applies to a marriage which was celebrated in England between an English domiciliary and a foreign domiciliary, whether the English domiciliary is the husband or the wife. It validates such a marriage if the foreign domiciliary has capacity and validly consents in accordance with English internal law, even though he lacks capacity

---

[55] [1969] 1 QB 1.
[56] See *Szechter v Szechter* [1971] P 286. See also *Way v Way* [1950] P 71, and *H v H* [1954] P 258.
[57] [1971] P 286.
[58] See Dicey & Morris, at p 683; and Cheshire & North, at p 647.
[59] See *Simonin v Mallac* (1860) 164 ER 917; *Ogden v Ogden* [1908] P 46; *Bliersbach v MacEwan* 1959 SC 43; and *Lodge v Lodge* (1963) 107 SJ 437.
[60] Cf the care with which, in *Szechter v Szechter* [1971] P 286, Sir Jocelyn Simon P considered whether there was duress in the English sense, as well as under Polish law, the domicile of both spouses.
[61] [1983] AC 145.

or does not validly consent under the law of his domicile.[62] It has been applied where the invalidating element under the law of the foreign domicile concerns consanguinity,[63] lack of parental consent (insofar as this is not regarded as a formality),[64] incapacity to marry out of one's religion or caste,[65] and consent to a sham marriage.[66] But, owing to the wording of the Marriage (Enabling) Act 1960, it does not apply where the marriage is saved by that Act from invalidation for affinity under English internal law.

The exception is evidently open to criticism as discriminating in favour of the lex fori, thus prejudicing the achievement of harmonised results in different countries, and creating 'limping' marriages (valid in one country, invalid in another). In its favour one could argue that the dual domicile doctrine leans unduly towards invalidation, and that the exception offers an admittedly less than ideal corrective.

Capacity to remarry

In order to enable a person who has already validly married to enter another valid monogamous marriage,[67] the prior marriage must first have been terminated by death, divorce or annulment. Problems may therefore arise where a different view as to the validity of a divorce or annulment is taken by English law from that taken by the law of a country where, at the time of the remarriage, the previously married person, or the other party to the remarriage, is domiciled.

The recognition in England of foreign divorces and annulments is now governed by Part II (ss 44–54) of the Family Law Act 1986, which entered into force on 4 April 1988. Section 50 of the 1986 Act specifies that, where a divorce or annulment has been granted by an English court, or a divorce or annulment is recognised in England by virtue of the 1986 Act, the fact that the divorce or annulment is not recognised elsewhere is not to preclude a former spouse from remarrying in England, nor to cause a remarriage of a former spouse, wherever celebrated, to be treated as invalid in England. This replaces a narrower provision contained in s 7 of the Recognition of Divorces and Legal Separations Act 1971, as amended by the Domicile and Matrimonial Proceedings Act 1973.[68] But, insofar as none of these enactments applies (perhaps by reason of the date of the divorce or annulment or the remarriage), *Perrini v Perrini*[69] and *Lawrence*

---

[62] See Dicey & Morris, Rule 70, Exception 3.

[63] See *Sottemayor v De Barros (No 2)* (1879) 5 PD 94.

[64] See *Ogden v Ogden* [1908] P 46.

[65] See *Chetti v Chetti* [1909] P 67.

[66] See *Vervaeke v Smith* [1981] Fam 77, CA; affirmed by the House of Lords on other grounds, [1983] 1 AC 145.

[67] For the situation where the second marriage is polygamous in nature, see under 'Polygamous marriages', pp 55–60 below.

[68] On this matter the 1986 Act implements Law Commission Report No 137 (1984), on *Recognition of Foreign Nullity Decrees and Related Matters*.

[69] [1979] 2 All ER 323.

v Lawrence[70] establish that the same principle operates at common law, and that the earlier contrary decisions in *R v Brentwood Registrar, ex parte Arias*[71] and *Padolecchia v Padolecchia*[72] were erroneous.

Thus English law is now fully committed to standing by its convictions when it grants or recognises a divorce or annulment. It will permit or recognise a remarriage of a former spouse, notwithstanding the non-recognition of the divorce elsewhere (in particular, at the domicile of the divorcee or his or her new partner). No doubt the same principle must also be applied to uphold the validity of a second marriage, where the prior marriage (rather than having been dissolved or annulled) is simply void ab initio under the English conflict rules on marriage, but is valid and subsisting under the conflicts law of the domicile of one or both of the parties to the second marriage at its celebration. This situation could arise where, for example, the latter law referred capacity to enter the first marriage to the law of the nationality rather than the domicile.

There is no English legislation on the converse problem: where a divorce or annulment is denied recognition in England, but is recognised at the domicile of the parties to a remarriage at the time thereof.[73] Some dicta in *Schwebel v Ungar*[74] and *Padolecchia v Padolecchia*[75] seem to suggest that a remarriage of a divorcee could be considered valid even though his prior divorce is denied recognition. But such a result is surely absurd. If the forum does not recognise the divorce, the person remains married to his or her first spouse. If it then upholds the remarriage, he or she will have two valid monogamous husbands or wives at the same time. The true rule must be that (conversely to s 50 of the 1986 Act), where a foreign divorce or annulment is denied recognition in England, the fact that the divorce or annulment is recognised elsewhere cannot enable a supposedly former spouse to remarry in England, nor to cause a monogamous remarriage of a supposedly former spouse, wherever celebrated, to be treated as valid in England.

Another problem concerning remarriage after divorce arises where a foreign law under which a divorce, which is recognised in England, is obtained, imposes some restriction on the capacity to remarry which, by dissolving the prior marriage, it creates. If such law precludes the former spouses from remarrying for a short period during which an appeal against the divorce decree is possible, such a restriction will be given full recognition by the English courts, regardless of the domiciles at or place of celebration of the remarriage.[76] On the other hand, an incapacity imposed by the law under which the divorce was obtained by way of penalty (for example, by preventing the guilty spouse from remarrying while the innocent one remains single) will be disregarded by the English

---

[70] [1985] Fam 106.
[71] [1968] 2 QB 956.
[72] [1968] P 314.
[73] The Law Commission resolutely turned a blind eye to this problem in its Report No 137 (1984).
[74] (1963) 42 DLR(2d) 622, Ontario CA, and (1964) 48 DLR(2d) 644, Supreme Court of Canada.
[75] [1968] P 314.
[76] See *Warter v Warter* (1890) 15 PD 152, and *Miller v Teale* (1954) 92 CLR 406.

courts, except perhaps where the remarriage takes place in the country imposing the penalty and at least one of the parties to it is then domiciled there.[77]

Non-consummation

Under English internal law a marriage is voidable if it has not been consummated owing to the inability of either spouse or the wilful refusal of the respondent. Other laws may, however, treat non-consummation differently; for example, as a ground for divorce rather than annulment.

In realistic terms annulment on these grounds in English law amounts to divorce under a misleading label, since non-consummation (and even the causative inability or refusal) is a post-nuptial fact,[78] and the decree of annulment has identical effects to a divorce decree.[79] Accordingly it is submitted (in accordance with the tentative preference of Dicey & Morris)[80] that, in an English petition for annulment, these grounds for relief (like grounds for divorce) should be governed exclusively by English law as the lex fori. Thus the English court would grant annulment on these grounds in accordance with English internal law whenever it has jurisdiction to entertain a petition for annulment; that is, on the basis of either spouse's domicile at, or habitual residence for a year up to, the presentation of the petition; and the domiciles of the parties at the time of the marriage, the intended matrimonial residence, and the place of celebration should be immaterial. No actual judicial decision reaches a result inconsistent with this view. Admittedly there are dicta in some cases favouring the law of the husband's domicile at the time of the marriage, or of the intended matrimonial residence.[81]

POLYGAMOUS MARRIAGES

Nature and governing law

Marriage, as known to English internal law (and to the laws of other Western, and many other, countries), is monogamous or exclusive in nature. Under such laws a person may have only one spouse at a time, and a prior subsisting marriage to which a person is party invalidates any further marriage which he or she may attempt to enter. Our previous discussion has largely assumed that the marriage in question is monogamous in nature.

---

[77] See *Scott v Attorney-General* (1886) 11 PD 128, as explained in *Warter v Warter* (1890) 15 PD 152.

[78] For example, the causative inability may arise from a road accident occurring on the journey from the church or register office to the honeymoon hotel.

[79] See the Matrimonial Causes Act 1973, s 16.

[80] Rule 79(3).

[81] See *Robert v Robert* [1947] P 164; *De Reneville v De Reneville* [1948] P 100; *Way v Way* [1950] P 71; *Ramsay-Fairfax v Ramsay-Fairfax* [1956] P 115; and *Ponticelli v Ponticelli* [1958] P 204. See also Dicey & Morris, Rule 79(3), suggesting that, if the lex fori as such is rejected, the reference should be to the petitioner's domicile at the time of the marriage.

In contrast polygamy (or, more accurately, polygyny) is permitted by the laws of some Asian or African countries, usually reflecting Islamic law or tribal custom. Such laws permit a man to have more than one wife at the same time, and do not invalidate a marriage simply because the husband is already married.[82] A polygamous marriage is one whose nature is governed by a law which admits polygamy. At a given moment such a marriage is either actually polygamous, in that the husband does in fact have more than one wife; or merely potentially polygamous, in that there is in fact only one wife, but the applicable law would permit the husband to take another wife despite the current marriage.[83] The laws of some countries provide for both monogamous and polygamous marriages, and distinguish them according to the religion of the parties or the form of the ceremony adopted.[84] Thus references to a monogamous or polygamous country must be understood as referring to the law of the country as applied to the particular marriage in question.

The nature of a marriage (as monogamous or polygamous) at its inception is governed by the law of the place of celebration, or the law of the husband's domicile, whichever is more favourable to monogamy. It has long been clear that a marriage celebrated in England or any other monogamous country is monogamous, regardless of the spouses' domiciles.[85] More recently the decision of the Court of Appeal in *Hussain v Hussain*[86] has established that a marriage is monogamous if at its celebration the husband is domiciled in England or some other monogamous country, even if it is celebrated in a polygamous country and the wife is domiciled there; as where the marriage takes place in Islamic form in Pakistan, between a man of Islamic faith, Pakistani origin, and English domicile of choice, and a woman of Islamic faith and Pakistani domicile.[87] On the other hand it is also clear that a marriage is polygamous at inception if it is so regarded both by the law of the place of celebration and the law of the husband's domicile at the time of the marriage, even if the wife is domiciled in a monogamous country.[88]

It is clear that a marriage which is monogamous at its inception cannot

---

[82] Polyandry, under which a woman may have several husbands simultaneously, appears to be very rare, and known only among very primitive communities. No cases involving it have come before English courts. Presumably the same principles would apply if such converse cases arose.

[83] Moreover 'wives' include female sex-partners whose status receives some legal recognition (such as 'tsipsis', secondary wives or concubines, under Chinese customary law applicable in Hong Kong), even if such status is lower than that of the primary wife (or 'tsai'), married in a more formal ceremony; see *Lee v Lau* [1967] P 14.

[84] See *Penhas v Eng* [1953] AC 304.

[85] See *Chetti v Chetti* [1909] P 67; *R v Hammersmith Registrar* [1917] 1 KB 634; *Baindail v Baindail* [1946] P 122; *Maher v Maher* [1951] P 342; and *Qureshi v Qureshi* [1972] Fam 173. The only explanation for the decision in *Radwan v Radwan (No 2)* [1973] Fam 35, that a marriage celebrated at the Egyptian consulate in Paris was polygamous, is that French law must have been taken to have referred its nature to Egyptian law, as that of the sending country of the consulate and the husband's nationality.

[86] [1983] Fam 26.

[87] See Stone [1983] Fam Law 76, and Dicey & Morris, Rule 72 and Exception thereto. See also *Ali v Ali* [1968] P 564. *Hussain v Hussain* impliedly overrules the scarcely comprehensible decision in *Re Bethell* (1888) 38 ChD 220.

[88] See *Risk v Risk* [1951] P 50; *Sowa v Sowa* [1961] P 70; and *Cheni v Cheni* [1965] P 85.

subsequently change its nature, even if the husband changes his domicile or religion and purports to enter a polygamous marriage with another woman;[89] and that, in the event of such a purported remarriage, intercourse by the husband with the subsequent 'wife' amounts to adultery against the monogamous wife, on which she can rely for the purpose of obtaining a divorce or other matrimonial relief.[90] It is probable, indeed, that considerations of certainty and coherence dictate that a subsisting monogamous marriage should invalidate a subsequent polygamous marriage for all purposes, as was recognised by the General Tax Commissioners in *Nabi v Heaton*,[91] though subsequent developments in that case were rather unsatisfactory: after the Crown had declined to rely on this point, their decision was affirmed on other grounds by Vinelott J,[92] and then reversed by consent in the Court of Appeal.[93] The point had been left open by the Privy Council, on appeal from the Gambia, in *Drammeh v Drammeh*,[94] while its earlier contrary ruling, on appeal from Sri Lanka, in *Attorney-General for Ceylon v Reid*[95] had emphasised the situation in Sri Lanka, where the personal law depended on religion and there was a constitutional right to change one's religion, and had reserved its position on the solution for English courts. On this problem the Law Commission, in its Report No 146 (1985), refused to recommend any legislation.

On the other hand, there are various ways in which a marriage which is polygamous at its inception may subsequently become monogamous:

(1) if, while it is potentially polygamous, an event occurs, such as a change of religion by the husband or the birth of a child, which has the effect, under the law of the place of celebration or the law of the husband's domicile at the time of the event, of precluding the husband from taking another wife during the subsistence of the marriage;[96]

(2) if, while the marriage is potentially polygamous, the spouses go through another marriage ceremony with each other in a monogamous country;[97]

(3) if, while the marriage is potentially polygamous, legislation precluding the husband from taking another wife during its subsistence comes into force in the country in which the marriage was celebrated or the husband is domiciled when the legislation comes into force;[98]

[89] See *Mehta v Mehta* [1945] 2 All ER 690; *Cheni v Cheni* [1965] P 85; *Parkasho v Singh* [1968] P 233; *Attorney-General for Ceylon v Reid* [1965] AC 720, and *Drammeh v Drammeh* (1970) 78 Ceylon Law Weekly 55.

[90] See *Attorney-General for Ceylon v Reid* [1965] AC 720; and *Drammeh v Drammeh* (1970) 78 Ceylon Law Weekly 55. Cf *Onobrauche v Onobrauche* (1978) 8 Fam Law 107, holding that where a man has two polygamous wives, intercourse with one does not constitute adultery against the other.

[91] [1981] 1 WLR 1052.

[92] [1981] 1 WLR 1052.

[93] [1983] 1 WLR 626.

[94] (1970) 78 Ceylon Law Weekly 55.

[95] [1965] AC 720.

[96] See the *Sinha Peerage Claim* [1946] 1 All ER 348, and *Cheni v Cheni* [1965] P 85.

[97] See *Ohochuku v Ohochuku* [1960] 1 WLR 183, as explained in *Cheni v Cheni* [1965] P 85 and *Parkasho v Singh* [1968] P 233.

[98] See *Parkasho v Singh* [1968] P 233, and *R v Sagoo* [1975] 2 All ER 926, involving respectively the Indian and the Kenyan Hindu Marriage Acts.

(4) if, while the marriage is potentially polygamous, the husband becomes domiciled in England or some other monogamous country.[99]

Presumably if a husband who has more than one polygamous wife acquires a domicile in a monogamous country, and subsequently all but one of those marriages terminate by divorce or death of the wives while the husband remains so domiciled, the remaining marriage will then become monogamous. But no such change in nature can occur while there are two subsisting polygamous marriages.[100]

Capacity for polygamy

'Capacity for polygamy' must be understood in a limited sense. It refers to the possible incapacitating effect of the fact that the marriage in question is polygamous in nature, taken with (if it be the case) the further fact that the husband is already married at the date of the marriage in question, so that the marriage is at inception actually (and not merely potentially) polygamous. Even if a marriage is polygamous in nature, capacity in terms of consanguinity, lack of age, or other factors which would be equally relevant if the marriage were monogamous, does not fall within the concept of 'capacity for polygamy', but remains governed by the dual domicile doctrine and its various exceptions,[101] in the same way as if the marriage were monogamous.

In an isolated (but clear and fully considered) decision, *Radwan v Radwan (No 2)*,[102] Cumming-Bruce J ruled that the dual domicile doctrine does not extend to capacity for polygamy, which is governed instead by the law of the intended matrimonial residence. He therefore upheld, in accordance with Egyptian law, as that of the intended matrimonial residence, a marriage celebrated before 1971 at the Egyptian consulate in Paris between a woman domiciled in England and a man who was domiciled in Egypt and was already polygamously married.[103] The decision was criticised by most commentators, but defended by a few, including the present writer.[104] However on reflection it no longer seems possible, in view of the approach adopted by the Court of Appeal in *Hussain v Hussain*,[105] to maintain that *Radwan* represents the law. The reasoning in *Hussain* effectively asserts that the dual domicile doctrine applies to capacity for polygamy, as well as to other aspects of capacity to marry.

---

[99] See *Ali v Ali* [1968] P 564, and *R v Sagoo* [1975] 2 All ER 926.
[100] See *Re Sehota* [1978] 1 WLR 1506.
[101] See 'Validity: Capacity and consent', pp 49–53 above.
[102] [1973] Fam 35.
[103] He added that in view of the saving made now by s 14(1) of the Matrimonial Causes Act 1973 (then s 4(1) of the Nullity of Marriage Act 1971) for choice of law rules which lead to the application of foreign law, the same result would be reached in the case of a similar marriage celebrated after July 1971.
[104] See [1983] Fam Law 76.
[105] [1983] Fam 26.

In the light of *Hussain v Hussain*,[106] the position where a person domiciled in England purports to marry in a polygamous country appears to be as follows:

(1) If the husband is already married, the purported marriage is rendered void by s 11(b) of the Matrimonial Causes Act 1973, which specifies that a marriage is void if at its celebration either party was already married, if the marriage was celebrated after July 1971, or under a common law rule of equivalent content, if it was celebrated before August 1971. If the husband (and not merely the wife) is domiciled in England, the marriage is probably monogamous (rather than actually polygamous) in nature;[107] but, whatever its nature, it is certainly void because, being married and domiciled in England, the husband lacks capacity to marry. If the wife and not the husband is domiciled in England, the marriage is actually polygamous, but void because of the wife's incapacity under the law of her domicile to marry a married man.

(2) If the spouses are both single, and the husband is domiciled in England, as in *Hussain v Hussain*[108] itself, the marriage is monogamous and valid. Probably the same applies if the husband is domiciled in another monogamous country and the wife is domiciled in England.

(3) If the spouses are both single, and the husband is domiciled in a polygamous country but the wife is domiciled in England, and the marriage is celebrated after July 1971, then the marriage is potentially polygamous and it is rendered void by s 11(d) of the Matrimonial Causes Act 1973, which specifies that a marriage celebrated after that date is void if it is an actually or potentially polygamous marriage entered into outside England and either spouse was at its celebration domiciled in England.

(4) If the spouses are both single, and the husband is domiciled in a polygamous country but the wife is domiciled in England, and the marriage is celebrated before August 1971, then although the marriage is potentially polygamous, it is probably valid. For, apart from s 11(d), which is inapplicable on account of the date, there is no convincing authority that English law incapacitates a single Englishwoman from marrying a single man, merely because the law of the husband's domicile and the place of celebration would permit him to marry an additional wife,[109] and no sensible reason why it should.

In its Report No 146 (1985) on polygamous marriages, the Law Commission has proposed legislation repealing s 11(d) and abolishing any rule preventing a person whose capacity is governed by English law from entering into a poten-

---

[106] [1983] Fam 26.
[107] Cf Dicey & Morris, Rule 72, Exception.
[108] [1983] Fam 26.
[109] The authorities once referred to by Dicey & Morris in favour of such a common law rule are: *Re Bethell* (1888) 38 ChD 220, which is open to criticism and is inconsistent with *Hussain v Hussain*; *Re Ullee* (1885) 53 LT 711, where the marriage took place in England and the husband was already married; *Lendrum v Chakravati* [1929] SLT 96, where the marriage took place in Scotland; and *Risk v Risk* [1951] P 50, where the decision was solely on the court's power to award matrimonial relief. Since the 11th ed (1987), Dicey's editors have abandoned the assertion of such a rule. See now 12th ed, Rule 75. See also Stone [1983] Fam Law 76.

tially polygamous marriage. The abolition would extend to existing marriages, subject to transitional savings for existing annulments, intervening marriages, and existing property or similar rights. The Law Commission considered that this would eliminate any distinction between monogamous and potentially polygamous marriages, but that is doubtful, for it overlooks the problem of the validity of a subsequent actually polygamous marriage. As argued above, a prior subsisting monogamous marriage does, while a prior subsisting potentially polygamous marriage does not, invalidate a subsequent actually polygamous marriage.[110]

Extent of recognition

In general, English law will now give similar effects, in the various contexts in which marriage is relevant, to a valid (actually or potentially) polygamous marriage as it gives to a valid monogamous marriage. As Dicey & Morris put it,[111] a valid polygamous marriage will be recognised in England as a valid marriage unless there is some strong reason to the contrary; that is, a strong reason peculiar to the particular issue in question. Much has changed since the 19th century, when there was a tendency to treat a polygamous marriage as non-existent for many purposes.

More specifically, until 1972 the English courts considered themselves unable to grant matrimonial relief (such as divorce, annulment, or even inter-spousal maintenance) in respect of a marriage of a polygamous nature, even if it was and had always been only potentially polygamous.[112] But this rule was abolished, even as regards actually polygamous marriages, by provisions of the Matrimonial Proceedings (Polygamous Marriages) Act 1972[113] which are now consolidated as s 47 of the Matrimonial Causes Act 1973. Moreover, as regards the substantive grounds on which an English divorce may be obtained by a polygamous wife, although intercourse by the husband with one actually polygamous wife does not constitute adultery against another polygamous wife,[114] his entry into a second polygamous marriage without the consent of the first polygamous wife usually amounts to unreasonable conduct towards her, at least if she is by then domiciled or habitually resident in England.[115]

Similarly a valid polygamous marriage will be effective to create proprietary rights under the Matrimonial Homes Act 1983,[116] and to make available the

---

[110] See text to notes 91–95 above.

[111] Rule 76.

[112] See *Hyde v Hyde* (1866) LR 1 P & D 130; *Risk v Risk* [1951] P 50; and *Sowa v Sowa* [1961] P 70. Cf *Iman Din v National Assistance Board* [1967] 2 QB 213, treating a valid polygamous marriage as sufficient to enable the authorities to reclaim from the husband the predecessor of income support provided to his wife and children.

[113] This implemented Law Commission Report No 42 (1971).

[114] See *Onobrauche v Onobrauche* (1978) 8 Fam Law 107, and Law Commission Report No 42, at para 50.

[115] See *Quoraishi v Quoraishi* [1985] FLR 780.

[116] See s 10(2).

summary procedure for the resolution of inter-spousal property disputes provided by s 17 of the Married Women's Property Act 1882.[117]

A valid subsisting polygamous marriage invalidates a subsequent monogamous marriage for civil purposes,[118] but will not support a criminal prosecution for bigamy,[119] though if the subsequent ceremony took place in England, the man could probably be convicted of making a false statutory declaration of single status, contrary to s 3 of the Perjury Act 1911.[120]

The children of a valid polygamous marriage count as legitimate for English purposes, and qualify as such to receive property under a succession governed by English law[121] (insofar as legitimacy remains relevant for such purposes).[122] But it is probable that, even after the entry into force of the Family Law Reform Act 1987 on 4 April 1988, children of an actually polygamous marriage will be unable to qualify as heirs for the purpose of inheriting titles of honour or property limited to devolve therewith.[123] In the sphere of child protection, a valid polygamous marriage prevents a child-wife from being in moral danger, so as to be subject to child care powers of local authorities, merely because she is cohabiting with her husband.[124]

A valid polygamous marriage will also be recognised for the purpose of enabling the wife to take property under a succession governed by English law; and if there are several polygamous widows of a deceased whose intestacy is governed by English law, the proprietary rights which English intestacy law confers on a surviving spouse will be divided between the widows.[125] A valid polygamous widow will also be able to claim financial provision as a widow under the Inheritance (Provision for Family and Dependants) Act 1975.[126]

A valid polygamous marriage is effective for the purpose of entitling the husband to a married man's tax allowance.[127] Conversely, the Immigration Act 1971 (as amended) provides for the deportation of persons other than British citizens if they belong to the family of a person who is deported, and defines family members as including two or more wives.[128] In addition, s 2 of the Immigration Act 1988 in effect denies the right of abode in the United Kingdom to a polygamous wife of a Commonwealth citizen if she has not been living in the

---

[117] See *Chaudry v Chaudry* [1975] 3 All ER 687, affirmed on other grounds [1976] 1 All ER 805.
[118] See *Baindail v Baindail* [1946] P 122.
[119] See *R v Sarwan Singh* [1946] 3 All ER 612, and *R v Sagoo* [1975] 2 All ER 926.
[120] See Dicey & Morris, at p 705.
[121] See the *Sinha Peerage Claim* [1946] 1 All ER 348, and *Bamgbose v Daniel* [1955] AC 107. Cf *Hashmi v Hashmi* [1971] 3 All ER 1253, recognising the legitimacy of children of an invalid marriage because they were legitimate under the law of the father's domicile.
[122] For the irrelevance of legitimacy in relation to English dispositions made and intestacies arising after 4 April 1988, see the Family Law Reform Act 1987, ss 1 and 18–19. For earlier dispositions, see the Family Law Reform Act 1969, ss 14 and 15.
[123] See the *Sinha Peerage Claim*, and s 19(4) of the Family Law Reform Act 1987.
[124] See *Mohammed v Knott* [1969] 1 QB 1.
[125] See *Coleman v Shang* [1961] AC 481, and the Penang cases [1920] AC 369, [1926] AC 529 and [1930] AC 346.
[126] See *Re Sehota* [1978] 1 WLR 1506.
[127] See *Nabi v Heaton* [1983] 1 WLR 626, reversing by consent [1981] 1 WLR 1052.
[128] See ss 3(5)(c) and 5(4).

United Kingdom and there is another wife of the husband who has been living in the United Kingdom.[129]

A polygamous wife's claim for benefits under the Social Security Act 1975 on the basis of her husband's contributions, and to child benefit, is regulated by SI 1975/561 and SI 1976/965. In general a valid polygamous marriage counts for such purposes as regards times when it is only potentially polygamous; but for the purpose of the wife's retirement pension, it is enough that the marriage was only potentially polygamous when she became entitled to the pension, and it is immaterial that the husband has subsequently taken another polygamous wife.

For the purposes of income support, housing benefit and family credit, unmarried couples are treated in the same way as married couples, but it is also specifically provided that 'partner', in relation to a claimant, includes each of two or more polygamous spouses of the claimant living in the same household with him.[130] In such cases full benefit is given in respect of the most needy of the polygamous wives, and some lesser benefit in relation to the other(s).[131] Applying the same principle in reverse, the Child Support Act 1991 largely ignores marital status, but (characteristically) its assessment regulations take care to penalise an actually polygamous household by reducing allowable housing costs.[132]

---

[129] See also SI 1988/1133.

[130] See SI 1987/1967, reg 2(1); SI 1987/1971, reg 2(1) and (3); SI 1987/1973, reg 2(1); and SI 1988/662, reg 1(2).

[131] See SI 1987/1967, reg 18; SI 1987/1971, reg 17; and SI 1987/1973, reg 46. See also SI 1987/1967, Sched 7; SI 1987/1971, regs 3(2), 11 and 18; and SI 1987/1973, reg 10(2).

[132] See SI 1992/1815, especially regs 1(2) and 17(c). See note 96, below and also text to Chapter 4.

4

MATRIMONIAL PROCEEDINGS

ENGLISH STATUS PROCEEDINGS

English jurisdiction

The international jurisdiction of the English High Court and divorce county courts to entertain proceedings concerning marital status is now governed by the Domicile and Matrimonial Proceedings Act 1973, s 5 and Sched 1, and the Family Law Act 1986, s 55. The 1973 Act regulates English jurisdiction to entertain proceedings for divorce, judicial separation, annulment of marriage, or presumption of death and consequential dissolution of marriage; and the 1986 Act applies the same jurisdictional principles to English proceedings for a declaration relating to marital status – that is, for a declaration that a marriage was valid at inception, or subsisted, or did not subsist, on a specified date, or that a divorce, annulment or separation obtained outside England is, or is not, recognised in England.[1]

Proceedings concerning marital status are excluded from the scope of the 1968 and Lugano Conventions on civil jurisdiction and judgments[2] by art 1[2](1) thereof, which refers to 'the status or legal capacity of natural persons'.[3] These Conventions do, however, extend to claims between spouses for maintenance or other financial provision, and they are taken into account when English jurisdiction to entertain claims for familial financial provision is examined later in this chapter.[4]

---

[1] Part III (ss 55–63) of the Family Law Act 1986, which entered into force on 4 April 1988, implements Law Commission Report No 132 (1984), on *Declarations in Family Matters*. Part III has replaced s 45 of the Matrimonial Causes Act 1973 and Ord 15, r 16 of the Rules of the Supreme Court 1965 (as amended). The powers conferred by Part III are exclusive; see s 58(4). Part III also deals (in ss 56 and 57) with declarations as to filial status; see Chapter 5, 'Children: filial relationships', below. Under Part III, if the relevant matters are proved by the applicant, the court must make the declaration sought unless to do so would manifestly be contrary to public policy; see s 58(1), and cf *Puttick v Attorney-General* [1980] Fam 1. A declaration under Part III binds the whole world, including the Crown, and the Attorney-General is entitled to intervene in Part III proceedings; see ss 58(2) and 59. But the declaration does not affect any final judgment or decree already pronounced; see s 60(3).

[2] On these Conventions, see Chapters 7–11 and 14, below.

[3] On this exclusion, see Chapter 7, under 'Subject-matter', pp 121–23 below.

[4] See under 'Familial financial provision', p 78 *et seq.* below.

In general, English jurisdiction to entertain proceedings concerning marital status exists if at least one of the spouses (whether the husband or the wife, the petitioner or the respondent) was domiciled in England at the institution of the proceedings, or had been habitually resident in England for the year up to such institution. Any of these four possible connections suffices to found English jurisdiction to entertain proceedings for a divorce or judicial separation,[5] for the annulment of a marriage,[6] or for a marital declaration.[7] In the case of proceedings for annulment or a marital declaration, it is also sufficient, where a spouse has died, that he was domiciled in England at his death, or had been habitually resident in England for the year up to his death.[8] But in the case of proceedings under s 19 of the Matrimonial Causes Act 1973 for a decree presuming that a spouse has died and dissolving the marriage, only the petitioning spouse's English domicile at or one-year habitual residence up to the institution of the proceedings is taken into account, and not the domicile or habitual residence of the allegedly deceased spouse.[9]

In general the connecting factor (a spouse's English domicile or one-year habitual residence) must exist at the institution of the proceedings in question. But if, while proceedings for divorce, judicial separation or annulment, over which the court has jurisdiction, are pending, other (supplemental or cross) proceedings for divorce, judicial separation or annulment are instituted in respect of the same marriage, the court is competent to entertain these other proceedings, even if meanwhile the connecting factor has ceased to exist.[10] Moreover this principle has full parasitic effect, so that (for example) a fourth proceeding will be competent if it is commenced while only the third proceeding is pending, the third having been competent only because commenced while the second was pending, and the second having been competent only because commenced while the original was pending; the institution of the original being the only time at which a sufficient connecting factor existed.

In English proceedings for divorce, judicial separation or annulment, the English courts also have wide powers under ss 22–24 of the Matrimonial Causes Act 1973 to make ancillary orders for financial provision or property adjustment between the spouses and their children.[11] In general the court's jurisdiction to entertain the principal proceedings concerning status automatically carries with it the further competence to make such ancillary orders.[12] For, although the 1968 and Lugano Conventions on civil jurisdiction and judgments[13] extend to

---

[5] See s 5(2) of the Domicile and Matrimonial Proceedings Act 1973.
[6] See s 5(3)(a) and (b).
[7] See s 55(2)(a) and (b) of the Family Law Act 1986.
[8] See s 5(3)(c) of the Domicile and Matrimonial Proceedings Act 1973, and s 55(2)(c) of the Family Law Act 1986.
[9] See s 5(4) of the Domicile and Matrimonial Proceedings Act 1973.
[10] See s 5(5) of the Domicile and Matrimonial Proceedings Act 1973.
[11] On orders as to child custody, made ancillarily in English matrimonial proceedings, see 'Child custody and abduction: English jurisdiction', in Chapter 5, p 94 *et seq.* below.
[12] See Dicey & Morris, Rule 88(1).
[13] See Chapters 7–11 and 14 below.

claims for maintenance, art 5(2) of those Conventions (and of Sched 4 to the Civil Jurisdiction and Judgments Act 1982) confer jurisdiction on a court of a contracting state (or a part of the United Kingdom) to entertain a maintenance claim against a defendant who is domiciled (in the sense used for the purposes of the Conventions) in another contracting state (or another part of the United Kingdom), if it is made ancillarily in proceedings concerning status and the court has jurisdiction under its own law to entertain the status proceedings. However there are some rare circumstances in which the Conventions can prevent an English court, properly seised of proceedings concerning matrimonial status, from also making ancillary financial orders, and these are considered under 'Familial financial provision', p 78 *et seq.* below.

Staying English matrimonial proceedings

Special provision is made by s 5(6) of and Sched 1 to the Domicile and Matrimonial Proceedings Act 1973 for the staying of English matrimonial proceedings in favour of proceedings which are concurrently pending elsewhere in respect of the same marriage. Section 5(6)(b) makes clear that these provisions are in addition to, and not in derogation from, the general discretion conferred on the English courts by the common law doctrine of forum non conveniens, to decline jurisdiction to entertain English proceedings on the ground that the matter could more appropriately be tried in a foreign court.[14] Thus in matrimonial cases the common law discretion remains available where proceedings have not yet been instituted in the appropriate foreign court,[15] but where there are simultaneously pending proceedings in England and elsewhere, as contemplated by Sched 1, the statutory provisions will prevail.

Paragraph 8 of Sched 1 requires the English court to stay English *divorce* proceedings if it appears, on application by a spouse, before the beginning of the trial on the merits, that:

(1) divorce or annulment proceedings in respect of the same marriage are pending (and not stayed) in another part of the British Islands (that is: Scotland, Northern Ireland, any of the Channel Islands, or the Isle of Man; but not Eire);

(2) the spouses last resided together, at or before the commencement of the English proceedings, in such other part; and

(3) at least one of them was habitually resident in that part throughout the year preceding the end of their last residence together before the English proceedings.[16]

---

[14] See *The Spiliada* [1987] 1 AC 460; and Chapter 8, under 'The mandatory character of Title II', p 149 below.

[15] The decision of Bush J in *Kapur v Kapur* [1984] FLR 920, that, in the absence of concurrent proceedings elsewhere, the English court has no power to decline matrimonial jurisdiction on grounds of hardship, apparent unfairness or similar considerations, ignores s 5(6)(b), and must be considered as per incuriam.

[16] See eg *Trezise v Trezise* (1991) *The Times*, 2 August.

Paragraph 9 of Sched 1 applies in other cases where, normally before the trial on the merits, in English proceedings for divorce, judicial separation, annulment, or a marital declaration, it appears that proceedings relating to the same marriage are pending outside England. The English court is then given a discretion to stay the English proceedings if it considers that the balance of fairness, including convenience, as between the spouses, makes it appropriate for the foreign proceedings to be disposed of before further steps are taken in the English proceedings. In considering this balance of fairness and convenience, the court must take account of all relevant factors, including convenience of witnesses and relative delay or expense.

In *de Dampierre v de Dampierre*,[17] the House of Lords ruled that the test of 'balance of fairness' under para 9 was similar to the general test for declining jurisdiction in favour of a foreign court laid down in *The Spiliada*.[18] Accordingly, applying para 9, they declined jurisdiction to entertain a wife's English divorce proceedings (apparently founded on the husband's habitual residence) in favour of the husband's concurrent French divorce proceedings, since both spouses were French nationals and the wife was no longer resident in England but in the United States, and in such circumstances it would not be unjust to deprive the wife of the more favourable English rules on financial provision.

The general power of the English courts to restrain a party by injunction from continuing to prosecute foreign proceedings which he has commenced, on the ground that their continuance would be oppressive,[19] extends to matrimonial proceedings. Thus in *Hemain v Hemain*,[20] where the spouses were French nationals but the matrimonial home had been in England, the Court of Appeal temporarily restrained the husband from prosecuting his French divorce proceedings until his English application for a stay of the wife's English divorce proceedings had been determined.

Choice of law in English matrimonial proceedings

In English matrimonial proceedings (as well as in any other English proceedings where such a question arises), the validity of a marriage is determined in accordance with the choice of law rules examined in Chapter 3 above. These in general refer formalities to the lex loci celebrationis, a person's capacity and consent to the law of his or her antenuptial domicile, and non-consummation to the lex fori.

Moreover the law which governs the relevant aspect of validity determines also the incidents of any invalidity which it imposes, for the purpose of classifying the marriage as void ab initio or merely voidable in the English sense; that is, as rendering the marriage open to collateral attack in any proceedings in which

---

[17] [1988] 1 AC 92.
[18] [1987] 1 AC 460. See Chapter 8, under 'The mandatory character of Title II', p 149 below.
[19] See *Société Nationale Industrielle Aerospatiale v Lee Kui Juk* [1987] AC 871; and pp 156–57 below.
[20] [1988] 2 FLR 388.

its existence is relevant, or as merely permitting direct attack by means of proceedings for annulment.[21] But the rule laid down by s 16 of the Matrimonial Causes Act 1973, that an English annulment of a voidable marriage has only prospective effect, probably applies regardless of any contrary rule of the law which governs the aspect of invalidity in question.[22]

With the exception of the validity of the marriage, all issues in English matrimonial proceedings are determined in accordance with English internal law. This includes the substantive grounds for divorce[23] or judicial separation; and the court's powers to award ancillary financial or proprietary relief, and ancillary relief relating to the custody of children. But in applying the vague rules of English internal law, referring to intolerable behaviour or good cause for separating, the laws and social customs of a foreign country with which the parties are connected may have some relevance.[24]

On capacity to remarry after an English divorce or annulment, see Chapter 3, 'Marriage', at pp 53–55 above.

RECOGNITION OF FOREIGN DIVORCES, SEPARATIONS AND ANNULMENTS

Introduction

The recognition in the United Kingdom of foreign divorces, legal separations and annulments of marriage is now governed by Part II (ss 44–54) of the Family Law Act 1986 ('the 1986 Act'), which entered into force on 4 April 1988. The 1986 Act implements most of the recommendations made by the Law Commission in their Report No 137 (1984) on *Recognition of Foreign Nullity Decrees and Related Matters*, though Parliament has departed from the Law Commission recommendations in respect of non-procedural divorces. The 1986 Act tidies up the earlier legislation on divorces and separations, and extends the revised legislation to annulments, whose recognition was previously governed by the common law.

As regards divorces and legal separations, the 1986 Act replaces the Recognition of Divorces and Legal Separations Act 1971 ('the 1971 Act'), as amended by the Domicile and Matrimonial Proceedings Act 1973 ('the 1973 Act'). The 1971 Act had implemented the Hague Convention of 1 June 1970 on the Recognition of Divorces and Legal Separations, with extensions and other provisions recommended by the Law Commission in their Report No 34 (1970), and the

---

[21] See *De Reneville v De Reneville* [1948] P 100; *Szechter v Szechter* [1971] P 286; and the Matrimonial Causes Act 1973, s 14.

[22] See Dicey & Morris, at p 725.

[23] See *Zanelli v Zanelli* (1948) 64 TLR 556, and the former s 46(2) of the Matrimonial Causes Act 1973, now repealed as unnecessary (see Law Commission Report No 48 (1972), at paras 103–108) by the Domicile and Matrimonial Proceedings Act 1973. Cf the Matrimonial Causes Act 1973, s 14 (on nullity).

[24] See *Quoraishi v Quoraishi* [1985] FLR 780; and Law Commission Report No 48, at para 105.

1986 Act continues its implementation.[25] As regards annulments, there was no earlier legislation, and the 1986 Act replaces the rules of common law. In general the 1986 Act treats divorces, legal separations and annulments in the same way.

Like the 1971 Act as amended by the 1973 Act, the 1986 Act provides for recognition throughout the United Kingdom (that is, in England and Wales, in Scotland, and in Northern Ireland).[26] As regards time, the 1986 Act applies to divorces, legal separations and annulments granted or obtained before its commencement date (4 April 1988), as well as to ones obtained subsequently, and operates so as to require or preclude (as appropriate) recognition in relation to times before as well as after that date, with the exceptions that it does not affect property to which a person became entitled before the commencement date, and it does not affect recognition of a divorce, separation or annulment whose recognition had been decided by a competent court in the British Islands before the commencement date.[27] There are, however, some savings which continue the recognition of certain 'old' divorces, separations and annulments in accordance with some former rules which are otherwise abolished.[28]

Part II of the 1986 Act is concerned only with recognition of a status decree (or equivalent) as such, and does not require recognition of findings of fault made in proceedings for divorce, legal separation or annulment, nor of maintenance, custody or other ancillary orders made in such proceedings.[29] Its provisions on capacity to remarry after a divorce or annulment have been considered in Chapter 3, 'Marriage' above.[30]

Under the 1986 Act four types of 'foreign' divorce, legal separation or annulment are effectively distinguished:

(1) 'British decrees': divorces, legal separations and annulments granted by a civil court in the British Islands, which comprise England and Wales, Scotland, Northern Ireland, the Channel Islands, and the Isle of Man (but do not include the Irish Republic);[31]

(2) 'internal non-procedural divorces': divorces obtained in the British Islands otherwise than by a decree granted by a civil court;

(3) 'overseas decrees': divorces, legal separations and annulments obtained by means of proceedings in a country outside the British Islands;

---

[25] Current parties in the Hague Convention include the United Kingdom, Australia, Italy, the Netherlands, Portugal, Denmark, Norway, Sweden, Finland, Switzerland, Cyprus and Egypt; see (1990) 29 ILM 1072.

[26] See s 54(1).

[27] See s 52(1) and (2), which are similar to s 10(4) of the 1971 Act.

[28] See s 52(4) and (5). The more important of these former rules will be mentioned at relevant points. Others relate to divorce decrees was registered under s 1 of the Indian and Colonial Divorce Jurisdiction Act 1926; divorces and annulments recognised under s 4 of the Matrimonial Causes (War Marriages) Act 1944; and overseas legal separations recognised under the Recognition of Divorces and Legal Separations Act 1971. But it is worth emphasising that there is no such saving for annulments recognised under the common law rules formerly applicable.

[29] See s 51(5), following s 8(3) of the 1971 Act.

[30] See pp 53–55 above.

[31] See Sched 1 to the Interpretation Act 1978.

(4) 'overseas non-procedural divorces': divorces obtained outside the British Islands without proceedings.

British decrees

By s 44(2) of the 1986 Act, a divorce, judicial separation or annulment granted at any date by a civil court in any part of the British Islands must be recognised in the other parts of the United Kingdom.[32]

Unlike in the case of overseas decrees, there is no requirement of a connecting factor between one of the spouses and the territory in which the decree was granted, and no power to refuse recognition on grounds of procedural unfairness or public policy. The sole exceptions to recognition of British decrees are specified by s 51(1) and (2), and relate to irreconcilability with a prior decision given or recognised in England, or to the absence of a subsisting marriage.[33]

Internal non-procedural divorces

By s 44(1) of the 1986 Act, no divorce or annulment obtained in the British Islands can be recognised in the United Kingdom unless it was granted by a civil court.[34] This covers religious divorces, such as a 'bare' talaq under classical Islamic Hanafi law,[35] or a 'gett' under Jewish law.[36] However a transitional provision permits the continued recognition of such a divorce, if it was obtained before 1974 and was recognised in the country or countries in which the spouses were domiciled at the time it was obtained.[37]

Overseas divorces, legal separations and annulments

Section 45 of the 1986 Act defines 'an overseas divorce, annulment or legal separation' as a divorce, annulment or legal separation obtained in a country outside the British Islands, and specifies that such a divorce, annulment or legal separation is to be recognised in the United Kingdom if, and only if, it is entitled to recognition under the normal provisions of Part II of the 1986 Act, or under the transitional provisions contained in s 52, or under some other statute.[38]

---

[32] This replaces s 1 of the 1971 Act, which was limited to decrees granted after 1971. The usual transitional provisions under Part II of the 1986 Act apply in relation to 'old' British divorce or separation decrees, even if granted before 1972; see s 52(1)–(3).

[33] These exceptions also apply to overseas decrees, and are considered under 'Overseas decrees: non-connectional exceptions', pp 74–5 below.

[34] This replaces s 16(1) of the 1973 Act.

[35] See text to note 42 below.

[36] See *Maples v Maples* [1988] Fam 14, decided under s 16 of the 1973 Act.

[37] See s 52(4) and (5)(a) of the 1986 Act, *Har-Shefi v Har-Shefi* [1953] P 220, and *Qureshi v Qureshi* [1972] Fam 173.

[38] Decrees on marital status are not within the scope of the Foreign Judgments (Reciprocal Enforcement) Act 1933 (considered in Chapter 14 below); see *Maples v Maples* [1988] Fam 14.

For an overseas divorce, annulment or legal separation to be recognised in the United Kingdom under the normal provisions of Part II, whether it was obtained by means of or without proceedings, s 46(1)(a) and (2)(a) require that it must be effective under the law of the country in which it was obtained.[39] Where a state comprises several territories in which different systems of law are in force in matters of divorce, annulment or legal separation, each territory is treated as a separate country for the purposes of Part II, except as regards recognition on the basis of a spouse's nationality.[40]

The 1986 Act distinguishes explicitly between overseas divorces, legal separations and annulments which were obtained by means of proceedings (here referred to as 'overseas decrees'), and overseas divorces which were obtained otherwise than by means of proceedings (here referred to as 'overseas non-procedural divorces'), and makes different provision for the two cases. Section 54(1) defines 'proceedings' as 'judicial or other proceedings', a phrase which was previously used, and caused difficulty, in s 2 of the 1971 Act. Parliament rejected the advice of the Law Commission to define 'proceedings' so as to include any acts by means of which a divorce is obtained, and the new provisions make it impossible now to maintain that that is the correct interpretation of 'proceedings'; an argument for which there was some authority and much reason in relation to]afo9 the earlier legislation.[41]

The Act presumably adopts the definition given by Oliver LJ in *Chaudhary v Chaudhary*,[42] that there are no 'proceedings' where the divorce results from an entirely private act of one or both of the spouses, even if witnesses to the act are required; some agency, whether lay or religious, established or recognised by the state, must have some function which is more than merely probative, though it need not have a power of veto. Thus there are no proceedings in the case of a 'bare talaq' under classical Islamic law of the Hanafi school, which is still applicable today in many Oriental countries, including Saudi Arabia, Dubai, India and the territory of Kashmir in Pakistan. Under that law a marriage between Moslems may be dissolved, with automatic and immediate effect,

---

[39] This accords with s 2(b) of the 1971 Act, but differs from the position at common law and under s 6 of the 1971 Act, under which:

(1) in the case of a judicial decree, ineffectiveness in the country of grant, with which a sufficient connecting factor existed, was disregarded if it was due to a mere error of procedure (as in *Pemberton v Hughes* [1899] 1 Ch 781) or of substantive law (as in *Merker v Merker* [1963] P 283), but not if it was due to impropriety in the appointment of the judge (as in *Adams v Adams* [1970] 3 All ER 572, and *McGill v Robson* (1972) 116 SJ 37) or to the lack of power of the particular court to grant the relevant type of relief (as in *Papadopoulos v Papadopoulos* [1930] P 55);

(2) in the case of a non-judicial divorce, recognition at the domicile sufficed, even if the divorce was not effective in the country where it was obtained (cf *Har-Shefi v Har-Shefi* [1953] P 220, and *Qureshi v Qureshi* [1972] Fam 173).

[40] See s 49. Cf the decision at common law in *Messina v Smith* [1971] P 322, recognising a Nevada divorce on the basis of the wife's real and substantial connection with the United States, since under the 'full-faith-and-credit' clause of the federal Constitution the divorce had to be recognised in all other states of the Union.

[41] See *Quazi v Quazi* [1980] AC 744; *Zaal v Zaal* (1982) 4 FLR 284; and Stone (1985) 14 Anglo-American Law Review 363.

[42] [1984] 3 All ER 1017.

simply by the husband solemnly pronouncing three times the word, 'talaq' (meaning 'I divorce you'), orally or in writing, in the presence of witnesses. The wife's consent is unnecessary, and she need not be present at the pronounce- ment of the talaq nor even be notified subsequently. As Oliver LJ explained, in the case of a 'bare talaq' there is no formality other than ritual performance, and no public or publicly recognised authority is involved at all, even by way of registration. Similarly there would be no proceedings, in the sense envisaged by the British legislation, where a divorce results automatically from a change of religion by one of the spouses.[43] On the other hand, a 'gett', under Jewish religious law, involves 'proceedings', since the necessary document must be delivered by the husband and accepted by the wife before a religious auth- ority.[44]

In modern times some Moslem countries, such as Pakistan (except Kashmir), while retaining the husband's right to dissolve a marriage by talaq, have imposed procedural requirements designed to protect wives. In Pakistan the Muslim Family Laws Ordinance 1961 requires a husband who has pronounced talaq to give written notice of the talaq, as soon as practicable, to a specified official, and to supply a copy of the notice to the wife. The official must then attempt to establish an arbitration council, including representatives of the spouses, with a view to bringing about a reconciliation and a consequent revo- cation of the talaq by the husband, but the spouses are not compelled to co- operate with the arbitration. The talaq does not dissolve the marriage immedi- ately on its pronouncement, and the marriage continues to subsist until 90 days after the notice is received by the official. But unless the husband meanwhile revokes the talaq, the marriage is automatically dissolved at the end of the 90- day period. Thus the husband can still insist on a divorce, despite the wife's objections and without satisfying any court or official that the marriage has broken down or that the wife has misbehaved in any way. Such a divorce may be referred to as an 'officially notified talaq'. The decision of the House of Lords in *Quazi v Quazi*[45] established that an officially notified talaq involved 'proceed- ings' within the meaning of ss 2 and 3 of the 1971 Act, and thus qualified for recognition as an overseas divorce thereunder if, for example, the talaq was pronounced in Pakistan by a husband of Pakistan nationality, and then notified to the appropriate official in Pakistan. Since there is no relevant change in the wording of the legislation, it follows that such a divorce now qualifies for recognition as an overseas decree under s 46(1) of the 1986 Act.

Subsequently in *Fatima v Home Secretary*[46] the House of Lords held that what might be called a 'transnational officially notified talaq' does not qualify for recognition as an overseas divorce under ss 2 and 3 of the 1971 Act. Such was the situation where a husband of Pakistan nationality pronounced talaq in

---

[43] See *Visvalingham v Visvalingham* (1979) 1 FLR 15, CA.
[44] See *Maples v Maples* [1988] Fam 14.
[45] [1980] AC 744.
[46] [1986] 1 AC 527; followed by the Court of Appeal in *Bashir v Zabu Nisar*, 21 April 1986.

England, and then sent notice of the talaq to an official in Pakistan. The decision emphasised that the pronouncement of the talaq was part of the proceedings, and seemed to require, for recognition as an overseas divorce under ss 2 and 3, that the entirety of the proceedings should have taken place in a foreign country in which the divorce was effective and with which one of the spouses had a connection specified by the British legislation; or at least that no part of the proceedings should have taken place within the British Islands.

As regards the *Fatima* type of situation, there are some differences between the wording of ss 2 and 3 of the 1971 Act and ss 45 and 46(1) of the 1986 Act,[47] and it is arguable that these would now justify a different solution,[48] to the effect that a procedural divorce could be *obtained in a country*, within the meaning of the 1986 Act, even if some of the proceedings by means of which it was obtained took place elsewhere. Otherwise the result would be that a transnational officially notified talaq could not now be recognised in the United Kingdom in any circumstances; not even on the basis of both spouses' domicile in the English sense, which was probably possible under s 6 of the 1971 Act.

The absurdity of the entirety doctrine adopted in *Fatima* becomes obvious, however, if it is taken literally and applied to judicial divorces. For it means that the English courts cannot recognise a divorce granted by, for example, a French court between spouses who are French by domicile, nationality and habitual residence, if the petition had been served in England or Germany on a respondent who was there on a short visit; or if evidence (for example, of adultery committed by the respondent at a London or Frankfurt hotel) were obtained by an English or German court for transmission to the French divorce court in pursuance of letters of request. It can hardly be denied that service of the petition, or the obtaining of evidence, are part of the proceedings by means of which the divorce was obtained. The only sensible course is for the House of Lords to overrule *Fatima*, or for any English court to declare it inapplicable in view of the revised wording of the 1986 Act, and adopt instead a test of where the proceedings were centred. In the case of a transnational officially notified divorce under Pakistan law, as in *Fatima*, the proceedings would be centred at the place where the official is based and receives notice of the talaq and should endeavour to pursue the reconciliation proceedings. Even on its own facts the decision in *Fatima* is indefensible.

---

[47] Section 2 of the 1971 Act referred to divorces which '(a) have been obtained by means of judicial or other proceedings in any country outside the British Isles; and (b) are effective under the law of that country.' Section 3 then required for recognition of such a divorce that 'at the date of the institution of the proceedings in the country in which [the divorce] was obtained' a specified connecting-factor should have existed between a spouse and 'that country'.

Section 45 of the 1986 Act contemplates a divorce 'obtained in a country outside the British Islands'. Section 46(1) then requires for recognition of such a divorce, if it was 'obtained by means of proceedings' (defined by s 54(1) as 'judicial or other proceedings'), that it should be 'effective under the law of the country in which it was obtained', and that at the relevant date (defined by s 46(3)(a) as 'the date of the commencement of the proceedings') a spouse should have had a specified connection with 'the country in which the divorce, annulment or legal separation was obtained'.

[48] See Dicey & Morris, at p 744. Cf Cheshire & North, at p 668.

Overseas decrees: connecting factors

As regards connecting factors, an overseas decree (that is, an overseas divorce, legal separation or annulment, obtained by means of judicial or other proceedings) qualifies for recognition if, at the date of the commencement of the overseas proceedings, at least one of the spouses (whether the husband or the wife, the petitioner or the respondent) was connected with the country in which the decree was obtained in any of four ways: by habitual residence; by domicile in the traditional English sense; by domicile in the sense used in family matters in the country where the decree was obtained; or by nationality.[49] Moreover findings of fact (for example, as to a spouse's habitual residence, his or her domicile under the law of the overseas country, or his or her nationality) which were made, expressly or by implication, in the overseas proceedings, and on the basis of which jurisdiction was assumed, are binding on the English courts if both spouses took part in the overseas proceedings, or appeared in them if they were judicial proceedings; and otherwise give rise to a rebuttable presumption of their correctness.[50]

As regards nationality, it is sufficient that the person was a national of the country in which the decree was obtained, even if he was also a British citizen or a national of a third country,[51] but a person is treated as a national of a colony or other dependent territory of the United Kingdom only if it has a law of citizenship or nationality separate from that of the United Kingdom and he is a citizen or national of that territory under that law.[52] In any event a decree can be recognised on the basis of a spouse's nationality of a state comprising several law districts only if it is effective throughout the state in question.[53]

Although the time at which a connecting factor must exist is normally the commencement of the overseas proceedings, where there were cross-proceedings it is sufficient for recognition of a decree obtained either in the original proceedings or in the cross-proceedings that a connecting factor had existed at the commencement of either the original proceedings or the cross-proceedings.[54] Further, where a recognised legal separation is converted in the same country into a divorce, the divorce will be recognised even if the connecting factor had disappeared in the interval.[55]

In respect of 'procedural' divorces and legal separations, the current rules on connecting factors under the 1986 Act differ from the former rules under the

---

[49] See s 46(1)(b), (3)(a) and (5). In the case of a decree of annulment granted after a spouse's death, it is sufficient that he was so connected at his death (instead of the commencement of the proceedings); see s 46(4).

[50] See s 48, which follows s 5 of the 1971 Act. See also *Cruse v Chittum* [1974] 2 All ER 940, where a finding by a Mississippi court, in granting a divorce, that the wife had been an actual bona fide resident of Mississippi for over a year up to the institution of the divorce proceedings, was considered equivalent to a finding of habitual residence, and, coupled with the fact that the wife was still resident in Mississippi a year after the decree, led to its recognition.

[51] See *Torok v Torok* [1973] 3 All ER 101.

[52] See s 54(2), following s 10(3) of the 1971 Act.

[53] See s 49(1) and (3)(a).

[54] See s 47(1), following s 4(1) of the 1971 Act.

[55] See s 47(2), following s 4(2) of the 1971 Act.

1971 Act (as amended by the 1973 Act), mainly in relation to recognition on the basis of domicile in the traditional English sense, which was formerly dealt with in s 6 of the 1971 Act, as amended by s 2 of the 1973 Act. It is now sufficient that the divorce or separation was obtained and is effective in a country in which one of the spouses was domiciled in the English sense, even if the other spouse was domiciled in that sense in another country which does not recognise the divorce or separation. On the other hand it is no longer sufficient that the divorce is recognised in the country in which both, or the countries in which each, of the spouses were domiciled in the English sense, if neither was domiciled in that sense in the country in which the divorce or separation was obtained. But by a transitional provision,[56] divorces or separations obtained before the commencement date of the 1986 Act continue to be recognised on this ground.

As regards annulments, the new rules under the 1986 Act differ from the common law rules formerly applicable in eliminating recognition on the basis of recognition in the country or countries in which the spouses were domiciled in the English sense of an annulment obtained elsewhere;[57] and in replacing the broad test of a spouse's real and substantial connection with the country in which the annulment was obtained[58] by more specific tests of habitual residence, nationality, or domicile under the law of the country where the annulment was obtained. Moreover there is no general saving continuing the recognition of 'old' annulments which were recognised under the formerly applicable common law.[59]

Overseas decrees: non-connectional exceptions

Section 51 of the 1986 Act specifies a number of grounds, not concerned with connecting factors, whose existence confers on the English courts a discretion to refuse recognition of an overseas decree.

First, by s 51(1), recognition may be refused if the decree was obtained at a time when it was irreconcilable with a decision determining the subsistence or validity of the same marriage, which had previously been given (whether before or after the commencement of Part II) by an English civil court, or given by a court elsewhere but recognised or entitled to be recognised in England. This exception also extends to British decrees and to overseas non-procedural divorces. There was no similar provision in the 1971 Act, but in *Vervaeke v Smith*[60] the House of Lords refused, effectively on grounds of public policy, to recognise a Belgian annulment of a marriage which an English court had previously held valid.

---

[56] See s 52(4) and (5)(b).
[57] See *Abate v Abate* [1961] P 29.
[58] See *Law v Gustin* [1976] 1 All ER 113, *Perrini v Perrini* [1979] 2 All ER 323, and *Vervaeke v Smith* [1981] 1 All ER 55, CA.
[59] Cf s 52(4) and (5).
[60] [1983] 1 AC 145.

Secondly, by s 51(2), recognition of a divorce or legal separation (but not an annulment) may be refused if the decree was obtained at a time when, according to English law (including its rules of private international law and the provisions of Part II), there was no subsisting marriage between the parties. Like the previous exception, this also extends to British decrees and to overseas non-procedural divorces. This provision corresponds to s 8(1) of the 1971 Act, except that under s 8(1) refusal of recognition was mandatory.

Thirdly, by s 51(3)(a)(i), recognition may be refused if the decree was obtained without such steps having been taken for giving notice of the proceedings to a spouse as, having regard to their nature and all the circumstances, should reasonably have been taken; or, by s 51(3)(a)(ii), if it was obtained without a spouse having been given (for a reason other than lack of notice) such opportunity to take part in the proceedings as, having regard to those matters, he should reasonably have been given. These provisions follow s 8(2)(a) of the 1971 Act. They are confined to overseas decrees, and do not extend to British decrees, nor to overseas non-procedural divorces.

In practice the courts have long been reluctant to refuse recognition on grounds of lack of notice,[61] though in *Macalpine v Macalpine*[62] recognition was refused where the petitioner had fraudulently denied knowledge of the respondent's address. As regards lack of opportunity to participate despite notice, in *Newmarch v Newmarch*[63] the court's discretion under the predecessor of s 51(3)(a)(ii) was held to be available where the wife's Australian solicitors had ignored clear and explicit instructions from her English solicitors to file an answer and defend, but in the result the discretion was exercised in favour of recognition, since it was considered that recognition would not prejudice the wife's financial interests. On the other hand recognition was refused in *Joyce v Joyce*,[64] where the wife's English solicitors had unsuccessfully sought to obtain an adjournment and the grant of legal aid in Quebec, and recognition would at that date (before the enactment of Part III of the Matrimonial and Family Proceedings Act 1984)[65] have prevented her from obtaining English relief in respect of the English matrimonial home.

Finally, by s 51(3)(b), recognition may be refused if it would be manifestly contrary to English public policy. This follows s 8(2)(b) of the 1971 Act. It extends to overseas non-procedural divorces, but not to British decrees.

As regards divorce, it is well established that recognition is not contrary to public policy merely because the substantive grounds for divorce on which the

---

[61] See *Igra v Igra* [1951] P 404, *Wood v Wood* [1957] P 254, *Hornett v Hornett* [1971] P 255, and *Law v Gustin* [1976] 1 All ER 113 – in none of which was recognition refused. See also *Re G* [1990] 2 FLR 325, [1990] Fam Law 23, on art 9(1)(a) of the European Convention on the Recognition and Enforcement of Decisions concerning Custody of Children and on the Restoration of Custody of Children, implemented by Part II of the Child Abduction and Custody Act 1985.
[62] [1958] P 35.
[63] [1978] 1 All ER 1.
[64] [1979] 2 All ER 156.
[65] See under 'English maintenance proceedings after a recognised foreign status decree', pp 82–84 below.

decree was based would not have been sufficient grounds for divorce under English internal law;[66] for example, today, desertion or separation for only one year. Similarly recognition cannot be refused because of fraud on the merits or because the foreign proceedings could be regarded as a sham.[67] Nonetheless some conceivable grounds for divorce, for example of a racial nature, may be so outrageous as to offend public policy.[68] Certainly recognition is likely to offend public policy sufficiently to make available the court's discretion if the petitioner had been compelled to seek the divorce as a result of duress, for example arising from political persecution.[69] Similarly public policy may be invoked against a divorce obtained without the petitioner's knowledge, she having been induced to sign the necessary document by the respondent's fraud that the document was of an entirely different nature, for example that it related to removal of the children from the country.[70]

In the case of an annulment, it is at least prima facie contrary to public policy to recognise an overseas decree annulling a marriage which is valid under English choice of law rules, at least if the marriage was celebrated in England and one of the spouses was domiciled in England at its celebration.[71] It seems from *Vervaeke v Smith*[72] that the English rule upholding a 'sham' marriage is one of public policy, overriding an overseas annulment, at least where the marriage was between a British citizen and a foreign national and their purpose was to enable the foreigner to acquire British nationality.

It must be emphasised that the effect of the existence of a ground specified by s 51 is only to confer a discretion on the English courts to refuse recognition. Moreover, in view of the policy against 'limping' marriages (subsisting in one country but not another) the courts are sparing in their denial of recognition on such grounds. Recognition is likely to be refused only in the interests of maintaining the coherence of the English conflict system, and in the rare cases where it is felt necessary to make a strong protest against plainly scandalous features of an overseas law. Often the court will grant recognition, despite lack of notice or

---

[66] See *Harvey v Farnie* (1882) 8 App Cas 43; *Bater v Bater* [1906] P 209; *Robinson-Scott v Robinson-Scott* [1958] P 71; *Manning v Manning* [1958] P 112; and *Indyka v Indyka* [1969] 1 AC 33.

[67] See *Bater v Bater* [1906] P 209, and *Re Meyer* [1971] P 298. Cf *Middleton v Middleton* [1967] P 62, where recognition was refused by reason of fraud as to the jurisdiction, but the decision should be considered obsolete.

[68] See *Re Meyer* [1971] P 298. Cf *Corbett v Corbett* [1957] 1 All ER 621, where the decision recognising an annulment given on racial or religious grounds is explicable on the ground of the wife respondent's approbation by remarriage.

[69] As in *Re Meyer* [1971] P 298. Cf *Igra v Igra* [1951] P 404, where the decision in favour of recognition is explicable by reason of the respondent husband's approbation by remarrying in reliance on the decree, and the wife petitioner's approbation by now seeking a declaration in favour of recognition.

[70] As in *Kendall v Kendall* [1977] 3 All ER 471.

[71] See *Ogden v Ogden* [1908] P 46; *Gray v Formosa* [1963] P 259; and *Lepre v Lepre* [1965] P 52 – in all of which these conditions were fulfilled and recognition was denied. Cf *Merker v Merker* [1963] P 283, where at the celebration of the marriage there was no English connection. While s 51(1) and (2), considered above, are not directly in point, they reflect the same policy as underlies decisions such as *Gray v Formosa*.

[72] [1983] 1 AC 145.

opportunity to be heard or other circumstances amounting to a denial of justice to one or both of the spouses, on the ground that the spouse or spouses unjustly treated have subsequently approbated the decree by remarrying in reliance on it,[73] or by petitioning for an English declaration in favour of its recognition;[74] or that the spouse unfairly treated abroad is opposing recognition solely for financial reasons, and recognition will not in fact prejudice her financial position.[75] Hence refusal of recognition on discretionary grounds is likely to be very rare, now that Part III of the Matrimonial and Family Proceedings Act 1984 has empowered the English courts in many cases to make English orders for financial provision after a recognised foreign divorce.[76]

Overseas non-procedural divorces

Part II of the 1986 Act makes explicit provision for overseas non-procedural divorces (that is, overseas divorces obtained otherwise than by means of judicial or other proceedings). As regards connecting factors, a very restrictive rule is adopted. At the date on which the divorce was obtained, at least one of the spouses must have been domiciled (either in the traditional English sense, or in the sense used in family matters by the law of the country where the divorce was obtained) in the country in which it was obtained, and the other spouse must have been domiciled (in either sense) either in that country or in another country whose law recognises the divorce, and neither spouse must have been habitually resident in the United Kingdom throughout the year up to the date on which the divorce was obtained.[77]

These rules effectively replace those formerly laid down by s 6 of the 1971 Act (as amended by the 1973 Act), and s 16(2) of the 1973 Act. They relax the requirement of domicile by allowing an alternative reference to domicile in the sense used in the country of the divorce, but tighten the requirement relating to habitual residence, by making the one-year habitual residence in the United Kingdom of either spouse, instead of both spouses, a barrier to recognition. Moreover the habitual residence barrier under s 16(2) of the 1973 Act only applied to divorces obtained after 1973. But a transitional provision permits the continued recognition of 'old' divorces which were recognised under such former provisions.[78]

As regards non-connectional factors, the exceptions specified in s 51(1) and (2) and 3(c), relating respectively to prior irreconcilable decisions, to the ab-

---

[73] As in *Igra v Igra* [1951] P 404.

[74] See *Igra v Igra* [1951] P 404, and *Hornett v Hornett* [1971] P 255. But it is not approbation to petition alternatively for such a declaration or an English divorce; see *Gray v Formosa* [1963] P 259, and *Macalpine v Macalpine* [1958] P 35.

[75] Compare *Newmarch v Newmarch* [1978] 1 All ER 1 with *Joyce v Joyce* [1979] 2 All ER 156.

[76] See under 'English maintenance proceedings after a recognised foreign status decree', pp 82–84 below.

[77] See s 46(2)(b) and (c), (3)(b), and (5). These provisions appear to have been overlooked by Butler-Sloss LJ (in interlocutory proceedings) in *Begum v Ali*, 21 May 1991.

[78] See s 52(4) and (5)(b).

sence of a subsisting marriage, and to public policy, extend to overseas non-procedural divorces; but the exceptions under s 51(3)(a)(i) and (ii), relating to lack of notice or opportunity to participate, do not.[79] In addition, s 51(3)(b) gives the English courts a discretion to deny recognition to an overseas non-procedural divorce if there is no official document certifying that the divorce is effective under the law of the country in which it was obtained; or, where one of the spouses was domiciled in another country at the date of the divorce, if there is no official document certifying that the divorce is recognised under the law of that other country. An official document is one issued by a person or body appointed or recognised for the relevant purpose under the law of the relevant country.[80] These provisions on official documents are new.

FAMILIAL FINANCIAL PROVISION

The 1968 and Lugano Conventions

The 1968 and Lugano Conventions,[81] by art 1[2](1), exclude individual status and capacity, and matrimonial property, from their scope. Thus they do not affect English jurisdiction to entertain proceedings for divorce, judicial separation, annulment of marriage, or a declaration as to marital status, as such;[82] nor do they affect proceedings under s 17 of the Married Women's Property Act 1882. On the other hand, it is clear from art 5(2) of the Conventions, and the decision of the European Court of Justice in *De Cavel v De Cavel (No 2)*,[83] that maintenance *is* within the scope of the Conventions, even when it is dealt with as an ancillary matter in proceedings primarily concerned with status, such as divorce proceedings; and that for this purpose 'maintenance' includes payments between divorced spouses which are intended to compensate for the disparity in their living standards created by the breakdown of the marriage, and which have to be fixed on the basis of their respective needs and resources. It is therefore submitted that any English order for financial provision (whether by way of periodical or of lump sum payments) or for property adjustment, between spouses and their children, which may be made in English proceedings for divorce, judicial separation or annulment under ss 22–24 of the Matrimonial Causes Act 1973, should be characterised as maintenance, and not as status or matrimonial property, for the purposes of the Conventions.[84]

---

[79] On all these exceptions, see under 'Overseas decrees: non-connectional exceptions', pp 74–7 above.

[80] See s 51(4).

[81] See Chapters 7–11 and 14 below.

[82] See 'English status proceedings', pp 63–6 above.

[83] Case 120/79, [1980] ECR 731.

[84] Cf Dicey & Morris, at p 786, where it is argued that a property adjustment order, made ancillarily to an English divorce, is not within the scope of the 1968 Convention, apparently because the proprietary rights which it creates are considered to arise directly from the dissolution of the marriage. This argument appears to overlook the discretionary character of such orders, their functional equivalence to lump sum orders, and their aim of redistributing resources in the light of needs.

In any event art 5(2) of the Conventions (and of Sched 4 to the Civil Jurisdiction and Judgments Act 1982) confer jurisdiction on the English courts to entertain maintenance proceedings against a defendant who is domiciled (in the Convention sense, approximately of substantial residence) in another contracting state (or another part of the United Kingdom), if the maintenance claim is made ancillarily in proceedings concerning personal status which the court is competent to entertain under English law.[85] Thus the traditional English rule that an English court, competently seised of proceedings for divorce, judicial separation or annulment, is automatically competent also to make orders for financial provision or property adjustment,[86] is largely unaffected by the Conventions.

More generally, however, it is unfortunate that there has been no English legislation seeking specifically to revise the prior English rules on maintenance jurisdiction, so as to integrate them with the Convention provisions into a coherent whole. As a result the current position concerning English maintenance jurisdiction is rather untidy.[87]

The 1968 and Lugano Conventions (and Sched 4 to the 1982 Act) introduce the curious features of enabling maintenance jurisdiction to be founded on the defendant's appearance without contesting the jurisdiction; and of enabling the parties to determine maintenance jurisdiction by explicit agreement thereon.[88] Moreover the general provisions of the Conventions on simultaneous proceedings in different contracting states in relation to similar or related claims extend to maintenance proceedings.[89] Otherwise the broad effect of the Conventions and Sched 4 on English maintenance jurisdiction is as follows:

(1) They confer such jurisdiction on the English courts if the defendant is domiciled in England, in the sense of substantial residence, as defined by art 52 of the Conventions and s 41 of the 1982 Act.[90]

(2) If the defendant is domiciled (in the Convention sense, as defined by art 52) in another contracting state or another part of the United Kingdom, they render the English courts competent if, and only if:

(a) the maintenance creditor is domiciled (in the Convention sense) in England;[91] or

(b) the maintenance creditor is habitually resident in England;[92] or

(c) the claim for maintenance made ancillarily in English proceedings is principally concerned with individual status (in other words: for

---

[85] The proviso that the status jurisdiction must not be based solely on the nationality of one of the parties is irrelevant to English jurisdiction.

[86] See Dicey & Morris, Rule 88(1).

[87] See Dicey & Morris, at pp 786–7.

[88] See arts 17 and 18; and Chapter 8, under 'Submission by appearance', and Chapter 11, under 'Jurisdiction clauses', pp 139–42 below.

[89] See arts 21–22; and Chapter 8, under 'Simultaneous actions in different countries', p 209 *et seq.* below.

[90] See art 2; and Chapter 8, under 'Domicile', pp 128–39 below.

[91] See art 5(2).

[92] See art 5(2); and on habitual residence, Chapter 2 above.

divorce, judicial separation, or annulment), and the court has jurisdiction under English law to entertain the status proceedings;[93] or

(d) an English order for interim maintenance is sought, pending full adjudication of the maintenance claim elsewhere within the contracting states.[94]

(3) If the defendant is not domiciled (in the Convention sense) within the contracting states, they remit questions relating to English maintenance jurisdiction to the English rules otherwise applicable.[95]

It seems probable that in English matrimonial proceedings where a wife is suing her husband for maintenance for their children, it is the wife, rather than the children, who constitutes the 'maintenance creditor' within the meaning of art 5(2); but that it is the child who constitutes the 'maintenance creditor' in non-matrimonial proceedings for his maintenance under Sched 1 of the Children Act 1989.

It is noteworthy that the Child Support Act 1991 is largely confined to situations which are purely internal to the United Kingdom, since s 44 of the Act excludes the jurisdiction of a child support officer if either the child, or the person with care (if an individual), or the absent parent, is not habitually resident in the United Kingdom. Thus, this disgraceful and wicked legislation[96] tolerates or perhaps encourages avoidance by emigration.

Various English maintenance proceedings

In view of art 5(2) of the 1968 and Lugano Conventions, the powers of the English courts to make ancillary orders for financial provision or property adjustment in proceedings for divorce, judicial separation, or annulment of marriage are largely unaffected by the Conventions. However such ancillary jurisdiction can be excluded by an explicit agreement (under art 17 of the Conventions), and by the existence of prior maintenance proceedings in another contracting state (under arts 21 and 22).

The Conventions have much greater effect on the jurisdiction of the English High Court and divorce county courts to entertain applications between spouses under s 27 of the Matrimonial Causes Act 1973, based on wilful neglect to maintain. Formerly, under s 6(1) of the Domicile and Matrimonial Proceedings Act 1973, the English courts had jurisdiction to entertain such proceedings if at their institution at least one of the spouses was domiciled in England, in the

---

[93] See art 5(2).
[94] See art 24; and Chapter 8, under 'Interim relief', pp 157–60 below.
[95] See art 4.
[96] These epithets were applied by Mrs Audrey Wise MP (see Hansard, Commons, 10 February 1994, at col 516). In the circumstances they may be considered unduly mild. The various obnoxious features of the legislation were well explored in the Commons' debates of 2 and 10 February 1994 (see Hansard, Commons, respectively at cols 941–86 and 483–555) and the Lords' debates of 1 and 9 February 1994 (see Hansard, Lords, respectively at cols 1217–41 and 1657–88).

traditional English sense of origin or permanent residence,[97] or if the applicant had been habitually resident in England for the year up to such institution, or if the respondent was resident in England at such institution. Now, however, s 6(1) only applies where the defendant is not domiciled (in the Convention sense) in any contracting state; and even then gives way to the Convention provisions on appearance, jurisdiction clauses, and simultaneous proceedings. If the defendant is domiciled (in the Convention sense) within the contracting states, English jurisdiction under s 27 is governed exclusively by the provisions outlined under the last heading.

The Conventions have a similar effect on the jurisdiction of the English magistrates' courts to entertain matrimonial maintenance proceedings under the Domestic Proceedings and Magistrates' Courts Act 1978. The English rules on jurisdiction under that Act, which are largely preserved by art 4 where the defendant is not domiciled (in the Convention sense) in any contracting state, create jurisdiction if the respondent is resident in England; or if the respondent is resident elsewhere in the United Kingdom, the applicant is resident in England, and the spouses last ordinarily resided together as man and wife in England.[98] Similarly the Conventions override the rules which now confer connectionally unlimited jurisdiction on the English courts to make non-matrimonial maintenance orders in respect of children under Sched 1 to the Children Act 1989.[99]

Again the Conventions in principle override the traditional English rules on the maintenance jurisdiction of magistrates' courts under special procedures involving the participation of courts of the two countries where the parties respectively reside: 'shuttlecock' procedures, where a provisional order is made by the English court, and confirmed by a foreign court, or vice versa;[100] and procedures involving the English court receiving an application for forwarding by diplomatic channels to a foreign court for decision, or vice versa.[101] But the Conventions give way where the special procedure is made available in pursuance of some other treaty between the United Kingdom and the relevant foreign country, such as the Hague Convention on the Recognition and Enforcement of Decisions relating to Maintenance Obligations (1973), or the United Nations Convention on the Recovery of Maintenance Abroad (1956).[102]

In general the English courts determine the merits of a maintenance or similar application in accordance with English internal law, but foreign law may be relevant in English proceedings for the confirmation or revocation of a foreign order under the shuttlecock procedures.[103]

---

[97] See Chapter 2 above.

[98] See Dicey & Morris, Rule 88(4)(a) and (b).

[99] See the Family Proceedings Rules 1991, r 10.6, and Dicey & Morris, Rule 97(1).

[100] See the Maintenance Orders (Facilities for Enforcement) Act 1920; the Maintenance Orders (Reciprocal Enforcement) Act 1972, Part I and s 40; and Dicey & Morris, Rule 88(4)(c), (d) and (f).

[101] See the Maintenance Orders (Reciprocal Enforcement) Act 1972, Part II and s 40; and Dicey & Morris, Rule 88(4)(e) and (f).

[102] See Dicey & Morris, Rule 88(4)(e)–(f) and (6). See also text to and note 120 below.

[103] See Dicey & Morris, Rule 88(7).

A further problem in relation to maintenance, especially with regard to orders for periodical payments, arises from the variable nature often possessed by such orders. According to the Schlosser Report,[104] under the 1968 and Lugano Conventions the court which originally made a maintenance order will not necessarily have jurisdiction to make a further order varying the amount of maintenance in the light of changed circumstances, such as a diminution of the value of the sum awarded owing to inflation. For the purpose of jurisdiction under the Conventions, an application for variation must be treated as a separate proceeding, and the necessary connecting factor must exist at the institution of the application for variation. Presumably, however, the obligation of recognition imposed by Title III of the Conventions requires that a court which is requested and is competent to vary a foreign order should determine the merits of the application in accordance with the law of the country in which the original order was made, and prevents a court from varying a foreign order which, under the law of the original country, is definitive.

English maintenance proceedings after a recognised foreign status decree

Part III (ss 12–27) of the Matrimonial and Family Proceedings Act 1984[105] empowers the English courts to make financial provision or property adjustment orders between spouses and their children[106] after a foreign divorce, annulment or legal separation has been obtained 'by means of judicial or other proceedings' in a country or territory outside the British Islands (that is: the United Kingdom, the Channel Islands and the Isle of Man) and is recognised in England.[107] In view of the reference to proceedings, it seems that Part III will not apply after a foreign divorce, such as a bare talaq, has been obtained without proceedings, within the meaning of Part II of the Family Law Act 1986.[108] But Part III applies even if the foreign decree was granted before its entry into force on 16 September 1985.[109]

Subject to the Conventions, s 15(1) confers jurisdiction on the English court to entertain an application under Part III if either of the spouses was domiciled in England (in the traditional sense of origin or permanent residence)[110] either at the date of the English application under Part III or at the date when the decree took effect in the foreign country in which it was obtained, or if either

---

[104] At pp 103–5.
[105] This implements Law Commission Report No 117 (1982) on *Financial Relief after Foreign Divorce.*
[106] The orders which may be made under Part III are the same as those which may be made under ss 23(1), 24(1) and 24A(1) of the Matrimonial Causes Act 1973 (as amended) ancillarily to the grant of an English divorce, separation or annulment; see s 17. In proceedings under Part III the court may also make interim orders for maintenance pending suit; see s 14. Provision is also made for the court to restrain or set aside transactions intended to defeat applications under Part III; see ss 23 and 24.
[107] See ss 12(1) and 27.
[108] See pp 69–73 and 77–8 above.
[109] See SI 1985/1316, and *Chebaro v Chebaro* [1987] Fam 127, CA.
[110] See Chapter 2, above.

spouse was habitually resident in England throughout the year up to either of those dates, or if either spouse had at the date of the application under Part III a beneficial interest in a former matrimonial home situated in England. Where, however, the court's jurisdiction is based solely on the existence of an English matrimonial home, the court cannot make an interim maintenance order, nor a final order for periodical payments, but only a property adjustment order in respect of, or a lump sum order limited to the value of, the respondent's interest in the English matrimonial home.[111]

However s 15(2) explicitly provides that these jurisdictional requirements are to give way to those imposed by Part I of the Civil Jurisdiction and Judgments Act 1982, which implements the 1968 and Lugano Conventions. Thus the tests laid down by s 15(1) are confined to cases where the defendant is not domiciled (in the Convention sense) within the contracting states; and even then give way to the Convention provisions on appearance, jurisdiction clauses, and simultaneous proceedings. If the defendant is domiciled (in the Convention sense) within the contracting states, English jurisdiction under Part III is governed exclusively by the Convention provisions outlined above.[112] This result could have been largely avoided if advantage had been taken of art 5(2) of the Conventions, by making financial relief under Part III ancillary to a declaration that the foreign divorce, separation or annulment is recognised in England; an option which the Law Commission strangely rejected.

In any event, by s 13, an application under Part III requires the court's leave, to be given on the basis that it considers there to be substantial ground for the application, though the existence of a financial order made by a foreign court does not prevent the English court from giving leave. Moreover, by s 16, before making a substantive order under Part III, the court must be satisfied that it would be appropriate for an English financial order to be made, having regard to all the circumstances of the case, including: the connections of the spouses with England, with the country of the decree and with other countries; any financial benefit which the applicant or a child has received or is likely to receive in consequence of the decree by virtue of an agreement or a foreign law; any financial order of a foreign court, and the extent to which it has been or is likely to be complied with; any right of the applicant to apply for financial relief abroad, and the reason for any omission so to apply; the availability of any English property in respect of which an English order could be made; the extent to which an English order is likely to be enforceable; and the length of time since the date of the decree. Once the English court is so satisfied, s 18 requires it, in exercising its powers under Part III, to proceed in the same way as in making an order ancillarily to an English divorce in accordance with ss 25 and 25A of the Matrimonial Causes Act 1973, though in considering the financial resources of the spouses and children it must take account of the extent to which any foreign financial order has been or is likely to be complied with.

[111] See ss 14(2) and 20. The court also has power under s 22 to transfer a statutory tenancy of a former matrimonial home as if it had itself granted a divorce.
[112] See under 'The 1968 and Lugano Conventions', pp 78–80 above.

In *Holmes v Holmes*[113] the Court of Appeal explained that the court should not grant leave under s 13 unless it considers that there is substantial ground for taking the view that it would be appropriate for an English order to be made, as envisaged by s 16. Moreover, while the purpose of Part III is to remedy hardships which formerly arose from failure by a foreign legal system to afford appropriate financial relief, the English courts will not assume jurisdiction on a wife's application under Part III simply because the English legislation on financial provision is more favourable to her than that of the country of the divorce, especially if in the circumstances of the case the country of the divorce is the natural forum for determination of her claim for financial provision. This approach is similar to that adopted by the House in *de Dampierre v de Dampierre*[114] in relation to the staying of English divorce proceedings in favour of concurrent proceedings abroad.

Enforcement of foreign maintenance orders[115]

In principle an overseas maintenance order can be enforced in England in accordance with the common law, in the same way as a personal judgment. But the common law regime requires that an overseas judgment should be final in the court which gave it, and many orders for periodical payments lack such finality because the original court has power to remit arrears.[116] It is often assumed that the same difficulty arises under the Foreign Judgments (Reciprocal Enforcement) Act 1933, but this seems to be a misconception, since the Act's definition of appeal deprives its requirement of finality of any content.[117] However the effect of s 11(2) of the 1933 Act, in excluding family law proceedings from its definition of personal actions, is that, in proceedings under the Act for the enforcement of an overseas maintenance order, jurisdictional review must be based on the common law rules of indirect jurisdiction applicable to family law proceedings, in accordance with s 4(2)(c), rather than the rules of indirect personal jurisdiction over personal actions laid down by s 4(2)(a).

In any event special regimes for the reciprocal enforcement of maintenance orders are made available by Part II of the Maintenance Orders Act 1950, as between the three parts of the United Kingdom; and by the Maintenance Orders (Facilities for Enforcement) Act 1920, and Part I of the Maintenance Orders (Reciprocal Enforcement) Act 1972, both as amended by the Maintenance Orders (Reciprocal Enforcement) Act 1992, in respect of orders made in

---

[113] [1989] Fam 47. See also *Z v Z* [1992] 2 FLR 291, Ewbank J.

[114] [1988] AC 92.

[115] This section should be read in conjunction with Chapter 14, 'Foreign Judgments', below.

[116] Compare *Harrop v Harrop* [1920] 3 KB 386, refusing enforcement on this ground, with *Beatty v Beatty* [1924] 1 KB 807, enforcing arrears under an order for periodical payments because the original court, while empowered to vary the order as regards future payments, could not remit arrears.

[117] See Chapter 14, under 'Finality in the original country', pp 320–21 below.

reciprocating countries outside the United Kingdom.[118] Countries so designated for the purpose of the 1972 Act[119] include:

(1) as parties to the Hague Convention of 2 October 1973 on the Recognition and Enforcement of Decisions relating to Maintenance Obligations: France, Germany, Italy, Luxembourg, Netherlands, Portugal, Switzerland, Norway, Sweden, Finland, the Czech Republic, Slovakia, and Turkey;[120] and

(2) by virtue of other arrangements for reciprocity: the Isle of Man; Gibraltar; Ireland; Malta; much of the United States, Canada and Australia; New Zealand; South Africa; Zimbabwe; Kenya; Tanzania; Ghana; India; Singapore; and Hong Kong.

In addition the 1968 and Lugano Conventions extend to European maintenance orders, so that the recognition and enforcement in the United Kingdom of orders made in other contracting states is governed by Title III of the Conventions. Of particular importance in relation to maintenance orders are arts 27(4) and 34[2], by which recognition and enforcement must be refused if the original court, in order to reach its judgment, decided a preliminary question concerning the status or capacity of an individual, matrimonial property, or succession on death in a way which conflicts with a rule of English private international law, and thereby reached a different result on the question from the one which would have been reached under the English rules of private international law. This proviso could apply, for example, where the foreign order awards maintenance ancillarily in divorce proceedings, and the divorce is for some reason denied recognition in England.

Also of significance is the ruling of the European Court of Justice in *Hoffmann v Krieg*,[121] that a judgment in respect of which an enforcement order has been made under the 1968 Convention cannot remain enforceable in the state addressed if its law precludes further enforcement for reasons outside the scope of the Convention, such as a subsequent and irreconcilable local judgment concerning personal status. More specifically, the Convention does not interfere with the local effects of a locally granted divorce, including the effects of the divorce in relation to the enforcement of a foreign maintenance order, even if the divorce is not recognised in the state of origin of the maintenance order. It is rather surprising that the court ruled that there was irreconcilability between a German maintenance order and a subsequent Dutch divorce, on the somewhat simplistic view that the maintenance order necessarily presupposed the existence of a matrimonial relationship. The ruling was, however, followed in *Macaulay v Macaulay*,[122] where the English Family Divisional Court refused to

---

[118] See Dicey & Morris, Rule 90(2)–(4).
[119] See SI 1974/556, 1975/2187, 1979/115, 1983/1125, 1993/591, and 1993/594.
[120] See SI 1993/593.
[121] Case 145/86, [1988] ECR 645.
[122] [1991] 1 WLR 179.

enforce an Irish maintenance order which had been followed by an English divorce.[123]

As regards procedure, an application for the enforcement in England of a European maintenance order under the 1968 or Lugano Conventions is transmitted through the Secretary of State to the magistrates' court within whose district the respondent is domiciled (in the Convention sense of substantially resident), or, if he is not domiciled in England, where he has assets. The first appeal is also determined by that magistrates' court, and the final appeal on a point of law is by way of case stated to the Family Division of the High Court.[124]

In the case of maintenance orders made in France, Germany, Italy, Luxembourg, Netherlands, Portugal or Switzerland, the substantive requirements of the Hague Convention of 1973 prevail over those of the 1968 and Lugano Conventions, in accordance with art 57.

---

[123] Cf *Bragg v Bragg* [1925] P 20; *Wood v Wood* [1957] P 254; *Qureshi v Qureshi* [1972] Fam 173; *Newmarch v Newmarch* [1978] Fam 79; and Stone [1988] 3 LMCLQ 383.

[124] See arts 32, 37, 40 and 41; and the 1982 Act, ss 5 and 6(3). Similarly, in Scotland or Northern Ireland, a European maintenance order is transmitted by the Secretary of State or the Lord Chancellor to the sheriff court or magistrates' court within whose district the respondent is domiciled or has assets; the appeal is dealt with by the same sheriff court or magistrates' court; and the final appeal lies to the Inner House of the Scottish Court of Session or to the Northern Irish Court of Appeal.

5

CHILDREN

FILIAL RELATIONSHIPS

Under this heading, unless otherwise indicated, 'child' refers to relationship and not age; in other words it is synonymous with 'son or daughter, of whatever age'.

The Family Law Reform Act 1987 ('the 1987 Act'), much of which entered into force on 4 April 1988,[1] has largely abolished the distinction between legitimate and illegitimate filial relationships, especially for proprietary purposes. Section 1(1) lays down the principle that, in the 1987 Act and other enactments passed or instruments made after its commencement on 4 April 1988, references to relationships are to be construed without regard to whether or not the parents of a child were at any time married to each other, and ss 18–21 apply this principle to settlements inter vivos and wills executed, and intestacies of persons dying, after 4 April 1988. This extends to dispositions referring to 'heirs' or otherwise creating entailed interests, but not to dignities or titles of honour or property limited to devolve therewith.[2]

Nonetheless s 1 of the 1987 Act retains for some purposes a distinction between what may conveniently be called marital and non-marital children, and s 1(2)–(4) in effect define a marital child (identified initially as 'a person whose father and mother were married to each other at the time of his birth') in terms of the prior law (including conflict rules) on legitimacy, legitimation and adoption. Thus, despite their diminished importance, the conflict rules on filial status will now be summarised. In these rules, 'domicile' has its traditional English sense (of origin or permanent residence).[3]

A person is a legitimate and marital child of his biological parents if:

(1) they were validly (or voidably) married to each other (in accordance with the English choice of law rules on the validity of marriage)[4] at his birth,

---

[1] See SI 1988/425.
[2] See s 19(2) and (4).
[3] See Chapter 2 above.
[4] See Chapter 3 above. A valid polygamous marriage will suffice: see the *Sinha Peerage Claim* [1946] 1 All ER 348, and *Bamgbose v Daniel* [1955] AC 107.

or at his conception, or at any moment between his birth and conception;[5] or

(2) at his conception his parents were parties to, or during the pregnancy they entered into, a void marriage with each other, and at the time of the conception or the subsequent purported marriage, one or both of them reasonably believed the marriage to be valid, and the father was domiciled in England at the child's birth or at the father's earlier death;[6] or

(3) he is regarded as having been legitimate at his birth by the law of the country or countries (other than England) in which each of his parents were domiciled at his birth,[7] or (probably) in which the father alone was so domiciled.[8]

A person is a legitimated and marital child of his biological parents if:

(a) they validly (or voidably) married each other after his birth, and at the subsequent marriage the father was domiciled either in England or in another country under whose law the child was legitimated by the subsequent marriage;[9] or probably if

(b) an event (other than the marriage of his parents), such as a declaration of recognition by his father, has occurred after his birth, which has the effect of legitimating him under the law of the country or countries in which the father was domiciled at the time of the child's birth and at the time of the event in question.[10]

A person is an adopted and marital child of his adoptive parent or parents, and is not a child of his biological parents (if different),[11] if he is adopted by means of:

(1) an adoption order made by an English court under the Adoption Act 1976 or earlier English legislation;[12]

(2) a court order made in Scotland, Northern Ireland, the Isle of Man, or any of the Channel Islands;[13]

(3) an overseas adoption: that is, an adoption of a description specified by statutory instrument and effected under the law of a country outside Great Britain;[14] or

---

[5] See the 1987 Act, s 1(2) and (4), and the Matrimonial Causes Act 1973, s 16.

[6] See the Legitimacy Act 1976, s 1 (as amended by the 1987 Act), and the 1987 Act, s 1(3)(a).

[7] See the 1987 Act, s 1(3)(d), and Re Bischoffsheim [1948] Ch 79, Bamgbose v Daniel [1955] AC 107, and Motala v Attorney-General [1990] 2 FLR 261 (reversed on other grounds, [1992] 1 AC 281).

[8] See the 1987 Act, s 1(3)(d), and Hashmi v Hashmi [1971] 3 All ER 1253. Cf Shaw v Gould (1868) LR 3 HL 55.

[9] See Re Wright (1856) 69 ER 920; Re Grove (1888) 40 ChD 216; Re Andros (1883) 24 ChD 637; Re Goodman (1881) 17 ChD 266; Re Grey [1892] 3 Ch 88; Legitimacy Act 1976, ss 2 and 3; and the 1987 Act, s 1(3)(b).

[10] See Re Luck [1940] Ch 864, and the 1987 Act, s 1(3)(b).

[11] See Adoption Act 1976, ss 12 and Part IV.

[12] See Adoption Act 1976, s 38(1)(a) and (b).

[13] See Adoption Act 1976, s 38(1)(c).

[14] See Adoption Act 1976, ss 38(1)(d) and 72(2).

(4) a foreign adoption recognised at common law: that is, an adoption which is recognised at common law on the ground that it was effected under the law of a country outside England in which the adoptive parent (or at least one of the adoptive parents) was domiciled.[15]

Declarations as to filial status

Part III of the Family Law Act 1986 now governs the jurisdiction of English courts to make declarations as to filial as well as marital status.[16] By ss 56 and 57 (as amended),[17] a person may apply to the English court for any of the following kinds of declaration:

- that a named person is or was his father or mother;
- that he is the legitimate child of his parents;
- that he has or has not become legitimated by subsequent marriage or otherwise;
- that he is, or is not, recognised as the adoptive child of a named person by virtue of an adoption effected outside the British Islands.

By ss 56(3) and 57(3), the English court has jurisdiction to entertain such an application if the applicant is domiciled in England (in the traditional sense of origin or permanent residence)[18] on the date of the application, or has been habitually resident in England throughout the year up to the application.

As in the case of marital declarations under Part III, if the relevant matters are proved by the applicant the court must make the declaration sought unless to do so would manifestly be contrary to public policy.[19] A declaration under Part III binds the whole world, including the Crown, and the Attorney-General is entitled to intervene in Part III proceedings.[20] But the declaration does not affect any final judgment or decree already pronounced.[21]

Bare declarations as to filial (or marital) status can be made only under Part III. But of course any English court is competent to determine status incidentally in any otherwise competent proceedings in which the question is relevant; for example, proceedings concerned principally with proprietary rights.

ADOPTION

Introduction

In England adoption is now governed largely by the Adoption Act 1976, which came fully into force on 1 January 1988.[22]

---

[15] See Adoption Act 1976, ss 38(1)(e).
[16] On declarations as to marital status, see Chapter 4, 'English status proceedings', pp 63–7 above.
[17] Section 56 is substituted by s 22 of the Family Law Reform Act 1987.
[18] See Chapter 2 above.
[19] See s 58(1).
[20] See ss. 58(2) and 59.
[21] See s 60(3).
[22] See SI 1987/1242.

The essence of adoption, as understood in English law, is the transfer of a child, for almost all purposes, from the family of his biological parents to that of an adoptive parent or parents, so that he ceases to be regarded as related to his biological relatives and is treated as a marital child of the adopter(s).[23] Under English internal law only a person who is under the age of 18 and has not been married can be adopted,[24] and adoption is effected by a court order made in proceedings in which the child's welfare is the principal consideration. Foreign laws may, however, permit the adoption of adults, or by non-judicial means, or for purposes other than the better upbringing of children. Unless, however, a foreign order or other act has the effect, under the foreign law in question, of transferring the adopted person from the family of his biological relatives to that of the adopter(s) for substantially all purposes, it cannot be recognised in England as an adoption.[25]

English adoptions

The jurisdiction of the English courts to make an adoption order is now governed by the Adoption Act 1976. Except in the very rare cases where a Convention adoption order is sought,[26] the English courts have jurisdiction to make an adoption order if the applicant (the proposed adoptive parent) or, in the case of an application by a married couple, one of the applicants, is domiciled in any territory within the British Islands (that is, England and Wales; Scotland; Northern Ireland; the Channel Islands; and the Isle of Man; but not the Irish Republic), and the child is not present in Scotland.[27] In addition s 13 requires that the child should have had his home with the applicant, or at least one of the applicants, throughout a period of, in some cases 13 weeks, in others 12 months, before the order is made, and that sufficient opportunities to see the child with the applicant, or with both applicants together, in the home environment should have been afforded to the adoption agency by which the child was placed or by the local authority within whose area the home is. These supervisory provisions will usually amount in practice to a further requirement of some degree of residence in England by applicant(s) and the child.[28] On the other hand the legislation deliberately omits to require that the child should have an English or British domicile. Moreover, in deciding whether to make an adoption order, the English court applies English internal law exclusively. However, in determining whether making the adoption order would promote the child's welfare (under s 6 of the 1976 Act), the court will take into account whether it would be recognised in other countries with which he is connected.[29]

---

[23] See the 1976 Act s 12 and Part IV.
[24] See the 1976 Act, ss 12(5) and 72(1).
[25] See Re Marshall [1957] Ch 507.
[26] See under 'Convention adoptions', pp 91–2 below.
[27] See the 1976 Act, ss 14(2)(a), 15(2)(a), and 62.
[28] See Re Y [1985] Fam 136. See also s 62(3), and s 72(1A), as substituted by the Children Act 1989.
[29] See Re B(S) [1968] Ch 204.

Convention adoptions

Rather unnecessarily, the Adoption Act 1976 also implements the Hague Convention of 15 November 1965 relating to the Adoption of Children,[30] to which only the United Kingdom, Austria and Switzerland are parties.[31] This provides for 'Convention adoptions', which are ordered in one contracting state and recognised in the other contracting states. Such an order must be applied for as such.[32]

English jurisdiction to make a Convention adoption order is now governed by s 17 of the Adoption Act 1976. For the English court to be competent to make a Convention adoption order:

(1) the adopter or adopters and the child must not all be United Kingdom nationals living in the United Kingdom;[33]

(2) the child must be a United Kingdom national or a national of another Convention country, and must also be habitually resident in the United Kingdom or another Convention country, and must not have been married;[34] and

(3) if the application is by one person, he must either:
   (a) be a national of another Convention country, and be habitually resident in Great Britain; or
   (b) be a United Kingdom national, and be habitually resident in the United Kingdom or another Convention country;[35]

(4) if the application is by a married couple, then either:
   (a) each spouse must be a United Kingdom national or a national of another Convention country, and both must be habitually resident in Great Britain; or
   (b) both must be United Kingdom nationals, and each must be habitually resident in the United Kingdom or another Convention country;[36]

(5) all these jurisdictional requirements must be satisfied both at the time of the application and when the order is made.[37]

In addition to these jurisdictional requirements, the legislation requires a measure of respect for foreign substantive rules. If the adopter, or both of the adopters, are nationals of another Convention country, the adoption must not be prohibited by a provision of the internal law of that country which is specified, in pursuance of the Convention, by statutory instrument.[38] If the child is not a

---

[30] See Cmnd 2615.
[31] See SI 1978/1431, and (1990) 29 ILM 1072.
[32] See Adoption Act 1976, s 17(1).
[33] See s 17(3), and SI 1978/1432, art 5.
[34] See ss 12(5) and 17(2); and SI 1978/1432, art 5.
[35] See s 17(5); and SI 1978/1432, art 5.
[36] See s 17(4); and SI 1978/1432, art 5.
[37] See s 17(1).
[38] See s 17(4), (5) and (8); and SI 1978/1431.

United Kingdom national, but is a national of another Convention country, the English court must apply any provisions of the internal law of that country relating to consents or consultations (other than consents of and consultations with the adopter and members of his family), and must satisfy itself that any such consent is given with full understanding of what is involved. The English court may, however, exercise any power which that law confers on an authority to dispense with such consents, subject to its giving a reasonable opportunity of communicating his opinion on the adoption to any person not resident in Great Britain whose attendance before such authority is required by that law.[39]

For present purposes, 'United Kingdom national' refers primarily to a British citizen. But a British Dependent Territories citizen, a British Overseas citizen, or a British National (Overseas), will also qualify in the rare cases where he also has a right of abode in the United Kingdom.[40]

In cases of dual nationality, one nationality is preferred and the others ignored, preference being given to United Kingdom nationality over any other nationality; to another Convention nationality over a non-Convention nationality; to the Convention nationality with which the person is most closely connected over another Convention nationality; and otherwise to the nationality with which the person is most closely connected.[41] But the English court is authorised to depart from these rules where it considers this appropriate.[42] A stateless person is treated as a national of the country in which he resides.[43] In relation to a state containing more than one legal system, its 'internal law' is to be ascertained by reference to any rule in force throughout the state indicating which of its systems is relevant in the instant case; or, if there is no such rule, it is the system most closely connected with the case.[44]

Recognition of foreign adoptions

Adoption orders made by Scottish, Northern Irish, Isle of Man or Channel Island courts are automatically recognised in England.[45]

Sections 38(1)(d) and 72(2) of the Adoption Act 1976, together with the Adoption (Designation of Overseas Adoptions) Order 1973,[46] provide for the recognition of 'overseas adoptions', currently defined as adoptions of children (persons who were under 18 and had not been married) effected in, and under the statutory law (as distinct from the customary or common law) of, a country outside Great Britain which is specified in Part I or Part II of the Schedule to the

[39] See s 17(6) and (7).
[40] See SI 1978/1432, art 7; the British Nationality Act 1981, s 51(3), as amended by the British Nationality (Falkland Islands) Act 1983, and by SI 1986/948; and the Immigration Act 1971, s 2 (as amended).
[41] See Adoption Act 1976, s 70(2).
[42] See s 70(3).
[43] See s 70(4).
[44] See s 71.
[45] See Adoption Act 1976, s 38(1)(b) and (c).
[46] SI 1973/19.

1973 Order. A large number of countries are so specified.[47] However s 53(2) and (3) of the 1976 Act now enable an overseas adoption to be denied recognition on grounds of public policy, or lack of competence on the part of the foreign authority which purported to authorise it (presumably under its own law). In the case of an overseas adoption made pursuant to the Hague Convention (referred to in the 1976 Act as a 'regulated adoption'), there are also elaborate provisions, based on the Convention, enabling the English High Court to annul the adoption on specified grounds (mainly relating to infringement of the law of the adoptee's nationality), if the adoptee or the adopter(s) are habitually resident in England.[48] There are also provisions for the recognition of, or exceptionally the denial of recognition to, decisions given in other Convention countries annulling an adoption made under the Convention, including one made in England.[49]

The recognition of foreign adoptions at common law is preserved by s 38(1)(e) of the Adoption Act 1976. Such recognition is granted if the adopter, or at least one of the adopters, was domiciled in the country under whose law the adoption was effected. Probably it is not also necessary that the child should have been resident there.[50] The normal public policy proviso of course applies.

For most purposes any adoption recognised in England has the same effects as an English adoption.[51] But only an adoption order made by a court in the United Kingdom is effective for the purpose of acquiring British citizenship.[52]

CHILD CUSTODY AND ABDUCTION

Under this heading, unless otherwise indicated, 'child' refers to a person under the age of 18. The term 'custody', in relation to children, has for some perverse reason been abandoned by the Children Act 1989, but without offering any equivalent single term having the same scope. Hence it is now necessary to use the term 'custody' generically, so as to refer to any matter concerning a child

---

[47] These include: Australia; Bahamas; Barbados; Bermuda; Botswana; British Virgin Islands; Canada; Cayman Islands; Cyprus; Dominica; Fiji; Ghana; Gibraltar; Guyana; Hong Kong; Jamaica; Kenya; Lesotho; Malawi; Malaysia; Malta; Mauritius; Montserrat; New Zealand; Nigeria; Pitcairn; St Christopher, Nevis and Anguilla; St Vincent; Seychelles; Singapore; Sri Lanka; Swaziland; Tanzania; Tonga; Trinidad and Tobago; Uganda; Zambia; Austria; Belgium; Denmark; Finland; France; Germany; Greece; Iceland; Ireland; Israel; Italy; Luxembourg; the Netherlands; Norway; Portugal; South Africa; Spain; Sweden; Switzerland; Turkey; and the United States of America.

[48] See ss 53(1) and 54(2).

[49] See ss 53(2)–(3) and 59(1).

[50] See *Re Valentine's Settlement* [1965] Ch 831. See also *R v Home Secretary ex parte Brassey* [1989] 2 FLR 486, [1989] Imm AR 258.

[51] See Adoption Act 1976, Part IV, especially s 38.

[52] See Adoption Act 1976, s 47(2); British Nationality Act 1981, s 1(5); and *R v Home Secretary ex parte Brassey* [1989] 2 FLR 486, [1989] Imm AR 258. However an overseas adoption (within the meaning of s 72(2) of the 1976 Act) is sufficient to create a right of abode in the United Kingdom under ss 2(1)(d) of the Immigration Act 1971 (as amended); see *Tahid v Home Secretary* [1991] Imm AR 157.

which can be dealt with by an English court by means of an order falling within the scope of s 8 of the Children Act 1989, whether the order would be described as a residence order, a contact order, a prohibited steps order, or a specific issue order, within the meaning of that section.[53]

English jurisdiction

Connecting factors

The jurisdiction of the English courts to determine proceedings concerning child custody is now governed by the Family Law Act 1986, Part I, Chapters I and II (ss 1–7), as amended by the Children Act 1989.[54] Part I of the 1986 Act implements a Report of the English and Scottish Law Commissions on *Custody of Children – Jurisdiction and Enforcement within the United Kingdom*.[55] A main aim of the Report and the 1986 Act is to resolve conflicts between courts of different parts of the United Kingdom. Thus Chapters III and IV of Part I deal respectively with Scottish and Northern Irish custody jurisdiction, and Chapter V with recognition and enforcement.

Under the 1986 Act, the English courts now have jurisdiction to entertain custody proceedings in several distinct cases: in connection with English matrimonial proceedings; by virtue of the child's habitual residence or presence in England; and by virtue of emergency.

The primary basis of English jurisdiction to entertain custody proceedings, conferred by s 2A of the 1986 Act, arises from the existence of English matrimonial proceedings (for divorce, judicial separation, or annulment) in respect of the marriage of the child's parents. In this situation custody jurisdiction follows from jurisdiction in the matrimonial proceedings, and thus depends on the English domicile or one-year habitual residence of either of the parents at or up to their institution.[56] If English matrimonial proceedings have been instituted and not dismissed, the English courts retain custody jurisdiction until the child

---

[53] Section 8(1) provides:

In this Act –
'a contact order' means an order requiring the person with whom a child lives, or is to live, to allow the child to visit or stay with the person named in the order, or for that person and the child otherwise to have contact with each other;
'a prohibited steps order' means an order that no step which could be taken by a parent in meeting his parental responsibility for a child, and which is of a kind specified in the order, shall be taken by any person without the consent of the court;
'a residence order' means an order settling the arrangements to be made as to the person with whom a child is to live; and
'a specific issue order' means an order giving directions for the purpose of determining a specific question which has arisen, or which may arise, in connection with any aspect of parental responsibility for a child.

[54] Part I of the 1986 Act entered into force on 4 April 1988. Most of the 1989 Act entered into force on 14 October 1991. References to Part I of the 1986 Act are to its provisions as so amended.
[55] Law Com 138 (1985).
[56] See Chapter 4, under 'English status proceedings', pp 63–7 above.

attains 18, even if a matrimonial decree has been granted and made absolute;[57] and if the matrimonial proceedings are dismissed after the beginning of the trial, a custody order may be made immediately on their dismissal, or on an application made on or before the dismissal. But English custody jurisdiction is excluded where an English decree of judicial separation has been granted, and Scottish or Northern Irish proceedings for divorce or nullity are pending or have led to the grant of a decree,[58] unless the Scottish or Northern Irish court has made an order declining custody jurisdiction or staying its custody proceedings on the ground that it would be more appropriate for custody to be determined in England. However the English court which is competent on this matrimonial basis may make an order declining custody jurisdiction on the ground that it would be more appropriate for custody to be determined elsewhere.

As a secondary basis, provided for by s 3 of the 1986 Act, the English courts have jurisdiction to entertain custody proceedings if at the date of the application[59] the child concerned is habitually resident in England, or is present in England and is not habitually resident in the United Kingdom. But this basis of English jurisdiction is excluded if Scottish or Northern Irish matrimonial proceedings in respect of the marriage of the child's parents are pending or have led to a decree, unless there is in force an order made by the Scottish or Northern Irish court declining custody jurisdiction or staying its custody proceedings on the ground that it would be more appropriate for custody to be determined in England.

Finally, on the basis of emergency, s 2(3)(b) of the 1986 Act enables an English court to determine custody under the inherent jurisdiction derived from wardship, if the child concerned is present in England at the date of the application,[60] and the court considers that the immediate exercise of its powers is necessary for his protection, even though he is habitually resident in Scotland or Northern Ireland.

Discretion to decline jurisdiction

By s 5(1), an English court which has jurisdiction to determine custody may refuse to do so if the matter has already been determined in proceedings elsewhere. By s 5(2), at any stage in English custody proceedings, the court may stay them if it appears that proceedings with respect to the same matters are continuing elsewhere, or that it would be more appropriate for those matters to be determined in proceedings to be taken elsewhere. Moreover s 5(4) saves common law powers to refuse an application or to grant a stay.

---

[57] See s 42(2).

[58] In the case of Scottish proceedings, the child must be under 16; see s 42(2) and (3).

[59] Where several applications are being determined together, the relevant date is that of the first application; and where there is no application, it is the date on which the court is considering whether to make the order; see s 7(c).

[60] See note 59 above.

In *Re H*,[61] Waite J refused to decline jurisdiction, and indeed restrained the continuance of parallel proceedings in Wisconsin, in a case where children habitually resident in England had been abducted by the father to Wisconsin and then returned under the Hague Convention on abduction. He held that under s 5(2) appropriateness, determined in accordance with the *Spiliada* principles,[62] remains decisive, even where there are parallel custody proceedings abroad, though in custody cases the welfare of the child is paramount and an agreement on jurisdiction concluded by the parents is of little weight. Moreover the child's habitual residence is important but not conclusive. In the result he based his decision partly on the children's habitual residence in England, but mainly the better opportunity of the father to participate in English litigation than that of the mother to participate in Wisconsin litigation.

Duration and variation of English orders

By s 6(1) and (2), an English custody order becomes inoperative if a Scottish or Northern Irish order dealing with the same matters comes into force, and the English courts lose the power to vary the English order in respect of such matters.

By s 6(3)–(5), an English court cannot vary an English custody order while matrimonial proceedings are continuing in Scotland or Northern Ireland in respect of the marriage of the parents of the child concerned, except where:

(1) the English order was made in connection with English proceedings for divorce, judicial separation or nullity in respect of the marriage of the child's parents, and those proceedings are continuing, and in the case of separation proceedings, the decree has not yet been granted; or

(2) there is in force an order made by the Scottish or Northern Irish court declining custody jurisdiction or staying its custody proceedings on the ground that it would be more appropriate for custody to be determined in England; or

(3) the English order was made under the inherent jurisdiction derived from wardship, and the child is present in England, and the court considers that the immediate exercise of its powers is necessary for his protection.

Choice of law, foreign orders and abduction

In English custody proceedings the court determines the substantive issues in accordance with English internal law, under which the main principle, now laid down by s 1(1) of the Children Act 1989, is that 'the child's welfare shall be the court's paramount consideration'. At one time the English courts applied the

---

[61] [1992] 2 FCR 205.

[62] See *The Spiliada* [1987] 1 AC 460, discussed in Chapter 8, under 'The mandatory character of Title II', p 149 *et seq.* below.

English welfare principle even in the face of a foreign custody order, and regarded such an order as merely a factor to be taken into account in determining what would be best for the child;[63] and this approach remains applicable except insofar as there is contrary legislation. Now, however, the Family Law Act 1986, Part I, Chapter V (ss 25–32), requires the English courts to recognise a Scottish or Northern Irish custody order as having the same effects as an English order, and to register and then enforce such orders; and Part II of the Child Abduction and Custody Act 1985, which implements the European Convention, signed at Luxembourg on 20 May 1980 on Recognition and Enforcement of Decisions concerning Custody of Children and on the Restoration of Custody of Children, requires the recognition and enforcement of orders made in many other European countries.

Moreover, even before 1985, the English courts were sometimes prepared in abduction cases to order the return of a child to the country from which he had been abducted after only a summary inquiry to ensure that such return would not be disastrous for him.[64] Now Part I of the Child Abduction and Custody Act 1985 implements the Hague Convention of 25 October 1980 on the Civil Aspects of International Child Abduction, whose main purpose is to secure, as between contracting states, upon a prompt application (which it facilitates), the almost automatic return of an internationally abducted child to the country of his habitual residence. Moreover the English courts now proceed by analogy with the Hague Convention in abduction cases to which it does not apply because the child has been abducted from a non-contracting state. Thus in such cases, since abduction is normally contrary to the interests of children, and custody should normally be determined by the courts of the child's habitual residence, an abducted child will be returned to that country if its courts would apply principles which are acceptable in English eyes, there are no contra-indications of the kinds indicated by art 13 of the Hague Convention, and there is no risk of persecution or discrimination.[65]

The Hague Convention on abduction

Part I of the Child Abduction and Custody Act 1985 implements the Hague Convention of 25 October 1980 on the Civil Aspects of International Child Abduction,[66] to which a substantial number of (mostly Western) countries have

---

[63] See *McKee v McKee* [1951] AC 352.

[64] See *Re H* [1966] 1 WLR 381; and *Re T* [1968] Ch 704. Cf *Re L* [1974] 1 WLR 250; and *Re C* [1978] Fam 105.

[65] See *G v G* [1991] 2 FLR 506; *Re F* [1991] Fam 25, where the Court of Appeal summarily ordered the return of a Jewish child to his habitual residence in Israel, then not yet a contracting state; *Re K*, 24 June 1991, summarily returning a child to Greece; *Re C*, 6 December 1991, summarily returning children to the Isle of Man; *Re S* [1993] 1 FCR 789, where the Court of Appeal remitted for consideration of points analogous to art 13 considerations; and *Re S*, 17 December 1992, where the Court of Appeal summarily returned Moslem children to Pakistan.

[66] Most of the text of the Convention appears as Sched 1 to the 1985 Act.

become party.[67] The Convention is confined to children under the age of 16.[68] Its main purpose is to secure, as between contracting states, upon a prompt application (which it facilitates), the almost automatic return of an internationally abducted child to the country of his habitual residence.[69] Thus the key connecting factor under the Convention is the habitual residence of the child in question (and, indirectly, that of a parent or other person entitled to custody of the child).[70]

By arts 3–5, the Convention in effect defines an international abduction (within the scope of its main provisions) as a wrongful removal of a child from, or a wrongful retention of a child outside, the territory of the contracting state in which he was habitually resident immediately before such wrongful removal or retention. For this purpose a removal or retention is regarded as wrongful if it infringed rights of custody which existed under the law of the state in which the child was habitually resident immediately before the removal or retention, and which were actually being, or would but for the removal or retention have been, exercised at that time.[71] 'Rights of custody' include rights relating to the care of the child's person, and in particular the right to determine his place of residence;[72] and it is immaterial whether such rights were attributed to an individual, or to an institution or other body; whether they were attributed to one person or to several persons jointly; and whether they arose by operation of law, by virtue of a judicial or administrative decision, by reason of a legally effective agreement, or otherwise. Moreover the Court of Appeal has held in *B v B*[73] that

---

[67] The current contracting states to the Hague Convention, in addition to the United Kingdom and eight other EC member states (France, Germany, the Netherlands, Luxembourg, Denmark, Ireland, Spain and Portugal), include the following countries: the United States, Canada, Australia, New Zealand, Norway, Sweden, Switzerland, Austria, Monaco, Hungary, Poland, Romania, Israel, Argentina, Belize, Ecuador, Mexico and Burkina. See Sched 1 to SI 1986/1159, as substituted by SI 1992/3199.

[68] See art 4.

[69] An additional but less important purpose is to promote the peaceful enjoyment internationally of rights of access (including the right to take a child for a limited period of time to a place other than his habitual residence), even in cases where no abduction has occurred; see arts 5 and 21.

[70] On the meaning of habitual residence, see Chapter 2 above.

[71] By art 14, in ascertaining whether there has been a wrongful removal or retention, the courts of the requested state are empowered to take notice directly of the law of, and of judicial decisions given in, the state of the habitual residence of the child, without recourse to the specific procedures for the proof of that law, or for the recognition of foreign decisions, which would otherwise be applicable. See also s 7 of the 1985 Act.

It is also contemplated by art 15 that a court of a contracting state may, before making an order for the return of a child under the Convention, request the applicant to obtain from the courts of the state of the child's habitual residence a decision that the removal or retention was wrongful within the meaning of the Convention, where such a decision may be obtained in that state. The central authorities of the contracting states must then so far as practicable assist the applicant to obtain such a decision. On the making of such declarations by British courts, see s 8 of the 1985 Act.

[72] Thus 'rights of custody', as referred to in the Convention, correspond to the kind of rights which would be conferred by a residence order, within the meaning of s 8 of the Children Act 1989. Similarly 'rights of access', under the Convention, correspond to the kind of rights which would be conferred by a contact order, under s 8.

[73] [1993] Fam 32.

a foreign court seised of a custody dispute itself constitutes a person, institution or other body having rights of custody, within the meaning of the Convention.

By arts 7–10, the Convention requires each contracting state to designate one or more central authorities (in the United Kingdom, the Lord Chancellor and the Secretary of State for Scotland),[74] which are to co-operate with each other to secure the prompt return of children under the Convention, by means including the institution of judicial proceedings and the provision of legal assistance. Anyone seeking such return may apply for assistance to a central authority of any contracting state. If a central authority which receives such an application has reason to believe that the child is in another contracting state, it must directly and without delay transmit the application to the central authority of that other contracting state, and the central authority of the state where the child is must take all appropriate measures in order to obtain the voluntary return of the child. Moreover art 11 requires the courts of contracting states to act expeditiously in proceedings for the return of children; and contemplates that a decision should normally be reached within six weeks from the commencement of proceedings. In the United Kingdom, applications under the Convention are assigned to the English and Northern Irish High Courts and the Scottish Court of Session.[75]

The key provision of the Convention is art 12[1], which requires that, where a child has been internationally abducted (as specified by arts 3–5), and, at the date of the commencement of proceedings before a court of the contracting state where the child is, a period of less than a year has elapsed from the date of the abduction, the court must order the return of the child forthwith. This mandatory obligation to order return is subject only to the limited exceptions specified by art 13, which operate where it is established or found that the person or body having the care of the child's person was not actually exercising the custody rights at the time of the removal or retention, or had consented to or subsequently acquiesced in the removal or retention; or that there is a grave risk that return would expose the child to physical or psychological harm or otherwise place the child in an intolerable situation; or that the child objects to being returned and has attained an age and degree of maturity at which it is appropriate to take account of his views. On these issues, the court must take into account information relating to the social background of the child provided by any competent authority of the child's habitual residence. Moreover, even where the proceedings have been commenced after the expiration of a one-year period from the abduction, art 12[2] requires that the court should still order the return of the child, unless one of the exceptions specified in art 13 applies, or it is demonstrated that the child has become settled in his new environment.

Ancillary rules applicable by the courts or authorities of the state to which the child has been abducted are laid down by arts 16–19. By art 16, after receiving notice of a wrongful removal or retention envisaged by arts 3–5, they are

---

[74] See s 3 of the 1985 Act.
[75] See s 4 of the 1985 Act.

precluded from deciding on the merits of rights of custody until it has been determined that the child is not to be returned under the Convention, or unless an application under the Convention is not lodged within a reasonable time following receipt of the notice.[76] By art 17, the fact that a decision relating to custody has been given, or is entitled to recognition, in the requested state is not a ground for refusing to return a child under the Convention, but the courts of the requested state may take account of the reasons for that decision in applying the Convention. By art 18, the Convention does not limit other powers to order the return of an abducted child. Finally art 19 makes clear that a decision under the Convention concerning the return of a child must not be regarded as a determination on the merits of any custody issue.

In general the English courts have fully respected the policy of the Convention in favour of returning abducted children, and accordingly have construed restrictively the exceptions specified by arts 12 and 13.[77] In particular they have frequently disregarded an abducting mother's assertion that she will not return with the children if their return is ordered. However, an unduly wide view of subsequent acquiescence by the innocent parent, within the meaning of art 13(1)(a), was adopted by a majority of the Court of Appeal (over the powerful dissent of Balcombe LJ) in Re A,[78] where Lord Donaldson MR and Stuart-Smith LJ found the father's letter to the abducting mother, written immediately after her secret departure, too clear to avoid a finding of acquiescence. On the other hand Lord Donaldson MR emphasised the limited consequences of such a finding, as merely giving rise to a judicial discretion, which should be exercised in favour of returning the child unless the circumstances made it more appropriate in the interests of the child that the merits of the custodial dispute should be determined by the courts of the country to which he had been abducted. Even this concession was, however, effectively abandoned by a differently constituted Court of Appeal (Brown P and Staughton and Scott LJJ) in Re A (No 2).[79] They affirmed a decision of Booth J, to whom the case had been referred back, which had paid lip-service to the purposes of the Convention but refused to return the children on seemingly minimal welfare grounds. The Court of Appeal specifically rejected the argument that, in the absence of any grave risk to the child, as contemplated by art 13(1)(b), the discretion permitted by art 13(1)(a) is limited to a consideration of the nature and quality of the acquiescence; in other words, whether the acquiescence is of such a character as to make it appropriate that the merits should be determined in the country to which the children have been abducted; and thus affirmed a decision rewarding the abductor and encouraging future abductions. The Court of Appeal also, rather shockingly, refused leave for a further appeal to the House of Lords.

It is submitted that (preferably, by way of interpretation of the concept of

[76] See also s 9 of the 1985 Act (as amended).
[77] See Re A [1988] 1 FLR 365; Evans v Evans [1989] 1 FLR 135; Re G [1989] 2 FLR 475; V v B [1991] 1 FLR 266; Re N [1991] 1 FLR 913; Re S [1991] 2 FLR 1; Re H, decided by the Court of Appeal on 16 July 1991; and Re A [1991] 2 FLR 241.
[78] [1992] Fam 106.
[79] [1993] Fam 1.

acquiescence; alternatively, in discretion) no account whatever should be taken of subsequent acts or words of the wronged parent unless it is clear that they are truly voluntary; and that in the case of acts or words of a wronged parent which were done or said shortly after he became aware of an unexpected abduction, and were not done as steps in judicial proceedings for which legal advice was available, such voluntariness can only exist where the acts or words were done or said in response to a credible offer by the abducting parent to return the child almost immediately if the wronged parent so desired. In this respect a little comfort may be drawn from the remark of Nicholls V-C in *Re AZ*,[80] that:

> the underlying objectives of the Convention require courts to be slow to infer acquiescence from conduct which is consistent with the parent whose child has been wrongly removed or retained perforce accepting, as a temporary emergency expedient only, a situation forced on him and which in practical terms he is unable to change at once. The Convention is concerned with children taken from one country to another. The Convention has to be interpreted and applied having regard to the way responsible parents can be expected to behave. A parent whose child is wrongly removed to, or retained in, another country is not to be taken as having lost the benefits the Convention confers by reason of him accepting that the child should stay where he or she is for a matter of days or a week or two. That is one edge of the spectrum.

Re AZ itself involved a very young marital child of an American father and an English mother. While the family were habitually resident in Germany, the mother, in breach of the father's joint custodial rights, retained the child in England during an agreed visit, by leaving the child in the care of the mother's sister, who shortly afterwards applied to the English court for a residence order. The father, an American serviceman who got on well with the aunt, was held to have acquiesced by filing an answer in the aunt's English custody proceedings explicitly agreeing with her plans for the child, and then executing a power of attorney enabling her to deal with the child's health, welfare and education, effective for a year, and giving her other useful papers, such as the child's birth certificate, even though a little later he instituted divorce proceedings in California in which he sought actual custody of the child, and some months later he made an application to the English court under the Hague Convention. In this case the Court of Appeal's finding of acquiescence seems justifiable, but the present writer would nonetheless have preferred a decision returning the child to Germany in the court's discretion under the Convention, since there is no reason to think that this would have harmed the child, and it would have underlined the policy of discouraging abduction. Perhaps the court was unduly impressed by the evident fact that the aunt was the most sensible and reliable adult involved.

Another deeply unsatisfactory decision, comparable with *Re A*, was given in *B v K*,[81] where Johnson J effectively rewarded an abducting mother by refusing to return against their wishes children aged nine and seven whom she had

---

[80] [1993] I FLR 682, CA.
[81] [1993] Fam Law 17.

indoctrinated against return. Fortunately this danger was clearly recognised by the Court of Appeal in *S v S*,[82] where Balcombe LJ emphasised that, if the court concluded that the child's views had been influenced by some other person, such as the abducting parent, or that the objection to return was because of a wish to remain with the abducting parent, then little or no weight should normally be given to those views, for any other approach would drive a coach and horses through the primary scheme of the Hague Convention. Nonetheless in *S v S* the Court of Appeal ultimately respected the strongly held wishes of a bright but (in the circumstances understandably) neurotic nine-year-old marital daughter of a French man and an English woman to be educated in England, on account of her greater linguistic ease in English. This decision seems to reflect perfectly the balance between considerations envisaged by the Convention.

The European Convention on recognition

Part II of the Child Abduction and Custody Act 1985 implements the European Convention on Recognition and Enforcement of Decisions concerning Custody of Children and on the Restoration of Custody of Children, signed at Luxembourg on 20 May 1980,[83] which provides for the reciprocal recognition and enforcement of custody orders between contracting states.[84] The Convention is confined to children under the age of 16, and further excludes a child who is entitled, under the law of his habitual residence or nationality or the internal law of the state addressed, to decide on his own place of residence.[85]

The European Convention applies to decisions given by a judicial or administrative authority of a contracting state, insofar as the decision relates to the care of the person of a child, including the right to decide on the place of his residence, or to the right of access to him.[86] Subject to specified exceptions, such a decision must be recognised in the other contracting states, and if it is enforceable in the state of origin, it must also be made enforceable in the other contracting states.[87] The Convention also applies to a decision, given in a contracting state after the removal across an international frontier of a child as to whose custody there was then no enforceable decision given in a contracting state, which relates to his custody and declares the removal to be unlawful.[88]

---

[82] [1993] 2 WLR 775.

[83] For the text of the European Convention as implemented, see Sched 2 to the 1985 Act.

[84] The current contracting states to the European Convention, in addition to the United Kingdom, comprise nine EC member states (France, Germany, Belgium, the Netherlands, Luxembourg, Denmark, Ireland, Spain and Portugal), and five other European countries (Norway, Sweden, Switzerland, Austria and Cyprus). See Sched 2 to SI 1986/1159, as substituted by SI 1992/1299.

[85] See art 1(a).

[86] See arts 1(b)–(c) and 11(1). By art 11(2), on recognising a decision concerning access, the competent authority of the state addressed may fix the conditions for its exercise, taking into account, in particular, relevant undertakings given by the parties. By art 11(3), where a decision on custody does not deal with access, or recognition of a decision on custody is refused, the central authority of the state addressed may apply to its courts for a decision on access at the request of a person claiming a right of access.

[87] See art 7.

[88] See art 12. On the making of such declarations by British courts, see s 23(2) of the 1985 Act.

Each contracting state must designate a central authority for the purposes of the Convention.[89] A person who is entitled under a custody decision given in a contracting state and seeks its recognition under the Convention may apply to the central authority in any contracting state, and the receiving central authority must forward the application directly and without delay to the central authority of the contracting state in which recognition is sought.[90] The latter must without delay take appropriate steps, including the institution of local judicial or administrative proceedings, to secure the recognition or enforcement of the decision;[91] and if recognition or enforcement of the foreign decision is refused, it may institute local proceedings concerning the substance of the case, and should then arrange for representation for the applicant therein.[92]

Enforcement of a foreign custody order under the Convention must be sought separately in each part of the United Kingdom, by means of an application for registration of the order in the English High Court, the Scottish Court of Session, or the Northern Irish High Court.[93] An order registered in England is enforceable in the same way as an English custody order.[94] While an application for registration is pending, interim relief is available in connection with the application, but the English courts cannot exercise their normal powers to make custody orders.[95]

Recognition and enforcement of the foreign decision can only be refused on one of the grounds specified in arts 9 and 10. Even then refusal is discretionary, and it firmly declared by art 9(3) that in no circumstances may the foreign decision be reviewed as to its substance. The grounds for refusal are as follows:

LACK OF NOTICE

Refusal of recognition is permitted by art 9(1)(a), where the decision was given in the absence of the defendant or his legal representative, and the defendant was not duly served with the instituting document in sufficient time to enable him to arrange his defence, unless the failure to effect service was due to the defendant's having concealed his whereabouts from the original applicant. The discretionary nature of this ground is demonstrated by *Re G*,[96] where a Belgian order granting custody to the father had been made without the mother having any knowledge of the application, because of a mistake by the Belgian court in sending the notice to a garbled version of her address in England.

---

[89] The central authorities in the United Kingdom are the Lord Chancellor and the Secretary of State for Scotland; see s 14 of the 1985 Act.

[90] See art 4.

[91] See art 5(1). On documents which should accompany a request to a judicial or other authority for recognition or enforcement, see art 13.

[92] See art 5(4).

[93] See ss 15(2)(b), 16, and 27(2) of the 1985 Act.

[94] See s 18. See also s 17, which provides for cancellation or variation of the registration of a foreign order in consequence of the order being revoked or varied in the original country.

[95] See ss 19 and 20.

[96] [1990] 2 FLR 325.

Nonetheless Booth J in her discretion recognised the order, since the mother could have raised the point in subsequent Belgian custody proceedings in which she took part, and in any event she had removed the child from Belgium in breach of a known prior order of the Belgian court.

LACK OF COMPETENCE

Refusal of recognition is permitted by art 9(1)(b), where the decision was given in the absence of the defendant or his legal representative, and the competence of the original court was not founded on one of the following connections: the habitual residence of the defendant; or the last common habitual residence of the child's parents, at least one parent being still habitually resident there; or the habitual residence of the child.

In addition, recognition may be refused under art 10(1)(c) if, at the time when the proceedings were instituted in the state of origin, either: (1) the child was a national of or habitually resident in the state addressed, and was neither a national of nor habitually resident in the state of origin; or (2) the child was a national of both the state of origin and the state addressed, and was habitually resident in the state addressed.

INCONSISTENT DECISIONS

Recognition may be refused, under art 9(1)(c), taken with art 1(d) and with s 15(3) of the 1985 Act, where the decision is incompatible with a custody decision which became enforceable in the state addressed before an improper removal of the child, unless the child had his habitual residence in the territory of the requesting state for one year before the removal. The following constitute an improper removal:

(1) a removal of a child across an international frontier in breach of a decision relating to his custody given and enforceable in a contracting state; or

(2) a failure to return a child across an international frontier at the end of a period of access or other temporary stay in a territory other than the one where custody is exercised; or

(3) a removal which is subsequently declared unlawful under art 12.

In addition, recognition may be refused under art 10(1)(d), where the decision is incompatible with another decision, which was either given in the state addressed, or was given in a third state and is enforceable in the state addressed, and (in either case) was given pursuant to proceedings begun before the submission of the request for recognition or enforcement, and (in addition) refusal is in accordance with the welfare of the child.

PUBLIC POLICY, CHANGED CIRCUMSTANCES AND WELFARE

Refusal of recognition is permitted by art 10(1)(a), where the effects of the decision are manifestly incompatible with the fundamental principles of the law relating to the family and children in the state addressed.

Refusal is also permissible, under art 10(1)(b), where by reason of a change in the circumstances (including the passage of time, but not including a mere change in the residence of the child after an improper removal), the effects of the original decision are manifestly no longer in accordance with the welfare of the child. For this purpose, art 15 requires the court addressed to ascertain the child's views unless this is impracticable having regard (in particular) to his age and understanding, and empowers it to request that any appropriate enquiries be carried out. This exception would seem however to offer an easy opportunity for abuse by the court addressed. Thus in *F v F*[97] Booth J saw fit to reward an abducting mother by invoking as a change of circumstance her subsequent willingness to concede some access to the father. More satisfactorily in *Re G*[98] the same judge showed a healthy scepticism towards the wishes unsurprisingly expressed by a child aged ten to stay with the abducting parent.

In addition to the grounds on which recognition may be refused altogether, art 10(2) permits the court addressed to adjourn proceedings for recognition or enforcement in the following cases: if an ordinary form of review of the original decision has been commenced; if proceedings relating to the custody of the child, commenced before the proceedings in the state of origin were instituted, are pending in the state addressed; or if another decision concerning the custody of the child is the subject of proceedings for enforcement or involving recognition.

By art 26, in relation to a state which has in matters of custody two or more systems of law of territorial or personal application, references to the law of a person's habitual residence or nationality are to the system of law determined by the rules in force in that state; or, if there are no such rules, to the system of law with which the person concerned is most closely connected. But references to the state of origin or to the state addressed are respectively to the territorial unit where the decision was given, or to the territorial unit where recognition or enforcement of the decision, or restoration of custody, is requested. However, by ss 15(2)(a) and 16(4)(a) of the 1985 Act, an English, Scottish or Northern Irish decision refusing to recognise a foreign custody order under arts 9 or 10 of the Convention has effect throughout the United Kingdom.

In the United Kingdom, the relationship between the Hague Convention on abduction and the European Convention on recognition is governed by s 16(4)(c) of the 1985 Act, by which a British court must refuse to register a foreign custody order under the European Convention and Part II of the Act, if an application in respect of the child under the Hague Convention and Part I of the Act is pending.

---

[97] [1989] Fam 1.
[98] [1990] 2 FLR 325.

6

CORPORATIONS AND INSOLVENCY

Corporations in general

For present purposes a corporation may be defined as an artificial entity which has legal personality. English law has long adopted a liberal approach to the recognition of foreign corporations. The creation of a corporation in a foreign country in accordance with its law is recognised in England, without any requirement that the creators, directors, shareholders, or activities of the corporation should have any other connection with the country of incorporation. Moreover a corporation is regarded as domiciled (in the traditional English sense) in the country in which it was incorporated,[1] and a foreign corporation, validly created and existing under the law of a foreign country, may sue and be sued in England.[2] As well as creation, issues concerning the fundamental capacity or internal management of a corporation are governed by the law of its country of incorporation,[3] and a dissolution or merger effected under that law is recognised in England.[4]

In these respects English law differs from that of most European countries, which refer corporate creation and status to the law of the country in which the entity has its actual headquarters. The European Community attempted to deal with this problem by a Convention on the Mutual Recognition of Companies and Bodies Corporate, signed on 29 February 1968,[5] but this Convention has not entered into force, and now seems unlikely to do so.[6]

Another connecting factor, the location of a corporation's actual head-

---

[1] See *Gasque v IRC* [1940] 2 KB 80; and Dicey & Morris, Rules 154(1) and 155.
[2] For recognition of an unusual type of corporation (a Hindu temple, having corporate status under Indian law), see *Bumper Development Corp v Metropolitan Police Commissioner* [1991] 4 All ER 638, [1991] 1 WLR 1362.
[3] See *Risdon Iron and Locomotive Works v Furness* [1906] 1 KB 49, holding that shareholders in an English limited liability company do not incur personal liability on its contracts, even where the contract is governed by a foreign law having a contrary rule; and *Carse v Coppen* [1951] SLT 145, holding in accordance with Scottish internal law (as it then stood) that a Scottish company could not create a floating charge over its English assets.
[4] See *National Bank of Greece and Athens v Metliss* [1958] AC 509, and *Adams v National Bank of Greece and Athens* [1961] AC 255. On the revivification of a dissolved foreign corporation for the purpose of winding it up in England, see the Insolvency Act 1986, ss 221(5)(a) and 225.
[5] See EC BullSupp 2/69.
[6] See Lasok & Stone, at pp 89–91.

quarters, has long been used in the United Kingdom for fiscal purposes,[7] and has now come to play an increasing role for conflict purposes.[8] It refers to the place where the central management and control of the corporation is in fact exercised; in effect, the place at which meetings of the board of directors (or equivalent managerial organ) are actually held.[9] Probably statutory references to a corporation's principal place of business (for example, in s 4(2)(a)(iv) of the Foreign Judgments (Reciprocal Enforcement) Act 1933) are to the same concept.[10]

Both connections (the place of incorporation and the location of the registered or equivalent office; and the location of the actual headquarters) are used in determining a corporation's domicile and seat for jurisdictional purposes under the 1968 and Lugano Conventions on civil jurisdiction and judgments and the Civil Jurisdiction and Judgments Act 1982. For most such purposes, s 42 of the 1982 Act specifies essentially that a corporation is domiciled and seated both in the country under whose law it was incorporated and in which it has its registered office or some other official address (one which it is required by law to register, notify or maintain for the purpose of receiving notices or other communications), and also in the country where its central management and control is exercised.[11] However s 43 provides a slightly different definition of a corporation's seat for the purpose of art 16(2) of the Conventions, which provides for exclusive jurisdiction over proceedings principally concerned with the validity of the constitution, the nullity or the dissolution of companies or other legal persons, or the decisions of their organs. Again in general a corporation is seated both in the country of its incorporation and in that of its actual headquarters, but a corporation incorporated under the law of a part of the United Kingdom is treated as seated exclusively in that part, even if its actual headquarters are located elsewhere.

The location of a corporate branch (or secondary establishment) is also important in relation to jurisdiction under Title II of the 1968 and Lugano Conventions,[12] and in cases where those Conventions remit English jurisdiction to English law,[13] and to the recognition and enforcement in England of judgments from countries other than contracting states to those Conventions.[14]

---

[7] See Dicey & Morris, Rule 154(2).
[8] See, for example, the Arbitration Act 1975, s 1.
[9] See *The Rewia* [1991] 2 Lloyd's Rep 325, CA. It seems likely, in the light of *Unit Construction v Bullock* [1960] AC 351, that the possibility, recognised by the House of Lords in *Swedish Central Ry v Thompson* [1925] AC 495, that the central management and control of a company may be divided or peripatetic, so as to make the company simultaneously resident in two countries for fiscal purposes, should now be regarded as obsolete.
[10] See *The Rewia* [1991] 2 Lloyd's Rep 325, CA.
[11] For fuller discussion see Chapter 8, under 'The central role of the defendant's domicile', p 128 *et seq.* below.
[12] See arts 5(5), 8[2] and 13[2] of the Conventions; and Chapters 7–11 below.
[13] See art 4 of the Conventions, and the Companies Act 1985, ss 691–698.
[14] See Chapter 14, below.

Winding up of companies

The jurisdiction of the English courts to wind up a company depends primarily on whether the company is regarded as solvent or insolvent, for the winding up of solvent companies falls within the scope of the 1968 and Lugano Conventions and is governed by art 16(2), while insolvent liquidation, and proceedings analogous thereto, are excluded from their scope by art 1[2](2).[15]

In the case of a solvent company, art 16(2) confers exclusive jurisdiction to entertain, inter alia, winding-up proceedings on the courts of the contracting state in which the company has its seat. By art 53[1], in order to determine that seat, the court seised must apply its own law, and in the United Kingdom s 43 of the 1982 Act specifies in effect that for the purpose of art 16(2):

(1) A company has its seat in the United Kingdom if either:
(a) it was incorporated under the law of a part of the United Kingdom; or
(b) its central management and control is exercised in the United Kingdom.

(2) A company has its seat in a particular part of the United Kingdom (such as England and Wales) if either:
(a) it was incorporated or formed under the law of that part; or
(b) it was incorporated under an enactment forming part of the law of more than one part of the United Kingdom, and it has a registered office situated in that part of the United Kingdom; or
(c) it was incorporated under the law of a country outside the United Kingdom, but its central management and control is exercised in that part.

(3) A company has its seat in another contracting state if either:
(a) it was incorporated under the law of that state; or
(b) its central management and control is exercised in that state; but not (in either case) if either:

---

[15] Parallel negotiations based on art 220[4] of the EC Treaty led to the emergence from a working group in June 1980 of a Draft Convention on Bankruptcy, Winding Up, Arrangements, Compositions and Similar Proceedings, together with a Report thereon; see EC BullSupp 2/82. For many years the Draft Convention has been shelved by the Council, but the Commission has recently endeavoured to revive the project. For a commentary on the Draft Convention, see Lasok & Stone, Chapter 10.

Meanwhile negotiations within the framework of the Council of Europe have led to the signature at Istanbul on 5 June 1990 of a Convention (No 136) on Certain International Aspects of Bankruptcy (including liquidation of insolvent companies). The Istanbul Convention is, however, very limited in scope, and deals principally with the recognition in one contracting state of the status and powers of a liquidator appointed in another contracting state. More precisely, it applies where a bankruptcy is opened in a contracting state, and then governs: (a) the exercise in other contracting states of certain powers of the liquidator; (b) the opening of secondary bankruptcies in other contracting states; and (c) the information to be given to creditors residing in other contracting states, and the lodgment of their claims. In particular, it does not regulate direct jurisdiction to open a primary bankruptcy, nor does it deal with most issues of choice of law or substantive law. Moreover it will give way to other existing or future conventions, and, as between EC member states, to rules of Community law. The United Kingdom has not ratified the Istanbul Convention. For a commentary thereon, see Güneysu, 'The New European Bankruptcy Convention', (1991) 11 YEL 295.

(c) it has its seat in the United Kingdom by virtue of incorporation under the law thereof;[16] or

(d) it is shown that the courts of the other contracting state would not regard it for the purposes of art 16(2) as having its seat there.

However, as regards the allocation of jurisdiction conferred on British courts by art 16(2) between the courts of the three parts of the United Kingdom, corporate winding-up proceedings are excluded from the scope of Sched 4 to the 1982 Act by s 17 and Sched 5, para 1. Instead the problem is in effect referred to the British rules which also govern the jurisdiction of the courts of a part of the United Kingdom to entertain winding-up proceedings in respect of insolvent companies, or of solvent companies not seated within the contracting states. But if a situation arose where such rules failed to confer jurisdiction on the courts for any part of the United Kingdom to entertain winding-up proceedings in respect of a solvent company seated in the United Kingdom, art 16(2) would operate to confer such jurisdiction on the courts of all three parts.

In the result, the English courts have jurisdiction to wind up a company which is registered in England, whether or not the company is solvent.[17] Conversely they lack jurisdiction to wind up a company which is registered in Scotland or Northern Ireland, again regardless of its solvency.[18] In the case of a company which is not registered in any part of the United Kingdom, the English courts have winding-up jurisdiction if:

(a) the company either has a principal place of business in England, or it does not have a principal place of business within the United Kingdom;[19] and

(b) if it is solvent, it does not have a seat in another contracting state to the 1968 or Lugano Conventions.[20]

Moreover an English court is not prevented from winding up a company incorporated outside the United Kingdom by the fact that the company has been dissolved or otherwise ceased to exist under the law of its country of incorporation.[21]

An English liquidation extends to foreign assets and liabilities.[22] In English winding-up proceedings, issues specific to such proceedings (such as priorities between creditors) are governed by English internal law, but issues which can arise in other contexts (such as the validity of a contract,[23] or, in the case of a

---

[16] Despite the attempt by s 43 to make a British seat by virtue of incorporation prevail over a seat in another contracting state by virtue of actual headquarters, it is probable that in such a situation art 23 of the Conventions would give primacy to the proceedings in the court first seised, and art 28 would require its judgment to be recognised in the country of the other seat. See Lasok & Stone, at pp 247–8; cf Dicey & Morris, Rule 157(1).

[17] See art 16(2) of the 1968 Convention, and s 117 of the Insolvency Act 1986.

[18] See Insolvency Act 1986, s 220(1)(b).

[19] See Insolvency Act 1986, ss 220 and 221.

[20] See art 16(2) of the 1968 and Lugano Conventions.

[21] See Insolvency Act 1986, ss 221(5)(a) and 225.

[22] See Dicey & Morris, Rule 159(1).

[23] See *Re Bonacina* [1912] 2 Ch 394.

company incorporated abroad, the identity of its shareholders)[24] remain governed by the law which would otherwise apply to them.[25]

Under s 426 of the Insolvency Act 1986, Scottish or Northern Irish court orders for or ancillary to winding up must be recognised and, in general, enforced in England, regardless of the existence of any connecting factor between the company and the original country. Similarly, by s 72 of the 1986 Act, and s 7 of the Administration of Justice Act 1977, a receiver appointed under Scottish or Northern Irish law in connection with a floating charge may exercise his powers in England.

In the case of a company incorporated outside the United Kingdom, English law recognises the authority to act on behalf of the company of a liquidator appointed under the law of the country of incorporation.[26] Similarly a receiver appointed under the law of the country of incorporation in connection with a floating charge may exercise his powers in England.[27]

Other proceedings under company law

Article 16(2) of the 1968 and Lugano Conventions confers exclusive jurisdiction on the courts of the contracting state in which a company, other legal person, or association of natural or legal persons has its seat, over proceedings (not based on insolvency) which have as their principal subject-matter the validity of the constitution, the nullity or the dissolution of the entity, or the validity or nullity of decisions of its organs.[28] Other proceedings under company law, not involving insolvency, are subject to the normal rules laid down by the Conventions, such as arts 5(1)[29] and 17.[30]

Article 16(2) clearly covers a petition for the winding up of a solvent company, and probably extends to a member's petition under s 459 of the Companies Act 1989, based on the allegation that the company's affairs are being conducted in a manner unfairly prejudicial to the member. This point was overlooked by the Court of Appeal in *Re Harrods (Buenos Aires) Ltd*,[31] which involved a member's petition, primarily for an order under s 459 that the controlling member should purchase the petitioner's shares, and in the alternative for winding up on the 'just and equitable' ground. But the House of Lords has now referred the case to the European Court of Justice, and the questions referred include whether proceedings under Part XVII of the Companies Act

---

[24] See *Re Banque des Marchands de Moscou* [1958] Ch 182.
[25] See Dicey & Morris, Rule 159(2).
[26] See Dicey & Morris, Rule 160.
[27] See *Cretanor Maritime Co Ltd v Irish Marine Management Ltd* [1978] 1 WLR 966, and Dicey & Morris, Rule 161(2).
[28] See *Newtherapeutics Ltd v Katz* [1991] Ch 226, where Knox J clarified art 16(2) in the light of the French and German texts.
[29] See Case 34/82 *Peters v South Netherlands Contractors' Association* [1983] ECR 987.
[30] See Case C-214/89 *Powell Duffryn v Petereit* [1992] 1 ECR 1745.
[31] [1991] 4 All ER 334, [1991] 3 WLR 397.

1985 (protection of members against unfair prejudice), or proceedings for the dissolution of a company, fall within art 16(2).[32]

Confusion is also apparent in Knox J's decision in *Newtherapeutics Ltd v Katz*.[33] He took the view that art 16(2) applied to an action brought by an English company against some of its former directors, complaining that in signing a contract, purportedly on its behalf, they had acted improperly because they had not been authorised by a meeting of the board. But it seems very doubtful that the act of some directors in signing a contract can be regarded as that of a corporate organ, within the meaning of art 16(2); and also that the validity or nullity, as distinct from the propriety, of the act is the principal question in proceedings seeking a pecuniary remedy against the individual directors who acted. Knox J proceeded to rule, less controversially, that an alternative complaint that in signing the contract the defendant directors had acted negligently in relation to the company's interests did not fall within art 16(2). Nonetheless he then treated the whole action as falling within art 16(2), on the ground that the former complaint constituted the main subject-matter of the action, since it was more likely to succeed. It seems impossible to find any warrant for this 'parasitic' approach in the Conventions. Finally, he ignored the elementary point that art 16 explicitly applies regardless of domicile, and dismissed the action as regards a defendant director who was domiciled outside the contracting states, on the wholly irrelevant ground that the action did not fall within any heading of RSC Ord 11, r 1(1).

As regards proceedings (other than for winding up) in respect of companies seated in the United Kingdom, the 1982 Act has implemented art 16(2) of the Conventions in a curious way. Although art 16(2) of Sched 4 to the 1982 Act allocates exclusive jurisdiction to the courts of the part of the United Kingdom in which the seat is located in the case of proceedings concerned with the validity of the constitution, the nullity, or the dissolution of a company, a different solution is adopted in the case of proceedings concerned with validity or nullity of decisions of corporate organs. For such proceedings art 5A of Sched 4 merely gives non-exclusive jurisdiction to the courts of the part of the United Kingdom containing the corporate seat, so that, for example, a plaintiff who wishes to challenge a decision of the board of directors is permitted to sue in another part of the United Kingdom where one or more of the defendant directors are domiciled.

As the European Court of Justice ruled in *Peters v South Netherlands Contractors' Association*,[34] other disputes under company law (not involving insolvency) may fall within art 5(1), as in the case of an action by a company against a shareholder to recover calls on shares. Thus such an action can be brought at the place where payment is due, often the registered office of the company, since the relationship between a company and its members is regarded as contractual for

---

[32] Case C-314/92 *Ladenimor v Intercomfinanz* [1992] OJ C219/4.
[33] [1991] Ch 226.
[34] See Case 34/82, [1983] ECR 987.

the purposes of the Conventions. Moreover in *Powell Duffryn v Petereit*[35] the court upheld, as complying with art 17, a jurisdiction clause contained in a company's articles of association and covering disputes between the company and shareholders as such. However in *Newtherapeutics Ltd v Katz*[36] Knox J held that a claim by a company against a director not domiciled within the contracting states and not having a service contract, for improper or negligent conduct as office-holder, was not a contractual claim within RSC Ord 11, r 1(1)(d).

Bankruptcy of individuals

Like proceedings for the winding up of insolvent companies, bankruptcy proceedings in respect of individuals are excluded from the scope of the 1968 and Lugano Conventions by art 1[2](2). English bankruptcy jurisdiction is now governed by s 265 of the Insolvency Act 1986, by which it is necessary and sufficient that the debtor is connected with England in one of the following ways:

(1)   that he is domiciled in England (in the traditional English sense of origin or permanent residence), presumably at the date of the presentation of the bankruptcy petition;
(2)   that he is personally present in England at the presentation of the petition;
(3)   that at any time during the three years preceding the presentation of the petition, he was ordinarily resident in England, or had a place of residence in England, or carried on business in England, whether personally or through an agent, and whether alone or as a partner.

In English bankruptcy proceedings, issues specific to such proceedings (such as priorities between creditors) are governed by English internal law,[37] though issues which can arise in other contexts (such as the validity of a contract) remain governed by the law which would otherwise apply to them.[38] The English bankruptcy rules do not discriminate against foreign creditors, or creditors under contracts governed by foreign law.[39]

English bankruptcy proceedings remain possible despite the existence of a foreign bankruptcy adjudication in respect of the same debtor.[40] On the other hand, English law endeavours to vest the debtor's property in his English trustee in bankruptcy, regardless of its location.[41] Within the United Kingdom this endeavour may be facilitated by the provisions for co-operation between the bankruptcy courts of its three parts, made by s 426 of the 1986 Act. An order for

---

[35] Case C-214/89, [1992] 1 ECR 1745.
[36] [1991] Ch 226.
[37] See Dicey & Morris, Rule 165.
[38] See *Re Bonacina* [1912] 2 Ch 394.
[39] See *Ex parte Melbourn* (1870) LR 6 Ch App 64, and *Re Kloebe* (1884) 28 ChD 175.
[40] See Dicey & Morris, Rule 163.
[41] See Insolvency Act 1986, ss 283, 306 and 436; and Dicey & Morris, Rule 164.

discharge in an English bankruptcy extends to debts arising under contracts governed by foreign law.[42]

Bankruptcy orders made by Scottish or Northern Irish courts must be recognised and, in general, enforced in England, regardless of the existence of any connecting factors between the debtor and the original country, and so as (for English purposes) to vest in the Scottish or Northern Irish trustee the debtor's property, wherever situated, including English land.[43] Equally a discharge of debts under a Scottish or Northern Irish bankruptcy is effective in England, regardless of what law governs the contract from which the debt arises.[44]

Bankruptcy orders made outside the United Kingdom are recognised in England if the debtor was domiciled in the original country, or submitted by appearance in the original proceedings, or (probably) if he was ordinarily resident or carried on business in the original country.[45] Such recognition of a foreign order extends to recognition of its effect under the foreign law of vesting the debtor's English movables in the trustee, but not his English land.[46] But a discharge of debts under such a bankruptcy is only effective in England if the debt arises from a contract which is governed by the law of the country of the bankruptcy, or of a third country which recognises the discharge.[47]

---

[42] See Insolvency Act 1986, s 281, and Dicey & Morris, Rule 166.
[43] See Insolvency Act 1986, s 426, and Dicey & Morris, Rules 167(1) and 168.
[44] See Dicey & Morris, Rule 173.
[45] See Dicey & Morris, Rule 167(2).
[46] See Dicey & Morris, Rules 169–170. In the case of successive bankruptcies of the same debtor in different countries (including parts of the United Kingdom), the earliest effective assignment of property to a trustee prevails over later assignments of the same property; see Dicey & Morris, Rule 171.
[47] See Dicey & Morris, Rule 172.

7

CIVIL JURISDICTION – INTRODUCTION

Direct international jurisdiction

In this and the next four chapters we shall examine the direct international jurisdiction of the English courts to entertain most types of civil proceeding. In the present context, 'international jurisdiction' refers to the power of a court to entertain a proceeding instituted before it, in view of the ways in which the parties to and the subject-matter of the proceeding are connected with the country to which the court belongs, and with other countries.

Rules which define or regulate the international jurisdiction of courts may be direct or indirect in nature. Rules of direct jurisdiction are applicable by a court for the purpose of determining *its own* jurisdiction to entertain proceedings which have been instituted before it. In accordance with such rules, the court seised will either accept jurisdiction and proceed to determine the substance of the dispute; or will decline jurisdiction, and leave the substantive dispute to be determined by a court of another country.

On the other hand, rules of indirect jurisdiction are applicable where a dispute has already been determined by a court of one country, and a court of another country is requested to recognise or enforce the judgment given by the original court. In accordance with such rules, the court addressed will determine whether it regards the original court as having been competent to determine the dispute, and will proceed to recognise, or refuse to recognise, the foreign judgment in the light of this determination.

This chapter and Chapters 8–11 below will deal with the direct jurisdiction of the English courts. The recognition and enforcement in England of foreign judgments, including the rules dealing with the indirect jurisdiction of foreign courts in connection with the recognition and enforcement of their judgments in England, will be considered in Chapter 14 below.

The Community Conventions

The direct jurisdiction of the English courts to entertain most types of civil proceeding is now governed principally by European Community law. More specifically, the principal legislation governing this matter is Title II of the

Brussels Convention of 27 September 1968 on Jurisdiction and the Enforcement of Judgments in Civil and Commercial Matters ('the 1968 Convention'),[1] as amended by three ancillary Conventions on accession thereto: the Luxembourg Convention of 9 October 1978 on Danish, Irish and British accession ('the 1978 Convention');[2] the Luxembourg Convention of 25 October 1982 on Greek accession ('the 1982 Convention');[3] and the Donostia–San Sebastián Convention of 26 May 1989 on Spanish and Portuguese accession ('the 1989 Convention').[4] These Conventions ('the Community Conventions') have the force of law in the United Kingdom by virtue of s 2 of the Civil Jurisdiction and Judgments Act 1982 ('the 1982 Act'), as amended by the Civil Jurisdiction and Judgments Act 1982 (Amendment) Orders 1989 and 1990.[5]

The Community Conventions, along with the Luxembourg Protocol of 3 June 1971 (hereafter 'the 1971 Protocol'),[6] which empowers the European Court of Justice to give preliminary rulings on their interpretation at the request of

---

[1] For the text of the 1968 Convention, as amended by the 1978, 1982 and 1989 Conventions, and currently in force in the United Kingdom, see [1990] OJ C189/2; or Sched 1 to the (British) Civil Jurisdiction and Judgments Act 1982, as substituted by SI 1990/2591. (For the original version, see [1978] OJ L304/36; for the 1978 version, [1978] OJ L304/77; and for the 1982 version, [1983] OJ C97/2.) For the Jenard Report (of the committee which negotiated the 1968 Convention), see [1979] OJ C59/1.

[2] For the text of the 1978 Convention, see [1978] OJ L304/1; or, as regards Titles V and VI, Sched 3 to the (British) Civil Jurisdiction and Judgments Act 1982. For the Schlosser Report (of the negotiating committee), see [1979] OJ C59/71.

[3] For the text of the 1982 Convention, see [1982] OJ L388/1; or, as regards Titles V and VI, Sched 3A to the (British) Civil Jurisdiction and Judgments Act 1982, added by SI 1989/1346. For the Evrigenis and Kerameus Report (of the negotiating committee), see [1986] OJ C298/1.

[4] For the text of the 1989 Convention, see [1989] OJ L285/1; or Sched 3B to the (British) Civil Jurisdiction and Judgments Act 1982, added by SI 1990/2591. For the Cruz, Real and Jenard Report (of the negotiating committee), see [1990] OJ C189/35.

[5] SI 1989/1346 and 1990/2591. For the implementation of the Conventions in the Irish Republic, see s 3(1) of the (Irish) Jurisdiction of Courts and Enforcement of Judgments (European Communities) Act 1988.

[6] For the text of the 1971 Protocol, as amended by the 1978, 1982 and 1989 Conventions, and currently in force in the United Kingdom, see [1990] OJ C189/25; or Sched 2 to the (British) Civil Jurisdiction and Judgments Act 1982, as substituted by SI 1990/2591. For the Second Jenard Report (of the negotiating committee), see [1979] OJ C59/66.

The 1971 Protocol initially entered into force in the original six member states on 1 September 1975. It is given the force of law in the United Kingdom by s 2 of the Civil Jurisdiction and Judgments Act 1982 (as amended). Decisions given by the European Court of Justice under the 1971 Protocol are, of course, binding on the English courts, subject only to the power of an appellate court to refer again to the European Court of Justice a point which has been the subject of a previous ruling, in the hope that it will reconsider its decision; see Cases 28–30/62 *Da Costa v Nederlandse Belastingadministratie* [1963] ECR 31; Case 283/81 *CILFIT v Italian Ministry of Health* [1982] ECR 3415; and s 3 of the Civil Jurisdiction and Judgments Act 1982. Section 3 also permits the British courts, in interpreting the Conventions, to take into account the Jenard, Schlosser, and Evrigenis and Kerameus Reports (cited in notes 1–4 above). See also s 4 of the (Irish) Jurisdiction of Courts and Enforcement of Judgments (European Communities) Act 1988.

appellate courts of contracting states,[7] are designed to harmonise the laws of the EC member states on the direct international jurisdiction of their courts to entertain most kinds of civil proceeding; and also on the related matter of the reciprocal recognition and enforcement in each member state of civil judgments given by the courts of the other member states.[8] They were negotiated on the basis of art 220(4) of the EC Treaty, and of art 3(2) of the three Acts of Accession, annexed to the Treaties of Accession to the Communities. They envisage the existence of strong mutual respect and trust between the courts of the various member states, and endeavour to allocate jurisdiction between them in a principled and convenient way, at least in cases where the defendant (or, in some cases, the subject-matter of the dispute) is regarded as 'belonging' to the Community, rather than the external world. Moreover, in the substantial case-law which has arisen under the 1971 Protocol, the European Court of Justice has with rare exceptions ruled that, in order to ensure, as far as possible, that the rights and obligations under the 1968 Convention of member states and private persons are equal and uniform, most of the concepts used in the Convention must not be interpreted as merely referring to the law of the country (or one of the countries) whose courts are involved, but must be construed independently and by reference to the objectives and scheme of the Convention, and to general principles stemming from the laws of the member states, viewed comparatively and as a whole.

At present the 1968 Convention is in force:

- in its 1982 version (that is, as amended by the 1978 and 1982 Conventions), in Germany,[9] Belgium, Denmark and Ireland;[10] and

---

[7] The principal difference between the 1971 Protocol and art 177 of the EC Treaty is that under the Protocol a court sitting at first instance has no power to request a preliminary ruling. It is therefore submitted that a first instance court is absolutely bound to follow or distinguish any relevant rulings previously given by the European Court of Justice.

Another novelty of the 1971 Protocol lies in the creation by art 4 of an additional procedure, whereby a reference to the European Court of Justice may be made by an *authority* of a contracting state if there is conflict between judgments given by courts of that state and a judgment given either by the European Court of Justice or by an appellate court of another contracting state. The judgments which give rise to such a reference must have become final, and the resulting ruling will not affect those cases, but will serve as a precedent for the future. So far, however, no references have been made under art 4.

[8] The reciprocal recognition and enforcement of judgments between EC member states is dealt with principally by Title III of the 1968 Convention (as amended); see Chapter 14 below.

[9] In reply to a question in the European Parliament relating to the application of the 1968 Convention to the territory of the former East Germany, the EC Commission stated on 31 March 1992 that, on acceding to the Federal Republic of Germany in accordance with art 23 of the latter's Basic Law, the five new districts became an integral part of Germany and thus automatically of the European Community. Accordingly, the 1968 Convention has applied fully to the new districts from the moment of their incorporation into the Federal Republic on 1 October 1990. See [1992] OJ C162/44.

Presumably the transitional provisions contained in art 54 of the 1968 Convention, and the corresponding provisions of the 1978, 1982 and 1989 Conventions, operate analogistically, with 1 October 1990 counting as the commencement date of the 1968 Convention for the eastern districts of Germany.

[10] Under art 32 of the 1989 Convention, that Convention will enter into force in relation to each of these states on the first day of the third month following its ratification. A Note from the Lord Chancellor's Department, published on 24 July 1991 in (1991) 88 LSG 28/36, disclosed that all

- in its 1989 version (that is, as further amended by the 1989 Convention), in the United Kingdom, France, Italy, the Netherlands, Luxembourg, Greece, Spain and Portugal.[11]

In the event of further accessions to the Community, the new member states will have to accept the 1968 Convention as a basis for negotiations with the other member states, and the necessary adjustments will be made by further accession conventions.[12] The member states have recently embarked on a review of the practical operation of the 1968 Convention.[13]

Title II (arts 2–24) of the 1968 Convention lays down rules of direct jurisdiction, applicable by a court of a contracting state for the purpose of determining its own jurisdiction to entertain proceedings which have been instituted before it. Most of the provisions of Title II define the connecting factors which are necessary and sufficient to confer direct jurisdiction on a court or the courts of a contracting state,[14] but a few of them regulate related issues, such as a court's duty in certain circumstances to decline jurisdiction of its own motion[15] or to ensure that the defendant has been properly notified of the proceedings,[16] and the course to be taken where proceedings concerning similar or related disputes are simultaneously pending in the courts of two or more contracting states.[17]

With minor exceptions, the rules laid down by Title II are of direct jurisdiction only, and not also of indirect jurisdiction, since arts 28[3] and 34 prevent a court of a contracting state, when requested under Title III to recognise or enforce a judgment given by a court of another contracting state, from reviewing the jurisdiction of the original court. The exceptions relate to insurance, certain consumer contracts, exclusive jurisdiction,[18] transitional cases,[19] and conven-

---

the EC member states had undertaken to ratify the 1989 Convention by the end of 1992, but in the result this deadline was not adhered to.

[11] The commencement dates of the Conventions were as follows:
  - (1) The 1968 Convention in its original form entered into force for France, Germany, Italy, Belgium, the Netherlands and Luxembourg on 1 February 1973.
  - (2) The 1978 Convention entered into force for those six states and Denmark on 1 November 1986; for the United Kingdom on 1 January 1987; and for Ireland on 1 June 1988. See SI 1986/2044.
  - (3) The 1982 Convention entered into force for those nine states and Greece on 1 October 1989. See SI 1989/1346, and (1991) 88 LSG 28/36.
  - (4) The 1989 Convention entered into force for France, the Netherlands and Spain on 1 February 1991; for the United Kingdom on 1 December 1991; for Luxembourg on 1 February 1992; for Italy on 1 May 1992; and for Greece and Portugal on 1 July 1992. See [1991] OJ C17/2 and C308/1; [1992] OJ C16/1, C64/1, and C144/1; (1991) 88 LSG 16/39; and (1992) 89 LSG 6/49, 15/35, 25/37 and 32/40.

[12] See art 63 of the 1968 Convention.

[13] See (1992) 89 LSG 39/43.

[14] Articles 2–18 and 24.

[15] Articles 19 and 20[1].

[16] Article 20[2]–[3].

[17] Articles 21–23.

[18] See arts 7–16 and 28[1]–[2].

[19] See art 54[3] of the 1968 Convention, art 34(3) of the 1978 Convention, art 12(2) of the 1982 Convention, and art 29(2) of the 1989 Convention.

tions between the contracting state addressed and a non-contracting state;[20] only in these exceptional cases may the court addressed review the jurisdiction of the original court, and refuse recognition of the judgment if it regards the original court as having been incompetent to determine the dispute. There are, however, grounds for refusing recognition where the defendant was not properly and timeously notified of the original proceedings,[21] or where irreconcilable judgments have been given by courts of different countries.[22]

The Lugano Convention

In addition to the Community Conventions, another Convention on Jurisdiction and the Enforcement of Judgments in Civil and Commercial Matters, designed in substance to extend the 1968 Convention to the European Free Trade Association (EFTA) countries, was opened for signature by the EC member states and the EFTA countries (Norway, Sweden, Finland, Iceland, Austria and Switzerland) at Lugano on 16 September 1988.[23] In accordance with art 61, the Lugano Convention entered into force between the United Kingdom and Switzerland on 1 May 1992,[24] and has since come into force for three more EFTA countries (Norway, Sweden, and Finland) and five more EC member states (France, Italy, The Netherlands, Luxembourg, and Portugal). It will enter into force for any other signatory state on the first day of the third month following its ratification. It is implemented in the United Kingdom by amendments to the Civil Jurisdiction and Judgments Act 1982, made by the Civil Jurisdiction and Judgments Act 1991.[25]

The relationship between the 1968 Convention and the Lugano Convention is regulated by art 54B of the Lugano Convention. Under art 54B(1) and (2), as regards their own direct jurisdiction, the courts of a country such as the United Kingdom, which is an EC member state and a contracting state to both the 1968 Convention and the Lugano Convention, must apply Title II of the 1968 Convention, rather than Title II of the Lugano Convention, except in each of the following cases, where they must instead apply Title II of the Lugano Convention:

(1) where the defendant is domiciled in an EFTA country which is a contracting state to the Lugano Convention;
(2) where art 16 of the Lugano Convention confers exclusive jurisdiction on the courts of an EFTA country which is a contracting state to the Lugano Convention;

---

[20] See arts 28[1]–[2] and 59.
[21] See art 27(2).
[22] See art 27(3) and (5).
[23] For the text of the Lugano Convention, see [1988] OJ L319/9; or Sched 3C to the (British) Civil Jurisdiction and Judgments Act 1982, added by the Civil Jurisdiction and Judgments Act 1991. For the Jenard and Möller Report (of the negotiating committee), see [1990] OJ C189/57.
[24] See SI 1992/745, and (1992) 89 LSG 7/12.
[25] Consequential amendments to the Rules of the Supreme Court 1965 have been made by SI 1992/1907.

(3) where there is a jurisdictional agreement between the parties which chooses a court or courts of an EFTA country which is a contracting state to the Lugano Convention, and which is effective under art 17 of the Lugano Convention; or

(4) where there are simultaneously pending proceedings in respect of similar or related disputes in courts of different contracting states to the Lugano Convention, one being an EC member state and the other an EFTA country.

There is, however, little difference between the provisions of Title II of the Lugano Convention and those of Title II of the 1968 Convention, especially in its 1989 version. On the other hand, neither the European Court of Justice nor any other entity is empowered to give generally authoritative rulings on the interpretation of the Lugano Convention. Instead the interpretation of the Lugano Convention is left to the national courts of the contracting states, and they are merely encouraged by the Second Protocol to, and the Second and Third Declarations made on signature of, the Convention to adopt similar solutions to each other and to the solutions reached under the 1968 Convention.[26]

Time and space

As regards direct jurisdiction, the principal transitional rule is laid down by art 54[1] of the 1968 Convention, along with art 34(1) of the 1978 Convention, art 12(1) of the 1982 Convention, and art 29(1) of the 1989 Convention, to the effect that any version of Title II of the 1968 Convention applies only to proceedings instituted after its entry into force in the forum state.[27] Thus in a given case the

[26] The Second Protocol to the Lugano Convention, on its Uniform Interpretation, recites in its Preamble that the negotiations which led to the conclusion of the Lugano Convention were based on the 1968 Convention, in the light of the rulings given by the European Court of Justice on the interpretation of the 1968 Convention up to the signature of the Lugano Convention. Article 1 of the Protocol requires the courts of a contracting state to the Lugano Convention, when applying and interpreting its provisions, to 'pay due account to' the principles laid down by decisions of courts of other contracting states concerning such provisions. The Second Protocol also establishes a system of exchange of information concerning judgments given under the Lugano Convention or the 1968 Convention through a central body, in the form of the Registrar of the European Court of Justice, and establishes a standing committee of representatives of the signatory states to exchange views on the functioning of the Lugano Convention and perhaps make recommendations for its revision. By the Second and Third Declarations made on signing the Lugano Convention, the EC member states recognised the appropriateness of the European Court of Justice, when interpreting the 1968 Convention, paying due account to case-law under the Lugano Convention, and the EFTA countries recognised the appropriateness of their courts, when interpreting the Lugano Convention, paying due account to the case-law of the European Court of Justice and the courts of the EC member states on provisions of the 1968 Convention which are substantially reproduced in the Lugano Convention.

[27] Similar provision is made by art 54(1) of the Lugano Convention. For minor transitional provisions, see art 54(3) of the 1968 Convention (consolidating art 35 of the 1978 Convention) and of the Lugano Convention, preserving British and Irish jurisdiction arising from a choice of law clause contained in a written contract concluded before the relevant commencement date; and art 54A of the 1968 Convention (consolidating art 36 of the 1978 Convention) and of the Lugano Convention, preserving Danish, Irish, Greek, Icelandic, Norwegian, Finnish and Swedish maritime jurisdiction founded on arrest for three years from the relevant commencement date.

crucial dates are simply that on which the instant proceeding was instituted, and those on which any version of the 1968 Convention entered into force for the forum state.

Accordingly, Title II of the 1968 Convention does not apply to an action which had been instituted in a court of a contracting state before the entry into force of the 1968 Convention for that state,[28] but does apply to an action which is instituted in a court of a contracting state after the commencement date of the Convention for that state, even if the cause of action sued on arose before that date.[29] Moreover the applicable version of Title II is the one which was in force in the forum state at the date on which the proceedings in question were instituted. Thus, for example, an English court must apply the 1978 version of Title II to actions instituted between January 1987 and September 1989; the 1982 version to proceedings instituted between October 1989 and November 1991; and the 1989 version to actions instituted in or after December 1991.

On the same principle, in applying Title II (which discriminates in favour of contracting states, and especially of defendants domiciled in a contracting state), a court must treat as other contracting states those, and only those, states which, at the date on which the proceeding in question was instituted, had entered into a contractual nexus with the forum state involving mutual obligations to apply some version of the 1968 Convention. Accordingly, in the case of an action instituted today, an English court must regard all the other EC member states as contracting states, since they are all contractually bound to the United Kingdom to apply either the 1982 or the 1989 version of the Convention. But there is still no relevant contractual nexus between, for example, Spain and Germany, and so the courts of each must regard the other as a non-contracting state.

The pre-1989 versions of the 1968 Convention contained elaborate provisions defining the territories of the contracting states to which the Convention applied. Thus art 60 (as amended by art 27 of the 1978 Convention) laid down a basic rule that the Convention applied to the European territories of the con-tracting states, and also to the French overseas departments and territories and Mayotte. Moreover it authorised the Netherlands and Denmark respectively by notified declaration to extend the Convention to the Dutch Antilles and to the Faroe Islands. As regards the United Kingdom, the Convention applied (as its European territories) to England and Wales, to Scotland, and to Northern Ireland; and the United Kingdom was authorised to extend it by notified declar-ation to one or more of the European territories for whose international relations it was responsible; that is, the Isle of Man, each of the Channel Islands, Gibral-tar, and the British Sovereign Base Areas of Akrotiri and Dhekelia in Cyprus.[30]

---

[28] Cf *The Volvox Hollandia* [1988] 2 Lloyd's Rep 361, where a majority of the English Court of Appeal took the view that, after the British commencement date, the English courts should take into account Title II of the 1968 Convention, and especially arts 21–23 on simultaneous actions, when exercising their discretion to assume or decline jurisdiction over actions instituted before that date.

[29] See Case 25/79 *Sanicentral v Collin* [1979] ECR 3423.

[30] See also ss 39 and 52(2) of the (British) Civil Jurisdiction and Judgments Act 1982.

No such declaration has been made by the United Kingdom, but in 1991 the Lord Chancellor's Department[31] disclosed that the Isle of Man and Gibraltar had requested that the 1968 Convention should be extended to them.

Curiously art 21 of the 1989 Convention has now deleted art 60 of the 1968 Convention, with the probable effect of enabling a contracting state to extend the 1968 Convention to any (even a non-European) territory for whose external relations it is responsible; so that, for example, the United Kingdom could now extend the Convention to the Falkland Islands or St Helena. Accordingly SI 1990/2591, by arts 10 and 11, has amended ss 39 and 52(2) of the 1982 Act so as to enable the 1968 Convention and the 1982 Act to be extended by Order in Council to any British colony, as well as to any of the Channel Islands or the Isle of Man. Like the 1989 version of the 1968 Convention, the Lugano Convention contains no provision defining the territories of the contracting states to which it applies.

Subject-matter

The material scope of the 1968 Convention is defined by Title I, art 1.[32] The general rule, laid down by art 1[1], is that the Convention applies to civil and commercial matters, whatever the nature of the court or tribunal, but does not extend, in particular, to revenue, customs or administrative matters. In other words, it applies to claims under private law, as distinct from public law, and thus does not apply to a dispute between a private person and a public authority which arises out of acts done by the public authority in the exercise of its powers as such.[33] On the other hand, art 5(4) makes clear that the Convention *does* apply to a civil claim in tort, even when it is made ancillarily to a prosecution in a criminal court.[34]

By way of exception, art 1[2] excludes the following matters from the scope of the Convention:

---

[31] See (1991) 88 LSG 28/36.

[32] Article 1 of the Lugano Convention is identical.

[33] See Case 29/76 *LTU v Eurocontrol* [1976] ECR 1541; Case 814/79 *Netherlands v Rüffer* [1980] ECR 3807; and Case C-172/91 *Sonntag v Waidmann* 21 April 1993, where the court ruled that a school-teacher supervising pupils is not a public authority acting as such, even where the school is in the public sector and the teacher's liability for negligence is covered by insurance governed by public law.

For British jurisdiction over claims by or against Eurocontrol (the European Organisation for the Safety of Air Navigation), see the Brussels Convention relating to Co-operation for the Safety of Air Navigation (1960) and amending Protocol (1981); the Multilateral Agreement relating to Route Charges (1981); the Civil Aviation Act 1982; the Civil Aviation (Eurocontrol) Act 1983; and RSC Ord 11, r 1(2)(b). See also *Irish Aerospace v Eurocontrol* [1992] 1 Lloyd's Rep 383.

[34] See Case C-172/91 *Sonntag v Waidmann* 21 April 1993, which involved a civil claim by relatives of a deceased pupil against a schoolteacher whose negligent supervision had caused the pupil's death, made ancillarily in a criminal prosecution of the teacher for manslaughter. See also art II of the Protocol annexed to the 1968 Convention, which entitles a defendant to appear and defend through a qualified representative, without appearing in person, in certain situations of this kind; and Case 157/80 *Rinkau* [1981] ECR 1391, which confines this right to criminal proceedings in which civil liability is in question, or on which civil liability could subsequently be based.

(1)   the status or capacity of individuals, matrimonial property, and succession on death;
(2)   bankruptcy, the winding up of insolvent corporations, and analogous proceedings;
(3)   social security; and
(4)   arbitration.

However, as art 27(4) indicates, and the ruling of the European Court of Justice in *Marc Rich v Impianti*[35] confirms, proceedings are excluded from the scope of the Convention by art 1[2] only where an excluded matter constitutes the principal subject-matter of the proceedings, and not where such a matter is involved merely as a subsidiary issue.[36] Thus, for example, the Convention applies to an action founded on a breach of contract, even if minority is raised as a defence, since the principal subject-matter of the action is the contract, and the defendant's capacity is only a subsidiary issue.

The exclusion of individual status and matrimonial property from a Convention designed for relationships of a primarily economic character is readily intelligible, but unfortunately the Convention does not exclude all matters governed by family law. In particular, as art 5(2) and the ruling of the European Court of Justice in *De Cavel v De Cavel (No 2)*[37] make clear, the 1968 Convention *does apply* to maintenance claims under family law, and does so even when the maintenance claim is made ancillarily in proceedings in which the principal claim is excluded from the Convention as a matter of status, such as divorce proceedings. In that ruling the court also took a wide view of the concept of maintenance, as covering payments between divorced spouses which are intended to compensate for the disparity in their living standards created by the breakdown of the marriage, and which have to be fixed on the basis of their respective needs and resources. On the other hand, in *De Cavel v De Cavel (No 1)*[38] the court took a wide view of the exclusion of matrimonial property, and ruled that this is not confined to property arrangements specifically and exclusively envisaged by certain national laws in the case of marriage, but extends to any proprietary relationships resulting directly from the matrimonial relationship or its dissolution.

Although the problem requires urgent clarification by the European Court of Justice, it is submitted that, on the basis of the existing rulings, the Convention should be applied to all English applications, made ancillarily in divorce proceedings, for financial provision or property adjustment orders between the spouses and their children, since in such applications the means and resources of the parties are crucial; but not to proceedings, such as ones under s 17 of the Married Women's Property Act 1882, in which existing proprietary rights,

---

[35] Case C-190/89, [1991] 1 ECR 3855.
[36] See also the Jenard Report [1979] OJ C59 at p 10; and the Schlosser Report [1979] OJ C59 at p 89.
[37] Case 120/79, [1980] ECR 731.
[38] Case 143/78, [1979] ECR 1055. See also Case 25/81 *CHW v GJH* [1982] ECR 1189.

arising from the ordinary law of property applicable regardless of any marital relationship, are dominant.[39] It is also submitted that the exclusion of succession does not extend to proceedings concerning a testamentary trust which has been perfected by transfer of the assets to the trustees, unless the proceedings involve a challenge to the validity or propriety of such transfer.[40]

The bankruptcy exclusion was construed by the European Court of Justice in *Gourdain v Nadler*,[41] following the Jenard and Schlosser Reports,[42] as referring to proceedings which, depending on the system of law involved, are based on the suspension of payments, the insolvency of the debtor, or his inability to raise credit, and which involve judicial intervention for the purpose either of compulsory and collective liquidation of assets, or simply of supervision. It seems that the exclusion extends to English proceedings for the winding up of a company by the court, whatever the ground on which the winding-up order is sought, if the company is in fact insolvent, as well as to cases where the ground for the order is the company's insolvency, but not to an English voluntary winding up, or winding up subject to judicial supervision, owing to the limited role of the court.[43] In *Gourdain v Nadler*,[44] the court also ruled that the bankruptcy exclusion extends to proceedings which derive directly from a bankruptcy or insolvent liquidation and are closely connected with the (main) bankruptcy or winding-up proceedings; such as an application by a liquidator, made under a provision of insolvency law and in the interest of the general body of creditors, to a court seised of corporate liquidation proceedings, for an order against a manager of the company in liquidation, requiring him to pay a sum into the company's assets, with a view to making good a deficiency presumed to be due to his mismanagement.

The exclusion of arbitration from the scope of the 1968 Convention by art 1[2](4) is designed to prevent conflict with the New York Convention of 10 June 1958 on the Recognition and Enforcement of Foreign Arbitral Awards,[45] to which all 12 EC member states except Portugal are now party.[46] Thus, as the European Court of Justice ruled in *Marc Rich v Impianti*,[47] the effect of art 1[2](4) is to exclude from the scope of Title II of the 1968 Convention judicial

---

[39] See, for further discussion, Lasok & Stone, at pp 172–9. Cf Dicey & Morris, at p 786, where it is argued that a property adjustment order, made ancillarily to an English divorce, is not within the scope of the 1968 Convention, apparently because the proprietary rights which it creates are considered to arise directly from the dissolution of the marriage.

[40] See Lasok & Stone, at pp 179–80. See also art 4 of the Hague Convention on the Law Applicable to Trusts and on their Recognition (1986), implemented in the United Kingdom by the Recognition of Trusts Act 1987, which distinguishes issues concerning a trust from preliminary issues relating to the validity of wills or of other acts by virtue of which assets are transferred to the trustee.

[41] Case 133/78, [1979] ECR 733 at 744.

[42] At pp 11–12 and 90.

[43] See the Schlosser Report at pp 90–91.

[44] Case 133/78, [1979] ECR 733.

[45] For its text, see [1958] JBL 396.

[46] See the Arbitration (Foreign Awards) Orders 1984–89: SI 1984/1168, 1987/1029, and 1989/1348.

[47] Case C-190/89, [1991] 1 ECR 3855.

proceedings before the courts of contracting states whose principal subject-matter is arbitration, such as an application to the English High Court under s 10(3) of the (English) Arbitration Act 1950 for an order appointing an arbitrator, even if the existence or validity of the arbitral agreement is in dispute. Similarly, as Hirst J had earlier indicated,[48] the exclusion also covers other English proceedings under RSC Ord 73, r 7(1), for the removal of an arbitrator, or for the remission or setting aside of an arbitral award, or by way of appeal from an arbitral award. Clearly it also covers judicial proceedings for the obtaining of evidence for use in arbitration proceedings, or for the enforcement of an arbitral award.

On the other hand the 1968 Convention applies in cases where a court of a contracting state is seised of an action on the merits, but the defendant requests it to decline jurisdiction in order to give effect to an arbitration agreement. For in such cases the principal subject-matter of the proceedings is the substantive liability, and the validity of the arbitration clause is merely an incidental issue. But if the arbitral agreement falls within the scope, and complies with the requirements, of art II of the New York Convention, art 57 of the 1968 Convention gives priority to the court's obligation to decline jurisdiction under the New York Convention, over its duty or power to exercise jurisdiction, which would otherwise arise under the 1968 Convention. Nonetheless, if the court should erroneously hold that the arbitration agreement is invalid, and therefore accept jurisdiction to determine the merits, its decisions, both as to the validity of the arbitration agreement and as to the merits, cannot be denied recognition in other contracting states under Title III of the 1968 Convention.[49] Thus s 32 of the 1982 Act, which endeavours to prevent recognition of a foreign judgment in the United Kingdom in such circumstances unless recognition is required by the 1968 Convention, can never apply to a judgment given in another contracting state, since the 1968 Convention will always require such recognition.

Other international conventions on particular matters

The relationship of the 1968 Convention with other international conventions which regulate direct jurisdiction (or the recognition or enforcement of foreign judgments) in relation to particular matters, and to which one or more contracting states to the 1968 Convention are party, is dealt with by art 57(1) and (2) of the 1968 Convention.[50] For this purpose it is immaterial whether the entry into

---

[48] [1989] ECC 198.

[49] See the Schlosser Report, at pp 92–3. The question of recognition, in the absence of submission by appearance, was, however, left open by the Court of Appeal in *Marc Rich v Impianti* [1992] 1 Lloyd's Rep 624.

[50] Article 57(2) was consolidated from art 25(2) of the 1978 Convention by the 1989 Convention. As regards direct jurisdiction, art 57(1) and (2) of the Lugano Convention contain provisions similar to art 57(1) and (2)(a) of the 1968 Convention. As to differences between art 57 of the 1968 and Lugano Conventions in relation to the recognition and enforcement of judgments given pursuant to conventions on particular matters, see Chapter 14 below.

force of the other convention, or its adoption by a contracting state, preceded or followed that of the 1968 Convention, but a contracting state which intends to accede to such a convention should first engage in consultations with the other contracting states.[51]

As regards direct jurisdiction, the general effect of art 57(1) and (2)(a) of the 1968 Convention is that, in a contracting state which has adopted another convention which regulates jurisdiction over a particular matter, in the event of conflict the provisions of the other convention prevail over Part II of the 1968 Convention. By way of exception, art 20 of the 1968 Convention, which requires a court in certain cases to examine its jurisdiction of its own motion and to stay its proceedings until adequate steps have been taken to notify the defendant of them, is specifically made applicable in any event. It also seems reasonably clear that arts 21 and 22 of the 1968 Convention, which deal with the problem of simultaneously pending actions in different contracting states in respect of similar or related claims, remain applicable in cases where jurisdiction is governed by another convention on a particular matter, except to the extent that the other convention contains an inconsistent provision dealing with simultaneous actions.[52]

Many of the other conventions which regulate direct jurisdiction over particular matters are concerned with international carriage or transport. They include:

- on carriage by air, the Warsaw Convention (1929), the Hague Protocol (1955), the Guadalajara Convention (1961), and the Montreal Protocols (1975);[53]
- on carriage by rail, the Berne Convention (1980);[54]
- on carriage of goods by road, the Geneva/CMR Convention (1956);[55]
- on carriage of passengers by road, the Geneva/CVR Convention (1973);[56]
- on bills of lading, art III(8) of the Hague–Visby Rules, as construed in *The Hollandia*;[57]
- on carriage of passengers by sea, the Athens Convention (1974);[58]

---

[51] See the Joint Declaration annexed to the 1968 Convention, and the Schlosser Report, at para 248.

[52] See *The Nordglimt* [1988] QB 183. Cf the Schlosser Report, at pp 139–41. The relationship between arts 21–22 and art 57 in respect of admiralty actions, one of which has been commenced in rem in accordance with the Brussels Convention on the Arrest of Seagoing Ships (1952), is the subject of one of the questions referred to the European Court of Justice by the English Court of Appeal in *The Maciej Rataj* [1992] 2 Lloyd's Rep 552, now pending as Case C-406/92.

[53] See the Carriage by Air Act 1961; the Carriage by Air Acts (Application of Provisions) Order 1967, SI 1967/480 (as amended by SI 1969/1083, 1979/931 and 1981/440); the Carriage by Air (Parties to Convention) Order 1988, SI 1988/243; the Carriage by Air (Supplementary Provisions) Act 1962; the Carriage by Air and Road Act 1979; and RSC Ord 11, r 1(2)(b).

[54] See Cmnd 8535 (1982), and the International Transport Conventions Act 1983.

[55] See the Carriage of Goods by Road Act 1965; SI 1967/1683 and 1980/697; and RSC Ord 11, r 1(2)(b). See also *Harrison & Sons Ltd v RT Steward Transport Ltd*, 30 July 1992.

[56] See the Carriage of Passengers by Road Act 1974.

[57] [1983] 1 AC 565. Cf *The Benarty* [1985] QB 325.

[58] See the Merchant Shipping Act 1979; the Carriage of Passengers and their Luggage by Sea (Interim Provisions) Order 1980, SI 1980/1092; the Carriage of Passengers and their Luggage by Sea (Parties to Convention) Order 1987, SI 1987/931; and RSC Ord 11, r 1(2)(b).

- on collisions at sea, the Brussels Convention on Certain Rules concerning Civil Jurisdiction in Matters of Collision (1952);[59]
- on the arrest of ships, the Brussels Convention relating to the Arrest of Seagoing Ships (1952);[60]
- on oil pollution, the Brussels Convention on Civil Liability for Oil Pollution Damage (1969)[61] and amending Protocol (1976);
- on liner conferences, the Geneva Convention (1974);[62]
- on employment of crew of ships or aircraft, the European Convention on Consular Functions (1967).[63]

Outside the transport sector, there are the Paris, Supplementary and Vienna Conventions (1960–63) and the Joint Protocol (1988), on liability for nuclear incidents.[64] Moreover art 57 probably extends to the New York Convention of 10 June 1958 on the Recognition and Enforcement of Foreign Arbitral Awards, to which all 12 EC member states except Portugal are now party. Article II of the New York Convention enables contracting parties to exclude judicial jurisdiction by means of a written agreement for arbitration, and requires the courts of a state which is a party to the New York Convention to give effect to such an arbitration clause by declining jurisdiction to entertain proceedings brought in contravention of the clause. Thus art 57 of the 1968 Convention ensures that the obligation to decline jurisdiction, arising from art II of the New York Convention, prevails over any obligation or power to exercise jurisdiction, which would otherwise arise under Part II of the 1968 Convention.

In the United Kingdom, s 9(1) of the Civil Jurisdiction and Judgments Act 1982 extends the effect of references in art 57 to other conventions, so as to include British legislation and rules of law implementing such other conventions. In *The Nordglimt*[65] Hobhouse J took the view that the 1982 Act indirectly incorporates into English law the jurisdictional provisions of conventions on particular matters, referred to in art 57, and thus rectifies any incompleteness or imperfection in the implementation of such conventions by earlier British legislation, but this was subsequently doubted by the Court of Appeal in *The Po*.[66] They held, however, that the effect of art 57 is to preserve English

---

[59] See Cmnd 8954 (1952); the Supreme Court Act 1981, s 22; RSC Ord 75, r 4; and *The Po* [1991] 2 Lloyd's Rep 206, CA. See also the Rhine Navigation Conventions (1868 and 1963), and the Supreme Court Act 1981, s 23.

[60] See Cmnd 8954 (1952); the Supreme Court Act 1981, s 21; *The Nordglimt* [1988] QB 183; *The Linda* [1988] 1 Lloyd's Rep 175; *The Deichland* [1990] QB 361, CA; and *The Prinsengracht* [1993] 1 Lloyd's Rep 41. See also the Rhine Navigation Conventions (1868 and 1963), and the Supreme Court Act 1981, s 23.

[61] See Cmnd 4403 (1970); the Merchant Shipping (Oil Pollution) Act 1971; the Merchant Shipping (Oil Pollution) (Parties to Convention) Order 1986, SI 1986/2225; and RSC Ord 75, rr 2(1)(c) and 4(1A).

[62] See EC Regulation 954/79 [1979] OJ L121/1; the Merchant Shipping (Liner Conferences) Act 1982; SI 1985/405 and 406; and RSC Ord 71, rr 40–44.

[63] See Cmnd 4403 (1970); and the Consular Relations Act 1968, s 4.

[64] See Cmnd 2514, 2515 and 2333 (1964) and Cm 774; and the Nuclear Installations Act 1965, s 17.

[65] [1988] QB 183.

[66] [1991] 2 Lloyd's Rep 206.

jurisdiction in cases where it is conferred on one ground by an unimplemented provision of a convention on a particular matter, and on another ground by a provision of traditional English law. Thus the English court remains competent to entertain an action against a shipowner who is domiciled in another contracting state to the 1968 Convention, where the action is in respect of a maritime collision and the ship is served but is not arrested because security is given. For service on the ship is sufficient under traditional English law, and it is sufficient under art 1(1)(b) of the Brussels Convention of 10 May 1952 on Civil Jurisdiction in Matters of Collision, to which the United Kingdom is a party, that arrest could have been effected and security has been furnished.

In addition art 57(3) of the 1968 Convention ensures that, in the event of conflict between the 1968 Convention and provisions as to jurisdiction (or recognition or enforcement of foreign judgments) in respect of particular matters contained in existing or future Community regulations or directives, the provisions of the regulation or directive will prevail. It seems, however, that no such regulations or directives yet exist. Moreover there is no corresponding provision in the Lugano Convention, and the EC member states have declared that they will ensure that such Community acts will respect the rules established by the Lugano Convention, and agreed that if a contracting state to the Lugano Convention considers that a provision contained in an act of a Community institution is incompatible with the Lugano Convention, the contracting states will promptly consider amending that Convention.[67]

The Community Patent Agreement, which was signed by the 12 EC member states at Luxembourg on 15 December 1989[68] but has not yet entered into force, is designed to create a new form of intellectual property right, to be known as a Community patent, amounting to a unitary patent covering the entire territory of the European Community. The territorial allocation of jurisdiction between the courts of the member states, and the reciprocal recognition and enforcement of judgments, in respect of actions involving a Community patent, will be governed in principle by the 1968 Convention, but subject to major modifications specified by arts 13, 14, 17, 34 and 36 of the Protocol on Litigation, and arts 67–69 of the revised Community Patent Convention, annexed to the Community Patent Agreement. The relevant provisions will be examined in Chapter 10 under 'Intellectual property: Community patents', pp 204–7 and in Chapter 14, below.

[67] See the Third Protocol to, and the first Declaration made on signature of, the Lugano Convention.
[68] For its text, see [1989] OJ L401/1.

8

CIVIL JURISDICTION – BASIC PRINCIPLES

A number of general (but not universal) principles are discernible as underlying Title II of the 1968 and Lugano Conventions:

(1)   that an action against a defendant who is domiciled in a contracting state should be brought in the courts of that state;

(2)   that a court before which a defendant appears, without contesting its jurisdiction, should thereby become competent;

(3)   that, in order to avoid the possibility of irreconcilable judgments, a court of a contracting state should decline jurisdiction in favour of a court of another contracting state which has been seised earlier of a similar or related dispute; but that otherwise a competent court, properly seised, should be bound to determine the dispute before it, regardless of the possibility that a court of another country might be better placed to do so;

(4)   that a court which is not competent to determine the merits of a dispute should nonetheless be able to grant provisional relief in circumstances of urgency;

(5)   that a court should not proceed to determine the merits of a dispute until it is satisfied that adequate steps have been taken to notify the defendant of the proceedings.

The central role of the defendant's domicile

Introduction

The principal connecting factor used by Title II of the 1968 and Lugano Conventions is the defendant's domicile at the institution of the proceedings. However the Conventions use a concept of domicile which differs radically from that adopted by traditional English law.[1] Broadly, for their purposes, domicile refers essentially, in the case of an individual, to a current residence which is of more than minimal actual or intended duration; and a company is considered as domiciled both at its registered office and also at its actual headquarters (if different).

---

[1] On the traditional English concept of domicile, which amounts to nationality disguised as permanent residence, see Chapter 2 above. The traditional concept remains applicable in the spheres of family law and succession on death, which are largely excluded from the scope of the 1968 Convention by art 1[2](1).

Under Title II of the 1968 Convention, the rules governing the existence of jurisdiction differ according to whether or not the defendant is domiciled in a contracting state. Where the defendant is domiciled in a contracting state, then:

(1) subject to rather limited exceptions (specified by arts 16 and 17), art 2 confers jurisdiction to entertain actions against him on the courts of that contracting state;

(2) subject to major exceptions (specified by arts 5–18 and 24), art 3 deprives the courts of the other contracting states of jurisdiction to entertain actions against him; and

(3) where a defendant domiciled in one contracting state is sued in a court of another contracting state and does not enter an appearance, art 20[1] requires the court to decline jurisdiction of its own motion unless it is satisfied that it has jurisdiction under one of the exceptions specified in the Convention.

As the European Court of Justice explained in *Handte v Traitements Mécano-Chimiques des Surfaces*,[2] the general rule in favour of the courts of the defendant's domicile reflects the Convention's purpose of strengthening the protection and security of persons established within the Community, and draws its rationale from the assumption that normally it is in the courts of his domicile that a defendant can most easily conduct his defence. The court also emphasised that the provisions enabling a defendant to be sued in a contracting state other than that of his domicile must be interpreted in such a way as to enable a defendant exercising normal caution reasonably to foresee the particular foreign court in which he may be sued. It is suggested, however, that the rationale for this preference for defendants over plaintiffs, a preference which has deep historical roots, goes beyond mere convenience in the conduct of litigation. Rather, it is linked with such general rules as that which places on the plaintiff the burden of proving his claim, and reflects a primordial legal assumption that complaints are presumptively unjustified, and that it is better, where the truth cannot be ascertained with reasonable certainty, that the courts should not intervene; that failure to rectify injustice is more tolerable than positive action imposing it. In the present context, this gives rise to a general rule that the plaintiff must establish his case to the satisfaction of the court in whose goodwill towards him the defendant would presumably have most confidence.

Where, however, the defendant is not domiciled in any contracting state, then, subject to limited exceptions (specified by arts 4(2) and 16–18),[3] art 4(1) of the 1968 Convention remits the jurisdiction of the courts of a contracting state to entertain actions against him to the law of the state whose court is seised.

Articles 2–4 and 20[1] of the Lugano Convention echo the corresponding provisions of the 1968 Convention. By virtue of art 54B of the Lugano Convention, for the courts of the United Kingdom, as an EC member state which is a party to both the 1968 Convention and the Lugano Convention, Title II of the

---

[2] Case C-26/91, 17 June 1992. [1992] 1 ECR 3967.

[3] For a further, prospective, exception to art 4, see arts 13 and 14 of the Protocol on Litigation annexed to the Community Patent Agreement, [1989] OJ L401, which is not yet in force.

Lugano Convention becomes applicable, instead of Title II of the 1968 Convention, mainly where the defendant is domiciled in an EFTA country, such as Switzerland, which is a contracting state to the Lugano Convention.

Although the Conventions are not explicit on the point, it seems clear that the relevant time as of which the defendant's domicile must be ascertained is that of the institution of the proceedings in question. It also seems probable that it is for the law of the court seised to decide whether its proceedings are to be regarded as instituted at the issue of the writ, or at its service.[4] It seems regrettable, however, that in the unusual cases where the defendant changes his domicile between the time when the cause of action arises and the time of the institution of the proceedings, the Conventions decline to offer the plaintiff the choice of suing at either of those domiciles. Provision of such an option might have enabled the Conventions to dispense with some of the less obviously appropriate options sometimes offered to a plaintiff by provisions such as art 5.

The provisions (such as art 2) of Title II of the 1968 Convention which confer jurisdiction over defendants who are domiciled in the forum state are indifferent as to the allocation of this jurisdiction among the courts for the various territories or districts of that state, and leave such allocation to the law of that state. In the United Kingdom this problem is addressed by s 16 of and Sched 4 to the Civil Jurisdiction and Judgments Act 1982, which apply in most cases where the defendant is domiciled in the United Kingdom.[5] Schedule 4 distributes jurisdiction among the courts for the three parts of the United Kingdom (England and Wales; Scotland; and Northern Ireland) by means of rules which are modelled on, but differ in some important respects from, those used by Title II of the 1968 Convention in allocating jurisdiction over defendants domiciled within the Community among the courts of the various contracting states. Moreover Sched 4 has been amended by the Civil Jurisdiction and Judgments Act 1982 (Amendment) Order 1993,[6] as from 1 April 1993, so as to take account of the 1989 Convention. So, in most respects, similar rules determine English jurisdiction over defendants domiciled in Scotland to those applicable to defendants domiciled in France.

Moreover the English rules to which art 4 of the 1968 Convention remits the determination of English jurisdiction over defendants who are not domiciled in any contracting state have been to some extent revised, in the light of Title II of the Convention, by amendments to the Rules of the Supreme Court 1965 made by SI 1983/1181, with a view to avoiding pointless distinctions between actions against, for example, defendants domiciled in France and defendants domiciled in the United States.

Nonetheless, it is necessary to distinguish, for the purpose of determining the existence of English jurisdiction over a defendant, according to where he is domiciled:

---

[4] Cf Case 129/83 *Zelger v Salinitri (No 2)* [1984] ECR 2397, on art 21.
[5] For types of proceeding which are excluded from Sched 4, see s 17 and Sched 5.
[6] SI 1993/603.

(1) If he is domiciled in England, the English courts have jurisdiction, subject to the limited exceptions specified by arts 16 and 17 of the 1968 Convention and by art 16 of Sched 4 to the 1982 Act.

(2) If he is domiciled in Scotland or Northern Ireland, the English courts lack jurisdiction, except in the many cases specified by arts 5–18 and 24 of Sched 4, or by Sched 5, to the 1982 Act, or by art 17 of the 1968 Convention.

(3) If he is domiciled in another EC member state, the English courts lack jurisdiction, except in the many cases where such jurisdiction is conferred by arts 5–18 and 24 of the 1968 Convention.

(4) If he is domiciled in an EFTA country which is a contracting state to the Lugano Convention, the English courts lack jurisdiction, except in the many cases where such jurisdiction is conferred by arts 5–18 and 24 of the Lugano Convention.

(5) If he is domiciled in any other country, or nowhere, then in general English jurisdiction is governed by English law, and the main provisions applicable are RSC Ords 10, 11 and 81 (as amended), and ss 691–98 of the Companies Act 1985; but the English provisions give way to arts 16–18 of the 1968 Convention, and to arts 16 and 17 of the Lugano Convention.

Defendants domiciled in England

By virtue of art 2 of the 1968 Convention, taken with art 2 of Sched 4 to the 1982 Act, the English courts have jurisdiction to entertain an action against a defendant who is domiciled in England, regardless of whether the subject-matter of the dispute has any connection with England. This applies to any action which falls within the scope of the Convention, with two exceptions: actions whose subject-matter (such as title to or tenancies of land; certain company law matters; the validity of entries in public registers; the validity or registration of officially granted intellectual property rights; or the enforcement of judgments) brings them within the exclusive jurisdiction of the courts of another contracting state under art 16 of the 1968 Convention or art 16 of the Lugano Convention, or of another part of the United Kingdom under art 16 of Sched 4 to the 1982 Act;[7] and actions which are subjected to the exclusive jurisdiction of courts of other contracting states by an express agreement between the private parties involved, operating under art 17 of the 1968 Convention or art 17 of the Lugano Convention.

Moreover Title II of the 1968 Convention is based on the principle that a competent court, properly seised of an action, is bound to accept jurisdiction and determine the dispute. It has no discretion to decline jurisdiction in favour of a court of another country on such grounds as that it considers that in the circumstances of the case the foreign court is a more appropriate forum for the

---

[7] See Chapter 10, under 'Exclusive jurisdiction', p 200 *et seq.* below.

determination of the dispute.[8] Thus the English courts must accept jurisdiction where the defendant is domiciled in England, even if it considers that the dispute could more appropriately be determined by a court outside the United Kingdom. Accordingly the English courts have accepted that under the Convention they have no power to decline jurisdiction on grounds of forum non conveniens in favour of a court of another contracting state. However, in *Re Harrods (Buenos Aires) Ltd (No 1)*[9] the Court of Appeal asserted that the Convention has not abolished the judicial discretion which existed under traditional English law to do so in favour of a court of a non-contracting state. But the House of Lords has now referred the *Harrods* case to the European Court of Justice.[10]

However the Convention does not prevent an English court in its discretion, arising under traditional English law and preserved by s 49 of the 1982 Act, from declining jurisdiction over a defendant domiciled in England in favour of a Scottish or Northern Irish court which is also competent under Sched 4 to the 1982 Act; for example, as the court for the place of performance of the relevant contractual obligation, or as the place where the relevant tort occurred. For art 2 of the Convention requires only that some court of the contracting state in which the defendant is domiciled should be able and willing to exercise jurisdiction, and is uninterested in the allocation of jurisdiction between courts for the various territories or districts of that state, so long as the law of that state does not take into account the defendant's nationality as such.

As already emphasised, 'domicile' has a special meaning for the purposes of the Conventions and the British implementing legislation, differing radically from its meaning under traditional English law. By art 52[1] of the 1968 Convention (and of the Lugano Convention), the court seised must apply its own law in order to determine whether an individual is domiciled in its own contracting state; and s 41 of the 1982 Act specifies that for present purposes an individual is domiciled in the United Kingdom, or in a part of the United Kingdom (that is: England and Wales; Scotland; or Northern Ireland), if he is resident therein and the nature and circumstances of his residence indicate that he has a substantial connection therewith.[11] In itself the reference to 'a substantial connection' is so vague as to be almost meaningless, since (according to context) 'substantial' can mean anything from 'total or almost total' to 'more than minimal'. However s 41(6) adds that an individual who is and has for the

---

[8] See the Schlosser Report, at paras 76–81; Lasok & Stone, at pp 280–85; and under 'The mandatory character of Title II', pp 149–57 below. This overrides the traditional English law, as developed in *The Spiliada* [1987] 1 AC 460.

[9] [1991] 4 All ER 334, [1991] 3 WLR 397; rejecting the views of Hobhouse J in *Berisford v New Hampshire Insurance* [1990] QB 631, and Potter J in *Arkwright v Bryanston* [1990] 2 QB 649. The Court of Appeal's decision in *Harrods* has been followed in *The Po* [1991] 2 Lloyd's Rep 206, CA, and by Hirst J in *Hamed El Chaity v Thomas Cook*, 5 May 1992.

[10] Case C-314/92 *Ladenimor v Intercomfinanz* [1992] OJ C219/4.

[11] It is also provided that an individual is domiciled in a part of the United Kingdom if he is resident in that part and the nature and circumstance of his residence indicate that he has a substantial connection with the United Kingdom as a whole, but not with any particular part. This possibility seems to lack any practical reality.

last three months or more been resident in the United Kingdom or a part thereof is rebuttably presumed to have a substantial connection therewith; and thus seems to indicate that the connection need not be much more than minimal. Presumably the test of substantiality should be understood in terms of duration, and both the currently existing and the intended future duration of the residence should be taken into account.

In *Daniel v Foster*[12] Sheriff Palmer, in the Dumbarton Sheriff Court, helpfully equated the references in s 41 to residence with ordinary or habitual residence, as explained in cases such as *Shah v Barnet London Borough Council*.[13] Accordingly for present purposes an individual can have more than one domicile at a given time, and it is enough to make him domiciled in a part of the United Kingdom that he has a place of business therein, which he frequently visits for a few days at a time, even though his main residence is in another part of the United Kingdom.

Neither art 52 of the 1989 version of the 1968 Convention, nor art 52 of the Lugano Convention, nor s 41 of the 1982 Act, makes any specific reference to domicile of dependence,[14] with the result that the existence and location of a domicile of dependence is now governed by the same choice of law rules as an independent domicile. Thus it seems that the existence of an English (or Scottish, or Northern Irish, or United Kingdom) domicile will in all cases be determined by the test of residence indicating substantial connection, as applied to the person whose domicile is in question himself. Even in the case of a newborn baby, the question will be whether he himself is resident in England in circumstances indicating a substantial connection with England, and the domicile and other connections of his parents or other custodians will be relevant merely as factual indications as to whether the baby himself is resident in and substantially connected with England.

In the case of a company or other corporation, or a partnership or other association (whether or not having legal personality), art 53[1] of the 1968 Convention (and of the Lugano Convention) specifies that domicile refers to the seat of the body, determined in accordance with the law of the court seised, and s 42 of the 1982 Act provides that for present purposes a corporation or association is seated and domiciled in England if *either*:

(1) it was incorporated or formed under the law of any part of the United Kingdom, *and* it has in England *either* its registered office, *or* some other official address (that is, an address which it is required by law to register,

---

[12] 1989 SLT (ShCt) 90, 1989 SCLR 378.

[13] [1983] 2 AC 309, HL. See Chapter 2 above.

[14] Article 52[3] in the pre-1989 versions of the 1968 Convention specified that, in derogation from the normally applicable choice of law rules laid down by art 52[1] and [2], the domicile of an individual had to be determined in accordance with the law of his nationality if by that law his domicile depended on that of another person or on the seat of an authority. However art 52[3] has been deleted by the 1989 Convention and is omitted from the Lugano Convention. For the difficulties and absurdities to which it was capable of giving rise, see Lasok & Stone, at pp 207–8.

notify or maintain for the purpose of receiving notices or other communications), *or* a place of business or other activity;[15] *or*

(2) its central management and control is exercised in England.

Corresponding tests are made applicable to corporate domicile in Scotland or Northern Ireland; and a corporation or association is domiciled in the United Kingdom if it is domiciled in any of the three parts.

However, by way of needless complication, s 43 of the 1982 Act lays down a slightly different definition of the seat of a corporation or association for the purposes of the exclusive jurisdiction over certain disputes under company law, provided by art 16(2) of the 1968 Convention (and art 16(2) of the Lugano Convention), and of the related provisions of Sched 4 to the Act. For these purposes, a corporation or association is seated in England if either:

(1) it was incorporated or formed under English law; *or*
(2) it was incorporated or formed under the law of more than one part of the United Kingdom, and either it has its registered office in England, or it does not have a registered office in the United Kingdom; *or*
(3) it was incorporated or formed under the law of a country outside the United Kingdom, but its central management and control is exercised in England.

Again, corresponding tests are made applicable to corporate domicile in Scotland or Northern Ireland; and a corporation or association is domiciled in the United Kingdom if it is domiciled in any of the three parts.

The concept of the place of central management and control (or, more simply, actual headquarters) of a corporation or association was clarified by the Court of Appeal in *The Rewia*,[16] which involved a one-ship company which was incorporated and had its registered office in Liberia, but whose directors were resident in Germany and held their meetings there, and whose ship was managed by agents in Hong Kong. The Court of Appeal held that the company was domiciled, for the purpose of the 1968 Convention, both in Liberia, as the place of its incorporation and registered office, and in Germany, as the place of its central management and control; and also that a contractual jurisdiction clause specifying the company's principal place of business referred to its most important place of business, rather than the place where most of its business was carried out, and thus amounted to the same thing as domicile by virtue of central management and control. Although in practice the company's agents in Hong Kong had a free hand in the day-to-day management of the vessel, their activities were subject to the control of the directors in Hamburg, which was the centre from which instructions were given when necessary, and ultimate control was exercised.

As *The Rewia* illustrates, the 1968 Convention (and the Lugano Convention) tolerate the possibility of multiplicity of domicile. However the structure of the

[15] For criticism of the width of this provision, see Lasok & Stone, at p 209.
[16] [1991] 2 Lloyd's Rep 325; reversing Sheen J, [1991] 1 Lloyd's Rep 69.

Conventions, and art 52 in particular, make it clear that if the defendant is domiciled in the forum state, its courts remain competent regardless of the fact (if it be such) that he is also domiciled elsewhere. If similar actions are commenced in two contracting states in both of which the defendant is domiciled, the court subsequently seised will have to decline jurisdiction in favour of the court first seised under art 21, in the same way as in cases where the concurrent jurisdiction is based on different grounds (as where one court is competent under art 2 on the basis of the defendant's domicile, and the other under art 5(1) as that of the place of performance of the relevant contractual obligation).

Where, however, a defendant is domiciled in more than one part of the United Kingdom, it will be open to a court of one such part in which he is domiciled, in its discretion under s 49 of the 1982 Act, to decline jurisdiction in favour of a court of another such part, even if no proceedings have yet been commenced in the latter court. This is because art 2 of the 1968 Convention is unconcerned with the allocation of jurisdiction between the various courts of the contracting state in which the defendant is domiciled, and arts 21 and 22 are not concerned with similar or related actions simultaneously pending in courts of the same contracting state; so the United Kingdom is free in such cases to retain the discretionary doctrine of forum non conveniens, and has done so by s 49 of the 1982 Act. The position is the same where the defendant is domiciled in the United Kingdom and the courts of two parts are competent on different grounds specified in Sched 4 to the 1982 Act; for example, one on the basis of the defendant's domicile under art 2 of Sched 4, and the other on the basis of the place of performance of the contractual obligation under art 5(1) of Sched 4.

Defendants domiciled in Scotland or Northern Ireland

If the defendant is not domiciled in England, but is domiciled in Scotland or Northern Ireland, the jurisdiction of the English courts to entertain actions against him is governed mainly by Sched 4 to the 1982 Act. The general rule, under art 3 of the Schedule, is that the English courts lack jurisdiction over such a defendant, but numerous exceptions, specified by arts 5–18 and 24 of Sched 4, confer such jurisdiction in a wide range of cases: for example, if the action is founded on a contractual obligation whose place of performance is in England, or on a tort which wholly or partly took place in England. Moreover, by art 20[1] of Sched 4, the English court must decline jurisdiction of its own motion if such a defendant does not enter an appearance, unless it is satisfied that the action falls within one of these exceptions.

The provisions of the Schedule are modelled to a large extent on those of Title II of the 1968 Convention, and thus are designed to place a Scottish defendant in a largely similar position, as regards English jurisdiction, to that of a French defendant. Nonetheless there are some important respects in which Sched 4 deliberately departs from the model offered by Title II. In particular Sched 4 contains no specific provisions for insurance or consumer contracts, and thus treats such contracts in the same way as ordinary contracts; and Sched 4 contains no provisions dealing with the situation where actions in respect of similar or related disputes are simultaneously pending in courts of different parts of the United Kingdom. Instead, where the courts of more than one part of the United Kingdom are competent to entertain an action in respect of a dispute, s 49 of the 1982 Act preserves the discretion of a competent court of one part to decline jurisdiction in favour of a competent court of another part, where it considers that the latter court would in all the circumstances be a more appropriate forum for the determination of the dispute, whether or not an action has also been commenced in the latter court.

The same concepts of domicile or seat are used by ss 41–43 to determine whether a person is domiciled or seated in Scotland or Northern Ireland, as for the determination of whether he is domiciled in England. If the defendant is domiciled in Scotland or Northern Ireland, the English courts, in determining whether they have jurisdiction to entertain an action against him, must ignore any other domicile he may have in a country outside the United Kingdom.

Defendants domiciled in other contracting states

If the defendant is not domiciled in the United Kingdom, the English courts, in determining their jurisdiction to entertain actions against him, must ascertain whether he is domiciled in any other contracting state to the 1968 Convention or to the Lugano Convention. If so, the general rule, laid down by art 3 of these Conventions, is that the English courts lack jurisdiction, but numerous important exceptions are laid down by arts 5–18 and 24 of the Conventions; for example, where the action is founded on the breach of a contractual obligation whose place of performance is in England, or on a tort which wholly or partly occurred in England. Moreover, by art 20[1] of the Conventions, the English court must decline jurisdiction of its own motion if such a defendant does not enter an appearance, unless it is satisfied that the action falls within one of these exceptions.

For the purpose of determining whether a defendant is domiciled in another contracting state, different approaches must be used according to whether he is an individual, or is a corporation or association. In the case of an individual, art 52[2] of the 1968 Convention (and of the Lugano Convention) requires that the English courts, in order to determine whether he is domiciled in another contracting state, must apply the law of the other contracting state in question. In other words, the English courts must determine whether he is domiciled in France in accordance with the French concept of domicile; whether he is domiciled in Germany in accordance with the German concept of domicile; whether he is domiciled in Switzerland in accordance with the Swiss concept of domicile; and so on. Moreover, in view of art 20[1], it seems the English court will have to ascertain the foreign concept of domicile of its own motion, where the defendant is not domiciled within the United Kingdom, he has not entered an appearance, and he is known to have some connection with another contracting state.

No difficulty can arise from a finding that he is domiciled in both France and

Germany, since what matters for English purposes is that he is domiciled in at least one other contracting state to the 1968 Convention, rather than in which one. It is probable, however, that if he were found to be domiciled both in Switzerland, in accordance with the Swiss concept of domicile, and also in Germany, in accordance with the German concept, art 54B(2)(a) of the Lugano Convention would have the effect of giving priority to the Swiss domicile, so that English jurisdiction would be determined under Title II of the Lugano Convention, rather than Title II of the 1968 Convention, insofar as they (in fact, very slightly) differ.

As art 52 recognises, the concept of an individual's domicile varies to some extent from one contracting state to another. Thus French and Luxembourg laws refer to the person's principal establishment, preferring a business to a domestic establishment, while Dutch law refers to his dwelling-place, and Italian law to the principal seat of his business and interests. Belgian law, however, refers to the place for which he is registered on the population registers, and German law recognises multiplicity of domicile and refers to any stable establishment.[17] In Ireland the Jurisdiction of Courts and Enforcement of Judgments (European Communities) Act 1988 specifies that, for the purpose of the 1968 Convention, an individual is domiciled in Ireland if (and only if) he is ordinarily resident therein.[18]

In the case of a corporation or association, art 53[1] of the 1968 Convention (and of the Lugano Convention) specifies that domicile refers to the seat of the body, determined in accordance with the law of the court seised. Thus the English courts, in determining for the purposes of the Conventions whether a corporation or association which is not domiciled within the United Kingdom is domiciled in another contracting state, will apply s 42(6) and (7) of the 1982 Act, which provide that a corporation or association is domiciled and seated in a state other than the United Kingdom if *either* it was incorporated or formed under the law of the state in question and has its registered office or some other official address there; *or* its central management and control is exercised there; *unless (in either case)* the state in question is another contracting state, and it is shown that the courts of that state would not consider it as seated there.[19]

However a special definition is adopted for the purpose of art 16(2) of the Conventions, which provides for exclusive jurisdiction of the seat over certain disputes under company law. For that purpose, s 43(6) and (7) of the 1982 Act provide that a corporation or association is regarded as seated in another contracting state if *either* it was incorporated or formed under the law of the state in

---

[17] See Droz, *Compétence Judiciaire et Effets des Jugements dans le Marché Commun*, at paras 344–9.

[18] See s 13(1) and Sched 5, Part I of the 1988 Act.

[19] Similar provision is made in Ireland by s 13 and Sched 5, Part III of the Jurisdiction of Courts and Enforcement of Judgments (European Communities) Act 1988, except that the third requirement is replaced by one preventing a corporation or association from being regarded in Ireland as seated in another contracting state if either: (1) it has its seat in Ireland by virtue of incorporation or formation under Irish law; or (2) it is shown that the courts of the other contracting state in question would not regard it for the purposes of art 16(2) of the 1968 Convention as having its seat in that state.

question, *or* its central management and control is exercised there; *and* it is not seated in the United Kingdom by virtue of incorporation or formation under the law of a part of the United Kingdom; *and* it is not shown that the courts of the other contracting state in question would not regard it for the purposes of art 16(2) as seated therein.

Defendants not domiciled in any contracting state

Where the defendant is not domiciled in any contracting state to the 1968 Convention or to the Lugano Convention, the jurisdiction of the English courts to entertain actions against him is in general remitted to English law by art 4 of the 1968 Convention. However art 4 gives way to a number of other provisions of the 1968 Convention or the Lugano Convention in certain cases: to arts 8–15, where the defendant is an insurer, or a supplier under a 'protected' consumer contract, and he has a secondary establishment in a contracting state from whose operations the dispute arises – he is then treated as domiciled in the state containing the secondary establishment; to art 16, on exclusive jurisdiction over certain matters, such as title to land, connected with a contracting state; and to arts 17 and 18, on submission by agreement or appearance to the jurisdiction of a court of a contracting state.

In cases governed by art 4 of the 1968 Convention, the English courts have jurisdiction to entertain an action, regardless of whether its subject-matter has any connection with England, if:

(1) the defendant is an individual, and he is served personally in England with the writ instituting the action while he is physically present in England, however brief his visit;[20] or

(2) the defendant is an individual, and the writ is delivered at or posted to his usual or last known address in England, and it comes to his knowledge, while he is present in England, within seven days of the delivery or posting;[21] or

(3) whether the defendant is a corporation, a partnership, or an individual, if he has a place of business in England.[22]

In addition, the English courts have jurisdiction in cases governed by art 4 if the cause of action is connected with England in one of the ways specified in RSC Ord 11, r 1(1), as amended by the Rules of the Supreme Court (Amendment No 2) 1983.[23] The 1983 Amendment removes some pointless distinctions between the position of defendants domiciled in other contracting states and defendants domiciled outside the Community, but the assimilation attempted is

---

[20] See art 3(2) of the 1968 Convention, and *Maharanee of Baroda v Wildenstein* [1972] 2 QB 283.

[21] See RSC Ord 10, r 1(2), as amended, and *Barclays Bank of Swaziland v Hahn* [1989] 1 WLR 506, [1989] 2 All ER 398, HL.

[22] See the Companies Act 1985, ss 691–698; and RSC Ord 81, as amended by SI 1983/1181, r 18. A partnership must be carrying on business in England in the name of the firm, and an individual must be doing so in a name other than his own personal name.

[23] SI 1983/1181.

limited. For example, it remains a sufficient basis of English jurisdiction, in cases governed by art 4, that the action is founded on a breach of a contract which was concluded in England.

In cases governed by art 4, the remission to the jurisdictional rules of the lex fori is wide enough to include rules permitting a competent court to decline jurisdiction in favour of a court of another country on the ground that the latter is regarded as better placed to determine the dispute, in view of the interests of the parties and the ends of justice. Accordingly s 49 of the 1982 Act, which preserves the traditional British doctrine of forum non conveniens to the extent that the Conventions permit, is operative in cases governed by art 4.

If a defendant is not domiciled in any contracting state, it will usually be unnecessary for the English courts to determine the country or countries, if any, in which he is domiciled. This question is, however, relevant for the purposes of art 59 of the 1968 Convention (and of the Lugano Convention), where the United Kingdom has concluded a convention for the reciprocal recognition and enforcement of judgments with a non-contracting state, and thereby given an undertaking not to recognise certain judgments given in other contracting states against defendants domiciled or habitually resident in the non-contracting state. So far the United Kingdom has concluded one such convention: the Ottawa Convention with Canada of 24 April 1984 providing for the Reciprocal Recognition and Enforcement of Judgments in Civil and Commercial Matters.[24] For such purposes, by ss 41(7) and 42(6) of the 1982 Act (and art IX(2)(b) of the Anglo-Canadian Convention), an individual defendant is regarded as domiciled in the relevant non-contracting state if he is resident in that state and the nature and circumstances of his residence indicate that he has a substantial connection with that state; and a corporation or association is regarded as so domiciled if either it was incorporated or formed under the law of the state in question and has its registered office or some other official address there, or its central management and control is exercised there.

Submission by appearance

Article 18 of the 1968 Convention confers jurisdiction, additional to that derived from other provisions, on a court of a contracting state before whom a defendant enters an appearance without contesting its jurisdiction, unless another court has exclusive jurisdiction by virtue of art 16 (for example, as a court of the situs of land whose title constitutes the subject-matter of the dispute). Similar provision is made by art 18 of the Lugano Convention, and by art 18 of Sched 4 to the 1982 Act, with savings for the corresponding art 16.

It is probable, in view of the analogy of art 17 and the history of the negotiations, that art 18 of the 1968 Convention derogates from art 4 and applies even where the defendant is not domiciled in any contracting state, as well as

---

[24] See Cmnd 9337 (1984), and SI 1987/468 (as amended by SI 1989/987, 1988/1304, 1988/1853, and 1987/2211).

where he is domiciled in another contracting state.[25] On the other hand, it seems unlikely that art 18 derogates from art 2, so as to override a rule of the law of the contracting state in which the defendant is domiciled, allocating jurisdiction between the courts for its territories or districts, but the point is unimportant in the United Kingdom, in view of the corresponding art 18 of Sched 4. In any event art 18 of the Conventions does not override rules of the law of the contracting state before whose court the defendant appears, allocating jurisdiction between its courts in terms of subject-matter. Thus, for example, appearance before an English industrial tribunal could not enable it to entertain contractual, as distinct from statutory, claims relating to a contract of employment.[26]

Article 18 of the 1968 Convention (and art 18 of the Lugano Convention) explicitly provide that appearance will not found jurisdiction 'where another court has exclusive jurisdiction by virtue of art 16' (of the same Convention). This refers primarily to cases where art 16 ascribes jurisdiction to the courts of another contracting state with which the relevant subject-matter is appropriately connected (for example, as the situs of the land whose title is disputed). But it seems probable that the proviso also applies where the defendant appears in a territorially inappropriate court of the appropriate contracting state, as where he appears in an English action concerned with title to Scottish land. Certainly in the United Kingdom art 18 of Sched 4 to the 1982 Act endeavours to ensure that the allocation of exclusive jurisdiction by art 16 of the Schedule cannot be overridden by the defendant's appearing in a court of an inappropriate part of the United Kingdom. On the other hand, the European Court of Justice has eliminated all doubts about the relationship between arts 17 and 18 of the 1968 Convention by ruling that appearance founds jurisdiction even where the parties had previously concluded an agreement designating some other court as exclusively competent in accordance with art 17.[27]

Although art 18 in terms excludes an appearance 'entered solely to contest the jurisdiction', the European Court of Justice has ruled in a series of cases[28] that a defendant may, without submitting to the jurisdiction, simultaneously raise defences as to both jurisdiction and merits, provided that his challenge to the jurisdiction is made no later than the submissions which under the procedural law of the court seised are regarded as the first defence addressed to the court; and in England Saville J has held that this applies even if the defendant also counterclaims and joins a third party.[29] But there will be submission by appear-

---

[25] See Droz, *Compétence Judiciaire et Effets des Jugements dans le Marché Commun* (1972), at paras 221 and 230–32.

[26] See also arts 13 and 14 of the Protocol on Litigation, annexed to the Community Patent Convention, [1989] OJ L401/1, not yet in force, by which art 18 of the 1968 Convention will apply to actions concerning infringement of a Community patent, but only if the court appeared in is one which is designated as a Community patent court.

[27] See Case 150/80 *Elefanten Schuh v Jacqmain* [1981] ECR 1671.

[28] Case 150/80 *Elefanten Schuh v Jacqmain* [1981] ECR 1671; Case 27/81 *Rohr v Ossberger* [1981] ECR 2431; Case 25/81 *CHW v GJH* [1982] ECR 1189; and Case 201/82 *Gerling v Treasury Administration* [1983] ECR 2503.

[29] *Rank Film Distributors v Lanterna* (1991), *Financial Times*, 14 June.

ance if the defendant, after unsuccessfully contesting the jurisdiction up to the court of last resort, then proceeds to file a defence on the merits.[30]

It is clear that in general it is for the law of the court seised to define the steps which will be regarded as constituting an appearance for the purposes of art 18. In England, the Rules of the Supreme Court 1965, as amended, no longer speak of a defendant 'entering an appearance', but of his 'acknowledging service of the writ'.[31] Such an acknowledgement is, however, equivalent to the entry of an appearance under the former practice, and undoubtedly constitutes the entry of an appearance for the purposes of art 18.[32] A defendant who wishes to contest the jurisdiction should file an acknowledgement of service containing a notice of intention to defend, and then apply to the court (usually by summons, supported by an affidavit verifying the facts relied on) under RSC Ord 12, r 8, for an order dismissing the action for lack of jurisdiction.[33] Additionally or alternatively he may apply for a stay of the English proceedings in favour of foreign proceedings,[34] or by reference to an arbitration clause,[35] or a foreign jurisdiction clause.[36] Where any such application under RSC Ord 12, r 8, or for a stay of proceedings, has been made, nothing done by the defendant (other than its withdrawal) before it has been finally disposed of will amount to submission, so as to found jurisdiction under art 18.[37]

On the other hand, in the absence of any such application and of any other indication that the defendant wishes to contest the jurisdiction, submission by appearance will occur if the defendant's solicitor endorses on the writ a statement accepting service;[38] or if the defendant applies for an order requiring the plaintiff to give security for costs;[39] or if the defendant applies for an order setting aside a default judgment and requiring the plaintiff to deliver a statement of claim;[40] or if the defendant applies for an order striking out one of several claims made in the action;[41] or if the defendant consents to the continuance of a *Mareva* injunction;[42] or if the defendant takes any other step in the proceedings which is unequivocally referable to an issue on the merits, in the sense that it is

---

[30] See *Marc Rich v Impianti* [1992] 1 Lloyd's Rep 624, English CA. Similarly if (after objecting to the jurisdiction) the defendant agrees to a settlement of the claim and participates in inviting the judge to make a consent order giving effect to the settlement; see per Scott J in *Adams v Cape Industries* [1991] 1 All ER 929; affirmed without consideration of this point, [1990] Ch 433, CA.

[31] See RSC Ord 12, as amended by SI 1979/1716.

[32] See RSC Ord 10, r 1(5), RSC Ord 12, r 8(7), and *The Messiniaki Tolmi* [1984] 1 Lloyd's Rep 266, CA.

[33] See RSC Ord 12, r 8(4), and *Carmel Exporters v Sea-Land Services* [1981] 1 WLR 1068, CA. For procedure in Scotland, see *British Steel v Allivane* [1988] ECC 405.

[34] See *Williams & Glyn's Bank v Astro Dinamico* [1984] 1 WLR 438, HL.

[35] See *Finnish Marine Insurance v Protective National Insurance* [1990] 1 QB 1078.

[36] See *The Sydney Express* [1988] 2 Lloyd's Rep 257.

[37] See *Hewden Stuart v Gottwald*, 13 May 1992, CA.

[38] See RSC Ord 10, r 1(4); *Manta Line v Sofianites* [1984] 1 Lloyd's Rep 14, CA; and *Sphere Drake v Sirketi* [1988] 1 Lloyd's Rep 139, CA.

[39] See *Lhoneux Limon v Hong Kong Banking Corp* (1886) 33 ChD 446.

[40] See *Fry v Moore* (1889) 23 QBD 395.

[41] See *The Messiniaki Tolmi* [1984] 1 Lloyd's Rep 266, CA.

[42] See *Esal v Pujara* [1989] 2 Lloyd's Rep 479, CA, distinguishing *Obikoya v Silvernorth* (1983) 133 NLJ 805, CA.

only necessary or useful if any objection to the jurisdiction has been waived.[43] However an application for an extension of time for serving a defence does not amount to submission,[44] and submission by appearance in one action cannot create jurisdiction over other, as yet uncommenced, actions against the same defendant by other plaintiffs in respect of related claims.[45]

Simultaneous actions in different countries

Articles 21–23 of the 1968 Convention (and of the Lugano Convention) deal with the problem of simultaneously pending actions in the courts of different contracting states in respect of similar or related disputes.[46] Article 21 deals with 'proceedings involving the same cause of action and between the same parties' and art 22 deals with 'related actions', defined by art 22[3] as actions which 'are so closely connected that it is expedient to hear and determine them together to avoid the risk of irreconcilable judgments resulting from separate proceedings'. Article 23 provides for conflicts of exclusive jurisdiction.

All these provisions are concerned with actions which are simultaneously pending in courts of different contracting states. If both actions are instituted in the same contracting state, the problem is impliedly remitted to the law of the contracting state in question, and in the United Kingdom the 1982 Act does not extend arts 21–23 of the Convention by analogy to actions in different parts of the United Kingdom. Instead Sched 4 omits any provision corresponding to arts 21–23, and s 49 leaves the matter to be dealt with under the more general principle of forum non conveniens. The Conventions also ignore the problem of simultaneous actions in a contracting state and a non-contracting state. Probably in such a case the contracting state may permissibly apply rules analogous to those laid down by arts 21–23.[47] On the other hand, the European Court of Justice made clear in *Overseas Union Insurance Ltd v New Hampshire Insurance Co*[48] that arts 21–23 apply regardless of the domicile of the parties to the actions, and even if the defendant is not domiciled in any contracting state. This decision also impliedly discredits the suggestion made by Hirst J in *Kloeckner v Gatoil*[49] that art 21 does not apply where the court subsequently seised has exclusive jurisdiction by virtue of an agreement between the parties under art 17.

Articles 21–23 are based on the principle of giving priority to the court 'first

[43] See *Rein v Stein* (1892) 66 LT 469; *Re Dulles's ST* [1951] Ch 842, CA; and *Williams & Glyn's Bank v Astro Dinamico* [1984] 1 WLR 438, HL.

[44] See *Hewden Stuart v Gottwald*, 13 May 1992, CA.

[45] See per Scott J in *Adams v Cape Industries* [1991] 1 All ER 929; affirmed by the Court of Appeal without consideration of this point, [1990] Ch 433.

[46] The 1989 Convention rephrases art 21 of the 1968 Convention, without change of substance, so as to accord with art 21 of the Lugano Convention.

[47] See Droz, *Compétence Judiciaire et Effets des Jugements dans le Marché Commun* (1972), at paras 329–30.

[48] Case C-351/89, [1991] 1 ECR 3317.

[49] [1990] 1 Lloyd's Rep 177. An appeal against this decision was abandoned after the Court of Appeal on 16 March 1990 upheld an order requiring security for costs.

seised', rather than on a judicial evaluation of the relative appropriateness or convenience of the two fora.[50] In the case of proceedings involving the same cause of action and between the same parties, art 21 imposes a mandatory obligation on the court subsequently seised, which must be performed of the court's own motion if necessary, initially to stay its own proceedings until the jurisdiction of the court first seised is established, and eventually, when such jurisdiction has been established, to decline jurisdiction in favour of that court.[51]

The initial stay is designed to cover such cases as the following. The plaintiff brings an action in a French court against a defendant domiciled in England, alleging that the place of performance of the relevant contractual obligation is within the French court's district, so as to render it competent under art 5(1). The defendant appears in the French court to contest its jurisdiction, alleging that the relevant place of performance is in England. Then, in order to protect his position, perhaps against a time-bar, the plaintiff responds by instituting proceedings in England in respect of the same claim before the French court has resolved the dispute as to its jurisdiction. In such a situation art 21 requires the English court to stay its proceedings until the French court has determined its own jurisdiction. If eventually the French court accepts jurisdiction, the English court must then decline jurisdiction and accordingly dismiss the English proceedings altogether. On the other hand, if the French court eventually declines jurisdiction, the English court will lift its stay and permit the English action to proceed. As Sheen J recognised in *Neste Chemicals v DK Line*,[52] it is not possible for a plaintiff, when commencing his first action, to reserve priority for a second action which he intends to commence elsewhere, for the Convention adopts a simple test of chronological priority.

As the European Court of Justice emphasised in *Overseas Union Insurance Ltd v New Hampshire Insurance Co*,[53] art 21 does not permit the second court, even where the jurisdiction of the first court is contested, itself to examine the jurisdiction of the first court, except possibly where the question is whether the second court has exclusive jurisdiction under art 16.

Clearly it is important for the purposes of art 21 to know the point at which a court is 'seised' of an action. This problem was considered by the European Court of Justice in *Zelger v Salinitri (No 2)*,[54] where the order of events was that a German writ was issued, then an Italian writ was issued and served, and finally the German writ was served. The court merely ruled that art 21 refers to definitive seisin, but that the question of whether a court is definitively seised at

---

[50] See *The Linda* [1988] 1 Lloyd's Rep 175.

[51] This is supplemented in England by RSC Ord 6, r 7(1)(b), and Ord 11, r 1(2)(a)(i), as amended, under which a writ can be served abroad without the court's leave only if it is indorsed with a statement that no proceedings involving the same cause of action are pending between the parties in another part of the United Kingdom or another contracting state.

[52] 29 January 1993; affirmed by CA (1994), *The Times*, 4 April.

[53] Case C-351/89, [1991] 1 ECR 3317.

[54] Case 129/83, [1984] ECR 2397.

the issue of the writ or at its service must be determined in accordance with the law of the country to which the court in question belongs. The court also noted that, from information placed before it, it appeared that a court of any of the original six member states would not be definitively seised until its writ was served. Subsequently, in *Dresser v Falcongate*[55] and *Neste Chemicals v DK Line*,[56] the English Court of Appeal has ruled that the position is similar in England: the issue of an English writ is not sufficient, and an English court is not definitively seised of a personal action until the writ is served on the defendant. In *Dresser* it was suggested that exceptions might exist where before service the court makes an interlocutory order, such as a *Mareva* injunction or an *Anton Piller* order, but the existence of such exceptions was subsequently rejected in *Neste*. Similarly in *The Freccia del Nord*[57] Sheen J ruled that an English court is not seised of an admiralty action in rem against a ship (not already in the custody of the court) until service or arrest, whichever occurs earlier.

In the case of actions which are related, in the sense that they are so closely connected that it is expedient to hear and determine them together to avoid the risk of irreconcilable judgments, but which involve different causes of action or are between different parties, art 22 confers discretion on the court subsequently seised. Article 22[1] permits the court subsequently seised, while both actions are pending at first instance, to stay its proceedings, so as to enable it to have the benefit of the first court's judgment before it reaches its own decision. It seems likely that this course will be useful only where the judgment of the first court will probably give rise to an estoppel which, under Title III of the Convention, will be binding on the second court in respect of an issue which it will have to determine. Precisely what estoppels will arise will be governed by the law of the first court, but in general personal judgments are binding only on the parties and those in privity with them. Article 22[2] permits the second court in the same circumstances to go further and decline jurisdiction altogether in favour of the first court, if certain additional conditions are met: that one of the parties applies for such an order, that the law of the country to which the first court belongs permits the consolidation of related actions, and that (independently of art 22)[58] the first court has jurisdiction to entertain both actions.

However in the case of related actions art 22 does not prevent the court subsequently seised from exercising its discretion in favour of proceeding to determine the action before it, without even waiting for the first court to give its decision. Indeed, in such a case, if the court subsequently seised is the first to give judgment, the court first seised will be bound, under Title III of the Convention, to give effect to estoppels which arise, under the law of the country of the court subsequently seised, from that court's judgment. Nonetheless, as

---

[55] [1992] QB 502; overruling the decision of Hirst J in *Kloeckner v Gatoil* [1990] 1 Lloyd's Rep 177. Cf the Schlosser Report, at para 182, and Dicey & Morris, *The Conflict of Laws*, (11th ed, 1987) at p 399.

[56] (1994) *The Times*, 4 April.

[57] [1989] 1 Lloyd's Rep 388.

[58] See (Case 150/80) *Elefanten Schuh v Jacqmain* [1981] ECR 1671.

Ognall J recognised in *Virgin Aviation v CAD Aviation*,[59] for the purpose of exercising its discretion under art 22, the court subsequently seised must not treat the legal system of one contracting state as superior or inferior to that of another, and a stay should not be refused on the ground that it would deprive one of the parties of a procedural advantage (such as the English procedure for obtaining summary judgment without trial under RSC Ord 14) which is available under the law of the court subsequently seised. In any event, as the European Court of Justice recognised in *Elefanten Schuh v Jacqmain*,[60] art 22 does not confer jurisdiction on a court to entertain an action in respect of which it is otherwise incompetent. In particular, it does not make good the deficiencies of art 6, which in some, but by no means all, cases empowers a court to entertain an action on the ground that it is related to another action of which the court is seised.

The importance of art 22 has been greatly reduced by the wide scope given to art 21 by the decision of the European Court of Justice in *Gubisch Maschinenfabrik v Palumbo*,[61] interpreting the reference in art 21 to 'proceedings involving the same cause of action and between the same parties'. The dispute involved the sale of a moulding machine by a German company to an Italian domiciliary. The seller brought an action in a German court claiming payment of the agreed price, and then the buyer brought an action in an Italian court claiming annulment of the contract on the ground that his offer to buy had been revoked before it was received by the seller, or alternatively for error or fraud, or, in the further alternative, claiming rescission for delay in delivery. On a reference from the Italian Court of Cassation, the European Court of Justice ruled that art 21 extends to a case where one party brings an action in a court of one contracting state claiming annulment or rescission of a contract at a time when an action brought by the other party, claiming enforcement of the contract, is pending in a court of another contracting state.

The court noted the purpose of arts 21–23, to prevent the existence of parallel proceedings in different contracting states which could result in irreconcilable judgments, and to pre-empt so far as possible the refusal of recognition of a foreign judgment under art 27(3) by reason of its irreconcilability with a judgment given between the same parties in the state addressed. It explained that art 21 applies to actions between the same parties, having the same cause and the same object. In the present case the parties were the same, and so was the cause, in the sense of the contractual relationship. The difficulty related to the object, since the first action sought enforcement of the contract, while the second sought its annulment or rescission. Nonetheless both actions centred on the binding force of the contract, and the claims in the second action could be viewed as merely a defence to the first, brought by way of a separate action in a

---

[59] (1990) *The Times*, 2 February. However the actions treated by Ognall J as 'related' and thus falling within art 22 seem on any view to have involved the same cause of action and thus to have fallen within art 21.

[60] Case 150/80, [1981] ECR 1671.

[61] Case 144/86, [1987] ECR 4861.

different contracting state. Thus the two actions should be regarded as having the same object, for formal identity of claims is unnecessary and separate determination of the actions would involve the risk that a decision of the first action upholding the contract might be refused recognition in the second state by virtue of an irreconcilable decision of a court of the second state annulling or rescinding the contract, a result which would be contrary to the purposes of the Convention.

Such reasoning perhaps overlooks the argument that, if the court subsequently seised had not been required to decline jurisdiction under art 21, and had not in its discretion declined jurisdiction or stayed its proceedings under art 22, the judgment first given, by whichever court, would have been binding on the other court in the normal way under Title III of the Convention, for Title III makes no exception to the obligation to grant recognition and enforcement to judgments given in other contracting states on account of the pendency of related proceedings in a court of the state addressed.[62]

In *The Maciej Rataj*,[63] the English Court of Appeal has referred to the European Court of Justice, among other questions, whether art 21 applies where, after goods carried by sea have been discharged in a damaged condition, the shipowner commences proceedings in a contracting state for a declaration of non-liability to cargo interests in respect of such damage, and the cargo claimants subsequently commence proceedings in another contracting state claiming damages against the shipowner in respect of such damage to their cargo. Neill LJ recognised that the *Gubisch* ruling implied an affirmative answer, but referred the question along with others which presented real difficulty. These include how the requirement of art 21 that the actions in the two countries should be between the same parties applies in multi-party situations; for example where cargo belonging to numerous owners is damaged in the course of a voyage. Possible solutions envisaged in the reference order are that art 21 applies only where there is a complete identity of parties between the two sets of proceedings; or only where all the parties to the second proceedings are also parties to the first proceedings; or whenever at least one of the plaintiffs and one of the defendants to the second proceedings are also parties to the first proceedings; or whenever the parties in the two proceedings are substantially the same. A further (and, it is submitted, correct) solution is that art 21 applies *insofar as* the claims are between common parties; that is, art 21 requires the second court to decline to entertain claims between persons who are parties in the first proceedings, and other connected claims are left to art 22.

Probably an admiralty action in rem against a ship, brought in one contracting state, and a personal action against the shipowner in respect of the same claim, brought in another contracting state, count as similar actions, falling within art 21, rather than related actions, falling within art 22, regardless of

---

[62] See Droz, *Compétence Judiciaire et Effets des Jugements dans le Marché Commun* (1972), at para 518.

[63] [1992] 2 Lloyd's Rep 552.

whether the action initially commenced in rem subsequently continues exclusively in rem (as where the shipowner fails to acknowledge service), or continues both in personam and in rem (as where the shipowner acknowledges service but does not obtain the release of the ship against security), or continues exclusively in personam (as where he not only acknowledges service but also obtains the release of the ship against security). For in *The Deichland*[64] the Court of Appeal held that an action in rem against a ship counts for the purpose of arts 2 and 3 of the 1968 Convention as an action against the shipowner or other person interested in the ship against whom the plaintiff would wish to proceed in personam if he entered an appearance, and it is difficult to suppose that the same does not apply for the purpose of art 21. Thus first instance decisions that art 22, rather than art 21, applies where an English action in rem is brought after a court of another contracting state has been seised of an action in personam against the shipowner in respect of the same claim, must be considered erroneous, even if this view is confined to the situation where the shipowner has not entered an appearance and the English action is continuing solely in rem – the view taken by Sheen J in *The Linda*[65] and *The Kherson*;[66] and a fortiori if it is extended to the situation where the shipowner has entered an appearance and the action is continuing solely in personam, or both in personam and in rem – the view of Hobhouse J in *The Nordglimt*.[67] The question has now been referred to the European Court of Justice by the Court of Appeal in *The Maciej Rataj*.[68] On the other hand the decision in *Gubisch* seems to justify the ruling of Sheen J in *The Linda*[69] that admiralty cross-claims between the same parties and arising from the same collision fall within art 21.

Simultaneous actions for infringement of intellectual property were considered in *LA Gear v Whelan*.[70] Mummery J held that art 21 does not apply to actions for passing off or trademark infringement in respect of acts done in different countries, even though both actions complain of the use of the same mark in relation to the same type of goods, since the subject-matter of each action is the mark registered, or the reputation and goodwill existing, in the country where the infringing acts were done. He also held, less convincingly, that an English action for infringement of a mark registered in the United Kingdom, and for passing off, by acts committed in the United Kingdom, was not 'related', within the meaning of art 22, to a prior Irish action for passing off, by use of the same mark on the same type of goods in Ireland, because 'it would not be possible, let alone expedient, for the two sets of proceedings to be heard and determined together in one country'. This was because, under the English doctrine of the locality of intellectual property actions announced in *Tyburn*

---

[64] [1990] QB 361.
[65] [1988] 1 Lloyd's Rep 175.
[66] [1992] 2 Lloyd's Rep 261.
[67] [1988] QB 183.
[68] [1992] 2 Lloyd's Rep 552.
[69] [1988] 1 Lloyd's Rep 175.
[70] [1991] FSR 670.

Productions v Conan Doyle,[71] the claim for infringement of the British registered mark could not be entertained by the Irish courts; and the English passing-off claim was so closely related to the registered-mark claim, the same acts of infringement being relied on, that there would be little advantage to the defendant in staying the English passing-off proceedings alone. It is submitted that the locality doctrine relied on is itself inconsistent with the 1968 Convention, since infringement actions are not mentioned in art 16; and that in any event the considerations relied on are relevant to the exercise, rather than the existence, of the court's discretion under art 22. On the other hand Saville J was clearly right in *Rank Film Distributors v Lanterna*[72] to hold that art 22 does not apply where the first proceedings are merely for protective relief, and the second proceedings are for determination of the merits of the dispute.

The concept of related actions, within the meaning of art 22, is the subject of one of the questions referred to the European Court of Justice by the Court of Appeal in *The Maciej Rataj*.[73] More specifically, the question envisages proceedings brought against a shipowner in one contracting state in respect of a claim by one group of cargo owners for damage to their portion of a bulk cargo carried under certain contracts of carriage, followed by separate proceedings in another contracting state against the same shipowner, involving essentially similar issues of fact and law, but brought by a different cargo owner and in respect of damage to its portion of the same bulk cargo, carried under separate contracts of carriage but on the same terms.

Article 23 supplements art 21 by providing that where actions come within the exclusive jurisdiction of several courts, a court subsequently seised must decline jurisdiction in favour of the court first seised. This situation is most likely to arise under art 16(2), which confers exclusive jurisdiction over certain matters of company law on the courts of the contracting state in which the company involved has its seat, for a company may be seated both in the country where it was incorporated and has its registered office, and also in another country in which its central management and control is actually exercised. Another case falling within art 23, on a possible interpretation of art 16(1), would be where the dispute concerns an easement benefiting land in one contracting state and burdening land in another contracting state. In any case of conflicting exclusive jurisdiction over a dispute, art 23 gives mandatory priority to the court first seised, and thus clearly implies that its judgment must be recognised in the other contracting states, including the other exclusively competent state.

In the case of actions involving a Community patent, under arts 13 and 34 of the Protocol on Litigation, annexed to the Community Patent Convention,[74] which is not yet in force, arts 21–23 of the 1968 Convention will operate subject

---

[71] [1991] Ch 75. See also Chapter 13, for discussion of choice of law in respect of actions for infringement of intellectual property.
[72] (1991) *Financial Times*, 14 June.
[73] [1992] 2 Lloyd's Rep 552.
[74] [1989] OJ L401/1.

to a proviso that, where the validity of the relevant Community patent is already in dispute before a Community patent court, or the Common Appeal Court, or the European Patent Office, another Community patent court or the European Patent Office should stay its own proceedings concerning the patent if a party so requests and there are no special grounds for continuing them.

In *Owens Bank v Bracco*[75] the Court of Appeal held that the 1968 Convention in general, and arts 21–23 in particular, do not apply to proceedings in a contracting state for the enforcement of a judgment given in a non-contracting state. Thus arts 21–23 did not apply where an English application for registration under Part II of the Administration of Justice Act 1920 of a judgment given by a St Vincent court was made while an application to an Italian court for enforcement in Italy of the St Vincent judgment was pending. Parker LJ considered, however, that, under a discretion conferred by traditional English law, the English court could have stayed its proceedings if an Italian decision likely to give rise to an issue estoppel (for example, as to whether the St Vincent judgment had been obtained by fraud) had been imminent, and if the English court considered that the issue could more appropriately be tried in Italy. On further appeal, the House of Lords referred such questions to the European Court of Justice, which ruled that Title II (as well as Title III) of the 1968 Convention, and arts 21–23 in particular, do not apply to proceedings, or issues arising in proceedings, in contracting states concerning the recognition and enforcement of judgments given in non-contracting states, thus endorsing the approach adopted by the Court of Appeal. It is perhaps surprising that arts 16(5) and 22 should have been excluded from application in such cases.

The mandatory character of Title II

As the Schlosser Report emphasises,[76] Title II of the 1968 Convention (and Title II of the Lugano Convention) are based on the principle, generally accepted in the laws of the Continental European countries, that a competent court, properly seised of an action, is bound to determine the dispute to which the action relates, and has no discretion to decline jurisdiction in favour of a foreign court which it considers a more appropriate forum for the determination of the dispute. Even the problem of actions simultaneously pending in courts of different contracting states in respect of similar or related disputes is dealt with largely by mandatory rules, for in the case of similar disputes art 21 *requires* the court subsequently seised to decline jurisdiction in favour of the court first seised. It is only in the case of dissimilar but related disputes that art 22 provides for judicial discretion, and then only on the part of the court subsequently seised.

In this respect the Conventions adopt the opposite approach to that of the

---

[75] [1992] 2 WLR 127. 2 AC 443, CA and HL; and Case C-129/92 [1994] 1 All ER 336, ECJ.
[76] At paras 76–81. See also Stone (1983) 32 ICLQ 477 at 496–9; and per Hirst J in *Aiglon Ltd v Gau Shan Co Ltd* [1993] 1 Lloyd's Rep 164, which involved art 6(1) of the Lugano Convention.

prior English law, which had come, in the 15 years preceding the British commencement date for the 1968 Convention, fully to adopt a doctrine of forum non conveniens, similar to one which had long been accepted in Scotland[77] and (with some differences) in the United States.[78] Under the British doctrine the exercise of international jurisdiction is discretionary, and a competent court, properly seised, will nonetheless decline jurisdiction in favour of a foreign court, if it is satisfied that the foreign court is also competent and that it is a more appropriate or suitable forum for the trial of the action, in the light of the interests of all the parties and the ends of justice.[79]

Such a doctrine had long been applied by the English courts in cases where the defendant was not present in England, and the plaintiff sought to subject him to English jurisdiction by obtaining the court's permission for service abroad under RSC Ord 11.[80] But until the 1970s it was considered that, where the defendant (or, in an admiralty action in rem, his ship) had been served in England while present there, the court had power to decline jurisdiction only if the plaintiff's choice of the English forum was (in a narrow sense) vexatious, oppressive or similarly abusive.[81] Subsequently, however, a broad doctrine of forum non conveniens was extended to cases where jurisdiction was founded on presence and service in England by a series of decisions of the House of Lords,[82] culminating in *The Spiliada*,[83] decided on 19 November 1986, where Lord Goff restated the English doctrine as follows:

(1) The basic principle is that an English court will decline jurisdiction on the ground of forum non conveniens where it considers that a court elsewhere is competent and is a more appropriate or suitable forum for the trial of the dispute, in the light of the interests of all the parties and the ends of justice.

(2) Where English jurisdiction arises from the presence and service in England of the defendant or his ship, the general burden rests on the defendant to persuade the English court to exercise its discretion to decline jurisdiction, by establishing that the foreign court is clearly or distinctly a more appropriate forum. However each party will have the evidential burden in relation to factors on which he relies. Moreover it will be sufficient for the defendant to satisfy the English court that prima facie the foreign court is clearly more appropriate, in

---

[77] See *La Société du Gaz de Paris v La SA de Navigation, 'Les Armateurs Français'*, 1926 SC(HL) 13, and Anton, *Private International Law* (1967), at pp 148–54.

[78] See eg *Gulf Oil Corp v Gilbert* 330 US 501 (1947), and *Piper Aircraft Co v Reyno* 454 US 235 (1981).

[79] See per Lord Goff in *The Spiliada* [1987] 1 AC 460.

[80] See eg *The Hagen* [1908] P 189; *Rosler v Hilbery* [1925] Ch 250; *Oppenheimer v Rosenthal* [1937] 1 All ER 23; *Kroch v Rossell* [1937] 1 All ER 725; *Buttes Gas v Hammer* [1971] 3 All ER 1025; and *Evans Marshall v Bertola* [1973] 1 WLR 349.

[81] See *Logan v Bank of Scotland (No 2)* [1906] 1 KB 141; *Egbert v Short* [1907] 2 Ch 205; *Re Norton's Settlement* [1908] 1 Ch 471; *St Pierre v South American Stores* [1936] 1 KB 382; and *Maharanee of Baroda v Wildenstein* [1972] 2 QB 283.

[82] See *The Atlantic Star* [1974] AC 436; *MacShannon v Rockware Glass* [1978] AC 795; *Castanho v Brown & Root Ltd* [1981] AC 557; *Trendtex v Crédit Suisse* [1982] AC 679; *The Abidin Daver* [1984] AC 398; and *The Spiliada* [1987] 1 AC 460.

[83] [1987] 1 AC 460.

the light of such factors as the availability of witnesses, the law governing the relevant transaction, and the residences and places of business of the parties, unless the plaintiff shows that to decline jurisdiction would amount practically to a denial of justice.

(3) Where English jurisdiction is founded on the English court's permission for service abroad under RSC Ord 11, similar factors (including the defendant's residence or place of business, and the jurisdictional basis under RSC Ord 11 relied on by the plaintiff) are relevant, but the burden rests on the plaintiff to persuade the English court that it is clearly the more appropriate forum for the trial of the dispute.[84]

(4) In both situations the English court may decline jurisdiction even though this will deprive the plaintiff of a legitimate advantage – in terms of, for example: damages awarded on a higher scale; a more complete procedure of discovery; a power to award interest; or a more generous limitation period – provided that it is satisfied that substantial justice will be done in the appropriate foreign forum. In this connection the English court may allow a plaintiff to keep the benefit of security obtained by commencing proceedings here, while at the same time declining jurisdiction to determine the substantive dispute.

(5) However practical justice requires that, where the plaintiff acted reasonably in commencing proceedings in England, and did not act unreasonably in failing to issue a protective writ in the appropriate foreign court within the limitation period applicable there, he should not be deprived of the benefit of having started proceedings within the limitation period applicable in England. Thus the appropriate order may be to make it a condition of declining jurisdiction that the defendant should waive a time-bar in the foreign jurisdiction.

It was also established by other decisions that an agreement between the parties, designating a court intended to have exclusive jurisdiction, has the effect of causing the designated court to be regarded prima facie as clearly the more appropriate forum.[85]

This exclusion of any such doctrine by the Conventions is surely to be welcomed in the interests of certainty, economy and efficiency. Litigation is an expensive method of settling disputes, and litigation to determine the appropriate forum is more wasteful than most, since a decision to decline jurisdiction hardly advances the solution of the dispute. Ideally the rules on the existence of jurisdiction should be as clear and involve as few disputable facts as possible, consistently with a reasonable allocation of jurisdiction; and jurisdictional grounds not requiring a

---

[84] In Ord 11 cases, the plaintiff must also satisfy the court that there is a good (or strongly arguable) case for the existence of the jurisdictional facts required by Ord 11, and also that, as to the merits, there is a serious question to be tried. Moreover, the latter requirement is separate from, and unrelated to, the question of *forum conveniers*. See *Seaconsar v Bank Markazi* [1993] 4 All ER 456, [1993] 3 WLR 756, HL.

[85] See *The Chaparral* [1968] 2 Lloyd's Rep 158; *The Eleftheria* [1970] P 94; *Mackender v Feldia* [1967] 2 QB 590; *Evans Marshall v Bertola* [1973] 1 All ER 992; *Carvalho v Hull Blyth* [1979] 3 All ER 280; *The El Amria* [1981] 2 Lloyd's Rep 119; *Trendtex v Crédit Suisse* [1982] AC 679; and *Hamed El Chaity v Thomas Cook*, 5 May 1992.

reasonable connection between the defendant or the subject-matter of the dispute and the court seised should be available only where a denial of justice cannot be avoided by any other means.[86] At least to the extent that the bases of jurisdiction accord with these ideals, it seems clearly desirable that efficiency should be promoted by *requiring* a court which is properly seised to proceed to determine the dispute, and prohibiting it from considering whether some other forum is in some way more suitable.

In reality, the Conventions do not invariably achieve a reasonable allocation of jurisdiction, especially where the defendant is not domiciled in a contracting state. Moreover, by way of exception to their general principle, and in addition to the judicial discretion explicitly conferred by art 22 in the case of simultaneous dissimilar but related actions, there are a number of situations in which the Conventions tolerate the existence of some judicial discretion, arising from the law of the court seised, to decline jurisdiction on grounds of forum non conveniens. In the United Kingdom, s 49 of the 1982 Act, which provides that nothing in the Act shall prevent a court in the United Kingdom from staying, sisting, striking out or dismissing any proceedings before it, on the ground of forum non conveniens or otherwise, where to do so is not inconsistent with the Conventions, authorises the British courts to make full use of such powers.[87] These situations will now be examined.

Where the defendant is not domiciled in any contracting state

Article 4 of the 1968 Convention remits jurisdiction to the national law of the court seised in most cases where the defendant is not domiciled within the contracting states,[88] and thus impliedly authorises a contracting state to permit its courts in such cases to decline jurisdiction in favour of another court, in accordance with a doctrine of forum non conveniens, whether the other court is a court for another part or district of the same contracting state, or is a court of another contracting state, or is a court of a non-contracting state. This exception in favour of judicial discretion is necessitated by the regrettable decision to retain the use of jurisdictional bases recognised by the lex fori but not involving a reasonable connection between the defendant or the cause of action and the court seised, against defendants not domiciled in a contracting state. Thus, in accordance with s 49 of the 1982 Act, the English courts retain their traditional

---

[86] See Stone (1983) 32 ICLQ 477 at 485–7.

[87] See also s 22, which ensures that Sched 8 will not prevent a Scottish court from declining jurisdiction on the ground of forum non conveniens; and, for England, the Rules of the Supreme Court (Amendment No 2) 1983, which retain the traditional rule that a High Court writ may be served abroad only with the leave of the court, granted at its discretion, except where the court's jurisdiction is conferred by the 1982 Act or by some other statute (eg one implementing a convention on a particular matter), rather than by the Rules of the Supreme Court (see rr 3 and 7 of the 1983 Rules, amending RSC Ord 6, r 7, and RSC Ord 11, r 1).

[88] There are exceptions in respect of insurance or consumer contracts, where the defendant insurer or supplier has a branch within the European Community (arts 8(2) and 13(2)); exclusive jurisdiction (art 16); jurisdiction clauses (art 17); and submission by appearance (art 18).

discretion to decline jurisdiction in most cases where the defendant is not domiciled within the contracting states.

Where the defendant is domiciled in the forum state

Article 2 of the 1968 Convention confers jurisdiction on the courts in general of the contracting state in which the defendant is domiciled, and requires that state to provide at least one court which is able and willing to determine the dispute. Subject to that, however, it permits the state of the defendant's domicile to allocate jurisdiction between the courts for its various territories or districts in almost any manner which it may choose.[89] Accordingly, the state may provide that in certain of such cases more than one of its courts shall be competent, and that one of its courts may then exercise discretion, in accordance with a doctrine of forum non conveniens, to decline jurisdiction in favour of another competent court of the same state, though not in favour of a court of another (whether contracting or non-contracting) state.[90]

Accordingly, in the United Kingdom Sched 4 to the 1982 Act allocates jurisdiction over a defendant who is domiciled in the United Kingdom between the English, the Scottish, and the Northern Irish courts, in such a way that in some cases both the courts of the part of the United Kingdom in which the defendant is domiciled, and the courts of another part (for example, those for the place of performance of the relevant contractual obligation, or for the place where a relevant tortious event occurred) are competent to determine a dispute. Section 49 of the Act then authorises a competent court of a part of the United Kingdom, in accordance with a doctrine of forum non conveniens traditionally accepted in its part, to decline jurisdiction in favour of a competent court of another part of the United Kingdom.

As far as the Conventions are concerned, the position is similar in other cases where Title II confers jurisdiction on the courts in general of a contracting state on some other basis than the defendant's domicile: as in the case of art 5(6), which refers to the domicile of the trust involved; art 14(1), which refers to the plaintiff consumer's domicile; and art 16, on exclusive jurisdiction. But in such cases the 1982 Act usually allocates such jurisdiction to the courts of a single part of the United Kingdom.[91]

Moreover, since Sched 4 fails to include any provisions analogous to arts 21–23 of the Conventions in relation to simultaneous similar or related actions

---

[89] The same applies to jurisdiction based on the defendant's domicile (or deemed domicile) over an insurance or protected consumer contract, under arts 8, 11 and 14.

[90] Cf *Re Harrods (Buenos Aires) Ltd (No 1)* [1991] 4 All ER 334, [1991] 3 WLR 397, where the English Court of Appeal, while accepting that under the 1968 Convention there is no power to decline jurisdiction over an English defendant on grounds of forum non conveniens in favour of a court of another contracting state, asserted that the Convention has not abolished the judicial discretion under traditional English law to do so in favour of a court of a non-contracting state. On appeal *Harrods* has now been referred by the House of Lords to the European Court of Justice, as Case C-314/92 *Ladenimor v Intercomfinanz* [1992] OJ C219/4.

[91] See s 10, and Sched 4, arts 5(6), 14(1) and 16.

in courts of different parts of the United Kingdom, the problem is left to be dealt with, whatever the defendant's domicile, in accordance with s 49, on the basis of traditional doctrines of forum non conveniens, which may lead the court first seised to decline jurisdiction in favour of the court subsequently seised.[92]

Where the defendant is domiciled in another contracting state

Where the Conventions confer jurisdiction on courts of one contracting state over a defendant who is domiciled in another contracting state, they usually single out the particular place within the non-domiciliary state whose courts are rendered competent. For example, art 5(1) and (3) confer jurisdiction over a defendant domiciled in another contracting state on the courts for the *place* of performance of the contractual obligation and the courts for the *place* where a relevant tortious event occurred. This means that if, for example, a French (or Swiss) domiciliary contracts to deliver goods in England, or causes a road accident in England, the competent British courts are the English courts, to the exclusion of the Scottish and Northern Irish courts. Moreover, in such a case the Conventions give the plaintiff, and not the courts, the choice of whether he should sue in England or in France (or Switzerland); and if he chooses to sue in England, the English courts are not permitted to decline jurisdiction in favour of the French (or Swiss) courts.[93] In such a case the only control which the English courts may exercise over the plaintiff's choice of forum is that they may transfer an English action between two English courts; in other words, between the High Court and a county court, or between two county courts.[94]

Reflex effect of arts 16, 17 and 21–23

Somewhat greater difficulty arises, however, in connection with the possible 'reflex effect', in favour of non-contracting states, of arts 16, 17 and 21–23 of the 1968 Convention (and of the Lugano Convention). The situations envisaged are:

(1)   where the subject-matter of an action falls within the material scope of art 16, but the relevant connection is with a non-contracting state; for example, where the action concerns title to land situated in New York; or

(2)   where there is an agreement, otherwise complying with art 17, designed to confer exclusive jurisdiction on a court or courts of a non-contracting state; or

(3). where similar or related actions are simultaneously pending in a court of a contracting state and a court of a non-contracting state, which was the court first seised.

It is clear that the Conventions do not *require* a contracting state to take any

---

[92] See *Castanho v Brown & Root* [1981] AC 557.

[93] See the Schlosser Report, at paras 76–78; and *Mercury Publicity v Loerke* (1991) *The Times*, 21 October, (1991) *Financial Times*, 13 November, English CA.

[94] See the Schlosser Report, at paras 80 and 81.

account of such factors. They do not, even impliedly, *require* contracting states to accord the same respect to such connections with non-contracting states as it expressly requires them to accord to such connections with each other.[95] On the other hand, it is equally clear that a contracting state is entirely free to authorise or even require its courts to take account of such connections, and accordingly decline jurisdiction in favour of a court of a non-contracting state, in cases where the defendant is domiciled outside the contracting states and jurisdiction is remitted to the lex fori by art 4.[96] The real difficulty is where the defendant is domiciled within the contracting states, and is sued in his domiciliary state or in a court of another contracting state which is competent under Title II of the Conventions, for example as the place of performance of the relevant contractual obligation or the domicile of a co-defendant.

It is submitted that, despite the undoubtedly discriminatory character of the Conventions, as shown especially by art 4, the purposes of arts 16, 17 and 21–23 (respectively: to respect the sovereignty and interests of the state which is recognised as having the predominant concern with the matter in question; to respect the freedom of the parties to regulate by agreement the manner in which their disputes should be settled; and to prevent litigation in different countries from giving rise to irreconcilable judgments) make it appropriate to construe these articles as impliedly permitting a contracting state to authorise or even require its courts to give the same or some lesser effect to such connections with non-contracting states as the articles require the contracting states to give to such connections with each other; rather than to interpret the Conventions as requiring such connections with non-member states to be wholly disregarded.[97]

If this view is accepted, the following consequences arise:

(1) The English courts continue to lack jurisdiction to entertain actions whose object is the determination of title to foreign land, and which are not based on a direct contractual or fiduciary relationship between the parties, even where the land is situated in a non-contracting state and the defendant is domiciled in England.[98]

(2) Equally, the English courts retain a discretion to decline jurisdiction so as to give effect to an exclusive jurisdiction clause in favour of a court of a non-

---

[95] See Droz, *Compétence Judiciaire et Effets des Jugements dans le Marché Commun* (1972), at paras 165–8, 216–18, and 329–30.

[96] See Stone (1983) 32 ICLQ 477 at 496–7.

[97] See Droz, *Compétence Judiciaire et Effets des Jugements dans le Marché Commun* (1972), at paras 165–8, 216–18, and 329–30. Unfortunately the reflex effect of art 21 was not accepted by Potter J in *Arkwright Mutual Insurance v Bryanston Insurance* [1990] 2 QB 649.

[98] For the lack of jurisdiction, see *Norris v Chambres* (1861) 3 De GF & J 583; *Deschamps v Miller* [1908] 1 Ch 856; and s 30 of the 1982 Act. For the exception for direct contractual or fiduciary relationships, see *Penn v Baltimore* (1750) 27 ER 1132; *Richard West & Partners Ltd v Dick* [1969] 2 Ch 424; *St Pierre v South American Stores* [1936] 1 KB 382; *Paget v Ede* (1874) LR 18 Eq 118; *British South Africa Co v De Beers* [1910] 2 Ch 502, reversed on other grounds, [1912] AC 52; *Arglasse v Muschamp* (1682) 23 ER 322, 369 and 438; *Cranstown v Johnson* (1796) 30 ER 952; *Razelos v Razelos* [1969] 3 All ER 929; *Re Courtney* [1835–42] All ER Rep 415; *Re Smith* [1916] 2 Ch 206; *Re Anchor Line* [1937] 1 Ch 483; and *Mercantile Investment Co v River Plate Co* [1892] 2 Ch 303. See further Chapter 15, under 'Immovable property: jurisdiction', p 354 et seq. below.

contracting state, provided that the clause satisfies the formal and other require-ments of art 17, and does not infringe arts 12, 15 and 16, of the Conventions.[99] In any event, where the defendant is not domiciled in a contracting state, it is enough that the clause complies with the requirements of English law (which do not require writing, nor that the clause should be confined to a particular legal relationship), and does not infringe art 16 of the Conventions.

(3) Similarly, the English courts retain a discretion to decline jurisdiction in favour of similar or in some circumstances related proceedings previously (or even, where the defendant is not domiciled in a contracting state, subsequently) instituted in a court of a non-contracting state.[100]

Arbitral agreements

Since art 57 of the 1968 Convention and of the Lugano Convention ensure that other conventions on particular matters will prevail over these Conventions, the English courts remain bound to decline jurisdiction in favour of arbitration where there is an international arbitration agreement complying with art II of the New York Convention of 10 June 1958 on the Recognition and Enforcement of Foreign Arbitral Awards and s 1 of the Arbitration Act 1975. It is less clear whether the effect of art 1[2](4) of the Conventions is to preserve their discretion under s 4(1) of the Arbitration Act 1950 to decline jurisdiction in support of a domestic arbitration agreement.

Restraining foreign proceedings

In addition to conferring a discretion on the English courts to decline jurisdic-tion to entertain English proceedings on grounds of forum non conveniens (discussed above), traditional English law has permitted the English courts to restrain a party by injunction from continuing to prosecute foreign proceedings which he has commenced. But, as the Privy Council ruled in *Soc Nationale Industrielle Aerospatiale v Lee Kui Jak*,[101] such an order will be granted much more cautiously than an order terminating English proceedings: the English court must be satisfied that the continuance of the foreign proceedings would be oppressive, and this normally requires not only that the English court should consider itself the natural forum for the determination of the dispute, but also that the continuance of the foreign proceedings would cause injustice to the defendant there (as by substantially prejudicing his position in connection with a related claim against a third person), and that the prevention of the foreign

---

[99] See the 1982 Act, s 49; RSC Ord 11, r 1; *The Eleftheria* [1970] P 94; *Mackender v Feldia* [1967] 2 QB 590; *Evans Marshall v Bertola* [1973] 1 All ER 992; *Carvalho v Hull Blyth* [1979] 3 All ER 280; and *Trendtex v Crédit Suisse* [1982] AC 679, affirming [1980] 3 All ER 721.

[100] See the 1982 Act, s 49; RSC Ord 11, r 1, as amended; *Castanho v Brown & Root* [1981] AC 557; and *The Abidin Daver* [1984] AC 398.

[101] [1987] AC 871.

proceedings would not unjustly deprive the plaintiff there of a legitimate advantage.

It seems clear that it would be contrary to the 1968 Convention or the Lugano Convention for an English court in any circumstances to restrain by injunction the continuance of proceedings in another contracting state in respect of a matter within the material scope of the Conventions.

Interim relief

By art 24 of the 1968 and Lugano Conventions and of Sched 4 to the 1982 Act, the English courts may grant such provisional, including protective, measures as may be available under English law, even if, under the Conventions or Schedule, the courts of another contracting state, or part of the United Kingdom, have jurisdiction as to the substance of the matter. Typically these provisions permit a court to make an order (such as a French *saisie conservatoire* or an English *Mareva* injunction) freezing assets belonging to the defendant and located in its territory, until the merits of the plaintiff's claim have been determined by a competent court elsewhere within the contracting states.

As the European Court of Justice ruled in *Reichert v Dresdner Bank (No 2)*,[102] art 24 is confined to measures designed to preserve the factual or legal status quo, with a view to protecting rights whose recognition is also sought from the court which is to determine the merits. Accordingly the provision does not extend to a 'pauline' action, for example under ss 423–425 of the (English) Insolvency Act 1986, whereby a creditor seeks the setting aside of a disposition which has been made by his debtor in fraud of creditors, since such relief involves altering the position of the debtor and the beneficiary under the disposition. The European Court of Justice has also on several occasions[103] emphasised that art 24 does not apply unless the substantive dispute, in respect of which the provisional measure is sought, falls within the material scope of the Convention as defined by art 1.

Article 24 is permissive rather than mandatory, and under the previously existing English law, as expounded by the House of Lords in *The Siskina*,[104] the English courts had no power to grant a *Mareva* injunction unless they had jurisdiction to determine the substantive dispute. This difficulty has, however, been removed by Part IV of the 1982 Act. First, s 24 of the Act empowers a British court to grant interim relief pending trial or appeal, even though the issue to be tried or appealed relates to its jurisdiction or there is a reference to the European Court of Justice under the 1971 Protocol. More importantly, s 25(1) empowers the English or Northern Irish High Court to grant interim relief in contemplation of proceedings which have been or are to be commenced in another contracting state or another part of the United Kingdom in respect of a

---

[102] Case C-261/90, 26 March 1992.
[103] See Case 143/78 *De Cavel v De Cavel (No 1)* [1979] ECR 1055; Case 120/79 *De Cavel v De Cavel (No 2)* [1980] ECR 731; and Case 25/81 *CHW v GJH* [1982] ECR 1189.
[104] [1979] AC 210. See also *Zucker v Tyndall Holdings* (1992) *Financial Times*, 8 July, CA.

matter which falls within the scope of the Conventions.[105] Section 25(2) adds a curious proviso that such an application may be rejected if the court considers that its incompetence in respect of the substantive dispute makes it inexpedient for it to grant the interim relief sought; a provision both unnecessary, in view of the discretionary character already possessed by provisional orders such as *Mareva* injunctions, and misconceived, since the lack of English jurisdiction to determine the merits has little bearing on the desirability of provisional measures against assets located in England. By s 25(3), the power to grant interim relief may be extended by Order in Council to cases where the substantive dispute is to be determined by a court outside the contracting states, or by arbitration, or where the subject-matter falls outside the scope of the Conventions. Such extensions are intended to proceed in stages and on a country-by-country basis;[106] but so far no such orders have been made. It has now been established that a *Mareva* injunction, granted by the English High Court under s 25 in support of proceedings in another contracting state or another part of the United Kingdom, can be served abroad without the court's leave, under RSC Ord 11, r 1(2), if the defendant is domiciled in a contracting state,[107] or under RSC Ord 11, r 1(1)(b), if he is not.[108] Moreover the significance of s 25 has been reduced by the decision of the House of Lords in *Channel Tunnel Group Ltd v Balfour Beatty Construction Ltd*,[109] that in any event the English court has power under s 37(1) of the Supreme Court Act 1981 to grant interim relief in support of any foreign arbitral or judicial proceedings, so long as it has, or apart from a jurisdiction or arbitration clause would have, jurisdiction to determine the substantive dispute.

Until 1988 *Mareva* injunctions were granted only in respect of assets situated in England, but the Court of Appeal has now established that in appropriate cases they may be granted in respect of foreign assets.[110] An order relating to foreign assets should, however, specify that it is to affect third parties in relation to acts abroad only as regards persons who are resident in England, have been given written notice at their English residence, and are able to prevent acts abroad which assist in infringement of the order, or to the extent that its recognition or enforceability has been established by a decision of the relevant foreign court.[111] In *Republic of Haiti v Duvalier*[112] the Court of Appeal upheld a

---

[105] For similar provision for Scotland, see s 27; and for Ireland, see its Jurisdiction of Courts and Enforcement of Judgments (European Communities) Act 1988, s 11.

[106] See s 25(4).

[107] See *Republic of Haiti v Duvalier* [1990] QB 202, CA.

[108] See *X v Y* [1990] QB 220, where Diamond QC emphasised that s 25 is designed to overrule *The Siskina* [1979] AC 210, and thus requires a fresh approach to the interpretation of RSC Ord 11.

[109] [1993] AC 334.

[110] See *Babanaft International v Bassatne* [1990] Ch 13; *Republic of Haiti v Duvalier* [1990] QB 202; and *Derby v Weldon (No 1)* [1990] Ch 48, and *(Nos 3 and 4)* [1990] Ch 65. Cf *Stadtwerke Essen v Trailigaz* [1988] ECC 291, where the Paris Court of Appeal held that art 24 enabled the French courts to appoint an expert to verify the operating conditions of a water-ozonisation plant in Germany, despite the absence of any urgency.

[111] See *Derby v Weldon (Nos 3 and 4)*, note 109 above.

[112] See note 109 above.

Mareva injunction affecting both English and foreign assets, granted in support of a French action against a defendant domiciled in France, but subsequently in *Rosseel v Oriental Commercial and Shipping*[113] the Court of Appeal explained that it is only in very exceptional circumstances (such as the involvement of an English solicitor in the administration of the defendant's assets, as had occurred in *Republic of Haiti v Duvalier*) that the English courts should grant a *Mareva* injunction in respect of foreign assets in support of foreign proceedings, judgments or awards.

In addition, s 26 of the 1982 Act gives further powers to an English (or Northern Irish) court, where it declines jurisdiction over admiralty proceedings, commenced in rem, in favour of a court elsewhere (whether or not within the contracting states) or of arbitration.[114] If property has been arrested, or bail or other security has been given to prevent or obtain release from arrest, the English court is authorised to retain the property arrested as security, or require the provision of equivalent security, for the satisfaction of an award or judgment, enforceable in England, which may be given in the proceedings in favour of which jurisdiction is declined. This extends to cases where under the Conventions an English court declines jurisdiction to entertain an admiralty action in rem in favour of an action in personam commenced earlier in another contracting state,[115] or of arbitration, and the English court will normally retain the ship or require equivalent security as if the merits were to be determined in the English action in rem.[116] Similarly in Scotland s 27 (which corresponds to s 25) has been construed as permitting the arrest of a ship in support of foreign proceedings in personam, if the applicant shows that he has a plausible cause of action under the foreign law.[117]

In *Denilauler v Couchet Frères*[118] the European Court of Justice ruled that a judgment granting provisional relief, which is obtained ex parte and is intended to be enforced without notice to the other party, is not enforceable in other contracting states under Title III of the 1968 Convention. Thus, where an ex parte freezing order is desired, it will usually be advisable for the plaintiff to apply to the courts of the country in which the property to be frozen is situated. In England the usual (though not invariable) procedure for obtaining a *Mareva* injunction in respect of English assets is by way of ex parte application, but in the case of foreign assets it will generally be advisable to proceed inter partes, especially as the order will not usually be regarded even in England as binding on third parties unless and until the court of the situs orders its enforcement.[119] Conversely, in *Mund & Fester v Hatrex*,[120] the European Court of Justice ruled

---

[113] [1990] 3 All ER 545.

[114] For the former English law, see *The Golden Trader* [1975] QB 348, and *The Rena K* [1979] QB 377.

[115] See *The Nordglimt* [1988] QB 183, read in the light of *The Deichland* [1990] QB 361, CA.

[116] See *The Bazias 3 and Bazias 4* [1993] 2 All ER 964, [1993] 2 WLR 854, CA.

[117] See *Clipper Shipping v SO Investment* [1989] ECC 216, Outer House of the Court of Session.

[118] Case 125/79, [1980] ECR 1553.

[119] See *Derby v Weldon (Nos 3 and 4)* [1990] Ch 65.

[120] Case C-398/92, decided on 10 February 1994; (1994) *Financial Times*, 22 February.

that, in view of the simplification in the reciprocal enforcement of judgments between member states which has been achieved by the 1968 Convention, art 7 of the EEC Treaty (on discrimination in relation to nationality) prevents a court of a member state, which is seised of an action on the merits, from granting protective measures against local assets more readily where the eventual judgment is likely to require enforcement in another member state than where it is likely to be enforced locally.

When the Community Patent Convention[121] enters into force, in the case of actions concerning the infringement of a Community patent, art 24 of the 1968 Convention will be excluded and replaced by arts 13(2) and 36 of the Protocol on Litigation, annexed to the Community Patent Convention, so that:

(1) any court of a contracting state to the Community Patent Convention (whether or not it is a Community patent court) will be able to grant, in respect of a Community patent, provisional or protective measures in accordance with its own law applicable to national patents, but with effect only in its own country, even if a Community patent court of another contracting state has sole competence to determine the merits of the dispute; and

(2) a Community patent court, which is competent to entertain an infringement action on grounds other than as the court for the place of the infringement complained of, will be able to grant provisional or protective measures which will have to be recognised and enforced, in accordance with Title III of the 1968 Convention, throughout the contracting states.

Service

The methods by which a writ instituting an action in one contracting state may be served on a defendant in another contracting state are regulated by art IV of the Protocol annexed to the 1968 Convention, and of the First Protocol annexed to the Lugano Convention. More fundamentally, art 20[2]–[3] of the Conventions require the original court to stay its proceedings until it is satisfied that a defendant who is domiciled in another contracting state has been effectively and timeously notified of their institution. In addition Title III of the Conventions require a court which is requested to recognise or enforce a judgment from another contracting state to refuse recognition if the defendant was not duly served with the writ in the original action in sufficient time to enable him to arrange for his defence and did not appear in the original action.

Methods of service

By art IV of the Protocols, a writ instituting an action in a court of one contracting state which needs to be served on a defendant in another contracting

---

[121] [1989] OJ L401/1.

state must either be transmitted in accordance with the procedures laid down in other conventions and agreements concluded between the contracting states, or by means of a new procedure, involving direct co-operation between the court officers of the states involved, created by art IV[2].

The most important of the other conventions referred to in art IV is the Hague Convention of 15 November 1965 on the Service Abroad of Judicial and Extrajudicial Documents in Civil or Commercial Matters, to which all the EC member states, with the exception of Ireland, are parties.[122] The Hague Convention (by art 2) requires each of its contracting states to designate a central authority to receive requests for service from other contracting states.[123] Under art 3, the authority or judicial officer competent under the law of the state in which the writ has been issued forwards to the central authority of the state in which service is to be effected two copies of a request in the form annexed to the Convention and of the writ to be served.[124] By art 4, if the central authority considers that the request does not comply with the Convention, it must promptly inform the applicant, specifying its objections. Otherwise, by art 5, the central authority must either itself serve the writ, or arrange to have it served by an appropriate agency; and such service must be effected either by a method prescribed by the internal law of the state addressed for the service of documents in internal actions on persons who are within its territory, or by a particular method which is requested by the applicant and is compatible with the law of the state addressed, or by delivery to the addressee, if he accepts it voluntarily and this is not incompatible with the law of the state addressed. Then, by art 6, the central authority, or another authority designated by it, must complete a certificate in the form annexed to the Convention, stating that the writ has been served and specifying the method, place and date of service and the person to whom the writ was delivered, and forward the certificate directly to the applicant; or if the writ has not been served, the certificate must set out the reasons preventing service. By art 13, the state addressed may refuse to comply with a valid request for service if it considers that compliance would infringe its sovereignty or security, but not on any other ground, such as that under its internal law it claims exclusive jurisdiction over the subject-matter of

---

[122] For the text of the Hague Convention, see Cmnd 3986 (1969). Of the EFTA countries, Finland, Norway and Sweden (but not Switzerland) are parties to the Hague Convention. Other parties include Turkey, Cyprus, the United States, Canada, Japan, Israel, Egypt, Pakistan, Botswana, Malawi, and Barbados. See (1990) 29 ILM 1072.

[123] The central authorities within the European Community are: in the United Kingdom, the Foreign Secretary; in France, Belgium, Denmark and Portugal, the Ministry of Justice; in Luxembourg, the *Parquet Général* of the Superior Court; in the Netherlands, the *procureur* of the Hague district court; in Italy, the registrar of the Rome Court of Appeal; in Greece, the Board of Administrative and Judicial Affairs in the Foreign Ministry; and in most regions of Germany, the Ministry of Justice, but in others the president of the regional court. Under art 18 the United Kingdom has designated as additional authorities the Senior Master of the (English) Supreme Court, the Crown Agent for Scotland, and the Registrar of the (Northern Irish) Supreme Court.

[124] In England the plaintiff lodges a request at the Central Office of the High Court, and the documents are sent by the Senior Master to the Parliamentary Under-Secretary of State at the Foreign Office for forwarding to the central authority of the state addressed. See RSC Ord 11, r 6(4)–(7).

the action or that its internal law would not permit a claim of the type in question; and in case of refusal, the central authority must promptly inform the applicant, stating the reasons. The Convention also (by art 9) permits a contracting state to use consular, or in exceptional circumstances diplomatic, channels to forward documents for the purpose of service to authorities of another contracting state which are designated by the latter for the purpose.[125]

The Hague Convention (by art 8) also permits a contracting state to effect service on a person abroad, without using any compulsion, directly through its diplomatic or consular agents. But a contracting state may declare that it is opposed to such service within its territory, unless the person to be served is a national of the state in which the writ originates, and within the European Community such declarations have been made by Belgium, France, Luxembourg, Germany and Portugal.

The Hague Convention (by art 10) also permits, in the absence of objection by the state of destination: the sending of writs by post directly to persons abroad; service effected as a result of a direct request from the judicial officers, officials, or other competent persons of the state of origin to the judicial officers, officials, or other competent persons of the state of destination; and service through the judicial officers, officials, or other competent persons of the state of destination at the direct request of the plaintiff. Within the European Community, Germany objects to all three methods; the United Kingdom to the second and third methods; and Denmark to the third method. In addition the Hague Convention (by art 11) permits two or more contracting states to agree to permit additional channels of transmission, such as direct communication between their respective authorities, and (by art 19) does not prejudice provisions of the internal law of a contracting state which permit additional methods of transmission of documents from abroad for service in its territory.

As permitted by art IV of the 1968 and Lugano Protocols, and art 11 of the Hague Convention, an English writ may also be served on a defendant in another contracting state to the 1968 or Lugano Conventions by a method provided for in a bilateral convention between the United Kingdom and the state of destination. Such bilateral conventions exist between the United Kingdom and each of the other EC member states, with the exception of Luxembourg and Ireland.[126] These conventions provide for service inter alia through the judicial authorities of the state of destination, and through the British consular authorities, though in Germany, Denmark, and Portugal consular service is not allowed if the addressee is a national of the state of destination.[127]

---

[125] Within the European Community, the authorities designated under art 9 are: in the United Kingdom, the central authority and the additional authorities (see note 122, above); in Belgium and Luxembourg, the central authority; in France, the *Procureur de la République* of the district in which the addressee resides; in the Netherlands, the *procureur* attached to the court within whose district service is requested; in Denmark, the judge or the president of the local court of first instance; in Germany, the central authority for the relevant region, and the president of the regional court; in Italy, the registrars of the first instance or intermediate appellate courts, and the process-servers of the first instance courts; in Greece and Portugal, none.

[126] See *The Supreme Court Practice 1991*, at para 11/6/2.

[127] See RSC Ord 11, r 6(2), and *The Supreme Court Practice 1991*, para 11/6/2.

A further procedure for service in another contracting state is made available by art IV[2] of the 1968 and Lugano Protocols, in addition to the methods provided for by the Hague Convention and the bilateral conventions between the relevant states, unless the state of destination objects to it by declaration. Under the new procedure, a writ may be sent by the appropriate public officers of the state in which it was issued directly to the appropriate public officers of the state in which the addressee is to be found; that is, to the registrars or the official process-servers (*huissiers*) of the court within whose area the defendant is residing or staying. The officer of the state of origin sends a copy of the writ to the officer of the state addressed who is competent to forward it to the addressee, and the writ is then forwarded to the addressee in the manner specified by the law of the state addressed. Such forwarding is recorded by a certificate sent directly to the officer of the state of origin.

The only EC member state which is not a party to the Hague Convention nor to a bilateral convention with the United Kingdom is Ireland. Accordingly, where an English writ has to be served on a defendant resident in Ireland, the new procedure specified in art IV[2] of the 1968 Protocol is mandatory and exclusive.

Duties of the original court

By art 20[2] of the 1968 and Lugano Conventions and of Sched 4 to the 1982 Act, a court of a contracting state, when seised of an action against a defendant who is domiciled in another contracting state or part of the United Kingdom and who has not entered an appearance, must stay its proceedings until it is shown that he has been able to receive the writ in sufficient time to enable him to arrange for his defence, or that all necessary steps have been taken to that end.[128] It seems clear, especially in the light of the case-law on art 27(2) of the 1968 Convention, which operates at the stage of recognition and enforcement of judgments,[129] that art 20[2] does not require that the defendant should have obtained actual knowledge of the action, but that technically valid service, in accordance with the law of the forum country or conventions binding on it, is not always sufficient. Rather, art 20[2] implies a Community law standard of reasonable efforts to notify, similar to those required in the United States under the 'due process' clause of the 14th Amendment to the American Constitution.[130] Personal service on an individual defendant, or postal service to his

---

[128] See also RSC Ord 13, r 7B, which requires an application for leave, supported by an affidavit showing compliance with art 20, before a default judgment can be obtained in the English High Court against a defendant domiciled elsewhere within the contracting states.

As regards actions for infringement of a Community patent, art 20[2] of the 1968 Convention will operate also in favour of a defendant who is not domiciled in any contracting state but has a secondary establishment in a contracting state other than that of the court seised. See art 13(3) of the Protocol on Litigation annexed to the Community Patent Convention, not yet in force, [1989] OJ L401/1.

[129] See Chapter 14, pp 339–42 below.

[130] See *Mullane v Central Hanover Bank & Trust Co* 339 US 306 (1950).

last-known address,[131] or delivery there through its letter-box or to an adult member of his household, should suffice, unless the address were known to have been permanently abandoned. Similarly, in the case of a company, service at or by post to a currently registered office, or some other place of business established by the company and not known to have been abandoned, should be sufficient. But newspaper advertisement should not be adequate unless the person had disappeared and could not be found by reasonable enquiries.[132]

By art 20[3] of the Conventions, art 20[2] is replaced by art 15 of the Hague Convention of 15 November 1965 on the Service Abroad of Judicial and Extrajudicial Documents in Civil or Commercial Matters, in cases where the writ had to be transmitted abroad in accordance with the Hague Convention. Since 11 of the 12 EC member states are now parties to the Hague Convention, it is art 15 thereof which will usually apply. By art 15(1), where a writ had to be transmitted abroad for the purpose of service and the defendant has not appeared, judgment must not be given until it is established either that the writ has been served by a method prescribed by the internal law of the state addressed for the service of documents in internal actions on persons within its territory, or that it has actually been delivered to the defendant or to his residence by another method provided for by the Hague Convention; and (in either case) that the service or delivery was effected in sufficient time to enable him to defend.

This requirement is qualified by art 15(2) of the Hague Convention, which permits a contracting state to declare that its courts may give judgment, even if no certificate of service or delivery has been received, if the document was transmitted by one of the methods provided for in the Hague Convention, and a period of not less than six months, considered adequate by the court in the particular case, has elapsed since the date of the transmission of the writ, and no certificate of any kind has been received, even though every reasonable effort has been made to obtain one from the competent authorities of the state addressed. Such declarations have been made by the United Kingdom, France, the Benelux countries, Denmark and Portugal; but not by Germany, Italy and Greece. Article 15(3), however, permits the court to order provisional measures in urgent cases.

In addition, where a writ had to be transmitted abroad for service under the Hague Convention and a judgment has been entered against a defendant who has not appeared, art 16 empowers the court to set aside the judgment despite the expiry of the time for appealing, if the defendant, without any fault on his part, did not have knowledge of the writ in sufficient time to defend, or of the judgment in sufficient time to appeal, and he has disclosed a prima facie defence to the action on the merits. Such an application must be filed within a reasonable time after the defendant has obtained knowledge of the judgment, and in addition a contracting state may impose a definite time-limit, of at least a year,

---

[131] See, however, *Re a Consignment of Italian Wine* [1988] ECC 159, where the German Supreme Court held that, under art 175 of the (German) Code of Civil Procedure, service by post is not permissible in German summary proceedings.

[132] Cf *Dobkin v Chapman* 236 NE2d 451 (1968).

running from the judgment. A one-year limitation period has been imposed by the United Kingdom, France, the Benelux countries, Denmark and Portugal, but none has been imposed by Germany, Italy or Greece.

Review in enforcement proceedings

Articles 27(2) and 34[2] of the 1968 and Lugano Conventions require a court of a contracting state, when requested to recognise or enforce a judgment given in another contracting state under Title III of the Conventions, to refuse recognition and enforcement if the judgment was given in default of appearance and the defendant was not duly served with the writ instituting the original action in sufficient time to enable him to arrange for his defence. These provisions are examined in Chapter 14, pp 339–42 below.

9

CIVIL JURISDICTION – ALTERNATIVE FORA

Articles 5–6A of the 1968 and Lugano Conventions specify a number of cases in which, by way of derogation from art 3, a defendant who is domiciled in one contracting state may be sued in another contracting state.[1] Their effect is to give the plaintiff a choice of suing in the state of the defendant's domicile, in accordance with art 2, or in a court of another contracting state with which a connection specified by arts 5–6A exists. The connections used in art 5 are between the cause of action and the forum made available, while those used in art 6 are between the cause of action in question and another cause of action which is the subject of another proceeding which is pending before that forum. In most of the cases listed in arts 5–6A jurisdiction is conferred, not on the courts in general of a state with which a specified connection exists, but on a particular court, within a contracting state, with which such a connection exists. Moreover the choice offered to the plaintiff by these provisions constitutes an absolute right, so that neither a court of the defendant's domicile nor a court rendered competent by arts 5–6A has any power to override the plaintiff's choice between such fora on grounds of appropriateness or convenience, however unreasonable, oppressive or downright malicious his choice may appear to be.

Where the defendant is domiciled in the United Kingdom, arts 5–6A of Sched 4 to the Civil Jurisdiction and Judgments Act 1982 largely echo the corresponding provisions of the Conventions, so as to offer a similar choice between courts of different parts of the United Kingdom. But in such cases s 49 of the 1982 Act ensures that a court of one part of the United Kingdom remains free to decline jurisdiction in favour of a concurrently competent court of another part of the United Kingdom, if it considers the latter to be a more appropriate forum for the determination of the dispute in the interests of justice.

Ordinary contracts

By art 5(1)[a][2] of the 1968 Convention, of the Lugano Convention, and of Sched 4 to the 1982 Act, the English courts have jurisdiction to entertain an

---

[1] Most of the cases dealt with in arts 5–6A are examined under the present heading, but art 5(2), on familial maintenance, is considered in Chapter 4 above.

[2] For convenience the first clause of the current art 5(1) will be referred to as art 5(1)[a].

action based on an ordinary contract, if the defendant is domiciled in another contracting state to the 1968 or Lugano Conventions, other than Luxembourg,[3] or in another part of the United Kingdom, and the place of performance of the relevant contractual obligation is located in England. In such a case the plaintiff has the choice of suing either at the defendant's domicile, in accordance with art 2 of the relevant Convention or Schedule, or in England, in accordance with art 5(1)[a] of the same instrument.

For present purposes, a contract counts as an ordinary contract, unless it is a contract of one of the following types:

(1) A contract of employment. These are now dealt with by art 5(1)[b], which uses the concept of place of performance, but defines it in a special way.

(2) A contract of insurance. These contracts are governed by arts 7–12A of the 1968 Convention and of the Lugano Convention, to the exclusion of art 5(1), though (by way of tiresome divergence) they count as ordinary contracts for the purpose of Sched 4 to the 1982 Act.

(3) A protected consumer contract. These are governed by arts 13–15 of the Conventions and the Schedule, to the exclusion of art 5(1).

(4) A tenancy of land. These are governed by art 16(1) of the Conventions and the Schedule, to the exclusion of art 5(1).

(5) A contract relating to matrimonial property or succession on death. These are excluded from the Conventions by art 1[2](1).

Almost every aspect of art 5(1)[a] has created difficulty, and it seems well arguable, on grounds both of principle and convenience, that the Conventions would be improved by its deletion, so as simply to refer ordinary contractual actions to the courts of the defendant's domicile in the absence of an explicit agreement on jurisdiction concluded between the contracting parties.[4]

Contractual matters

Even the concept of a contract has given rise to three rulings by the European Court of Justice. These have established that the concept must be construed independently of any particular national law, that it extends to any relationship which is substantially similar to relationships which are undoubtedly contrac-

---

[3] See art I[1] of the Protocol annexed to the 1968 Convention. See also art IA of the First Protocol annexed to the Lugano Convention, which permits Switzerland to make a reservation enabling it to refuse, until the end of 1999, to recognise judgments given in other contracting states on the basis of art 5(1) against defendants domiciled in Switzerland. For this purpose a company is regarded as domiciled in Switzerland if it has both its registered office and its effective centre of activities there.

[4] See Stone (1983) 12 Anglo-American Law Review 52, and Lasok & Stone, at pp 220–21.

tual, and that it requires privity, in the sense of a transaction between the parties whereby the defendant has voluntarily undertaken an obligation towards the plaintiff. Thus in *Peters v South Netherlands Contractors' Association*[5] the court ruled that art 5(1)[a] applied to an action brought by an incorporated association of building contractors against one of its members for sums payable by virtue of the constitution of the association, in conjunction with decisions taken by its organs; and in *Arcado v Haviland*[6] the court solemnly confirmed that art 5(1)[a] applied to an action brought by an independent commercial agent against a manufacturer, claiming payment of commission due under, and damages for the wrongful repudiation of, an agency contract between them. More interestingly, in *Handte v Traitements Mécano-Chimiques des Surfaces*[7] the court ruled that art 5(1)[a] does not extend to a claim by an ultimate purchaser of a product against a manufacturer who was not the direct seller to the plaintiff, based on defects in the product or its unfitness for its intended purpose. The court emphasised that, where goods are subject to a chain of sales, the liabilities of the various sellers may differ, and the manufacturer may be unaware of the identity or domicile of the ultimate purchaser. Moreover the non-contractual characterisation of such liability accorded with the laws of most of the contracting states.

The place of performance of the obligation in question

The European Court of Justice established in *De Bloos v Bouyer*[8] that if the action is based on a single contractual obligation, then the obligation in question, for the purpose of art 5(1), is the contractual obligation on which the action brought is based.[9] Thus, in the case of a contract for the sale of goods, the place of performance of the seller's obligations relating to the quality of the goods supplied is the place at which the goods in question were delivered to the buyer.[10] On the other hand, where a seller sues for the price of goods supplied, the relevant obligation is the buyer's obligation to pay the price, and the place

---

[5] Case 34/82, [1983] ECR 987.
[6] Case 9/87, [1988] ECR 1539.
[7] Case C-26/91, 17 June 1992. [1992] 1 ECR 3967.
[8] Case 14/76, [1976] ECR 1497.
[9] A suggestion made by the court in *De Bloos* (at para 17) that a claim to damages could in some cases be based on an independent contractual obligation to pay damages, rather than merely constituting a remedy for breach of a primary obligation to perform some other act, seems to have been abandoned in Case 9/87 *Arcado v Haviland* [1988] ECR 1539.
[10] See *Thompson Hayward v Sirena* [1988] ECC 319, French Court of Cassation; *Re a Consignment of Italian Wine* [1988] ECC 159, German Supreme Court; and *Hewden Stuart v Gottwald*, 13 May 1992, English Court of Appeal (applying German law as the proper law of the contract). Cf the decision of the Frankfurt Court of Appeal on reference back in *Tessili v Dunlop* (23 March 1977; noted in the Digest of Case-Law relating to the European Communities, published by the European Court, D Series, Case I-5.1.2–B9), which proceeded to assume jurisdiction on the ground that the place of performance for a claim for rescission was the buyer's place of business, where the goods to be returned had become situated.

where the goods were delivered is in itself irrelevant.[11] Similarly, where a contract between issuing and confirming banks in relation to a letter of credit provides for reimbursement through a third bank, the place of performance of the issuing bank's obligation to reimburse the confirming bank is at the specified place of business of the third bank.[12]

If the plaintiff makes in the same action several claims, based on different obligations arising from the same contract, the European Court of Justice ruled in *Shenavai v Kreischer*[13] that art 5(1) must be read as conferring jurisdiction to entertain all such claims on the courts for the place of performance of the most important of the contractual obligations on which any of these claims are based. It must be emphasised that this does not mean that one must look for the principal or characteristic obligation under the contract as a whole, but for the most important of the obligations on which the plaintiff's claims in the action are based. For example, if a seller of goods delivered sues the buyer for the price and also for damages for breach of a contractual term prohibiting resale in a specified market, the principal or characteristic obligation under the contract is clearly the seller's obligation to deliver the goods, but no claim by the plaintiff in the action is based on failure to deliver or improper delivery. Rather, the relevant point for present purposes is that the buyer's obligation to pay the price is more important than his obligation not to resell in the prohibited manner, and accordingly the court for the place of payment will be competent to entertain an action based on both these obligations.

The ruling in *Shenavai v Kreischer* was applied in England in *Union Transport v Continental Lines*,[14] where a charterer sued a shipowner for failing to nominate or provide a vessel. The House of Lords (per Lord Goff) held that the principal of these obligations was the obligation to nominate; and thus the English court was competent, since the nomination should have been received by the charterer in England, where it resided, even though it was in Florida that the vessel should have been made available for loading the cargo.[15] Two further points, not addressed by the House of Lords, were usefully clarified by the Court of Appeal (per Lloyd LJ). First, that in some cases where an action is based on several obligations, it would be artificial or arbitrary to select one of them as the principal obligation, and in that event the decision in *Shenavai* does not require the court to do so. Secondly, that the doctrine of principal obligation adopted in *Shenavai* is, from a plaintiff's viewpoint, enabling rather than

---

[11] See Case C-288/92 *Custom Made Commercial Ltd v Stawa Metalbau GmbH*, 29 June 1994; *Nienaber v Impex-Euro* [1988] ECC 150, Italian Supreme Court; and *Mercury Publicity v Loerke* [1993] ILPR 142, English CA, which involved a claim for money due under a contract of commercial agency.

[12] See *Royal Bank of Scotland v Cassa di Risparmio delle Provincie Lombard* (1992) *Financial Times*, 21 January, English CA.

[13] Case 266/85, [1987] 1 ECR 239.

[14] [1992] 1 All ER 161, [1992] 1 WLR 15, HL; affirming [1991] 2 Lloyd's Rep 48, CA.

[15] See also *Rank Film Distributors v Lanterna* (1991) *Financial Times*, 14 June, where the licensor under an exclusive film-exploitation agreement was suing for the agreed licence fee, and also for a much smaller sum for materials (such as copies of the films) supplied, and Saville J (following *Shenavai*) held that the principal obligation was to pay the licence fee.

restrictive, and does not prejudice the competence, under *De Bloos*, of a court which is seised of several claims arising from the same contract to entertain those among them which are based on obligations whose places of performance are located within its territory, even if the place of performance of the principal among the obligations sued on is located elsewhere.

This last point was apparently overlooked in *Gascoine v Pyrah*,[16] which involved a contractual claim by an English intending purchaser of a French horse against a German veterinary surgeon for negligence in examining, assessing and reporting on the condition of the horse. Southwell QC (in the English High Court) declined jurisdiction under art 5(1) on the ground that the principal obligation sued on was properly to assess the x-rays taken, and the assessment took place at the defendant's domicile in Germany. It is submitted that he should have entertained the action insofar as it was based on a breach of contract comprising the delivery in England of a negligently prepared report. His decision was later reversed on other grounds.[17]

Some confusion exists as to the right approach where an exclusive distributor sues the manufacturer for infringing the agreed exclusivity or repudiating the contract. It is submitted that the better view, which accords with the decisions of the Belgian Court of Cassation in *Knauer v Callens*[18] and *Audi-NSU v Adelin Petit*,[19] is that the relevant place of performance is the territory in respect of which the contract granted exclusive rights to the distributor. The Belgian approach seems more convincing than the decision of the English Court of Appeal in *Medway Packaging v Meurer Maschinen*,[20] that the principal obligation involved in a repudiation of an exclusive distribution contract is the obligation to give reasonable notice of termination at the distributor's place of business, and that the obligation to respect exclusivity is equally performable in the countries of both parties. Even less convincing is the decision of a French Court of Appeal in *Vauth v Lindig*,[21] that the place of performance of a manufacturer's obligation to continue, rather than terminate, a contract of exclusive agency, is at the manufacturer's own domicile.

As the European Court of Justice ruled in *Tessili v Dunlop*,[22] once the relevant obligation has been identified, the place of its performance must be determined, for the purpose of art 5(1)[a], by reference to the substantive law which governs the obligation under the choice of law rules of the country whose court is seised.[23] The relevant choice of law rules of most of the member states,

---

[16] (1991) *The Times*, 26 November, (1991) *The Independent*, 11 December.
[17] 25 May 1993, CA.
[18] [1978] I Pas Belge 871.
[19] (1979) 94 Journal des Tribunaux 625.
[20] [1990] 2 Lloyd's Rep 112.
[21] [1989] ECC 212.
[22] Case 12/76, [1976] ECR 1473.
[23] The applicable substantive law will usually be the internal law of a particular country, but it could be a uniform law specified in a treaty, such as the Uniform Law on International Sales, annexed to a Hague Convention of 1 July 1964; see Case C-288/92 *Custom Made Commercial Ltd v Stawa Metalbau GmbH*, 29 June 1994.

including the United Kingdom, have now been to a large extent harmonised by the EC/Rome Convention of 19 June 1980 on the Law Applicable to Contractual Obligations.[24] Thus for the purposes of art 5(1)[a] the English courts will usually apply the proper law of the contract in question to determine the content of the (sole or principal) obligation on which the action is based, including the place where that obligation should have been performed; but in the case of 'old' contracts, concluded before the commencement of the 1980 Convention for the United Kingdom on 1 April 1991, the proper law will be ascertained in accordance with the traditional English choice of law rules, while in the case of 'new' contracts, concluded after March 1991, it will be ascertained in accordance with the 1980 Convention. It is worth emphasising, however, that the harmonisation of choice of law rules by the 1980 Convention does not eliminate the discriminatory effects which arise under *Tessili* from differences in national substantive laws; for example as to the presumptive place for payment of the price in the absence of an explicit contractual term.[25]

Equally, as the European Court of Justice ruled in *Zelger v Salinitri (No 1)*,[26] it is for the national law which governs the contract to determine the formal validity of an express agreement as to the place of performance of an obligation. The formal requirements laid down by art 17 for clauses which deal with jurisdiction as such are not applicable by analogy to clauses which specify a place of performance, at any rate if the clause embodies a real intention that the performance should actually be carried out at the specified place.

Disputed facts

The European Court of Justice ruled in *Effer v Kantner*[27] that jurisdiction under art 5(1)[a] is not excluded merely because the defendant denies the facts from which such jurisdiction would arise; for example, where he denies the existence of the contract sued on, perhaps by asserting that the person who purported to conclude it as his agent had authority to do so.

It is not entirely clear how far a court, in determining its jurisdiction under provisions of the Convention such as art 5(1)[a], should investigate or decide disputed facts which are relevant to the existence of such jurisdiction. The English courts have usually followed the same approach as they have long used in relation to similar questions in the context of Ord 11 of the Rules of the Supreme Court, whereby it is necessary and sufficient for the plaintiff to produce evidence satisfying the court that there is a good (or strongly) arguable

---

[24] For its text, see [1980] OJ L266, or Sched 1 to the Contracts (Applicable Law) Act 1990, or App 3 to Lasok & Stone. The 1980 Convention is examined in Chapter 12 below.

[25] See *Mercury Publicity v Loerke* (1991) *The Times*, 21 October, (1991) *Financial Times*, 13 November, English CA, involving the English rule that, unless otherwise agreed, a debt is payable at the creditor's residence, and the corresponding German rule, referring to the debtor's residence. See also *Hewden Stuart v Gottwald*, 13 May 1992, English CA.

[26] Case 56/79, [1980] ECR 89.

[27] Case 38/81, [1982] ECR 825.

case for the existence of the relevant jurisdictional facts.[28] The English practice, if not dictated by the Conventions, at least seems consistent with the policies underlying them.

Defendants not domiciled in a contracting state

Article 5(1)[a] does not apply if the defendant is not domiciled in any contracting state to the 1968 or Lugano Conventions. In such cases English jurisdiction over an action based on an ordinary contract is in general remitted to English law by art 4 of the 1968 Convention, and the High Court will then be competent if any of the following connections exists:

(1) if the defendant is present or has a place of business in England;[29]
(2) if the breach of contract on which the action is based was committed in England;[30]
(3) if the contract was concluded in England,[31] or was concluded for the defendant by or through an agent residing or carrying on business in England;[32] or
(4) if the proper law of the contract, which in general governs the substantive rights and obligations of the parties thereunder, is English law.[33]

Obviously the second of these cases is similar to art 5(1)[a] of the Conventions, but the third and fourth retain a much wider jurisdiction over 'outsiders' than the Conventions permit in the case of defendants domiciled in other contracting states. Moreover, subject to arts 8[2] and 13[2] of the Conventions, these bases of jurisdiction over 'outsiders' extend to contracts of employment, insurance contracts, and protected consumer contracts. Service abroad under RSC Ord 11, r 1(1)(d) and (e), is not, however, possible where the alleged

---

[28] See *Horni v Korner* [1951] AC 869; *Tesam Distribution v Shuh Mode* (1989) *The Times*, 24 October, CA; *Medway Packaging v Meurer Maschinen* [1990] 2 Lloyd's Rep 112, CA; *Mercury Publicity v Loerke* [1993] ILPR 142, CA; *New England Reinsurance Corp v Messoghios Insurance Co* [1992] 2 Lloyd's Rep 251, CA; *Rank Film Distributors v Lanterna* (1991) *Financial Times*, 14 June, Saville J; *The Agia Skepi* [1992] 2 Lloyd's Rep 467, Saville J; and (now most importantly) *Seaconsar v Bank Markazi* [1993] 4 All ER 456, [1993] 3 WLR 756, HL. Cf. *Attock Cement v Romanian Bank for Foreign Trade* [1989] 1 WLR 1147, CA; and *Overseas Union Insurance v Incorporated General Insurance* [1992] 1 Lloyd's Rep 439, CA.

The requirement of a good arguable case is somewhat more demanding than that of a showing of the existence of a serious question which warrants trial, which is the test under Ord 11 in relation to facts which are relevant to the merits but not to jurisdiction (see *Seaconsar v Bank Markazi* [1993] 4 All ER 456, [1993] 3 WLR 756, HL); but under art 5(1)[a] such facts are immaterial at the jurisdictional stage.

[29] See *Maharanee of Baroda v Wildenstein* [1972] 2 QB 283; RSC Ord 10, r 1(2), and Ord 81, as amended; *Barclays Bank of Swaziland v Hahn* [1989] 1 WLR 506, [1989] 2 All ER 398, HL; the Companies Act 1985, ss 691–698; and Chapter 8 above, under 'Defendants not domiciled in any contracting state', pp 138–9.

[30] See RSC Ord 11, r 1(1)(e), as amended.

[31] See RSC Ord 11, r 1(1)(d)(i), as amended.

[32] See RSC Ord 11, r 1(1)(d)(ii), as amended.

[33] See RSC Ord 11, r 1(1)(d)(iii), as amended.

contract is not between the parties to the litigation, or where the plaintiff is seeking a declaration that he is not party to a contract purportedly concluded on his behalf by an unauthorised agent.[34]

Transitional provisions

Transitional provisions now contained in art 54[3] of the 1968 and Lugano Conventions,[35] and Sched 13, Part II, para 1(2) to the 1982 Act, preserve the jurisdiction of the English courts to entertain actions against defendants domiciled in another contracting state or another part of the United Kingdom concerning contracts entered into before the relevant commencement date, where the parties had agreed before that date that the contract should be governed by English law.[36] If the defendant is domiciled in another contracting state, the agreement choosing English law must have been made explicitly and in writing;[37] but if he is domiciled in Scotland or Northern Ireland, the agreement may have been made orally or by implication. These transitional provisions are not confined to 'ordinary' contracts, but extend to contracts of employment, insurance contracts, and protected consumer contracts.

Torts and non-contractual restitutionary obligations

Article 5(3) of the 1968 Convention, of the Lugano Convention, and of Sched 4 to the 1982 Act, confer jurisdiction on the English courts to entertain an action based on a tort or a non-contractual restitutionary obligation, if the defendant is domiciled in another contracting state, or in another part of the United Kingdom, and the harmful event occurred in England.[38] In such a case the plaintiff has the choice of suing either at the defendant's domicile, in accordance with art 2 of the Conventions or of Sched 4, or in England, in accordance with art 5(3).

---

[34] See *Finnish Marine Insurance v Protective National Insurance* [1990] 1 QB 1078.

[35] Article 54[3] of the 1968 Convention is consolidated from the 1978 Convention by the 1989 Convention.

[36] These provisions also preserve any corresponding jurisdiction of the Scottish, Northern Irish, and Irish courts.

[37] See *New Hampshire Insurance Co v Strabag Bau* [1992] 1 Lloyd's Rep 361, where the English Court of Appeal held that it was not enough, in the case of a German defendant, that a written contract impliedly but clearly indicated a choice of English law as its proper law.

[38] Article 5(3) of Sched 4 to the 1982 Act also refers explicitly to a threatened wrong, and confers jurisdiction if the harmful event is likely to occur in England. It is submitted that a corresponding rule must be considered as implied in art 5(3) of the Conventions. Cf the Schlosser Report [1979] OJ C59 at para 134.

By art 5(4) of the Conventions and of Sched 4, a court seised of criminal proceedings also has jurisdiction to entertain against a defendant domiciled elsewhere within the contracting states a civil claim for damages or restitution which is based on an act giving rise to the criminal proceedings, to the extent that the court has jurisdiction under its own law to entertain civil proceedings. However it is thought that there are no circumstances in which an English criminal court has power under English law to entertain a civil claim, within the meaning of art 5(4). The powers of English courts to make restitution or compensation orders are merely a minor feature of the sentencing process, and are designed neither to respect nor to prejudice the full civil rights of the victim. Similarly it appears that art 5(4) has no operation in Scotland; see *Davenport v Corinthian Motor Policies at Lloyds* [1991] SLT 774.

The deliberate ambiguity[39] in the concept, 'the harmful event', used in art 5(3) has to a large extent been resolved by the decision of the European Court of Justice in *Bier v Mines de Potasse d'Alsace*,[40] where a Dutch horticulturalist brought an action (in English terms, for nuisance) in a Dutch court against a French mining company, claiming damages for the discharge of saline waste into the Rhine by the defendant in France, which had caused damage to the plaintiff's plantations in the Netherlands and necessitated expensive remedial measures. On a reference by the Hague Court of Appeal, the European Court of Justice ruled that, where the place of the allegedly wrongful conduct and the place of the resulting injury are not identical, art 5(3) must be construed as referring to both places, so as to give the plaintiff the option of suing at either of them.

Where the defendant is not domiciled in any contracting state, so that jurisdiction is remitted by art 4 of the 1968 Convention to the law of the country whose court is seised, RSC Ord 11, r 1(1)(f) now confers jurisdiction on the English High Court over a claim founded on a tort if either the damage was sustained in England, or it resulted from an act committed in England. Clearly this formula is designed to produce similar effects to art 5(3).

Torts involving physical injury or damage

It is clear that the decision in *Bier* above is not confined to nuisance against land, but extends to any kind of tort involving physical injury to person or property, including personal injury claims against manufacturers of defective goods. Thus in general, in cases of physical injury or damage, it is enough to found jurisdiction under art 5(3) that any substantial element of the acts and events constituting the tort, up to and including the sustaining of the initial physical injury by the plaintiff or his property, took place within the territory or district for which the court sits. Such an interpretation accords with the reasoning of the Irish Supreme Court in *Grehan v Medical Inc*,[41] where it upheld Irish jurisdiction (under pre-accession Irish legislation referring to an 'action founded on a tort committed' in Ireland) over an American manufacturer of an allegedly defective component of a heart valve, which had been used in medical treatment of the plaintiff in Ireland. It also accords with the decision of the English Court of Appeal in *Hewden Stuart v Gottwald*,[42] where it upheld English jurisdiction under art 5(3) over a German company which had in Germany redesigned a crane and manufactured the redesigned parts, and supplied them ex-works there to an English company for re-assembly in England; the crane had later collapsed while in use in England.

Some limits on the width of the general rule are, however, indicated by two decisions of the European Court of Justice. First, it may reasonably be inferred

[39] See the Jenard Report [1979] OJ C59 at p 26.
[40] Case 21/76, [1976] ECR 1735.
[41] [1988] ECC 6.
[42] 13 May 1992.

from *Dumez Bâtiment and Tracona v Hessische Landesbank*[43] that a court would not be competent under art 5(3) merely because consequential financial loss occurred within its district as a result of physical injury or damage sustained elsewhere in consequence of allegedly wrongful conduct committed elsewhere. It is also submitted that the court for the place of consequential physical injury, arising from initial physical injury elsewhere caused by conduct elsewhere, would not have jurisdiction under art 5(3). Thus, for example, if a man domiciled in England were injured in a road accident in Belgium, caused by the negligence of a driver domiciled in Belgium, and were then rushed to a hospital in the Netherlands, and later died there, with the result that his widow and children, who were also domiciled in England, suffered loss of income, and grief, in England, neither the Dutch nor the English courts would be competent to entertain claims by the deceased or his estate or family against the driver.

Secondly, in *Handte v Traitements Mécano-Chimiques des Surfaces*[44] the European Court of Justice, in ruling that, in the case of a chain of sales, a claim by an ultimate purchaser against a manufacturer is not a contractual matter, falling within art 5(1), emphasised that the provisions of Title II which derogate from the general rule in favour of the courts of the defendant's domicile must be interpreted in such a manner as to permit a defendant exercising normal caution reasonably to foresee the particular court (of a contracting state other than that of his domicile) in which he may be sued. This suggests that, for example, a manufacturer of a defective product may not be subject to the jurisdiction of the court for the place where physical injury arises from the use of the product, if its commercial marketing by the manufacturer and others in his chain of commercial distribution had taken place elsewhere, and the product had only reached the place of injury by being taken there for use by the ultimate purchaser.[45]

Torts involving purely financial loss

Where only financial loss (and no physical injury or damage) has resulted from the defendant's allegedly tortious conduct, it seems that competence under art 5(3) based on the place of injury is confined to the court for the place where the initial financial loss was sustained by the immediate victim, to the exclusion of the court for the place where further, consequential financial loss was sustained, whether by the immediate victim or by another, indirect victim. For three-party situations such a limitation was laid down by the European Court of Justice in *Dumez Bâtiment and Tracona v Hessische Landesbank*,[46] so as to prevent a French parent company from bringing an action in France against a German bank whose withdrawal of credits to a German property developer had led to the halting of a building programme in Germany, and thereby caused the plaintiff's Germany subsidiary to become insolvent, and the plaintiff itself to suffer conse-

43 Case C-220/88, [1990] 1 ECR 49.
44 Case C-26/91, [1992] 1 ECR 3967.
45 See also *World-Wide Volkswagen v Woodson* 444 US 286 (1980).
46 Case C-220/88, [1990] 1 ECR 49.

quential financial loss in France. A similar approach had been adopted earlier in a two-party situation by the German Supreme Court in *Re a Consignment of Italian Wine*,[47] where it ruled against German jurisdiction to entertain an action brought by a German buyer of wine against an Italian seller, alleging tortious infringement of EC Regulations concerning the composition of wine, since it considered that the harmful event had occurred in Italy, where the wine and its documentation had been delivered by the defendant to the plaintiff, and not in Germany, where the plaintiff had incurred expense in respect of transport costs in returning the wine to Italy.

Subject to that limitation, the approach adopted for the purposes of RSC Ord 11, r 1(1)(f) by the English Court of Appeal in *Metall und Rohstoff v Donaldson Lufkin & Jenrette*,[48] seems equally appropriate for art 5(3) of the Convention. On this basis it is enough either that some significant damage has been sustained in England, or that, looking at the tort alleged in a common-sense way, damage has resulted from substantial and efficacious acts of the defendant committed in England (even if other substantial and efficacious acts have been committed elsewhere). Accordingly English jurisdiction was upheld in respect of an action for inducing breaches of contract against an American defendant who, by acts of inducement committed largely in New York, had caused its subsidiary to commit breaches of commodity contracts with the plaintiff. The most significant of these breaches had taken place in England, and it was in England that the plaintiff had suffered loss, by not receiving payments and warrants and by having its accounts closed.

In *Minster v Hyundai*[49] Steyn J (in the English High Court) upheld English jurisdiction under art 5(3) to entertain a claim, based on the principles announced in *Hedley Byrne v Heller*,[50] for financial loss caused by an allegedly negligent false statement (as to the conformity of goods with the terms of a contract of sale) made by the defendant to an intermediary (the seller) abroad, and then forwarded by the intermediary to the plaintiff buyer in England, and relied on by the plaintiff in England (in authorising payments to the seller abroad). The actual decision seems justified, but the reasoning of Steyn J, invoking the test of where in substance the tort had occurred, used in the English case-law on the pre-Convention version of RSC Ord 11,[51] seems too restrictive in view of the rulings of the European Court of Justice.

Less satisfactory is the decision of Southwell QC (in the English High Court), against the existence of English jurisdiction under art 5(3), in *Gascoine v Pyrah*.[52] This involved a claim for negligence made by an English purchaser of a French horse against a German veterinary surgeon, who had been engaged to

---

[47] [1988] ECC 159.
[48] [1990] QB 391, [1989] 3 All ER 14, [1989] 3 WLR 563.
[49] [1988] 2 Lloyd's Rep 621.
[50] [1964] AC 465.
[51] For such case-law on tortious statements, see *Diamond v Bank of London and Montreal* [1979] QB 333, CA, and *The Albaforth* [1984] 2 Lloyd's Rep 91, CA; not following *Cordova v Victor* [1966] 1 WLR 793.
[52] (1991) *The Times*, 26 November, (1991) *The Independent*, 11 December.

examine and report on the condition of the horse before the purchase. The defendant had examined and x-rayed the horse in France, assessed the x-rays and written his report in Germany, and delivered his report to the plaintiff in England. In reliance on the report the plaintiff had proceeded to purchase the horse, with delivery and payment taking place in France; and had then brought it to England, where its poor condition became apparent and further expenditure was incurred. Southwell QC took the view that the central allegation in tort was the defendant's failure to use due care in Germany in the examination of the x-rays and the preparation of the report, and the damage took place primarily in France. While it is agreed that the consequential financial loss incurred in England would not create English jurisdiction, it is submitted that the delivery in England of the defendant's report by the defendant to the plaintiff or his agent should have been held sufficient to create English jurisdiction under art 5(3). His decision was later reversed on other grounds.[53]

Defamation

As regards defamation, in *Shevill v Presse Alliance*[54] the English Court of Appeal held that it was sufficient to found English jurisdiction under art 5(3) that the publication complained of in the action had taken place in England, even if it had been accompanied by a much wider publication, which was not complained of in the action and which had taken place abroad. Accordingly they accepted jurisdiction to entertain an action brought by an English plaintiff for a libel, in which the defamatory statements related to conduct asserted to have occurred in France, and which had been published in a French evening newspaper, which had a circulation of 200,000 copies in France and 250 copies in England, since the plaintiff had limited her claim to the copies which had been published in England. Subsequently, the House of Lords has referred the case to the European Court of Justice, whose ruling is awaited.

Infringement of intellectual property rights

It is clear that art 5(3) applies to any kind of tort, including the infringement of an intellectual property right, such as a trademark. Moreover art 5(3) operates to confer jurisdiction on the courts for the place of an allegedly infringing act, even if the defendant relies on a licence arising from a contract over which those courts otherwise lack jurisdiction.[55] Similarly, arts 14(5) and 17(2) of the Protocol on Litigation, annexed to the Community Patent Convention,[56] when in force, will permit the holder of a Community patent to sue for its infringement in the courts of the member state in which the infringement was committed or

---

[53] 25 May 1993, CA.
[54] [1992] 1 All ER 409, [1992] 2 WLR 1. Cf *Kroch v Rossell* [1937] 1 All ER 725, and *Pillai v Sarkar* [1994] *The Times*, 21 July, French J.
[55] See *Re Jurisdiction in Contract and Tort* [1988] ECC 415, German Supreme Court.
[56] [1989] OJ L401.

threatened, but only in respect of infringements committed or threatened within that state.

Contribution between tortfeasors

In *Santa Fe v Gates*,[57] the English Court of Appeal held that, as regards jurisdiction under art 5(3) to entertain a claim for contribution made by one tortfeasor against another under the Civil Liability Contribution Act 1978, the relevant acts or events are the ones which constitute a 'harmful event' in relation to the victim's claims against the tortfeasors.[58]

Restitutionary obligations

In *Kalfelis v Schröder, Münchmeyer, Hengst & Co*,[59] the European Court of Justice held that art 5(3) extends beyond torts so as to cover any action asserting a non-contractual liability, including a claim for restitution based on unjust enrichment, but that a court which is properly seised of tortious or restitutionary claims under art 5(3) is not thereby rendered competent to deal also with related contractual claims.[60] Probably, however, the inclusion of restitutionary claims, while extending to claims which either are unconnected with any contract or which, as in *Kalfelis* itself, arise from the initial invalidity or illegality of a contract, does not extend to restitutionary claims which arise from, and amount to a remedy for, a breach of contract, as where a buyer who has rejected goods for breach of a promissory condition seeks to recover back the price paid.[61]

A pending reference to the European Court of Justice by the English Court of Appeal, in *Kleinwort Benson v Glasgow District Council*,[62] concerns the application of art 5(1) and (3) to an action in restitution to recover or trace money lent under an ultra vires contract. At first instance (sub nom *Barclays Bank v Glasgow District Council*)[63] Hirst J ruled that such an action fell outside the scope both of art 5(1) and of art 5(3) of Sched 4 to the 1982 Act. It is submitted that he was right in respect of art 5(1), since this is confined to actions based on an arguable assertion that there is a *valid* contract; but wrong on art 5(3), which does, according to the decision in *Kalfelis*, extend to restitution as well as tort. Admittedly the phrase, 'the harmful event', is infelicitous when applied to

---

[57] Decided on 16 January 1991.

[58] Cf *Engdiv v Trentham* [1990] SLT 617, where Lord Prosser, in the Scottish Court of Session, took the view that a claim for contribution between persons liable to a third party for the same injury constitutes a contractual matter, falling within art 5(1), if the liability to the third party of the defendant to the contribution claim arises from the breach of a contract between them.

[59] Case 189/87, [1988] ECR 5565.

[60] On the latter point, *Kalfelis* was followed by the English Court of Appeal in *Hewden Stuart v Gottwald*, 13 May 1992.

[61] See Case 14/76 *De Bloos v Bouyer* [1976] ECR 1497; considered at p 168 above.

[62] Referred by a decision on 18 May 1993.

[63] [1992] 3 WLR 827.

restitution, but the difficulty disappears when one applies the tort rules analogistically, so that, in the case of restitution, a court becomes competent if any of the acts or events from which the liability arguably arises (other than an act or event which was merely consequential on an enrichment which had already been completed elsewhere) took place within its district.

The European Court of Justice ruled in *Reichert v Dresdner Bank (No 2)*[64] that a 'Pauline' action under French law, whereby a creditor seeks to have set aside a disposition of property made by his debtor, on the ground that it was made for the purpose of defrauding creditors, does not fall within art 5(3). The court emphasised that in such an action rescission is sought not only against the fraudulent debtor, but also against the beneficiary under the fraudulent disposition, and that he is liable to restore the property not only where he acted in bad faith, but also where he acted in good faith but did not provide consideration. While these features no doubt indicate that such an action is not an action in tort, it is difficult to see why they prevent its being an action in restitution.

Where the defendant is not domiciled in any contracting state, RSC Ord 11, r 1(1)(d)(i), on contracts made in England, has been construed as extending to an action seeking payment on a quasi-contractual basis, and for this purpose the quasi-contract is regarded as made where the money claimed by the plaintiff was received by the defendant.[65] In addition RSC Ord 11, r 1(1)(t), added by SI 1990/1689, now gives the English High Court jurisdiction to entertain a claim against a defendant not domiciled in any contracting state for money had and received, or for an account or other relief against him as constructive trustee, if his alleged liability arises from acts committed in England, whether those acts were committed by the defendant or by anyone else.

Secondary establishments

Article 5(5) of the 1968 Convention, of the Lugano Convention, and of Sched 4 to the 1982 Act, confer jurisdiction on the English courts to entertain actions against a defendant who is domiciled in another contracting state, or another part of the United Kingdom, if the defendant has a secondary establishment[66] which is situated in England, and the dispute arises from the operations of the English establishment.

These provisions do not apply where a defendant who is not domiciled in any contracting state sets up a secondary establishment in England. In such a case, in general art 4 remits the jurisdiction of the English courts to English law, and English law then confers jurisdiction on the High Court on the ground that the defendant has a place of business in England, whether the defendant is a company, a partnership or an individual, and whether or not the dispute arises

---

[64] Case C-261/90, 26 March 1992. [1992] 1 ECR 2149.

[65] See *Re Jogia* [1988] 1 WLR 484, and *Finnish Marine Insurance v Protective National Insurance* [1990] 1 QB 1078.

[66] The phrase, 'secondary establishment', is here used as a synonym for the inelegant phrase, 'branch, agency or other establishment', used in the legislation.

from the operations of the English establishment.[67] However, by way of exception, arts 8[2] and 13[2] of the Conventions require that where an insurer, or a supplier under a protected consumer contract, is not domiciled in any contracting state, but has a secondary establishment in a contracting state, and the dispute arises from the operations of the secondary establishment, he should be treated for the purposes of the Conventions as domiciled in the contracting state in which the secondary establishment is situated.

The concept of a secondary establishment, within the meaning of art 5(5), was construed restrictively in early decisions of the European Court of Justice. In *Somafer v Saar-Ferngas*[68] the court explained generally that the concept implies an apparently permanent place of business, which constitutes an extension of a parent body, and which has a management and is materially equipped to negotiate business with third parties, so that the latter, though knowing of the legal link with the parent body, whose head office is abroad, do not have to deal directly with the parent body but may transact business at the extension. More specifically, in *De Bloos v Bouyer*[69] the court ruled that an exclusive distributor of a manufacturer's products does not constitute a secondary establishment of the manufacturer, since it is an essential characteristic of a secondary establishment, within the meaning of art 5(5), that the secondary establishment should be subject to the direction and control of the parent body. In *Blanckaert & Willems v Trost*,[70] the court ruled, very specifically, that an independent commercial agent who merely negotiates business, and whose legal status leaves him basically free to arrange his own work and decide what proportion of his time to devote to the principal's interests, and whom the principal may not prevent from also representing others competing in the same manufacturing or marketing sector, and who, moreover, merely transmits orders to the principal without being involved in either their terms or their execution, is not a secondary establishment of the principal within the meaning of art 5(5).

More recently, however, the court ruled, in *Schotte v Parfums Rothschild*,[71] that one member of a group of companies may act as a secondary establishment of another member of the group for the purposes of art 5(5), at least if the companies have similar names and a common management, and in the relevant transaction one of the companies contracts explicitly on behalf of the other; for in such circumstances third parties who do business with the establishment should be entitled to rely on the appearance created. It is unclear how far this ruling indicates a more liberal approach to art 5(5): for example, whether the court would now be willing to reconsider the situation where the companies do not have similar names or common management or belong to the same group,

---

[67] As to companies, see the Companies Act 1985, Part XXIII, Chapter I; and as to partnerships and individuals, see RSC Ord 81 (as amended).

[68] Case 33/78, [1978] ECR 2183.

[69] Case 14/76, [1976] ECR 1497.

[70] Case 139/80, [1981] ECR 819.

[71] Case 218/86, [1987] ECR 4905. Cf *Adams v Cape Industries* [1990] Ch 433, CA, refusing to pierce the corporate veil in the context of the recognition of an American judgment under English common law.

but, at least as regards transactions relating to the relevant type of product, one of them acts exclusively and explicitly as agent for the other.

In *Somafer v Saar-Ferngas*[72] the court also considered generally the concept of operations, within the meaning of art 5(5), and adopted a restrictive approach. It ruled that the provision is confined to three types of litigation: actions relating to rights and obligations concerning the management, in a strict sense, of the establishment, such as ones concerning the situation of the building where it is located or the local engagement of staff to work there; actions relating to undertakings which have been entered into at the establishment in the name of the parent body and which must be performed in the contracting state in which the establishment is located; and actions concerning non-contractual obligations arising from the activities in which the establishment has engaged on behalf of the parent body at the place where it is located. Possibly the later decision in *Schotte v Parfums Rothschild*,[73] although itself concerned with the concept of a secondary establishment rather than the concept of operations, may indicate that the court would now consider adopting a wider interpretation of the latter concept also, with a view to respecting reasonable expectations of third parties. Certainly it is difficult to see why the court for the district in which a secondary establishment is located should not be competent to entertain any action against the principal body in respect of a claim which arises from anything done anywhere by members of the staff attached (solely or principally) to the secondary establishment.

Trusts

By art 5(6) of the 1968 and Lugano Conventions[74] and of Sched 4, taken with s 10(2) of the 1982 Act, the English courts have jurisdiction over a defendant who is domiciled in another contracting state or part of the United Kingdom, where he is sued as settlor, trustee or beneficiary of a trust which was created by the operation of a statute, or by a written instrument, or orally and evidenced in writing, and the trust is domiciled in England. For this purpose, a trust is regarded as domiciled in England if and only if English law is the system of law with which the trust has its closest and most real connection.[75]

Where the defendant is not domiciled in any contracting state, or the subject-matter is outside the scope of the 1968 Convention, RSC Ord 11, r 1(1)(j) (as amended) confers jurisdiction on the English High Court to entertain a claim for the execution of the trusts of a written instrument, being trusts which ought to

[72] Case 33/78, [1978] ECR 2183.
[73] Case 218/86, [1987] ECR 4905.
[74] Article 5(6) of the 1968 Convention was inserted by the 1978 Convention.
[75] See art 53[2] of the 1968 Convention (added by the 1978 Convention) and of the Lugano Convention, and s 45 of the 1982 Act. Similarly in Ireland a trust is regarded as domiciled there if (but only if) Irish law is the system of law with which the trust has its closest and most real connection; see s 13(3) and Sched 5, Part V, of the (Irish) Jurisdiction of Courts and Enforcement of Judgments (European Communities) Act 1988.

be executed according to English law and of which the defendant in question is a trustee, or for any relief or remedy which might be obtained in such an action. An earlier requirement that the trust property had to be situated in England[76] has now been deleted by the 1983 amendment,[77] but RSC Ord 11 differs from art 5(6) in excluding statutory trusts, and in taking full account of a choice of law clause contained in the trust instrument.

All these provisions and others (such as art 2 of the 1968 Convention, conferring jurisdiction on the courts of the defendant's domicile) give way, however, to art 17[2] of the 1968 and Lugano Conventions,[78] which enable a trust instrument expressly to confer jurisdiction on a specified court of a contracting state, or the courts of a specified contracting state, over proceedings brought against a settlor, trustee or beneficiary, involving their mutual relations or rights or obligations under the trust, with the result that the chosen court or courts will have exclusive jurisdiction. Somewhat redundantly, art 17[2] of Sched 4 to the 1982 Act makes supplementary provision, where the defendant is domiciled in the United Kingdom, for a trust instrument to choose a court or the courts of a part of the United Kingdom, but with non-exclusive effect. On the other hand, a jurisdiction clause is void if it purports to exclude the jurisdiction of courts which have exclusive jurisdiction under art 16 of the Conventions or of Sched 4.[79]

The exclusion by art 1[2](1) of the 1968 and Lugano Conventions of 'wills and succession' from the scope of the Conventions would, on the orthodox interpretation, confine all the above-mentioned provisions of the Conventions and the 1982 Act to trusts which are created or arise inter vivos, rather than by will.[80] But it seems more reasonable to construe the exclusion narrowly, so as to render the Conventions applicable to testamentary trusts, where the action is brought after the execution of an assent by the personal representatives, transferring the property to the trustees, unless the action involves an attack on the validity of the assent; for at that stage the testamentary character of the trust is of merely historical significance.

In the case of trusts of land, arts 5(6) and 17[2] of the Conventions (and of Sched 4 to the 1982 Act), and, indeed, other provisions (such as art 2 of the 1968 Convention, conferring jurisdiction on the courts of the defendant's domicile) give way to art 16(1)(a) of the Conventions (and the Schedule), which confer exclusive jurisdiction on the courts of the situs over proceedings whose principal subject-matter is rights in rem in land. It seems, however, that art 16(1)(a) should be applied only where it is sought in the action to establish or enforce the trust against a third party, such as a subsequent purchaser or donee, who was not involved in its creation and has not voluntarily accepted appointment as a

---

[76] See the former RSC Ord 11, r 1(1)(e); *Winter v Winter* [1894] 1 Ch 421; and *Official Solicitor v Stype Investments* [1983] 1 WLR 214.

[77] See SI 1983/1181.

[78] Article 17[2] of the 1968 Convention was added by the 1978 Convention.

[79] See art 17[3] of the Conventions and of Sched 4.

[80] See the Schlosser Report, at paras 52 and 112.

trustee.[81] In any event it is clear that art 5(6) does not apply to purely constructive trusts, such as those which arise from estate contracts.[82]

Admiralty

As the Schlosser Report explains,[83] little attention was given to admiralty actions when the 1968 Convention was originally negotiated, but this omission was rectified in the 1978 Convention. Thus the 1968 Convention, in its original form, contained no provision dealing specifically with admiralty actions in rem. Since, however, most of the member states (including the United Kingdom) were parties to the Brussels Convention of 10 May 1952 on the Arrest of Seagoing Ships ('the Arrest Convention'),[84] it was possible for the 1978 Convention (in art 25) to provide for jurisdiction to entertain admiralty actions in rem mainly by means of an agreed interpretation of art 57 of the 1968 Convention, which regulates the relationship between the 1968 Convention and other international conventions which deal with jurisdiction or recognition and enforcement of judgments in respect of particular matters. Article 25 of the 1978 Convention has now been consolidated into art 57 of the 1968 Convention by the 1989 Convention.

As regards direct jurisdiction, art 57 of the 1968 and Lugano Conventions now provide that the Conventions are not to affect other conventions to which the contracting states are or become parties and which, in relation to particular matters, govern jurisdiction or the recognition or enforcement of judgments, and accordingly that the Conventions do not prevent a court of a contracting state which is a party to a convention on a particular matter from assuming jurisdiction in accordance with that convention, even where the defendant is domiciled in another contracting state which is not a party to that convention, but that the court must in any event apply art 20 of the Conventions, on examining its jurisdiction of its own motion and on ensuring that the defendant is properly notified of the action.

Thus the jurisdiction of the English High Court, under s 21 of the Supreme Court Act 1981, to entertain an admiralty action in rem against a ship which has been arrested in England, is not prejudiced by the 1968 and Lugano Conventions, since such jurisdiction is conferred by the Arrest Convention.[85] Moreover s 26 of the 1982 Act enables an English or Northern Irish court which declines jurisdiction over admiralty proceedings to retain security for an award

---

[81] See Chapter 15, under 'Immovable Property: Jurisdiction', pp 354–60, below.
[82] See the Schlosser Report, at para 117.
[83] At pp 108–11.
[84] Cmd 8954. The Arrest Convention is now implemented in England by s 21 of the Supreme Court Act 1981 and s 28 of the County Courts Act 1984.
[85] Transitional provisions for arrest by Danish, Irish and Greek courts, pending the accession of those countries to the Arrest Convention, are now spent. A similar transitional concession, operating for up to three years from accession to the Lugano Convention, is provided for Iceland, Norway, Finland and Sweden by art 54A thereof.

or judgment to be made or given elsewhere. In *The Nordglimt*[86] Hobhouse J construed the 1982 Act as rectifying any deficiencies in earlier British implementation of other conventions such as the Arrest Convention, but this was subsequently doubted by the Court of Appeal in *The Po*.[87] In *The Deichland*[88] the Court of Appeal held that for the purposes of arts 2 and 3 of the 1968 Convention an action in rem against a ship counts as an action against the shipowner or other person interested in the ship (such as a demise charterer) against whom the plaintiff would wish to proceed in personam if he entered an appearance. Unfortunately it also held that art 7 of the Arrest Convention, which confers jurisdiction on the courts of the country where the ship is arrested, does not apply where no arrest occurs because the usual undertakings designed to prevent arrest are given by the shipowner's insurers. But, as Sheen J made clear in *The Prinsengracht*,[89] jurisdiction certainly arises where the shipowner acknowledges the issue of the writ under RSC Ord 75, r 3(b), or provides bail.

In *The Nordglimt*[90] Hobhouse J also held that art 21 of the 1968 Convention, on similar actions, does not apply where there is simultaneously pending in a court of one contracting state an action in rem against a ship, and in a court of another contracting state a personal action against the shipowner in respect of the same claim, since the shipowner is not a party to the action in rem unless and until he submits by appearance. Subsequently in *The Linda*[91] and *The Kherson*[92] Sheen J has taken the same view where the shipowner has not entered an appearance in the action commenced in rem, but not where he has entered an appearance therein, so that that action is continuing at least partly in personam. But it seems clear that the decision of the Court of Appeal in *The Deichland*,[93] that for the purposes of arts 2 and 3 of the 1968 Convention an action in rem against a ship counts as an action against the shipowner or other person interested in the ship (such as a demise charterer) against whom the plaintiff would wish to proceed in personam if he entered an appearance, must also apply for the purpose of art 21. In any event the question has now been referred to the European Court of Justice by the Court of Appeal in *The Maciej Rataj*.[94] In any event it is now established that for the purpose of arts 21 and 22 an English court is not seised of an action in rem against a ship (not already in the custody of the court) until service or arrest (whichever occurs earlier).[95]

The Arrest Convention is concerned only with actions against ships, and does not provide for actions against a cargo or freight. Hence art 5(7) of the 1968 and

---

[86] [1988] QB 183.
[87] [1991] 2 Lloyd's Rep 206.
[88] [1990] QB 361.
[89] [1993] 1 Lloyd's Rep 41.
[90] [1988] QB 183.
[91] [1988] 1 Lloyd's Rep 175.
[92] [1992] 2 Lloyd's Rep 261.
[93] [1990] QB 361.
[94] [1992] 2 Lloyd's Rep 552.
[95] See *The Freccia del Nord* [1989] 1 Lloyd's Rep 388.

Lugano Conventions[96] and of Sched 4 confers jurisdiction on the English courts over a defendant domiciled in another contracting state or part of the United Kingdom to entertain a dispute concerning the payment of remuneration claimed in respect of the salvage of a cargo or freight, if the cargo or freight in question has been arrested under the court's authority to secure such payment, or could have been so arrested, but bail or other security was given; provided that the defendant is claimed to have an interest in the cargo or freight, or to have had such an interest at the time of the salvage. Apparently art 5(7) authorises actions in personam as well as actions in rem.[97]

Article 57 also preserves jurisdiction conferred by the Brussels Convention of 10 May 1952 on Civil Jurisdiction in Matters of Collision ('the Collision Convention'),[98] to which the United Kingdom, among others, is a party.[99] In *The Po*[100] the Court of Appeal held that the effect of art 57 is to preserve English jurisdiction in cases where it is conferred both by an unimplemented provision of the Collision Convention and a continuing provision of traditional English law – as where a collision action is brought in rem, and the ship is served but not arrested because security is given. Service on the ship is sufficient under traditional English law, and it is sufficient under art 1(1)(b) of the Collision Convention that arrest could have been effected and security has been furnished. Thus the effect of art 57 is to preserve English jurisdiction in such (combined) circumstances, even if the owner of the defendant ship is domiciled in another contracting state.

Since the Convention of 10 October 1957 on Limitation of Liability of Owners of Seagoing Ships does not deal with judicial jurisdiction, it was necessary for the 1968 Convention to make provision for jurisdiction to entertain admiralty limitation actions. Hence art 6A of the 1968 and Lugano Conventions[101] provide that, where by virtue of the Conventions a court of a contracting state has jurisdiction in actions relating to liability arising from the use or operation of a ship, that court, or any other court substituted for the purpose by the internal law of that state, shall also have jurisdiction over claims for limitation of such liability; and art 6A of Sched 4 to the 1982 Act makes similar provision for the jurisdiction of the courts of a part of the United Kingdom over defendants domiciled in other such parts. The effect is to enable a shipowner to bring a limitation action at his own domicile.[102]

Article VB to the Protocol annexed to the 1968 Convention (as amended)

---

[96] Article 5(7) of the 1968 Convention was added by the 1978 Convention.
[97] See *The Deichland* [1990] QB 361.
[98] Cmd 8954.
[99] The Collision Convention is implemented in England by the Supreme Court Act 1981, s 22, and RSC Ord 75, r 4.
[100] [1991] 2 Lloyd's Rep 206.
[101] Article 6A of the 1968 Convention was added by the 1978 Convention.
[102] See *The Volvox Hollandia* [1988] 2 Lloyd's Rep 361. But a suggestion by Kerr LJ at 372–73, apparently based on art 21, that a shipowner could not commence a limitation action at his domicile under art 6A after a claimant had commenced a liability action in another member state (eg under art 5(3)), seems questionable.

withdraws disputes between the master and a member of the crew of a ship registered in Denmark, Ireland, Greece or Portugal, concerning remuneration or other conditions of service, from the jurisdiction of the courts of other contracting states, in favour of the diplomatic or consular officers of the state of registration. In such a case, the court seised must stay its proceedings until it is established that the appropriate diplomatic or consular officer has been notified; and must decline jurisdiction, of its own motion if necessary, if the officer has exercised powers in the matter accorded by a consular convention, or (in the absence of such a convention) if within the permitted time he raises objection to its exercising jurisdiction. Similar provision is made in respect of ships registered in Iceland, Norway, and Sweden by art Vb of the First Protocol annexed to the Lugano Convention. The United Kingdom has frequently concluded consular conventions relating to such disputes.[103]

Ancillary jurisdiction

The Conventions to a large extent respect the principle that, in order to reduce the expense and inconvenience of litigation and the risk of irreconcilable judgments, it is desirable that related disputes should be decided by the same court and in the same proceedings. Positively, art 6 of the 1968 and Lugano Conventions, and of Sched 4 to the 1982 Act, confer on a court which is competently seised of an action additional or ancillary jurisdiction to entertain a related claim against a person domiciled in another contracting state or part of the United Kingdom, whether it is a claim by a plaintiff against an additional defendant, a claim by a defendant against a third party, or a counterclaim by a defendant against a plaintiff, even if the court would not have had jurisdiction to entertain the additional claim in its own right.[104] Negatively, arts 21–23 of the Conventions deal with the problem of similar or related actions, simultaneously pending in courts of different contracting states, by requiring or permitting the court subsequently seised to decline jurisdiction or stay its proceedings in favour of the court first seised.[105] But the grant by art 6 of ancillary jurisdiction is incomplete, for it does not enable a court properly seised of one claim by a plaintiff against a defendant to entertain also a related claim by the same plaintiff against the same defendant, and art 22 does not make good this deficiency, for its sole effect is to permit a court to stay its proceedings or decline jurisdiction in favour of a court of another contracting state, and not to confer any additional jurisdiction to entertain a related claim.[106] This difficulty was one of the reasons which induced the European Court of Justice to adopt, in the

---

[103] See the Consular Relations Act 1968, s 4; and Dicey & Morris, p 562.

[104] Under art 13 of the Protocol on Litigation, annexed to the Community Patent Convention, [1989] OJ L401/1, not yet in force, art 6 of the 1968 Convention will apply to actions concerning the infringement of a Community patent, with the slight modification that a person who is not domiciled in any contracting state but has a secondary establishment in a contracting state will be treated as domiciled in that state.

[105] See Chapter 8, under 'Simultaneous actions in different countries', pp 142–9 above.

[106] See Case 150/80 *Elefanten Schuh v Jacqmain* [1981] ECR 1671.

context of employment, a strained interpretation of the then current version of art 5(1).[107]

Co-defendants

Where there are a number of defendants and they are domiciled in different contracting states or parts of the United Kingdom, art 6(1) of the Conventions and of Sched 4 confer jurisdiction on the courts for the district in which any one of the defendants is domiciled. Article 6(1) does not explicitly define the necessary degree of connection between the claims against the various defendants, but in *Kalfelis v Schröder, Münchmeyer, Hengst & Co*[108] the European Court of Justice ruled that the definition of 'related actions' given in art 22(3), that is, ones which are so closely connected that it is expedient to hear and determine them together to avoid the risk of irreconcilable judgments resulting from separate proceedings, applies by analogy.

This test seems to resemble closely the test for 'necessary or proper parties' under Ord 11, r 1(1)(c) of the (English) Rules of the Supreme Court (as amended), under which the liability of both defendants must depend on the same investigation, though their liabilities may be either cumulative or alternative.[109] Thus in *Gascoine v Pyrah*[110] the English Court of Appeal permitted an English purchaser of a French horse, who was suing his English agent who had acted in the purchase, to join as a codefendant under art 6(1) a German veterinary surgeon who had been engaged to examine and report on the condition of the horse; the claims against both defendants being for negligence in advising in favour of the purchase.

Article 6(1) does not apply where the defendant to be added is not domiciled within the contracting states, but in such a case RSC Ord 11, rr 1(1)(c) and 4(1)(d), as amended, confer jurisdiction on the English High Court where in the action a claim is brought against a person duly served in England or elsewhere, and a person abroad is a necessary or proper party thereto, provided that there is a real issue between the plaintiff and the person duly served which the plaintiff may reasonably ask the court to try. The 'real issue' test replaces the former requirements that the cause of action against the existing defendant should be bona fide or plausible and not (on undisputed facts) doomed to fail in law,[111] and that the existing defendant should not be merely a subordinate and secondary defendant against whom the court could only make a subsidiary order after the liability of the defendant to be added had been established,[112] but this change appears essentially verbal. More importantly, the amendment ensures

[107] See Case 133/81 *Ivenel v Schwab* [1982] ECR 1891.
[108] Case 189/87, [1988] ECR 5565.
[109] See *Massey v Heynes* (1881) 21 QBD 330, and *Croft v King* [1893] 1 QB 419. See also *The Rewia* [1991] 1 Lloyd's Rep 69, Sheen J; reversed [1991] 2 Lloyd's Rep 325, CA.
[110] 25 May 1993, CA; reversing Southwell QC, (1991) *The Times*, 26 November, (1991) *The Independent*, 11 December.
[111] See *Witted v Galbraith* [1893] 1 QB 577, *The Brabo* [1949] AC 326, and *Multinational Gas v Multinational Services* [1983] Ch 258.
[112] See *Rosler v Hilbery* [1925] Ch 250.

that it is sufficient that one of the defendants is domiciled, even if not present, in England.

In *The Rewia*[113] the English Court of Appeal ruled that, by analogy with the new RSC Ord 11, r 1(1)(c), a plaintiff relying on art 6(1) must show that there is a real issue which he may reasonably ask the court to try as to whether the English defendant is liable. Accordingly they declined jurisdiction over a German shipowner, who had been joined as co-defendant in an action brought by a cargo owner against an English charterer for breach of a bill-of-lading contract, since as a matter of construction of the bill of lading, which could and should be decided at a preliminary stage, it was not seriously arguable that the charterer was liable.

In *Barclays Bank v Glasgow District Council*,[114] Hirst J rejected an argument that art 6(1) of Sched 4 applied where numerous separate actions in restitution had been brought in England by various banks against various English or Scottish local authorities, seeking to recover or trace money lent under ultra vires contracts, even though the actions involved common issues, and the court had stayed most of the actions to await the determination of a few 'lead' actions. He rightly doubted whether art 6(1) could extend beyond cases where the same plaintiff sues several defendants in a single action. In any event the 'lead action' procedure would not involve the court in hearing and determining the actions together, within the meaning of art 22. Moreover the difficult legal problems involved and the large sums at stake made it almost inevitable that the disputes, unless settled, would ultimately be taken to the House of Lords, and its decision would eliminate any possibility of irreconcilability between English and Scottish decisions involving different defendants. As regards art 6(1) Hirst J's decision was later approved by the Court of Appeal.[115]

Third-party proceedings

By art 6(2) of the Conventions and of Sched 4, an English court, when properly seised of an action brought by a plaintiff against a defendant, is given additional jurisdiction to entertain third-party proceedings instituted by the defendant against a third person who is domiciled in another contracting state or part of the United Kingdom, unless the original action was instituted solely with the object of removing the third party from the jurisdiction of the court otherwise competent in his case. It will be noticed that, unlike in the case of co-defendants, the primary jurisdiction need not be based on the defendant's domicile, but could be based, for example, on art 5(1)[116] or even art 4. However art 6(2) permits the court seised to apply its own procedural law on the admissibility of third-party proceedings, provided that they do not prejudice the

---

[113] [1991] 2 Lloyd's Rep 325, CA; reversing [1991] 1 Lloyd's Rep 69, Sheen J.
[114] [1992] 3 WLR 827.
[115] See *Kleinwort Benson v Glasgow District Council*, 18 May 1993, where the Court of Appeal referred points concerning art 5(1) and (3) to the European Court of Justice.
[116] See Case C-365/88 *Kongress Agentur Hagen v Zeehaghe* [1990] 1 ECR 1845.

effectiveness of the Convention, for example by preventing such proceedings against third parties who are domiciled or resident in other member states.[117] Where the defendant and the third party are an insured and his insurer, or vice versa, art 6(2) does not apply, but art 10(1) and (3) make similar provision.

Article 6(2) does not apply where the third party is not domiciled in any contracting state. In such a case jurisdiction over him is remitted to the lex fori by art 4. Formerly, English law treated third-party proceedings as a separate action for the purposes of jurisdiction,[118] but now the amended Rules of the Supreme Court 1965 enable a third party to be joined as a necessary or proper party to the original action, in the same way as a co-defendant.[119]

Counterclaims

By art 6(3) of the 1968 and Lugano Conventions and of Sched 4 to the 1982 Act, an English court, when properly seised of an action brought by a plaintiff who is domiciled in another contracting state or part of the United Kingdom, is given additional jurisdiction to entertain a counterclaim which arises from the same contract or facts as those on which the original claim is based. This jurisdiction extends to insurance and consumer contracts.[120] It may, however, be excluded by a contrary agreement complying with art 17 of the 1968 or Lugano Conventions.[121] The restriction to counterclaims arising from the same contract or facts seems unfortunate. No such restriction was accepted in traditional Scottish law, which adopted the cogent argument that it is unjust to pursue a claim against a person while withholding what is owed to him on any, even an unrelated, ground,[122] and traditional English law probably left the matter to the court's discretion.[123] Where the plaintiff against whom the counterclaim is made is not domiciled in any contracting state, art 6(3) does not apply, and jurisdiction is largely remitted to the lex fori in accordance with art 4. In such cases the English courts retain a discretion to admit even unconnected counterclaims.

Property

The additional bases of jurisdiction over defendants domiciled in other contracting states offered by arts 5–6A of the 1968 and Lugano Conventions do not

---

[117] See Case C-365/88 *Kongress Agentur Hagen v Zeehaghe* [1990] 1 ECR 1845. Special provision is made by art V of the 1968 Protocol and of the First Lugano Protocol in relation to German, Spanish, Austrian and Swiss third-party proceedings, which have a limited character in that they operate to preclude the third party from disputing matters decided in the action between the plaintiff and the defendant, but do not enable the defendant to obtain, in the same proceedings, affirmative relief against the third party.

[118] See RSC Ord 16, r 3(4), prior to the 1983 amendment.

[119] See the current RSC Ord 16, r 3(4), as amended by SI 1983/1181, r 14.

[120] See arts 11[2] and 14[3] of the Conventions, and art 14[3] of Sched 4.

[121] See Case 23/78 *Meeth v Glacetal* [1978] ECR 2133.

[122] See Anton, *Private International Law* (1967), at pp 131–8.

[123] See RSC Ord 15, rr 2 and 5(2), and *Factories Insurance v Anglo-Scottish Insurance* (1913) 29 TLR 312.

include any basis founded on the presence or arrest of movable property situated within the forum's district, even where title to the property in question constitutes the subject-matter of the proceedings. However, art 59 of the Conventions, which offer some protection to defendants domiciled or habitually resident outside the contracting states from the enforcement in one contracting state of judgments given in other contracting states pursuant to excessive jurisdictional bases,[124] recognise that jurisdiction based on the location of property is not in reality excessive if the dispute is connected with the property. In view of this, art 5(8) of Sched 4 to the 1982 Act, in allocating jurisdiction over defendants domiciled in the United Kingdom between the courts for its three parts, confers non-exclusive jurisdiction on the courts for a part of the United Kingdom in which the relevant property is situated, if the proceedings concern a debt secured on immovable property, or concern proprietary or possessory rights in, or rights of security over, or seek authority to dispose of, movable property, and this applies even in the case of disputes involving protected consumer contracts.[125] However the relevant movable property must be situated in the part of the United Kingdom whose court is seised at the commencement of the action, and not merely at an earlier time when the cause of action arose.[126] Moreover in England similar jurisdiction over defendants not domiciled within the contracting states is now provided for by RSC Ord 11, r 1(1)(i).

---

[124] See Chapter 14 below.
[125] See Sched 4, art 13.
[126] See *Barclays Bank v Glasgow District Council* [1992] 3 WLR 827, Hirst J; subsequently referred on other points by the Court of Appeal to the European Court of Justice as *Kleinwort Benson v Glasgow District Council*, 18 May 1993.

IO

CIVIL JURISDICTION – PROTECTIVE OR EXCLUSIVE JURISDICTION

PROTECTIVE JURISDICTION

The 1968 and Lugano Conventions lay down special rules for three types of contract (insurance contracts, certain consumer contracts, and contracts of employment), with a view to protecting the party expected to have occupied a weaker bargaining position when entering into the contract.

Insurance contracts

Section 3 (arts 7–12A) of Title II of the 1968 and Lugano Conventions regulates jurisdiction to entertain an action based on a contract of insurance, largely to the exclusion of the other provisions of Title II.[1] These provisions are based on the idea that, when entering into an insurance contract, the policy-holder is in a weaker position than the insurer, and therefore needs and deserves special protection. Accordingly the policy-holder is given a wide choice of fora in which to sue the insurer, while the insurer is generally required to sue the policy-holder at the latter's domicile, and contracting out of these provisions in advance of the dispute arising is allowed only in exceptional cases.

No explicit definition of insurance is offered, but it is clear that all types of insurance (as generally understood) are covered, and that the policy-holder is compelled to accept (and, in reality, pay for) the special protection provided, regardless of whether he is in reality in a weak position; for example, where a major manufacturer insures his factories against fire with a small syndicate at Lloyd's.[2] Only in the case of marine and aviation insurance has this approach been qualified, as a result of British pressure, and then only by lifting the restriction on contracting out. Since it is the existence of an insurable interest which distinguishes insurance from wagering, the European Court of Justice will have to provide guidance as to how the existence of an insurable interest should be determined for the purpose of ascertaining the scope of Section 3, and

[1] See art 7, which makes savings for arts 4 and 5(5).
[2] See *New Hampshire Insurance Co v Strabag Bau* [1992] 1 Lloyd's Rep 361, where the English Court of Appeal accepted, in view of the Schlosser Report, that the Convention provisions on insurance are not confined to insurances taken out for domestic or private purposes.

it is suggested that for this purpose an autonomous but wide definition of the concept would be appropriate.

The protective provisions apply only if the defendant is domiciled, or treated as domiciled, within the contracting states.[3] However, by art 8[2], an insurer who is not so domiciled under the normal rules on domicile applicable for the purposes of the Conventions, but who has a secondary establishment in a contracting state, out of operations of which the dispute arises, is treated as domiciled in the state in which the secondary establishment is situated.[4] But there is no corresponding provision in relation to a policy-holder or other insured or beneficiary. If the defendant is neither domiciled nor treated as domiciled within the contracting states, English jurisdiction to entertain an action based on a contract of insurance is remitted to English law by art 4, and English law then treats the contract in the same way as an 'ordinary' contract.

Moreover, where the defendant is domiciled (or treated as domiciled) in the United Kingdom, Sched 4 to the 1982 Act deliberately makes no special provision for insurance contracts, corresponding to that made by the Conventions, with the result that jurisdiction to entertain an action based on a contract of insurance is allocated between the English, Scottish and Northern Irish courts in accordance with the same provisions as apply to 'ordinary' contracts. This omission has led the Inner House of the Scottish Court of Session to hold, in *Davenport v Corinthian Motor Policies at Lloyds*,[5] that a victim of a Scottish road accident, who had successfully sued the driver in Scotland and thereby gained a right of direct action against the driver's English insurer under s 151 of the Road Traffic Act 1988, could not bring her direct action in Scotland, since the claim under s 151 was considered not to be a claim in tort within art 5(3) of Sched 4, but a purely statutory claim. The decision seems to involve a total misunderstanding of the ruling of the European Court of Justice in *Kalfelis v Schröder, Münchmeyer, Hengst & Co*,[6] which established that art 5(3) of the Conventions extends beyond claims in tort to cover restitutionary claims and, in general, claims based on any non-contractual and non-familial obligation.

Under arts 8–10 of the 1968 and Lugano Conventions, the English courts have jurisdiction to entertain an action which is based on a contract of insurance, and is brought against an insurer who is domiciled (or treated as domiciled) within the contracting states, in each of the cases listed below. These rules apply whether the action is brought by the policy-holder (that is, the person who as principal concluded the contract with the insurer, or his universal successor, such as his executor or trustee in bankruptcy); or by some other insured or beneficiary under the insurance policy (such as a member of the

---

[3] See art 7, saving art 4.

[4] Similar provision is made by art 13[2] in the case of a supplier under a protected consumer contract; and, for actions concerning the infringement of a Community patent, by art 13(3) of the Protocol on Litigation annexed to the Community Patent Agreement, [1989] OJ L401. In the latter case the dispute need not be connected with the operations of the secondary establishment in question.

[5] [1991] SLT 774.

[6] Case 189/87, [1988] ECR 5565.

policy-holder's family, whose liability arising from his driving of the policy-holder's car is covered by a policy of motor insurance, or in whose favour a declaration of trust of the benefit of a life policy has been made by the policy-holder); or by a third-party victim of a tort, liability for which is covered by the policy, and who has a right of direct action against the insurer under the law which governs the availability of such direct actions according to English choice of law rules.[7] The cases in which the English courts have jurisdiction to entertain proceedings against an insurer under arts 8–10 are as follows:

(1) if the defendant insurer is domiciled in England;[8]

(2) if the defendant insurer is not domiciled in England, but has a secondary establishment in England, and the dispute arises from the operations of the English establishment;[9]

(3) if the defendant insurer is domiciled in Scotland or Northern Ireland, or is not domiciled within the contracting states but is treated as domiciled in Scotland or Northern Ireland by virtue of having therein a secondary establishment from whose operations the dispute has arisen, and the place of performance of the sole or main obligation under the contract of insurance on which the action is based is located in England;[10]

(4) if the defendant insurer is domiciled in another contracting state, or is not domiciled in any contracting state but is treated as domiciled in another contracting state by virtue of having therein a secondary establishment from whose operations the dispute has arisen, and the policy-holder is domiciled in England;[11]

(5) if the defendant is a co-insurer, and is either domiciled in another contracting state, or is not domiciled in any contracting state but is treated as domiciled in another contracting state by virtue of having therein a secondary establishment from whose operations the dispute has arisen, and an action against the leading insurer is pending in the English court;[12]

(6) if the defendant insurer is domiciled in another contracting state, or is not domiciled in any contracting state but is treated as domiciled in another contracting state by virtue of having therein a secondary establishment from whose operations the dispute has arisen, and the insurance is liability insurance or insurance of immovable property, or of both movable and immovable property

---

[7] See art 10[2]. The relevant English choice of law rules are obscure, especially as (unlike, among the contracting states, France, Belgium, the Netherlands, Luxembourg, Spain, and Switzerland) the United Kingdom is not a party to the Hague Convention of 4 May 1971 on the Law Applicable to Road Traffic Accidents. By art 9 of that Convention, a victim has a direct claim against a liability-insurer if such a claim is recognised either: (1) by the law applicable to the victim's claim against the insured; or (2) by the internal law of the country of the accident; or (3) by the law which governs the insurance contract.

[8] Article 8[1](1) of the Conventions, and art 2 of Sched 4 to the 1982 Act.

[9] Articles 5(5), 7, 8[1](1) and 8[2] of the Conventions, and s 44 and Sched 4, arts 2 and 5(5), of the 1982 Act.

[10] See arts 8[1](1) and 8[2] of the Conventions, and s 44 and Sched 4, art 5(1), of the 1982 Act.

[11] Articles 8[1](2) and 8[2] of the Conventions.

[12] Articles 8[1](3) and 8[2] of the Conventions.

where both are adversely affected by the same contingency, and the harmful event occurred in England;[13]

(7) as a third party, joined by an insured who is a defendant in English proceedings brought by a victim of a tort, liability for which is covered by the policy, if the insurer so joined is domiciled in another contracting state, or is not domiciled in any contracting state but is treated as domiciled in another contracting state by virtue of having therein a secondary establishment from whose operations the dispute has arisen.[14]

On the other hand, the Conventions severely restrict jurisdiction to entertain an action brought by an insurer against a policy-holder or other insured or beneficiary who is domiciled in a contracting state. The English courts are competent to entertain such an action only where:

(1) the defendant is domiciled in England;[15] or
(2) the defendant has a secondary establishment in England, and the dispute arises from the operations of the English establishment;[16] or
(3) the defendant is domiciled in Scotland or Northern Ireland, and the place of performance of the sole or main obligation under the contract of insurance on which the action is based is located in England.[17]

To prevent circumvention of these protective rules, arts 12 and 12A invalidate any agreement on jurisdiction over insurance, except in the following cases:

(1) where the agreement on jurisdiction was entered into after the dispute had arisen;[18]

(2) insofar as it enables the policy-holder, an insured or a beneficiary to sue in an additional court or courts;[19]

(3) where it chooses a court or the courts of a contracting state in which at its conclusion both the policy-holder and the insurer were domiciled or habitually resident, to the exclusion of the courts for the place of a possible harmful event abroad, unless such an agreement is contrary to the law of the chosen state;[20]

(4) where it is concluded with a policy-holder who is not domiciled within the contracting states, except insofar as the insurance is compulsory under the law of a contracting state, or the insurance relates to immovable property situated in a contracting state;[21]

(5) insofar as the contract of insurance to which the agreement relates covers

---

[13] Articles 8[2] and 9 of the Conventions.
[14] Articles 8[2] and 10[1] of the Conventions.
[15] See art 11[1] of the Conventions, and Sched 4, art 2, of the 1982 Act.
[16] See arts 5(5), 7 and 11[1] of the Conventions, and Sched 4, art 5(5), of the 1982 Act.
[17] See art 11[1] of the Conventions, and Sched 4, art 5(1), of the 1982 Act.
[18] Article 12(1).
[19] See art 12(2).
[20] See art 12(3). It seems clear that British law contains no such curious prohibition.
[21] See art 12(4). For the cases in which the various EC member states require insurance to be obtained, see the Schlosser Report, at para 138.

maritime or air risks, other than personal injury to passengers and loss of or damage to their baggage.[22]

In *Charman v WOC Offshore*,[23] Hirst J held that the last exception does not extend to cases where the insurance and the jurisdiction agreement cover both marine and non-marine risks, unless the non-marine risks are merely ancillary to the marine risks. Thus he ruled invalid an English jurisdiction clause in respect of an insurance of equipment for use in reconstructing a breakwater in Algeria. He was prepared to treat as the subject of a marine risk any item of equipment which had a certificate of seaworthiness, but the instant insurance and agreement also covered major items of land-based or harbour equipment (such as caterpillar tractors and harbour boats).

The Convention provisions on insurance are, however, subject to a saving, specified in art 11[2], enabling a defendant (whether an insurer, or a policy-holder, insured or beneficiary) to make a counterclaim, arising from the same contract or facts, in the court in which the original action is pending; and the acceptance by art 12(1) of agreements on jurisdiction concluded after the dis-pute has arisen necessarily implies that jurisdiction over insurance also arises in accordance with art 18 where a defendant (whether an insurer, or a policy-holder, insured or beneficiary) enters an appearance without contesting the court's jurisdiction.

Protected consumer contracts

Like Section 3 on insurance, Section 4 (arts 13–15) of Title II of the 1968 and Lugano Conventions regulates jurisdiction to entertain actions based on certain consumer contracts (hereafter 'protected consumer contracts'), largely to the exclusion of the other provisions of Title II.[24] Similarly these provisions are based on the idea (perhaps more justifiable in this case) that the consumer is in

---

[22] See arts 12(5) and 12A. Article 12(5) permits to an agreement on jurisdiction 'which relates to a contract of insurance in so far as it covers one or more of the risks set out in Article 12A', and art 12A specifies the following risks:

   (1) Any loss of or damage to
      (a) sea-going ships, installations situated off-shore or on the high seas, or aircraft, arising from perils which relate to their use for commercial purposes;
      (b) goods in transit other than passengers' baggage where the transit consists of or includes carriage by such ships or aircraft.
   (2) Any liability, other than for bodily injury to passengers or loss of or damage to their baggage,
      (a) arising out of the use or operation of ships, installations or aircraft as referred to in point 1(a) above insofar as the law of the Contracting State in which such aircraft are regis-tered does not prohibit agreements on jurisdiction regarding insurance of such risks;
      (b) for loss or damage caused by goods in transit as described in point 1(b) above.
   (3) Any financial loss connected with the use or operation of ships, installations or aircraft as referred to in point 1(a) above, in particular loss of freight or charter-hire.
   (4) Any risk or interest connected with any of those referred to in points (1) to (3) above.

[23] [1993] 1 Lloyd's Rep 378.
[24] See art 13[1], which makes savings for arts 4 and 5(5).

an economically weaker and legally less experienced position than the supplier,[25] and therefore needs and deserves special protection. Accordingly the consumer is given a choice of fora in which to sue the supplier, while the supplier is generally required to sue the consumer at the latter's domicile, and contracting out of these provisions in advance of the dispute arising is allowed only in exceptional cases.

A protected consumer contract, as defined by art 13 of the Conventions, is as follows. First, the contract must be concluded by a person ('the consumer') for a purpose which can be regarded as being outside his trade or profession.[26] Thus the consumer must be a private final consumer, not acting in the course of a business or profession, and not a company, contracting to receive financial services.[27] It appears to be implied that the other party, the supplier, must be acting in the course of a trade or profession. Secondly, the contract must be either: for the sale of goods on instalment credit terms;[28] or for a loan repayable by instalments or for any other form of credit, made to finance the sale of goods;[29] or otherwise for the supply of goods, or for the supply of services[30] other than transport.[31] Finally, in the case of a contract for the supply of goods without credit, or for the supply of services, the conclusion of the contract must have been preceded by a specific invitation addressed to the consumer, or by advertising, in the state of his domicile, and he must have taken in that state the steps necessary for the conclusion of the contract on his part.[32]

Curiously Sched 4 to the 1982 Act, which allocates jurisdiction between the English, Scottish and Northern Irish courts where the defendant is domiciled (or treated as domiciled) in the United Kingdom, contain provisions similar to arts 13–15, but uses a slightly different definition of a protected consumer contract. As regards contracts for the supply of goods without credit, or for the supply of services, Sched 4 makes no reference to invitation or advertising, but requires that the consumer should have taken his necessary steps in the part of the United Kingdom in which he was domiciled. As a result rare cases may occasionally arise where the contract is a protected consumer contract for the purposes of the Conventions, but an 'ordinary' contract for the purposes of Sched 4, or conversely. In what follows such cases will be ignored.

The protective provisions apply only if the defendant is domiciled, or treated as domiciled, within the contracting states.[33] However, as in the case of an insurer, by art 13[2] a supplier who is not so domiciled under the normal rules on domicile applicable for the purposes of the Conventions, but who has a

---

[25] See Case C-89/91 *Shearson Lehman Hutton v TVB*, 19 January 1993, at para 18.
[26] Article 13[1], opening clause.
[27] See Case C-89/91 *Shearson Lehman Hutton v TVB*, 19 January 1993, following Case 150/77 *Bertrand v Ott* [1978] ECR 1431.
[28] Article 13[1](1).
[29] Article 13[1](2).
[30] Article 13[1](3).
[31] Article 13[3].
[32] Article 13[1](3)(a) and (b).
[33] See art 13[1], opening clause, saving art 4.

secondary establishment in a contracting state, out of whose operations the dispute has arisen, is treated as domiciled in the state in which the establishment is situated. If the defendant is not domiciled, and not treated as domiciled, within the contracting states, English jurisdiction to entertain an action based on a consumer contract is remitted to English law by art 4, and English law then treats the contract in the same way as an 'ordinary' contract.

The English courts have jurisdiction under Section 4 of the Conventions to entertain an action based on a protected consumer contract, brought by the consumer against the supplier, if the supplier is domiciled in England;[34] or if the supplier has a secondary establishment in England, and the dispute arises from the operations of the English establishment;[35] or if the supplier is domiciled (or treated as domiciled, by virtue of having a secondary establishment from whose operations the dispute has arisen) in another contracting state or part of the United Kingdom, and the consumer is domiciled in England.[36] If the action is brought by the supplier against the consumer, the consumer must be domiciled in England.[37]

Article 15 of the Conventions renders invalid any agreement as to jurisdiction which is inconsistent with arts 13 and 14, with three exceptions: where it was entered into after the dispute had arisen; insofar as it enables the consumer to sue in additional courts; or where it confers jurisdiction on the courts of the contracting state in which both the consumer and the supplier were at its conclusion domiciled or habitually resident, and it is not contrary to the law of that state.[38] In the United Kingdom, art 15 of Sched 4 to the 1982 Act makes corresponding provision invalidating jurisdictional agreements inconsistent with arts 13 and 14 of the Schedule.

The Convention provisions on protected consumer contracts are, however, subject to a saving, specified in art 14[3], enabling a defendant (whether a supplier or a consumer) to make a counterclaim, arising from the same contract or facts, in the court in which the original action is pending; and the acceptance by art 15(1) of agreements on jurisdiction concluded after the dispute has arisen necessarily implies that jurisdiction over a protected consumer contract also arises in accordance with art 18 where a defendant (whether a supplier or a consumer) enters an appearance without contesting the court's jurisdiction.

Contracts of employment

The 1968 Convention in its 1989 version, the Lugano Convention, and Sched 4 to the 1982 Act, as amended by SI 1993/603, contain, in arts 5(1)[b][39] and

---

[34] Article 14[1] of the 1968 Convention, and of Sched 4 to the 1982 Act.

[35] Articles 5(5) and 13[1]-[2] of the 1968 and Lugano Conventions and of Sched 4 to the 1982 Act.

[36] Articles 13[2] and 14[1] of the 1968 and Lugano Conventions, and ss 10 and 44, and Sched 4, art 14[1], of the 1982 Act.

[37] Article 14[2] of the 1968 and Lugano Conventions, and of Sched 4 to the 1982 Act.

[38] British law has no objection to the agreements referred to in art 15(3); see Stone (1983) 32 ICLQ 477 at 483-4.

[39] For convenience the second clause of art 5(1) is here referred to as art 5(1)[b].

17[5], explicit provisions for actions involving a contract of employment. Their principal effect is to confer jurisdiction on the courts for the place where the employee habitually carries out his work under the contract, and their main purpose is to protect the employee, in view of his probable unequal bargaining power, by ensuring for him the protection of collective agreements and statutory safeguards applicable at the place where he mainly works. Accordingly, as was ruled by the European Court of Justice in *Shenavai v Kreischer*,[40] and followed by the English Court of Appeal in *Mercury Publicity v Loerke*,[41] for present purposes the concept of a contract of employment must be construed restrictively, and confined to cases involving a personal relationship of master and servant, thus excluding a contract for professional services (for example, those of an architect or lawyer, engaged as an independent contractor to carry out a particular task), and a fortiori excluding a commercial contract whereby a company obtains exclusive rights to canvass in its country for advertising in a foreign newspaper.

The pre-1989 versions of the 1968 Convention deliberately made no specific reference to contracts of employment, with the result that they fell within the general scope of the Convention, as a civil or commercial matter,[42] and the particular scope of art 5(1), as a contractual matter.[43] However the European Court of Justice, in *Ivenel v Schwab*,[44] *Shenavai v Kreischer*,[45] and *Six Constructions v Humbert*,[46] adopted a special interpretation of art 5(1) in relation to contracts of employment, to the effect that in the case of such contracts the relevant place of performance, for the purpose of art 5(1), was always the place, if any, at which the employee habitually performed his work under the contract; and accordingly no court was competent under art 5(1) if the employee habitually worked outside the contracting states, or if there were no single country in which his work was habitually and mainly performed.[47] However the protective effect of the court's rulings was limited by the absence of any provision in those versions of the Convention invalidating a jurisdiction clause contained in a contract of employment.[48]

The protective policy adopted by the court has now been accepted and carried forward by explicit provisions in the 1989 version of the 1968 Convention, and in the Lugano Convention. Minor differences between the current version of the 1968 Convention and the Lugano Convention are partly explained by the fact that the decision of the European Court of Justice in *Six Constructions v Humbert*[49] was given after the completion of the negotiations resulting in the

---

[40] See Case 266/85, [1987] I ECR 239.
[41] [1993] ILPR 142.
[42] See Case 25/79 *Sanicentral v Collin* [1979] ECR 3423.
[43] See Case 133/81 *Ivenel v Schwab* [1982] ECR 1891.
[44] See note 43 above.
[45] Case 266/85, [1987] I ECR 239.
[46] Case 32/88, [1989] ECR 341.
[47] See Case 32/88 *Six Constructions v Humbert* [1989] ECR 341.
[48] See Case 25/79 *Sanicentral v Collin* [1979] ECR 3423.
[49] Case 32/88, [1989] ECR 341.

Lugano Convention, but before the completion of those resulting in the 1989 Convention. In the result, the English courts now have jurisdiction to entertain an action relating to a contract of employment in each of the following cases:

(1) if the defendant (whether the employer or the employee) is domiciled in England;[50]

(2) if the defendant (whether the employer or the employee) is domiciled in another contracting state to the 1968 Convention or the Lugano Convention or in another part of the United Kingdom, and the employee habitually carries out his work in England;[51]

(3) if the action is brought by the employee against the employer, and the defendant employer is domiciled in another contracting state to the 1968 Convention, or in another part of the United Kingdom, and the employee does not habitually carry out his work in any one country, and the business establishment of the employer which engaged the employee was or is now situated in England;[52]

(4) if the defendant (whether the employer or the employee) is domiciled in another contracting state to the Lugano Convention, and the employee does not habitually carry out his work in any one country, and the place of business of the employer through which the employee was engaged was situated in England;[53] or

(5) in accordance with the ordinary rules on jurisdiction over defendants domiciled within the contracting states, relating to secondary establish-

---

[50] Article 2 of the 1968 Convention and of Sched 4 to the 1982 Act.

[51] Article 5(1)[b] of the 1968 Convention (as amended by the 1989 Convention), of the Lugano Convention, and of Sched 4 to the 1982 Act (as amended by SI 1993/603). See also, on earlier versions of art 5(1) of the 1968 Convention: Case 133/81 *Ivenel v Schwab* [1982] ECR 1891; Case 266/85 *Shenavai v Kreischer* [1987] 1 ECR 239; and Case 32/88 *Six Constructions v Humbert* [1989] ECR 341.

The concept of the place of habitual work was clarified by the European Court of Justice in Case C-125/92: *Mulox v Geels*, decided on 13 July 1993, (1993) *Financial Times*, 20 July. The court ruled that where an employee works in more than one contracting state, the relevant place is the place at or from which he has principally worked. Thus a French court was competent to entertain an action claiming damages for wrongful dismissal, brought against an English company by its former international-marketing manager, a Dutch national, since he had worked for the defendant from an office in France, where he also resided, and had returned to that office after each business trip abroad; and by the time of the dismissal, he had come to work exclusively in France. See also *Re a Sales Agent's Contract* [1988] ECC 273, where the German Supreme Court had earlier held that, in the case of a commercial traveller who works from his residence, which is located within the area assigned to him, on behalf of a company domiciled in another contracting state, his residence constitutes the relevant place.

[52] See art 5(1)[b] of the 1968 Convention, as amended by the 1989 Convention, and of Sched 4 to the 1982 Act, as amended by SI 1993/603. In limiting this jurisdictional base to actions brought by, and not against, the employee, the amendment reflects the court's reasoning in Case 32/88 *Six Constructions v Humbert* [1989] ECR 341.

[53] Lugano Convention, art 5(1)[b]. In enabling this base to be used in actions brought by the employer, as well as actions brought by the employee, this provision is capable of producing anti-protective effects. Such effects were rejected by the European Court of Justice in Case 32/88 *Six Constructions v Humbert* [1989] ECR 341, a decision on the original version of the 1968 Convention, given after the negotiation, and with knowledge of the terms, of the Lugano Convention.

ments, co-defendants, third parties, counterclaims, or submission by appearance.[54]

In addition art 17[5] of the 1968 Convention in its 1989 version, and of the Lugano Convention, add force to the policy of employee protection by invalidating agreements as to jurisdiction in respect of contracts of employment unless the agreement on jurisdiction was made after the dispute had arisen. The 1989 Convention, but not the Lugano Convention, makes an exception insofar as the agreement gives the employee an additional forum in which to sue.

The special provisions on employment are limited to cases where the defendant is domiciled in a contracting state. If he is not so domiciled, in general art 4 remits English jurisdiction to English law, and RSC Ord 11 treats employment contracts in the same way as ordinary contracts.

EXCLUSIVE JURISDICTION

Article 16 of the 1968 and Lugano Conventions, and of Sched 4 to the 1982 Act, confers exclusive jurisdiction over proceedings which are principally concerned with certain kinds of subject-matter. These rules are overriding in character. They apply regardless of domicile,[55] appearance,[56] or contrary agreement between the parties to the dispute.[57] A court seised contrary to art 16 must decline jurisdiction of its own motion,[58] and a judgment given in contravention of art 16 must be refused recognition in the other contracting states.[59]

Title to or tenancies of land

Article 16(1) of the 1968 and Lugano Conventions, and of Sched 4 to the 1982 Act, confers exclusive jurisdiction over proceedings which are principally concerned with rights in rem in, or tenancies of, immovable property on the courts of the contracting state or part of the United Kingdom in which the land is situated. There is a limited exception for certain tenancies of short duration. These provisions are considered in Chapter 15 below.[60]

Company law

Proceedings relating to the winding up of insolvent companies or other legal persons, and analogous proceedings, are excluded from the scope of the 1968

---

[54] That is, under arts 5(5), 6 and 18 of the Conventions and of Sched 4. In view of art 5(1)[b], art 5(5) appears to add little in employment cases.

[55] See art 16 itself.

[56] See art 18.

[57] See art 17[3].

[58] See art 19.

[59] See arts 28(1) and 34[2]; and Chapter 14 below.

[60] Under 'Immovable property: Jurisdiction', pp 354–60.

and Lugano Conventions by art 1[2](2). Other proceedings under company law fall within the scope of the Conventions, and art 16(2) confers exclusive jurisdiction on the courts of the contracting state in which a company, other legal person, or association of natural or legal persons has its seat, over proceedings which have as their principal subject-matter the validity of the constitution, the nullity, or the dissolution of the entity, or the validity or nullity of decisions of its organs.[61] Other proceedings under company law are subject to the normal rules laid down by the Conventions, such as arts 5(1)[62] and 17.[63] These matters are considered in Chapter 6 above.

Intellectual property

Article 16(4) of the 1968 and Lugano Conventions deal with proceedings principally concerned with the registration or validity of patents, trademarks, designs, or other similar rights required to be deposited or registered, and confer exclusive jurisdiction on the courts of the contracting state in which the deposit or registration has been applied for, has taken place, or is under the terms of an international convention deemed to have taken place.

In the United Kingdom, these provisions ensure that the British courts have exclusive jurisdiction over proceedings principally concerned with grant, registration or validity in relation to a patent granted by, or a patent application made to, the British Patent Office under Part I of the Patents Act 1977;[64] a design registered or applied for under the Registered Designs Act 1949 (as amended by Part IV of the Copyright, Designs and Patents Act 1988); a trademark registered or applied for under the Trade Marks Act 1938; or a grant or application under the Plant Varieties Acts 1964 and 1983. Since such rights are granted for the whole of the United Kingdom, proceedings of this kind are excluded from Sched 4 to the 1982 Act by para 2 of Sched 5, with the result that the plaintiff has the choice of suing in the courts of any part of the United Kingdom.[65]

On the other hand art 16(4) does not apply to copyright, since this arises automatically from creation, fixation or publication, without the need for or possibility of any official grant; nor, for the same reason, to the rights in performances, and the unregistered design rights, created by Parts II and III of the Copyright, Designs and Patents Act 1988. Moreover, as the European Court of Justice ruled in *Duijnstee v Goderbauer*,[66] it does not apply to a dispute between an employer and an employee relating to their mutual rights in respect of an invention made by the employee, since such issues are governed by the

---

[61] See *Newtherapeutics Ltd v Katz* [1991] Ch 226, where Knox J clarified art 16(2) in the light of the French and German texts.

[62] See Case 34/82 *Peters v South Netherlands Contractors' Association* [1983] ECR 987.

[63] See Case C-214/89 *Powell Duffryn v Petereit* [1992] 1 ECR 1745.

[64] See *Napp Laboratories v Pfizer* [1993] FSR 150, applying art 16(4) to a petition for revocation.

[65] See the Patents Act 1977, s 132; the Registered Designs Act 1949, ss 45–47; and the Civil Jurisdiction and Judgments Act 1982, s 17 and Sched 5, para 2.

[66] Case 288/82, [1983] ECR 3663.

contract of employment and the law governing it, rather than by the law of the country of the patent application and grant.[67]

Since art 16(4) is confined to proceedings principally concerned with *registration or validity*, actions for infringement of intellectual property rights remain governed by the general provisions of Title II of the Conventions. Thus the plaintiff will often have a choice between the courts of the defendant's domicile (under art 2) and the courts of the place of infringement (under art 5(3)).[68] Hence it is plain beyond peradventure that the continued refusal of the English courts, dating from *Potter v Broken Hill*,[69] and demonstrated by *Def Lepp Music v Stuart-Brown*,[70] *James Burrough Distillers v Speymalt Whisky Distributors*,[71] *Tyburn Productions v Conan Doyle*,[72] and *LA Gear v Whelan*,[73] to entertain actions for infringements committed abroad of intellectual property rights granted or recognised by the law of the country where the allegedly infringing acts were committed, contravenes Title II of the Conventions.

It seems probable that, where an action for infringement of an officially granted intellectual property right is brought in a country other than that of the grant (for example, if it is brought at the defendant's domicile, in accordance with art 2), the defendant will be able to attack the validity of the grant *by way of mere defence* in the court seised of the infringement action, if the law of the granting country permits such a defence in infringement actions brought in its own courts. But art 16(4) will prevent the making of an application for revocation of the grant, even by way of counterclaim in an action for infringement, elsewhere than in the state of the grant.

European patents

The European Patent Convention, signed at Munich on 5 October 1973,[74] has established a European Patent Office, seated at Munich, and empowered it to grant, on a single application, a 'bundle' of national patents, usually in common form, for such of the participating countries as are designated in the application. The Convention is not a Community, but a more general European, instrument. It entered into force on 1 June 1978. Current parties to it include the United Kingdom and nine other EC member states (the exceptions being Ireland and

---

[67] See art 60(1) of the European Patent Convention, and the annexed Protocol on Jurisdiction and the Recognition of Decisions in respect of the Right to the Grant of a European Patent, especially arts 4 and 5(2); the Community Patent Convention, art 69(4)(b); and the Patents Act 1977, ss 43(2) and 82.

[68] See *Re Jurisdiction in Contract and Tort* [1988] ECC 415, where the German Supreme Court also held that the courts for the place of an allegedly infringing act are competent under art 5(3), even if the defendant relies on a licence arising from a contract over which those courts otherwise lack jurisdiction.

[69] (1906) 3 CLR 479, affirming [1905] VLR 612.

[70] [1986] RPC 273.

[71] [1991] RPC 130.

[72] [1991] Ch 75.

[73] [1991] FSR 670.

[74] For its text, see [1974] ILM 270.

Portugal), and four other west European countries (Austria, Sweden, Switzerland and Liechtenstein; the latter two being treated as a unit). It is implemented in the United Kingdom by the Patents Act 1977, which refers to a patent for the United Kingdom comprised in a bundle granted by the European Patent Office as a European patent (UK).

In relation to patents granted by the European Patent Office, other than Community patents governed by the Community Patent Convention,[75] art 16(4) of the 1968 and Lugano Conventions is supplemented by art VD of the annexed Protocols, so as to confer exclusive jurisdiction over proceedings principally concerned with the registration or validity of such patents, granted for one or more of the contracting states, on the courts of a contracting state, insofar as the patent is granted for that state. Article VD is designed to make it clear that, in the case of a European patent, jurisdiction belongs to each contracting state for which a grant has been made, as regards the validity or registration of the patent for its territory, and not to the German courts in respect of the whole 'bundle'.[76] Thus the British courts have exclusive jurisdiction over post-grant proceedings concerned with the validity of a European patent (UK), in the same way as over similar proceedings relating to a patent granted by the British Patent Office.

On the other hand, pre-grant proceedings concerning an application for a European patent are brought before tribunals within the European Patent Office, and not before national courts, unless the dispute concerns ownership of the invention, in which case jurisdiction is allocated between national courts by the Protocol on Jurisdiction and the Recognition of Decisions in respect of the Right to the Grant of a European Patent, annexed to the European Patent Convention. The Protocol is implemented in the United Kingdom by ss 82 and 83 of the Patents Act 1977.

Under the Protocol, the court competent to determine disputes as to ownership, arising between application for and grant of a European patent, and otherwise than between employer and employee, may be determined by a written agreement between the parties to the dispute. Otherwise jurisdiction over such a dispute belongs to the courts of the participating country in which the applicant for the European patent has his residence or principal place of business; or if the applicant's residence or place of business is outside the participating countries, then to the courts of the other party's residence or principal place of business. If the dispute is between employer and employee, the competent court may again be determined by a written agreement between the parties to the dispute, but subject to a proviso that the agreement must be valid under the law which governs the contract of employment. In the absence of a valid agreement between the parties, jurisdiction over an employer–employee dispute belongs to the courts of the country in which the employee was mainly employed, or, if there is no determinable place of main employment,

---

[75] See under the next sub-heading below.
[76] See the Schlosser Report, at para 173.

the country of the employer's place of business to which the employee was attached. If no court would otherwise be competent, as a last resort the Protocol confers jurisdiction on the German courts. The Protocol also regulates the problem of simultaneous proceedings in different states, by requiring the court subsequently seised normally to decline jurisdiction in favour of the court first seised, and requires with minor exceptions that a final decision given in a participating country should be recognised in other participating countries.

Community patents

The original version of a Community Patent Convention was signed by the EC member states in 1975,[77] but was never brought into force. A revised version was signed by the member states at Luxembourg on 15 December 1989,[78] but has not yet entered into force, since ratification by all 12 member states is required. The Convention is designed to supplement the European Patent Convention by creating a unitary patent for the entire territory of the European Community, which will be known as a Community patent. Such a patent will be governed by the provisions of the European Patent Convention on such issues as patentability, and by the Community Patent Convention on such issues as revocation and infringement, largely to the exclusion of national law. It will be capable of transfer, revocation or lapse only in respect of the entire territory of the Community. A Community patent will be granted by the European Patent Office to a successful applicant who has so requested, along with patents for non-member states, such as Switzerland, which have acceded to the European Patent Convention and are designated in the application.

Under the revised Community Patent Convention and its annexed Protocol on Litigation, each member state will have to designate a limited number of its courts of first and second instance as 'Community patent courts', which (to the exclusion of other courts) will have jurisdiction to entertain actions concerning the infringement of a Community patent.[79] For the United Kingdom the Annex to the Protocol on Litigation specifies the English Patents Court (within the Chancery Division), the Outer House of the Scottish Court of Session, and the Northern Irish High Court, as Community patent courts of first instance; and the English and Northern Irish Courts of Appeal, and the Inner House of Scottish Court of Session, as Community patent courts of second instance. The validity of a Community patent will be open to attack by means of opposition or revocation proceedings before tribunals within the European Patent Office, or in a Community patent court by way of a counterclaim for revocation made by a defendant in an action for infringement. A Community patent court which is properly seised of an action for infringement will also be competent to entertain

---

[77] See [1976] OJ L17.
[78] See [1989] OJ L401.
[79] More fully: actions for infringement, for threatened infringement, for a declaration of non-infringement, or for compensation for use between publication and grant; and counterclaims for revocation. See arts 1 and 15 of the Protocol on Litigation.

a counterclaim for revocation. Neither art 16 of the 1968 Convention, nor art VD of the annexed Protocol, will apply to a Community patent.

From a judgment of a Community patent court of first instance, appeal will lie to a Community patent court of second instance in the same member state. More radically, however, the Protocol on Litigation will also establish at Community level a 'Common Appeal Court'. If an appeal (other than an interlocutory appeal) to a Community patent court of second instance involves questions as to the validity or effect of a Community patent, other than questions remitted by the Convention to national law, the court of second instance will have to refer the case to the Common Appeal Court for decision of such questions. On the reference the Common Appeal Court will determine the questions of validity or effect referred, giving a ruling on both facts and law, and its decision will be binding in the further proceedings in the case; for example in the court of second instance to which the case will revert for disposal of the appeal.[80] In addition to its role in receiving such references, the Common Appeal Court will hear appeals from the Revocation or Patent Administration Divisions of the European Patent Office. But references from national courts concerning the allocation of jurisdiction over actions relating to Community patents between the courts of the various member states will be made to the European Court of Justice, and not to the Common Appeal Court.

The allocation of jurisdiction over actions concerning the infringement of a Community patent between the Community patent courts of the various member states will be governed by Title II of the 1968 Convention, as greatly modified by arts 13, 14, 17 and 34 of the Protocol on Litigation annexed to the Community Patent Convention. Conversely art 13 of the Protocol will ensure that a judgment of a Community patent court will qualify for recognition and enforcement in the other contracting states in accordance with Title III of the 1968 Convention.

The general rules laid down by arts 2–4 of the 1968 Convention, whereby jurisdiction belongs to the courts of the contracting state in which the defendant is domiciled, or if he is not domiciled in any contracting state, is remitted to the law of the forum state, will be replaced, pursuant to arts 13(2), 14(1)–(3) and 17(1) of the Protocol on Litigation, by rules which confer jurisdiction:

- primarily on the courts of the contracting state in which the defendant is domiciled;
- secondly, if the defendant is not domiciled in any contracting state, on the courts of the contracting state in which the defendant has a secondary establishment;
- thirdly, if the defendant does not have even a secondary establishment in any contracting state, jurisdiction is conferred on the courts of the contracting state in which the plaintiff is domiciled;
- fourthly, if the plaintiff too is not domiciled in any contracting state, on the

[80] See arts 22, 23(1) and 36(3) of the Protocol on Litigation.

courts of the contracting state in which the plaintiff has a secondary establishment;

- finally, if both parties do not have even a secondary establishment in any contracting state, on the courts of the contracting state in which the Common Appeal Court has its seat.

The courts thus designated will have jurisdiction over infringements committed in any contracting state. The Protocol on Litigation will also (by arts 13(2), 14(5) and 17(2)) replace the alternative bases of jurisdiction specified by art 5 of the 1968 Convention by an option enabling the plaintiff to sue in the courts of the contracting state in which the relevant infringing act was committed or threatened, but such jurisdiction will be limited to infringements committed or threatened within that state.

In addition the Protocol (by art 13(3)) adopts the general principle that a person who is not domiciled in any contracting state but has a secondary establishment in a contracting state should be treated as domiciled in the state in which the secondary establishment is located, and this will affect the operation of arts 6, 17 and 20 of the 1968 Convention (respectively on multiple parties; jurisdiction clauses; and examination of jurisdiction of the court's own motion and notification of the defendant). Otherwise (under arts 13(2) and 14(4) of the Protocol) arts 17 and 18 of the 1968 Convention (respectively on jurisdiction clauses and submission by appearance) will operate in their normal way, provided that the court chosen or appeared in is a Community patent court.

As regards simultaneous actions in respect of similar or related claims, arts 21–23 of the 1968 Convention will operate subject to art 34 of the Protocol on Litigation, which will apply where the validity of the same Community patent is already in dispute before a Community patent court, or in the Common Appeal Court, or in the European Patent Office. In such a case, a Community patent court or the European Patent Office will have to stay its own proceedings concerning the patent (other than proceedings for a declaration of non-infringement) at the request of a party if, after hearing the other parties, it finds that there are no special grounds for continuing them.

Moreover art 24 of the 1968 Convention, on interim relief, will be excluded and replaced by arts 13(2) and 36 of the Protocol on Litigation. Any court of a contracting state (whether or not it is a Community patent court) will be able to grant, in respect of a Community patent, provisional or protective measures in accordance with its own law as applicable to national patents, but with effect only in its own country, even if a Community patent court of another contracting state has sole competence to determine the merits of the dispute; and a Community patent court which is competent on grounds other than as the place of infringement will have sole power to grant provisional or protective measures which will qualify for recognition and enforcement in accordance with Title III of the 1968 Convention throughout the contracting states.

By arts 66–74 of the revised Community Patent Convention, proceedings concerning a Community patent or application, but not involving infringement, will be subject to the jurisdiction of the ordinary courts and authorities of the contracting states, rather than of the Community patent courts. In general such proceedings will be subject to the 1968 Convention and will be dealt with in the same way as similar proceedings involving national patents granted in the competent state; though in such proceedings the court must treat a granted patent as valid, or grant a stay until the European Patent Office has determined a pending application.[81] However the 1968 Convention will be modified as follows:

(1) Article 67(a) of the Community Patent Convention will confer exclusive jurisdiction over proceedings relating to compulsory licences on the courts and authorities of the contracting state in whose territory the licence will operate.

(2) Article 67(b) will confer exclusive jurisdiction over disputes as to title between an employer and an employee, on the courts and authorities of the contracting state whose law governs this matter under art 60(1) of the European Patent Convention; that is, the law of the country in which the employee was mainly employed, or if there is no determinable place of main employment, the country in which the employer's place of business to which the employee was attached was located; and will invalidate a contrary agreement on such jurisdiction unless it is permissible under the law governing the contract of employment.

(3) By art 68(3), disputes for which there would otherwise be no competent court within the contracting states will be subject to the jurisdiction of the German courts.

(4) By art 69, if irreconcilable decisions on title to a Community patent are given by courts of different contracting states in proceedings between the same parties, the decision of the court first seised will prevail, even in the state where the contrary decision was given.

Enforcement of judgments

Article 16(5) of the 1968 and Lugano Conventions, and of Sched 4 to the 1982 Act, confer exclusive jurisdiction over proceedings concerned with the enforcement of judgments on the courts of the contracting state, or the part of the United Kingdom, in which the judgment has been or is to be enforced. It might have been supposed that these provisions, which are evidently based on a desire to respect the sovereignty of the country of enforcement, would apply both to judgments of the courts of the country of enforcement and to judgments given elsewhere, whether or not within the contracting states, but in *Owens Bank v Bracco*[82] the European Court of Justice has ruled that Title II (as well as Title III) of the 1968 Convention does not apply to proceedings in contracting states concerning the recognition and enforcement of judgments given in non-contracting states. Fortunately, however, the former English rule which

---

[81] See arts 72–73.
[82] Case C-129/92, [1994] 1 All ER 336, ECJ. See also [1992] 2 AC 443, CA and HL.

prevented the English courts from entertaining an action at common law (as distinct from an application for registration under a statute), seeking the enforcement in England of a foreign judgment, unless the court had personal jurisdiction over the judgment debtor on bases such as his presence, domicile or submission,[83] has been abrogated by English legislation. The current version of RSC Ord 11, r 1(1)(m), gives the English High Court jurisdiction to entertain proceedings for the enforcement of a foreign judgment or arbitral award, even though the defendant and the underlying claim have no connection with England.

In *AS-Autoteile Service v Mahle*,[84] the European Court of Justice ruled that an action to oppose enforcement, such as that provided for by art 767 of the German Code of Civil Procedure, falls within art 16(5) of the Convention; but that art 16(5) does not enable a party who brings an action to oppose enforcement in the courts of the state of enforcement to plead a set-off between the judgment in question and a claim which the courts of the state of enforcement would lack jurisdiction to entertain if it were the subject of an independent action.

More generally the court explained in *Reichert v Dresdner Bank (No 2)*[85] that the essential purpose of art 16(5) is to enable the courts of the country of execution to apply their own rules in relation to the acts of the enforcing authorities. Thus the provision is confined to disputes arising from measures of execution, especially measures against land or movable property. Accordingly the court rejected an absurd argument that art 16(5) enabled a creditor to bring a 'pauline' action, seeking the setting aside of a disposition of property made by his debtor in fraud of creditors, in the country in which the asset transferred was situated. Such an action no doubt aims to assist the creditor in the ultimate enforcement of his debt, but it is not concerned with a dispute arising from measures taken in execution of a judgment.

---

[83] See Stone [1983] 1 LMCLQ 1 at 5.
[84] Case 220/84, [1985] ECR 2267.
[85] Case C-261/90, [1992] 1 ECR 2149.

II

CIVIL JURISDICTION – FORUM CLAUSES

JURISDICTION CLAUSES

Article 17 of the 1968 and Lugano Conventions authorise parties to existing or potential disputes to enter into an agreement specifying the court or courts which will be competent to determine such disputes, and regulate the validity and effect of such agreements (generally referred to as 'jurisdiction clauses').[1] Article 17 is a complex provision.[2] It has given rise to a substantial case-law, and has been amended by the 1978 Convention and again by the 1989 Conven-

---

[1] On art 17[2], which deals with provisions on jurisdiction contained in trust instruments, see Chapter 9, under 'Trusts', pp 181–2 above.
[2] In its 1989 version, it read as follows:

[1] If the parties, one or more of whom is domiciled in a Contracting State, have agreed that a court or the courts of a Contracting State are to have jurisdiction to settle any disputes which have arisen or which may arise in connection with a particular legal relationship, that court or those courts shall have exclusive jurisdiction. Such an agreement conferring jurisdiction shall be either–
(a) in writing or evidenced in writing, or
(b) in a form which accords with practices which the parties have established between themselves, or
(c) in international trade or commerce, in a form which accords with a usage of which the parties are or ought to have been aware and which in such trade or commerce is widely known to, and regularly observed by, parties to contracts of the type involved in the particular trade or commerce concerned.
Where such an agreement is concluded by parties, none of whom is domiciled in a Contracting State, the courts of other Contracting States shall have no jurisdiction over their disputes unless the court or courts chosen have declined jurisdiction.
[2] The court or courts of a Contracting State on which a trust instrument has conferred jurisdiction shall have exclusive jurisdiction in any proceedings brought against a settlor, trustee or beneficiary, if relations between these persons or their rights or obligations under the trust are involved.
[3] Agreements or provisions of a trust instrument conferring jurisdiction shall have no legal force if they are contrary to the provisions of Articles 12 or 15, or if the courts whose jurisdiction they purport to exclude have exclusive jurisdiction by virtue of Article 16.
[4] If an agreement conferring jurisdiction was concluded for the benefit of only one of the parties, that party shall retain the right to bring proceedings in any other court which has jurisdiction by virtue of this Convention.
[5] In matters relating to individual contracts of employment an agreement conferring jurisdiction shall have legal force only if it is entered into after the dispute has arisen or if the employee invokes it to seise courts other than those for the defendant's domicile or those specified in Article 5(1).

tion. It endeavours to regulate fully the formal validity, and partly the essential validity, of jurisdiction clauses; and in general gives exclusive effect to a valid jurisdiction clause.

Formal validity

As regards formal validity, the original version of art 17[1] of the 1968 Convention required simply that an agreement as to jurisdiction must be made or evidenced in writing. Then the 1978 version made it alternatively sufficient, in international trade or commerce, for the agreement to be made in a form which accorded with practices in that trade or commercial sphere of which the parties were or should have been aware.[3] Now, in the 1989 version of the 1968 Convention, and in the Lugano Convention, art 17[1] specifies that an agreement on jurisdiction must be either:

(a) [made] in writing or evidenced in writing, or
(b) [made] in a form which accords with practices which the parties have established between themselves, or
(c) in international trade or commerce, [made] in a form which accords with a usage of which the parties are or ought to have been aware and which in such trade or commerce is widely known to, and regularly observed by, parties to contracts of the type involved in the particular trade or commerce concerned.

Paragraph (a) follows the wording of the original version. Paragraph (b) reflects a doctrine, apparently based on some swollen concept of good faith, which had been announced by the European Court of Justice in interpreting the original version.[4] Paragraph (c) endeavours to clarify the amendment made by the 1978 Convention.

The European Court of Justice has given nine rulings on the formal validity of jurisdiction clauses under art 17, mostly on the original version. It began by adopting a fairly strict approach to the requirement of writing,[5] but has since come to adopt an increasingly relaxed approach.[6] In view of this relaxation, it is thought that there is little, if any, difference in effect between the formal

---

[3] Cf *The Rewia* [1991] 1 Lloyd's Rep 69, where Sheen J seems to have misunderstood the alternative character of the 1978 addition. He also considered that a clause in a bill of lading referring to the carrier's principal place of business did not accord with international commercial practice, because the bill did not identify the carrier or his principal place of business, but this approach seems to confuse form with content. His decision was reversed by the Court of Appeal on other grounds, [1991] 2 Lloyd's Rep 325.

[4] See Case 25/76 *Segoura v Bonakdarian* [1976] ECR 1851; Case 71/83 *Russ v Haven* [1984] ECR 2417; and Case 313/85 *Iveco Fiat v Van Hool* [1986] ECR 3337.

[5] See Case 24/76 *Estasis Salotti v RÜWA* [1976] ECR 1831 at 1840–41; and Case 25/76 *Segoura v Bonakdarian* [1976] ECR 1851 at 1860.

[6] See Case 71/83 *Russ v Haven* [1984] ECR 2417; Case 221/84 *Berghoefer v ASA* [1985] ECR 2699; Case 313/85 *Iveco Fiat v Van Hool* [1986] ECR 3337; and Case C-214/89 *Powell Duffryn v Petereit* [1992] 1 ECR 1745. Cf the views of Advocate-General Lenz in Case C-288/92 *Custom Made Commercial Ltd v Stawa Metalbau GmbH*, 8 March 1994; in its judgment of 29 June 1994, the court found it unnecessary to address art 17.

requirements specified by the three successive versions of art 17. Thus the following analysis is in general regarded as applicable to all three versions.

It is clear that an agreement on jurisdiction must be explicit, and can never be implied.[7] On the other hand, where there is a contract in writing, signed by both parties, incorporation by reference (including by a chain of references) is possible, but the reference (or all the references in the chain) must be express, and reasonable steps must have been taken by the party relying on incorporation to bring the contents of incorporated clause to the knowledge to the other party (for example, by sending a copy him of the document to be incorporated at a suitable time prior to the signature of the contract), unless it can reasonably be assumed that the latter is already familiar with its terms (for example, where the document contains standard terms recommended by a trade association to which both parties belong).[8]

In the absence of a contract in writing signed by both parties, it is usually sufficient if one of the parties sends or hands to the other a document purporting to confirm the conclusion of an oral contract on terms contained or properly incorporated (in the sense explained above) in the confirmatory document, and the recipient fails to inform the confirmer of his objection to the confirmatory document within a reasonable time after receiving it. Despite the stricter approach once adopted by the European Court of Justice,[9] the later case-law indicates that it is now immaterial whether in fact the prior oral contract contained an express term specifically on jurisdiction, or an express term incorporating a document containing a jurisdiction clause, or made no reference whatever to jurisdiction, or even had no existence at all.[10] In any event, where a written agreement between the parties, containing a jurisdiction clause, has expired but has been tacitly renewed by the parties, and the renewal of the substantive agreement is valid under the applicable national law, so that the earlier agreement serves as the basis for their continued relations, the jurisdiction clause also will continue to operate in connection therewith.[11]

More specifically, a clause dealing with jurisdiction over disputes between a company and its shareholders, contained in the constitutional documents of the company (such as its articles of association), which have been validly adopted under the relevant national law, and lodged in a place accessible to shareholders or entered in a public register, satisfies the formal requirements of art 17.[12]

---

[7] See Case 24/76 *Estasis Salotti v RÜWA* [1976] ECR 1831 (on the original version); and *New Hampshire Insurance Co v Strabag Bau* [1992] 1 Lloyd's Rep 361, CA (on the 1978 version). See similarly per Scott J in *Adams v Cape Industries* [1991] 1 All ER 929 (affirmed by the Court of Appeal without consideration of this point, [1990] Ch 433) on the recognition of foreign judgments under English common law.

[8] See Case 24/76 *Estasis Salotti v RÜWA* [1976] ECR 1831; and *Harvey v Ventilatorenfabrik Oelde*, (1992) *Financial Times*, 11 November, CA (under RSC Ord 11). ·

[9] See Case 25/76 *Segoura v Bonakdarian* [1976] ECR 1851.

[10] See Case 71/83 *Russ v Haven* [1984] ECR 2417; Case 221/84 *Berghoefer v ASA* [1985] ECR 2699; and Case 313/85 *Iveco Fiat v Van Hool* [1986] ECR 3337. See also *The Sydney Express* [1988] 2 Lloyd's Rep 257.

[11] See Case 313/85 *Iveco Fiat v Van Hool* [1986] ECR 3337.

[12] See Case C-214/89 *Powell Duffryn v Petereit* [1992] 1 ECR 1745.

As regards third parties, a jurisdiction clause which has been validly agreed on between the original parties to a contract also operates in favour of and against a third person who under the applicable national law has succeeded to the rights and obligations of one of the parties under the contract (for example, a subsequent holder of a bill of lading).[13] More generally, where a contract (for example, of insurance) is concluded wholly or partly for the benefit of a third party, he may take advantage of a jurisdiction clause which is validly agreed on between the contracting parties and is intended to operate in his favour.[14] Normally, however, a jurisdiction clause contained in a substantive contract only binds the parties to that contract.[15] On the other hand, there seems no warrant in art 17 for the view adopted by the English Court of Appeal (per Bingham LJ) in *Dresser v Falcongate*,[16] that a jurisdiction clause contained in a bill of lading could not be binding between a bailor and a sub-bailee, because their mutual relationship was not contractual, but rather a consensual 'bailment on terms'. The terms of such a bailment surely amount to an agreement between the parties to it, within the meaning of art 17.

The formal requirements specified by art 17 are exhaustive. It is not open to a member state to require additional formalities, such as that a jurisdiction clause be expressed in a particular language.[17] Presumably, however, if a party abusively chose to use a language which he knew the other would not understand, there would be no 'agreement', under a Convention standard, independent of any particular national law, within the meaning of art 17.

Article 17 is qualified by art I(2) of the 1968 and first Lugano Protocols, which give special protection to persons domiciled in Luxembourg, by making an agreement on jurisdiction valid with respect to such a person only if he has expressly and specifically so agreed. As construed by the European Court of Justice in *Porta-Leasing v Prestige International*,[18] this requires that the provision on jurisdiction must be contained in a clause which is exclusively devoted to jurisdiction, and the Luxembourg domiciliary must specifically sign the jurisdiction clause. His signature of the whole contract, which contains the jurisdiction clause, is not sufficient, though it is not necessary for the jurisdiction clause to be contained in a separate document from the contract to which it relates. Thus special care must be taken if it is desired to bind a Luxembourg domiciliary by a jurisdiction clause.

A jurisdiction clause which falls within the scope of art 17 and fails to satisfy the formal requirements imposed thereby is, in general, void for all purposes. By way of exception, it may, however, have some effect insofar as the Conventions remit jurisdiction to a national law which has less strenuous formal

---

[13] See Case 71/83 *Russ v Haven* [1984] ECR 2417.
[14] See Case 201/82 *Gerling v Treasury Administration* [1983] ECR 2503.
[15] See *Stadtwerke Essen v Trailigaz* [1988] ECC 291, where the Paris Court of Appeal held that a jurisdiction clause contained in a construction contract was not binding on a sub-contractor.
[16] [1992] QB 502.
[17] See Case 150/80 *Elefanten Schuh v Jacqmain* [1981] ECR 1671.
[18] Case 784/79, [1980] ECR 1517.

requirements. Thus English law, apart from the Conventions, imposes no formal requirements on jurisdiction clauses, and accordingly an English court continues to have a discretion to respect a jurisdiction clause which does not satisfy the formal requirements of art 17, if the defendant is not domiciled within the contracting states, so that jurisdiction is remitted to the lex fori by art 4.[19] Again, where the defendant is domiciled in the United Kingdom, art 2 refers the allocation of jurisdiction between its three parts to British law, and by art 17 of Sched 4 to the 1982 Act, a jurisdiction clause which does not satisfy the formal requirements of the Conventions, but does satisfy those of the law of the part of the United Kingdom whose court or courts are chosen, confers at least non-exclusive jurisdiction on the chosen court(s). For this purpose English law imposes no formal requirements, but Scottish law, following the Conventions, requires an agreement made or evidenced in writing or made in a form according with trade or commercial practices of which the parties were or should have been aware.[20]

Other aspects of validity

As regards the permissible scope of a jurisdiction clause, art 17[1] of the Conventions and of Sched 4 to the 1982 Act authorise an agreement relating to 'any disputes which have arisen or which may arise in connection with a particular legal relationship'.[21] Thus it is clear that a jurisdiction clause may cover potential, as well as existing, disputes, and that the disputes need not relate to contractual, as distinct from delictual, proprietary or even familial support claims. But, by analogy with arts 6(3) and 22[3], the reference to disputes arising from a particular legal relationship should probably be construed as limiting the permissible scope of a jurisdiction clause to a particular transaction or incident. Accordingly it will be permissible for a contract to contain a jurisdiction clause referring to 'any dispute arising from or in connection with this contract or anything done in connection with its negotiation, conclusion, performance, non-performance or purported performance, and whether the claim is based on a contractual obligation or on the law of tort or restitution';[22] and it will be permissible for drivers whose vehicles have collided to make an agreement on jurisdiction over 'all claims between us arising from the collision'; but not to include in a long-term exclusive distributorship agreement a jurisdiction clause extending to disputes relating exclusively to an individual sale contract

---

[19] See RSC Ord 11, r 1(1)(d)(iv); *The Chaparral* [1968] 2 Lloyd's Rep 158; *The Eleftheria* [1970] P 94; *Mackender v Feldia* [1967] 2 QB 590; *Evans Marshall v Bertola* [1973] 1 All ER 992; *Carvalho v Hull Blyth* [1979] 3 All ER 280; and *Trendtex v Crédit Suisse* [1982] AC 679.

[20] See the 1982 Act, Sched 8, para 5(2).

[21] Despite the reference to 'disputes', the suggestion by Sheriff Boyle in *British Steel v Allivane* [1988] ECC 405, that art 17 does not apply where it appears to the court seised that there is no dispute on the merits seems clearly misconceived.

[22] Cf *The Sennar* [1985] 1 WLR 490, where the House of Lords gave effect to an issue estoppel arising from a Dutch judgment, to the effect that a jurisdiction clause contained in a bill of lading covered claims in tort as well as claims in contract.

entered into in pursuance of the umbrella agreement. However in *Powell Duffryn v Petereit*,[23] the European Court of Justice accepted that the relationship between a company and its shareholders as such was sufficiently particular.

As regards special types of subject-matter, art 17[3] of the Conventions provides that agreements conferring jurisdiction shall have no legal force if they are contrary to art 12 or 15, on insurance and protected consumer contracts, or if the courts whose jurisdiction they purport to exclude have exclusive jurisdiction by virtue of art 16. Probably the Conventions leave it to the law of a contracting state on which art 16 confers exclusive jurisdiction to regulate the permissibility of a jurisdiction clause which varies the normal allocation of such jurisdiction between its courts. In any event, in the United Kingdom arts 16 and 17(3) of Sched 4 to a large extent make analogous provision in respect of arts 15 and 16 of the Schedule. In addition art 17[5] of the 1968 Convention in its 1989 version, of the Lugano Convention, and of Sched 4 as amended by SI 1993/603, now invalidate jurisdiction clauses relating to contracts of employment, except where the jurisdiction clause is agreed on after the dispute has arisen or insofar as it offers additional fora to a plaintiff employee.

As the European Court of Justice made clear in *Sanicentral v Collin*,[24] the Conventions prevent a contracting state from imposing additional restrictions relating to the subject-matter in respect of which a jurisdiction clause is permitted; for example, by refusing, before the entry into force of the 1989 Convention, to recognise a jurisdiction clause contained in a contract of employment. The court also explained that, in view of art 54(1) of the 1968 Convention, by which the Convention applies to proceedings instituted after its entry into force, a jurisdiction clause which fulfils the requirements of art 17 is effective if the action is instituted after the commencement date of the Convention, even if the jurisdiction clause was contained in a contract which was made and broken before that date, and even if the national law in force prior to the Convention in the country seised of the action did not permit jurisdiction clauses in respect of contracts of the relevant type. No doubt the same principle applies in respect of subsequent versions of art 17 and their commencement dates for the forum state.

Problems as to the possible invalidity of a jurisdiction clause by reason of lack of consent, owing to such factors as fraud or other misrepresentation, mistake, duress or other improper pressure, will probably be remitted to the national law which is applicable according to the choice of law rules of the court seised, since the EC/Rome Convention of 19 June 1980 on the Law Applicable to Contractual Obligations[25] by art 1(2)(d) excludes jurisdiction clauses from its scope, and the European Court of Justice is unlikely to wish to create substantive rules at Community level on such questions.[26] The European Court of Justice might usefully emphasise, however, that an alleged mistake or misrepresentation can

[23] Case C-214/89, 10 March 1992, (1992) *The Times*, 15 April.
[24] Case 25/79, [1979] ECR 3423.
[25] [1980] OJ L266. See Chapter 12 below.
[26] Cf Case 12/76 *Tessili v Dunlop* [1976] ECR 1473, on art 5(1).

be relevant only where it affects consent to the jurisdiction clause itself, as distinct from the substantive contract containing the jurisdiction clause.[27]

Effects

Article 17[1] of the Conventions envisages a jurisdiction clause, complying with the requirements discussed above, which chooses 'a court or the courts' of a contracting state. Then, provided that at least one of the parties to the agreement on jurisdiction is domiciled in a contracting state,[28] art 17[1] confers on the chosen court or courts exclusive jurisdiction over disputes falling within the scope of the agreement. This is qualified by art 17[4], which adds that if the agreement on jurisdiction was concluded for the benefit of only one of the parties, that party retains the right to bring proceedings in any other court which has jurisdiction by virtue of the Conventions. It is submitted that, although the text of art 17[1] is a model of reticence on the point, it should be enough that a party was domiciled in a contracting state either at the time when the agreement on jurisdiction was concluded, or at the time of the institution of the action in which the agreement is relied on.

If none of the parties was domiciled within the contracting states, art 17[1] deprives the courts of the other contracting states of jurisdiction over disputes within the scope of the agreement, unless the chosen court or courts have declined jurisdiction. But the chosen courts must determine their jurisdiction in accordance with their own law, as remitted to by art 4; and where the English High Court is chosen, it will, in its discretion, accept jurisdiction unless the defendant establishes strong grounds showing that it would be unjust to do so.[29]

As regards the effects of a jurisdiction clause, the European Court of Justice has paid little attention to the wording of art 17, and instead adopted a liberal interpretation, designed to respect the intention of the parties. In *Meeth v Glacetal*[30] which involved a contract of sale between French and German parties containing a clause specifying that an action must be brought in the defendant's country, the court construed art 17 as enabling such a 'reciprocal' jurisdiction clause to be effective to achieve its purpose. The court added that whether such a clause will prevent a court seised in accordance therewith from entertaining a related set-off or, it seems, counterclaim, depends on the con-

---

[27] Cf *Heyman v Darwins* [1942] AC 356. See also *Anterist v Crédit Lyonnais* [1988] ECC 1, where the German Supreme Court recognised that '[a]n (international) jurisdiction clause which is intended to relate to all disputes concerning the relations between the parties to a contract normally also covers disputes concerning the validity and existence of the contract'.

[28] As regards actions concerning the infringement of a Community patent, a jurisdiction clause will operate in accordance with art 17 of the 1968 Convention, provided that the chosen court is a Community patent court; and for this purpose a person who is not domiciled in any contracting state, but has a secondary establishment in a Contracting State, will be treated as domiciled in that state. See arts 13 and 14 of the Protocol on Litigation, annexed to the Community Patent Convention, [1989] OJ L401/1, not yet in force.

[29] See RSC Ord 11, r 1(1)(d)(iv), and *The Chaparral* [1968] 2 Lloyd's Rep 158.

[30] Case 23/78, [1978] ECR 2133.

struction of the jurisdiction clause. It is submitted that a jurisdiction clause should be construed as excluding such a set-off or counterclaim only where the clause expresses so absurd an intention with unmistakable clarity.

In the light of *Meeth*, there can be no doubt that a clause which clearly expresses an intention to confer non-exclusive jurisdiction on a specified court (for example: 'without prejudice to the rights of each party to sue in any court which is otherwise competent, each hereby agrees that the other shall be entitled to sue him in the English High Court') is effective under art 17 to achieve its purpose, and in *Kurz v Stella Musical*[31] Hoffmann J so held. No doubt art 17 implies that a jurisdiction clause must be presumed to be intended to create exclusive jurisdiction unless the clause indicates a contrary intention with reasonable clarity.[32]

Similarly, as the European Court of Justice ruled in *Anterist v Crédit Lyonnais*,[33] art 17[4] will apply only where the jurisdiction clause shows with reasonable clarity that it was not intended to prevent one of the parties from suing in other competent courts. It is not enough that the parties were domiciled in different contracting states, and the clause selects one of those states. The clause must either explicitly indicate the party in whose favour it was made, or it must specify the courts before which each of the parties may sue the other, but give one of them a wider choice of courts than the other.

Article 17 envisages a choice of 'a court or the courts' of a contracting state. Thus one may choose a specific court, such as the English High Court, the Paris Commercial Court, or the Hamburg Landgericht (a court of first instance). Such a choice is advisable, since it eliminates the problem of finding the territorially appropriate court within the chosen state. It is clear that the chosen court need not otherwise have *territorial* competence, though one cannot override the member state's rules allocating competence over categories of subject-matter between different types of court; for instance, by attempting to confer jurisdiction over a non-commercial matter on a French commercial court, or to confer jurisdiction over a commercial contract on a British industrial tribunal.[34]

If, on the other hand, one merely chooses the courts in general of a specified contracting state, it will be for the law of that state to determine which of its courts shall be competent. It is submitted that in such a case the chosen state is bound to provide at least one competent court, and that if it lacks any applicable

---

[31] [1992] Ch 196.

[32] See *Sohio v Gatoil* [1989] 1 Lloyd's Rep 588, where the English Court of Appeal took the view that a jurisdiction clause in a commercial contract of sale should normally be construed as exclusive.

[33] Case 22/85, [1986] ECR 1951. The case involved a guarantee given to a French bank, on the bank's standard form, by a German domiciliary in respect of liabilities of a French company. The guarantee contained a clause specifying that the court within whose district the branch of the bank involved in the transaction was situated, in casu the Sarreguemines court in France, should have exclusive jurisdiction to determine all matters relating to the performance of the agreement, whichever party were the defendant. The bank, however, attempted to bring an action on the guarantee in the German court within whose district the guarantor was domiciled.

[34] See the Jenard Report, at p 38.

rule for selecting that court or courts, all its courts become territorially competent.[35] Indeed, such a result is provided for in Scotland by para 5(4) of Sched 8 to the 1982 Act. It seems regrettable that the 1982 Act does not include a provision that a clause which merely chooses the courts of the United Kingdom or of England generally should be normally construed as referring to the English High Court.[36]

Since art 17 is based on the principle of party autonomy, it does not prevent parties who have concluded an agreement on jurisdiction from subsequently concluding a further agreement varying or rescinding the earlier agreement. Similarly, as the European Court of Justice ruled in *Elefanten Schuh v Jacqmain*[37] and *Spitzley v Sommer Exploitation*,[38] if in contravention of a valid agreement on jurisdiction one of the parties brings an action, or makes a counterclaim, against the other party to the agreement in a court other than the court or courts agreed on, but the other party enters an appearance without contesting the jurisdiction, art 18 prevails over art 17 and the court seised has jurisdiction.

Where a jurisdiction clause choosing an English court or the English courts does not satisfy the formal requirements of art 17 of the Convention, but the defendant is domiciled in the United Kingdom, it will at least be effective under art 17 of Sched 4 to the 1982 Act to confer non-exclusive and discretionary jurisdiction on the chosen English court or courts.[39] The position is similar, under art 4 of the 1968 Convention and RSC Ord 11, r 1(1)(d)(iv), where the defendant is domiciled outside the contracting states.

Choice of an external court

Article 17 of the Conventions in terms envisages only cases in which the court or courts chosen are those of a contracting state. Moreover, since Title II of the Conventions is in general mandatory in character, at first sight it might appear that a court which is competent, for example under art 2 as the court of the defendant's domicile, is bound to ignore completely a jurisdiction clause which purports to confer exclusive jurisdiction on a court of a non-contracting state. So rigid a view is not, however, generally accepted,[40] and it is submitted that the proper conclusion is that a contracting state is free to allow its courts to decline jurisdiction in order to give effect to a jurisdiction clause which would have been

---

[35] Cf the Jenard Report, at p 37.

[36] See Stone (1983) 32 ICLQ 477 at 484.

[37] Case 150/80, [1981] ECR 1671.

[38] Case 48/84, [1985] ECR 787.

[39] The non-exclusive character of art 17 of Sched 4 was noted by Sheriff Boyle in *British Steel v Allivane* [1988] ECC 405, but his judgment overlooks the primacy of art 17 of the Convention, even in cases where both parties are domiciled in the United Kingdom and the agreement chooses the courts of a part thereof.

[40] See Droz, *Compétence Judiciaire et Effets des Jugements dans le Marché Commun* (1972), at paras 216–18.

effective under art 17 but for the fact that the chosen court or courts are courts of a non-member state.[41]

Accordingly, in view of the traditional English practice, the English courts will, in their discretion, decline jurisdiction in the face of an agreement, otherwise complying with art 17, for the exclusive jurisdiction of a non-member state, unless the plaintiff establishes strong grounds which make it unjust to give effect to the agreement.[42] This view gains some support from *The Rewia*,[43] where in the explicit exercise of discretion Sheen J refused to decline jurisdiction, conferred by art 6(1) of the Convention, over a German co-defendant, despite an agreement choosing the Hong Kong courts, mainly because to respect the jurisdiction clause would have caused related claims against different defendants to be heard in different countries. However on appeal his decision was reversed on other grounds.[44]

Where the defendant is not domiciled within the contracting states, there is no doubt that a contracting state is entitled, under art 4 of the Conventions, to permit its courts to decline jurisdiction by reference to an agreement for the jurisdiction of a non-contracting state, even if the jurisdiction clause does not satisfy the requirements of art 17, unless it contravenes arts 12, 15 or 16.

Article 17 is concerned only with agreements which choose a court or courts; that is, a regular judicial body established as part of the public authority of a state. Private arbitration is excluded from the scope of the Conventions by art 1[2](4), but arbitration clauses are regulated by the New York Convention of 10 June 1958 on the Recognition and Enforcement of Foreign Arbitral Awards, to which all the EC member states except Portugal are now party.

ARBITRATION CLAUSES

Despite the reference in art 220(4) of the EC Treaty to securing the reciprocal recognition and enforcement of arbitration awards, as well as of judgments of courts and tribunals, it has proved unnecessary for a convention on arbitration to be concluded at Community level, since the problem is adequately dealt with by more general international conventions. In particular, all of the present member states, with the exception of Portugal, are now parties to the New York Convention of 10 June 1958 on the Recognition and Enforcement of Foreign

---

[41] Cf *Re a Swiss Jurisdiction Clause* [1988] ECC 172, where the German Supreme Court disregarded an alleged agreement between German domiciliaries for exclusive Swiss jurisdiction as infringing art 38(2) of the (German) Code of Civil Procedure, which allows agreements on jurisdiction to be concluded before the dispute has arisen only if at least one of the parties is not domiciled in Germany.

[42] See *The Eleftheria* [1970] P 94; *Mackender v Feldia* [1967] 2 QB 590; *Evans Marshall v Bertola* [1973] 1 All ER 992; *Carvalho v Hull Blyth* [1979] 3 All ER 280; and *Trendtex v Crédit Suisse* [1982] AC 679.

[43] [1991] 1 Lloyd's Rep 69.

[44] [1991] 2 Lloyd's Rep 325, CA.

Arbitral Awards ('the New York Convention'),[45] which is implemented in the United Kingdom by the Arbitration Act 1975.

The New York Convention was negotiated within the framework of the United Nations, and has been ratified or acceded to by a very large number of countries, widely spread geographically and reflecting a wide variety of legal and political traditions.[46] By art VII(2), it supersedes between its contracting states the Geneva Protocol of 24 September 1923 on Arbitration Clauses and the Geneva Convention of 26 September 1927 for the Execution of Foreign Arbitral Awards, which had been negotiated under the auspices of the League of Nations.[47] Hence the relationship between the EC member states, other than Portugal, is now governed by the New York Convention, to the exclusion of the Geneva Protocol and Convention. Otherwise the New York Convention does not prejudice provisions more favourable to recognition and enforcement contained in other conventions or in the national law of the state addressed.[48]

The New York Convention deals with the recognition and enforcement of both arbitration agreements and arbitral awards. Arbitration agreements are regulated by art II, which is designed to replace the Geneva Protocol of 1923, and which appears to have been a last-minute addition. Both art II of the New York Convention and the Geneva Protocol are now implemented in the United Kingdom by ss 1 and 7(1) of the Arbitration Act 1975. Most of the provisions of the New York Convention are concerned primarily with awards, and are designed to replace the Geneva Convention of 1930.[49]

As regards scope, art I of the New York Convention makes it clear that it is immaterial whether the parties are individuals or corporate bodies, and whether the arbitrator was appointed for the particular dispute or was a permanent arbitral body to which the parties submitted. Article I(3) permits a contracting state, by declaration, to confine its application of the Convention to disputes arising from legal relationships, whether contractual or not, which are regarded as commercial under its own law, and such reservations have been made by

---

[45] For its text, see Cmnd 6419, or [1958] JBL 396.

[46] See SI 1984/1168 and 1989/1348. Parties to the New York Convention include: Australia; Algeria; Antigua and Barbados; Argentina; Austria; Bahrain; Belize; Benin; Botswana; Bulgaria; Burkina Faso; Cambodia; Cameroon; Canada; Central African Republic; Chile; China; Colombia; Costa Rica; Cuba; Cyprus; Dominica; Djibouti; Ecuador; Egypt; Finland; Ghana; Guatemala; Haiti; Holy See; Hungary; India; Indonesia; Israel; Japan; Jordan; Kenya; Korea; Kuwait; Madagascar; Malaysia; Mexico; Monaco; Morocco; New Zealand; Niger; Nigeria; Norway; Panama; Peru; Philippines; Poland; Romania; Russia; San Marino; Singapore; South Africa; Sri Lanka; Sweden; Switzerland; Syria; Tanzania; Thailand; Trinidad and Tobago; Tunisia; United States of America; and Uruguay.

[47] For the text of the Geneva Protocol and Convention, see the Schedules to the Arbitration Act 1950. Portugal (as well as all the other EC member states) is now a party to the Geneva Protocol and Convention, so these now govern the relations between Portugal and each of the other member states.

   The following non-member states are party to the Geneva Protocol and Convention, but not to the New York Convention: Bahamas; Bangladesh; Grenada; Guyana; Malta; Mauritius; Pakistan; Saint Christopher and Nevis; St Lucia; Western Samoa; and Zambia. See SI 1984/1168 and 1989/1348.

[48] See art VII(1).

[49] On the recognition and enforcement of foreign arbitral awards, see Chapter 14 below.

many states, including (within the European Community) France, Denmark and Greece. Such reservations can create major difficulties when made by a state, such as India, whose law contains no clear distinction between commercial and non-commercial matters,[50] and it seems unfortunate that the Convention does not require a state which makes such a reservation to accompany it with a binding definition of the distinction between commercial and non-commercial matters drawn by its law. Apart from such a reservation, the Convention applies to disputes concerning any matter, whether a contract, a tort or any other legal relationship, provided only that the matter is capable of settlement by arbitration under the law of the state addressed.[51] It seems clear, however, that the Convention does not apply to disputes between states governed by public international law.

As regards arbitration agreements, unlike the Geneva Protocol,[52] the New York Convention does not specify any international element as required to make art II applicable, so that, on a literal reading, a contracting state would be bound to apply art II even in purely domestic cases. Such a result would be perfectly intelligible, since the possibility can never be ruled out (at the time when the agreement is made, or when a court is requested to decline jurisdiction in pursuance of the agreement) that a subsequent change in a party's residence or in the location of his assets may make it necessary to enforce the award abroad. In practice, however, implementing legislation in some contracting states, including the United Kingdom, has confined the operation of art II to cases involving some foreign element specified by the legislation. Thus, by s 1 of the Arbitration Act 1975, the British courts are not bound to decline jurisdiction pursuant to an arbitration agreement in accordance with art II, but have a discretion to do so under s 4(1) of the Arbitration Act 1950, if the arbitration agreement does not provide, expressly or by implication, for arbitration outside the United Kingdom, and none of the parties is, being an individual, a national of or habitually resident in, or, being a corporation, incorporated in or centrally managed and controlled in, a state other than the United Kingdom.[53] Such a restriction may not be justified by the Convention, but it is unlikely to provoke protests from other contracting states.

Article II of the New York Convention provides for the recognition and enforcement of arbitration agreements which fulfil its requirements. A court of a contracting state must recognise the validity of such an agreement; and, more

---

[50] See *Indian Organic Chemicals v Chemtex Fibres* (1978) 65 All India Reporter, Bombay Section, 108.

[51] See arts II(1) and V(2)(a).

[52] The Geneva Protocol applied only where the parties were 'subject to the jurisdiction of', ie resident in, different Contracting States, but it was immaterial where the arbitration was to take place; see art 1.

[53] Cf the American implementing Act, 9 US Code, Chapter 2, which by s 202 excludes from the scope of the Convention an agreement arising out of a relationship which is entirely between American citizens, or corporations incorporated or having their principal place of business in the United States, unless it involves property located abroad, or envisages performance or enforcement abroad, or has some other reasonable relation with one or more foreign states.

specifically, when seised of an action in respect of a matter which falls within the scope of such an agreement, if any of the parties so requests, the court must refer the parties to arbitration. In other words it must enforce the agreement by declining jurisdiction to entertain the action brought in breach of it. Such dismissal is mandatory, in contrast with the judicial discretion conferred by traditional English law.[54] The Convention does not, however, prevent a court which declines jurisdiction over the merits, in accordance with art II, from granting or maintaining protective relief in support of the arbitration. Thus where the English courts stay under art II an admiralty action in rem in which a ship has been arrested, they will normally retain the ship or require equivalent security under s 26 of the Civil Jurisdiction and Judgments Act 1982.[55] Similarly, on staying a personal action, they may (under s 37(1) of the Supreme Court Act 1981) grant or maintain a *Mareva* injunction,[56] or, indeed, any other type of interlocutory injunction (including one requiring a party to continue performance of the alleged contractual obligation which is the subject-matter of the dispute to be arbitrated); but in its discretion the English court will usually refuse interlocutory relief which would effectively pre-empt the decision of a foreign arbitrator, and will be reluctant to grant interlocutory relief unless some good reason for its being sought from the English court, rather than the court of the country of the arbitration, is shown.[57]

Article II deals expressly with formal validity. The agreement must be in writing, and 'agreement in writing' is defined as including an arbitral clause in a contract, or a separate agreement for arbitration alone, being (in either case) either signed by the parties or else contained in an exchange of letters or telegrams. In view of the *inclusive* character of the definition, other tangible messages which are unsigned but of ascertainable origin, such as telexes or communications by electronic mail, may also suffice. Indeed in *Zambia Steel & Building Supplies v Clark & Eaton*[58] the Court of Appeal accepted as sufficient an agreement concluded by the oral acceptance of a written offer. Nor can there be serious doubt that incorporation by express reference is acceptable, though the Italian courts have frequently invoked the analogy of arts 1341 and 1342 of their Civil Code, which require specific approval, and refused to accept such incorporation,[59] and have sometimes even referred the issue to the law of the country where the contract was made and which was regarded as governing the contract.[60] It seems clear that, in the interest of uniformity and commercial

---

[54] See s 4(1) of the Arbitration Act 1950, which remains applicable in purely internal cases.

[55] See *The Bazias 3 and Bazias 4* [1993] 2 All ER 964, [1993] 2 WLR 854, CA.

[56] See *The Rena K* [1979] QB 377.

[57] See *Channel Tunnel Group Ltd v Balfour Beatty Construction Ltd* [1993] AC 334.

[58] [1986] 2 Lloyd's Rep 225.

[59] See eg *Miserocchi v Agnesi* (1972) 8 Rivista di Diretto Internazionale Privato e Processuale 564; *Menaguale v Intercommerce* (1980) 16 Rivista etc 34; *SEV-Scherk Enterprises v Soc des Grandes Marques* (1978) 14 Rivista etc 772; and *Junakovik v Seagull Shipping* (1976) 99 Il Foro Italiani I 1496.

[60] See eg *Begro v Lamberti* (1977) 13 Rivista etc 89; *Brisighello v Chemapol* (1978) 14 Rivista etc 94; and *Total v Lauro* (1978) 14 Rivista etc 118.

convenience, the requirement of writing should be given an autonomous interpretation governed by public international law, rather than read as impliedly referring to the forum's choice of law rules. But, since there is no international tribunal which has power routinely to resolve problems of interpretation of the New York Convention, parties from other countries who are seeking to conclude arbitration agreements with persons resident in Italy would be well advised to take the same care to obtain a specific signature to the arbitration clause as parties seeking to make agreements on judicial jurisdiction with persons domiciled in Luxembourg.

Apart from formalities, art II of the New York Convention specifies that the arbitration agreement must be confined to 'differences ... between [the parties] in respect of a defined legal relationship', a requirement similar to one contained in art 17 of the 1968 Convention, which in fact was derived from the New York Convention.[61] Article II also repeats the main provision of the Geneva Protocol, by stipulating that it is immaterial whether the differences 'have arisen' before or 'may arise' after the agreement is concluded.[62] On the other hand art II limits its operation to disputes 'concerning a subject matter capable of settlement by arbitration', and delphically[63] eliminates the obligation to decline jurisdiction where the court 'finds that the [arbitration] agreement is null and void, inoperative or incapable of being performed'.

As regards arbitrability, the analogy of art V(2) indicates clearly that the court seised of an action in breach of an arbitration agreement must apply its own internal law for the purpose of determining whether the subject-matter of the dispute is capable of settlement by arbitration within the meaning of art II. However, in view of the emphatic declaration in art II that the dispute may be existing or potential, it seems clear that a matter must be regarded as arbitrable, for the purposes of the Convention, if the relevant law would permit the arbitration of disputes concerning the matter in question where the arbitration agreement was made after the dispute had arisen. Where this is so, art II overrides any rule of the national law which refuses to respect arbitration agreements concerning such matters when they relate to future disputes.

It follows from this that arts 12 and 15 of the 1968 and Lugano Conventions, which restrict agreements affecting jurisdiction in respect of insurance and protected consumer contracts only in the case of future disputes, cannot in any way invalidate, or justify a national law in disregarding, arbitration agreements relating to these matters and falling within the scope of the New York Convention, even in the case of future disputes. However, this view was in effect rejected by the Belgian Court of Cassation in *Audi NSU v Adelin Petit*,[64] which

---

[61] See the Jenard Report, at p 37.

[62] Article II(1). Before 1923, courts were often willing to give effect to arbitration agreements concluded after the dispute had arisen, but reluctant to do so in the case of agreements relating to possible future disputes. The principal aim of the 1923 Protocol was to ensure the effectiveness of arbitration clauses relating to future disputes.

[63] Per Lord Mustill in *Channel Tunnel Group Ltd v Balfour Beatty Construction Ltd* [1993] AC 334.

[64] (1979) 94 Journal des Tribunaux 625.

involved Belgian legislation invalidating agreements excluding Belgian jurisdiction made between a Belgian exclusive distributor and a foreign manufacturer prior to the termination of the exclusive dealing contract.

It is submitted that the reference in art II(3) to the possibility of an arbitration agreement being 'null and void' should be read as not referring to formal validity or arbitrability, which are separately dealt with in art II itself; but to such matters as offer and acceptance, mistake, misrepresentation, improper pressure, and personal incapacity. By analogy with art V(1)(a), such questions of essential validity, with the exception of capacity, should be referred to the law expressly or impliedly chosen by the parties, or failing any indication of such a choice, to the law of the country where the award is to be made; while capacity should be referred to the law applicable thereto under the forum's choice of law rules.

The reference in art II(3) to the possibility of an arbitration clause being 'inoperative' seems to refer to cases to which, on its true construction, ascertained in accordance with the law governing its essential validity, the clause does not apply, perhaps owing to an unexpected change of circumstances.[65] On the other hand, the impossibility of performing the arbitration agreement simply requires factual appraisal, and relates to difficulties such as the existence of hostilities or natural disasters at the agreed seat of the arbitration.[66]

Finally, the proviso whereby the court seised is required to decline jurisdiction only 'at the request of one of the parties' must be understood as remitting to the lex fori the timeliness of the request. Accordingly s 1(1) of the Arbitration Act 1975, and RSC Ord 12, require the defendant to apply for a stay of the proceedings by summons, after acknowledging service but before delivering any pleadings or taking any other steps in the proceedings. The 1975 Act, however, exempts the court from its obligation to decline jurisdiction where it is 'satisfied ... that there is not in fact any dispute between the parties with regard to the matter agreed to be referred',[67] and this is in practice construed as referring to cases where the defendant's contentions appear so hopeless as not to merit trial, a test analogous to that applied on applications for summary judgment under RSC Ord 14.[68] But there is little doubt that, so construed and applied, the Act does not accurately implement the Convention.

---

[65] Cf *Carvalho v Hull Blyth (Angola)* [1979] 1 WLR 1228.
[66] Cf Dicey & Morris, at p 598.
[67] Section 1(1).
[68] See *Channel Tunnel Group Ltd v Balfour Beatty Construction Ltd* [1993] AC 334.

12

CONTRACTS

INTRODUCTION

The 1980 Convention

Until recently choice of law in respect of contracts was governed in English courts largely by the traditional rules of English common law. Now, however, the traditional English rules in this sphere (and those of nine other EC member states) have been largely replaced by the EC Convention, opened for signature at Rome on 19 June 1980, on the Law Applicable to Contractual Obligations ('the 1980 Convention').[1]

This Convention entered into force on 1 April 1991 for the United Kingdom, along with France, Germany, Italy, Belgium, Luxembourg, Denmark and Greece; on 1 September 1991 for the Netherlands; and on 1 January 1992 for Ireland.[2] It is implemented in the United Kingdom by the Contracts (Applicable Law) Act 1990.

By art 17, the 1980 Convention does not apply to contracts concluded before its commencement date for the forum state. Thus the traditional rules retain importance transitionally, and it will be some time before a substantial case-law, clarifying the 1980 Convention and establishing the extent to which the Conven-

---

[1] For the text of the 1980 Convention, see [1980] OJ L266, or Sched 1 to the (British) Contracts (Applicable Law) Act 1990. For an official commentary, see the Guiliano and Lagarde Report on the 1980 Convention, [1980] OJ C282. The Report may be considered by the British courts as a guide to assist in the interpretation of the 1980 Convention; see the 1990 Act, s 3(3)(a).

The 1980 Convention is supplemented by a Convention on Greek Accession, signed at Luxembourg on 10 April 1984 ('the 1984 Convention'), but the latter serves only to permit Greek accession and add an authentic Greek text, without making substantive changes. The 1984 Convention entered into force, along with the 1980 Convention, on 1 April 1991. For the text of the 1984 Convention, see [1984] OJ L146, or Sched 2 to the 1990 Act.

Further negotiations will be necessary on Spanish and Portuguese accession to the 1980 Convention.

Unlike the 1968 Convention on Jurisdiction and the Enforcement of Judgments in Civil and Commercial Matters (examined in Chapters 7–11 above and 14 below), the 1980 Convention is not based directly on art 220 of the EC Treaty, but arises from a 'voluntary' decision of the member states to attempt further harmonisation in the sphere of private international law.

[2] See art 29 of the Convention; [1991] OJ C52/1; SI 1991/707; (1991) 88 LSG 16/35 and 28/36; and (1992) 31 ILM 245. The 1980 Convention had been implemented in advance of its entry into force by Germany and Denmark.

tion departs from the traditional rules, develops. However, even before such a case-law has developed, it seems already clear that the differences between the solutions adopted by the 1980 Convention and those of traditional English law are far less important than the similarities.

The 1980 Convention specifies, by art 18, that in its interpretation and application, regard should be had to the international character of its rules and to the desirability of achieving uniformity in their interpretation and application. Moreover, in pursuance of the second Joint Declaration annexed to the Convention, two Protocols empowering the European Court of Justice to give preliminary rulings on its interpretation were signed on 19 December 1988,[3] but owing to delays in ratification, have not yet entered into force.[4] Under these Protocols, a preliminary ruling may be requested, at its discretion, by an appellate court of a contracting state; even in the case of a court of last resort, the making of a reference will be discretionary.[5]

The 1980 Convention applies regardless of reciprocity, since art 2 provides that any law specified by the Convention must be applied whether or not it is the law of a contracting state. Indeed, the 1980 Convention almost entirely avoids the discriminatory character for which the 1968 Convention is rightly infamous.[6]

More generally, art 1(1) of the 1980 Convention specifies that the choice of law rules laid down by the Convention apply to contractual obligations in any situation involving a choice between the laws of different countries, and art 19(1) adds that each territory of a state (such as the United Kingdom) which comprises several territories having distinct laws in respect of contracts (as is the case in respect of England and Wales, of Scotland, and of Northern Ireland) must be treated as a separate country for the purposes of the Convention. However art 19(2) permits such a state not to apply the Convention to conflicts solely between the laws of its own territories.[7] Fortunately the Contracts (Applicable Law) Act 1990 rejects this invitation to pointless complication.

Exclusions from the 1980 Convention

The material scope of the 1980 Convention is, however, restricted to a fairly limited extent by art 1(2)–(4), which excludes certain types of transaction, certain terms, and certain issues from the ambit of the Convention, and thus remits them to the traditional conflict rules of the court seised.

---

[3] See [1989] OJ L48; or Sched 3 to the 1990 Act.

[4] See (1991) 88 LSG 18/33.

[5] See art 2 of the First Protocol. Under art 3, there will also be a procedure whereby in certain circumstances a non-judicial authority of a contracting state may request a ruling; this parallels art 4 of the 1971 Protocol on the interpretation of the 1968 Convention on civil jurisdiction and judgments.

[6] A minor exception is the exclusion from the scope of the 1980 Convention by art 1(3) of contracts of insurance of risks located within the Community.

[7] See, similarly, Council Directive 88/357, art 7(1)(i), on non-life insurance; and art 4(3) of Council Directive 90/619, on life insurance.

As regards types of transaction, perhaps the most important exclusion is made by art 1(3) and (4), which refer to contracts of insurance (other than re-insurance) covering risks situated within the European Community. Instead the matter is regulated by Council Directive 88/357,[8] in the case of non-life insurance, and Council Directive 90/619,[9] in the case of life insurance.

The exclusion by art 1(2)(c) of obligations arising under bills of exchange, cheques, or promissory notes, or under other negotiable instruments insofar as the obligations arise from the negotiable character of the instrument, reflects the special character of such instruments. Such a document is designed to crystallise a definite obligation in precise terms, with a view to ease of transfer, and the normal choice of law rules adopted by the Convention, which would permit the taking into account of connections not apparent on the face of the instrument, would clearly be unsuitable. Such instruments are, moreover, subject to special conflict rules both in the United Kingdom[10] and in the Continental countries,[11] and though the content of these special rules appears far from ideal, very little litigation seems to arise from them.[12]

The exclusion by art 1(2)(g) of 'the constitution of trusts and the relationship between settlors, trustees and beneficiaries' seems designed merely to remove any possible misunderstanding by Continental courts that trusts form part of the law of obligations, rather than the law of property or associations.

Another exclusion, laid down by art 1(2)(b), covers contractual obligations relating to succession on death, to matrimonial property, or to rights and duties arising out of a family relationship, parentage, marriage or affinity, including maintenance obligations in respect of illegitimate children. This exclusion, taken with the exclusion by art 1(2)(a) of questions of individual status or capacity, seems designed to cover all contracts which fall within the sphere of family law,[13] and to avoid the perverse distinction between maintenance and matrimonial property made by the 1968 Convention on jurisdiction and judgments.[14] These exclusions reflect the focus of the Convention on 'ordinary', arm's length, if not necessarily commercial, transactions.

Whatever the type of contract, art 1(2)(d) excludes the validity and interpretation of arbitration or jurisdiction clauses from the scope of the Convention, apparently because such questions are already to a large extent dealt with by art 17 of the 1968 Convention on civil jurisdiction and judgments, or by arts II and V of the New York Convention of 1958 on the Recognition and Enforcement of Foreign Arbitral Awards. Even so, there seems little reason for excluding the 1980 Convention from questions not thus dealt with; for example, the effect of fraud or mistake on the validity of a jurisdiction clause. In any event, the

---

[8] [1988] OJ L172.
[9] [1990] OJ L330.
[10] See the Bills of Exchange Act 1882, s 72.
[11] See the Geneva Conventions of 7 June 1930 and 19 March 1931, For the Settlement of Certain Conflicts of Laws in Connection with (respectively) Bills of Exchange or Cheques.
[12] See Lasok & Stone, p 352.
[13] See the Guiliano and Lagarde Report, at p 10.
[14] See Chapter 7, under 'Subject-matter', pp 120–4 above.

exclusion does not extend to the substantive contract containing an arbitration or jurisdiction clause. Nor does it prevent such a clause from being taken into account in determining the proper law of the substantive contract under arts 3 and 4 of the Convention.[15]

Other exclusions relate to particular issues, rather than types of transaction or clause. They relate to: individual status or capacity;[16] questions governed by company law, such as the creation, by registration or otherwise, legal capacity, internal organisation or winding up of companies and other bodies, and the personal liability of officers and members as such for the obligations of a company or body;[17] the question whether an agent is able to bind a principal, or an organ to bind a company or other body, to a third party;[18] and evidence and procedure.[19] These exclusions reflect the conception that, even where there is a contract involved, the issues in question should not be regarded as contractual for choice of law purposes. Some of them will be considered more fully, in connection with the scope of the proper law, later in this chapter.

Other international conventions

By arts 20 and 21, the 1980 Convention is not to prejudice the application of:

(1) provisions which are contained in existing or future acts of European Community institutions, or in national laws harmonised in implementation of such acts, and which, in relation to particular matters, lay down choice of law rules relating to contractual obligations;

(2) other international conventions to which a contracting state to the 1980 Convention is, or becomes, a party.

However arts 23 and 24 impose procedural safeguards before a member state, for which the 1980 Convention has entered into force, accedes to a multilateral convention, a principal aim of which is to lay down rules of private international law concerning any matter governed by the 1980 Convention. The member state in question must notify the other member states through the Secretary-General of the EC Council, and then wait for six months, during which another member state may request consultations, or for a year if consultations are requested but agreement is not reached, before amending its law so as to accord with the other multilateral convention. However this procedure need not be followed if another contracting state to the 1980 Convention or one of the European Communities is already a party to the multilateral convention, or if its object is to revise a convention to which the state concerned is already a party, or if it is a convention concluded within the framework of the EC Treaties. A similar

---

[15] See the Guiliano and Lagarde Report, at p 12.
[16] Article 1(2)(i).
[17] Article 1(2)(e).
[18] Article 1(2)(f). On these questions, see Dicey & Morris, Rules 156 and 199.
[19] Article 1(2)(h).

consultation procedure is applicable under art 23 in other cases where a member state, for which the 1980 Convention is in force, wishes to adopt a new choice of law rule in regard to a particular category of contract within the scope of the 1980 Convention, but the delay for consultations is then two years instead of one year.

Other multilateral conventions which deal principally with choice of law in the contractual sphere include:

(1)   the Hague Convention of 15 June 1955 on the Law Applicable to International Sales of Goods,[20] which entered into force in 1964 and is now in force between France, Italy, Belgium, Denmark, Norway, Sweden, Finland, Switzerland and Niger (but not the United Kingdom);

(2)   the Hague Convention of 14 March 1978 on the Law Applicable to Agency, which has not yet entered into force; and

(3)   a revised Hague Convention, adopted on 30 October 1985, on the Law Applicable to Contracts for the International Sale of Goods,[21] which is designed to replace the 1955 Convention, but which has not yet entered into force.

Other international conventions harmonise substantive rules on particular types of contract, and specify the transnational scope of the substantive rules in question, so as to override the normal choice of law rules. Sometimes poor drafting of such provisions on territorial scope causes problems. Thus the (British) Carriage of Goods by Sea Act 1924, implementing the Hague Rules on bills of lading, merely made the Rules applicable to shipments from the United Kingdom, with the result that they could be avoided, as regards English courts, by choosing English law to govern a shipment from another contracting state.[22] But now the (British) Carriage of Goods by Sea Act 1971, implementing the Hague–Visby Rules, has made them applicable to shipments from either the United Kingdom or another contracting state, with the result that in the case of such a shipment they override a choice of a foreign proper law.[23]

Also noteworthy is art VIII(2)(b) of the International Monetary Fund Agreement signed at Bretton Woods in 1944, by which exchange contracts which involve the currency of an IMF member state and which contravene exchange control regulations of that state, maintained or imposed consistently with the IMF Agreement, are rendered unenforceable in other member states. This provision is implemented in the United Kingdom by the Bretton Woods Agreements Act 1945 and Order 1946.[24] Since the breakdown of the system of fixed parities in the early 1970s, art VIII(2)(b) has been construed narrowly. Thus a contract is an 'exchange contract' only when it provides for the exchange of one

---

[20] For its text, see (1952) 1 AJCL 275.
[21] For its text, see (1985) 24 ILM 1573.
[22] See *Vita Food Products v Unus Shipping* [1939] AC 277, overruling *The Torni* [1932] P 78.
[23] See *The Hollandia* [1983] 1 AC 565.
[24] SR & O 1946/36.

currency for another, and not (for example) for the sale of goods, or insofar as it is a monetary transaction in disguise.[25]

The nature of the choice of law problem for contracts

Contracts connected with more than one country may conveniently be referred to as transnational contracts.[26] Determination of the law which governs the substantive rights and obligations of the parties under such contracts is one of the most important issues in private international law. Such contracts constitute the channel for international trade. They give rise to a substantial quantity of litigation. They also present factual patterns of almost infinite complexity and variation.

It seems appropriate first to identify some of the possible factual complexities. These relate to the residences of the parties; the places of negotiation, conclusion and performance; the terms of the contract; and the content of the various connected laws.

As regards parties, typically the parties to a transnational contract reside or carry on business in different countries. Moreover, more than one place of business of one of the parties may have been involved in the formation or performance of the contract.

As regards formation, the contract may have been negotiated by communications between the respective places of business of the parties, and the determination of its place of conclusion may involve the application of rules which differ as between the connected laws to facts which may be in dispute.

As regards performance, the place of performance of a transnational contract is not necessarily the same for all the obligations under the contract. Even if a principal or characteristic obligation is identifiable, its place of performance may not have been specified in the contract, and the implied or default location may differ according to the various connected laws. Or the contract may give one of the parties a choice of places at which to perform or require performance.

As regards terms, a transnational contract may contain an express clause ('a choice of law clause') specifying the law by which the parties intended that the contract should be governed. Or the contract may contain a jurisdiction or arbitration clause ('a forum clause'), specifying the forum by which disputes connected with the contract were intended to be determined. Or the contract may be expressed in a standard form which had been drafted in contemplation of the law of its country of origin. Moreover, the chosen law, the specified forum, or the origin of the standard form used, may be that of, or located in, a country otherwise lacking any apparent connection with the contract.

On the substantive issues, one connected law, but not another, may contain rules rendering the contract, or one or more of its terms, invalid, or may even

---

[25] See *Wilson Smithett & Cope v Terruzzi* [1976] QB 683, and *United City Merchants v Royal Bank of Canada* [1983] 1 AC 168.

[26] See per Lord Diplock in *Amin Rasheed v Kuwait Insurance Co* [1984] 1 AC 50.

prohibit performance under criminal penalty. Or one of the connected laws may suffer from insufficient development, and thus offer no ascertainable solution to many of the issues which may arise in relation to contracts of the relevant kind.

The dominant policies

In view of such factual complexities, most systems of private international law have given priority in this sphere to the policies of respecting and effectuating the expectations of the contracting parties, in accordance with the primary objective of contract law; of promoting certainty, predictability, commercial convenience, and (hopefully) uniformity of results, regardless of forum; and thus of facilitating the conduct and promoting the growth of international trade and commerce.[27] Such considerations underlie the traditional approach in the United Kingdom, elsewhere in the European Community, and indeed almost everywhere world-wide, and not surprisingly have also inspired the 1980 Convention.

Accordingly the 1980 Convention largely accords with the traditional English law in adopting the following general approach to choice of law in respect of transnational contracts:

(1) A contract, as an economic unity, should normally be governed in most respects by a single law (in traditional English terminology, 'the proper law of the contract').[28]

(2) However this general principle does not preclude the adoption for a particular type of issue (such as formal validity, the existence or validity of consent, or the remedies to be available) of a special choice of law rule, more appropriate in view of the nature of the issue in question, derogating to some extent from the normal reference to the proper law.[29]

(3) The proper law of a contract should be determined, if possible, by reference to an agreement between the parties; and accordingly:

(a) a choice of law clause, purporting to specify the governing law, agreed to by the parties, should be respected, even if the chosen law is otherwise apparently unconnected with the contract; and

(b) in the absence of an explicit agreement between the parties as to the governing law, an implied agreement thereon should be inferred and respected, if such an inference can reasonably be drawn.[30]

(4) In the absence of even an implied choice by the parties, a test of closest connection should be used to provide a default solution.[31]

(5) In any event, it is the internal law of the legal system expressly or

---

[27] See, on choice-influencing considerations, the American Law Institute's *Restatement, Second, Conflict of Laws* (1971), s 6.
[28] See the 1980 Convention, arts 3(1) and 4(1).
[29] See the 1980 Convention, arts 8–11 and 14.
[30] See the 1980 Convention, art 3.
[31] See the 1980 Convention, art 4.

impliedly agreed on by the parties, or the internal law of the country most closely connected, which applies as the proper law, and not the choice of law rules contained in that legal system, which might refer to the law of some other country; renvoi is excluded in determining the proper law.[32]

In substantive contract law, the 20th century has seen a trend towards restricting the freedom of parties to make whatever agreement suits them, in order to grant protection to parties in a weaker bargaining position, and to safeguard public interests in such matters as currency stability. Accordingly, some limited but significant derogations from the general proper law approach are made by the 1980 Convention (and by the traditional English law), by way of special choice of law rules for certain types of contract, designed to protect parties in a weaker bargaining position, such as consumers or employees;[33] and by way of savings designed to accord some respect to the interest of a country in having its mandatory rules applied in cases for which it asserts particular concern;[34] as well as by way of the traditional saving permitting the forum country to invoke its stringent public policy against foreign substantive rules which it considers outrageous in content.[35] On the whole, however, it is the general approach, which seeks to safeguard party expectations by respecting their choice of the governing law, which remains dominant, and the exceptions, designed to achieve other objectives, continue to have relatively limited scope and importance.

Structure

In view of the structure of the 1980 Convention, it seems convenient to focus on types of contract according to their substantive nature, and to deal first with 'ordinary' contracts; that is, all contracts whose substantive nature brings them within the scope of the 1980 Convention, with the exception of consumer or employment contracts, some of which are governed by special rules under arts 5 and 6.

In relation to 'ordinary' contracts, it is convenient to consider in turn: the rules for determining the proper law; the rules on the extent to which particular issues, as such, may be governed by some law other than the proper law; and

---

[32] See art 15 of the 1980 Convention; and, similarly, under traditional English law, *Re United Railways of Havana* [1960] Ch 52, CA, and *Amin Rasheed v Kuwait Insurance Co* [1984] 1 AC 50, HL. See also, similarly, arts 2 and 3 of the Hague Convention (1955) on the Law Applicable to International Sales of Goods, and art 15 of the Hague Convention (1985) on the Law Applicable to Contracts for the International Sale of Goods.

However the exclusion of renvoi does not in itself prevent respect for self-limiting rules, whereby a proper law confines the application of certain of its substantive rules to contracts entirely domestic to, or connected in some particular way with, its territory; as exemplified by the Dutch rule applied in *Sayers v International Drilling* [1971] 3 All ER 163, or the British rules laid down by ss 26 and 27(1) of the Unfair Contract Terms Act 1977.

[33] See the 1980 Convention, arts 5 and 6.

[34] See the 1980 Convention, arts 3(3), 7, and 22(1)(a).

[35] See the 1980 Convention, art 16; and similarly, under traditional English law, *Kaufman v Gerson* [1904] 1 KB 591.

finally the derogations from the proper law designed to reflect interests of other legal systems, or to safeguard the stringent public policy of the forum.

Then we shall consider in turn various 'non-ordinary' types of contract: consumer contracts, for some of which special rules are laid down by art 5 of the 1980 Convention; employment contracts, for which special rules are laid down by art 6 of the Convention; and, finally, insurance contracts, for some of which special rules are laid down by other EC legislation.

ASCERTAINMENT OF THE PROPER LAW

Express choice

Under the 1980 Convention, as under the traditional English law,[36] the proper law of a contract is determined primarily by reference to any express agreement on choice of law concluded by the parties to the contract. Only in the absence of any, or any valid, express choice is reference made, secondarily, to implied choice or closest connection. Thus art 3(1) of the 1980 Convention specifies that a contract is to be governed by the law chosen by the parties, and that the choice may be expressed by the terms of the contract.[37] Usually any express choice of law will be made by a clause contained in the contract as concluded, but art 3(2) permits an express choice to be agreed on after the conclusion of the contract (so as to replace the proper law resulting from a previous express or implied choice or from the closest connection), though such a subsequent choice will not prejudice the formal validity of the contract, nor adversely affect the rights of third parties.[38] It also seems consistent with the policy of the Convention to accept an express choice agreed on before the contract, so that, for example, a long-term distribution agreement could effectively provide that particular contracts of sale subsequently concluded between the same parties pursuant to the agreement should be governed by a specified law, unless the particular contract should otherwise provide.

The wide scope of the freedom of choice which the Convention confers on the parties is made clear by art 1(1), which specifies that (within the scope of the Convention) its choice of law rules are applicable 'in any situation involving a

---

[36] See *R v International Trustee* [1937] AC 500; *Vita Food Products v Unus Shipping* [1939] AC 277; *Co Tunisienne de Navigation v Co d'Armement Maritime* [1971] AC 572; and *Amin Rasheed v Kuwait Insurance Co* [1984] 1 AC 50.

[37] In full, art 3(1) provides: 'A contract shall be governed by the law chosen by the parties. The choice must be express or demonstrated with reasonable certainty by the terms of the contract or the circumstances of the case. By their choice the parties can select the law applicable to the whole or a part only of the contract.'

[38] In full, art 3(2) provides: 'The parties may at any time agree to subject the contract to a law other than that which previously governed it, whether as a result of an earlier choice under this Article or of other provisions of this Convention. Any variation by the parties of the law to be applied made after the conclusion of the contract shall not prejudice its formal validity under Article 9 or adversely affect the rights of third parties.'

choice between the laws of different countries', and art 3(3), which provides for an automatic saving in favour of the mandatory rules of the country most closely connected, but only where, apart from the parties' choice of law, or of law and jurisdiction, the contract is exclusively connected with a single country.[39] In view of art 3(3), it seems clear that there is no category of 'purely domestic' contracts to which the Convention does not apply at all.[40]

In cases falling within art 3(3), the parties' choice is not invalidated altogether, but the chosen law operates subject to all mandatory rules of the otherwise exclusively connected country. It does so, however, even if the policy underlying the relevant mandatory rule is minimal. Thus a promise in writing, signed in England, to make a gift in England, would fall foul of the English doctrine of consideration, despite the inclusion of a clause choosing Italian law, which does not require consideration for an agreement in writing; even though the parties could easily have avoided the problem by including a nominal consideration or using a formal deed. It is unclear whether the traditional English law included a rule similar to art 3(3), but in any event the situation envisaged is negligible in occurrence and importance. It is submitted that art 3(3) should be construed very restrictively: in particular, the foreign origin of the goods should take a contract of sale outside art 3(3) even if it is concluded between parties resident in the importing country and performed there; and even if it is a consumer contract, since art 5 provides adequate protection for the consumer.[41]

It is clear from arts 1(1) and 3(3) that the Convention (like the traditional English law) permits the parties to choose a law which has no other apparent connection with the contract.[42] The freedom to choose an unconnected law is justifiable in terms of commercial convenience: the rules of the chosen law may be well developed and familiar to the parties, while those of all the connected laws may be obscure or a matter for speculation; or it may be convenient to use

---

[39] In full, art 3(3) provides: 'The fact that the parties have chosen a foreign law, whether or not accompanied by the choice of a foreign tribunal, shall not, where all the other elements relevant to the situation at the time of the choice are connected with one country only, prejudice the application of rules of the law of that country which cannot be derogated from by contract, hereinafter called "mandatory rules".' See similarly, for non-life insurance contracts, Directive 88/357, art 7(1)(g).

On other derogations from the proper law, in favour of mandatory rules of some other law, see art 7 of the 1980 Convention, considered later in this chapter under 'Mandatory rules', pp 260–4 below.

[40] Cf Young [1991] LMCLQ 314 at 315.

[41] Cf Young [1991] LMCLQ 314 at 320.

[42] On this aspect of the traditional English law, see especially *Vita Food Products v Unus Shipping* [1939] AC 277, where the Privy Council (on appeal from Nova Scotia) upheld an express choice of English law in a bill-of-lading contract for the carriage of herrings from Newfoundland to New York in a Nova Scotian ship. Lord Wright specifically rejected an argument that, since the transaction allegedly had no connection with English law, the choice could not seriously be taken, and emphasised that connection with English law was not as a matter of principle essential. See also per Lord Atkin in *R v International Trustee* [1937] AC 500; and per Lord Diplock in *Co Tunisienne de Navigation v Co d'Armement Maritime* [1971] AC 572, and *Amin Rasheed v Kuwait Insurance Co* [1984] 1 AC 50. See also, for certain non-life insurance contracts, Directive 88/357, art 7(1)(f).

the same law for associated transactions (such as a chain of sales of the same goods), even though the connection with the other transactions is not immediately apparent from the contract.

It is also clear from arts 1(1) and 3(3) that under the Convention (as well as under the traditional English law) a choice made by the parties remains effective even though their purpose in making it was to avoid mandatory rules of the law of the country with which the contract is most closely connected. The Convention does not adopt the French doctrine of *fraude à la loi*, under which (outside the contractual sphere) a French court will disregard connections which have been deliberately manipulated by parties for the purpose of evading the law otherwise applicable. Such a safeguard would be unintelligible in the context of a choice of law rule which gives primacy to the parties' intentions, for it would be conceptual nonsense to envisage parties attempting to evade their own intentions!

In the contractual sphere it was once argued in Dicey & Morris[43] for an English doctrine invalidating an express choice if the parties' purpose in adopting it was to evade mandatory rules of the law most closely connected with the contract, but this suggestion lacked any support from English decisions, and was eventually abandoned by Dicey's editors.[44] Such a doctrine of evasion was, however, introduced, in one limited context, by s 27(2)(a) of the (British) Unfair Contract Terms Act 1977, in relation to choices of foreign law designed to evade the mandatory controls on exemption clauses imposed by that Act. This provision is not expressly repealed by the Contracts (Applicable Law) Act 1990, but it seems incompatible with the 1980 Convention, even when account is taken of art 7(2).[45]

Like the traditional English law, the Convention contains (in art 16)[46] a proviso enabling a court to refuse to apply the foreign law otherwise applicable where its application would conflict with a stringent public policy of the forum country. Usually the public policy proviso will come into play on account of the obnoxious content of the substantive rules contained in the proper law, but it seems at least theoretically possible that the quality of an express choice may itself infringe the forum's stringent public policy. Although the question is likely to remain entirely hypothetical, there is much to be said for the view of Mann[47] that an express choice should be disregarded if the choice is absurd, capricious or wholly unreasonable, in that, not only does the contract have no, or no substantial, connection with the country whose law is chosen, but there is no sensible reason of any kind by reference to which the choice can be justified,

---

[43] See 9th ed (1973), at p 730.

[44] See 11th ed (1987), at pp 1172–3.

[45] See, further, on art 7(2) and on the 1977 Act, later in this chapter under 'Mandatory rules', pp 260–4.

[46] Article 16 provides: 'The application of a rule of the law of any country specified by this Convention may be refused only if such application is manifestly incompatible with the public policy ("ordre public") of the forum.'

[47] See FA Mann (1950) 3 ILQ 60 and 597, explaining *Vita Food Products v Unus Shipping* [1939] AC 277.

so that the only inference possible is that the choice was designed simply to hinder the determination of any litigation concerning the contract.

On this basis, a choice of any law which has a substantial connection with the contract cannot be regarded as wholly unreasonable; nor can a choice, in a transnational commercial contract, of any reasonably well-developed law of a Western country, even if the chosen law is otherwise unconnected with the contract. For in the latter case parties may reasonably choose to invoke a law whose rules are well established and easily discoverable, and which they may regard as neutral between them (including in terms of ease of access to legal advice). An example of a capricious or absurd choice might be a choice of Iranian law in a contract for the sale of goods by an English seller to a French buyer, all negotiations and performances taking or expected to take place in England or France, and there being no connection with Iran whatever, even as a contemplated place of further export of the goods. As the example indicates, the likelihood of businessmen making such a choice in normal commercial circumstances is a theoretical, rather than a realistic, possibility.

It is clear from arts 1, 4 and 19 of the Convention that the proper law, whether chosen by the parties or determined by reference to closest connection, must be the law of a country, in the sense of a territory having its own legal rules on contracts.[48] Thus one cannot choose EC law,[49] or public international law, or general principles of law recognised by civilised nations, since these do not contain a set of detailed rules of contract law.[50]

Similarly, it seems clear that parties are limited, in choosing the proper law, to the laws of countries which exist at the time of the choice, but that they cannot limit their choice to the content of a law as it exists at the time of contracting or some other specified date, and must accept subsequent changes in its substantive rules which the chosen law makes applicable to existing contracts, except insofar as such retroactive effects may infringe a stringent public policy of the forum.[51] Thus parties cannot validly choose ancient Roman law, as disclosed in Justinian's Digest. Nor can they effectively choose French law as it stands at the date of contracting; probably in this case the proviso will be disregarded, and the clause will then operate as a normal choice of French law, including subsequent changes whose recognition does not infringe the forum's

---

[48] Lord Wright's requirement in *Vita Food Products v Unus Shipping* [1939] AC 277, that an express choice must be *legal*, can be understood in the same sense.

[49] See arts 181 and 215(1) of the EC Treaty, whereby a contract between the Community and a private person is governed by its proper law, even when the dispute comes before the European Court of Justice pursuant to a jurisdiction clause.

[50] See Dicey & Morris, at pp 1218–19. Cf *Deutsche Schachtbau- und Tiefbohrgesellschaft mbH v Ras Al Khaimah National Oil Co* [1990] AC 295, CA (reversed by the House of Lords on other grounds), holding that the use of 'internationally accepted principles of law governing contractual relations' in a foreign arbitration did not prevent the enforcement of the award in England under the New York Convention on the Recognition and Enforcement of Foreign Arbitral Awards (1958) and the Arbitration Act 1975.

[51] See *R v International Trustee* [1937] AC 500, where the House of Lords gave effect to American legislation adopted in 1933, invalidating gold clauses contained in contracts concluded in 1917; and Dicey & Morris, at p 1219.

stringent public policy. Nor can they choose German law as it stood at 1 January 1933.[52]

Since art 3 refers to a choice *by the parties*, it seems probable that (as under traditional English law) the parties cannot confer on one of them a unilateral power subsequently to designate the proper law.[53] On the other hand there seems no reason why they should not be allowed to agree on a contingent substitution: for example, that a contract of loan should be governed by Swiss law, but if Swiss law should be altered so as to impose restrictions on the chargeable rate of interest, then German law should apply instead.[54]

Under the Convention (as under the traditional English law) a choice of law clause, like any other contractual term, will be void for uncertainty if the court, applying the principles of contractual interpretation contained in its own substantive law, is unable to identify 'with reasonable certainty' which law is the one that the parties intended to choose. Such a situation arose, in the view of a minority of the House of Lords, in *Co Tunisienne de Navigation v Co d'Armement Maritime*,[55] which involved a tonnage contract between a French shipowner and a Tunisian shipper for the carriage of oil between two Tunisian ports. The contract permitted the carrier to use ships owned, controlled or chartered by him, but the contract was expressed on a standard form designed for a voyage charterparty, and contained a clause choosing the law of the flag of the vessel carrying the goods. The majority in the House of Lords, relying on a finding that the parties contemplated that the carrier would, at least primarily, use his own ships, which all flew the French flag, managed to construe the choice of law clause as referring to the law of the flag of the vessels owned by the carrier, and thus to French law. If a choice of law clause is void for uncertainty, it is nonetheless probably effective to eliminate the possibility of an implied choice, so the test of closest connection will operate.

Article 3(1) explicitly accepts that a choice of law clause may select the law applicable to *a part* of the contract, rather than the whole.[56] But partial choices have been rare and should not be encouraged, since they are likely to lead to confusion or to an arbitrary imbalance between the parties' obligations. Hence it

---

[52] Apparently such clauses were commonly used during the Cold War period in trading contracts between English and East German undertakings, but disputes under the contracts in question never came before English courts or arbitrators. Probably such a clause, agreed to before German reunification in 1989, would have been wholly ineffective as a choice of law, if tested under the principles of the 1980 Convention or those of traditional English law. See Cohn, *Manual of German Law*, Vol II (2nd ed, 1971), at para 8.52.

[53] See *The Armar* [1981] 1 All ER 498, [1981] 1 WLR 207; *The Mariannina* [1983] 1 Lloyd's Rep 12; and *The Stolt Marmaro* [1985] 2 Lloyd's Rep 428. Cf Dicey & Morris, at pp 1220–22.

[54] See *The Iran Vojdan* [1984] 2 Lloyd's Rep 380; and Dicey & Morris, at pp 1220–22.

[55] [1971] AC 572.

[56] The possibility of scission was also accepted in traditional English law; see per Lord MacDermott, dissenting, in *Kahler v Midland Bank* [1950] AC 24 at 42, relying on the existence of unusual and compelling circumstances.

The Convention also seems impliedly to admit the possibility of incorporation by express reference of the terms of an enactment from one country into a contract governed by the law of another country, so as to remain unaffected by the subsequent repeal or amendment of the enactment in its country of origin. As to this practice, see Dicey & Morris, at pp 1222–3.

would be desirable that the courts should discover and respect a partial choice only where the intention to split is clear, and the scission contemplated produces intelligible results. This is unlikely to be the case unless there are in effect two severable and independent contracts (for example, to deliver beer at Hamburg in July for payment in marks there on delivery, and to deliver cocoa at Los Angeles in August for payment in dollars there on delivery), which merely for convenience have been incorporated in the same document. A similar approach seems appropriate in relation to scission by implied choice, or by closest connection under the second sentence of art 4(1).

By art 3(4), the existence and validity of the parties' consent to a choice of law clause are referred to the choice of law rules laid down by arts 8, 9 and 11, which also govern the same issues in relation to contracts as a whole and their substantive terms. The relevant issues include the conclusion of an agreement by means of offer and acceptance; the existence and effect on consent of misrepresentation or undue pressure; compliance with formalities; and individual capacity. It seems convenient to postpone consideration of the operation of arts 8, 9 and 11 in respect of choice of law clauses to be dealt with later in this chapter, along with the discussion of their more general effects, under 'The scope of the proper law', pp 247–51.

Implied choice and closest connection – generally

In the absence of an express choice, art 3 of the Convention (like the traditional English law) directs the court to consider next whether an implied choice of law by the parties can be ascertained. It is sufficient under art 3 that the parties' choice, though not expressed in the contract, is 'demonstrated with reasonable certainty by the terms of the contract or the circumstances of the case'.[57] It seems arguable that the Convention encourages the discovery of an implied choice somewhat more readily than the traditional English law, as declared by Lord Diplock, for the House of Lords, in *Amin Rasheed v Kuwait Insurance Co*,[58] since Lord Diplock required a 'necessary' implication, rather than one merely 'demonstrated with reasonable certainty'.

Broadly, however, it seems clear that the Convention agrees with the traditional English law in its post-war phase in adopting a fairly restrictive approach to the discovery of an implied choice. Some clear indication, usually arising from differences between the connected laws affecting the validity of the contract or relating to their adequacy in a supplementary role, or from the presence in the contract of a forum clause, is required to enable an implied choice to be discovered.

The Convention (like the traditional English law, in its post-war develop-

---

[57] See, similarly, Directive 88/357, art 7(1)(h), on non-life insurance contracts. Cf art 2(2) of the Hague Convention (1955) on the Law Applicable to International Sales of Goods, which requires a 'designation . . . unambiguous[ly] result[ing] from the provisions of the contract', and art 7(1) of the Hague Convention (1985) on the Law Applicable to Contracts for the International Sale of Goods, which requires a 'choice . . . clearly demonstrated by the terms of the contract and the conduct of the parties, viewed in their entirety'.

[58] [1984] 1 AC 50.

ment) accepts that in some cases there will be no choice of law, express or implied, by the parties. In that event (and also to the extent that a partial choice by the parties leaves the remaining part of the contract without a governing law), art 4(1) of the Convention selects as the proper law 'the law of the country with which [the contract] is most closely connected',[59] and art 4(2)–(4) lays down a number of rebuttable presumptions as to closest connection. The most important of these is laid down by art 4(2), in favour of the law of the country of the residence (in various senses, depending on a number of distinctions) at the time of the conclusion of the contract of the party who is to effect the performance which is characteristic of the contract.[60]

The Guiliano and Lagarde Report[61] makes clear that it is the supply of goods or services (rather than the receipt of or payment for them) which constitutes the characteristic performance, so the presumption amounts to a systematic preference for the law of the seller's, rather than the buyer's, country. By art 4(5), the presumptions as to closest connection are rebuttable by reference to 'the circumstances as a whole', and the presumption in favour of the characteristic performer's residence is excluded where such performance cannot be determined – for example, in a contract to barter guns for butter, or for the sale and lease-back of equipment.[62]

---

[59] In full, art 4(1) provides: 'To the extent that the law applicable to the contract has not been chosen in accordance with Article 3, the contract shall be governed by the law of the country with which it is most closely connected. Nevertheless, a severable part of the contract which has a closer connection with another country may by way of exception be governed by the law of that other country.'

The last sentence admits the possibility of severance between the laws of countries with which different parts of the contract are most closely connected, but it is submitted that, to prevent confusion or arbitrary imbalance between the parties' obligations, a court should carry out such a severance only where the scission contemplated would produce sensible results, and that this is unlikely to be the case unless there are in effect two independent contracts which, merely for convenience, have been incorporated in the same document.

Article 7(1)(h) of Directive 88/357, on non-life insurance, is similar to art 4(1) of the 1980 Convention.

[60] In full, art 4(2) provides: 'Subject to the provisions of paragraph 5 of this Article, it shall be presumed that the contract is most closely connected with the country where the party who is to effect the performance which is characteristic of the contract has, at the time of conclusion of the contract, his habitual residence, or, in the case of a body corporate or unincorporate, its central administration. However, if the contract is entered into in the course of that party's trade or profession, that country shall be the country in which the principal place of business is situated or, where under the terms of the contract the performance is to be effected through a place of business other than the principal place of business, the country in which that other place of business is situated.'

The reference in art 4(2) to the time of the conclusion of the contract, along with the provision by art 3(2) for an express or implied choice by an agreement concluded subsequent to the contract, confirm the rule in traditional English law (see eg *Co Tunisienne de Navigation v Co d'Armement Maritime* [1971] AC 572) that connections which come into existence after the conclusion of the contract are irrelevant except in support of an argument that there was a subsequent implied agreement to vary the proper law; an argument which will scarcely ever succeed.

[61] [1980] OJ C282 at p 20.

[62] The latter example is usefully suggested by Young [1991] LMCLQ 314 at 322–3. His further suggestion that the same applies to a distribution agreement, under which the buyer has obligations to market the goods supplied, is much more doubtful. It seems likely that the marketing activities of the distributor should be regarded as characteristic of the contract.

In the absence of both express and implied choice, the traditional English law also adopted a test of closest connection. But, unlike the reference by art 4 of the Convention to the law of the *country most closely connected*, traditional English law (as ultimately clarified in *Amin Rasheed v Kuwait Insurance Co*)[63] referred to the *law most closely connected*.[64] The difference may be important, for (as is clear from Lord Wilberforce's speech in *Amin Rasheed*) the test of *the law most closely connected* is effectively equivalent to the wide doctrine of implied choice by the parties applied by English law in the pre-war period. Before the decision of the Privy Council in *Bonython v Australia*,[65] the English courts had long spoken simply in terms of intention, express or implied.[66] Under the earlier law it was conclusively presumed that the parties to a transnational contract had at least impliedly agreed on the governing law, and the only problem (in the absence of express choice) was to identify the law which should be taken to have been impliedly chosen. After *Bonython* it became accepted that in some cases no intention could be ascribed to the parties, and recourse must then be had to a test of closest connection, but the focus ultimately established on the law, rather than the country, most closely connected finally restored the wider doctrine of implied choice under a pseudonym.

A test of closest connection supposedly avoids the legal fiction of ascribing to the parties an intention which in fact they never formed, and its introduction paralleled similar developments in the English domestic law of contract; for example, in the doctrine of frustration. But in truth it is wholly misleading to regard the doctrine of implied, or even express, choice as subjective. In *Vita Food Products v Unus Shipping*[67] the real reason for the presence of the English law clause in the contract may well have been that a drunken captain inadvertently used an obsolete form, but of course (save in the most exceptional circumstances, amounting to non est factum) such facts are entirely irrelevant, the parties being conclusively taken to have deliberately adopted the terms of the document used. Similarly in the case of implied choice, evidence of what the parties actually had in mind is totally irrelevant and inadmissible. An implied choice is discovered by inference from what the parties said or wrote in

---

[63] [1984] 1 AC 50.

[64] For a time it was doubtful under English law whether one should search for the law, or for the country, with which the contract was most closely connected. In *Bonython v Australia* [1951] AC 201, Lord Simonds referred to the law most closely connected, but in *Re United Railways of Havana* [1961] AC 1007, Lord Denning referred to the country most closely connected. Subsequently Lord Denning adopted the opposite view in *Miller v Whitworth* [1970] AC 583, endorsing McNair J's preference in *Rossano v Manufacturers' Life Insurance Co Ltd* [1963] 2 QB 352 for the law most closely connected. Then when *Miller v Whitworth* went to the House of Lords, [1970] AC 583, Lord Hodson proposed a combined reference to the country and law most closely connected. Eventually in *Amin Rasheed v Kuwait Insurance Co* [1984] 1 AC 50, the House of Lords unequivocally resolved the controversy in favour of the law most closely connected, and, as Lord Wilberforce's speech demonstrates, this amounted to the wide, pre-war, test of implied intention wearing a modern, if unattractive, disguise. See Stone [1984] 3 LMCLQ 438.

[65] [1951] AC 201.

[66] See eg *R v International Trustee* [1937] AC 500.

[67] [1939] AC 277.

concluding the contract, considered in the light of circumstances then existing and known to, and contingent events expected by, both of them.

The advantage of the law impliedly chosen by the parties (as such, or disguised as the law most closely connected) over the country most closely connected is that the former gives perspective to the inquiry. One asks what hypothetical sensible persons, concluding this contract, would have agreed on had they considered the question, with such knowledge of the surrounding circumstances, and such expectations as to future events, as were at the conclusion of the contract actually shared by the real parties, and with such knowledge as to the content of the connected laws as could then have been obtained by reasonable inquiry of competent lawyers practising in the relevant countries. On this basis one seeks a law suitable for the contract actually concluded: a law which will uphold its validity and provide detailed supplementary rules to solve problems not specifically regulated by its terms. It is difficult to see any other perspective which can offer any useful way of evaluating the importance of the various connections. Unfortunately the reference to the *country most closely connected*, in art 4 of the Convention, seems designed to discourage courts from adopting the appropriate perspective, while offering no other overall perspective, except such as can be inferred from a group of rebuttable, rather arbitrary, and incomplete presumptions. Hopefully the English courts at least will feel able to construe the reference in art 4 to the law of the country most closely connected as substantially according with the traditional English approach.[68]

The use by art 4 of presumptions as to closest connection also conflicts with the English experience that presumptions were of little value in this context. After an earlier flirtation with various conflicting presumptions, by the end of the 19th century English law had been led by experience to abandon the attempt to use rebuttable presumptions, based on such factors as the place of contracting, the place of performance, or, in contracts of affreightment, the flag of the ship carrying the goods. However some 'guidelines of common sense and last resort' remained discernible for use in cases where, after evaluating the connections as a whole without the aid of any presumption, no other implied choice or closest connection emerged.

Again it is submitted that the Convention represents a backward step in this matter. Systematic preference for the law of the supplier's country seems essentially arbitrary. Moreover it is not even likely to achieve certainty, predictability and uniformity of results regardless of forum, since it operates only by way of a rebuttable presumption of uncertain strength, which gives way, not only to a choice of law clause, but also to the discovery of an implied choice of law or a more closely connected country. It seems not unlikely that in many cases courts of the supplier's country will follow the presumption, while on similar facts

---

[68] Cf Young [1991] LMCLQ 314 at 321, who considers it difficult to discern a clear trend in the traditional English case-law placing greater emphasis on the internal features of the contract (such as its terminology) than on such connections as the residences of the parties.

courts of the recipient's country will find an implied choice or closest connection displacing the presumption in favour of their own law.[69]

Implied choice and closest connection – particular factors

Validation and supplementation

Validation is probably the strongest indicator of an implied choice under art 3 of the Convention, as under the traditional English law. It has long been recognised that parties should be taken to have chosen a connected law which accepts the validity of the whole of the contract, in preference to one which would invalidate the contract or a term. A long line of English case-law emphasises this factor[70] or at least reaches results consistent with it.[71] Occasionally an English court has discounted this factor on the ground that the parties were unaware of the invalidating rule,[72] but such an objection seems unprincipled. A few English decisions have allowed the factor of validation to be outweighed by a cluster of connections, including a forum clause, with the invalidating law,[73] but this approach was eventually criticised by Lord Wilberforce in *Co Tunisienne de Navigation v Co d'Armement Maritime*.[74]

Akin to the feature of validation is that of adequate supplementary content. As the House of Lords recognised in *Amin Rasheed v Kuwait Insurance Co*,[75] especially in the case of a highly technical contract embodied in an elaborate standard form, parties should be taken to have chosen a connected law which is familiar with the type of contract, and contains well-established detailed rules for interpreting and supplementing its express terms, rather than another connected law whose rules for such contracts, as they stand at the time of contracting, are a matter for the broadest speculation. Thus, although the use of a standard form of English origin is not in itself an important connection with English law if the form has become commonly used in transactions otherwise unconnected with England,[76] it is otherwise if at the time of contracting the other potentially applicable law lacks any detailed rules for interpreting the

---

[69] Young [1991] LMCLQ 314 at 323 argues that the presumptions laid down by art 4 are so weak that they will only operate as a 'tie-breaker', providing a solution where the connections with various countries would otherwise be regarded as equal. If this is so, their value (as well as their potential for harm) will be almost negligible.

[70] See, for example, *Peninsular Line v Shand* (1865) 16 ER 103, and *Re Missouri Steamship Co* (1889) 42 ChD 321, on the validity of exemption clauses; and *Hamlyn v Talisker Distillery* [1894] AC 202, and *Spurrier v La Cloche* [1902] AC 445, on the validity of arbitration clauses.

[71] See *Sayers v International Drilling* [1971] 3 All ER 163, and *Coast Lines v Hudig & Veder* [1972] 2 QB 34.

[72] See *British South Africa Co v De Beers* [1910] 2 Ch 502, CA, which involved the English rule against clogging the equity of redemption. Eventually the House of Lords upheld the contract on a narrower interpretation of the English domestic rule: [1912] AC 52.

[73] See *Royal Exchange Assurance v Vega* [1902] 2 KB 384, CA, and *Maritime Insurance v Assecuranz* (1935) 52 LILR 16. Both cases involved English rules invalidating marine insurance policies.

[74] [1971] AC 572 at 598.

[75] [1984] 1 AC 50.

[76] See *The Adriatic* [1931] P 241, *Co Tunisienne de Navigation v Co d'Armement Maritime* [1971] AC 572, and *Coast Lines v Hudig & Veder* [1972] 2 QB 34. Earlier decisions to the contrary, such as *The Industrie* [1894] P 58, are now obsolete.

contract. Such was the situation in *Amin Rasheed*, where a marine insurance policy, in a standard form of English origin, was issued by a Kuwaiti insurance company in favour of a Liberian company in respect of a vessel trading in the Persian Gulf. Since at the time of contracting Kuwait law lacked any detailed rules on marine insurance, and its Commercial Code merely provided for the court to decide in accordance with custom and equity, the House of Lords (per Lord Diplock) held that in these circumstances the use of the form of English origin necessarily implied a choice of English law.

The use of a standard form is also a strong indication of an implied choice of the law of its country of origin if the form had previously been used only in contracts of an internal character, as in *Miller v Whitworth*,[77] where a standard form which had hitherto been used only for building work to be performed in England was in the instant case used for a construction contract between a Scottish builder and the English owner of premises in Scotland.

Forum clauses

Under the Convention, as under the traditional law, a forum clause constitutes a very strong indication of an implied choice of the law of the chosen forum as the proper law of the contract. 'Forum clause' means a clause specifying a court which is to have jurisdiction over disputes arising from the contract, or a clause which provides for such disputes to be determined by arbitration, and either specifies the place where the arbitration proceedings are to be held, or otherwise indicates the procedural law which is to be used in the arbitration proceedings (for example, by providing for arbitration in accordance with the (English) Arbitration Act 1950).[78]

As regards weight, in *Co Tunisienne de Navigation v Co d'Armement Maritime*,[79] the House of Lords indicated that a forum clause gives way to the factor

---

[77] [1970] AC 583.

[78] An arbitration clause which gives no indication of either the place or the method of arbitration is obviously no indication of any proper law; see *Miller v Whitworth* [1970] AC 583. Somewhat similarly, little weight attaches to a clause which merely gives one of the parties an option to sue in a specified court, as in *The Stolt Marmaro* [1985] 2 Lloyd's Rep 428.

[79] [1971] AC 572. The case involved a tonnage contract between a French shipowner and a Tunisian shipper for the carriage of a specified quantity of oil between two Tunisian ports over a specified period. It was expressed on an inappropriate standard form of English origin, designed for a voyage charterparty, but no vessel was named, and it was specified instead that the carriage should be effected in vessels owned, controlled or chartered by the carrier. The form contained a clause purporting to choose the law of the flag of the vessel carrying the goods, and also a London arbitration clause. There was no difference between French and Tunisian laws in relation to carriage by sea, but both differed in some respects from English law.

The House of Lords held unanimously that the proper law of the contract was French law. The majority (Lords Morris, Dilhorne and Diplock) construed the choice of law clause as referring to French law, since the parties had contemplated that, at least primarily, the carrier would use his own vessels, all of which flew the French flag. It was irrelevant that he actually used a number of chartered ships, flying a picturesque variety of flags, since his own ships proved to be too small for the purpose, for conduct subsequent to the conclusion of the contract could only be taken into account when it amounted to a new contract or gave rise to an estoppel. The minority (Lords Reid and Wilberforce) held the flag clause to be meaningless and inapplicable in the circumstances, but nonetheless held that the proper law was French law.

of validation,[80] and also gives way if all other substantial connections are with a single other country and law[81] (or possibly with several countries whose laws in the relevant sphere are identical); but otherwise, in the absence of a choice of law clause, the law indicated by a forum clause will become the proper law.[82] For this purpose the residence of a party is always a substantial connection, so that if (as in *Tzortzis v Monark Line*)[83] the parties reside in different countries, a forum clause will be decisive, whether it chooses a forum belonging to one of those countries or (as in *Tzortzis*) a neutral forum in a third country. Insubstantial connections include the use of an 'internationalised' standard form, the language in which the contract is expressed, and the currency of account or payment. It is probable that the Convention contemplates a similar approach.

Related contracts

In some cases the fact that a contract is ancillary to another contract (whether between the same or different parties) may justify the inference of an implied choice, subjecting the ancillary contract to the same law as governs the principal contract. Such an implication is likely in the case of a guarantee,[84] but not in the case of a letter of credit or a performance bond.[85]

In addition weight may be sometimes attached to the fact that a contract is one of a group of similar contracts between one party (for example, as employer or principal) and numerous others (for example, as employees or agents). This factor tends towards the law of the residence of the party common to all the similar contracts.[86]

The characteristic performer's residence

Where there is no express or implied choice, art 4(1) of the 1980 Convention applies as the proper law the law of the country with which the contract is most closely connected, and art 4(2)–(4) provides a number of presumptions as to closest connection. Article 4(5) makes it clear that these presumptions are

---

[80] See per Lord Wilberforce at 598, disapproving *Maritime Insurance v Assecuranz* (1935) 52 LILR 16.

[81] Cf art 3(3) of the 1980 Convention.

[82] The House of Lords disapproved earlier indications (in *Kwik Hoo Tong v Finlay* [1927] AC 604, and *Tzortzis v Monark Line* [1968] 1 WLR 406) that a forum clause should be given even greater weight.

[83] [1968] 1 WLR 406.

[84] See *Broken Hill Pty v Xenakis* [1982] 2 Lloyd's Rep 304.

[85] See *Attock Cement v Romanian Bank for Foreign Trade* [1989] 1 WLR 1147, [1989] 1 All ER 1189, CA.

[86] See *Sayers v International Drilling* [1971] 3 All ER 163, CA, and *Mercury Publicity v Loerke* [1993] ILPR 142, CA.

CONTRACTS

incomplete and rebuttable: '[Article 4(2)] shall not apply if the characteristic performance cannot be determined, and the presumptions in [art 4(2)–(4)] shall be disregarded if it appears from the circumstances as a whole that the contract is more closely connected with another country.' It is far from clear how strong the presumptions are intended to be, how easily they can be rebutted.

The main presumption, laid down by art 4(2),[87] is in favour of the law of the country of the relevant residence of the characteristic performer at the time of contracting. The relevant residence of the characteristic performer is elaborately defined:

> in general, in the case of an individual, one looks to his habitual residence;
> in general, in the case of a company or association, one looks to its central administration;
> but if the characteristic performer enters into the contract in the course of his trade or profession, one looks to his principal place of business, unless the contract requires his characteristic performance to be effected through another of his places of business;
> and if the characteristic performer enters into the contract in the course of his trade or profession, and the contract requires his characteristic performance to be effected through one of his places of business other than his principal place of business, one looks to his secondary place of business through which the contract requires his characteristic performance to be effected.

However, in view of the merely presumptive character of the reference to the characteristic performer's residence, the precise definition of his relevant residence is probably of little real significance. Moreover, it seems that under the Convention, as under the traditional English law, where one of the parties is a public authority, its residence has no more, but no less, importance than the relevant residence of a private entity would have had if the entity had occupied the same contractual position.

It is clear from the Guiliano and Lagarde Report[88] (though not from the text of the Convention itself)[89] that it is the supply of goods or services, rather than

---

[87] In full, art 4(2) provides: 'Subject to the provisions of [art 4(5)], it shall be presumed that the contract is most closely connected with the country where the party who is to effect the performance which is characteristic of the contract has, at the time of conclusion of the contract, his habitual residence, or, in the case of a body corporate or unincorporate, its central administration. However, if the contract is entered into in the course of that party's trade or profession, that country shall be the country in which the principal place of business is situated or, where under the terms of the contract the performance is to be effected through a place of business other than the principal place of business, the country in which that other place of business is situated.'

In view of the explicit reference in art 4(2) to residence 'at the time of conclusion of the contract', the assertion in the Guiliano and Lagarde Report (at p 20) that, in determining the closest connection, account may be taken of factors which supervened after the conclusion of the contract, is puzzling. Such an approach would disappoint expectations and cause arbitrary results, as well as contradicting the traditional English rules.

[88] See at p 20.

[89] See Lasok & Stone, pp 362–3.

the receipt of or payment for them, which constitutes the characteristic performance, so the presumption amounts to an arbitrary preference, of uncertain strength,[90] for the law of the seller or other supplier's country.[91] In contrast, a contract to barter guns for butter, or hotel accommodation for advertising, will lack any determinable characteristic performance, and thus under art 4(5) there will be no available presumption.

The presumption in favour of the supplier's residence does not apply to certain types of contract:

- contracts relating to land, for which art 4(3) provides a presumption in favour of the lex situs;
- contracts of carriage of goods, for which art 4(4) provides a more limited presumption in favour of the carrier's residence;
- 'protected' consumer contracts, governed by art 5; and
- contracts of employment, governed by art 6.

Although traditional English law (as ultimately developed) had abandoned presumptions in this sphere, some guidelines of common sense and last resort, applicable where no other persuasive solution is apparent, can be discerned from the English case-law. Thus, in substantial accord with art 4(2), where the parties were resident in the same country at the conclusion of the contract, the English case-law would, as a guideline of last resort, apply the law of the common residence, even if the principal place of performance were elsewhere.[92] But where the parties resided in different countries, the traditional English guideline of last resort would look to the place of principal performance,

---

[90] Contrast the firm rules laid down by the Hague Convention of 15 June 1955 on the Law Applicable to International Sales of Goods (1952) 1 AJCL 275, to which France, Italy, Belgium, Denmark, Norway, Sweden, Finland, Switzerland, and Niger (but not the United Kingdom) are parties. By art 3, in the absence of express or implied choice by the parties, and subject to certain specified exceptions, a sale is governed by the law of the country where the vendor has his habitual residence at the time when he receives the order; or if the order is received by a branch office of the vendor, by the law of the country where such branch is located. By way of exception, a sale is governed by the law of the country in which the buyer has his habitual residence, or has the branch which gives the order, if the order is received in that country by the seller or his agent or other representative; and a sale at an exchange or a public auction is governed by the law of the country where the exchange is located or the auction takes place.

[91] A similar but more elaborate approach is adopted by the Hague Convention of 30 October 1985 on the Law Applicable to Contracts for the International Sale of Goods (1985) 24 ILM 1573, which has not yet entered into force. In the absence of express or implied choice by the parties, art 8 lays down rebuttable presumptions, generally in favour of the law of the seller's place of business; but in favour of the law of the buyer's place of business if the contract was negotiated and concluded between parties present there, or expressly requires delivery there, or resulted from a call for tenders by the buyer. However the presumptions give way where another law is 'manifestly more closely connected' with the contract, having regard to the circumstances as a whole, including any business relationships between the parties. But in the case of auction sales and sales on a commodity or other exchange, art 9 permits party choice only to the extent that the law of the place of the auction or exchange permits, and otherwise applies that law.

[92] See *Jacobs Marcus v Credit Lyonnais* (1884) 12 QBD 589, and *Zivnostenska Bank v Frankman* [1950] AC 57.

rather than the residence of the principal or characteristic performer, if they differed.[93] Often, however, they would concur.[94] The one clear advantage possessed by the Convention's reference to residence is that it avoids difficulties arising from the uncertain or multiple character which may be possessed by the place of (even principal or characteristic) performance as such.[95]

Contracts for the carriage of goods (including single voyage charter-parties and other contracts whose main purpose is the carriage of goods) are governed by art 4(4), which excludes the general presumption in favour of the character-istic performer's residence arising from art 4(2), and offers a presumption in favour of the law of the country of the carrier's principal place of business at the time the contract is concluded, but only if it is also the country in which either the place of loading, or the place of discharge, or the principal place of business of the consignor is situated. In the absence of any such concurrence, no pre-sumption applies. The traditional English guideline of last resort for a contract for the carriage of goods by sea, between parties resident in different countries, referred to the law of the flag of the vessel involved.[96]

Contracts concerning land

By art 4(3), to the extent that the subject-matter of the contract is a right in, or a right to use, immovable property, there is a presumption in favour of the lex

[93] See *R v International Trustee* [1937] AC 500, applying New York law to a dollar loan which was raised by the British government from the American public through a New York issuing house in 1917, and which was repayable and secured in New York; *Re United Railways of Havana* [1961] AC 1007, applying Pennsylvanian law to dollar-denominated debentures issued by an English company, which ran a railway in Cuba, to raise funds for the purchase of rolling-stock; the debentures were issued through a New York issuing house, but the trustee was a Pennsyl-vanian company and the principal sum was repayable in Pennsylvania; and *Power Curber v National Bank of Kuwait* [1981] 1 WLR 1233, holding that a bank's letter of credit is normally governed by the law of the place of payment against documents, even if the bank is not resident there.

[94] As in *Chatenay v Brazilian Submarine Telegraph Co* [1891] 1 QB 79, involving a contract of agency; in *Benaim v Debono* [1924] AC 514, involving an fob sale; and in *Hewden Stuart v Gottwald*, 13 May 1992, which involved a contract between a German company and an English company, whereby a German company undertook to redesign in Germany, and there to manu-facture and supply ex-works the redesigned parts for, a crane which it had earlier manufactured and supplied. Although it also undertook to test the crane in England after reassembly by the English purchaser, the Court of Appeal held that the proper law was German law, emphasising the place of principal performance.

The limited force of the guideline is illustrated by *Mercury Publicity v Loerke* [1993] ILPR 142, where the Court of Appeal considered that, in the case of a contract granting exclusive rights to canvass for advertisements to be published in a newspaper, the fact that in negotiating the contract the agent had come to the principal's place of business, leaving the area in which the agent himself resided and in which he intended to operate his agency, was a factor in favour of the law of the country where the principal had his place of business and the contract was made, as was the fact that the contract was one of 15 similar contracts between the principal and other agents in various countries with different systems of law.

[95] For an example of multiple places of performance, see *Bonython v Australia* [1951] AC 201, applying Queensland law to debentures issued by the Queensland government in respect of a loan, over half of which was raised in London, the rest being raised in Australia. The holders had the option of repayment in any of three Australian cities or in London.

[96] See *Lloyd v Guibert* (1865) LR 1 QB 115; *The Assunzione* [1954] P 150; and *Coast Lines v Hudig & Veder* [1972] 2 QB 34.

situs. A similar English guideline of last resort existed in the case of a contract for the transfer or creation of an interest in land if the parties were resident in different countries.[97] But if the parties resided in the same country, the law of the common residence was likely to be preferred to the lex situs,[98] and in such circumstances it is not unlikely that the presumption under art 4(3) will be found to be rebutted.

THE SCOPE OF THE PROPER LAW

Under the 1980 Convention, as under the traditional English law, most issues relating to a contract are usually governed by its proper law. Thus art 8(1) provides that '[t]he existence and validity of a contract, or of any term of a contract, shall be determined by the law which would govern it under this Convention if the contract or term were valid', and art 9 makes it sufficient for a contract to satisfy the formal requirements of the proper law. By art 10(1), the proper law governs 'in particular: (a) interpretation; (b) performance; (c) within the limits of the powers conferred on the court by its procedural law, the consequences of breach, including the assessment of damages in so far as it is governed by rules of law; and (d) the various ways of extinguishing obligations, and prescription and limitation of actions'. In addition, by art 14(1) the proper law applies to the extent that it contains, in the law of contract, rules which raise presumptions of law or determine the burden of proof.

However the Convention specifies various exceptions where a given type of issue is affected by a law other than the proper law. Thus the various types of issue will now be considered in turn. All the rules now considered must be read subject to the exceptions made by arts 3(3), 7 and 16, in relation to mandatory rules or public policy, which will be examined subsequently.

Essential validity and formation

Article 8(1) of the 1980 Convention lays down a general rule that the existence and validity of a contract, or of any term of a contract, must be determined by the law which would govern it under the Convention if the contract or term were valid. This may conveniently be referred to as the putative proper law.[99]

As regards essential validity, art 8(1) accords with the traditional English case-law, which has applied the (putative) proper law both in relation to questions involving the essential validity of the contract as a whole (for example,

---

[97] See *Mount Albert BC v Australasian Life Insurance Soc* [1938] AC 224, applying New Zealand law to debentures issued by a New Zealand local authority in favour of a Victorian company carrying on business in Australia and New Zealand. The loan was repayable in Victoria, but was charged on the rateable land in the borrower's district.

[98] See *Re Courtney* [1835–42] All ER Rep 415; *British South Africa Co v De Beers Consolidated Mines* [1910] 2 Ch 502 (reversed on other grounds, [1912] AC 52); *Mercantile Investment Co v River Plate Co* [1892] 2 Ch 303; *Re Smith* [1916] 2 Ch 206; and *Re Anchor Line* [1937] 1 Ch 483.

[99] See Dicey & Morris, Rule 178.

so as to uphold a contract unsupported by consideration,[100] or to invalidate a contract for infringement of exchange restrictions),[101] and in relation to the validity of particular terms (for instance: exemption clauses,[102] clauses which restrict competition,[103] no-challenge clauses in respect of registered trade-marks,[104] clauses fixing rates of interest,[105] and gold value clauses).[106] However it is in relation to essential validity that the provisos in favour of the forum's mandatory rules and its stringent public policy, under arts 7(2) and 16 of the Convention, have most importance, and amount to major derogations from the operation of the proper law.[107]

Article 8(1) extends to formation, so that in general (and, again, in accordance with the traditional English law)[108] the putative proper law determines such issues as the existence of a sufficient offer and acceptance or other formative acts,[109] and whether a party's consent is invalidated by mistake, misrepresentation, non-disclosure or improper pressure. Thus in general the putative proper law determines whether a contract has been validly formed by a sufficient offer and acceptance: for example if the letter of acceptance is lost in the post;[110] or if an offer, expressed to remain open for a specified time, is purportedly accepted during that time despite an intervening attempted revocation; or if an offeror remains silent in the face of a purported acceptance which attempts to vary the terms of the original offer. Again the putative proper law in general determines the effect of non-fraudulent misrepresentation or failure to disclose material facts,[111] or of economic pressure,[112] though a stringent English policy may well be invoked under art 16 against a foreign rule which denies relief against non-economic pressure or fraud.[113]

However in relation to formation art 8(2) provides a sensible exception to art

---

[100] See *Re Bonacina* [1912] 2 Ch 394, involving an Italian promise to pay a debt which had been released by bankruptcy.
[101] See *Kahler v Midland Bank* [1950] AC 24 and *Zivnostenska Bank v Frankman* [1950] AC 57.
[102] See *Peninsular Line v Shand* (1865) 16 ER 103; *Re Missouri Steamship Co* (1889) 42 ChD 321; *Vita Food Products v Unus Shipping* [1939] AC 277; *Sayers v International Drilling* [1971] 3 All ER 163; and *Coast Lines v Hudig & Veder* [1972] 2 QB 34.
[103] *Apple Corps Ltd v Apple Computer Inc* [1992] FSR 431; *South African Breweries Ltd v King* [1900] 1 Ch 273. Cf *Rousillon v Rousillon* (1880) 14 ChD 351, on respect for mandatory rules of the lex fori.
[104] *Apple Corps Ltd v Apple Computer Inc* [1992] FSR 431.
[105] See *Mount Albert BC v Australasian Life Ins Soc* [1938] AC 224.
[106] See *R v International Trustee* [1937] AC 500.
[107] On these provisos, see under 'Public policy and mandatory rules', pp 256–66 below.
[108] See Dicey & Morris, Rule 178. Cf Jaffey (1975) 24 ICLQ 603.
[109] See *Albeko v Kamborian Shoe Machine Co* (1961) 111 LJ 519; *The Parouth* [1982] 2 Lloyd's Rep 351, CA; and *Union Transport v Continental Lines* [1992] 1 WLR 15, HL.
[110] See *Albeko v Kamborian Shoe Machine Co* (1961) 111 LJ 519.
[111] See *Mackender v Feldia* [1967] 2 QB 590.
[112] See *Trendtex v Crédit Suisse* [1982] AC 679; and *Dimskal Shipping Co v International Transport Workers Federation, The Evia Luck* [1992] 2 AC 152, where a majority of the House of Lords (per Lord Goff; with Lord Templeman dissenting) applied English law, as the expressly chosen proper law of a contract concluded by foreigners abroad, to allow avoidance of a contract concluded under economic pressure (by way of 'blacking' in the context of an industrial dispute) which was legitimate under the law of the country, Sweden, where it was exerted.
[113] See *Kaufman v Gerson* [1904] 1 KB 591, and *Mackender v Feldia* [1967] 2 QB 590.

8(1), by enabling a party to rely on the law of his habitual residence to establish that he did not consent, if it appears from the circumstances that it would not be reasonable to determine the effect of his conduct in accordance with the putative proper law.[114] This would probably apply where, for example, an English resident ignores an offer (or counter-offer) received from abroad and governed by a foreign law under which silence is treated as consent. Presumably (by analogy with art 4(2)) the reference to habitual residence should be construed, in the case of a party (especially a company) acting in the course of business, as referring to his place of business whose staff were engaged in the relevant negotiations; and in the case of a company or unincorporated body not acting in the course of business, to its central administration.

Article 8 of the Convention is extended by art 3(4) so as to cover the existence and essential validity of the parties' consent to an express or implied choice of the applicable law. Thus (subject to the proviso by art 8(2) in favour of a party's habitual residence) the law specified in a choice of law clause will determine whether the choice of law clause itself was agreed to by means of sufficient acts of offer and acceptance, and whether a party's consent to that clause was invalidated by factors such as misrepresentation. Then, if the choice of law clause is valid under the law which it specifies, that law will also determine whether the substantive contract as a whole, and each of its particular substantive terms, are valid in the same respects. While logical objections could be made to such a 'boot-strap' approach, it is thought that the solution adopted is sufficiently intelligible, and that the proviso in art 8(2) should be adequate to protect the legitimate expectations of a party who denies having agreed to a choice of law clause invoked by the other party.[115]

Formal validity

By art 9(1)–(3) of the 1980 Convention, a contract is formally valid if it satisfies either the formal requirements of either:

(1)   its proper law; or
(2)   the law of the country where it was concluded; or
(3)   where it was concluded between persons (or agents) who were in different countries, the law of one of those countries.

This rule of alternative reference reflects a policy of facilitating the conclusion of

---

[114] In traditional English law such an exception was supported by commentators such as Wolff, *Private International Law* (2nd ed, 1950), at p 439, and Dicey & Morris (11th ed, 1987), at pp 1198–201, but had not been specifically considered by the courts.

[115] Dicey & Morris, at p 1251, raise the problem of negotiations involving a 'battle of forms', each containing a different choice of law clause. In this situation the proper course, in the view of the present writer, is first to determine whether there is a contract on the terms of the first-issued form, taking into account its choice of law clause in accordance with arts 3(4) and 8; and then whether there is (also) a contract on the terms of the second-issued form, taking similar account of its choice of law clause. If one concludes thereby that there are two mutually inconsistent contracts, the later-formed contract supersedes the earlier to the extent of the inconsistency.

transactions, and accords with or (as regards the last alternative) develops the traditional English law.[116]

By art 14(2), a contract may be proved by any mode of proof which is recognised by the law of the forum or by any of the laws which is referred to in art 9 and under which the contract is formally valid, provided that such mode of proof can be administered by the forum. This deals with the problem raised by the procedural characterisation by traditional English law of the (English) Statute of Frauds 1677, which now requires written evidence of a contract to guarantee a liability of a third party. By procedural characterisation, the Statute of Frauds had been made applicable in English actions involving contracts concluded abroad and governed by foreign law.[117] The Convention, while not interfering directly with such procedural characterisation, overrides its effect, by requiring the acceptance of oral evidence in accordance with a foreign proper law or lex loci actus which upholds the formal validity of the contract.

By way of exception to the general rules on formal validity,[118] art 9(6) of the 1980 Convention subjects a contract whose subject-matter is a right in or a right to use immovable property to the mandatory formal requirements of the law of the country where the property is situated, if by that law those requirements are imposed irrespective of the country where the contract is concluded and of its proper law. Probably such mandatory requirements include those now imposed by s 2 of the (English) Law of Property (Miscellaneous Provisions) Act 1989,[119] under which a contract for the sale or other disposition of an interest in land can only be made in writing complying with the section, since the section should probably be construed as designed to apply to contracts for the disposition of English land, even when concluded abroad and governed by foreign law.

Capacity

Capacity to contract is largely excluded from the scope of the 1980 Convention by art 1(2)(a) and (e).[120] There is merely a provision, by art 11, that '[i]n a contract concluded between persons who are in the same country, [an individual] who would have capacity under the law of that country may invoke his incapacity resulting from another law only if the other party to the contract was aware of this incapacity at the time of the conclusion of the contract or was not aware thereof as a result of negligence'. This reflects an exception invented by French case-law in

---

[116] See *Guépratte v Young* (1851) 4 De G & Sm 217, and *Van Grutten v Digby* (1862) 31 Beav 561. Similar provision to art 9 of the 1980 Convention is made by art 11 of the Hague Convention (1985) on the Law Applicable to Contracts for the International Sale of Goods.

[117] See *Leroux v Brown* (1852) 12 CB 801.

[118] For another exception, relating to 'protected' consumer contracts, see art 9(5), considered under 'Protected consumer contracts', pp 266–70 below.

[119] This replaces s 40 of the Law of Property Act 1925, which required written evidence (or part performance) of a contract for the disposition of land.

[120] Article 1(2)(a) refers to 'questions involving the status or legal capacity of natural persons', and art 1(2)(e) to 'questions governed by the law of companies and other bodies corporate or unincorporate such as the creation, by registration or otherwise, legal capacity, internal organisation or winding up of companies and other bodies corporate or unincorporate and the personal liability of officers and members as such for the obligations of the company or body'.

1861[121] to a general rule referring capacity to the law of the nationality of the person whose capacity is at issue. In view of the general rules of English law, the exception created by art 11 is of minor importance.

Under English law, there is a special rule for capacity to enter into a marriage settlement, a type of transaction wholly excluded from the 1980 Convention by art 1(2)(b), whereby each party's capacity is governed by the law of his or her domicile.[122] English law also has a special rule for contracts for the disposition of land, whereby capacity is governed by the lex situs.[123]

In the case of other contracts, it is probably sufficient under English law for the parties (whether individual or corporate) to have capacity under the proper law of the contract, ascertained in the normal way and thus with full account taken of even an express choice by the parties.[124] This reflects a desire to respect the expectations of the undoubtedly capable party, and to facilitate international trade, in which incapacitating rules are viewed as a tiresome nuisance, which a person should be permitted to avoid by contemplating a different law. It is probably alternatively sufficient, if an individual lacks capacity under the proper law, for him to have capacity by the law of his domicile;[125] or, in the case of a company, for it to have capacity under the law of its country of incorporation.[126] The rationale for this alternative reference to the personal law is that there is no need to be more royalist than the Queen: incapacities are presumably imposed in order to protect immature, weak-minded or otherwise inadequate persons (or corporate members), and only the personal law can have an interest in imposing protection sufficient to justify burdening international commerce. Insofar as an issue, such as capacity, is excluded from the scope of the Convention, but is referred by the traditional English conflict rules to the proper law, it seems clear that the reference must now be understood as to the proper law as determined in accordance with the Convention.[127]

Interpretation, performance and discharge

The 1980 Convention specifies, by art 10(1)(a), (b) and (d), that (in general) the proper law governs interpretation, performance, and the various ways of ex-

---

[121] See *De Lizardi v Chaise*, Sirey 61.1.305 (1861), a decision of the Chambre des Requêtes of the Court of Cassation.

[122] See *Re Cooke's Trusts* (1887) 56 LT 737; *Cooper v Cooper* (1888) 13 App Cas 88; and *Viditz v O'Hagan* [1900] 2 Ch 87.

[123] See *Bank of Africa v Cohen* [1909] 2 Ch 129.

[124] See *Male v Roberts* (1800) 3 Esp 163; *McFeetridge v Stewarts & Lloyds* 1913 SC 773; *Charron v Montreal Trust* (1958) 15 DLR(2d) 240; and especially *Bodley Head v Flegon* [1972] 1 WLR 680, which explicitly respects a choice of law clause, while assuming that the issue concerned personal capacity. Cf Dicey & Morris, Rule 181(1), referring to the law most closely connected, rather than the proper law normally ascertained; and Rule 156, insisting, without convincing reasons or authority, that a company must have capacity under both the proper law of the contract and the law of its country of incorporation.

[125] Cf Dicey & Morris, Rule 181(1), which refers to the person's domicile and residence.

[126] Cf Dicey & Morris, Rule 156, which insists, without convincing reasons or authority, that a company must have capacity under both the proper law of the contract and the law of its country of incorporation.

[127] See Young [1991] LMCLQ 314 at 318.

tinguishing obligations.[128] In addition art 14(1) specifies that the proper law also applies to the extent that it contains, in the law of contract, rules which raise presumptions of law or determine the burden of proof.[129] However some derogation from art 10(1) is made by art 10(2), which provides that, in relation to the manner of performance and the steps to be taken in the event of defective performance, regard must be had to the law of the country in which performance takes place.

The operation of the main rule applying the proper law to questions of interpretation, performance and discharge is exemplified by the decision of the Privy Council in *Mount Albert BC v Australasian Assurance Soc*,[130] where a contract of loan was governed by New Zealand law but the loan was made repayable in Victoria. Although Victorian law, the lex loci solutionis, attempted by legislation to reduce the rate of interest which the debtor needed to pay in order to discharge the debt (but without prohibiting payment of the full amount of interest as agreed), the Privy Council held that interest remained payable in full in accordance with the New Zealand proper law. Similarly it is for the proper law to determine whether a contract has been frustrated by factual difficulties in its performance arising after its conclusion;[131] and whether a contract is affected by subsequent legislation abrogating gold value clauses, or imposing a moratorium on payments, depends on whether the legislation forms part of the proper law.[132] However, as will be seen, public policy considerations may intervene where the law of the place of performance prohibits the carrying out of the agreed performance under criminal penalty,[133] or in relation to the effect on contracts of the outbreak of a war involving the United Kingdom.[134]

Again it is for the proper law to resolve ambiguities such as arise where a contract specifies the money of account (in which a debt is measured) by means of a name (such as pounds, dollars or francs) which is capable of referring to the currencies of several countries; though it by no means follows that the proper law will resolve the ambiguity in favour of its own currency, even if that is one of those so named.[135] However, once it is established from the express terms of the contract or from its interpretation under the proper law that a debt is measured in (say) Canadian dollars, it will be for the law of the currency (in this case, Canadian law) to supply the definition of the tokens which represent units of its currency;[136] this may be regarded as a splitting of the proper law by implied

---

[128] See Dicey & Morris, Rule 180.
[129] For a similar approach in traditional English law, see *Re Cohn* [1945] Ch 5.
[130] [1938] AC 224.
[131] See *Jacobs v Crédit Lyonnais* (1884) 12 QBD 589.
[132] See *R v International Trustee* [1937] AC 500, applying American legislation abrogating gold-value clauses to a contract governed by New York law; and *National Bank of Greece and Athens v Metliss* [1958] AC 509, and *Adams v National Bank of Greece and Athens* [1961] AC 255, holding English contracts unaffected by Greek moratoria.
[133] See under 'Criminal prohibition by the law of the place of performance', pp 258–60 below.
[134] See *Ertel Bieber v Rio Tinto* [1918] AC 260.
[135] See eg *Bonython v Australia* [1951] AC 201.
[136] See eg *Pyrmont v Schott* [1939] AC 145.

choice under art 3 of the 1980 Convention. On the other hand, the Convention probably does not alter the rather mean-spirited approach under traditional English law,[137] whereby it is the 'main' proper law, rather than the law of the currency of account, which determines whether a debt should be increased by way of revalorisation after a currency collapse. It is also for the proper law to determine by interpretation the respective obligations of the parties to a contract of sale in relation to the obtaining of any necessary export licence, if the contract is silent on the point.[138]

The proviso by art 10(2), requiring the law of the place of performance to be taken into account in relation to the manner of performance and the steps to be taken in the event of defective performance, seems to reflect Lord Wright's remark in *Mount Albert* that the law of the place of performance may regulate the minor details of performance, but not so as to affect the substance of the obligation. It is presumably based on the supposed intention of the parties, and no doubt applies to such questions as what are normal business hours, within which delivery should be effected under a contract of sale.[139] Some further light on the scope of art 10(2) may be found in the Hague Conventions, 1955 and 1985, on the sale of goods.[140] In the absence of express contrary agreement, the law of the country of inspection of goods delivered governs (under the 1955 Convention, art 4) the form of, periods for, and notifications concerning such inspection, and the measures to be taken in case of refusal of the goods; or (under the 1985 Convention, art 13) the modalities and procedural requirements for such inspection. Probably it is also for the law of the place of payment to determine whether, where a contractual debt is expressed in a currency other than that of the place of payment, the debtor has the option (in the absence of an express agreement to the contrary) of paying by means of local currency of equivalent value, instead of paying in the currency of account itself.[141]

Procedure and remedies

By art 1(2)(h), the 1980 Convention largely excludes from its scope 'evidence and procedure', thus leaving them to be governed by the lex fori in accordance with English and other traditional laws. The exclusion is explicitly made subject to art 14(1), which makes applicable rules of the proper law, contained in the law of contract, which raise presumptions of law or determine the burden of proof; and to art 14(2), which enables a contract to be proved by any mode of proof which is recognised either by the law of the forum, or by any law which is made applicable to its formal validity by art 9, and under which it is

---

[137] See *Anderson v Equitable Life* (1926) 134 LT 557.
[138] See *Pound v Hardy* [1956] AC 588.
[139] See Dicey & Morris, at p 1262.
[140] Hague Convention (1955) on the Law Applicable to International Sales of Goods, (1952) 1 AJCL 275; and Hague Convention (1985) on the Law Applicable to Contracts for the International Sale of Goods, (1985) 24 ILM 1573.
[141] See Dicey & Morris, at p 1263.

formally valid, provided that such mode of proof can be administered by the forum.[142]

The exclusion is also subject to art 10(1)(c), which specifies that, within the limits of the powers conferred on the court by its procedural law, the proper law governs the consequences of breach, including the assessment of damages insofar as it is governed by rules of law. It seems clear that the saving for limits on the forum's powers under its own procedural law will ensure that English courts will not be required to follow a foreign proper law to the length of making available non-monetary remedies, such as orders for specific performance, in circumstances where English law would limit the plaintiff to monetary remedies; for example, because specific performance would necessitate continuing judicial supervision.[143]

On the other hand, the Convention seems to encourage the application of the proper law to the greatest extent practicable in connection with the assessment of damages. It thus confirms the decision in *D'Almeida v Becker*,[144] where Pilcher J accepted that the proper law governs questions of remoteness of damage and of the admissibility of heads of damage, and accordingly applied Portuguese law to determine whether a seller could recover from his defaulting buyer a sum which the seller had had to pay as damages to his own supplier, this being an uncontemplated but direct and unavoidable consequence of the defendant's breach. No doubt the existence and extent of an innocent party's duty to mitigate his loss is also governed by the proper law. Moreover the frequent assertion by English courts that the 'mere quantification of damages' is a procedural matter governed by the lex fori must now be construed narrowly, as confined to the problem of putting a monetary value on a head of damage which the proper law admits, but for the monetary evaluation of which the proper law provides no rule which is sufficiently definite to enable it to be applied in practice by courts elsewhere. Such a situation is most likely to arise in relation to the quantification of heads such as pain and suffering in personal injury cases.

Time-limits for bringing actions

By art 10(1)(d), the Convention specifies that the proper law governs (as well as the various ways of extinguishing obligations) prescription and limitation of actions. Thus whether an action concerning a contract has been commenced within the applicable time-limit is treated as a substantive question, to be determined in accordance with the proper law of the contract. A similar approach, not confined to contractual matters, had already been introduced in England by the Foreign Limitation Periods Act 1984,[145] which largely

---

[142] On art 14(2), see under 'Formal validity', pp 249–50 above.

[143] See Dicey & Morris, at p 1264.

[144] [1953] 2 QB 329. See also *Boys v Chaplin* [1971] AC 356, a decision on tort, considered in Chapter 13 below.

[145] For a fuller discussion of the 1984 Act, see Stone [1985] 4 LMCLQ 497.

implemented Law Commission Report No 114 (1982) on the Classification of Limitation in Private International Law.[146] Before the 1984 Act English law had resolutely insisted on treating time-limits for bringing actions as a matter of procedure, governed by the lex fori.

Although the basic rule laid down by s 1 of the 1984 Act, subjecting time-limitation to the law which governs the substantive matter to which the action relates, accords with art 10(1)(d) of the 1980 Convention, this basic rule is qualified by a number of other provisions of the 1984 Act, and in relation to contractual actions these qualifications will now give way to the 1980 Convention insofar as they are inconsistent therewith:

(1) The 1984 Act, by s 2, contains its own saving for English public policy, and further declares it inconsistent with public policy to apply a foreign rule on time-limitation if to do so would cause undue hardship to one of the parties. On this basis, in *Jones v Trollope Colls*,[147] a personal injury action arising from a road accident in Pakistan, the Court of Appeal refused to apply the one-year limitation period under Pakistan law against an American plaintiff who had been long hospitalised and had been led by the defendant to believe that her claim would be met by its insurers. Section 2 of the 1984 Act seems compatible with art 16 of the 1980 Convention.

(2) The 1984 Act, by s 1(3), makes applicable the English rule that it is the issue of the writ, rather than (for example) its service, which constitutes the commencement of an English action for limitation purposes, even where limitation is governed by a foreign law which has a different rule.[148] This seems justifiable under the 1980 Convention by virtue of the exclusion of procedure under art 1(2)(h).

(3) The 1984 Act, by s 2(3), requires the English courts to disregard any foreign rule under which time does not run while a party is absent from a given country. This is based on a strong English policy against such 'tolling-through-absence' rules,[149] and seems justifiable under art 16 of the 1980 Convention.

(4) Conversely, the 1984 Act, by s 2(4), retains, even where limitation is otherwise governed by foreign law, the operation of British legislation preventing the running of time where a party is or has been an enemy, or detained in enemy territory, during a war to which the United Kingdom is a party. This is clearly justifiable under art 16 of the 1980 Convention.

(5) The 1984 Act, by s 4(3), preserves English discretion to grant or refuse equitable relief, such as specific performance or an injunction, by reference to English conceptions of acquiescence or unreasonable delay, even where the substantive dispute is governed by foreign law. Such relief must be refused if a

---

[146] Cmnd 8570 (1982). See also the Law Commission's earlier Working Paper No 75 (1980).
[147] (1990) *The Times*, 26 January.
[148] See also s 5 of the 1984 Act, on the commencement of English arbitration proceedings.
[149] For judicial hostility to such rules in the United States, see *George v Douglas Aircraft*, 332 F2d 73 (1964).

definite limitation period is applicable to such relief under the foreign law and has expired; but otherwise the foreign law is merely to be taken into account in the exercise of the English discretion. Insofar as this provision could lead to the grant of such relief in England in circumstances where it clearly would not be granted in the country of the proper law, it is difficult to see how such a result could be justified under the 1980 Convention.

Consequences of nullity

Article 10(1)(e) of the 1980 Convention provides for the application of the proper law to 'the consequences of nullity of the contract'. However the United Kingdom has made a reservation under art 22 excluding the application of art 10(1)(e) in this country.[150] Yet the basic idea of the provision is clearly correct: coherence requires that the law which imposes invalidity, usually the proper law, should be allowed also to determine its consequences – for example, as regards the restoration of or payment for benefits received. Similar considerations underlie s 1 of the Law Reform (Frustrated Contracts) Act 1943, which makes the Act, which deals with the consequences of frustration, applicable to contracts governed by English law. Moreover in *Dimskal Shipping Co v International Transport Workers Federation, The Evia Luck*,[151] the House of Lords applied English law as the expressly chosen proper law of a contract entered into under economic pressure between foreigners abroad, not only to establish the illegitimacy of the economic pressure and the resulting invalidity of the contract, but also the existence of a consequential restitutionary right to recover back money paid under the contract. So it seems that the British reservation excluding art 10(1)(e) has little real effect.

PUBLIC POLICY AND MANDATORY RULES

The 1980 Convention (by arts 3(3), 7 and 16) derogates from its main rule, referring most contractual issues to the proper law, by including a traditional proviso permitting the forum to insist on respect for its own stringent public policy, and also a number of further provisos causing or permitting the proper law to be overridden in favour of mandatory rules of the lex fori or the law of a third country.

Stringent public policy of the lex fori

Traditional English conflict law, and the conflict law of other countries, make an exception to all choice of law rules, in the contractual and other spheres, by excluding the application of an otherwise applicable foreign law if the content

---

[150] See the Contracts (Applicable Law) Act 1990, s 2(2).
[151] [1992] 2 AC 152.

of its relevant substantive rules is such that their application would contravene a stringent public policy of the forum country. In such cases the corresponding rule of the internal lex fori is substituted. Such a proviso is adopted by art 16 of the 1980 Convention, which permits a court to refuse to apply a rule of the proper law (or of some other law which is applicable to some issue under the Convention) if such application is manifestly incompatible with the public policy (or *ordre public*) of the forum.

The public policy proviso (under art 16 and under traditional English law) refers primarily to the rare cases where the relevant foreign rule (as applied to the substantive facts) departs so radically from English concepts of fundamental justice that its application would be intolerably offensive to the English judicial conscience, even where all the connecting factors (except as to the forum seised) are with the country of the rule.[152] An example in the contractual sphere is *Kaufman v Gerson*,[153] which involved a promise by a wife to repay money misappropriated by her husband, made in response to a threat to prosecute the husband for the misappropriations. The contract was exclusively connected with France, was governed by French law, and was valid thereunder. The Court of Appeal nonetheless refused to enforce the contract, on the ground that the English rule invalidating contracts made under that kind of pressure reflected a fundamental principle of justice which ought to be universally respected.[154]

It is also worth emphasising that in principle the public policy proviso against oppressive foreign rules can apply against a rule which unreasonably invalidates a contract, as well as against one which unreasonably upholds a contract.

In addition to its operation against foreign rules having oppressive content, art 16 appears to preserve two more specific features of the traditional English law on public policy:

(1) The rule of English public policy preventing the application of any foreign rule differing from the English substantive rules as to the effect on existing contracts of the outbreak of a war to which the United Kingdom is a party.[155]

(2) The rules of English public policy designed to prevent the English courts from encouraging or requiring parties to perform acts abroad whose performance would contravene the criminal law of the country where the performance would take place.

The last-mentioned rules must now be examined more closely.

---

[152] See per Simon P in *Cheni v Cheni* [1965] P 85; a case on the validity of a marriage rather than a contract.

[153] [1904] 1 KB 591.

[154] Cf *Lemenda Trading Co Ltd v African Middle East Petroleum Co Ltd* [1988] 1 QB 448, where Phillips J applied the English rule, invalidating contracts for the exercise of influence with a public authority in return for a reward to be concealed from the authority to be influenced, to a contract governed by English law for the influencing of an official in Qatar, whose law contained a similar rule invalidating such contracts.

[155] See *Ertel Bieber v Rio Tinto* [1918] AC 260.

Criminal prohibition by the law of the place of performance

It is probable that art 16 preserves, as a matter of manifest public policy, the traditional English rules that the English courts will not enforce (even by awarding damages for breach):

(1) a contract entered into with a common intention that it should be performed in defiance of a known prohibition imposed by the law of the place of such intended performance; or

(2) a contractual obligation whose agreed performance would necessitate the commission abroad of an act which is in fact at the date of the agreed performance prohibited by the criminal law of the country in which the contract requires the act to be performed;

(3) even if (in either case) the proper law is that of a third country, and that law regards the obligation as valid and enforceable despite the prohibition.

Some limits on these rules must be emphasised. First, they require a criminal prohibition. If, as in *Mount Albert BC v Australasian Assurance Soc*,[156] the law of the place of performance purports merely to release an obligation, rather than to prohibit its performance under penalty, the obligation will continue to operate as agreed in accordance with the proper law. Secondly, it is only the law of the place of the agreed or intended performance of the prohibited obligation to which the rules refer; illegality under the law of the place of contracting, or the law of a party's residence or nationality, as such, is irrelevant.[157]

Thirdly, for the rules to apply, the prohibited act must be an act of performance. It is enough that the contract necessarily requires the act to be done by way of its performance; or alternatively that the act is one of the possible modes of performance, and is the one which the parties, at the time of contracting, with knowledge of the prohibition, intended should be followed.[158] But it is not enough that the prohibited act is merely a preliminary or preparatory step which a party may need to take in order to reach a position from which he can carry out the contractually required performance.[159] Thus in *Kleinwort v Ungarische Baumwolle*[160] the Court of Appeal enforced a promise by a Hungarian bank to an English bank, under a contract governed by English law, to provide cover in London for certain bills, although it was known to the parties that the Hungarian bank would not be able to fulfil its promise without committing in Hungary breaches of Hungarian exchange prohibitions

---

[156] [1938] AC 224. See text to note 130 above.
[157] See *Re Missouri Steamship Co* (1889) 42 ChD 321; *Vita Food Products v Unus Shipping* [1939] AC 277; *Kleinwort v Ungarische Baumwolle* [1939] 2 KB 678; *Toprak v Finagrain* [1979] 2 Lloyd's Rep 98; and *Bodley Head v Flegon* [1972] 1 WLR 680.
[158] See per Robert Goff J in *Toprak v Finagrain* [1979] 2 Lloyd's Rep 98, affirmed more briefly by the Court of Appeal.
[159] See per Staughton J in *Libyan Arab Foreign Bank v Bankers Trust* [1988] 1 Lloyd's Rep 259.
[160] [1939] 2 KB 678; followed on similar facts in *Toprak v Finagrain* [1979] 2 Lloyd's Rep 98.

unless the Hungarian central bank authorised the payments. The parties had never actually intended that the Hungarian bank should commit offences in Hungary; rather, they had contemplated that if the central bank's consent were refused, the promisor would fail to pay, but would in effect be in breach of an absolute warranty that such permission would be granted. Similarly in *Libyan Arab Foreign Bank v Bankers Trust*[161] Staughton J enforced payment of a large credit in dollars established by a Libyan bank with the English branch of an American bank, despite American executive orders forbidding the debtor to pay, since the contract was governed by English law and enabled the creditor to require payment in cash in London. Again in *Bodley Head v Flegon*,[162] Brightman J upheld a power of attorney signed by a Russian author in Russia, but expressly governed by Swiss law, empowering a Swiss lawyer to arrange publication of the author's works in the West, since it did not require anything to be done in Russia, even though the export of the text of the works from Russia would contravene Russian law.

The first limb of the public policy rule is applicable, however, where the parties' actual common object or intention at the time of contracting was that the contract should be performed by means of an act done in defiance of a known criminal prohibition imposed by the law of the country where the act was intended to be performed. In such circumstances the entire contract will be regarded as illegal and unenforceable in England, even if the unlawful intention is concealed by the documentation and revealed only by oral testimony. Such a situation arose in *Foster v Driscoll*,[163] which involved a conspiracy to ship whisky into the United States during 'prohibition', and *Regazzoni v Sethia*,[164] where a contract expressed in the documents as a sale cif Genoa was in fact intended to be performed by exporting the goods from India in breach of an Indian prohibition on exports destined ultimately for South Africa. Although these cases involved contracts governed by English law, there is little doubt that the same result would be reached in such situations even if the contract were governed by the law of a third country, and regardless of the view taken by that law. It seems likely that an analogous result would be reached where the guilty intention to perform in defiance of a known prohibition was possessed by one, but not the other, of the parties: the guilty party would then be unable to enforce the contract at all, but (unless performance would inevitably require breach of the prohibition in the country where it was imposed, in which case a variation on the second limb of the rule would apply) the innocent party would be able to do so.

The second limb of the public policy rule applies where there was no guilty intention satisfying the first limb, but, unknown to the parties, there in fact existed at the time of contracting, or there came into force between the time of

---

[161] [1988] 1 Lloyd's Rep 259. See also *Libyan Arab Foreign Bank v Manufacturers Hanover Trust (No 2)*, [1989] 1 Lloyd's Rep 608.
[162] [1972] 1 WLR 680.
[163] [1929] 1 KB 470.
[164] [1958] AC 301.

contracting and the time for performance, in a country where the contract necessarily required an act of performance to be done, a criminal prohibition against the doing of that act. In such a case, if the contract is governed by English law, and the illegality is supervening, then at least the obligation whose performance is prohibited will be pro tanto frustrated and discharged. Such a situation arose in *Ralli v Naviera*,[165] which involved a charter-party governed by English law for a voyage from India to Spain. The contract provided for payment of freight in Spain on arrival, but during the voyage a Spanish decree came into force prohibiting payment or receipt of freight at a rate exceeding a statutory limit, which was lower than the agreed rate. The Court of Appeal held that, under English law as the proper law, the supervening Spanish decree had the effect of frustrating the obligation to pay the contractual freight insofar as it exceeded the statutory limit.

Probably a similar result would have followed if the prohibition had existed at the time of contracting, but had not come to the knowledge of the parties until after the voyage had commenced. If, however, the prohibition had become known to the parties before any substantial performance had been carried out, it would seem proper to regard the entire contract as frustrated; for example, if in *Ralli* the prohibition had come into force and come to the knowledge of the parties before the loading had commenced.

If, however, the proper law were that of a third country, it is probable that in cases of 'innocent' illegality, the English courts would respect a rule of the foreign proper law which substituted for the prohibited obligation a similar obligation to be performed in a different country where its performance was not prohibited. An example would be the *Ralli* situation, with the variation that the proper law was German, and German law substituted an obligation to pay the excess freight in Hamburg or London. But if a foreign proper law were to insist on maintaining the obligation to perform in the original country, in defiance of the prohibition there, that would produce a situation contrary to stringent English public policy, and English law would insist on discharging the obligation as if the contract were governed by English law.[166]

Mandatory rules

The 1980 Convention, by art 3(3), defines 'mandatory rules' as ones 'which cannot be derogated from by contract'; in other words, substantive rules which, under the law containing them, apply (at least in cases purely internal to the country in question) despite any contractual term attempting to provide for a contrary result, and invalidate any such contrary term. Mandatory rules may be contrasted with suppletive rules, which are designed merely to supplement and resolve ambiguities in the terms of a contract, and thus give way to a contractual term providing for a different solution.

---

[165] [1920] 2 KB 287.
[166] See FA Mann (1937) 18 BYIL 97.

Under the general rules laid down by the Convention, a contract is subject to both the mandatory and the suppletive rules of its proper law, since arts 8–10 provide for the application of the proper law to essential and formal validity and interpretation. However, in addition to the classical public policy proviso specified by art 16, the Convention derogates from its general rules by a number of provisions which require or permit the application of mandatory rules of a law other than the proper law, so as to override the control normally enjoyed by the proper law, and to make the proper law operate subject to the mandatory rules of the other law. In the case of 'ordinary' contracts,[167] the relevant provisions are contained in arts 3(3) and 7.

First, art 3(3) applies where all relevant connections, other than a choice of law, or of forum and law, are connected with a single country. In such a case the chosen law operates subject to all the mandatory rules of the country otherwise exclusively connected, including ones whose underlying policy is of minimal strength (such as the English doctrine of consideration).[168] The very narrow scope of this provision makes it of small practical importance.

Much more importantly, art 7 provides:

(1) When applying under this Convention the law of a country, effect may be given to the mandatory rules of the law of another country with which the situation has a close connection, if and in so far as, under the law of the latter country, those rules must be applied whatever the law applicable to the contract. In considering whether to give effect to these mandatory rules, regard shall be had to their nature and purpose and to the consequences of their application or non-application.[169]

(2) Nothing in this Convention shall restrict the application of the rules of the law of the forum in a situation where they are mandatory irrespective of the law otherwise applicable to the contract.[170]

However the United Kingdom has exercised its right under art 22(1)(a) to make a reservation enabling it not to apply art 7(1).[171] Most British commentators have approved the making of this reservation. The present author, however, is inclined to regard it as on balance ill-advised.

The rationale of art 7 is best understood in terms of the concept of interest analysis, isolated by Brainerd Currie,[172] and the various choice influencing

---

[167] On protected consumer contracts, and employment contracts, see arts 5 and 6, examined under 'Certain particular contracts', pp 266–73 below.

[168] See also, to similar effect, Directive 88/357, art 7(1)(g), on non-life insurance.

[169] See also, for provisions with similar effect to art 7(1) of the 1980 Convention: art 7(2) of Directive 88/357, on non-life insurance; and art 4(4) of Directive 90/619, on life insurance.

[170] See also, for provisions with similar effect to art 7(2) of the 1980 Convention: art 7(2) of Directive 88/357, on non-life insurance; art 4(4) of Directive 90/619, on life insurance; and art 17 of the Hague Convention (1985) on the Law Applicable to Contracts for the International Sale of Goods.

[171] See the Contracts (Applicable Law) Act 1990, s 2(2).

[172] See his *Selected Essays on the Conflict of Laws* (1963).

factors specified in s 6 of the American Law Institute's *Restatement, Second Conflict of Laws* (1971). For art 7 aims to offer some respect to the policies of a country or legal system which claims an interest in invalidating a contract governed by another law, but proceeds cautiously where the invalidating law is not that of the forum. It recognises that there are some circumstances in which the policies of supporting party expectation and facilitating international commerce, which underlie the proper law doctrine, should give way to policies underlying an invalidating substantive rule contained in the law of another country with which the contract is connected in a matter such as to make the furtherance of the invalidating policies of particular importance.

The basic idea of interest analysis is that a country or legal system may be said to have a substantial interest in the application to a transnational situation of a rule contained in its internal law, if a policy or purpose which the substantive rule is designed to promote or achieve would be furthered to a substantial extent by the application of the substantive rule in the determination of the case in question, in view of the factual connections between the parties, acts and events involved in the case and the country in question. The fundamental aim of art 7 is to achieve a reasonable compromise between according a measure of respect for a substantial interest possessed by a country in the application of an invalidating substantive rule contained in its law, and safeguarding adequately the general choice of law policies favouring party expectations and the convenient conduct of international trade. In a sense, what is at issue is protectionism, though of a technically legal rather than an economic character.

Where the invalidating substantive rule belongs to the lex fori, art 7(2) gives a free hand to that law (by legislation or judicial decision) to define and insist on safeguarding its own interests. Where the invalidating rule belongs to a law other than that of the forum, art 7(1), unless excluded by reservation, entrusts a discretionary power to the court seised, where a foreign law has asserted an interest in having one of its mandatory rules applied in certain circumstances to contracts governed by other laws. The forum is invited to evaluate the legitimacy of the asserted interest, and to weigh it against the considerations (such as unfair surprise to the party prejudiced by the invalidating rule) which favour adherence to the proper law. In this connection, it may be expected that a court will seldom choose to invalidate in support of a foreign interest unless its own law has a broadly similar invalidating rule, and would assert a similar interest in a situation connected with its own country in a broadly similar way. The achievement of such a result in such cases may be considered to advance international legal co-operation and harmony.

As matters stand, art 7(2) operates to cover cases where English law insists on promoting its own interests in applying its own mandatory rules so as to invalidate a contract governed by foreign law. The opportunity offered by art 7(1) to qualify the refusal by traditional English law to accord similar respect to similar foreign interests in analogous cases has for the time being been declined.

It must of course be emphasised that the intervention of English mandatory rules to further specific English interests has always been and remains exceptional; the general rule is that even mandatory English rules apply only to contracts governed by English law. Moreover, the most important cases in which English law asserts an interest in overriding a foreign proper law involve consumer or employment contracts, and are now governed (at least mainly) by arts 5 and 6 of the Convention, rather than art 7.[173]

In the present context English courts have not usually spoken the language of interest analysis,[174] but have referred instead to public policy, where the English invalidating rule belongs to the common law; or to statutory wording or interpretation, where the mandatory rule is contained in an English statute. Nonetheless it is clear that one is concerned here with a relational, rather than a universalist, public policy,[175] since the existence of appropriate connections with England is undoubtedly crucial; and it is submitted that the terminology of interest analysis offers the most useful method of explanation, comprehension, and useful development.

Examples of the process may be seen in the following rulings:

(1) that the common law rule against champerty, which invalidates a contract by which a person who has no legitimate interest in a dispute agrees to finance litigation in return for a share of the proceeds, applies whenever the litigation to be financed is to take place in an English court, even if the champertous agreement is governed by foreign law;[176]

(2) that the common law rule against unreasonable restraint of trade applies to a contract prejudicing trade which would take place in England, even if the anti-competitive contract is governed by a foreign proper law;[177]

(3) that the former rule invalidating an agreement on familial maintenance where it purported to exclude English judicial discretion over maintenance did not apply where the agreement was concluded in contemplation of foreign divorce proceedings and was subsequently approved (with qualifications) by the foreign divorce court;[178]

(4) that, on account of its explicit wording, wartime legislation imposing exchange control invalidated contracts to borrow foreign currency, entered into in circumstances of personal emergency by British subjects involuntarily trapped in enemy territory, save possibly in the case of borrowings by British servicemen in the course of escape from internment as prisoners of war in enemy hands;[179]

---

[173] See under 'Certain particular contracts', p 266 et seq. below.
[174] See, however, in the context of tort, the speeches of Lords Hodson and Wilberforce in *Boys v Chaplin* [1971] AC 356; discussed in Chapter 13 below.
[175] Cf the universalist public policy asserted in cases such as *Kaufman v Gerson* [1904] 1 KB 591; considered under 'Stringent public policy of the lex fori', pp 256–7 above.
[176] See *Grell v Levy* (1864) 143 ER 1052, and *Re Trepca Mines* [1963] Ch 199.
[177] See *Rousillon v Rousillon* (1880) 14 ChD 351.
[178] See *Addison v Brown* [1954] 2 All ER 213.
[179] See *Boissevain v Weil* [1950] AC 327; a truly shocking decision.

(5) by a Scottish court, that a Scottish enactment on hire purchase, which required a copy of the contract to be sent to the hirer within 14 days, should be construed so as to apply whenever the hirer had signed the agreement in Scotland, even if the finance company was English and had accepted the offer in England, and the contract was to be performed in England and contained an English law clause;[180]

(6) by the High Court of Australia, on appeal from New South Wales, that a New South Wales statute regulating deposits paid and interest charged under hire-purchase contracts was confined to contracts technically concluded in New South Wales, and thus did not apply where a hirer resident in New South Wales executed the agreement at the finance company's branch office there, but the finance company subsequently executed the agreement at its head office in Victoria.[181]

An example of a case where art 7(1) might have had useful effect if it had not been excluded by reservation would be a champertous agreement, governed by American law, for the financing of litigation to take place in New Zealand; it being assumed that American law has no objection to champerty, while New Zealand law, like English internal law, objects to such an arrangement as increasing the risk of deception of courts by false evidence. As matters stand, an English action for a share of the spoils obtained from the champertously maintained New Zealand litigation would probably succeed, in application of the American proper law. The English invalidating rule would be inapplicable because the litigation champertously maintained was not brought in England, and thus it was not the English courts which were put at increased risk of deception by false evidence; and the similar New Zealand rule would be inapplicable because it belonged to neither the proper law nor the lex fori. Under art 7(2), if not excluded by reservation, the English court could have applied the New Zealand invalidating rule and rejected the claim.

In the sphere of non-consumer contracts,[182] the question arises whether art 7(2) of the 1980 Convention will preserve the operation of s 27(2)(a) of the Unfair Contract Terms Act 1977. This specifies in effect that the controls imposed by the Act on the validity of exemption clauses are applicable if: the proper law is foreign by express or implied choice, but the country of closest connection is a part of the United Kingdom, and an express or implied choice of a foreign law was imposed wholly or mainly for the purpose of evading the 1977 Act. The Contracts (Applicable Law) Act 1990, which implements the 1980 Convention, does not expressly repeal s 27(2)(a). On the other hand, the only provision of the Convention which could conceivably permit the maintenance of such a provision is art 7(2), and art 7(2) seems designed to preserve forum

---

[180] See *English v Donnelly* 1958 SC 494. This type of situation is now governed by art 9(5) of the 1980 Convention.

[181] See *Kay's Leasing v Fletcher* (1964) 116 CLR 124.

[182] As regards the operation of the Unfair Contract Terms Act 1977 in relation to consumer contracts, see under 'Protected consumer contracts', pp 266–70 below.

conflict rules based on objective connections, rather than on nebulous concepts such as evasive purpose.

Self-limiting rules

As we have seen, art 7 of the Convention enables a contract in some cases to be invalidated by mandatory rules belonging to a law other than the proper law, where the invalidating law asserts an interest in an expanded operation. A converse problem concerns self-limiting (or self-denying) rules:[183] that is, where a legal system chooses to limit the transnational scope of certain of its own substantive rules (usually mandatory rules), either by declaring such rules inapplicable to all transnational contracts, or confining them to transnational contracts which are connected in specified ways with its territory. The result is that there will be some transnational contracts which are governed by the law of the country in question, but to which some of its mandatory rules, which apply to contracts purely internal to that country, are rendered inapplicable. Traditional English law respected self-limiting rules contained in a foreign proper law.[184] It seems that, with the exception of protected consumer contracts and employment contracts,[185] the 1980 Convention does not intervene against the maintenance of self-limiting rules.

Two such rules are laid down in the (British) Unfair Contract Terms Act 1977, so as to exclude certain transnational contracts from the scope of the controls on the validity of exemption clauses imposed by the 1977 Act. First, s 26 makes such an exclusion in respect of international supply contracts, even if the proper law of the contract is English, Scottish or Northern Irish law. The definition of an international supply contract for this purpose is adapted from art 1 of the Uniform Law on International Sales, annexed to a Hague Convention of 1964 and minimally implemented in the United Kingdom by the Uniform Laws on International Sales Act 1967, and is as follows:

(1) the contract must be for the sale of goods, or must be one under which possession or ownership of goods passes (such as hire, hire purchase or barter); and

(2) the contract must have been made between parties whose places of business (or if they had none, their habitual residences) were in different states; and either:

    (a) at the conclusion of the contract the goods must have been in the course of carriage from one state to another, or the contract must have required such carriage to take place subsequently; or

---

[183] See FA Mann (1972–73) 46 BYIL 117, and Dicey & Morris, at pp 19–21 and 25–6. It is not clear why Dicey's editors have now chosen to draw a distinction between 'self-limiting' and 'self-denying' rules, nor in what the difference between the two categories is supposed to consist.

[184] See *Sayers v International Drilling* [1971] 3 All ER 163, involving Dutch rules which invalidated exemption clauses contained in internal, but not transnational, employment contracts.

[185] See under 'Certain particular contracts', p 266 *et seq.* below.

(b) the acts of offer and acceptance must have been done in different states; or

(c) the contract must have provided for the goods to be delivered in a state other than the state where the acts of offer and acceptance were done.[186]

Secondly, s 27(1) of the 1977 Act excludes the operation of the controls imposed by the Act where the proper law is English, Scottish or Northern Irish, but this is so by virtue of an express or implied choice, and the country of closest connection is a country outside the United Kingdom.[187]

CERTAIN PARTICULAR CONTRACTS

Articles 5 and 6 of the 1980 Convention seek to protect a party in a weaker bargaining position by making special provision respectively for certain consumer contracts, and for individual contracts of employment.[188]

For similar reasons, art 1(3) and (4) exclude from the scope of the 1980 Convention contracts of insurance (other than re-insurance) covering risks situated within the European Community. Instead the matter is regulated by Council Directive 88/357,[189] in the case of non-life insurance, and Council Directive 90/619,[190] in the case of life insurance.

Protected consumer contracts

Scope

To fall within the scope of art 5, a contract must be a consumer contract, defined in substantive terms, and must also fulfil certain territorial requirements, so as to become what can conveniently be referred to as a 'protected consumer contract'.

As regards substantive characteristics, art 5(1) requires, positively, that the contract must either have as its object the supply of goods or services to a person (referred to as 'the consumer') for a purpose which can be regarded as being outside his trade or profession, or must be for the provision of credit for that object. It seems clear that this implies that the supplier should be (or at least appear to the consumer to be) acting in the course of a trade or profession, and the Guiliano and Lagarde Report notes a majority view in the negotiating committee that 'normally' the supplier must so act.[191] It indicates also that the purchaser must not be acting 'primarily' within his trade or pro-

---

[186] The Act speaks of delivery 'to', but this is clearly a slip for 'in'.
[187] For criticism of this provision, see FA Mann (1978) 27 ICLQ 661.
[188] For a perceptive and thorough analysis of arts 5 and 6, see Morse (1992) 41 ICLQ 1.
[189] [1988] OJ L172.
[190] [1990] OJ L330.
[191] [1980] OJ C282 at 23.

fession; and must not hold himself out as so acting; and that a sale of securities is excluded. Negatively, art 5(4)(a) and (5) exclude a contract of carriage, other than a contract for the supply of a combination of travel and accommodation for an inclusive price (in other words, a package tour).[192]

As regards territorial requirements, art 5(2) requires, positively, that at least one of the following conditions must be satisfied:

(1) the conclusion of the contract must have been preceded by a specific invitation addressed to the consumer in the country of his habitual residence or by advertising there, and he must have taken in that country all the steps necessary on his part for the conclusion of the contract; or

(2) the supplier or his agent must have received the consumer's order in the country of the consumer's habitual residence; or

(3) the contract must be for the sale of goods, and the consumer must have travelled from the country of his habitual residence to another country and there given his order, and his journey must have been arranged by the seller for the purpose of inducing the consumer to buy.

Negatively, art 5(4)(b) and (5) exclude a contract for services (other than a package tour) to be supplied exclusively in a country other than that of the consumer's habitual residence.[193] It seems reasonably clear that the Convention contemplates that for its purposes a consumer can only have one habitual residence at a given moment.[194]

As regards the reference in the first alternative offered by art 5(2) to advertising in the country of the consumer's habitual residence, the Guiliano and Lagarde Report suggests that the advertising must have been aimed specifically at that country, though it also contemplates that an advertisement in a special special European edition of a magazine of American origin would suffice.[195] However it is submitted that it should be sufficient for this purpose that the advertisement came to the attention of the consumer in his country through normal commercial channels, that it induced him to enter into the negotiations which led to the conclusion of the contract, and that nothing done by the consumer caused the supplier reasonably to suppose that such was not the case. In any event it seems necessary that the advertisement should have been a factor actually inducing the consumer to enter into the contract.

There is also some ambiguity in the further requirement of the first alternative, that the consumer should have taken in his country all the steps necessary on his part for the conclusion of the contract. Surely it should be enough that he posts his offer in his own country, and heads it as from his own address there, even if he had written the order while on a visit to another country.

The reference in the second alternative offered by art 5(2) to an agent of the

---

[192] For criticism of this exclusion, see Morse (1992) 41 ICLQ 1 at 5.
[193] For criticism of this exclusion, see Morse (1992) 41 ICLQ 1 at 5.
[194] Cf Morse (1992) 41 ICLQ 1 at 9.
[195] [1980] OJ C282 at 24.

supplier is intended to include anyone acting on his behalf, including staff manning a stand at a short-term exhibition.[196]

On the other hand, it seems proper to regard art 5 as inapplicable in any case where the consumer's conduct (however honest his intentions) misleads the supplier as to the country of the consumer's habitual residence; as could be the case where the consumer, when placing an order, requests delivery at an address of a relative resident in a different country from the consumer himself.

Effects

In the case of a protected consumer contract (within the scope of art 5), three special choice of law rules apply.[197] First, by art 5(3), in the absence of an express or implied choice of law by the parties in accordance with art 3, the law of the consumer's habitual residence becomes the proper law. The tests of closest connection and characteristic performer's residence, laid down for other cases by art 4, are wholly excluded in the case of protected consumer contracts.

Secondly, by art 5(2), if there is an express or implied choice of law by the parties in accordance with art 3, the choice remains effective to designate the proper law, but the proper law operates subject to the mandatory rules for the protection of the consumer contained in the law of his habitual residence. The effect of this is to give the consumer the cumulative benefit of the protective rules of the chosen law and the law of his habitual residence; on any given issue, the protective rule contained in whichever of the two laws is more favourable to him prevails. Moreover, unlike under art 7,[198] it is irrelevant whether, apart from the Convention, the law containing the mandatory rules would have insisted on their application to contracts governed by foreign law.[199]

On the other hand, it seems clear that the mandatory rules of the law of the consumer's country which are made to override a chosen proper law by art 5(2) are confined to ones whose purpose is to protect consumers as such, or weaker parties more generally as such.[200] Thus they do not extend to mandatory rules whose purpose is to safeguard a public interest other than the protection of weaker contracting parties from exploitation by parties in a stronger bargaining position, even where the rule would, if applied, have the effect of

---

[196] See the Guiliano and Lagarde Report, at p 24.
[197] Harmonisation at Community level of substantive law on consumer contracts has now begun with the adoption of Directive 93/13, on unfair terms in consumer contracts, [1993] OJ L95/29, which has to be implemented by the end of 1994. Puzzlingly, in view of the 1980 Convention, the Directive contains a choice of law provision in art 6(2), which requires member states to ensure that a consumer does not lose the protection granted by the Directive through a choice of the law of a country outside the Community as the proper law, if the contract has a close connection with the territory of the member states.
[198] See under 'Mandatory rules', pp 260–4 above.
[199] See Morse (1992) 41 ICLQ 1 at 8.
[200] See Morse (1992) 41 ICLQ 1 at 8.

benefiting the consumer; examples of such non-protective rules include ones prohibiting the supply of narcotics or sawn-off shotguns in the interests of public health or safety, or restricting the availability of credit with a view to countering inflation.[201] Even more clearly, art 5(2) does not make applicable mandatory rules of the consumer's country whose purpose is to protect suppliers; for example, by imposing a penal rate of interest on defaulting buyers.

It also seems reasonably clear that, in the case of a protected consumer contract (within the meaning of art 5), one cannot have recourse to art 7 for the purpose of making applicable mandatory rules whose purpose is to protect consumers, or weaker parties generally, and which belong to a law which is neither the proper law nor the law of a protected consumer's habitual residence. For, at least in the case of protected consumer contracts, art 5 seems designed to operate as a definitive regulation of the circumstances and manner in which it is proper to override the proper law in the interests of consumer protection.[202] Indeed, it also seems likely, for similar reasons, that art 7 cannot be used to invoke consumer-protective mandatory rules, for example of the law of the consumer's habitual residence, in cases where the contract is (substantively) a consumer contract, but is not (territorially) a protected consumer contract, within the scope of art 5. On the other hand, recourse to art 7 seems permissible, even in the case of a protected consumer contract, for the purpose of introducing mandatory rules of a law other than the proper law which are based on policies other than the protection of consumers or weaker parties.

Thirdly, by art 9(5), in the case of a protected consumer contract, the formal validity of the contract is governed exclusively by the law of the consumer's habitual residence. This bilateralises and develops the Scottish decision in *English v Donnelly*,[203] which gave overriding effect to a modern Scottish enactment requiring consumers to be supplied with copies of agreements which they had signed, in cases where the consumer had signed the agreement in Scotland, even if the consumer's offer had been accepted by the supplier in England and contained a clause choosing English law.

The ultimate effect of art 5 in relation to the United Kingdom is to develop and bilateralise the rule laid down by s 27(2)(b) of the Unfair Contract Terms Act 1977, which made applicable the controls imposed by the 1977 Act on the validity of exemption clauses, despite an express or implied choice of foreign law, if in the making of the contract one of the parties dealt as consumer, he was then habitually resident in the United Kingdom, and the steps necessary for the making of the contract on his part were taken in the United Kingdom.

The Contracts (Applicable Law) Act 1990, which implements the 1980 Convention, does not expressly repeal the mandatory provisions of s 27(2), nor the self-limiting provisions of ss 26 and 27(1), of the 1977 Act,[204] but it seems to

---

[201] Cf *Kay's Leasing v Fletcher* (1964) 116 CLR 124; see text to note 181 above.

[202] Cf Morse (1992) 41 ICLQ 1 at 10.

[203] 1958 SC 494.

[204] On the anti-evasion rule of s 27(2)(a), and the self-limiting rules of ss 26 and 27(1), see pp 264–6 above.

do so by implication in the case of all contracts which are (substantively) consumer contracts, whether or not they are (territorially) protected consumer contracts, within the meaning of art 5. For, it is submitted, art 5 is designed to establish a definitive solution, exclusive of art 7 as well as any national legislation relating to choice of law, to the question of what mandatory rules designed to protect a weaker party should be applied, and in what circumstances, to a consumer contract; and the continued operation of ss 26 or 27 in relation to any consumer contract could have the effect of either denying or ensuring the application of British mandatory rules designed to protect weaker parties in a manner inconsistent with the objectives underlying art 5.

Employment contracts

Again in the interest of protecting weaker parties, art 6 of the 1980 Convention makes special provision for individual contracts of employment. Here, however, the contracts affected are indicated solely in substantive, rather than territorial, terms; but no actual definition is specified, and the question arises whether the concept should be construed as having an autonomous meaning under Community law, to be elaborated by the European Court of Justice, or by way of reference to some national law involved (such as the lex fori, or the law which would be applicable if the contract *were* an employment contract). Despite the contrary arguments of Morse,[205] it is submitted that an autonomous Community meaning is preferable. This need not involve any distortion; for if the contract is an employment contract under the Community cóncept, and the choice of law rules laid down in art 6 therefore apply to identify the law which is, or whose mandatory rules are, applicable, this will not require an applicable law which does not regard the contract as an employment contract (but as, say, a contract for professional services) to apply its substantive rules as if it were an employment contract, but only to apply its substantive rules which it considers applicable to a contract having the character which it ascribes to the instant contract.

In the absence of an express or implied choice under art 3, the proper law of a contract of employment is ascertained in accordance with art 6(2), to the exclusion of art 4. By art 6(2), rebuttable presumptions are laid down in favour of:

(a) the law of the country in which the employee habitually carries out his work in performance of the contract, even while he is temporarily employed in another country;[206] or

---

[205] (1992) 41 ICLQ 1 at 12–13.

[206] For the use of somewhat similar connections (such as the country where the employee 'ordinarily works' or 'wholly or mainly works' under the contract) in traditional English law, see: the Employment Protection (Consolidation) Act 1978, ss 141 and 153, and *Wilson v Maynard Shipbuilding Consultants* [1978] QB 665; the Equal Pay Act 1970, ss 1 and 10 (as amended); the Sex Discrimination Act 1975, ss 6 and 10; the Race Relations Act 1975, ss 4 and 8; and the Patents Act 1977, s 130.

(b) if he does not habitually carry out his work in any one country, the law of the country in which the place of business through which he was engaged is situated.[207]

But these presumptions are rebuttable in favour of the law of the country most closely connected with the contract, as indicated by the circumstances as a whole.

It is submitted that, as with 'ordinary' contracts, the proper law must be ascertained in the light only of the situation at the date of contracting, and not in the light of subsequent developments (unless they amount to a new agreement). More specifically, in determining where, if anywhere, an employee habitually works under a contract, and also in determining the country of closest connection with the contract, attention should be focused on what the parties agreed or contemplated at the time of contracting. If they then agreed and contemplated that the employee would be moved from one country to another from time to time as the employer's business should require, it cannot be said that he ever has any habitual place of work, even if in fact he works in the same country for 30 years from contracting until dismissal; and in such a case the length of the actual work does not relevantly increase the degree of connection of the contract with the country where it takes place.[208]

It may be wondered why the specified connections (of habitual working, or engaging establishment) give rise only to presumptions, rather than to firm rules eliminating any consideration of closest connection. The concealed rationale may relate to the relative protectiveness of the various connected laws. If the place of habitual work is within the Community (or in some other First World country, such as Sweden or the United States), the first presumption is very unlikely to be rebutted. But if a person resident (at the time of contracting) in a First World country is employed by a company which is also resident in the same or another First World country, but the place of habitual work is a Third World country, the presumption may readily be rebutted in favour of the law of the common residence of the parties, or if they reside in different countries, the residence of the employer.

Moreover, by art 6(1), an express or implied choice of law by the parties has effect subject to the mandatory rules for the protection of the employee con-

---

[207] Morse (1992) 41 ICLQ 1 at 19 suggests persuasively that art 6(2)(b) refers to a place of business of the employer having some permanence. See also Case 33/78 *Somafer v Saar-Ferngas* [1978] ECR 2183, on art 5(5) of the 1968 Convention.

Cf *Sayers v International Drilling* [1971] 1 WLR 1176, where the Court of Appeal held that a contract for the employment of an Englishman as an oil-rig worker by a Dutch subsidiary of an American company, under which he could be required to work anywhere in the world except the United Kingdom, and was in fact sent to work in Nigerian waters, was impliedly governed by Dutch law, even though he had been recruited at an English place of business of an English sister company of the Dutch company. Accordingly s 1(3) of the (British) Law Reform (Personal Injuries) Act 1948, which invalidates clauses in employment contracts excluding the employer's liability for personal injuries suffered by the employee, was held not to apply. A similar result would now seem justifiable on the basis of closest connection, whether or not the presumption under art 6(2)(b) would initially apply.

[208] Cf Morse (1992) 41 ICLQ 1 at 17–18, who prefers to take account of the place of actual work.

271

tained in the law of the country with which the contract is most closely connected, ascertained in accordance with or by rebuttal of the presumptions specified in art 6(2). As in the case of consumer contracts, it is irrelevant under art 6(1) whether, apart from the Convention, the law containing the mandatory rules would have insisted on their application to contracts governed by foreign law,[209] but the mandatory rules referred to by art 6(1) seem to be confined to ones whose purpose is to protect employees, or weaker parties generally, as such, and not to extend to ones which have some other purpose (such as prohibiting certain types of activity, such as the manufacture of narcotics, in the public interest), but which would, if applied, have the effect of benefiting the employee. Even more clearly, the reference does not extend to mandatory rules designed to protect employers; for example, by ensuring a right to dismiss, or make deductions from pay, in certain circumstances. Equally, the exhaustive character of art 6 in relation to the issues with which it purports to deal must prevent the use of art 7 to invoke mandatory employee protective rules from any law other than the proper law or the law of the country of closest connection. However it seems permissible to invoke art 7 so as to enable the application of mandatory rules which are not designed to protect employees (including in some cases, in view of the absence of a specific provision analogous to art 9(5), ones concerned with the formal validity of the contract), and which are contained in a law other than the proper law, or even in a law other than that of the country of closest connection.[210]

The policy of offering a reasonable but predictable measure of employee protection which underlies art 6 seems to require that its provisions should extend to claims in tort between employer and employee arising from things done or omitted in the course of purported performance of the contract of employment, and especially to personal injury claims, as if they were claims founded on the contract, so as to override whatever choice of law rules would normally be applied by the forum to tort claims.[211] The propriety of such an interpretation is to some extent confirmed by the Guiliano and Lagarde Report,[212] which states that the mandatory rules referred to consist not only of provisions relating to the contract of employment itself, but also provisions concerning industrial safety and hygiene, even though they are regarded in some member states as provisions of public law; and that art 6 extends to void contracts and de facto employment relationships. A contrary view is taken by Morse,[213] though he admits that it would lead to a lack of uniformity in the application of the Convention.

[209] See Morse (1992) 41 ICLQ 1 at 14.
[210] Cf Morse (1992) 41 ICLQ 1 at 16-17, whose view that art 7(2) can be used to invoke mandatory employee protective rules of the lex fori as such leads immediately into unnecessary difficulties.
[211] On this basis there would be no justification for a decision such as was given by a Scottish court in *Brodin v Seljan* [1973] SLT 198, applying the law of the forum and the place of the accident to invalidate an exemption clause relating to the employer's liability for personal injuries, even though the contract of employment, as a seaman on a foreign ship, was for habitual work outside the forum country and was governed by foreign law.
[212] [1980] OJ C282 at 25-6.
[213] Morse (1992) 41 ICLQ 1 at 20.

For similar reasons, it is confidently submitted (contrary to the views of Morse)[214] that art 6 must be read as overriding any self-limiting rule contained in a given law which would, on territorial grounds, prevent mandatory employee protective rules belonging to that law from applying in a case where art 6 makes that law the proper law of the contract, or makes the mandatory rules of that law override a proper law chosen by the parties. Thus, for example, art 6 will eliminate the self-limiting rule contained in s 141 of the (British) Employment Protection (Consolidation) Act 1978, whereby the British provisions on unfair dismissal are excluded if the employee ordinarily works outside Great Britain, so as to make those provisions applicable whenever the proper law, or the law of the country of closest connection, is English or Scottish law.

Insurance contracts

Article 1(3) and (4) of the 1980 Convention exclude from its scope contracts of insurance (other than re-insurance) covering risks situated within the European Community. Instead the matter is regulated by Council Directive 88/357,[215] in the case of non-life insurance, and Council Directive 90/619,[216] in the case of life insurance.

The location of the risk

Article 1(3) of the 1980 Convention referred the determination of the location of a risk to the law of the court seised, but this reference has since been overridden by the harmonisation effected by the directives. The following rules as to the location of an insured risk or commitment are laid down by art 2(d) of Directive 88/357 and art 2(e) of Directive 90/619:

(1)   In the case of an insurance of buildings, or buildings together with their contents, the risk is located where the property is situated.
(2)   In the case of insurance of vehicles of any type, the risk is located in the country of registration.
(3)   In the case of policies for up to four months covering travel or holiday risks, the risk is located in the country where the policy-holder took out the policy.
(4)   In all other cases covered by the non-life directive, and in the case of life insurance, the risk or commitment is located in the country of an individual policy-holder's habitual residence, or of a corporate policy-holder's establishment to which the contract relates.

[214] (1992) 41 ICLQ 1 at 14–15.
[215] [1988] OJ L172. By art 32, this directive had to be implemented by the member states by 30 June 1990. It has been implemented in the United Kingdom by SI 1990/1333, reg 6, adding s 94A and Sched 3A to the Insurance Companies Act 1982.
[216] [1990] OJ L330. This had to be implemented by the member states by 20 May 1993; see art 30.

Risks located outside the Community

If the risk is not located within the Community, under the definitions of location specified by the directives, or if the contract is of re-insurance, the choice of law rules laid down by the 1980 Convention apply. The parties are then free to choose the governing law, expressly or by implication, in accordance with art 3 of the Convention, and in default of choice the law of the country of an establishment of the insurer involved in the transaction will normally apply under art 4.[217] As in the case of 'ordinary' contracts, the proper law may give way to mandatory rules or public policy, under arts 3(3), 7 or 16 of the Convention.

Non-life risks located within the Community

Choice of law rules for non-life insurance contracts falling within the scope of Directive 88/357 and covering risks located within the Community are laid down by art 7 of the directive.

Under art 7(1), the proper law is determined as follows:

(1) If the risk relates to damage to or loss of ships, boats, aircraft, railway rolling-stock, or goods in transit or baggage (irrespective of the form of transport), or to liability arising out of the use of ships, boats, or aircraft (including carrier's liability), then the parties are free to choose any law as the proper law.[218] But in this case (as under art 3(3) of the 1980 Convention) a choice of an unconnected law to govern a contract otherwise exclusively connected with a single member state will give way to mandatory rules of the law of the member state with which the contract is otherwise exclusively connected.[219]

(2) Otherwise, if the policy-holder's habitual residence or central administration are located in the same member state as the risk, the internal law of that state becomes the proper law, but if the conflict rules of that state allow, the parties are free to choose another law as the proper law.[220] Again a choice of an unconnected law to govern a contract otherwise exclusively with a single member state will give way to mandatory rules of the law of the member state with which the contract is otherwise exclusively connected.[221]

(3) Otherwise, the parties are given a limited choice. Primarily, they may choose between the law of the member state in which the risk is located and the law of the country of the policy-holder's habitual residence or central administration.[222] Further, if the policy-holder pursues a commercial or industrial activity or a liberal profession, and the contract covers two or more risks

---

[217] See, to similar effect, *Amin Rasheed v Kuwait Insurance Co* [1984] 1 AC 50.
[218] See Directive 88/357, art 7(1)(f), and Directive 73/239 (as amended), art 5(d)(i) and Annex, point (a), classes 4, 5, 6, 7, 11 and 12.
[219] Article 7(1)(g).
[220] Article 7(1)(a).
[221] Article 7(1)(g).
[222] Article 7(1)(b).

which relate to such activities and are located in different member states, the freedom of choice extends to the laws of each member state in which any of the risks is located, as well as to that of the country of the policy-holder's habitual residence or central administration.[223] The freedom further extends to choosing some other law, if the conflict rules of a member state whose own law may be chosen so permit.[224] Lastly, if the risks covered by the contract are limited to events occurring in a member state other than the member state where the risk is located, the freedom of choice further extends to the law of the state of the events covered.[225]

(4) Any choice permitted by the above rules must (as under art 3(1) of the 1980 Convention) be expressed or demonstrated with reasonable certainty by the terms of the contract or the circumstances of the case.[226]

(5) Where the above rules permit party choice, but no effective choice has been made by the parties, the contract is governed by the law of the country, among those between which party choice is permitted, with which it is most closely connected, and there is a rebuttable presumption of closest connection with the member state in which the risk is situated.[227]

(6) Provision is also made for states comprising several territories having separate systems of contract law, similar to that of art 19 of the 1980 Convention.[228]

However art 7(2) of the Directive makes the following derogations from the control of the proper law:

(1) Similarly to art 7(2) of the 1980 Convention, it permits the forum to apply its own mandatory rules in international situations where, apart from the directive, it would have been bound to do so.

(2) Somewhat similarly to art 7(1) of the 1980 Convention, it permits a member state to apply mandatory rules of the law of the member state in which the risk is situated, or of the member state imposing an obligation to take out insurance, in international situations where the law containing the mandatory rule requires its application. But if the contract covers risks situated in more than one member state, the contract must be severed for this purpose.

In addition, art 7(3) permits the forum to invoke its own stringent public policy, and art 8(4)(c) permits a member state to derogate from art 7 in the case of a compulsory insurance contract, so as to provide that the law of the state which imposes the obligation to take out insurance will become the proper law of the contract.

---

[223] Article 7(1)(c).
[224] Article 7(1)(d).
[225] Article 7(1)(e).
[226] Article 7(1)(h).
[227] Article 7(1)(h); which also permits severance, in the same way as art 4(1) of the 1980 Convention.
[228] Article 7(1)(i).

Life risks located within the Community

The position is rather simpler in the case of life insurance contracts where the commitment is located within the Community. Under art 4 of Directive 90/619, the law of the member state of the commitment becomes the proper law. Party choice of some other law is permitted only where the conflict rules of the state of commitment so permit, or in favour of the law of the nationality of an individual policy-holder who is a national of one member state but is habitually resident in another member state. However the forum is permitted to apply its own rules, or those of the member state of the commitment, insofar as they are otherwise mandatory, regardless of the proper law, and also to invoke its own stringent public policy.

13

TORT

Introduction

As Lord Wilberforce put it in *Boys v Chaplin:*[1]

> A tort takes place in France: if action is not brought before the courts in France, let other courts decide as the French courts would. This has obvious attraction. But there are ... disadvantages.

Fundamentally, the main problem to be addressed in this area is whether suitable exceptions can be devised to the almost inevitable basic rule referring tort liability to the law of the country in which the tort took place. To merit adoption, such exceptions need to reduce the disadvantages arising from that rule, but without preventing the basic rule from achieving its legitimate purposes, and without introducing other disadvantages (such as excessive uncertainty).

In respect of tort (unlike contract), the English choice of law rules have not been harmonised by EC legislation,[2] nor by other international agreements,[3] but remain based on specifically English case-law.[4] The leading authority is the decision of the House of Lords in *Boys v Chaplin*,[5] which involved a road accident in Malta, in which the plaintiff, a pillion passenger on a motor scooter, was injured as a result of the negligent driving of a car by the defendant. Both parties were British servicemen stationed in Malta but normally resident in England, and the defendant was insured, against claims arising from his driving, in England by an English company. The main issue was whether the plaintiff could recover damages for pain and suffering in accordance with Eng-

---

[1] [1971] AC 356.

[2] It was originally intended that what eventually became the 1980 Convention on the Law Applicable to Contractual Obligations, [1980] OJ L266, should also contain provisions on choice of law in respect of torts; see art 10 of the 1972 Preliminary Draft, (1973) 21 AJCL 587. But in 1978 it was decided to confine the instant negotiations to contracts.

[3] The United Kingdom is not a party to the Hague Convention of 4 May 1971 on the Law Applicable to Traffic Accidents, (1968) 16 AJCL 589, nor to the Hague Convention of 2 October 1973 on the Law Applicable to Products Liability, (1973) 21 AJCL 150, (1972) 11 ILM 1283.

[4] Changes have, however, been proposed by the English and Scottish Law Commissions in their Report on *Choice of Law in Tort and Delict*, Law Com 193 (1990).

[5] [1971] AC 356, affirming [1968] 2 QB 1, CA.

lish law, or whether damages must be confined to pecuniary loss in accordance with Maltese law.

The House of Lords (comprising Lords Hodson, Guest, Donovan, Wilberforce and Pearson) unanimously (and in agreement with a majority of the Court of Appeal and with the judge of first instance) held that damages for pain and suffering should be awarded in accordance with English law. Unfortunately, however, five separate speeches were read, and the views of first preference expressed in the House of Lords disclose no line of reasoning justifying the result reached for which there is a majority at all essential points. Similarly in the Court of Appeal Lords Denning and Upjohn had disagreed totally on the reasons by which they reached the same result,[6] and at first instance Milmo J had relied on an authority[7] which was subsequently rejected by a majority in both the House of Lords and the Court of Appeal. Fortunately, however, the most perceptive of the speeches in the House, that of Lord Wilberforce, with whom Lord Hodson substantially agreed, and with whom Lord Pearson was prepared to concur by way of second preference, has been followed in subsequent decisions.[8] We shall therefore proceed on the basis that the speech of Lord Wilberforce in *Boys* represents the current law.

On this basis, the grounds for the decision in *Boys* are as follows:

(a) Although the mere quantification of damages under the admissible heads is a matter of procedure governed by the lex fori, the admissibility of a head of damage is a matter of substance, and in a personal injury action pain and suffering is a separate head of damage from pecuniary loss.[9]

(b) In an English action in tort in respect of acts and events which occurred abroad, the general rule as to choice of law in respect of substantive issues requires double actionability under both English law, as the lex fori, and under the lex loci delicti, the law of the country in which the acts and events in question occurred. Thus if the defendant properly establishes by pleading and proof any substantive respect in which the lex loci delicti is more favourable to him than the corresponding rule of English domestic law, the

---

[6] Only Diplock LJ, dissenting in the Court of Appeal, would have decided the issue in favour of the defendant.

[7] *Machado v Fontes* [1897] 2 QB 231.

[8] See *Sayers v International Drilling* [1971] 1 WLR 1176, per Lord Denning MR; *Church of Scientology v MPC* (1976) 120 SJ 690, per Bridge LJ; *Coupland v Arabian Gulf Oil Co* [1983] 1 WLR 1136, per Hodgson J (almost summarily affirmed by the Court of Appeal); *Armagas v Mundogas* [1986] AC 717, per Robert Goff and Dunn LJJ in the Court of Appeal (affirmed by the House of Lords without consideration of choice of law); and *Johnson v Coventry Churchill International Ltd* [1992] 3 All ER 14, Kay QC in the High Court; and *Red Sea Insurance v Bouygues* (1994) *The Times*, 21 July, PC (per Lord Slynn).

[9] This proposition was adopted by Lords Wilberforce, Hodson and Pearson (in the House of Lords), as well as by Lord Denning and Diplock LJ (in the Court of Appeal). But contrary views were adopted by Lord Donovan (in the House of Lords) and Lord Upjohn (in the Court of Appeal), who considered all questions relating to the remedy to be procedural; and by Lord Guest, who accepted the admissibility of heads of damage as substantive, but regarded pain and suffering and pecuniary loss as mere elements in the quantification of a single head of damage, comprising the bodily injury.

plaintiff will succeed on that issue only to the extent that liability exists both under English domestic law and under the lex loci delicti.[10] In the words of Lord Wilberforce:[11]

> The broad principle should surely be that a person should not be permitted to claim in England in respect of a matter for which civil liability does not exist, or is excluded, under the law of the place where the wrong was committed. This non-existence or exclusion may be for a variety of reasons and it would be unwise to attempt a generalisation relevant to the variety of possible wrongs. But in relation to claims for personal injuries one may say that provisions of the lex [loci] delicti, denying, or limiting, or qualifying recovery of damages because of some relationship of the defendant to the plaintiff, or in respect of some interest of the plaintiff (such as loss of consortium) or some head of damage (such as pain and suffering) should be given effect to. I can see no case for allowing one resident of Ontario to sue another in the English courts for damages sustained in Ontario as a passenger in the other's car, or one Maltese resident to sue another in the English courts for damages in respect of pain and suffering caused by an accident in Malta. I would, therefore, restate the basic rule of English law with regard to foreign torts as requiring actionability as a tort according to English law, subject to the condition that civil liability in respect of the relevant claim exists as between the actual parties under the law of the foreign country where the act was done.

(c) But the general rule is subject to exception, where clear and satisfying grounds justifying the adoption of some other solution are shown. In particular, the lex loci delicti will be excluded, and English law alone will be applied, if:

(1) the parties are substantially connected with England and not with the country where the acts and events occurred, and

(2) in view of this lack of connection between the parties and its territory, the lex loci delicti has no substantial interest in having its rule, differing from the corresponding English rule, applied as between the parties in question.[12]

Thus, in the instant case, the connection of the parties with England, their lack of connection with Malta, and the absence of any Maltese interest in denying the award of damages for pain and suffering between parties lacking any substantial

---

[10] This proposition was accepted in the House by Lords Wilberforce, Hodson and Guest; but rejected by Lord Donovan and, in his first-preference views, Lord Pearson. It was also accepted in the Court of Appeal by Lord Denning and by Diplock LJ, dissenting, but rejected by Lord Upjohn.

[11] [1971] AC at 389.

[12] The concept of interest analysis derives essentially from the writings of Brainerd Currie; see his *Selected Essays on the Conflict of Laws* (1963). It has been very influential in American courts since the decision of the New York Court of Appeals in *Babcock v Jackson* [1963] 2 Lloyd's Rep 286.

connection with Malta, justified the application of the exception so as to permit the award of damages for pain and suffering in accordance with English law.[13]

As Lord Wilberforce put it:[14]

> Given the general rule, as stated above . . ., as one which will normally apply to foreign torts, I think that the necessary flexibility can be obtained from that principle which represents at least a common denominator of the United States decisions, namely, through segregation of the relevant issue and consideration whether, in relation to that issue, the relevant foreign rule ought, as a matter of policy or . . . science, to be applied. For this purpose it is necessary to identify the policy of the rule, to enquire to what situations, with what contacts, it was intended to apply; whether not to apply it, in the circumstances of the instant case, would serve any interest which the rule was devised to meet. This technique appears well adapted to meet cases where the lex [loci] delicti either limits or excludes damages for personal injury; it appears even necessary and inevitable. No purely mechanical rule can properly do justice to the great variety of cases where persons come together in a foreign jurisdiction for different purposes with different pre-existing relationships, from the background of different legal systems. It will not be invoked in every case or even, probably, in many cases. The general rule must apply unless clear and satisfying grounds are shown why it should be departed from and what solution, derived from what other rule, should be preferred. If one lesson emerges from the United States decisions it is that case-to-case decisions do not add up to a system of justice. Even within these limits this procedure may in some instances require a more searching analysis than is needed under the general rule. But unless this is done, or at least possible, we must come back to a system which is purely and simply mechanical.
>
> I find in this approach the solution to the present case. The tort here was committed in Malta; it is actionable in this country. But the law of Malta denies recovery of damages for pain and suffering. Prima facie English law should do the same: if the parties were both Maltese residents it ought surely to do so; if the defendant were a Maltese resident the same result might follow. But in a case such as the present, where neither party is a Maltese resident or citizen, further enquiry is needed rather than an automatic application of the rule. The issue, whether this head of damage should be allowed, requires to be segregated from the rest of the case, negligence or otherwise, related to the parties involved and their circumstances, and tested in relation to the policy of the local rule and of its application to these parties so circumstanced. So segregated, the issue is whether one British subject, resident in the United Kingdom, should be prevented from recovering, in accordance with English law, against another British subject, similarly situated, damages for pain and suffering which he cannot recover under the rule of the lex [loci] delicti. This issue must be stated, and examined, regardless of whether the injured person has or has not also a recoverable claim under a different heading (e.g., for expenses actually incurred) under that law. This Maltese law cannot simply be rejected on grounds of public policy, or some general conception of justice. For it is one thing to say or presume that domestic rule is a just rule, but quite another, in a case where a foreign element is involved, to reject a foreign rule on any such general ground. The foreign rule must be evaluated in its application.

---

[13] Reasoning along these lines was adopted by Lords Wilberforce and Hodson, and by way of second preference, Lord Pearson, in the House of Lords, and by Lord Denning in the Court of Appeal. It was, however, rejected by Lords Guest and Donovan in the House; and by Lord Upjohn and Diplock LJ in the Court of Appeal.

[14] [1971] AC at 391–2.

The rule limiting damages is the creation of the law of Malta, a place where both respondent and appellant were temporarily stationed. Nothing suggests that the Maltese State has any interest in applying this rule to persons resident outside it, or in denying the application of the English rule to these parties. No argument has been suggested why an English court, if free to do so, should renounce its own rule. That rule ought, in my opinion, to apply.

Lord Wilberforce rightly recognised, though he did not fully explain, that the purpose of the Maltese rule denying the award of damages for pain and suffering could not have been to encourage reckless driving, or to ensure that accident victims should live in poverty or on social security, but must have been to protect defendants and their insurers from supposedly excessive financial burdens. That purpose would not have been furthered by application of the Maltese rule in the instant case, where the defendant was a British serviceman stationed temporarily in Malta but normally resident in England, and insured in England by an English company. On the other hand the policies of financial protection and respect for personality, which underlie the English rule awarding damages for pain and suffering, had relevant application in favour of a plaintiff who was a British serviceman temporarily stationed abroad but normally resident in England, even though the accident happened abroad.

The role of the lex fori

The general rule adopted in *Boys v Chaplin*, requiring double actionability on every substantive issue under the lex fori and the lex loci delicti, reflects and clarifies the rule adopted about a century earlier by the Court of Exchequer Chamber in *Phillips v Eyre*,[15] which was the leading authority during the intervening period. There Willes J explained that, to found a suit in England for a wrong alleged to have been committed abroad, two conditions had to be fulfilled: the first, that the wrong must have been of such a character that it would have been actionable if committed in England; and the second, that the act must not have been justifiable by the law of the place where it was done. This rule had meanwhile been approved and applied by the House of Lords in *Carr v Fracis Times*.[16] However it was the second limb of the rule, referring to the lex loci delicti, rather than the first, referring to the lex fori, which was at issue in *Phillips v Eyre* and *Carr v Fracis Times*, as well as *Boys v Chaplin*.

The first limb derives from the decision of the Privy Council, reversing the English Court of Admiralty, in *The Halley*.[17] There the Privy Council dismissed a claim against a shipowner for damage resulting from a collision caused by the negligent navigation of his ship by a compulsory pilot, since at that date such vicarious liability did not exist under English internal law, even though the collision had occurred in Belgian waters and such liability did exist under Belgian

[15] (1870) LR 6 QB 1.
[16] [1902] AC 176.
[17] (1868) LR 2 PC 193.

law. The first limb is also explicable historically, by reference to the manner in which the English court originally overcame jurisdictional difficulties and asserted its competence to entertain actions based on foreign torts: by means of a legal fiction that the acts and events had occurred in England.[18] In the period between *Phillips v Eyre* and *Boys v Chaplin*, the rule in *The Halley* (or the first limb of the rule in *Phillips v Eyre*) was applied by the Scottish Court of Session in *McElroy v McAllister*,[19] so as to reject a claim for damages for loss of expectation of life, which was then recognised by English law, the lex loci delicti, but not by Scottish law, the lex fori; and by the High Court of Australia, on appeal from the Australian Capital Territory, in *Anderson v Eric Anderson Radio & TV Pty Ltd*,[20] so as to reject a claim altogether on account of the plaintiff's contributory negligence, in accordance with the lex fori, although this was a ground for apportionment under New South Wales law, the lex loci delicti. Since *Boys v Chaplin* it has again been applied by the Scottish Court of Session in *Mitchell v McCullough*,[21] so as to reject, in an action for an assault committed in the Bahamas, claims under Bahamian law for losses suffered by a company of which the plaintiff was a director, and by members of the plaintiff's family, since such losses were not recoverable under Scottish internal law. It has, however, been rejected (along, indeed, with the second limb) by the Irish Supreme Court in *Grehan v Medical Inc*.[22]

The requirement of actionability under English internal law, although explicable historically and well established, is utterly devoid of merit, and the Law Commissions have recommended its abrogation by legislation.[23] The flagrant injustice to which it can give rise is most obvious where it enables an English defendant to escape liability to a foreigner for acts done and injuries sustained in the foreigner's country. It is difficult to say whether the English rule, giving the benefit of English law to any defendant, regardless of whether he has any connection with England, is better or worse than the corresponding German rule, which guarantees the benefit of German law to a defendant who is a German national. Perhaps the question is without meaning: the English rule evinces generalised wrong-headedness, while the German rule reduces the scope of the error, but does so by means of unprincipled discrimination. It is interesting, however, that in *Grehan v Medical Inc*,[24] Walsh J in the Irish Supreme Court, in

---

[18] See *Mostyn v Fabrigas* (1774) 98 ER 1021, upholding a plea that the acts had taken place 'at Minorca, to wit at London, in the parish of St Mary le Bow, in the ward of Cheap'!

[19] 1949 SC 110.

[20] (1966) 114 CLR 20.

[21] [1976] SLT 2.

[22] [1988] ECC 6.

[23] See their Report on *Private International Law: Choice of Law in Tort and Delict*, Law Com 193, Scottish Law Com 129 (1990), at paras 2.6–2.11 and 4.1(1), and cl 1 of the appended draft Tort and Delict (Applicable Law) Bill. The recommendation was provisionally foreshadowed in their Working Paper 87, Consultative Memorandum 62 (1984).

The recommendation for legislative abrogation is subject to savings relating to English public policy; foreign penal, revenue, and other public laws; overriding English enactments; and procedure. See paras 3.55 and 4.1(9) of the Report; and cl 4 of the appended draft Bill.

[24] [1988] ECC 6.

criticising the first limb of the English rule, emphasised that it required the application of the lex fori even where the only connection with the forum country was that the defendant had moved there after the tort was committed. He also emphasised that it placed the victim of a foreign tort in a far worse position than the victim of a breach of a foreign contract. It is also noteworthy that any such general reference to the lex fori as such was rejected in the United States as long ago as 1918.[25]

The fundamental absurdity of the reference to the lex fori is most apparent in actions complaining of the infringement abroad of foreign intellectual property rights, where it requires the action to be dismissed if a corresponding property right does not exist in England (as where no parallel patent has been obtained here),[26] or if liability arises from a wider definition in the foreign country of the acts which infringe the right (as where, for example, the foreign law makes it infringement of a patent to import or sell an *indirect* product of a patented process). Indeed, ludicrous decisions at first instance in both England and Scotland have gone so far as to hold that the territorial restrictions expressed in the British legislation on copyright and registered trademarks prevent the entertainment here in any circumstances of an action for an infringement, in a country to which the corresponding British legislation does not extend, of a copyright recognised by, or trademark registered in, the country in question, even if the defendant's acts would have amounted to the infringement of a parallel British copyright or registered trademark in the same ownership, if they had been committed in the United Kingdom.[27] It seems clear that such a conclusion is based on a misunderstanding of the nature of the reference to the lex fori, whose rules, under the formula announced in *Phillips v Eyre* and subsequently reiterated, have to be applied *as if the defendant's acts complained of had been committed in England*. An even more radical and indefensible approach in the intellectual property sphere was adopted by Vinelott J in *Tyburn Productions v Conan Doyle*,[28] to the effect that the ancient distinction between transitory and local actions, which before the Civil Jurisdiction and Judgments Act 1982 prevented the English courts from entertaining actions for trespass or other torts against foreign land, still prevents them from entertaining actions concerned with the validity or infringement of foreign patents, copyrights, registered trademarks, or other intellectual property rights.[29] He seems to have overlooked the abrogation of any such jurisdictional

---

[25] See *Loucks v Standard Oil Co of New York* 120 NE 198 (1918); a decision of Cardozo J.

[26] As in *Potter v Broken Hill* [1905] VLR 612; affirmed on other grounds, (1906) 3 CLR 479.

[27] See (on copyright) per Browne-Wilkinson J in *Def Lepp Music v Stuart-Brown* [1986] RPC 273; and (on trademarks) per Lord Coulsfield in *James Burrough Distillers v Speymalt Whisky Distributors* [1991] RPC 130. In the latter case a parallel trademark was registered in the United Kingdom in favour of a company associated with the plaintiff company, rather than the plaintiff itself, but the decision did not rely on this technical difference in ownership. See also *Norbert Steinhardt v Meth* (1960) 105 CLR 440.

[28] [1991] Ch 75; relying on *Potter v Broken Hill* (1906) 3 CLR 479, and *Norbert Steinhardt v Meth* (1961) 105 CLR 440.

[29] He admitted, however, that 'an action for passing-off is an application of the tort of misrepresentation and the court can grant an injunction to restrain passing-off in a foreign jurisdiction if the threatened conduct of the plaintiff is unlawful in that jurisdiction'; citing *Alfred Dunhill v Sunoptic* [1979] FSR 337.

rule, in relation to actions for infringement, by the 1968 Convention on Jurisdiction and the Enforcement of Judgments in Civil and Commercial Matters.

The facts of *Boys v Chaplin* did not present a good opportunity for reconsideration of the first limb of the general rule, but its approval may reasonably be considered to be the weakest part of that decision, and, indeed, the only serious flaw in the speech of Lord Wilberforce. Fortunately, however, the decision introduced an exception to the rule requiring double actionability; and, although initially it may not have been wholly clear, the decision appears to have contemplated that the exception should permit departure from either or both of the limbs of the general rule, whenever 'clear and satisfying grounds' for preferring some other solution are shown. For Lord Wilberforce admitted that the traditional English rule 'bears a parochial appearance, that it rests on no secure doctrinal principle, that outside the world of the English speaking common law it is hardly to be found'. Moreover, in rejecting an argument for the substitution of a rule referring simply to the lex loci delicti, partly on account of difficulties and injustices which had driven the American courts to abandon such a rule as a universal solvent, and to qualify it by means of a principle of 'contacts' or 'interests', he explained that such a qualification could equally well be added to the existing English rule.

Similarly Lord Hodson concluded his speech[30] by adopting the principle stated by the American Law Institute's *Restatement, Second, Conflict of Laws* (1971), that rights and liabilities of parties with respect to an issue in tort should be determined by the internal law of the state which, as to that issue, has the most significant relationship to the occurrence and the parties; that separate rules should apply to different kinds of torts; and that the importance of the respective contacts should be evaluated in the context of the particular issue, the nature of the tort, and the purposes of the tort rules involved; and that controlling effect is given to the law of the country which, because of its relationship with the occurrence and the parties, had the greater concern with the specific issue raised in the litigation. Moreover Lord Pearson accepted[31] that, whatever general rule should be adopted, some exception would be required in the interests of justice.

Thus *Boys v Chaplin* itself indicates that the exception can override the reference in the general rule to the lex fori, as well as or instead of overriding its reference to the lex loci delicti. Moreover, this has now been confirmed by the decision of the Privy Council, per Lord Slynn, in *Red Sea Insurance v Bouygues*,[32] upholding a direct action by a loss insurer in its own name in accordance with the Saudi Arabian lex loci, although no such right of action existed under the Hong Kong lex fori.

In view of the indefensible character of the requirement of actionability under the lex fori as such, it is submitted that clear and satisfying grounds for adopting another solution, usually the application of the lex loci delicti alone, should readily

---

[30] [1971] AC at 380.
[31] [1971] AC at 406.
[32] (1994) *The Times*, 21 July.

be found. More specifically, the lex fori should be resorted to only in the rare cases where either:

(1) the content of the relevant foreign law is so intolerably offensive to the English judicial conscience that a stringent English public policy precludes its application by an English court in any circumstances, regardless of connecting factors;[33] or

(2) both parties lack any substantial connection with the country where the acts and events on which the claim is based occurred, but have a substantial connection with England (or one has a substantial connection with England, and the other with a third country whose law is not materially different from English law), and the law of the country where the acts and events occurred has no substantial interest in the application of its substantive rules between the parties in question, in view of the purposes underlying those rules and the parties' lack of connection with its territory.

It is well established that, in litigation founded on tort as well as other matters, procedure is governed by the lex fori, and in *Boys v Chaplin* it was accepted that the mere quantification of damages under heads recognised as admissible by the law or laws governing substance is procedural. This seems an over-simplification. The function of the rule on procedure is to avoid burdening the parties and the court with the trouble, inconvenience or dislocation of attempting to apply foreign rules on matters which concern the conduct of the proceedings, and which either are unlikely to affect the result, or in respect of which departure from the English method would require the court to conduct itself in an unfamiliar and undesirable manner. The archetypal procedural rule is as to the size of the paper on which pleadings should be typed, but the category extends to such matters as the availability of a jury trial and the respective roles of judge and jury.

The procedural category should not be used as an excuse for applying the lex fori so as to achieve a desired result, though this was not infrequently done in America in the period prior to *Babcock v Jackson*,[34] when the accepted rule was that liability in tort was governed by the lex loci delicti. Such abuses occurred, for example, in *Grant v McAuliffe*,[35] where a Californian court evaded the rule in favour of the lex loci delicti by characterising as procedural (or alternatively as a matter of estate administration) the question whether liability in tort survives the death of the wrongdoer, so as to be enforceable against his estate; and in *Kilberg v Northeast Airlines*,[36] where a New York court disregarded as procedural (or alternatively as contravening its public policy) a statutory limit on the maximum amount recoverable for a wrongful death. In particular, an issue should not be regarded as procedural unless there would be real inconvenience in attempting to

---

[33] A possible example might be if the lex loci delicti denied any right to use reasonable force in resisting an unlawful arrest by public officers.

[34] [1963] 2 Lloyd's Rep 286.

[35] 264 P2d 944 (1953).

[36] 172 NE2d 526 (1961).

apply foreign law (as in the case of vague foreign rules for quantifying non-patrimonial losses, such as pain and suffering, or loss of bodily facility), or unless doing so would unacceptably distort the method by which English litigation is conducted (as in the case of American rules requiring jury trial of personal injury claims). Certainly a foreign rule which specifies a fixed monetary limit on the maximum amount of damages which can be awarded for a particular type of claim should not be considered procedural, since there is no serious inconvenience or difficulty in applying such a limit, the result is greatly affected, and the method of trial is not affected at all.[37] Nor, it is submitted, despite the decision of Hodgson J in *Coupland v Arabian Gulf Petroleum Co*,[38] should a foreign rule that social security benefits should not be deducted from a plaintiff's loss of earnings be disregarded as procedural; for omitting to make the deduction actually simplifies the judicial task.

The common law rule which formerly characterised time-limits for bringing actions as procedural has been rightly abrogated by the Foreign Limitation Periods Act 1984, subject to provisos for public policy or undue hardship.[39] In *Jones v Trollope Colls*,[40] the Court of Appeal construed 'undue hardship' as referring simply to hardship which is excessive, or greater than the circumstances warrant. Accordingly, in a personal injury action brought by an American plaintiff against English defendants about two years after the road accident from which the claim arose had occurred in Pakistan, they disregarded the one-year limitation period under Pakistan law, because the plaintiff had been incapacitated in hospital in Germany for much of the one-year period, and had been led by one of the defendants to believe that her claim would be met by its insurers.

The role of the lex loci delicti

Although in *Phillips v Eyre*,[41] the leading authority prior to *Boys v Chaplin*,[42] Willes J (for the Court of Exchequer Chamber) deferred to *The Halley*[43] in requiring actionability under English domestic law, he recognised the primary role of the lex loci delicti, by emphasising that the civil liability arising out of a wrong derives its birth from the law of the place, and that its character is determined by that law. Accordingly he specified, as the second limb of his general rule as to the conditions necessary to found a suit in England for a wrong alleged to have been committed abroad, that the act must not have been justifiable by the law of the place where it was done.

This recognition of the primacy of the lex loci delicti seems justifiable in terms of interest analysis, territorial sovereignty, party expectations, and general

[37] See *Reich v Purcell* 432 P2d 727 (1967).
[38] [1983] 2 All ER 434; affirmed without consideration of this point, [1983] 3 All ER 226, CA.
[39] See Stone [1985] 4 LMCLQ 497.
[40] (1990) *The Times*, 26 January.
[41] (1870) LR 6 QB 1.
[42] [1971] AC 356.
[43] (1868) LR 2 PC 193.

conceptions of justice. For a country usually has a substantial interest in regulating acts and consequences which take place within its territory, and disregard for that interest can be resented as an infringement of its territorial sovereignty. Moreover people generally tend to view law in territorialist terms (though they tend to focus primarily on the criminal law), and thus to expect that both their primary conduct (in avoiding dangerous or prohibited behaviour) and their secondary conduct (in obtaining suitable insurance cover) will be judged or should be guided by the law of the place where they are acting or intending to act.

In *Phillips v Eyre*[44] itself the court applied the second limb of the general rule by dismissing an action for assault and false imprisonment in respect of acts committed in Jamaica, then a British colony, by the governor in the suppression of a rebellion, on the ground that the acts in question had been validly, albeit retroactively, legalised by an Act of Indemnity adopted by the Jamaican legislature. Similarly the availability of 'police power' or 'public authority' defences under the lex loci delicti to actions for intentional interference with the plaintiff's person or property had been recognised earlier in *Blad's Case*,[45] *Mostyn v Fabrigas*,[46] *Dobree v Napier*,[47] and *R v Leslie*,[48] and was recognised subsequently in *Carr v Fracis Times*.[49] Indeed, subject only to the possible operation of a stringent English public policy against scandalous foreign rules, it seems clear that, on grounds of interest analysis and territorial sovereignty, the lex loci delicti must be allowed to regulate the use of force for public purposes in its territory, regardless of whether the parties are foreigners.

The second limb has also led to the rejection of claims for unintentional injuries, where the relevant claim was not recognised by the lex loci delicti. Thus a fatal accident action was dismissed by the Privy Council in *Canadian Pacific Ry v Parent*,[50] where the Quebec lex fori gave the victim's widow an independent claim in respect of his death, but the Ontario lex loci delicti rejected her claim because liability to her deceased husband had been excluded by a contractual term. Similarly in *Walpole v Canadian Northern Ry*[51] and *McMillan v Canadian Northern Ry*,[52] the Privy Council, on appeal from Saskatchewan, which had abolished the doctrine of common employment, rejected claims by an employee or an employee's dependants against the employer in respect of accidents which had occurred in British Columbia or Ontario, whose laws had retained or extended the doctrine. Under the second limb it was not enough to support a tort action elsewhere that the lex loci delicti provided a statutory claim for a limited sum by way of workman's compensation, whether payable from a public fund, or payable

[44] (1870) LR 6 QB 1.
[45] (1673) 36 ER 991.
[46] (1774) 98 ER 1021.
[47] (1836) 132 ER 301.
[48] (1860) 29 LJMC 97.
[49] [1902] AC 176.
[50] [1917] AC 195.
[51] [1923] AC 113.
[52] [1923] AC 120.

by the employer after determination by a specialist tribunal, for such claims were not tortious in character. Similarly in *Naftalin v LMS Ry*[53] and *McElroy v McAllister*,[54] Scottish courts rejected claims under Scottish law for solatium in respect of the wounded feelings of the surviving relatives of men killed in English accidents, since such claims were not then recognised by English law. Again in *MacKinnon v Iberia Shipping*,[55] a Scottish court rejected a claim for the victim's own pain and suffering resulting from an accident in Dominica, under whose law only pecuniary loss was recoverable.

On the other hand, in *Machado v Fontes*[56] the English Court of Appeal, in an obvious and perhaps wilful misinterpretation of the second limb of the rule in *Phillips v Eyre*, equated 'not justifiable' with 'wrongful' and 'justifiable' with 'innocent', and thus proceeded to uphold in accordance with English law an action for a libel published in Brazil, although no civil liability existed under Brazilian law, since the act amounted to a crime there.[57] The court added that all aspects of the assessment of damages were procedural and governed by the lex fori. A similar decision was given subsequently by the Supreme Court of Canada, on appeal from Quebec, in *McLean v Pettigrew*,[58] upholding in accordance with Quebec law a claim by a gratuitous passenger against his driver for negligent driving in Ontario, despite the immunity from such claims conferred by the Ontario 'guest statute', since the driving in question amounted to the offence of careless driving under Ontario law, although the driver had been prosecuted but acquitted in Ontario.[59] Fortunately *Machado v Fontes*[60] has been overruled by the House of Lords in *Boys v Chaplin*,[61] and in view of *Walpole v Canadian Northern Ry*[62] and *McMillan v Canadian Northern Ry*[63] it seems clear that the second limb of the rule in *Phillips v Eyre* requires liability in tort (and not some other type of civil liability, such as for breach of contract) under the lex loci delicti.[64]

In *Metall und Rohstoff v Donaldson Lufkin & Jenrette*,[65] the Court of Appeal seem to have considered that if the tort took place in England, English law would

---

[53] 1933 SC 259.
[54] 1949 SC 110.
[55] 1955 SC 20.
[56] [1897] 2 QB 231.
[57] The sufficiency of criminality under the lex loci had earlier been suggested by dicta in *Scott v Seymour* (1862) 158 ER 865, and by dicta of Cockburn CJ at first instance in *Phillips v Eyre* (1869) LR 4 QB 225.
[58] (1945) 2 DLR 65.
[59] See also *Brown v Poland* (1952) 6 WWR(NS) 368, where cross-claims between drivers arose from an accident in Montana caused by the negligence of both drivers, one of whom had also committed the offence of crossing the centre line while passing. An Alberta court apportioned the claim against that driver in accordance with the Alberta lex fori, but dismissed the cross-claim in accordance with the Montana lex loci.
[60] [1897] 2 QB 231.
[61] See per Lords Wilberforce, Hodson and Guest; with Lords Donovan and Pearson dissenting on this point.
[62] [1923] AC 113.
[63] [1923] AC 120.
[64] Cf Cheshire & North, at p 539.
[65] [1990] 1 QB 391.

always and exclusively apply. But no argument based on the exception (about to be considered) was presented in that case.

The role of law of the country to which the parties belong

As has been seen, the decision of the House of Lords in *Boys v Chaplin*[66] has established an exception to the general rule requiring actionability, on each substantive issue, under both the lex fori and the lex loci delicti. Lord Wilberforce considered that the exception should be available whenever clear and satisfying grounds for preferring some other particular solution were demonstrated. He then proceeded to exclude application of the Maltese lex loci delicti, in favour of the English lex fori, on the ground that both of the parties were British servicemen, habitually resident in England, and that Maltese law had no interest in the application of its rule denying liability for pain and suffering as between such parties. Similarly Lord Hodson applied English law on the ground of its greater concern to regulate the issue between the parties. Thus it is clear that the exception is based, at least primarily, on interest analysis, a concept which was isolated by an American academic, Brainerd Currie,[67] and which has been frequently utilised by American courts since the breakthrough decision in *Babcock v Jackson*,[68] where the New York Court of Appeals abandoned the rigid rule in favour of the lex loci delicti which had prevailed in the United States at least for the previous half-century.[69] Currie's may be seen as the most important contribution to conflicts theory in the 20th century.

Interest analysis involves focusing on the particular substantive rules which conflict, and ascertaining their purposes. A country or its legal system is regarded as interested in the application of a substantive rule contained in its law, in preference to a conflicting rule contained in the law of another country, in a particular case if one or more of the purposes or policies which its rule is designed to achieve or promote would be furthered by the application of its rule, in preference to the conflicting rule contained in the other connected and possibly applicable law, in the case in question, in view of the connections of the parties and the acts and events involved with its territory. Of course one is not concerned with the actual intentions of the legislator, but with the objective function of the rule: a rule should be regarded as designed to achieve those results which, as compared with the conflicting rule, it is likely to achieve, and which could reasonably be regarded as desirable.[70]

The concept may usefully be illustrated by reference to American cases involving the operation in relation to road accidents of various rules granting a special

---

[66] [1971] AC 356.
[67] See his *Selected Essays on the Conflict of Laws* (1963), especially Chapter 4.
[68] 191 NE2d 279 (1963).
[69] See *Alabama Great Southern Railroad Co v Carroll* 11 So 803 (1892); *Slater v Mexican National Railroad* 194 US 120 (1904); and *Loucks v Standard Oil Co of New York* 120 NE 198 (1918). Cf *Mertz v Mertz* 3 NE2d 597 (1936).
[70] It is misunderstanding of the objective nature of the inquiry into the purposes of rules which has led some English commentators to reject interest analysis; see eg Fawcett (1984) 47 MLR 650.

immunity from ordinary liability for negligently caused injury. The cases deal mainly with 'guest statutes', which reduce the standard or eliminate the duty of care owed by a driver to his gratuitous passenger,[71] or with statutes setting a low maximum amount which may be recovered for wrongful death (in English terms, fatal accidents).[72] The same analysis of interests is equally applicable where the special immunity rule excludes liability for pain and suffering, as in *Boys v Chaplin*;[73] or exempts a charitable body from liability;[74] or excludes liability between members of a family.[75]

At least in the case of road accidents, a special immunity of any of these types is not designed to encourage 'exciting' driving or other risk-taking conduct, nor to ensure that accident victims live in poverty or on social security, but to protect the defendant and his insurers from supposedly excessive or unjustifiable financial burdens. Hence a country having such a rule is not interested in applying it merely because the accident happened within its territory. It is disinterested unless the defendant was habitually resident, or had his relevant place of business, or his vehicle was registered or insured, there. On the other hand a country which rejects such a special immunity and maintains ordinary principles of liability for negligence aims thereby both to deter careless conduct and to protect the financial position of accident victims. Thus such a country is interested in application of its rule on deterrent grounds if the wrongful conduct takes place within its territory; and is interested on compensatory grounds if the injury is received, or the victim is habitually resident, there.

As Lord Wilberforce, though not Brainerd Currie, recognised, interest analysis alone is not acceptable as a complete solution to choice of law in tort or other areas.[76] On its own it creates too much uncertainty and unpredictability and encourages forum shopping. Two laws may have substantial but conflicting interests, or no law may be interested, and Currie's reversion to the lex fori in such cases[77] has little merit. Moreover, it would outrage the most basic principles of conflicts justice to increase the liability of a defendant who acted and caused injury in his own country, merely because the plaintiff happened to be a foreigner; or

---

[71] See eg *Babcock v Jackson* 191 NE2d 279 (1963); *Tooker v Lopes* 249 NE2d 394 (1969); *Cipolla v Shaposka* 267 A2d 854 (1970); *Milkovitch v Saari* 203 NW2d 408 (1973); *Neumeier v Kuehner* 286 NE2d 454 (1972); *Labree v Major* 306 A2d 808 (1973).

[72] See eg *Reich v Purcell* 432 P2d 727 (1967); *Hurtado v Superior Court* 522 P2d 666 (1974); *Rosenthal v Warren* 475 F2d 438 (1973).

[73] [1971] AC 356. See also *Bryant v Silverman* 703 P2d 1190 (1985), where an Arizona court applied the law of Arizona, to which the parties belonged, so as to allow the award of damages for non-pecuniary injuries in respect of a fatal accident in Colorado, whose law confined fatal accident awards to pecuniary losses.

[74] See eg *Schultz v Boy Scouts of America* 480 NE2d 679 (1985); though this was neither a road accident case nor a satisfactory decision.

[75] See eg *Haumschild v Continental Casualty* 95 NW2d 814 (1959); and *Corcoran v Corcoran* [1974] VR 164.

[76] Cf *Grehan v Medical Inc* [1988] ECC 6, where the Irish Supreme Court rejected both limbs of the rule in *Phillips v Eyre*, on the ground that it was capable of producing arbitrary decisions, in favour of a rule of sufficient flexibility to respond to the individual issues arising in and the social and economic dimensions of each case.

[77] See his *Selected Essays on the Conflict of Laws* (1963), especially Chapter 4.

conversely to reduce the entitlement of a plaintiff who was injured in his own country by acts committed there, merely because the defendant happened to be a foreigner.[78] On the other hand, as Currie rightly recognised, the idea of applying the law having the *greater interest or concern* seems impracticable, since no intellectually defensible method can be devised for the weighing of the conflicting interests of laws which, ex hypothesi, have chosen to give priority to different objectives; and attempts to do so tend to degenerate into preference for the forum's rule, subjectively perceived (whether overtly or covertly) as more accordant with substantive justice.[79]

Moreover, in most cases the lex loci delicti *does* have a substantial interest in the application of its rule; and even where it does not, application of its rule accords with the instinctive expectations of ordinary people as to the territoriality of law, and cannot be regarded as positively unjust. All that can be said against the lex loci delicti, apart from cases where its content is obnoxious or where the location of the events is truly fortuitous (in the sense of unexpected and unintended by both parties, as where a plane crashes on landing after being hijacked or diverted to avoid bad weather), is that in some cases its application does not provide the best solution.

Hence the appropriate rule, which accords with many of the leading American decisions and seems compatible with the decision and dicta in *Boys v Chaplin*,[80] is that in general tort liability should be governed by the lex loci delicti, but that there should be an exception in favour of the law of the country (or countries) to which the parties belong, where:

(1) neither party is strongly connected with the country of the occurrence, and both are strongly connected with the same other country (or with two other countries whose relevant rules are identical with each other's but different from those of the country of the occurrence);[81] and

(2) in view of the parties' lack of connection with the country of the occurrence, and the nature and purposes of the conflicting rules, that country has no substantial interest in the application of its rules as between them, in preference to those of their own country.

In cases involving road accidents and special immunities of the types mentioned above, this approach leads to the following results:

(1) If the accident happens in an ordinary liability country, its law should be applied so as create liability, even if both parties belong to an immunity country. For in such a case the lex loci delicti has both a deterrent and a compensatory

---

[78] See Jaffey (1982) 2 LS 98.

[79] Cf Leflar (1966), 41 NYULR 267, who raises preference for the better substantive rule into an independent determinative consideration. 'That way chaos lies'!

[80] [1971] AC 356.

[81] For cases involving parties from different countries but with equivalent laws, see *Pfau v Trent Aluminium Co* 263 A2d 129 (1970); *Chila v Owens* 348 FSupp 1207 (1972); *Gross v McDonald* 354 FSupp 378 (1973). All these cases rejected the lex loci delicti's guest statute in favour of the ordinary negligence rule common to the different countries to which the parties respectively belonged. See also *Reich v Purcell* 432 P2d 727 (1967), similarly rejecting the lex loci delicti's quantum limit on wrongful death awards.

interest.[82] A fortiori if one of the parties belongs to the country of the occurrence, even if it is the defendant, who would benefit from the law of the plaintiff's country.[83]

(2) If the accident happens in an immunity country, but both parties belong to an ordinary liability country, liability should be imposed in accordance with the law of the parties' country. For in such a case the lex loci delicti is disinterested, and the law of the parties' country is interested in protecting the financial interests of the plaintiff.[84]

(3) But if the accident occurs in an immunity country and the defendant belongs to that country, he must be allowed the benefit of its law, even if the plaintiff belongs to an ordinary liability country. For the laws have conflicting interests, and it would be unjust to a defendant acting and causing injury in his own country to deprive him of the benefit of its law.[85] The same must apply where the defendant belongs, not to the country of the accident, but to another country whose law provides for the same immunity.[86]

(4) If the accident occurs in an immunity country and the plaintiff belongs to that country but the defendant belongs to an ordinary liability country, so that each party would benefit if the other's law were applied, both laws are disinterested and there seems no adequate reason for departing from the lex loci delicti.[87]

---

[82] See eg *Milkovitch v Saari* 203 NW2d 408 (1973), where, in the case of a Minnesota accident involving Ontario parties, a Minnesota court refused to apply the Ontario guest statute, and allowed recovery for ordinary negligence under Minnesota law.

[83] See *Hurtado v Superior Court* 522 P2d 666 (1974), where a Californian court refused to limit in accordance with Mexican law the damages recoverable for the wrongful death of a Mexican resident, arising from an accident in California for which a Californian resident was responsible.

[84] See *Babcock v Jackson* 191 NE2d 279 (1963), and *Tooker v Lopes* 249 NE2d 394 (1969), where New York courts allowed recovery for ordinary negligence between New Yorkers in respect of Ontario or Michigan accidents, despite an Ontario guest statute, which eliminated any duty of care, and a Michigan guest statute, which required gross negligence; *Reich v Purcell* 432 P2d 727 (1967), where a California court allowed full recovery to an Ohio plaintiff from a Californian defendant in respect of a Missouri accident, despite a low statutory limit on maximum recovery under Missouri law; *Corcoran v Corcoran* [1974] VR 164, where a Victorian court allowed recovery under its own law between Victorian spouses in respect of a road accident in New South Wales, whose law did not permit inter-spousal tort claims; and *Boys v Chaplin* [1971] AC 356 itself.

[85] See *Cipolla v Shaposka* 267 A2d 854 (1970), where a Pennsylvanian court applied a Delaware guest statute in favour of a Delaware defendant against a Pennsylvanian plaintiff; and dicta of Lords Hodson and Wilberforce in *Boys v Chaplin* [1971] AC 356, at 379, 392.

Cf the indefensible decision to the contrary in *Rosenthal v Warren* 475 F2d 438 (1973), where a federal Court of Appeals, sitting as a New York court, deprived a Massachusetts doctor of the benefit of a Massachusetts maximum limit on wrongful death awards as against the dependants of a New York patient treated in Massachusetts.

[86] See *Pryor v Swarner* 445 F2d 1272 (1971).

[87] See *Neumeier v Kuehner* 286 NE2d 454 (1972), where a New York court applied an Ontario guest statute to an Ontario accident involving an Ontario passenger and a New York driver.

This is the most controversial case. In *Labree v Major* 306 A2d 808 (1973), the opposite result was reached by a Rhode Island court, essentially on the view that such immunities should be limited as much as possible and should not apply unless an immunity country is interested. Similarly in *Erwin v Thomas* 506 P2d 494 (1973), an Oregon court applied Oregon law to allow a Washington wife to recover against an Oregon driver for loss of her husband's consortium owing to his injury in a Washington accident, although Washington law rejected claims of this type.

Since in cases involving special immunities from liability for road accidents the plaintiff succeeds if either the lex loci delicti or the law of the country to which the parties belong admits his claim,[88] it might be suggested that a simple rule of alternative reference should be adopted, and interest analysis dispensed with. But this would be unacceptable, since it overlooks other types of issue to which the lex loci delicti should be applied, even where the parties both belong to another country whose law favours the plaintiff.

This is especially the case where the issue concerns legal justification for intentional interference with the plaintiff's person or property by reference to police or other public powers. For example, if an arrest takes place in France, respect for French sovereignty, as well as the need for certainty, requires that the grounds which justify arrest, the manner in which an arrest should be effected, the amount of force which may properly be used in effecting an arrest, and the remedies open to a person unlawfully arrested, should be referred to French law – even if, for example, the person arrested is an Englishman and the person who makes the arrest is an English policeman who has been summoned through Interpol to assist the French police. The interest of the lex loci delicti in regulating the deliberate use of force within its borders is so strong that it should only be overridden by a stringent public policy against scandalous or unconscionable rules.[89] Moreover it seems inappropriate, in the absence of a stringent public policy of the forum, to impose a greater liability, in accordance with some other law, for acts which the actor was *required* to perform by the law of the place at which he acted.

It must also be noted, as was recognised in *The Halley*,[90] that even where liability is governed by some other law, rules of conduct imposed by the lex loci delicti must be taken into account as data relevant to the application of vague standards of liability contained in the governing law. For example, even if English law supplies the applicable duty and standard of care as between two English drivers whose vehicles collide on a German road, in determining, as required by English law, which of them was negligent, it must be recognised that in Germany it is proper to drive on the right rather than the left side of the road. To similar effect, art 7 of the Hague Convention of 4 May 1971 on the Law Applicable to Traffic Accidents requires that, whatever the applicable law, in determining liability account must be taken of rules relating to the control and safety of traffic which were in force at the time and place of the accident.

More generally, whenever the purpose of the rule of the lex loci delicti is, at least partly, to influence conduct, then (subject only to a stringent public policy against

---

[88] The decision of the Court of Appeal in *Church of Scientology v Metropolitan Police Commissioner* (1976) 120 SJ 690, suggests that a similar result pattern may apply to vicarious liability, even in cases other than road accidents. That is, it may be sufficient if vicarious liability exists either under the lex loci delicti or the law of the country to which the parties belong. The case involved the vicarious liability of an English chief constable for an alleged libel published in Germany by English police officers in a report to a German police authority.

[89] See per Lord Denning MR in *Hesperides Hotels v Aegean Turkish Holidays* [1978] QB 205, which involved a similar issue, as to the lawfulness of requisitioning of land by a public authority. The choice of law question was not considered in the House of Lords, [1979] AC 508.

[90] (1868) LR 2 PC 193.

unconscionable rules) the lex loci delicti's interest should be respected. In particular, it is submitted that the lex loci delicti should always determine whether the plaintiff's contributory negligence has the effect of barring recovery altogether, or merely of causing apportionment of damages, or is wholly irrelevant to recovery, for whichever rule is chosen by a legal system, the choice reflects, at least in part, a policy as to the best distribution of the burden of taking precautions with a view to preventing accidents, and thus the country of the accident has a conduct oriented interest in the application of its rule.[91] Somewhat similarly, since the aim of awarding exemplary or punitive damages is by definition to punish and deter undesirable conduct, the availability of such an award should be referred to the lex loci delicti, even if the parties belong to another country.[92]

Since the exception depends upon the parties belonging to the same country (or to countries having equivalent laws), rules are needed to identify the country to which a party belongs. Clearly such rules must reflect the interests involved, but they should also be designed to achieve the maximum certainty and to avoid disappointing reasonable expectations of parties or their insurers. It is therefore suggested that, for present purposes, in general an individual should be regarded as belonging to the country of his habitual residence, and a company to the country containing its place of business the staff of which were (wholly or mainly) involved in the acts and events which gave rise to the claim. However, by way of exception, a person involved in a road accident as a driver, the employer of a driver, or the owner of a vehicle, should be regarded as belonging to the country in which the vehicle which he or his employee was driving, or of which he was the owner, was registered.[93] And, by way of further and overriding exception, a diplomat or military serviceman should be regarded as belonging to the country which he serves, rather than the country in which he is stationed, if his involvement is otherwise than as a driver in a road accident, or, where he is involved in a road accident as a driver, if his motor insurance was issued in the country which he serves.[94]

Further complications arise where several (actual or potential) plaintiffs and/or defendants are involved in the same incident. Such a situation arose in *Tooker v Lopez*,[95] where careless driving in Michigan by a New York driver caused the deaths of herself and one of her passengers, who was also habitually resident in New York, and serious injury to another passenger, who was habitually resident in Michigan. A New York court upheld a claim by the survivors of the New York passenger, applying the New York ordinary negligence rule in preference to the

---

[91] Cf *Sabell v Pacific Intermountain Express Co* 536 P2d 1160 (1975), where a Colorado court applied its own apportionment rule to an accident in Iowa between Colorado residents, in preference to the Iowa rule under which the plaintiff's negligence would have provided a complete defence.

[92] Cf *Bryant v Silverman* 703 P2d 1190 (1985), where an Arizona court applied its own law, so as to allow the award of exemplary damages, in a fatal accident action between Arizona residents in respect of an accident in Colorado, despite their unavailability in fatal accident cases under Colorado law.

[93] See *Babcock v Jackson* [1963] 2 Lloyd's Rep 286; and *Tooker v Lopez* 249 NE2d 394 (1969).

[94] See *Boys v Chaplin*, especially per Lord Denning MR in the Court of Appeal, [1968] 2 QB 1 at 24.

[95] *Tooker v Lopez* 249 NE2d 394 (1969).

Michigan guest statute requiring gross negligence. The Michigan passenger did not make a claim, but the subsequent New York decision in *Neumeier v Kuehner*[96] indicates that the Michigan guest statute would have been applied against her if she had. It is thought that such discrimination is intolerable, and that the only principled solution is to adhere to the lex loci delicti unless all persons who were involved in the incident, and in relation to whose mutual rights and obligations the connected laws conflict, belong to the same country (or to countries having equivalent laws).[97]

This view gains some support from *Re Paris Air Crash of 3 March 1974*,[98] where a plane belonging to a Turkish airline crashed in France, killing 346 occupants, who came from 12 states of the USA and 24 other countries. In an action against the Californian manufacturer, a Californian court applied Californian law. While it might have been better to have applied Turkish law, as that of the registration of the aircraft, it seems clear, in terms of both justice and convenience, that in such cases a single law must be applied to the claims of all the passengers, regardless of their various residences.

Another kind of complication arises where the lex loci delicti differs from the law of the country to which the parties belong in respect of more than one issue; especially if, were each such issue to be considered alone, the lex loci delicti would be seen as interested in having its rule prevail on one, but not on another, of these issues. Again it is submitted, on grounds both of principle and convenience, that (at least in general) a single law should govern all the issues; and accordingly that if the lex loci delicti is interested in having any one of its rules applied in preference to a conflicting rule of the country to which the parties belong, then the rules of the lex loci delicti should usually prevail on all the issues. Otherwise we will get absurd results, such as allowing a child passenger to recover against a parent driver on proof of ordinary negligence, when one of the connected laws would reject the claim on grounds of inter-familial immunity and the other would reject it under a guest statute.[99]

---

[96] 286 NE2d 454 (1972).

[97] It is conceded that if, for example, all but one of the persons involved belong to the same country (not being the country of the accident), but the remaining person belongs to the country of the accident, the law of the country to which the other persons belong can properly be applied as between them if there is no difference between the two laws which is capable of affecting the rights and obligations of the person who belongs to the country of the accident. A concrete example would be a collision in a country having a guest statute between a car registered in, and containing a passenger from, an ordinary liability country, and a car registered in the country of the collision, but containing no passenger. The guest issue cannot affect the rights or liabilities of the driver from the country of the collision, even to the passenger in the other car; so it is acceptable to allow the claim of the passenger against his own driver in accordance with the law of the country to which they belong.

Further exceptions to the rule proposed are not ruled out, if they can be justified in a principled way; but it is thought that they cannot be identified in advance and must wait for actual fact law patterns to arise.

[98] 399 FSupp 732 (1975).

[99] Cf *Lillegraven v Tengs* 375 P2d 139 (1962), where an Alaskan court allowed a claim by an Alaskan passenger against an Alaskan vehicle-owner arising from an accident in British Columbia, by combining the British Columbian rule making a vehicle-owner liable for the negligence of anyone driving with his consent, with the longer Alaskan time-limit for bringing actions.

An important application of the law of the country to which the parties belong was made by Kay QC (in the High Court) in *Johnson v Coventry Churchill International Ltd*,[100] where an English construction worker had sustained personal injury as a result of the collapse of a rotten plank at a building site in Germany where he was working as an employee of an English company, which supplied temporary labour to German construction companies. He had been recruited in England to work in Germany for a 13-week period, and his contract of employment with the defendant expressly chose English law as its proper law. Under German law the liability of an employer to an employee for negligently caused industrial accidents had been abolished, so as to leave compensation to social security law, but (apparently in accordance with EC Regulation 1408/71) the plaintiff was affiliated to the English, and not the German social security system. Kay QC held the English employer liable, applying English law in accordance with the exception envisaged by Lord Wilberforce in *Boys v Chaplin*.[101]

He explained that the German rule 'was introduced as part of social security legislation to improve benefits payable to injured workmen whilst avoiding the need to inquire into questions of fault in such circumstances. Doubtless the contributions made by German employers towards state benefits reflect such a policy and the fact that they are freed of the responsibility to compensate employees for injury arising from fault on their part. It would seem therefore that there is nothing in the policy underlying the foreign rule that was ever intended to have any application to the case of an English citizen working for an English employer.' In view especially of the social security position, application of the German rule in the circumstances of this case would not serve any interest which the rule was devised to meet, and in all the circumstances English law had the most significant relationship with the occurrence and the parties. Moreover application of English law to this situation would not introduce an undesirable element of uncertainty, but would afford protection to English employees working abroad for English companies in countries of whose laws they could be expected to have little knowledge.

This decision seems entirely acceptable as an application of *Boys v Chaplin*, if one assumes that the choice of law problem should have been addressed in terms of tort. It is, however, submitted that tort liabilities arising between contracting parties from things done or omitted in the course of the purported performance of the contract should be treated for choice of law purposes as contractual liabilities; and, indeed, that where the contract was concluded after March 1991, the 1980 Convention on the Law Applicable to Contractual Obligations, implemented by the Contracts (Applicable Law) Act 1990, so requires.[102]

---

[100] [1992] 3 All ER 14.
[101] [1971] AC 356.
[102] See Chapter 12 above.

The Hague Convention on Traffic Accidents

The United Kingdom is not a party to the Hague Convention of 4 May 1971 on the Law Applicable to Traffic Accidents,[103] but the Convention is in force in five EC member states[104] and a few other European countries.[105] The Convention applies regardless of reciprocity, and even where it leads to the application of the law of a non-contracting state, but it gives way to other international conventions dealing with special fields.[106]

For the purpose of delimiting the scope of the Convention, art 1(2) defines a traffic accident as 'an accident which involves one or more vehicles, whether motorised or not, and is connected with traffic on the public highway, in grounds open to the public or in private grounds to which certain persons have a right of access'. However the Convention is effectively confined to claims against drivers, vehicle-owners and pedestrians, since art 2(1) and (2) excludes from its scope 'the liability of manufacturers, sellers or repairers of vehicles' and 'the responsibility of the owner, or of any other person, for the maintenance of a way open to traffic or for the safety of its users'.

A further exclusion, by art 2(3), covers 'vicarious liability, with the exception of the liability of an owner of a vehicle, or of a principal, or of a master'. This exclusion seems aimed at the vicarious liability of parents for the acts of their children, recognised in some legal systems. Also excluded, by art 2(3)–(5), are recourse actions among persons liable, recourse actions and subrogation involving insurers, and actions or recourse actions by or against social insurance institutions or public automobile guarantee funds. On the other hand, the Convention does apply to, and lays down specific rules on, direct actions by accident victims against liability insurers.[107]

Article 3 of the Convention lays down a general rule in favour of the internal law of the country where the accident occurred, but arts 4 and 5 make an exception in certain cases in favour of the internal law of the country[108] in which the vehicle or vehicles involved in the accident were registered, and art 10 contains the usual proviso permitting refusal to apply foreign rules whose content makes their application 'manifestly contrary to public policy'. By art 6, the country in which a vehicle was habitually stationed is substituted for the country of its registration, if it was unregistered, or if it was registered in more than one country, or if neither its owner, nor its possessor, nor its driver was habitually resident in the country of registration.

The Convention seeks to ensure unity in the applicable law where there are

---

[103] (1968) 16 AJCL 589.
[104] France, Belgium, Luxembourg, the Netherlands and Spain.
[105] Including Austria and Switzerland. See (1990) 29 ILM 1072.
[106] See arts 11 and 15.
[107] See art 9.
[108] Although arts 3–5 speak of the *state* of the accident or registration, art 12 provides that a territory forming part of a non-unitary state is to be considered a state if it has its own law on civil non-contractual liability arising from traffic accidents. However art 13 permits a non-unitary state to ignore the Convention in the case of accidents occurring, and involving only vehicles registered, within its territory.

several potential defendants, by specifying that where more than one vehicle was involved in an accident, the exception in favour of the law of the registration applies only if all the vehicles involved were registered in the same country,[109] and that if one or more pedestrians were involved in the accident and may be liable, the law of the registration applies only if all such pedestrians were habitually resident in the country of the registration.[110] But if these conditions are fulfilled, the Convention tolerates diversity in the law applicable to various plaintiffs, by applying the law of the registration to claims by the following persons:

(1) regardless of the claimant's habitual residence, claims by drivers, vehicle-owners, and owners of goods carried in a vehicle, other than goods belonging to or in the care of a passenger;[111]

(2) claims by passengers who were not habitually resident in the country in which the accident occurred, and claims in respect of goods carried in a vehicle and belonging to or in the care of such a passenger;[112]

(3) claims by pedestrians who were habitually resident in the country of the registration, including claims for damage to their personal belongings.[113]

Otherwise, however, the law of the country of the accident applies – for example, to claims by a passenger who was habitually resident in the country of the accident, or by a pedestrian who was habitually resident either in the country of the accident or in a third country.[114]

Article 8 specifies that the law applicable under arts 3–5 governs, in particular, the basis and extent of liability; the grounds for exemption from liability, any limitation of liability, and any division of liability; the existence and kinds of compensatable injury; the kinds and extent of damages; the assignability and inheritability of a right to damages; the persons entitled to compensation for their own injuries; the liability of a master or principal for the acts of his servant or agent; and time-limits for actions, including the commencement, interruption or suspension of the limitation period. However art 7 requires that, whatever the applicable law, in determining liability account must be taken of rules relating to the control and safety of traffic which were in force at the time and place of the accident.

Article 9 deals with direct actions by a victim against the liability insurer of a person liable. It provides in effect that such a remedy shall be available if it is available under either: (a) the law applicable under arts 3–5; or (b) the law of the country where the accident occurred; or (c) the law governing the contract of insurance.

The Convention seems to merit two severe criticisms. It ignores the content of the conflicting rules, and consequently disregards the legitimate interests of the

[109] Article 4(b).
[110] Article 4(c).
[111] Articles 4(a)(i) and 5(2).
[112] Articles 4(a)(ii) and 5(1).
[113] Articles 4(a)(iii) and 5(3).
[114] Article 3 and the final clause of art 4(a).

country of the accident where its law is more favourable to recovery than the law of the registration; and it discriminates between victims of the same accident according to their respective habitual residences.

Torts occurring in more than one country

So far we have assumed that all the acts and events on which the claim is based occurred in one country. But obviously it is possible for the defendant's conduct to take place in one country and the plaintiff's injury in another, and more complicated situations, in which either the conduct, or the injury, or both, takes place in more than one country, can readily be envisaged. The problem of determining the lex loci delicti for purposes of choice of law in such cases has been addressed by two decisions of the Court of Appeal, in *Armagas v Mundogas*[115] and *Metall und Rohstoff v Donaldson Lufkin & Jenrette*,[116] which have adopted the analogy of the confused case-law on jurisdiction under the former version of RSC Ord 11, prior to its amendment in connection with accession to the 1968 Convention. Accordingly the rule is that the lex loci delicti is the law of the country in which the tort was in substance committed. In *Metall und Rohstoff v Donaldson Lufkin & Jenrette*[117] the Court of Appeal ruled further that if the tort was in substance committed in England, then English law is exclusively applicable, without any possibility of exception in favour of, for example, the law of the country to which both parties belong. But if the tort was in substance committed abroad, the exception to the general rule requiring double actionability, in favour of the law of the country to which both parties belong, will no doubt apply in a similar way to the situation where the entirety of the tort occurred in a single foreign country.

Under the test of the country where the tort was in substance committed, the authorities indicate that the tort of deceit (or analogous negligent misrepresentation) is committed at the place where the false statement is received and acted on.[118] In a case of inducing multiple breaches of contract, the tort is in substance committed in the country where the most important breaches induced were committed by the person induced and the resulting losses were incurred by the plaintiff. Thus in *Metall und Rohstoff v Donaldson Lufkin & Jenrette*,[119] where American defendants, by acts of inducement committed largely in New York, had caused their subsidiary to commit breaches of commodity contracts with the plaintiff, the most significant of which had taken place in England, and it was in England that the plaintiff had suffered damage, by not receiving payments and warrants and by having its accounts closed, as a matter of substance the torts had

---

[115] [1986] AC 717.
[116] [1990] QB 391.
[117] [1990] QB 391.
[118] See *Armagas v Mundogas* [1986] AC 717; a decision of the Court of Appeal on (inter alia) choice of law, affirmed by the House of Lords without consideration of choice of law. See also, on jurisdiction under the former RSC Ord 11, *Diamond v Bank of London & Montreal* [1979] QB 333, and *Cordoba Shipping v National State Bank* [1984] 2 Lloyd's Rep 91. The contrary decision in *Cordova v Victor* [1966] 1 WLR 793 is obsolete.
[119] [1990] QB 391.

taken place in England, and it was therefore immaterial that the claim was time-barred under New York law. As regards defamation, at least in cases of a single publication to one person, the tort will be regarded as committed at the place of publication; that is, where the defamatory communication (such as a letter) is received by the third party to whom it is published.[120]

As regards product liability, the English decisions on where a tort is in substance committed indicate that, where a manufacturer is sued by a consumer or bystander injured by a defective product, the tort will be regarded as committed in the country where the injury was sustained, at least if the product had been marketed in that country by the manufacturer or in accordance with his intentions.[121] Moreover in the United States Kozyris[122] has cogently argued that the place of production should be considered unimportant, and the place of distribution should normally be decisive. So perhaps the reference should be to the place of business (of the manufacturer or some other dealer) at which the goods were last marketed through commercial channels in accordance with the defendant's intention before the injury. Some support for this approach may be drawn from two American decisions. In *Boudreau v Baughman*,[123] the designer of a chair, a resident of North Carolina, was sued by a guest of the ultimate purchaser for injuries sustained in Florida. The defendant had sold the design to a furniture manufacturer, also resident in North Carolina, which had manufactured the chair and sold it to a furniture store in Florida, which in turn had sold it to the plaintiff's Floridan hosts. A North Carolina court applied the law of Florida, as that of the place of sale, distribution, delivery, and use of the product, as well as the place of injury, and thus having the most significant relationship to the claim. In *McCrossin v Hicks Chevrolet*,[124] a District of Columbia court applied its own law to impose strict liability on a manufacturer of a car purchased by the plaintiff from a dealer within the District, even though the plaintiff purchaser was resident in Maryland and the car caught fire there.

The Hague Convention on Products Liability

France, the Netherlands, Luxembourg, Spain and Norway, but not the United Kingdom, are parties to the Hague Convention of 2 October 1973 on the Law

---

[120] See *Bata v Bata* [1948] WN 366, decided under the former version of RSC Ord 11.

[121] See *Distillers Co v Thompson* [1971] AC 458; *Moran v Pyle* (1973) 43 DLR(3d) 239; and *Castree v Squibb* [1980] 1 WLR 1248. The contrary decision in *Monro v American Cyanamid* [1944] KB 432 is now obsolete.

[122] 'Values and Methods in Choice of Law for Products Liability: A Comparative Comment on Statutory Solutions' (1990) 38 AJCL 475.

[123] 368 SE2d 849 (1988). See also *Schmidt v Driscoll Hotel* 82 NW2d 365 (1957), where a Minnesota court applied its own dramshop Act to hold a Minnesota tavern-keeper, who had sold liquor to a drunk, liable to a Minnesota resident who was injured by the drunk in Wisconsin. Cf *Bernhard v Harrah's Club* 546 P2d 719 (1976), where a Californian court applied Californian law to hold a Nevada tavern-keeper who had supplied liquor to an intoxicated Californian patron liable for injuries to a Californian resident sustained in a road accident in California caused by the negligent driving of the patron on her way home. The court emphasised that the Nevada tavern had actively solicited in California for the custom of Californian residents.

[124] 248 A2d 917 (1969).

Applicable to Products Liability.[125] Its material scope is elaborately defined by arts 1–3, to the following effect:

(1) The Convention applies to the liability of manufacturers and certain other persons 'for damage caused by a product, including damage in consequence of a misdescription of the product or of a failure to give adequate notice of its qualities, its characteristics or its method of use'.[126]

(2) 'Product' includes natural and industrial products, either new or manufactured, and whether movable or immovable, though a contracting state can make a reservation excluding raw agricultural products.[127]

(3) 'Damage' covers personal injury, damage to property, and purely economic loss, except that damage to the product itself, and consequential economic loss, are excluded unless associated with other damage.[128]

(4) The Convention applies to the liability of manufacturers of a finished product or a component part of a product, producers of a natural product, suppliers of a product, persons such as repairers or warehousemen included in the commercial chain of preparation or distribution of a product, and agents or employees of any such persons.[129]

(5) The Convention does not, however, apply as between persons between whom the property in, or the right to use, the product was transferred.[130]

The Convention lays down (in arts 4–7) a complicated set of choice of law rules which utilise five connecting factors, usually in combination: the place of injury; the habitual residence of the direct victim; the principal place of business of the defendant; the place of acquisition of the product by the direct victim; and the reasonable foreseeability or otherwise to the defendant that the product or the defendant's products of the same type would be made available in a country through commercial channels. The rules which emerge are as follows, and applied in the following order:

(1) If the habitual residence of the direct victim and the principal place of business of the defendant are in the same country, the law of that country applies.[131]

(2) Otherwise if the habitual residence of the direct victim and the place of acquisition by the direct victim are in the same country, the law of that country applies, unless the defendant establishes that he could not reasonably have foreseen that the product or his products of the same type would be made available in that country through commercial channels.[132]

[125] For its text, see (1973) 21 AJCL 150, (1972) 11 ILM 1283. For parties, see (1990) 29 ILM 1072.
[126] Article 1(1).
[127] Articles 2(a) and 16(1)(2).
[128] Article 2(b).
[129] Article 3.
[130] Article 1(2).
[131] Article 5(a).
[132] Articles 5(b) and 7.

(3) Otherwise if the place of injury and the principal place of business of the defendant are the same country, the law of that country applies.[133]

(4) Otherwise if the place of injury and either the habitual residence of the direct victim or the place of acquisition by the direct victim are in the same country, the law of that country applies, unless the defendant establishes that he could not reasonably have foreseen that the product or his products of the same type would be made available in that country through commercial channels.[134]

(5) Otherwise the plaintiff has a choice between the law of the place of injury and the law of the defendant's principal place of business, unless the defendant establishes that he could not reasonably have foreseen that the product or his products of the same type would be made available in the country of injury through commercial channels.[135]

(6) Finally, as a last resort, the law of the defendant's principal place of business applies.[136]

In every case it is the internal law of the connected country which is made applicable, and not its choice of law rules. The rules apply regardless of reciprocity, and even where they lead to the application of the law of a non-contracting state.[137] There is, however, the usual proviso permitting refusal to apply foreign rules whose content makes their application 'manifestly incompatible with [the forum's] public policy',[138] and the Convention gives way to other international conventions dealing with special fields.[139]

The scope of the law applicable under the Convention is specified by art 8, to the effect that it determines, in particular, the basis and extent of liability; the grounds for exemption from liability, and any limitation or division of liability; the kinds of compensatable injury; the form and extent of compensation; the assignability and inheritability of a claim; the persons entitled to compensation for their own injuries; the liability of an employer or principal for the acts of his servant or agent; the burden of proof, insofar as the rules of the applicable law thereon pertain to the law of liability; and time-limits for actions, including the commencement, interruption or suspension of the limitation period.[140] However art 9 permits consideration of the rules of conduct and safety prevailing in the country where the product was introduced into the market.

The Convention in form refers to the law of a connected *state*, but by art 12 each territory forming part of a non-unitary state and having its own rules on product liability is treated as a state for the purpose of the Convention. However art 13 permits a non-unitary state not to apply the Convention in cases where a unitary

---

[133] Article 4(b).
[134] Articles 4(a) and (c) and 7.
[135] Articles 6 and 7.
[136] Articles 6 and 7.
[137] Article 11.
[138] Article 10.
[139] Article 15.
[140] But art 16(1)(1) permits a state to make a reservation excluding rules on time-limits.

state would not have to apply foreign law under the Convention. Thus, for example, if the United States were to become party to the Convention, it would not have to apply French law (under rule (6) above) in a case where the defendant manufacturer was French, the product was foreseeably acquired by the victim through commercial channels in New York, but he suffered the injury at his habitual residence in California.[141]

It is difficult to see any merit in the complicated rules laid down by the Convention. Why the defendant's principal place of business should be important is far from clear, and the significance attached to the commercial marketing of the defendant's products *of the same type* deprives a manufacturer or supplier of the ability effectively to charge different prices in different markets so as to reflect different costs owing to different levels of product liability. It is difficult to see any circumstances in which the rules laid down by the Convention would produce better results than a rule referring simply to the place of business (of the defendant or an intermediate dealer) from which the product was last supplied in the course of business in accordance with the defendant's intention before it caused the injury.

Torts connected with contracts

Although the matter is unsettled, it is submitted that tort claims between parties to a contract arising in connection with the negotiation or performance of the contract should be treated as contractual for choice of law purposes, and thus in general governed by the proper law of the contract, ascertained in accordance with the 1980 Convention.[142] This would accord with the parties' expectations and their probable or reasonably imputed intention of choosing a law to govern their entire relationship in respect of the transaction, rather than the merely contractual aspects of it in some technical sense. Of course the control of the proper law of the contract would give way to the provisions of arts 5–7 of the 1980 Convention for the protection of consumers, employees, or overriding English interests in the usual way.

This submission derives some support from the decision of the Court of Appeal in *Sayers v International Drilling*,[143] where the majority tested the validity and effectiveness of an exemption clause by reference to the proper law of the contract, despite the fact that the plaintiff was asserting a claim in tort for negligently causing personal injury. The later case of *Coupland v Arabian Gulf Petroleum Co*[144] involved no difference between the connected laws which was regarded as substantive. Moreover the submission would have provided an easy solution in *Johnson v Coventry Churchill International Ltd*,[145] by giving the employee the benefit of English law as the expressly chosen proper law of the contract.

---

[141] See Reese (1973) 21 AJCL 149 at 150.
[142] See Chapter 12 above.
[143] [1971] 1 WLR 1176.
[144] [1983] 1 WLR 1136.
[145] [1992] 3 All ER 14. See the text to note 99 above.

In their 1990 Report, the Law Commissions were divided in their views on the issue of contractual defences to tort claims, and recommended no legislation on the question.[146]

The Law Commission Report

In their Report on *Private International Law: Choice of Law in Tort and Delict*,[147] the English and Scottish Law Commissions have broadly adopted one of the two models for reform suggested in their earlier Consultation Paper.[148] They recommend non-retroactive legislation extending to the whole of the United Kingdom,[149] abolishing the existing rule requiring double actionability under the lex fori as such and the lex loci delicti,[150] and replacing it with a rule referring primarily to the lex loci delicti, but with an exception in favour of the law most substantially connected with the tort. More precisely, the law prima facie applicable would be:

(1)   in cases of personal injury, death or damage to property, that of the country where the person or property was when injured or damaged;[151]
(2)   in other cases, that of the country in which the most significant elements in the sequence of events constituting the tort occurred.[152]

But the law ultimately applicable would be that of the country with which the tort had the most substantial connection, in view of the connections of the parties as well as those of the events constituting or connected with the tort and their surrounding circumstances and consequences:

(a)   where there is no law prima facie applicable, because the case is not one of personal injury, death or damage to property, and there is no single country in which the most significant elements in the sequence of events occurred; or
(b)   by way of displacement of the law prima facie applicable, where such displacement would produce a substantially more appropriate solution.[153]

Renvoi would be explicitly excluded,[154] and a single law is envisaged as governing all issues between the same parties, but different laws might govern claims between different parties arising from the same incident.[155] Section 1(2) of the Foreign Limitation Periods Act 1984, and corresponding legislation for Northern

[146] See note 146 below, at paras 3.49–3.50.
[147] Law Com 193, Scot Law Com 129 (1990).
[148] Working Paper No 87, Consultative Memorandum 62 (1984).
[149] See paras 3.58–3.59; and cl 6 of the appended draft Tort and Delict (Applicable Law) Bill.
[150] See paras 2.11 and 4.1(1); and cl 1 of the appended draft Bill.
[151] See paras 3(6) and 4.1(2); and cl 2(1) and (2) of the appended draft Bill.
[152] See paras 3.10 and 4.1(4); and cl 2(3)(a) of the appended draft Bill.
[153] See paras 3.9–3.12 and 4.1(5); and cl 2(3)–(5) of the appended draft Bill.
[154] See para 3.56; and cl 2(6) of the appended draft Bill. This accords with the Hague Convention of 2 October 1973 on the Law Applicable to Products Liability.
[155] See paras 3.52–53. This approach accords with that of the Hague Convention of 4 May 1971 on the Law Applicable to Traffic Accidents.

Ireland, would be repealed as no longer needed in view of the abolition of the rule in *The Halley*.[156]

Some derogations in favour of the lex fori are, however, proposed:

(1) The law of a part of the United Kingdom would alone apply, if all, or the most significant, elements of the allegedly wrongful conduct took place in that part. This is designed, inter alia, to protect an English manufacturer from liability under foreign law for environmental damage abroad caused by emissions from his English factory.[157] It would, of course, have the opposite effect in cases where English law was more 'environmentally friendly' than that of the country where the damage occurred.

(2) The law of the part of the United Kingdom in which the action was brought would alone apply in cases of defamation, slander of title or goods, malicious falsehood, or invasion of privacy, in respect of a statement published outside the United Kingdom, if the publication of the statement took such a form that a publication also occurred within the United Kingdom, or was simultaneous with or subsequent to a separate publication of a similar statement within the United Kingdom.[158] This is designed to protect freedom of speech within the United Kingdom, but would seem to extend to cases where a few copies of a foreign newspaper were published in England, or to any broadcast from abroad received in England.

(3) There would be savings relating to:

(a) public policy;

(b) foreign penal, revenue or other public laws;

(c) overriding English statutes; and

(d) procedure.[159]

It will be noted that no guidelines are offered to assist in the application of the central concepts on which the proposed rules are based: as to the most significant events, the most substantial connection, or whether one solution is substantially more appropriate than another. Indeed, in the earlier Consultation Paper, the Law Commissions specifically rejected interest analysis and every other known principle which could give relative significance to the various connections. Except for the welcome (but excessively qualified) proposal to eliminate reference to the lex fori from the general rule, the Report may be seen as a failure to offer any meaningful solution to the problems addressed.

---

[156] See cl 5 of the appended draft Tort and Delict (Applicable Law) Bill.
[157] See paras 3.14–3.19 and 4.1(6); and cl 3(1) of the appended draft Bill.
[158] See paras 3.28–3.33 and 4.1(7); and cl 3(2) and (5) of the appended draft Bill.
[159] See paras 3.55 and 4.1(9); and cl 4 of the appended draft Bill.

14

FOREIGN JUDGMENTS

INTRODUCTION

Types of judgment

In this chapter we shall examine the rules relating to the recognition and enforcement in England of foreign personal judgments. For this purpose a personal judgment may be defined as a judgment which determines a claim which is based on the law of non-familial obligations (that is, the law of contract, tort, or restitution; but not family law) or of movable property, and is for particular relief against a specific person.[1] The proprietary effects of foreign personal and other judgments are, however, considered in Chapter 15; and the treatment in England of foreign judgments of a specialised character (decrees and orders under family law,[2] and judgments relating to the collective liquidation of an estate)[3] are dealt with in other chapters. The last part of this chapter deals with the recognition and enforcement in England of foreign arbitral awards.

Enforcement and mere recognition

A judgment given in one country may receive effect in another country by way of mere recognition, or by way of enforcement. Enforcement of a foreign personal judgment implies that a personal judgment has been given by a court of one country ('the original country') which orders a person to perform some particular act (such as the payment of a definite sum of money to another person), or not to perform some particular act (such as not to disturb his

---

[1] This definition reflects the Foreign Judgments (Reciprocal Enforcement) Act 1933, s 11(2) of which in effect defines 'personal judgment' as excluding a judgment given in connection with a matrimonial matter, the administration of the estate of a deceased person, a bankruptcy, the winding up of a company, a lunacy, or the guardianship of a minor, and s 4(2)(b) of which in effect excludes from the concept a judgment whose subject-matter is land, and a judgment in rem whose subject-matter is movable property.

[2] See Chapter 4 on decrees concerning matrimonial status, and orders for financial or proprietary relief under family law; and Chapter 5 on decrees concerning filial status, and orders relating to the custody or adoption of children.

[3] See Chapter 6 on bankruptcy and corporate liquidation, and Chapter 15 on administration of a deceased's estate.

neighbour's sleep by excessive noise), and that steps are taken by the courts or authorities of another country ('the country addressed') with a view to securing compliance with the obligation imposed by the judgment.

Enforcement involves recognition, but mere recognition (without enforcement) of a foreign personal judgment is also possible. Mere recognition implies that the judgment, whether or not it ordered a person to perform (or not to perform) some particular act, is given conclusive effect in the country addressed in respect of questions which it decided, but without steps being taken by the courts or authorities of the country addressed with a view to securing compliance with any obligation imposed by the judgment. In some cases mere recognition is all that is necessary or possible: for example, where the judgment has rejected a claim as unfounded, but without awarding costs; or where the judgment has upheld a claim and awarded a sum of money, but the sum has since been paid as ordered. Mere recognition, if granted, will prevent the claimant from reviving in the country addressed a claim which has been rejected, or accepted but in his opinion to an inadequate extent, by the foreign judgment.

The precise estoppels which arise from a judgment may differ from one law to another. It seems inherent in the very concept of recognition that, at least in general, mere recognition must involve giving a foreign judgment the same conclusive effects as to causes of action and issues determined, and persons affected, as it has in the original country under its law, and not the same effects as the law of the country addressed would give to a similar judgment given by its own courts. In the context of the 1968 Convention, this principle has been accepted by the European Court of Justice in *Hoffmann v Krieg*,[4] as well as in the Jenard Report.[5] In the United States it is explicitly adopted by the statute implementing the 'full-faith-and-credit' clause of the American Constitution, 28 US Code s 1738.[6]

In purely English conflicts law this principle may derive some support from the decision of the House of Lords in *The Sennar (No 2)*,[7] giving effect (prior to British accession to the 1968 Convention) to an issue estoppel arising from a Dutch judgment, so as to construe a jurisdiction clause contained in a bill of lading as covering claims in tort as well as claims in contract. Moreover, while in *House of Spring Gardens Ltd v Waite*[8] the Court of Appeal, in the context of the enforcement of an Irish judgment at common law, appears to have taken account only of English concepts of privity of interest, there was no evidence,

---

[4] Case 145/86, [1988] ECR 645. It was also accepted by the German Supreme Court, in the context of the bilateral convention between Germany and Switzerland, in *Re the Enforcement of a Swiss Maintenance Agreement* [1988] ECC 181 at 187.

[5] [1979] OJ C59 43. Cf the Schlosser Report, which reserved its opinion ([1979] OJ C59 at 127–8).

[6] Cf *Hart v American Airlines* 304 NYS2d 810 (1969), where, despite this legislation, a New York court felt able to derive from a Texas judgment unusual issue estoppels in favour of non-parties, in accordance with New York, but not Texas, law.

[7] [1985] 1 WLR 490. See also Spencer-Bower and Turner, *The Doctrine of Res Judicata* (2nd ed, 1969); and Stone [1983] 1 LMCLQ 1 at 23–6.

[8] [1991] 1 QB 241.

and even less ground for imagining, that Irish law would have denied the effect given to the relevant Irish judgment by the English court.[9] Again the decision of the House of Lords in *Republic of India v India Steamship Co Ltd*,[10] on recognition of an Indian judgment in the light of s 34 of the Civil Jurisdiction and Judgments Act 1982, throws little light on this question, since there was nothing to suggest that the Indian rules on the scope of cause of action estoppel differed from the English rules.

Enforcement regimes

There are five distinct regimes applicable to the enforcement in England of foreign personal judgments. Since their respective scope depends mainly on the country of origin of the judgment, it is convenient to speak of British judgments (given in another part of the United Kingdom); European judgments (given in a contracting state to the 1968 or Lugano Conventions on Jurisdiction and the Enforcement of Judgments in Civil and Commercial Matters); and overseas judgments (given in a country which is not a contracting state to those Conventions).

The enforcement in each part of the United Kingdom of judgments given in its other parts is now governed by Part II, s 18 and Scheds 6 and 7, of the Civil Jurisdiction and Judgments Act 1982.

The enforcement in the United Kingdom of judgments given in the other EC member states is now governed by (mainly, Title III of) the 1968 Convention on Jurisdiction and the Enforcement of Judgments in Civil and Commercial Matters, as amended by the Accession Conventions of 1978, 1982 and 1989.[11] Similarly, the enforcement in the United Kingdom of judgments given in EFTA countries which are contracting states to the Lugano Convention of 16 September 1988 on Jurisdiction and the Enforcement of Judgments in Civil and Commercial Matters is now governed by the Lugano Convention.[12] The 1968 and Lugano Conventions are implemented and supplemented in the United Kingdom by the Civil Jurisdiction and Judgments Acts 1982 (as amended) and 1991.

There are three distinct regimes which govern the enforcement in the United Kingdom of judgments given in a country which is not a party to the 1968 and Lugano Conventions: those provided for respectively by the common law, the Administration of Justice Act 1920, and the Foreign Judgments (Reciprocal Enforcement) Act 1933. The 1920 and 1933 Acts apply to judgments given in a

---

[9] The Court of Appeal seems to have overlooked the point that, since the date of the second judgment of the Irish Supreme Court was 10 June 1988, the question of privity in connection with that judgment should have been governed by the 1968 Convention as amended, which had entered into force between the United Kingdom and Ireland on 1 June 1988.

[10] [1993] AC 410.

[11] For the current text of the 1968 Convention, see [1990] OJ C189/2, or Sched 1 to the Civil Jurisdiction and Judgments Act 1982, as substituted by Sched 1 to SI 1990/2591.

[12] For its text, see [1988] OJ L319/9, or Sched 3C to the Civil Jurisdiction and Judgments Act 1982, added by the Civil Jurisdiction and Judgments Act 1991, Sched 1. For its parties, see Chapter 7, pp 118–19 above.

country to which, on account of reciprocity, the Act in question has been applied by Order in Council, while the common law applies to judgments from countries to which these Acts do not apply. However all three regimes applicable to overseas judgments reflect the traditional English approach, and are substantially similar to each other, but radically different from the regimes now applicable to British or European judgments.

Some features are common to all five regimes on enforcement. They all involve an application to an English court, by the party seeking enforcement, for a suitable English judgment or order. The common law regime involves the bringing of an ordinary action in an English court, pleading the foreign judgment and seeking the entry of a similar English judgment. The other four regimes involve an application to an English court for an order that the foreign judgment be registered for enforcement. Under all five regimes, once an English judgment or registration order has been obtained and has become final, the same measures of actual execution (such as a writ of fieri facias against chattels, or a garnishee order against debts, belonging to the judgment debtor) are available as in the case of a similar English judgment.[13] As regards enforceable judgments within its scope, each regime is exclusive, not only of enforcement of the judgment under the other regimes, but also of an English action based on the original claim.[14] To qualify for enforcement in England under any of the five regimes, the judgment must be enforceable in the original country.[15]

In the case of overseas judgments, all three traditional regimes are confined to permitting the enforcement of judgments which award a definite sum of money. Thus an overseas judgment awarding an indefinite sum (such as £10,000 less

[13] See the 1920 Act, s 9(3); the 1933 Act, s 2(2); the 1982 Act, s 4(3), Sched 5 para 6, and Sched 6 para 6; Case 119/84 *Capelloni and Aquilini v Pelkmans* [1985] ECR 3147; and Case 148/84 *Deutsche Genossenschaftsbank v Brasserie du Pecheur* [1986] 2 CMLR 496. See also, in Ireland, s 6(1) of the (Irish) Jurisdiction of Courts and Enforcement of Judgments (European Communities) Act 1988.

As regards the enforcement of maintenance orders under the 1968 and Lugano Conventions, see the 1982 Act, s 5(4), (5A) and (7).

On the costs of the English enforcement proceedings, see the 1920 Act, s 9(3)(c); the 1933 Act, s 2(6); and the 1982 Act, s 4(2). Cf s 8(2) of the Irish Act.

As to interest on money judgments, see the 1933 Act, s 2(2)(c) and (6), and the 1982 Act, s 7 and Sched 11, Part II; and RSC Ord 71, r 28(1)(b). In Ireland, see s 8 of the 1988 Act.

On the conversion of foreign currency, see *Miliangos v Frank* [1976] AC 443; or, as regards maintenance orders, s 8 of the 1982 Act (and, in Ireland, s 9 of the 1988 Act). See also *Re the Enforcement of a Swiss Maintenance Agreement* [1988] ECC 181, a decision of the German Supreme Court involving a Swiss index-linked maintenance order.

[14] See the 1933 Act, s 6; Case 42/76 *De Wolf v Cox* [1976] ECR 1759; the 1982 Act, ss 18(8) and 34; and *Republic of India v India Steamship Co Ltd* [1993] AC 410. By way of exception, it is possible to obtain enforcement at common law of a judgment to which the 1920 Act applies, but in such a case the applicant will usually be refused costs of the common law enforcement action; see the 1920 Act, s 9(5).

[15] See, as regards the common law, per Russell LJ in *Colt Industries v Sarlie (No 2)* [1966] 1 WLR 1287; the 1920 Act, s 9(1), which makes registration subject to the English court's discretionary finding that in all the circumstances enforcement here would be 'just and convenient'; the 1933 Act, s 2(1)(b); the 1982 Act, Sched 6, paras 3(b) and 4(1)(b), and Sched 7, paras 3(b) and 4(1)(b); and the 1968 Convention, arts 31 and 47. A dubious exception seems to permit enforcement at common law despite a stay of execution in the original country on account of the judgment debtor's bankruptcy; see *Berliner Industriebank v Jost* [1971] 2 All ER 1513.

costs to be, but not yet having been, taxed), or an overseas judgment imposing an obligation to perform, or abstain from performing, some act other than the payment of money (such as an order for the specific performance of a contract, or an injunction against a threatened tort) cannot be enforced in England.[16] It is, however, otherwise in the case of British or European judgments, which are enforceable under the 1982 Act or the 1968 or Lugano Conventions, if they either award a definite sum of money or grant non-monetary relief.[17]

To be enforceable in England, an overseas or European judgment must not be for payment of a fine or tax.[18] It may, however, be a judgment given by a criminal court in ancillary civil proceedings, awarding compensation to a victim who has intervened in a prosecution to claim damages,[19] or even a judgment awarding exemplary damages in respect of a civil claim.[20]

Regimes governing mere recognition

As regards mere recognition, overseas judgments are governed by the common law and s 34 of the 1982 Act, even if the original court is one to which, as regards enforcement, the 1920 Act or the 1933 Act applies.[21] Section 34 eliminates a former restriction on the effects of recognition, whereby recognition did not prevent a person entitled under an unsatisfied but enforceable money judgment from suing in England on the original claim. In effect it extends to foreign judgments the doctrine of merger, whereby a plaintiff's cause of action merges in a judgment in his favour upholding the cause of action, and ceases to have any separate existence.[22]

---

[16] See *Sadler v Robins* (1801) 1 Camp 253; *Beatty v Beatty* [1924] 1 KB 807; the 1920 Act, ss 9(1) and (3) and 12(1); and the 1933 Act, ss 1(2) and 2.

[17] See the Schlosser Report, at p 132, and *EMI Records v Modern Music Karl-Ulrich Watterbach* [1992] 1 QB 115.

[18] See *Huntington v Attrill* [1893] AC 150; *Rossano v Manufacturers' Life* [1963] 2 QB 352; the 1920 Act, ss 9(2)(f) and 12(1); the 1933 Act, s 1(2)(b); and the 1968 and Lugano Conventions, art 1[1].

[19] See *Raulin v Fischer* [1911] 2 KB 83; the 1933 Act, ss 2(5) and 11(1); and the 1968 and Lugano Conventions, arts 1[1] and 5(4), and their (first) annexed Protocols, art 2.

[20] See *General Textiles v Sun & Sand Agencies* [1978] 1 QB 279.

[21] In the case of overseas judgments to which the 1933 Act applies, s 8 of that Act makes some provision for mere recognition, but probably does not alter the results otherwise reached under the common law.

[22] See *Republic of India v India Steamship Co Ltd* [1993] AC 410, where the House of Lords held that for the purposes of s 34 a cargo-owner's claims against a shipowner under bills of lading in respect of goods lost, and of goods damaged, as a result of the same incident during the voyage, were comprised in the same cause of action, but that s 34 gives way to waiver, estoppel by representation, or contrary agreement between the parties. Cf *Black v Yates* [1992] 1 QB 526, where Potter J construed s 34 as not preventing a minor, who was habitually resident in England, and who had obtained damages under a Spanish judgment, from suing again in England on the same cause of action with a view to obtaining additional damages, in view of the English policy that a minor should not be bound by proceedings which are against his interests. Such an approach is defensible, if at all, only as an application of the public policy proviso. Less controversially, Potter J also ruled that a foreign judgment in respect of a dependency claim arising from a fatal accident did not bar a subsequent English action on behalf of the deceased's estate for lost expectation of life, since the widow, who was a plaintiff in both courts, had not purported to act on behalf of the estate in the foreign proceedings. See also *Midland International Trade Services v Al-Sudairy* (1990) *Financial Times*, 2 May.

Similarly the mere recognition of British judgments is governed by the common law and s 34 of the 1982 Act, subject to the exception that, in the case of British judgments, s 19 of the 1982 Act eliminates jurisdictional review. On the other hand the 1968 and Lugano Conventions govern mere recognition, as well as enforcement, of European judgments.

THE VARIOUS ENFORCEMENT REGIMES

Overseas judgments

As we have seen, three distinct but traditional regimes (under the common law, the Administration of Justice Act 1920, and the Foreign Judgments (Reciprocal Enforcement) Act 1933) apply to the enforcement in England of overseas money judgments. The three regimes are very similar to each other, and their respective scope depends mainly on the country of origin of the judgment.

Under the common law regime, the party seeking enforcement brings an ordinary action in an English court, pleading the foreign judgment and seeking the entry of an English judgment to similar effect. In clear cases the procedure under RSC Ord 14 for obtaining an English judgment summarily, without a full trial, may be used. Under the 1920 and 1933 Acts, the party entitled applies to the High Court for an order that the foreign judgment be registered for enforcement.

Procedure for obtaining a registration order under the 1920 Act or the 1933 Act is governed by RSC Ord 71, Part I, rr 1–12. Such applications are dealt with by a judge or master of the Queen's Bench Division. The application may be made ex parte, but it must be supported by an affidavit exhibiting the judgment and, where relevant, an English translation, and verifying that the requirements for registration are satisfied. After registration has been ordered, notice must be served on the judgment debtor, and he may apply, by summons supported by affidavit, to have the registration set aside. Actual execution of a registered judgment is not possible until the period for making an application to have the registration set aside has expired, and if such an application is made, until it has been finally determined.[23]

Under all three regimes the English court will review the jurisdiction of the original court under the English rules of indirect jurisdiction, and will refuse enforcement if the foreign court lacked competence under those rules. Other available defences are that the judgment was obtained by fraud; that the defendant abroad was not properly notified of the foreign proceedings; and that enforcement would contravene a stringent English public policy.[24] The three regimes differ, however, in their requirements concerning the finality of the judgment in the original country.[25]

The common law governs the enforcement of overseas judgments to which no

[23] See the 1920 Act, s 9(4); the 1933 Act, s 2(2); and RSC Ord 71, r 10.
[24] See under 'Substantive requirements', pp 326–4 below.
[25] See under 'Finality in the original country', pp 320–1 below.

other regime is exclusively applicable. Thus it applies, for example, to the enforcement of judgments given in the United States; but not to the enforcement of judgments to which the 1933 Act[26] or the 1968 or Lugano Conventions[27] apply. It is possible to seek enforcement at common law of a judgment falling within the 1920 Act, but an applicant who does so will usually be refused costs of the English enforcement action.[28]

Part II of the Administration of Justice Act 1920 governs the enforcement of judgments given by the superior courts of the numerous Commonwealth countries to which the Act has been extended, on the basis of reciprocity, by Order in Council. These include Australia (except for its Capital Territory), New Zealand, the Falkland Islands, Jamaica, Trinidad, Ghana, Nigeria, Kenya, Tanzania, Uganda, Zimbabwe, Zambia, Malawi, Botswana, Sri Lanka, Malaysia, Singapore, Hong Kong, Cyprus, Malta, and Gibraltar. But it cannot now be extended to additional countries.[29]

The Foreign Judgments (Reciprocal Enforcement) Act 1933 governs the enforcement of judgments given by courts of Commonwealth or foreign countries to which it has been extended, on the basis of reciprocity, by Order in Council.[30] It now applies to Guernsey,[31] Jersey,[32] the Isle of Man,[33] most of Canada,[34] the Australian Capital Territory,[35] India,[36] Pakistan,[37] Austria,[38] Norway,[39] Israel,[40] Suriname[41] and Tonga.[42] It also applies, as regards judgments concerning matters which are outside the scope of the 1968 Convention,[43] to France, Germany, Italy, Belgium, and the Netherlands.[44] The Act also applies to judgments given outside the United Kingdom in pursuance of

---

[26] See s 6.
[27] See Case 42/76 *De Wolf v Cox* [1976] ECR 1759.
[28] See s 9(5) of the 1920 Act.
[29] See s 7(1) of the 1933 Act, and SR & O 1933/1073.
[30] If a judgment falls within the scope of the 1933 Act, s 6 prevents enforcement by action at common law. The 1933 Act does not apply to judgments on marital status, such as a declaration of recognition of a non-judicial divorce; see *Maples v Maples* [1988] Fam 14.
[31] See SI 1973/610.
[32] See SI 1973/612.
[33] See SI 1973/611.
[34] See SI 1987/468 (as amended by SI 1987/2211, 1988/1304, 1988/1853, and 1989/987), by art 3 of which the 1933 Act is made applicable to the Federal Court of Canada and the courts of the following provinces or territories: British Columbia, Manitoba, New Brunswick, the Northwest Territories, Nova Scotia, Ontario, Prince Edward Island, Saskatchewan, and the Yukon Territory.
[35] See SI 1955/559.
[36] See SI 1958/425.
[37] See SI 1958/141.
[38] See SI 1962/1339.
[39] See SI 1962/636.
[40] See SI 1971/1039.
[41] See SI 1981/735.
[42] See SI 1980/1523.
[43] See art 56(1), and Cases 9 & 10/77: *Bavaria Fluggesellschaft Schwabe and Germanair Bedarfsluftfahrt v Eurocontrol* [1977] ECR 1517.
[44] See respectively: SR & O 1936/609; SI 1961/1199; SI 1973/1894; SR & O 1936/1169; and SI 1969/1063 and 1977/2149.

certain international conventions dealing with carriage by rail[45] or road,[46] air navigation services,[47] oil pollution,[48] or nuclear incidents,[49] in any country (other than the United Kingdom) which is a party to the relevant convention.[50] However s 1(2A) of the 1933 Act, added by the 1982 Act, excludes from enforcement under the 1933 Act a judgment for the enforcement of a judgment given in a third country.

British judgments

Part II (s 18 and Scheds 6 and 7) of the Civil Jurisdiction and Judgments Act 1982 governs the enforcement in England of judgments of Scottish or Northern Irish courts or tribunals (except Northern Irish magistrates' courts).[51] Schedule 6 applies to judgments awarding a definite sum of money, and Sched 7 to judgments awarding non-monetary relief. These provisions are exclusive, since s 18(8) prevents the enforcement at common law of a judgment to which Sched 6 applies. They do not, however, apply to provisional or protective measures, other than interim payment orders.[52] Nor do they apply to a British judgment ordering the registration for enforcement of a European or overseas judgment under the 1920 Act, the 1933 Act, or the 1968 or Lugano Conventions.[53]

The procedure under Scheds 6 and 7 is for the party seeking enforcement to obtain from the original court a certificate of a money judgment, or a certified copy and certificate of a non-money judgment, and then to make an ex parte application to the English High Court for registration of the certificate or judg-

---

[45] See the Berne Convention concerning International Carriage by Rail (1980), Cmnd 8535 (1982); and the International Transport Conventions Act 1983, s 6.

[46] See the Geneva Convention on the Contract for the International Carriage of Goods by Road (1956), Cmnd 3455; the Carriage of Goods by Road Act 1965, s 4; the Geneva Convention on the Contract for the International Carriage of Passengers and Luggage (1973); and the Carriage of Passengers by Road Act 1974, s 5.

[47] See the Multilateral Agreement relating to Route Charges (1981); and the Civil Aviation Act 1982, s 74A, inserted by the Civil Aviation (Eurocontrol) Act 1983.

[48] See the Brussels Convention on Civil Liability for Oil Pollution Damage (1969), Cmnd 4403 (1970), and amending Protocol (1976); and the Merchant Shipping (Oil Pollution) Act 1971, s 13(3).

[49] See the Paris Convention on Third Party Liability in the Field of Nuclear Energy (1960), as amended in 1964, Cmnd 2514 (1964); and the Nuclear Installations Act 1965, s 17(4), (5) and (5A), as amended by the Energy Act 1983, s 31.

[50] See further under 'Conventions on particular matters', pp 324–6 below. The argument advanced tentatively in Dicey & Morris, under Rule 55, that other international conventions (on carriage by air, or carriage of passengers by sea) which contain rules of direct international jurisdiction, but are silent as to recognition and enforcement of foreign judgments, have the effect of substituting their bases of direct jurisdiction as the applicable grounds of indirect jurisdiction for the purposes of recognition and enforcement under the 1933 Act or the common law, seems hard to accept.

[51] These provisions have, since 1987, replaced the Judgments Extension Act 1868 and the Inferior Courts Judgments Extension Act 1882. For transitional provisions, see the 1982 Act, Sched 13, Part II, paras 2 and 3.

[52] See s 18(5)(d).

[53] See s 18(7).

ment. After registration the other party may apply to have the registration set aside on the ground that it was effected contrary to the relevant Schedule.

The regime for British judgments differs radically from those applicable to overseas judgments, in that British judgments are exempted from the usual requirements that the foreign court should have been competent under the English rules of indirect jurisdiction, that the foreign proceedings should have complied with minimum standards of procedural fairness, that the judgment should not be for payment of a tax,[54] and that its enforcement should not infringe English public policy. But a British non-money judgment cannot be registered in England under Sched 7 if compliance with it would involve a breach of English law.[55]

Mere recognition (without enforcement) of British judgments is governed by the common law, together with ss 19 and 34 of the 1982 Act. Section 19 eliminates jurisdictional review where mere recognition of a British judgment is sought, and s 34 enables a recognised foreign judgment to be invoked as a defence to an English action in respect of the same claim, even where the foreign judgment upheld the claim and has not been satisfied.

European judgments

Title III of the 1968 Convention provides for the recognition and enforcement in each contracting state of judgments given by courts of the other contracting states. Similarly Title III of the Lugano Convention provides for the reciprocal recognition and enforcement of judgments between its contracting states, where one of the states involved is an EC member state and the other is an EFTA country, or both are EFTA countries.[56,57] Article 25 of the Conventions defines 'judgment' as a decision given by a court or tribunal of a contracting state, and specifies that the name given to a judgment (such as decree, order, decision, or writ of execution) is immaterial, and that Title III extends to a decision of a court officer determining costs.[58]

To qualify for enforcement under Title III, it is not necessary that the judgment should have awarded a sum of money. It is sufficient that the judgment has imposed some obligation which is enforceable in the original country,[59] whether the obligation is to pay a definite sum of money, or to take or abstain from some other action (as in the case of a decree of specific performance of a contract, or an injunction against the commission of a tort). Moreover

---

[54] However a British judgment imposing a fine is not enforceable in other parts of the United Kingdom; see s 18(3)(b).

[55] See Sched 7, para 5(5).

[56] See the Lugano Convention, art 54B(1) and (2)(c).

[57] For parties to the Lugano Convention, see Ch 7, pp 118–19 above.

[58] Article VA to the (first) Protocol annexed to the Conventions adds that 'court' includes the Danish, Icelandic, and Norwegian administrative authorities when dealing with maintenance; and the Finnish ulosotonhaltija/overexekutor when dealing with civil or commercial matters. See the Schlosser Report at pp 93–4.

[59] See art 31.

the requirement of enforceability in the original country does not apply to mere recognition. On the other hand, in *Owens Bank v Bracco*[60] the European Court of Justice (in agreement with the English Court of Appeal) ruled that the 1968 Convention does not apply to proceedings, or issues arising in proceedings, in contracting states concerning the recognition and enforcement of judgments given in non-contracting states. Thus Title III is confined to an original judgment on the merits, and does not extend to a judgment authorising enforcement of a judgment given in a third country.

As regards subject-matter, Title III of the 1968 Convention and Lugano Convention are confined to judgments which are principally concerned with matters which fall within the scope of the Conventions as defined by art 1.[61] Since arbitration is excluded from the scope of the Conventions by art 1[2][4], Title III is inapplicable to the recognition or enforcement, not only of arbitral awards, but also of judgments based on or principally concerned with such awards, such as a judgment authorising enforcement of, or varying or setting aside, an arbitral award. Moreover, as the European Court of Justice ruled in *Hoffmann v Krieg*,[62] a judgment in respect of which an enforcement order has been made under the 1968 Convention cannot remain enforceable in the state addressed if its law precludes further enforcement for reasons outside the scope of the Convention, such as a subsequent and irreconcilable local judgment concerning personal status. More specifically, the Convention does not interfere with the local effects of a locally granted divorce, including the effects of the divorce in relation to the enforcement of a foreign maintenance order, even if the divorce is not recognised in the state of origin of the maintenance order. Title III also gives way to other multilateral conventions which contain provisions on recognition or enforcement of judgments in respect of particular matters, in accordance with art 57.

As regards time, Title III applies fully where the action in which the judgment was given was instituted after the entry into force of the 1968 Convention or the Lugano Convention between the state of origin and the state addressed, and does not apply at all where the judgment was given before that date. In the intermediate case where the original action was instituted before the relevant commencement date but the judgment was given after that date, Title III applies, but subject to a proviso for the review of the jurisdiction of the original court by the court addressed.[63] As regards the United Kingdom, the relevant commencement date is 1 January 1987 in relation to French, German, Italian, Belgian, Dutch, Luxembourg, or Danish judgments; 1 June 1988 in relation to Irish judgments; 1 October 1989 in relation to Greek judgments; 1 December 1991 in relation to Spanish judgments; 1 July 1992 in relation to Portuguese judgments; and 1 May 1992 in relation to Swiss judgments.

---

[60] Case C-129/92, [1994] 1 All ER 336, ECJ; [1992] 2 AC 443, CA and HL.
[61] See Chapter 7, under 'Subject-matter', pp 121–4 above.
[62] Case 145/86, [1988] ECR 645.
[63] See the 1968 Convention, art 54; the 1978 Convention, art 34; the 1982 Convention, art 12; the 1989 Convention, art 29; and the Lugano Convention, art 54.

Title III provides for both recognition and enforcement of judgments, and both defines the substantive requirements for, and regulates the procedure for obtaining, recognition or enforcement. The same substantive requirements apply to mere recognition and to enforcement, except that for enforcement there is an additional requirement that the judgment should be enforceable in the original country.[64] The substantive requirements take the form of limited exceptions to a general rule requiring recognition and enforcement. Articles 29 and 34[3] prohibit the court addressed from in any circumstances reviewing the substance or merits of the judgment, and in most cases art 28 prevents the court addressed from reviewing the jurisdiction of the original court. But by arts 27 and 34[2] recognition and enforcement must be refused if the judgment is a default judgment and the defendant was not duly and timeously served with the originating document; or if recognition is contrary to the public policy of the state addressed; or if the judgment decided an incidental question of individual status or capacity, matrimonial property, or succession, in a manner contrary to the conflict rules of the state addressed; or in certain cases if the judgment is irreconcilable with another judgment.[65]

As regards procedure, art 26 enables mere recognition to be invoked incidentally whenever relevant, and also enables an interested party to apply for a declaration of recognition by means of the enforcement procedure. As regards enforcement, the procedure for obtaining a declaration of enforceability, or in the United Kingdom an order authorising registration for enforcement,[66] is elaborated by arts 31–49, and the European Court of Justice has ruled that this procedure is exclusive.[67] A separate and independent application for registration must be made in each part of the United Kingdom (that is: England and Wales; Scotland; and Northern Ireland) in which registration for recognition or enforcement is sought.[68]

The initial application for enforcement is made ex parte by an interested party, and a prompt decision should be given on such an application.[69] This decision is subject to an inter partes appeal, lodged under arts 36 and 37 by the

---

[64] See arts 27–29, 31 and 34.

[65] These exceptions are examined under 'Substantive requirements', pp 326–41 below.

[66] See art 31[2] of the Conventions; and RSC Ord 71, rr 30 and 31. For supplementary British legislation, see the 1982 Act, ss 4–8, 11–12 and 40, and RSC Ord 71, rr 25–36.

[67] See Case 42/76 De Wolf v Cox [1976] ECR 1759.

[68] See art 31[2] of the Conventions; the 1982 Act, ss 4 and 5; and the Schlosser Report, at p 132.

[69] See arts 31 and 34; and RSC Ord 71, rr 27 and 28(1)(d)(i).

On the documentary evidence required from a party seeking recognition or enforcement, see arts 33 and 46–49 of the Conventions; the 1982 Act, ss 11 and 12; and RSC Ord 71, rr 28, 35 and 36. In Ireland, see ss 1(2), 10 and 12 of the (Irish) Jurisdiction of Courts and Enforcement of Judgments (European Communities) Act 1988.

On the applicant's obligation to give an address for service, see art 33[2]; the Jenard Report, at p 50; the Schlosser Report, at p 134; and Case 198/85 Carron v Federal Republic of Germany [1987] 1 CMLR 838. On his exemption from giving security for costs, see art 45, and RSC Ord 71, r 29. On his entitlement to legal aid for the ex parte application, see art 44 of the Conventions, the Jenard Report, at p 54, and the 1982 Act, s 40.

For service of the decision given on the application, see arts 35 and 36, and RSC Ord 71, r 32.

party against whom enforcement is sought,[70] in the normal case where the ex parte decision authorised enforcement, or under art 40 by the applicant for enforcement, in the less usual case where the ex parte decision refused to authorise enforcement.[71] The decision on the inter partes appeal is subject to a single further appeal on a point of law only.[72] Partial enforcement may be applied for or granted where the judgment dealt with several matters.[73]

In England, except in the case of a maintenance order, the initial application for an order that a European judgment be registered for enforcement is made to the High Court, where it will normally be dealt with by a master of the Queen's Bench Division, and the first appeal (whether by the respondent to or the applicant for enforcement) will be determined by a judge of that Division.[74] The final appeal lies to the Court of Appeal or alternatively, under the 'leapfrog'

[70] On the time for lodging the appeal, see art 36 of the Conventions, and RSC Ord 71, rr 32 and 33.

[71] By art 40(2), the party against whom enforcement is sought must be summoned to appear, and if he fails to appear, art 20(2) and (3) (on staying proceedings until proper steps have been taken to notify the defendant in sufficient time to enable him to arrange for his defence) apply, even where he is not domiciled in any contracting state. This applies even where the initial application was rejected solely because the documents required by arts 46 and 47 were not produced at the proper time; see Case 178/83 *Firma P v Firma K* [1984] ECR 3033. See also RSC Ord 71, r 33.

[72] See arts 37(2) and 41.

The further appeal lies only against a decision which terminates the proceedings in the lower court, and not against an interlocutory decision made by the lower court prior to the conclusion of its proceedings; see Case 258/83 *Brennero v Wendel* [1984] ECR 3971. Moreover the further appeal cannot be brought in respect of a decision under art 38 (such as one refusing, despite an appeal in the original country, to stay the proceedings in the country addressed, but requiring the enforcing party to give security), even if the same judgment also disposes entirely of the intermediate appeal; see C-183/90 *Van Dalfsen v Van Loon* [1991] 1 ECR 4743.

[73] See art 42.

[74] See arts 32, 37 and 40; and RSC Ord 32, rr 11 and 12, and RSC Ord 71, rr 26 and 33(1).

A similar arrangement operates in Scotland, Northern Ireland, and Ireland: both the initial application and the first appeal (whether by the respondent to or the applicant for enforcement) will be determined by the Court of Session or the High Court. In Ireland the initial application will be determined by the Master of the High Court; see s 5 of the (Irish) Jurisdiction of Courts and Enforcement of Judgments (European Communities) Act 1988.

At the other extreme, in Italy both the initial application and the first appeal (whether by the respondent to or the applicant for enforcement) will be determined by a court which is normally one of intermediate appeal.

The most obviously natural judicial order in this matter is adopted for France, Germany, Luxembourg, Denmark, Greece, Spain and Portugal: the initial application is made to a court of first instance, and the first appeal, whether by the respondent to or the applicant for enforcement, lies to a court of intermediate appeal.

In Belgium and the Netherlands, the initial application and a first appeal by the respondent against an ex parte enforcement order are dealt with by a court of first instance, but a first appeal by the applicant against an ex parte refusal to make an enforcement order lies to a court of intermediate appeal.

Under the Lugano Convention, in Switzerland the initial application is made to a different judge, the *juge de la mainlevée* or the *juge cantonal d'exequatur compétent*, according to whether the judgment orders payment of money or some other performance; but in any event the first appeal lies to the *tribunal cantonal*.

procedure, to the House of Lords.[75] In the case of a maintenance order, the application is transmitted by the Secretary of State to the magistrates' court within whose district the respondent is domiciled, or, if he is not domiciled in England, has assets; the first appeal is also determined by that court; and the final appeal is by way of case stated to the High Court.[76]

In *Deutsche Genossenschaftsbank v Brasserie du Pecheur*,[77] the European Court of Justice construed art 36 as preventing any appeal *against an enforcement order* by an interested third party, such as another creditor of the judgment debtor, but accepted that interested third parties may take proceedings to challenge *measures of execution* in accordance with the law of the state addressed. Similarly, as the court ruled in *Sonntag v Waidmann*,[78] the further appeal provided for by art 37[2] against an intermediate decision in favour of enforcement cannot be brought by an interested third party.

In *Hoffmann v Krieg*,[79] the European Court of Justice ruled that, in general, where a respondent fails to raise by way of an appeal under art 36 an objection which could have been so raised, he cannot subsequently raise that objection at the stage of actual enforcement, and similarly that such an objection cannot be raised of the court's own motion at the stage of actual enforcement. But, by way of exception, such preclusion does not apply where it would have the result of compelling a court to disregard a local judgment on a matter excluded from the scope of the Convention (such as a decree of divorce) because it is not recognised in the state of origin of the foreign judgment.

By art 39, an ex parte declaration of enforceability enables the applicant to take protective measures against the respondent's property, but definitive enforcement is delayed until the appeal inter partes has become time-barred or has been disposed of.[80] In *Capelloni and Aquilini v Pelkmans*,[81] the European

---

[75] See the 1982 Act, s 6(1) and (2). In Scotland the final appeal lies simply to the Inner House of the Court of Session.

[76] See arts 32, 37, 40 and 41; and the 1982 Act, ss 5 and 6(3).

Similarly, in Scotland or Northern Ireland, a European maintenance order is transmitted by the Secretary of State or the Lord Chancellor to the sheriff court or magistrates' court within whose district the respondent is domiciled or has assets; the appeal is dealt with by the same sheriff court or magistrates' court; and the final appeal lies to the Inner House of the Scottish Court of Session or to the Northern Irish Court of Appeal.

A rather different solution has been adopted in the Irish Republic, where application for enforcement of a maintenance order (like any other judgment) is made to and determined by the Master of the High Court. But in the case of an order for maintenance by way of periodical payments, the actual measures of enforcement are taken by the District Court for the district in which the maintenance debtor resides, except that the Master of the High Court may, on application by the maintenance creditor, order that arrears existing at the making of the enforcement order should be treated as payable under an ordinary judgment. See art 32 of the Conventions, and ss 1(1), 5, 6(2) and 7 of the (Irish) Jurisdiction of Courts and Enforcement of Judgments (European Communities) Act 1988. See also s 7(3) and (4), on the effect of enforcement orders in respect of European judgments varying or revoking maintenance orders in respect of which enforcement orders have been made.

[77] Case 148/84, [1986] 2 CMLR 496.

[78] Case C-172/91, 21 April 1993.

[79] Case 145/86, [1988] ECR 645.

[80] See also the 1982 Act, ss 4(4) and 5(5), and RSC Ord 71, r 34.

[81] Case 119/84, [1985] ECR 3147.

Court of Justice noted that the purpose of art 39 is to enable the party who has obtained an enforcement order, but who cannot yet proceed to take enforcement measures, to prevent the respondent from disposing of his property in the meantime so as to impede or prevent future enforcement.[82] It recognised, however, that art 39 confines itself to stating the principle that the applicant may proceed with protective measures during the relevant period, and leaves points not specifically dealt with to the procedural law of the court addressed, insofar as its procedural rules do not conflict with the principles expressly or impliedly laid down by the Convention, and in particular by art 39. Consequently art 39 overrides requirements under the procedural law of the state addressed, whereby a party who has obtained an enforcement order cannot proceed directly with protective measures against the respondent's property, but must obtain a further order from the court addressed specifically authorising him to do so; or whereby provisional measures are limited to a shorter period than the time for lodging and determining an appeal under art 36; or whereby a party who has taken protective measures must obtain a confirmatory judgment in respect of the measures taken. However the Convention does not prevent the respondent from complaining, in accordance with national procedures, of irregularities or abuses which he alleges to have occurred in the course of the execution of the protective measures. Probably in England art 39 entitles a judgment creditor to obtain, as a protective measure, a *Mareva* injunction or an order for payment into court, without showing urgency or a risk that assets will be dissipated or removed.[83]

European authentic instruments and court settlements

Title III of the 1968 and Lugano Conventions is supplemented by Title IV, arts 50 and 51, which provides for the enforcement in a contracting state, by means of the procedures specified in Title III, of 'authentic instruments' drawn up or registered, and litigational settlements approved by courts, in other contracting states.[84] The instrument or settlement must be enforceable (without a confirmatory judgment) in the state of origin, and its enforcement must not be contrary to the public policy of the state addressed.[85]

Authentic instruments are familiar in the Continental countries. Such an instrument is one which is drawn up by a public officer, such as a notary, signed

---

[82] See also the Jenard Report, at p 50.

[83] See the Jenard Report, at p 52, the Schlosser Report, at pp 134–5, and the 1982 Act, s 4. See also s 11(3) of the Irish Act, by which an application in Ireland for an enforcement order may include an application for protective measures of types which the court has power to grant in proceedings which, apart from the Conventions, are within its jurisdiction, and the enforcement order will then include a provision granting the protective measures applied for.

[84] See also s 13 of the 1982 Act, and SI 1993/604.

[85] In *Re the Enforcement of a Swiss Maintenance Agreement* [1988] ECC 181, the German Supreme Court indicated (in the context of the German–Swiss bilateral convention) that where the approval of an agreement (in casu, a maintenance agreement between divorcing spouses) is subject to the court's control as to its compliance with substantive legal rules, a court order approving it amounts to an ordinary judgment, rather than the judicial approval of a settlement.

by the parties in his presence, and witnessed by him, thus establishing an especially formal and probative record of the transaction, and enabling a party in whose favour an obligation evidenced by the instrument is undertaken to proceed directly to measures of execution on the basis of the instrument, as if it were a judgment, without bringing an action before a court. Thus art 50 applies mainly to notarial instruments which evidence an immediate obligation to pay a definite sum of money, and which usually contain a statement of direct enforceability.[86] Authentic instruments are unknown in English internal law, but in Scotland an instrument establishing a clearly defined contractual obligation can be entered in a public register, and an extract from the register will be enforceable by execution in the same way as a judgment, and will fall within art 50.[87]

Authentic instruments and judicially approved litigational settlements differ from judgments in that they lack the conclusive effect of res judicata and, being contractual in nature, can be rendered invalid by such factors as mistake, misrepresentation, incapacity or prohibited purpose. Title IV recognises the lack of conclusiveness by providing only for enforcement, and not mere recognition. But there is room for doubt as to the proper course to be taken by the court addressed of enforcement proceedings under Title IV if the respondent puts forward a serious argument that the instrument or settlement is invalid. Droz[88] argues that in such a case the court addressed should stay its proceedings, and perhaps meanwhile permit provisional enforcement, or enforcement conditional on the applicant providing security, so as to enable the respondent to bring an action for the annulment of the instrument or settlement in a court which is competent to entertain such an action under Title II of the Convention. He accepts, however, that this course would not be appropriate if the attack is based on a matter, such as the incapacity of an individual, which is excluded from the scope of the Conventions by art 1[2](1).

Finality in the original country

The various regimes differ in their requirements concerning the finality of the judgment in the original country. At one extreme, an overseas judgment cannot be registered for enforcement under the 1920 Act if the respondent satisfies the English court that an appeal is pending in the original country, or that he is entitled and intends to appeal there.[89] Somewhat similarly, a British judgment will be registered for enforcement under Part II of the 1982 Act only on production to the court addressed of a certificate issued by the original court stating that the time for appealing in the original country has expired without an appeal being lodged, or an appeal has been finally disposed of;[90] and after registration,

---

[86] See Droz, *Compétence Judiciaire et Effets des Jugements dans le Marché Commun* (1972), ss 606–16.

[87] See the Schlosser Report, at p 136.

[88] See note 86 above, at ss 618–24 and 628.

[89] See s 9(2)(e).

[90] See Sched 6, paras 3(a) and 4(1)(b); and Sched 7, paras 3(a) and 4(1)(b).

if the court addressed is satisfied by the unsuccessful party that he is entitled and intends to apply in the original country for the setting aside or quashing of the judgment, it may stay enforcement on such terms as it thinks fit, for a period reasonably sufficient to enable such application to be disposed of.[91]

Less demandingly, to qualify for recognition or enforcement at common law, an overseas judgment (other than a judgment given in default of appearance) must be final in the original court, in the sense that it constitutes res judicata in the court by which it was given and cannot be reviewed by means of any proceedings in that court,[92] but this requirement may be inapplicable to default judgments.[93] On the other hand the pendency or possibility of an appeal to a higher court in the original country does not prevent recognition or enforcement at common law, though a judgment will not be enforceable here if enforcement in the original country has been stayed pending appeal.[94]

At first sight the 1933 Act seems to follow the common law, since s 1(2)(a) (as amended by Sched 10 to the 1982 Act) explicitly requires finality in the original country, except in the case of judgments for an interim payment. But other provisions of the 1933 Act appear to deprive the requirement of finality of all content. For s 1(3) specifies that a judgment counts as final even if in the original country an appeal against it is pending or is still admissible, and s 11(1) defines 'appeal' as including any proceeding by way of discharging or setting aside a judgment, or an application for a new trial or a stay of execution. Since this definition apparently includes an application for review made to the very court which gave the judgment, it seems that in all cases the possibility that the judgment may be set aside or varied in the original country falls to be dealt with under s 5, whereby, on an application by the respondent after registration of a judgment, the English court has a discretion to set aside the registration on the ground that an appeal in the original country is pending, or is admissible and intended, or to adjourn the respondent's application for a period reasonably sufficient to enable the applicant to take the necessary steps to have the foreign appeal disposed of, and also to impose appropriate terms. The English court remains free, however, to permit immediate and unconditional enforcement despite the pendency of a foreign appeal, and is likely to do so where it considers that the respondent is engaged in unmeritorious procedural manoeuvrings for purposes of delay.[95]

In the case of a European judgment, there is no requirement that the judg-

---

[91] See Sched 6, para 9; and Sched 7, para 8.

[92] See *Nouvion v Freeman* (1889) 15 App Cas 1; *Harrop v Harrop* [1920] 3 KB 386; and *Beatty v Beatty* [1924] 1 KB 807. Thus Slade LJ was right in *Adams v Cape Industries* [1990] Ch 433, to say (citing *Pemberton v Hughes* [1899] 1 Ch 781), in relation to recognition and enforcement at common law, that the English courts are 'generally' not concerned with whether the original court was competent under its own rules on international jurisdiction. The exception is where a breach by the original court of such rules has the effect of making its judgment wholly void, and thus not final, in the original country.

[93] See *Vanquelin v Bouard* (1863) 143 ER 817 at 828.

[94] See *Colt Industries v Sarlie (No 2)* [1966] 1 WLR 1287.

[95] See *General Textiles v Sun & Sand Agencies* [1978] 1 QB 279.

ment should be in any sense final in the original country.[96] With two exceptions, interlocutory judgments, as well as judgments given at the conclusion of a trial, have to be recognised and enforced under Title III. The first exception is that interlocutory decisions which are not intended to govern the legal relationships of the parties, but to arrange the further conduct of the proceedings, such as orders for the taking of evidence, are not within the scope of Title III.[97] The second arises from the ruling of the European Court of Justice in *Denilauler v Couchet Frères*,[98] that judgments authorising provisional or protective measures, which are delivered without the defendant having been summoned to appear, and which are intended to be enforced without prior service, do not fall within the scope of Title III. That case involved a *saisie conservatoire*, ordered by a French court under art 48 of the French Code of Civil Procedure, for the freezing of a bank account in Germany, but the decision is equally applicable to an English *Mareva* injunction obtained by the usual ex parte procedure. Title III applies, however, to a *Mareva* injunction obtained by means of a summons inter partes.[99]

In *EMI Records v Modern Music Karl-Ulrich Watterbach*,[100] Hobhouse J refused, in reliance on *Denilauler*, to enforce under Title III an injunction, apparently against infringement of copyright, which had been granted by a German court under a procedure whereby the injunction took effect immediately on its issue, without service, and would remain in force until the court, on the defendant's application, set it aside. He considered that *Denilauler* excluded all ex parte orders from enforcement under Title III, except where the order would only take effect after it had been served on the defendant and he had been given a reasonable opportunity to appear before the court and dispute the making of the order.

A European judgment remains recognisable and enforceable under Title III despite the pendency or availability of any form of appeal or review in the original country, whether in a higher court or in the court which gave the judgment. Provision is, however, made by arts 30 and 38 whereby a court addressed is given a discretion to stay its proceedings, where an ordinary appeal is pending or admissible in the original country. By art 30[1], a court in which mere recognition is sought may stay its proceedings if an ordinary appeal against the judgment has been lodged in the original country, and art 30[2] gives an additional power to stay such proceedings where the judgment was given in Ireland or the United Kingdom and enforcement in the original country is suspended by reason of an appeal. By art 38[1], a court seised of an inter partes appeal against an ex parte decision authorising enforcement is given a discretion

---

[96] See the Jenard Report, at p 43, and the Schlosser Report, at p 126.

[97] See the Schlosser Report, at pp 126-7. As to such matters, see the Hague Conventions on Civil Procedure (1954), Service Abroad (1965), and the Taking of Evidence Abroad (1970). The United Kingdom is a party to the 1965 and 1970 Conventions.

[98] Case 125/79, [1980] ECR 1553.

[99] See per Browne-Wilkinson V-C in *Derby v Weldon* (1988) *The Times*, 15 November; affirmed and extended by the Court of Appeal on other grounds, [1990] Ch 65.

[100] [1992] 1 QB 115.

to stay its proceedings, if an ordinary appeal has been lodged in the original country or the time for such an appeal has not expired. In the latter case, the court addressed may also specify a time within which such an appeal must be lodged. Article 38[2] extends these powers of the court addressed, where the judgment was given in the United Kingdom or Ireland, so as to be exercisable in connection with any, however extraordinary, form of appeal there. Although art 30 expressly refers only to an appeal which has actually been lodged, the analogy of art 38 indicates that art 30 should be construed as permitting a stay where the time for an ordinary appeal has not yet expired and a party intends to lodge such an appeal.[101]

The European Court of Justice ruled in *Industrial Diamond Supplies v Riva*[102] that in arts 30 and 38 'ordinary appeal' refers to any appeal which may result in the annulment or amendment of the judgment, and whose lodging is bound by a period laid down by law and commencing by virtue of the judgment. Thus an appeal to the highest court in the original country (in casu, to the Italian Court of Cassation) may count as an ordinary appeal for present purposes. It also seems clear that an application to the court which gave the judgment (for example, an application to set aside a default judgment and proceed with a trial of the merits) may count as an ordinary appeal if there is a time-limit, running from the judgment, for such applications.[103] But, as Phillips J held in *Interdesco v Nullifire*,[104] an application in France known as a *recours en revision*, to set aside a judgment on the ground that it was procured by fraud, is not an 'ordinary appeal', since such an application could be filed at any time after the judgment, but within two months of the applicant's becoming aware of the facts relied on.

The court addressed can stay its proceedings under art 38 only if the respondent applies for a stay, and in any event art 38 only confers a discretion. If the pending or proposed appeal appears hopeless, the court addressed may properly refuse to take it into account and simply dismiss the appeal against the enforcement order. Moreover, as Diamond QC explained in *Petereit v Babcock International Holdings Ltd*,[105] a stay should not be granted more or less automatically, but only where appropriate for the purpose of protecting the respondent against the risk that, if his appeal in the original country were to succeed, he would be unable to enforce the decision on appeal and would be deprived of the fruits of his success by reason of a previous unconditional enforcement of the judgment appealed from. In any event, during a stay under art 38, provisional measures of enforcement remain available under art 39.

The scope of the power to stay has been greatly reduced by the European Court of Justice's ruling in *Van Dalfsen v Van Loon*,[106] that a party seeking a

---

[101] See the Jenard Report, at pp 46–7.
[102] Case 43/77, [1977] ECR 2175.
[103] See the Schlosser Report, at pp 129–30.
[104] [1992] 1 Lloyd's Rep 180.
[105] [1990] 1 WLR 350.
[106] Case C-183/90, [1991] 1 ECR 4743.

stay under art 38[1] can only rely on arguments which he was unable to make before the original court. In *SISRO v Ampersand Software*,[107] the English Court of Appeal has referred to the European Court of Justice questions as to the relationship between art 38 and arts 27 and 28.[108]

Article 38[3] empowers a court hearing an appeal against an enforcement order also to make enforcement conditional on the provision of such security as it shall determine. In *Brennero v Wendel*[109] the European Court of Justice ruled that this power can only be exercised in a judgment which finally disposes of the respondent's appeal, and not by way of an interim order in the course of the proceedings in the appeal, but also indicated that the power can be exercised even where there is no appeal in the original country, in order to protect the respondent in case his further appeal in the country addressed succeeds.

In some Continental countries, a court which grants an injunction also fixes a periodic penalty payment in the event of non-compliance, but the court has power to reduce the amount of the penalty subsequently. To deal with this form of procedure, art 43 provides that a judgment which orders a periodic payment by way of penalty is enforceable in the other contracting states only if the amount of the payment has been finally determined by the courts of the original country. Despite a contrary suggestion in the Schlosser Report,[110] it seems clear that art 43 does not prevent an English court from enforcing a French injunction, to which the French court has coupled a periodic penalty payment, by measures which ignore the penalty payment, such as committal or sequestration.

Conventions on particular matters

Article 57(1) of the 1968 and Lugano Conventions make those Conventions give way to any convention to which a contracting state is or becomes a party, and which deals with jurisdiction, or recognition and enforcement, in relation to a particular matter, and art 57(2) of the 1968 Convention[111] specifies certain consequences of this rule. As regards recognition and enforcement, art 57(2)(b) of the 1968 Convention[112] provides that a judgment given in a contracting state in the exercise of jurisdiction provided for in a 'particular convention' must be recognised and enforced in the other contracting states in accordance with Title III of the 1968 Convention, and that where a 'particular convention' to which both the state of origin and the state addressed are parties lays down conditions for the recognition or enforcement of judgments, those conditions will apply, but in any event the provisions of Title III which concern the procedures for

---

[107] (1993) *The Times*, 29 July.
[108] The reference is now pending as Case C-432/93.
[109] Case 258/83, [1984] ECR 3971.
[110] At p 132.
[111] Article 57(2), (3) and (5) of the Lugano Convention correspond to art 57(2) of the 1968 Convention.
[112] Article 57(3) and (5) of the Lugano Convention correspond to art 57(2)(b) of the 1968 Convention.

recognition and enforcement may be applied. The Lugano Convention adds, by art 57(4), a proviso enabling a contracting state to deny recognition and enforcement of judgments given in other contracting states against persons domiciled in the state addressed in pursuance of 'particular conventions' to which the state addressed is not a party, unless the judgment would otherwise be recognised under its law.

Thus the combined effect on recognition and enforcement of the 1968 Convention and a 'particular convention' appears to be as follows. If the 'particular convention' deals only with direct jurisdiction, or if it has been adopted only by the state of origin and not by the state addressed, Title III applies to judgments given in pursuance of the 'particular convention' in the same way as it applies to other judgments, and the 'particular convention' has no effect at the stage of recognition and enforcement. If, on the other hand, the 'particular convention' deals with recognition and enforcement, and it has been adopted both by the state of origin and the state addressed, then, insofar as there is conflict between the substantive requirements for recognition and enforcement laid down by the 'particular convention' and those contained in Title III of the 1968 Convention, the requirements of the 'particular convention' prevail; but as regards procedure for obtaining recognition or enforcement, the applicant is entitled to proceed in the manner provided for by Title III, and if the 'particular convention' also provides for a procedure, the applicant has the option of using either the procedure provided for by Title III or that provided for by the 'particular convention'.[113]

Hence, for example, if an applicant wishes to obtain enforcement in England of a French judgment which is based on a contract for the international carriage of goods by road, falling within the scope of the Geneva Convention of 1956 (to which the United Kingdom and France are parties), he may use the procedure specified in art 31 et seq of the 1968 Convention, but (in derogation from arts 28 and 34 of the 1968 Convention) the English court will have to review the jurisdiction of the French court in accordance with art 31 of the Geneva Convention.[114] Probably, however, in such a case the applicant for enforcement can no longer proceed in accordance with the Foreign Judgments (Reciprocal Enforcement) Act 1933, despite the extension by s 9(1) of the Civil Jurisdiction and Judgments Act 1982 of references in Title VII (in particular, art 57) of the 1968 Convention to other conventions (in particular, the 'particular conventions' to which art 57 applies), so as to include references to British legislation implementing such other conventions (in particular, the Foreign Judgments (Reciprocal Enforcement) Act 1933 as applied by the Carriage of Goods by Road

---

[113] See the Schlosser Report, at pp 139–41.

[114] Article 31(1) of the Geneva Convention confers jurisdiction on a court of a contracting state designated by agreement of the parties to the contract of carriage, and on the courts of a contracting state within which the defendant is ordinarily resident, or has his principal place of business, or his branch or agency through which the contract of carriage was made, or the goods were taken over by the carrier, or the place designated for delivery is situated. Article 31(3) explicitly prohibits the re-opening of the merits by the court addressed.

Act 1965). For the procedure under the 1933 Act was made available by s 4 of the 1965 Act, rather than being specified in the Geneva Convention itself. Thus the Geneva Convention does not require derogation from the normal rule that the enforcement procedure under Title III of the 1968 Convention is exclusive.

SUBSTANTIVE REQUIREMENTS

Review of the merits

The general rule under all five regimes is that the English court cannot review the substance or merits of the foreign decision. It is not open to the English court to consider whether the original court made some error in determining the underlying dispute, whether the error alleged is of fact or of law (and whether of English or foreign law, of substantive or conflicts law). This applies under all three of the traditional regimes applicable to overseas judgments.[115] However the traditional English regimes on overseas judgments make a major exception for judgments obtained by fraud, by requiring the English court to review the merits of the underlying dispute in order to ascertain the existence of fraud, even where the party alleging fraud relies on evidence which he placed or could have placed before the foreign court.[116] The exception has been qualified by the Court of Appeal's ruling in *House of Spring Gardens v Waite*,[117] in the context of enforcement at common law, that the exception for fraud cannot be invoked where the claim that the foreign judgment had been obtained by fraud had been litigated and rejected in a second, separate action in the foreign country, and the second judgment was not itself impeachable in England on any ground.

As regards the enforcement of British judgments, Part II of the 1982 Act suppresses substantive review without qualification. In the event of fraud, the remedy must be sought in the original country. At most the court addressed may stay the enforcement proceedings in consequence of an application or appeal in the original country.[118]

As regards European judgments, arts 29 and 34[3] of the 1968 and Lugano Conventions specify that under no circumstances may a judgment be reviewed as to its substance by a court in which recognition or enforcement is sought, though art 27(4) makes an exception in respect of judgments involving the decision of a preliminary question of individual status or capacity, matrimonial

---

[115] See *Godard v Gray* (1870) LR 6 QB 139; *Henderson v Henderson* (1844) 115 ER 111; *Ellis v McHenry* (1871) LR 6 CP 228; the Administration of Justice Act 1920, s 9(2) and (3); and the Foreign Judgments (Reciprocal Enforcement) Act 1933, ss 2(1)–(2) and 4(1).

[116] See *Abouloff v Oppenheimer* (1882) 10 QBD 295; *Vadala v Lawes* (1890) 25 QBD 310; the 1920 Act, s 9(2)(d); the 1933 Act, s 4(1)(a)(iv); *Syal v Heyward* [1948] 2 KB 443; and *Owens Bank v Bracco* [1992] 2 AC 443.

[117] [1991] 1 QB 241.

[118] See Sched 6, paras 3, 5, 9 and 10; and Sched 7, paras 3, 5, 8 and 9.

property, or succession, in a manner inconsistent with the conflicts law of the country addressed. These provisions limit the scope of the public policy proviso contained in art 27(1). Thus, as the English Court of Appeal recognised in *SISRO v Ampersand Software*,[119] the application to European judgments of the traditional English exception for fraud would contravene the Conventions, and, in general at least, the remedy for fraud must be sought in the original country. On the other hand it seems permissible for the court addressed to invoke the public policy proviso against recognition in the rare situation where there is cogent newly discovered evidence, but the law of the original country denies any possibility of proceedings to re-open the judgment.

Jurisdictional review

Overseas judgments

Under the three traditional English regimes, an overseas personal judgment will not be recognised or enforced unless the original court is regarded as having had jurisdiction over the respondent – the person against whom the overseas judgment is invoked – or his privy, under the relevant English rules of indirect jurisdiction. The burden of establishing the existence of such indirect jurisdiction lies on the party seeking recognition or enforcement.[120]

The English rules of indirect personal jurisdiction differ, but only slightly, as between the common law, the 1920 Act, and the 1933 Act. In broad terms, under all three systems the only connections giving rise to indirect jurisdiction over a person are: (a) his residence (in varying senses) in the original country[121] at the institution of the action there; or (b) his submission to the jurisdiction of the original court, either by express agreement to such jurisdiction, or by

---

[119] (1993) *The Times*, 29 July; following the Schlosser Report, at p 128; and approving *Interdesco v Nullifire* [1992] 1 Lloyd's Rep 180, Phillips J. In *SISRO* the Court of Appeal referred another point to the European Court of Justice, where the case is now pending as Case C-432/93.

[120] See *Adams v Cape Industries* [1990] Ch 433, CA.

[121] In *Adams v Cape Industries* [1990] Ch 433, the Court of Appeal inclined tentatively to the view that, in the case of a judgment given by an American federal district court in the exercise of jurisdiction arising from diversity of residence of the parties (as well as in the case of a judgment of such a court given in the exercise of jurisdiction arising from the character of the cause of action as governed by federal law), the relevant original country, within which the defendant's residence or lack of residence is material, is the United States as a whole, rather than the particular state within the Union in and for which the court is sitting; so that for English purposes the defendant's residence in Illinois would subject him to the 'diversity' jurisdiction of the federal district court for Texas, Alaska or Hawaii. This view is surprising in view of the federal Supreme Court's rulings in such cases as *Erie Railroad v Tompkins* (1938) 304 US 64, *Klaxon v Stentor* (1941) 313 US 487, and *Guaranty Trust v York* 326 US 99 (1945), that in diversity cases a federal district court must (except on certain questions governed by the Federal Rules of Procedure; and subject to federal constitutional requirements which are applicable to both federal and state courts) act as a court of the state in which it is sitting, and accordingly must apply the law of that state (including its choice of law rules) in determining all questions of substance and some questions of procedure, and in particular must determine its territorial jurisdiction to entertain an action by reference to connections of the defendant and the cause of action with, and in accordance with the law of, the state in which it is sitting.

appearance in the original action.[122] It is not enough that some or all of the acts and events which gave rise to the cause of action occurred in the original country, and that an equivalent connection with England would have conferred direct jurisdiction on the English courts.[123]

RESIDENCE

Where the respondent is an individual, the reference to his 'residence', as a basis of indirect jurisdiction, must be understood as follows:

(1) At common law, it refers simply to his physical presence in person in the original country, however transiently, at the institution of the action there.[124] It is not enough that he was carrying on business there through an agent.[125]

(2) Under the Administration of Justice Act 1920, s 9(2)(b) makes it necessary and sufficient either that he was ordinarily resident in the original country, or that he was carrying on business there.

(3) Under the Foreign Judgments (Reciprocal Enforcement) Act 1933 it is probable that s 4(2)(a)(iv), which merely speaks of his residence, should be understood as referring simply to his physical presence in person, however transiently, so as to accord with the common law. However s 4(2)(a)(v) makes it alternatively sufficient that he had an office or place of business in the original country, provided that the action was in respect of a transaction effected through or at that office or place.

Where the respondent is a corporation, the meaning of the reference to its presence or residence in the original country, as a basis of indirect jurisdiction for the purposes of the common law (and the 1920 Act), was elucidated by the Court of Appeal in *Adams v Cape Industries*[126] as follows:

(1) Residence requires that the corporation should have been carrying on

---

[122] See *Schibsby v Westenholz* (1870) LR 6 QB 155; *Singh v Rajah of Faridkote* [1894] AC 670; *Emanuel v Symon* [1908] 1 KB 302; *Adams v Cape Industries* [1990] Ch 433; the 1920 Act, s 9(2)(a) and (b); the 1933 Act, ss 4(1)(a)(ii), (2)(a), and 11(2); and the 1982 Act, ss 32 and 33. Earlier dicta (in eg *Emanuel v Symon*) that the defendant's nationality would suffice to found jurisdiction at common law are now discredited; see eg per Slade LJ in *Adams v Cape Industries*.

[123] See note 124 above, and *Turnbull v Walker* (1892) 67 LT 767, *Re Trepca Mines* [1960] 1 WLR 1273, and *Sidmetal v Titan* [1966] 1 QB 828.

[124] See *Carrick v Hancock* (1895) 12 TLR 59, approved by the Court of Appeal in *Adams v Cape Industries* [1990] Ch 433, where Slade LJ said that 'in the absence of any form of submission to the foreign court, [its] competence depends on the physical presence of the defendant in the country concerned at the time of suit', and that 'the temporary presence of a defendant in the foreign country will suffice provided at least that it is voluntary (i.e. not induced by compulsion, fraud or duress)'. Thus 'the voluntary presence of an individual in a foreign country, whether permanent or temporary and whether or not accompanied by residence, is sufficient to give the courts of that country territorial jurisdiction over him under our rules of private international law'. However he explicitly left open whether residence without presence would suffice.

[125] See *Blohn v Desser* [1962] 2 QB 116.

[126] [1990] Ch 433.

business (or, in the case of a non-trading corporation, other corporate activities) in the original country at a definite and reasonably permanent place.[127] Thus a corporation is resident in a country if it has a fixed place of business of its own there (whether as owner, lessee or licensee) and for more than a minimal period of time has carried on its own business from such premises by its servants or agents.[128]

(2) But a corporation may be resident in a country even though it has no fixed place of business of its own there, if an agent acting on its behalf has for more than a minimal period of time been carrying on the corporation's business (as opposed to his own business) at or from some fixed place of business in the country.

(3) To determine whether the business carried on by an agent should be regarded as his own business or as that of the corporation necessitates an investigation both of the activities and functions of the agent and of the relationship between him and the corporation.[129] Many matters are relevant in this investigation, but no single one is conclusive. They include the contributions, if any, made by the corporation to the financing of the business carried on by the representative; how he is remunerated; the degree of control exercised by the corporation over the running of the business conducted by the representative; whether he reserves part of his accommodation or staff for conducting business related to the corporation; whether he displays its name at his premises or on his stationery, in such a way as to indicate that he is a representative of it; what business, if any, he transacts as principal exclusively on his own behalf; whether he makes contracts with third parties in the name of the corporation, or otherwise in such manner as to bind it, and if so, whether he requires specific authority in advance before binding the corporation to contractual obligations. Though not in itself conclusive, it is of great importance whether the agent has authority to enter into contracts on behalf of the corporation without submitting them to the corporation for approval;[130] and the fact that a representative never makes contracts in the name of the corporation or otherwise in such manner as to bind it is a powerful factor pointing against the residence of the corporation.

(4) The same principles apply where a parent company is alleged to have carried on business through the agency of a subsidiary company. Even though they may be said to constitute a single economic unit, each of the companies in a group is a separate legal entity, and there is no presumption that a subsidiary is

---

[127] See also *Littauer Glove v Millington* (1928) 44 TLR 746; and the 1920 Act, s 9(2)(b).

[128] See also the following cases on earlier rules as to English jurisdiction over foreign corporations: *Newby v Von Oppen* (1872) LR 7 QB 293; *Haggin v Comptoir d'Escompte de Paris* (1889) 23 QBD 519; *La Bourgogne* [1899] P 1 and [1899] AC 431; and *Dunlop v Cudell* [1902] 1 KB 342.

[129] See also *Vogel v Kohnstamm* [1973] 1 QB 133 (on enforcement at common law); and *Sfeir v National Insurance Co of New Zealand* [1964] 1 Lloyd's Rep 330 (on enforcement under the 1920 Act); and the following cases on earlier rules as to English jurisdiction over foreign corporations: *Okura v Forsbacka Jernverks* [1914] 1 KB 715; *Saccharin Corp v Chemische Fabrik Von Heyden* [1911] 2 KB 516; *Thames and Mersey Marine Insurance Co v Societa di Navigazione a Vapore del Lloyd Austriaco* (1914) 111 LT 97; *Grant v Anderson* [1892] 1 QB 108; *The Princesse Clementine* [1897] P 18; *The Lalandia* [1933] P 56; and *The Holstein* [1936] 2 All ER 1660.

[130] See also *Jabbour v Custodian of Israeli Absentee Property* [1954] 1 WLR 139.

carrying on the business of its parent as its agent. A parent company is entitled to arrange the affairs of its group in such a way that the business carried on in a particular country is the business of its subsidiary and not its own, and the court will not 'pierce the corporate veil' merely because the parent's purpose was to reduce its own exposure to the jurisdiction of the foreign court.

In the instant case, the Court of Appeal concluded that an English parent company was not resident in Illinois through a subsidiary incorporated and carrying on business there, mainly because, although the main function of the subsidiary was to assist in the marketing in the United States of asbestos sold by its sister companies, and for such services it was remunerated by way of commission on sales, paid to it by the sister companies, it had no general authority to bind the parent to any contractual obligations, and it never in fact, even with prior authority from the parent, effected any transaction in such a manner that the parent thereby became subject to contractual obligations to any person.

In contrast, for the purposes of the 1933 Act, s 4(2)(a)(iv) and (v) require that a respondent company should have had, in the original country, either its principal place of business, or a secondary office or place of business through or at which the transaction involved in the original action was effected.

In any event, s 32 of the 1982 Act prevents residence from creating indirect jurisdiction by an overseas court over an individual or a company under any of the three regimes, if the original action was brought in defiance of a valid agreement for arbitration or for the exclusive jurisdiction of the courts of another country, unless the agreement was incapable of being performed for reasons not attributable to the plaintiff's fault; and for this purpose the English court is not bound by findings of the original court.

SUBMISSION

Under all three regimes for overseas judgments, indirect jurisdiction over a non-resident may arise from his submission, by agreement[131] or appearance.

As regards submission by agreement, it is well established that an agreement on jurisdiction must be explicit and can never be implied.[132] On the other hand an explicit agreement on jurisdiction may take the form of a clause contained in a standard form contract, such as the articles of association of a company,[133] or it may be constituted by an informal expression of consent to accept the jurisdiction.[134] It may contemplate exclusive or non-exclusive jurisdiction, and it may

---

[131] See *Emanuel v Symon* [1908] 1 KB 302; *Feyerick v Hubbard* (1902) 71 LJKB 509, which involved a jurisdiction clause contained in a patent assignment contract; the 1920 Act, s 9(2)(b); and the 1933 Act, s 4(2)(a)(iii).

[132] See *Singh v Rajah of Faridkote* [1984] AC 670; *Emanuel v Symon* [1908] 1 KB 302; and *Vogel v Kohnstamm* [1973] 1 QB 133. Contrary dicta in *Blohn v Desser* [1962] 2 QB 116, and *Sfeir v National Insurance Co of New Zealand* [1964] 1 Lloyd's Rep 330, are now discredited.

[133] See *Copin v Adamson* (1874) LR 9 Ex 345 and (1875) 1 ExD 17.

[134] See *General Textiles v Sun & Sand Agencies* [1978] 1 QB 279.

refer to the courts in general of a specified country, or to a particular court, and in the latter case it will not confer jurisdiction on other courts of the same country.[135]

As regards submission by appearance, it is enough that the respondent appeared as plaintiff or counterclaimant in the original proceedings.[136] Thus a plaintiff in a foreign action is regarded as submitting to the jurisdiction of the original court, not only as regards his own claim, but also in respect of any counterclaim which the original court permits to be made against him in the same proceedings by a person whom he has sued. Similarly a defendant who counterclaims is regarded as submitting to the jurisdiction of the original court in respect of the plaintiff's claim against him as well as his own counterclaim against the plaintiff.

There is also submission by appearance on the part of a defendant in a foreign action who voluntarily appears in the original action without counterclaiming,[137] and the appearance may be either at first instance or on appeal.[138] However s 33(1) of the 1982 Act requires that, to found indirect jurisdiction under any of the three regimes applicable to overseas judgments, the appearance should be on the merits, and not for the limited purposes of contesting the jurisdiction of the original court, requesting it to decline jurisdiction in favour of arbitration or of adjudication in another country,[139] or of protecting, or obtaining the release of, property seized, or threatened with seizure, in the foreign proceedings. Probably the reference to actual or threatened seizure of property should be construed as confined to seizure before judgment for the purpose of founding jurisdiction or providing security, as distinct from seizure after judgment in execution.[140]

European judgments

In the case of European judgments, arts 28[3] and 34[2] of the 1968 Convention, and arts 28[4] and 34[2] of the Lugano Convention, explicitly preclude the court addressed from reviewing the jurisdiction of the original court, save in certain exceptional cases specified elsewhere in the Conventions. Thus the general rule under the Conventions is that it is for the original court to determine whether it has jurisdiction in accordance with Title II, and its decision upholding its jurisdiction is binding on the courts of the other contracting states when recognition or enforcement is sought under Title III. In this respect the Conventions depart from the usual international practice, and even from the practice in the

---

[135] See *General Textiles v Sun & Sand Agencies* [1978] 1 QB 279.

[136] See *Emanuel v Symon* [1908] 1 KB 302; the 1920 Act, s 9(2)(b); and the 1933 Act, s 4(2)(a)(ii).

[137] See *Emanuel v Symon* [1908] 1 KB 302; the 1920 Act, s 9(2)(b); and the 1933 Act, s 4(2)(a)(i).

[138] See *General Textiles v Sun & Sand Agencies* [1978] 1 QB 279.

[139] This overrules the decisions at common law in *Harris v Taylor* [1915] 2 KB 580, and *Henry v Geoprosco* [1976] 2 QB 726, and aligns the position at common law and under the 1920 Act with the position already existing under the 1933 Act.

[140] Cf the common law decisions in *De Cosse Brissac v Rathbone* (1861) 158 ER 123, *Voinet v Barrett* (1885) 55 LJQB 39, and *Guiard v De Clermont* [1914] 3 KB 145.

United States in respect of judgments given in a sister state.[141] The approach adopted by the Conventions is apparently based on the close relationship between the contracting states and their strong mutual confidence in each others' courts.

The consequence of this approach is that a defendant who is sued in a court which he considers to lack jurisdiction should, in his own interests, appear in the original court for the purpose of contesting its jurisdiction. Although in cases where another contracting state has exclusive jurisdiction, or the defendant is domiciled in another contracting state and does not appear, the original court is required by arts 19 and 20(1) to consider its jurisdiction of its own motion, it is not unlikely that, if the defendant fails to appear and place his evidence and arguments before the court, it will reach an erroneous decision in favour of its competence, and that decision will not be open to review when recognition or enforcement is sought in another contracting state.

The exceptions, where the Conventions require the court addressed to review the international jurisdiction of the original court, and refuse recognition if it lacked jurisdiction under Title II, are as follows:

(1) Where the dispute falls within the Sections of Title II which deal with insurance, protected consumer contracts, or exclusive jurisdiction.[142] The rationale seems to be a fear that otherwise the policies of protecting policyholders and consumers, and respecting the interests of the state of exclusive jurisdiction, might have been undermined.

(2) Where the respondent is domiciled or habitually resident in a non-member state between which and the state addressed there is a bilateral convention entered into in pursuance of art 59 of the 1968 Convention.[143]

(3) Where the original action was instituted before, but the judgment was given after, the entry into force of the Conventions between the state of origin and the state addressed.[144]

Additional exceptions under the Lugano Convention permit jurisdictional review in the following cases:

(1) Where the respondent is domiciled in an EFTA country, and the court of origin based its jurisdiction on a ground on which is contrary to the Lugano Convention, and the judgment is not entitled to recognition in the state addressed apart from the Convention.[145]

---

[141] See eg *Milliken v Meyer* 311 US 457 (1940), *McGee v International Life Insurance Co* 355 US 220 (1957), and *Hanson v Denckla* 357 US 235 (1958). Cf *Baldwin v Iowa State Traveling Men's Assoc* 283 US 522 (1931), and *Durfee v Duke* 375 US 106 (1963).

[142] Article 28[1].

[143] Articles 28[1] and 59.

[144] Article 54.

[145] Articles 28[2] and 54B(3). In addition art Ia of the Protocol annexed to the Lugano Convention permits Switzerland to make a reservation enabling it, until the end of 1999, to refuse to recognise judgments where the jurisdiction of the original court was based only on art 5(1) of the Convention, and the defendant was domiciled in Switzerland at the introduction of the original action. For this purpose a company is regarded as domiciled in Switzerland if it has both its registered office and its effective centre of activities there.

(2)   Where the original court assumed jurisdiction in pursuance of a convention on a particular matter to which the state addressed is not a party, and the respondent is domiciled in the state addressed, unless the judgment is otherwise entitled to recognition under the law of the state addressed.[146]

But the significance of most of the exceptions is reduced almost to vanishing point by a supplementary rule, laid down by art 28[2] of the 1968 Convention and art 28[3] of the Lugano Convention, that for these purposes, except in relation to the transitional exception, the court addressed is bound by the findings of fact on which the original court based its jurisdiction.

BILATERAL CONVENTIONS UNDER ART 59

Article 59 of the 1968 and Lugano Conventions authorise a contracting state to conclude a convention with a non-contracting state on the recognition and enforcement of judgments, and therein to undertake an obligation not to recognise certain judgments given in other contracting states against defendants domiciled or habitually resident in the non-contracting state. Accordingly a Convention between the United Kingdom and Canada, providing for the Reciprocal Recognition and Enforcement of Judgments in Civil and Commercial Matters, was signed at Ottawa on 24 April 1984 and entered into force on 1 January 1987.[147] It contains, in art IX, an undertaking in favour of Canadian domiciliaries and habitual residents of the type authorised by art 59 of the 1968 and Lugano Conventions.[148] The effect of art 59 and the Anglo-Canadian Convention will be that a British court will refuse to recognise or enforce a judgment of a court of another contracting state to the 1968 or Lugano Conventions if the following conditions are fulfilled:

(1)   The defendant was domiciled or habitually resident in Canada, semble at the institution of the action in which the judgment was given, 'domicile' having the meaning adopted by the 1982 Act.[149] Probably the domicile or habitual residence need not be in a Canadian province or territory desig-

---

[146] Articles 28[2] and 57(4).

[147] For its text, see Cmnd 9337 (1984) or the Schedule to the Reciprocal Enforcement of Foreign Judgments (Canada) Order 1987, SI 1987/468. This Order (as amended by SI 1989/987, 1988/1304, 1988/1853, and 1987/2211) implements the provisions of the Anglo-Canadian Convention for reciprocal recognition and enforcement by applying Part I of the Foreign Judgments (Reciprocal Enforcement) Act 1933 (as amended by the Civil Jurisdiction and Judgments Act 1982) to judgments given in a civil or commercial matter by the Federal Court of Canada or any court of the following territories: British Columbia, Manitoba, New Brunswick, the Northwest Territories, Nova Scotia, Ontario, Prince Edward Island, Saskatchewan or the Yukon Territory. It is, however, noteworthy that the Order does not make provision for the recognition or enforcement in the United Kingdom of judgments given in Quebec.

[148] The undertaking is implemented in the United Kingdom by s 9(2) of the 1982 Act, and art 7(b) of SI 1987/468.

[149] See art IX(2) of the Anglo-Canadian Convention, and ss 41(7) and 42(6) of the 1982 Act.

nated by Canada as one to which the Anglo-Canadian Convention extends, but could be in Quebec.[150]

(2) The original action was held by the original court to fall within art 4 of the 1968 or Lugano Conventions, in that, in view of arts 52 and 53, the defendant was not domiciled in any contracting state, and no provision of Title II derogating from art 4 (such as arts 8(2), 16, 17 or 18) was applicable. Accordingly the original court considered itself required by art 4 to determine its jurisdiction in accordance with its own law, including its rules conferring excessive jurisdiction, modified solely by art 4(2), whereby a plaintiff domiciled in the original country receives the same jurisdictional advantages as if he were its national.

(3) The only basis on which the original court had jurisdiction under its own law[151] must have been one of the excessive bases specified in art 3[2], such as the defendant's nationality, or the plaintiff's nationality, domicile or residence, or the situation or seizure of property.

(4) If the original court founded its jurisdiction on the presence or seizure of property situated in its territory, the action must not have been based on a claim to or involving that property, or to a debt secured on that property.

THE TRANSITIONAL SITUATION

Jurisdictional review is required in the transitional situation where the judgment was given after the date on which the 1968 or Lugano Convention entered into force between the state of origin and the state addressed, but the action in which it was given was instituted before that date.[152] Title III does not apply at all if the judgment was given before the relevant commencement date, and applies fully if the original action was instituted after that date.[153] In the transitional case, Title III applies, but subject to the proviso that the original court must have had jurisdiction, either under the rules provided for in Title II of the Convention, or under those provided for in a convention between the state of origin and the state addressed which was in force when the original action was instituted.[154] The relevant version of Title II is the one which entered into force between the state of origin and the state addressed on the date that the Convention entered into force between them, and in reviewing jurisdiction by reference to Title II one must treat as contracting states the states which were or became parties to the Convention on that date. The other conventions referred to are the bilateral conventions which are listed in art 55 and accordingly replaced by the

---

[150] See art IX(1) of the Anglo-Canadian Convention, and SI 1987/468. Cf arts I(c), II(1) and XII of the Anglo-Canadian Convention.

[151] See the Jenard Report, at p 61.

[152] For the various commencement dates, see Chapter 7, under 'Time and space', pp 119–21 above.

[153] See the 1968 Convention, arts 54[1] and 56[1]; the 1978 Convention, art 34(1)-(2); the 1982 Convention, art 12(1); the 1989 Convention, art 29(1); and the Lugano Convention, art 54[1] and 56[1].

[154] See the 1968 Convention, art 54[2]; the 1978 Convention, art 34(3); the 1982 Convention, art 12(2); the 1989 Convention, art 29(2); and the Lugano Convention, art 54[2].

1968 or Lugano Conventions, and to the conventions on particular matters referred to in art 57 and accordingly given priority over the 1968 and Lugano Conventions.

Prior to its accession to the 1968 Convention the United Kingdom was a party to bilateral conventions with France, Belgium, West Germany, Italy, and the Netherlands, and these conventions had effect under the Foreign Judgments (Reciprocal Enforcement) Act 1933, s 4(2) and (3) of which lays down rules of indirect jurisdiction. Thus, in the case of a French judgment given after 1986 in an action instituted before 1987 in respect of a dispute not falling within the scope of a convention on a particular matter, the English court will now recognise and enforce the judgment in accordance with Title III of the 1968 Convention as amended, provided that the French court had jurisdiction, either under the rules contained in Title II of the 1968 Convention, as amended by the 1978 Convention, applied on the fictitious assumption that the United Kingdom had been a contracting state to the 1968 Convention at the institution of the French action, or under the rules contained in s 4 of the 1933 Act. In the case of an Irish judgment given in 1989 in an action commenced in 1987, there being no bilateral convention, the jurisdictional review would be based solely on Title II as amended.

Since the Convention was not in fact in force in both states at the institution of the original action, the original court will not have applied Title II, or at any rate will not have treated the state addressed as a contracting state, so the special provision for jurisdictional review is necessary to prevent recognition and enforcement of judgments founded on excessive bases of jurisdiction against defendants domiciled in the state addressed, and for the same reason there is no provision that in the transitional case the court addressed must accept the findings of fact relevant to jurisdiction made by the original court. But it seems doubtful whether the complicated provisions for the transitional case are really worthwhile. It would surely have been simpler, and involved little derogation from the objectives of the Conventions, if Title III had been made applicable only where the original action had been instituted after the relevant commencement date.

British judgments

All possibility of jurisdictional review is excluded where recognition or enforcement of a judgment given in one part of the United Kingdom is sought in another part of the United Kingdom under Part II of the 1982 Act.[155]

Public policy

The recognition and enforcement in England of overseas and European judgments is subject to a proviso that recognition of the judgment must not be

---

[155] See s 19 (on mere recognition), and Scheds 6 and 7 (on enforcement). The position was similar under earlier legislation: see *Wotherspoon v Connolly* (1871) 9 Macph 510, and *Laughland v Wansborough Paper* [1921] 1 SLT 341.

contrary to English public policy. The proviso in favour of English public policy operates under the common law,[156] the 1920 Act,[157] the 1933 Act,[158] and the 1968 and Lugano Conventions.[159] But English public policy cannot be invoked against the enforcement of a Scottish or Northern Irish judgment under Part II of the 1982 Act.

The 1968 and Lugano Conventions in effect crystallise one aspect of public policy, by specifying in arts 27(4) and 34[2] that recognition or enforcement in England of a European judgment must be refused if the original court, in order to reach its judgment:

(1)   decided a preliminary question concerning the status or capacity of an individual, matrimonial property, or succession on death – matters which, when they form the principal subject-matter of proceedings, exclude them from the scope of the Convention by virtue of art 1[2](1); and

(2)   decided that question in a way which conflicts with a rule of English private international law; and

(3)   thereby reached a different result from that which would have been reached by the application to such questions of the English rules of private international law.

This special proviso could apply, for example, where the judgment upholds a defence of minority to a claim for damages for breach of contract, by applying the law of the defendant's nationality or domicile, when an English court would have rejected the defence, by applying the law governing the contract. It could also apply where the foreign judgment awards maintenance ancillarily in divorce proceedings, and the divorce is for some reason denied recognition in England. In the case of an overseas judgment, such situations fall to be dealt with under the general public policy proviso, which leaves the English court a power of appreciation, rather than imposing a firm obligation to refuse recognition in such cases.[160]

Another crystallisation of English public policy is found in s 5 of the Protection of Trading Interests Act 1980, which prevents the enforcement at common law or under the 1920 or 1933 Acts of an overseas judgment for multiple damages. Even the unmultiplied element of the damages awarded, representing the actual loss found by the foreign court to have been sustained, is rendered unenforceable in England. Section 6 goes further by enabling in certain circumstances a person who has satisfied, or suffered enforcement abroad of, an overseas judgment for multiple damages, to sue in England for recoupment of the

---

[156] See eg *Re Macartney* [1921] 1 Ch 522.

[157] See s 9(1) and (2)(f).

[158] See s 4(1)(a)(v).

[159] See arts 27(1) and 34[2].

[160] Cf *Gray v Formosa* [1963] P 259, and *Lepre v Lepre* [1965] P 52, where public policy was invoked against the recognition of foreign decrees annulling marriages which were valid under the English conflict rules.

multiple element paid or enforced.[161] In view of the 1980 Act, an English court would probably invoke public policy against the enforcement under the 1968 or Lugano Conventions of a European judgment awarding multiple damages, at least as regards the multiple element of the amount awarded. But there appears to be no English policy against the enforcement of foreign judgments awarding exemplary or aggravated damages, for example where the defendant has perversely refused to meet a clearly justified claim, if no multiplication is involved,[162] unless perhaps the amount awarded is entirely irrational.[163]

More generally, it seems clear that the public policy proviso should be construed narrowly, and in particular that it should not be used to rectify supposed deficiencies in legislative provisions which endeavour to deal specifically with a particular type of objection. Thus in the case of European judgments, it would be improper to invoke public policy in order to review the merits of the judgment (in the face of arts 29 and 34[3]); or in order to criticise the choice of law rules used in the judgment in respect of its principal subject-matter, falling within the scope of the Convention (in the face of the specific, but limited, rule laid down by art 27(4)). Indeed art 28[3] of the 1968 Convention, and art 28[4] of the Lugano Convention, specifically forbid the use of public policy to extend jurisdictional review. On the other hand, it is possible to identify five types of situation in which English public policy may properly be invoked against recognition of a European or overseas judgment.

The first is where the English court considers that recognition of the judgment would be unconscionable because of the outrageous character of the substantive rule applied by the original court. Examples might be where the judgment has upheld and enforced a contract to pay a fee to an assassin for carrying out an assassination, or a contract to pay a prostitute a fee for her services. At one time it was considered that a maintenance order against the father of a non-marital child, lasting beyond the child's minority, fell into this category,[164] but a more tolerant approach to such an order may be expected today.

The second type of situation is where recognition of the judgment would be contrary to the political interests of the United Kingdom in the conduct of its economic or foreign policies. Examples might be where the judgment upholds and enforces a contract whose conclusion was prohibited by British exchange control legislation,[165] or a contract which amounts to a conspiracy to commit acts in a foreign country which are criminally prohibited in the country where they are intended to be performed, such as a contract to smuggle goods into a country which prohibits the import of goods of that nature.[166]

The third type of situation is where, despite proper notification of the insti-

---

[161] See also s 7, which provides for the reciprocal enforcement of foreign 'recoupment' judgments. On ss 5–7 of the 1980 Act, see Stone [1983] 1 LMCLQ 1 at 16–17.

[162] See *General Textiles v Sun & Sand Agencies* [1978] 1 QB 279.

[163] See *Adams v Cape Industries* [1990] Ch 433.

[164] See *Re Macartney* [1921] 1 Ch 522.

[165] See *Boissevain v Weil* [1950] AC 327; which did not, however, involve a foreign *judgment*.

[166] See *Foster v Driscoll* [1929] 1 KB 470, and *Regazzoni v Sethia* [1958] AC 301; neither of which, however, involved a foreign judgment.

tution of the original action,[167] the respondent was in some other way denied a reasonable opportunity to present his case, or was otherwise prejudiced by the use by the foreign court (perhaps in breach of its own law) of a procedure which is considered seriously unfair by English standards.[168] Such denial of a hearing could occur, for example, where the plaintiff in the foreign action, having agreed to allow extra time for filing a defence, proceeds to obtain a default judgment in breach of the agreement.[169]

The seriously unfair procedure followed by the original court was one of the grounds on which the Court of Appeal refused, in *Adams v Cape Industries*,[170] to enforce at common law a judgment of an American federal court, given against a defaulting defendant in a personal injury action brought by numerous plaintiffs. The American court, in unexpected breach of its own procedural law, had assessed damages without receiving evidence of the particular injuries sustained by the individual plaintiffs. It had instead fixed an average amount for all the plaintiffs, and left it to their counsel to distribute the total award so arrived at between them. An argument that the defendant should have applied to the American court to have the judgment set aside on the ground of this procedural irregularity, an application which would have succeeded if made timeously, rather than raising the objection in England when enforcement here was sought, was rejected on the ground that the defendant had not been aware of the method of assessment used until enforcement in England was threatened. Slade LJ conceded, however, that if a foreign law were to provide for the plaintiff to serve a notice specifying a sum claimed as damages, and then for a default judgment then to be entered for that sum without proof or judicial assessment, such a procedure would usually be considered unobjectionable, provided that, after due allowance had been made for differences between the foreign law and English law in levels of award and in substantive law, the amount of the actual award was not irrational.

Slade LJ also took the view that, even if the only procedural impropriety related to the assessment of damages, the judgment creditor could not invoke the foreign judgment for the purpose merely of establishing liability, so as to obtain an English judgment under which damages would be assessed by the English court, even though he considered that such a result would 'get closer to substantial justice' than total dismissal of the claim. Why such limited recognition should be impossible is far from clear.

The fourth type of case is where cogent evidence has been discovered since the judgment was given, but there is no effective way of having the matter reopened in the original country.[171]

---

[167] This matter being dealt with specifically by the 1920 Act, s 9(2)(c); the 1933 Act, s 4(1)(a)(iii); and the 1968 and Lugano Conventions, art 27(2). See under the next heading, below.

[168] See *Jacobson v Frachon* (1927) 44 TLR 103, and *Adams v Cape Industries* [1990] Ch 433.

[169] See *Levin v Gladstein* 55 SE 371 (1906), and *Restatement, Second, Conflict of Laws* (1971), s 115.

[170] [1990] Ch 433.

[171] See *Interdesco v Nullifire* [1992] 1 Lloyd's Rep 180, and *SISRO v Ampersand Software* (1993) *The Times*, 29 July, where the Court of Appeal made a reference to the European Court of Justice, now pending as Case C-432/93.

The fifth type of case is where there are irreconcilable judgments given by courts of different countries, and there is no specific enactment or rule available dictating which of them should prevail.[172]

Inadequate notice of the original action

All the regimes on recognition and enforcement of overseas or European judgments make an exception for judgments given in default against a defendant who was not adequately notified of the original action, but a British judgment cannot be denied enforcement under Part II of the 1982 Act on this ground.

In the context of recognition at common law, Atkin LJ said in *Jacobson v Frachon*[173] that the foreign court must have given notice to the litigant that it was about to proceed to determine his rights, and must also have afforded him an opportunity of substantially presenting his case.[174] It may be, however, that service in a form authorised by an agreement between the parties will always satisfy the common law.[175] Under the 1920 Act, s 9(2)(c) prevents enforcement if the judgment debtor, being the defendant in the original proceedings, was not duly served with the process of the original court and did not appear. Under the 1933 Act, s 4(1)(a)(iii) requires the registration of a judgment to be set aside if the English court is satisfied that the judgment debtor, being the defendant in the original court, did not receive notice of the proceedings there in sufficient time to enable him to defend them and did not appear, even if process was duly served on him in accordance with the law of the original country.

In the case of European judgments, arts 27(2) and 34[2] of the 1968 and Lugano Conventions require recognition and enforcement to be refused where the judgment was given in default of appearance and the defendant was not duly served with the document which instituted the proceedings in sufficient time to enable him to arrange for his defence, and art 46(2) requires an applicant for recognition or enforcement of a default judgment to produce a document which establishes that the party in default was served with the document instituting the proceedings.

This protection at the stage of recognition or enforcement is in addition to that conferred in the original action by art 20[2] and [3] of the 1968 and Lugano Conventions and art 15 of the Hague Convention of 15 November 1965 on the Service Abroad of Judicial and Extrajudicial Documents in Civil or Commercial Matters, to which all the present EC member states except Ireland are parties. These provisions require the original court to stay its proceedings:

(1) where the defendant is domiciled in another contracting state to the 1968 or Lugano Conventions, and the instituting document did not have to be trans-

---

[172] See under 'Irreconcilable judgments', pp 342–4 below.
[173] (1927) 138 LT 386 at 392.
[174] Denial to a party of a substantial opportunity to be heard, arising otherwise than from failure adequately to notify the defendant of the proceedings, could make recognition or enforcement contrary to public policy, within the meaning of s 9(1) of the 1920 Act, s 4(1)(a)(v) of the 1933 Act, or art 27(1) of the 1968 or Lugano Conventions. See under 'Public policy', pp 335–9 above.
[175] See *Copin v Adamson* (1874) LR 9 Ex 345 and (1875) 1 ExD 17.

mitted abroad in accordance with the 1965 Convention, until it is shown that he has been able to receive the instituting document in sufficient time to enable him to arrange for his defence, or that all necessary steps have been taken to that end; or

(2) where the instituting document had to be transmitted abroad in accordance with the 1965 Convention, and the defendant has not appeared, until it is established that the document was served by a method prescribed by the internal law of the state to which it was transmitted, or was actually delivered to the defendant or to his residence by another method provided for by the 1965 Convention, in sufficient time to enable him to defend, or (by way of exception) until a period of at least six months, considered adequate by the court in the particular case, has elapsed since the document was transmitted in accordance with the 1965 Convention, and no certificate of any kind has been received, despite all reasonable efforts to obtain one, from the authorities of the receiving state.

The cumulative protection of the defendant at both stages was confirmed by the European Court of Justice in *Pendy Plastic Products v Pluspunkt*.[176] A Dutch writ against a German defendant had been transmitted to Germany for service in accordance with the 1965 Convention, and the Dutch court had given a default judgment after receiving a certificate from a German court that service had not been possible since the defendant was no longer resident at the address given, and the plaintiff was now seeking to enforce the Dutch judgment in Germany. The European Court of Justice ruled that the court addressed may refuse recognition and enforcement under art 27(2), even though the original court had considered itself satisfied, in accordance with art 20[3] of the 1968 Convention and art 15 of the 1965 Convention, that the defendant had had an opportunity to receive service of the instituting document in sufficient time to enable him to make arrangements for his defence. It is, however, important to note that, as the European Court of Justice confirmed in *Debaecker and Plouvier v Bouwman*,[177] the protection of art 27(2) at the stage of recognition and enforcement extends to every defendant, regardless of his domicile or residence, whereas the protection of art 20 of the 1968 or Lugano Convention and art 15 of the 1965 Convention, at the stage of the original action, is confined to a defendant who is domiciled in another contracting state to the 1968 or Lugano Convention, or resident in a state which is a party to the 1965 Convention.

In *Denilauler v Couchet Frères*,[178] which involved an attempt to enforce in Germany a French order, known as a *saisie conservatoire*, similar to an English *Mareva* injunction, freezing a bank account in Germany, the European Court of Justice ruled that judgments authorising provisional or protective measures, which are delivered without the defendant having been summoned to appear, and which are intended to be enforced without prior service, are outside the

[176] Case 228/81, [1982] ECR 2723.
[177] In Case 49/84, [1985] ECR 1779.
[178] Case 125/79, [1980] ECR 1553.

scope of Title III of the Convention. This is because arts 27(2), 46(2) and 47(1) cannot be applied to such judgments without distorting their substance and scope; because the whole of the Convention is designed to ensure that the procedural rights of the defence are observed; and because such judgments require particular judicial care, and the courts of the state where the assets to be frozen are located are best able to evaluate the relevant circumstances and impose suitable conditions. The court recognised, however, that provisional measures ordered in adversary proceedings may be enforceable under Title III of the Convention, and in *Derby v Weldon*[179] Browne-Wilkinson V-C recognised that Title III applies to an English *Mareva* injunction obtained by means of a summons inter partes.

Various aspects of art 27(2) were clarified by the European Court of Justice in *Klomps v Michel*:[180]

(1) A default judgment remains within the scope of art 27(2), even though the defendant has subsequently applied to the original court to have it set aside, if his application has been dismissed because it was made beyond the applicable time-limit.

(2) The instituting document referred to in art 27(2) is the document whose service enables the plaintiff, under the law of the original country, to obtain, in the event of default by the defendant, a judgment capable of being recognised or enforced under the Convention.

(3) In determining whether the defendant was given sufficient time to arrange for his defence, only the time available for taking steps to prevent the issue of a judgment in default which is enforceable under the Convention may be taken into account.

On the other hand, in *Sonntag v Waidmann*[181] the European Court of Justice emphasised that art 27(2) does not apply if the defendant had entered an appearance in the original proceedings. Moreover, where a civil claim is made ancillarily in a criminal prosecution, there is a sufficient appearance in relation to the civil claim if the defendant answers the criminal charges, but not the civil claim, through a lawyer whom he has chosen, and the lawyer is present when the court deals orally with the civil claim.

The decision of the European Court of Justice in *Klomps v Michel*[182] established that the requirement in art 27(2) of due service refers to service in accordance with the law of the original country and the treaties binding on it. Thus a default judgment not preceded by such service – for example, because

---

[179] (1988) *The Times*, 15 November; affirmed and extended by the Court of Appeal on other grounds, [1990] Ch 65.

[180] Case 166/80, [1981] ECR 1593. This case involved enforcement in the Netherlands of a German judgment given in summary proceedings for the recovery of a debt, known as *mahnverfahren*. Cf *Martens Confectie v Sartex* [1989] ECC 209, a decision of the Hague Court of Appeal involving enforcement in the Netherlands of an Italian judgment obtained ex parte under a summary procedure known as the *procedimento d'ingiunzione*.

[181] Case C-172/91, 21 April 1993.

[182] See note 182 above.

the documents served were not accompanied by a translation, as in *Lancray v Peters & Sickert*[183] – must be refused recognition, even if the notification was sufficient to enable the defendant to arrange for his defence, unless under the law and treaties of the original country the irregularity has been cured by subsequent acts. Similarly, as ruled in *Minalmet v Brandeis*,[184] a default judgment must be refused recognition under art 27(2) if the originating document was not duly served, even if the defendant later became aware of the judgment and failed to make use of the avenues of appeal available under the procedural law of the state of origin.

Moreover *Klomps v Michel*[185] and *Debaecker v Bouwman*[186] have established that the requirement of sufficient time to arrange for one's defence requires that the method of notification used (as well as amounting to due service) must, within the limits of practicability, be such that it is reasonably likely to inform the defendant or his agents of the proceedings, as well as requiring that the period of time between such notification and the entry of judgment in default must be reasonably sufficient to enable the filing of a defence. Thus, even if the original court has held, in separate adversary proceedings, that service had been duly effected, the court addressed still has to examine whether there was sufficient time for the defendant to arrange for his defence;[187] and where, as in *Debaecker v Bouwman*, after the defendant has deliberately disappeared without leaving a forwarding address, due service has been effected on a public official, but the plaintiff then discovers the defendant's new address, he must notify the defendant at that address before proceeding to obtain a default judgment.

Irreconcilable judgments

As the European Court of Justice explained in *Hoffmann v Krieg*,[188] judgments are irreconcilable with each other where they involve mutually exclusive consequences; in other words, insofar as they give rise to conflicting estoppels between the same persons. It proceeded, however, to rule, rather surprisingly, that there was irreconcilability between a German maintenance order and a subsequent Dutch divorce, on the questionable assumption that the maintenance order necessarily presupposed the existence of a matrimonial relationship.[189]

Considerations of logic and coherence require that where two judgments are

---

[183] Case C-305/88, [1990] I ECR 2725.
[184] Case C-123/91, [1992] I ECR 5661.
[185] See note 182 above.
[186] Case 49/84, [1985] ECR 1779.
[187] See *Klomps v Michel*, note 182 above.
[188] Case 145/86, [1988] ECR 645.
[189] This ruling was, however, followed in *Macaulay v Macaulay* [1991] I WLR 179, where the English Family Divisional Court refused to enforce an Irish maintenance order which had been followed by an English divorce. Cf *Bragg v Bragg* [1925] P 20; *Wood v Wood* [1957] P 254; *Qureshi v Qureshi* [1972] Fam 173; *Newmarch v Newmarch* [1978] Fam 79; and Stone [1988] 3 LMCLQ 383.

irreconcilable with each other, at least one of them must be refused recognition or effect. Hence, insofar as the problem is not solved by specific legislation, recourse must be had to general concepts such as public policy.[190] The general trend of both British and European law is to prefer a local judgment to an irreconcilable foreign judgment; and as between irreconcilable foreign judgments from different countries, to prefer the earlier judgment.

Irreconcilability between a local judgment and a foreign judgment

A foreign judgment will be refused recognition insofar as it is irreconcilable with a judgment given in the country addressed, regardless of the order in time in which the judgments were given. In relation to overseas judgments, this appears to be the position at common law,[191] under the 1920 Act,[192] and under the 1933 Act.[193]

As regards European judgments, arts 27(3) and 34[2] of the 1968 and Lugano Conventions provide that a judgment given in a contracting state must not be recognised or enforced in another contracting state if it is irreconcilable with a judgment given in a dispute between the same parties in the state addressed. There is no requirement in art 27(3) that the judgments should have been given in respect of the same cause of action. Presumably the reference in art 27(3) to the same parties should be construed purposively so as to include their privies, so that the provision will apply where, for example, one action to recover a contractual debt was brought by the original creditor and the other by his assignee. But the local judgment must be an actual judgment, and not merely a court settlement falling within Title IV of the Conventions.[194]

Irreconcilability between foreign judgments from different countries

Where the irreconcilable judgments are from different foreign countries, s 4(1)(b) of the 1933 Act gives preference to the earlier judgment by permitting the court addressed to set aside the registration of an overseas judgment if it is satisfied that the matter in dispute in the proceedings in the original court had previously to the date of the judgment in the original court been the subject of a final judgment by a competent court. The position at common law, and under the 1920 Act, was for a long time obscure, but now, in *Showlag v Mansour*,[195] the analogy of the 1933 Act has prevailed. There the Privy Council, on appeal

---

[190] However in *Hoffmann v Krieg*, note 190 above, the European Court of Justice explained that under the 1968 Convention the public policy proviso contained in art 27(1) cannot be used in relation to conflicts between a judgment of the state addressed and a judgment of another contracting state, since this type of problem is dealt with by art 27(3).

[191] See *Vervaeke v Smith* [1983] 1 AC 145; *Man v Haryanto* [1991] 1 Lloyd's Rep 429, CA; Wolff, *Private International Law* (2nd ed, 1950), para 248; and Stone [1983] 1 LMCLQ 1.

[192] See s 9(1).

[193] See s 4(1)(a)(v) and (b).

[194] 2 June 1994.

[195] (1994) *The Times*, 29 March.

from Jersey, faced with a conflict between an earlier English and a later Egyptian judgment, held (per Lord Keith) that where there were two competing foreign judgments, each of which had been pronounced by a competent court, and was final and otherwise unimpeachable, then the earlier in time had to be recognised to the exclusion of the later, unless there were circumstances connected with the obtaining of the second judgment which made it unfair for the party relying on the first judgment to do so.

Article 27(5) of the 1968 and Lugano Conventions requires a European judgment to be refused recognition if it is irreconcilable with an earlier judgment given in a non-contracting state involving the same cause of action and between the same parties, and the overseas judgment fulfils the conditions necessary for its recognition in the state addressed. In the United Kingdom, the latter clause simply means that the overseas judgment must comply with the substantive requirements for recognition at common law or under s 8 of the 1933 Act, and does not require that its recognition should have been established by proceedings in the United Kingdom.[196] No doubt the restriction in art 27(5) to judgments between the same parties should be construed liberally, as in the case of art 27(3), to include privies (such as successors in title), but the restriction to judgments involving the same cause of action leaves unsolved the problem of conflicting issue (as distinct from cause of action) estoppels.

The 1968 and Lugano Conventions contain no provision specifically directed to the position of a court of a contracting state which is faced with irreconcilable European judgments given by courts of two other contracting states. Perhaps it was hoped that the provisions of Title II on simultaneous actions, and those of Title III itself, would ensure that this situation would hardly ever arise, but they do not guarantee that it never will. Droz argues that the judgment first given should prevail,[197] and this seems acceptable as a basic rule. On the other hand, it is submitted that the third court should prefer the second judgment where the second judgment refused to recognise the first judgment on grounds specified in arts 27 or 28 which are not in any way specific to the second state – for example, for lack of proper notification, under art 27(2), or for infringement of exclusive jurisdiction, under arts 16 and 28. Moreover it seems arguable that the second judgment should be preferred where the second court was not aware of the first judgment, since the parties may then be considered to have waived their rights under the first judgment.[198]

ARBITRAL AWARDS

As with foreign judgments, there are several regimes which govern the recognition and enforcement in England of foreign arbitral awards. We shall, how-

[196] See the Schlosser Report, at para 205.
[197] *Compétence Judiciaire et Effets des Jugements dans le Marché Commun*, at paras 519–23. Cf the preference given to the later judgment under the 'full-faith-and-credit' clause of the United States' Constitution, as construed in *Treinies v Sunshine Mining Co* 308 US 66 (1939).
[198] Cf Spencer-Bower and Turner, *The Doctrine of Res Judicata* 1348 (2nd ed, 1969), at paras 383–86.

ever, focus mainly on the regime provided for by the New York Convention of 10 June 1958 on the Recognition and Enforcement of Foreign Arbitral Awards,[199] and implemented by the Arbitration Act 1975.[200] The New York Convention, which was negotiated within the framework of the United Nations, and has been ratified or acceded to by a large number of countries with a wide variety of political and legal traditions, including all the EC member states except Portugal.[201]

As between its contracting states, the New York Convention replaces the Geneva Protocol of 24 September 1923 on Arbitration Clauses and the Geneva Convention of 26 September 1927 for the Execution of Foreign Arbitral Awards,[202] but otherwise it does not prejudice provisions more favourable to recognition and enforcement contained in other conventions or in the national law of the state addressed.[203] Thus the Geneva Protocol and Convention, as implemented by the Arbitration Act 1950, remain applicable, however, to the recognition and enforcement in England of certain awards made in countries which are parties to that Convention but not to the New York Convention;[204] and the common law regime remains available in favour of recognition and enforcement, even where the award falls within the New York or Geneva Conventions.[205]

The scope of the New York Convention, as regards awards,[206] is defined by art I. It applies to the recognition and enforcement of arbitral awards made in a state other than the state where recognition or enforcement of the award is sought, and also to awards which are not considered as domestic awards in the

---

[199] For its text, see Cmnd 6419, or [1958] JBL 396.

[200] The 1975 Act does not schedule the text of the Convention, but paraphrases its provisions in the body of the Act.

[201] The parties to the New York Convention include Australia; Algeria; Antigua and Barbados; Argentina; Austria; Bahrain; Belgium; Belize; Benin; Botswana; Bulgaria; Burkina Faso; Cambodia; Cameroon; Canada; Central African Republic; Chile; China; Colombia; Costa Rica; Cuba; Cyprus; Denmark; Dominica; Djibouti; Ecuador; Egypt; Finland; France; Germany; Ghana; Greece; Guatemala; Haiti; Holy See; Hungary; India; Indonesia; Ireland; Israel; Italy; Japan; Jordan; Kenya; Korea; Kuwait; Luxembourg; Madagascar; Malaysia; Mexico; Monaco; Morocco; Netherlands; New Zealand; Niger; Nigeria; Norway; Panama; Peru; Philippines; Poland; Romania; Russia; San Marino; Singapore; South Africa; Spain; Sri Lanka; Sweden; Switzerland; Syria; Tanzania; Thailand; Trinidad and Tobago; Tunisia; United States of America; and Uruguay. See SI 1984/1168 and 1989/1348.

[202] For their text, see the Schedules to the Arbitration Act 1950.

[203] See art VII; and the Arbitration Act 1975, ss 2 and 6.

[204] The following countries are party to the Geneva, but not the New York, Conventions: Bahamas; Bangladesh; Grenada; Guyana; Malta; Mauritius; Pakistan; Portugal; Saint Christopher and Nevis; St Lucia; Western Samoa; and Zambia. See SI 1984/1168 and 1989/1348.

[205] On the common law regime, see Dicey & Morris, Rules 61–63. Where there is an overseas or British judgment based on or otherwise authorising enforcement of an award, it is also possible to seek enforcement in England under the Administration of Justice Act 1920, the Foreign Judgments (Reciprocal Enforcement) Act 1933, or Part II of the Civil Jurisdiction and Judgments Act 1982; see Dicey & Morris, Rules 66–67. But art I[2](4) of the 1968 and Lugano Conventions prevents the recognition or enforcement thereunder of a European judgment based on or authorising enforcement of an award.

[206] On art II of the Convention, which deals with the recognition and enforcement of arbitral agreements, see Chapter 11, under 'Arbitration clauses', pp 218–23 above.

state where recognition or enforcement is sought,[207] but a contracting state is permitted to make a reservation restricting its application of the Convention to awards made in other contracting states, and such reservations have been made by many states, including the United Kingdom.[208] It seems clear that a state which makes such a reservation is not bound to apply the Convention to awards made in its own territory, even when it considers the award not to be a domestic award but to be made under the procedural law of another contracting state.[209] Article I also makes it clear that it is immaterial whether the parties are individuals or corporate bodies, and whether the arbitrator was appointed for the particular dispute or was a permanent arbitral body to which the parties submitted. It seems clear, however, that the Convention does not apply to disputes between states governed by public international law.

The reference to non-domestic awards takes account of the acceptance by many conflict systems, including the English system, that the procedure used in an arbitration need not invariably be that provided for by the internal law of the country in which the arbitration proceedings are conducted.[210] Thus a purposive construction of the Convention (taking account especially of arts V(1)(e) and VI) would exclude its application in cases where the award, although made elsewhere, is regarded as domestic in the state addressed, in the sense that it considers that the arbitral procedure was governed by its own law. However in *Hiscox v Outhwaite*,[211] which involved an award signed by the arbitrator in France after proceedings conducted in England in accordance with English procedure, the House of Lords (per Lord Oliver) felt unable to avoid the conclusion that an award is made when it is (actually and purportedly) signed by the arbitrator, at any rate in the absence of something in the arbitration agreement or the rules under which the arbitration is conducted requiring some further formality before the award becomes effective. However, in substantial agreement with the views of Lord Donaldson MR, dissenting in the Court of Appeal, the House of Lords deprived this construction of any practical effect by

---

[207] Cf the Geneva Convention, which was confined to awards made in a contracting state between persons 'subject to the jurisdiction of' (that is, resident in) different contracting states.

[208] Within the European Community, such reservations have also been made by Ireland, France, Germany, Belgium, the Netherlands, Denmark, and Greece.

[209] Another permissible reservation by a contracting state confines its application of the Convention to disputes arising from legal relationships, whether contractual or not, which are regarded as commercial under its law. Such reservations have been made by many states, including (within the Community) France, Denmark and Greece; but not by the United Kingdom. Difficulties and absurdities may arise if such a reservation is made by a state, such as India, whose law contains no clear distinction between commercial and non-commercial matters; see *Indian Organic Chemicals v Chemtex Fibres* (1978) 65 All India Reporter, Bombay Section, 108.

[210] See *Miller v Whitworth* [1970] AC 583. As Lord Mustill explained in *Channel Tunnel Group Ltd v Balfour Beatty Construction Ltd* [1993] AC 334: 'Certainly there may sometimes be an express choice of a curial law which is not the law of the place where the arbitration is to be held: but in the absence of an explicit choice of this kind, or at least some very strong pointer in the agreement to show that such a choice was intended, the inference that the parties when contracting to arbitrate in a particular place consented to having the arbitral process governed by the law of that place is irresistible.'

[211] [1992] 1 AC 562, reversing [1991] 3 All ER 124, CA, and restoring [1991] 2 Lloyd's Rep 1, Hirst J.

ruling further that, in view of arts V(1)(e) and VI of the Convention, the fact that an award falls within the scope of the Convention, and is prima facie entitled to recognition and enforcement thereunder, because it was made in another contracting state, does not prevent the courts of the country under whose procedural law it was made from exercising their normal supervisory powers over the award; including, in England, the power to authorise and entertain an appeal against the substance of the award for error of law.

Article III of the New York Convention requires each contracting state to recognise arbitral awards within its scope as binding and to enforce them, under the conditions laid down in arts IV–VI. In general the state addressed should apply its own rules of procedure, but must not impose substantially more onerous conditions, or higher fees or charges, than are imposed on the recognition or enforcement of domestic arbitral awards. By art IV, a party applying for recognition or enforcement under the Convention must, at the time of his application, supply the duly authenticated original award or a duly certified copy of it; the original arbitration agreement or a duly certified copy of it; and if the award or agreement is not in an official language of the country addressed, a certified translation into such a language.

The substantive exceptions to recognition and enforcement are exhaustively defined by arts V and VI. They may conveniently be classified under four headings:

(1) invalidity or inadequate scope of the arbitration agreement;[212]
(2) procedural deficiencies in the arbitration proceedings;[213]
(3) invalidity of the award in the country of origin;[214] and
(4) non-arbitrability of subject-matter, and public policy of the state addressed.[215]

The wording of art V makes it clear that, except for non-arbitrability and public policy (which may be raised by the court addressed of its own motion), the burden of establishing the existence of a ground for refusal of recognition and enforcement rests on the party opposing recognition ('the respondent'). The only burden which rests on the applicant for recognition or enforcement is to produce the documents specified in art IV, and to satisfy the court, by reference to these documents or otherwise, that the award falls within the scope of the Convention, as defined by art I. If he fulfils these requirements, the court is bound to recognise and enforce the award, unless the respondent proves the existence of a ground for refusal under art V, or the court, of its own motion, invokes art V(2), which relates to the non-arbitrability of the subject-matter and to the public policy of the state addressed. Article V also makes it clear that, where a ground for refusal is established, the court is not bound to refuse recognition and enforcement, but has a discretion, and thus may accord

---

[212] Article V(1)(a) and (c); implemented by the 1975 Act, s 5(2)(a), (b) and (d), and (4).
[213] Article V(1)(b) and (d); implemented by s 5(2)(c) and (e).
[214] Articles V(1)(e) and VI; implemented by s 5(2)(f) and (5).
[215] Article V(2)(a) and (b); implemented by s 5(3).

recognition and enforcement, despite the establishment of a ground for refusal, if it considers that the irregularity is a mere technicality and the objection lacks substantial merit.[216] In view of this, the grounds for attack may properly be construed broadly in case of doubt, leaving it to the courts' discretion to ensure that they are not abused.

Invalidity or inadequate scope of the arbitration agreement

Article II of the Convention envisages an arbitration agreement in writing, and specifies that it may be contained in a substantive contract or may be a separate agreement, but that it must be signed by the parties or contained in an exchange of letters or telegrams,[217] and art IV(1)(b) requires an applicant for recognition or enforcement of an award to produce a copy of such an agreement at the time of his application. Hence, in the absence of a written agreement complying with art II, the application will fail in limine. If the original arbitration agreement is made orally, but both parties subsequently appear before the arbitrator and submit to his jurisdiction, the (more or less) formal pleadings exchanged in the arbitration proceedings will often fulfil the requirement of writing; but if there are no such pleadings, the award cannot be enforced under the Convention, for its wording and objectives (including certainty and commercial convenience) leave no room for an exception based on estoppel or good faith. On the other hand, if the arbitral agreement satisfies the formal requirements of art II, it is not open to a contracting state to require other or more onerous formalities.

Article V(1)(a) authorises the court addressed to refuse recognition of an award if the respondent establishes that the parties to the arbitration agreement were under some incapacity under the law applicable to them (according to the conflict rules of the state addressed);[218] or that the arbitration agreement is not valid under the law to which the parties subjected it or, failing any indication thereon, under the law of the country where the award was made. This formula seems to permit implied as well as express choice by the parties, and thus will normally lead to the law indicated by the arbitration clause as the law intended to govern the arbitral procedure, or, where the clause gives no indication of the intended curial law, to the law which was eventually used in the arbitration proceedings as their curial law, which will usually, though not invariably, coincide with that of the country where the award was made. The law so ascertained will govern the essential validity of the arbitration agreement in relation to issues such as misrepresentation, mistake, or improper pressure. But, in view of arts II and V(2)(a), it seems clear that art V(1)(a) does not extend to questions concerning arbitrability of subject-matter, and that for the purposes of art V(1)(a) any national rule which discriminates against arbitration agreements concluded before the dispute arose must be ignored.

---

[216] See Dicey & Morris, at p 624.
[217] See Chapter 11, under 'Arbitration clauses', pp 218–23 above.
[218] For the English choice of law rules on individual capacity to contract, see Chapter 12, under 'The scope of the proper law: Capacity', pp 250–1 above.

Article V(1)(c) deals with the scope of an arbitration agreement. It authorises the court addressed to refuse recognition if the respondent establishes that the award deals with a difference not contemplated by or not falling within the terms of the submission to arbitration, or if the award contains decisions on matters beyond the scope of the submission to arbitration, subject to a proviso that, if the decisions on matters submitted to arbitration can be separated from those not so submitted, the part of the award which contains decisions on matters submitted to arbitration may be recognised and enforced. It is thought that the references to 'the submission to arbitration' include, but are not confined to, the original arbitration agreement. They also include any further agreement as to the scope of the arbitration which is implied by the conduct of the parties in the course of the arbitral proceedings. No doubt, in interpreting the original arbitration agreement to determine its scope, the court addressed must apply the law which governs the essential validity of the agreement under art V(1)(a).

Procedural deficiencies in the arbitral proceedings

Article V(1)(b) enables the court addressed to refuse recognition of an award where the respondent establishes that he was not given proper notice of the appointment of the arbitrator or of the arbitration proceedings, or was otherwise unable to present his case; and art V(1)(d) enables it to do so where he establishes that the composition of the arbitral authority, or the arbitral procedure, was not in accordance with the agreement of the parties, or, failing such agreement, with the law of the country where the arbitration took place.

As regards proper notice and inability to be heard, the court addressed will no doubt have regard to what is acceptable under its own law of civil procedure and the treaties (especially those on recognition of foreign judgments) to which its state is a party.[219] Thus service in a manner which complies with the law governing the arbitral proceedings will not automatically satisfy these requirements. On the other hand, although the absence of proper notice is not automatically cured where the defendant appears in the arbitral proceedings, a respondent who appears and defends, despite very short notice, will have a heavy burden to discharge in persuading the court addressed that the procedure was so unjust as to justify refusal of recognition. In any event a court may, in its discretion, accord recognition even where, perhaps because it is rather demanding in its procedural standards, it finds a lack of proper notice or other opportunity to be heard; for example, if the respondent did not receive notice because he was in hiding from his creditors, or was refused a hearing because of his offensive conduct before the arbitrator and his refusal to apologise and undertake not to repeat the offence.

As regards the composition of the arbitral authority, and the arbitral procedure generally, under art V(1)(d) the court addressed is instructed to consider

[219] See under 'Substantive requirements: Inadequate notice', pp 339–42 above.

first the terms of the arbitration agreement, and only where they are silent is it to refer to the law of the country where the arbitration took place. It should not consider the validity of the agreed terms under any law, but should treat them as valid, leaving any attack on their validity to the courts of the country of origin. If, however, the arbitral agreement is silent on a question of procedure, recourse must be had by the court addressed to 'the law of the country where the arbitration took place'.

The need for art V(1)(d) seems questionable, and it is submitted that the court addressed should, in its discretion, apply this provision sparingly; that is, only where it is satisfied that the infringement is not merely technical but has led to real injustice. Indeed, in such a case, the court will probably be willing to refuse recognition on other grounds, such as lack of proper service or other opportunity to be heard (under art V(1)(b)) or infringement of its public policy (under art V(2)(b)). In any event, a party dissatisfied with the arbitral proceedings can always attack the award in its country of origin in accordance with the law of that country, and arts V(1)(e) and VI offer him derivative protection, ancillary to an attack in the country of origin, in other contracting states.

Invalidity in the country of origin

Article V(1)(e) enables the court addressed to refuse recognition if the award has not yet become binding on the parties, or if it has been set aside or suspended by a competent authority of the country in which, or under the law of which, it was made. This is supplemented by art VI, which applies where an application for setting aside or suspension has been made to such an authority. In such a case, the court addressed may, if it considers proper, adjourn its decision on the enforcement of the award, and may also, on the application of the party claiming enforcement, order the respondent to give security.

The meaning of 'binding', for the purposes of art V(1)(e), is obscure. The expression replaces a requirement of the Geneva Convention that the award should be 'final', and appears to be intended to overrule decisions given in some countries, not including the United Kingdom,[220] by which 'finality' could only be proved by producing a decision of a court of the relevant country authorising enforcement of the award.[221] It is submitted that an award should be considered 'binding', for the purposes of the New York Convention, unless it is proved that in the country of origin it would be treated as non-existent, in the sense that it would be ignored in all judicial proceedings, without the need for a judgment setting it aside.[222]

The relevant country, for the purposes of arts V(1)(e) and VI, is referred to as

---

[220] See *Union Nationale des Coopératives Agricoles v Catterall* [1959] 2 QB 44.

[221] The demand for an enforcement order from a court of the country of origin has, however, sometimes been made under the New York Convention; see eg a decision of the Basle Court of Appeal of 6 September 1968, 64 Schweizerische Juristen-Zeitung 378.

[222] Cf *De Reneville v De Reneville* [1948] P 100, and the American Law Institute's *Restatement, Second, Conflict of Laws* (1971), s 92.

'the country in which, or under the law of which, th[e] award was made'. This clearly recognises that many systems of private international law, including the English, accept that the procedure in an arbitration is only presumptively governed by the law of the country in which the arbitration takes place, and that it is open to the parties to conduct arbitration proceedings in one country but in accordance with the procedural law of another country.[223] The meaning of the 'or' in art V(1)(e) is far from clear, but it is submitted that the provision should be read as specifying as the relevant country: 'the country under whose law the award was made, ascertained in accordance with the private-international-law rules of the country whose court is addressed, it being understood that in some countries these rules refer invariably, and in other countries presumptively, to the law of the country in which the award was made'.

Non-arbitrable subject-matter and forum public policy

Article V(2) enables the court addressed to refuse recognition where it finds, whether at the invitation of a party or of its own motion, either that the subject-matter of the difference is not capable of settlement by arbitration under its own law, or that the recognition or enforcement of the award would be contrary to its own public policy. Article II makes it clear that a country can only consider a matter as non-arbitrable, for the purposes of the Convention, if it will not accept the validity of an agreement for arbitration in respect of the matter, even if the agreement is made after the dispute has arisen. The public policy proviso in the New York Convention will no doubt have a limited operation, similar to that of the corresponding proviso in relation to the recognition of foreign judgments.[224] It is not contrary to English public policy to enforce a Swiss award given under an ICC arbitration clause, using as the proper law governing the substantive obligations of the parties 'internationally accepted principles of law governing contractual relations',[225] even though in an arbitration whose curial law is English the arbitrator must apply the law of the particular country whose law would have been applied by the English court.

---

[223] See note 211 above.
[224] See under 'Substantive requirements: Public policy', pp 335–9 above.
[225] See *Deutsche Schachtbau- und Tiefbohrgesellschaft mbH v Ras Al Khaimah National Oil Co* [1990] AC 295, CA (reversed by the House of Lords on other grounds).

15

PROPERTY

In this chapter various conflict issues relating to property will be considered. First we shall address the classification of property as movable or immovable, and the rules for assigning property rights to a particular location. Then we shall consider in turn the rules on jurisdiction and choice of law in relation to immovable property (land), and on choice of law in relation to dealings inter vivos with various types of movable property (chattels; negotiable instruments; and ordinary intangibles). Finally we shall examine the conflict rules concerning succession on death, trusts, and matrimonial property.

NATURE AND LOCATION

The distinction between realty and personalty, which was central to English internal property law before 1926, but is of minimal importance in English internal property law today, is not important in the conflict of laws. Instead, for conflict purposes a distinction is drawn between movable and immovable property. The distinction is of particular importance in relation to succession on death, where in general movables are governed by the law of the deceased owner's last domicile, while immovable property is in general governed by the law of the country in which it is situated, the lex situs.

In essence immovable property means land, but whether a type of interest in land (such as a lease, a mortgage, or a beneficial interest behind a trust for sale) is treated as movable or immovable is referred to the law of the country in which the land in question is situated, the lex situs.[1] All interests in English land are treated as immovable, including a lease,[2] a mortgage and the debt secured

---

[1] See *Freke v Carbery* (1873) LR 16 Eq 461; *Re Hoyles* [1911] 1 Ch 179; *Re Berchtold* [1923] 1 Ch 192; *Macdonald v Macdonald* 1932 SC(HL) 79; and *Re Cutliffe* [1940] 1 Ch 565.
[2] See *Freke v Carbery* (1873) LR 16 Eq 461; *Duncan v Lawson* (1889) 41 ChD 394; and *Pepin v Bruyère* [1900] 2 Ch 504.

thereby,[3] a rentcharge,[4] a beneficial interest behind a trust for sale which has not yet been executed,[5] and investments (at least if situated in England) which represent the proceeds of sale of English settled land.[6] Like English mortgages, Scottish heritable bonds are immovable;[7] though a debt secured both by a Scottish heritable bond and also by an English mortgage, or even an English money bond, has been treated as movable.[8] Whether a tangible object associated with land (such as title deeds, keys to a building, cattle on a farm, or a ramp attached to a quay) is treated as part of the land, and thus as immovable, is governed by the lex situs of the object.[9]

Any interest in land is situated where the land lies.[10] Chattels are situated where they are in fact located at the relevant time. Simple contract debts are situated at the debtor's residence, even if payable elsewhere; and if the debtor has several residences, the debt is situated at the residence of the debtor at or through which it is expressly or impliedly made payable or would be paid in the ordinary course of business.[11] But a debt due under a deed or other specialty is situated where the deed is and not where the debtor resides,[12] unless it is secured by a mortgage of land, in which case it is situated where the land lies.[13] Negotiable instruments transferable by delivery, or endorsement and delivery, are situated where the instrument is located at the relevant time,[14] but corporate shares transferable by registration are situated where the register is kept.[15]

---

[3] See *Re Hoyles* [1911] 1 Ch 179, approved in *Macdonald v Macdonald* 1932 SC(HL) 79. Cf *Haque v Haque (No 2)* (1965) 114 CLR 98, treating a mortgage of Australian land as movable for purposes of succession.

[4] See *Chatfield v Berchtoldt* (1872) LR 7 Ch App 192.

[5] See *Re Berchtold* [1923] 1 Ch 192. Cf *Re Piercy* [1895] 1 Ch 83, where the decision upholding successive trusts of the proceeds of sale of Italian land is best explained on the basis of a renvoi from Italian law to English law as the lex patriae.

[6] See s 75(5) of the Settled Land Act 1925, and *Re Cutliffe* [1940] Ch 565. Cf *Midleton v Cottesloe* [1949] AC 418, holding that s 75(5) does not affect the situs for fiscal purposes.

[7] See *Johnstone v Baker* (1817) 56 ER 780; *Jerningham v Herbert* (1829) 38 ER 851; *Allen v Anderson* (1846) 67 ER 870; *Re Fitzgerald* [1904] 1 Ch 573 at 588; *Re Berchtold* [1923] 1 Ch 192 at 201; *Macdonald v Macdonald* 1932 SC(HL) 79 at 84 and 86; and Anton, *Private International Law* (1967), at p 389.

[8] See *Duchess of Buccleuch v Hoare* (1819) 56 ER 777, and *Cust v Goring* (1854) 52 ER 151. Cf Anton, *Private International Law* (1967), at p 389.

[9] See *Ex parte Rucker* (1834) 3 Dea & Ch 704; the Schlosser Report [1979] OJ C59/71 at para 168; and *Bell v Exxtor Group*, 23 July 1992, Sheen J, affirmed by the Court of Appeal, 24 February 1993.

[10] See *Chatfield v Berchtold, Freke v Carbery, Re Hoyles, Re Berchtold* and *Macdonald v Macdonald*, notes 1 and 4 above.

[11] See *New York Life Insurance Co v Public Trustee* [1924] 2 Ch 101; *Re Wagg's Claim* [1956] Ch 323 at 342–4; *Jabbour v Custodian of Israeli Absentee Property* [1954] 1 WLR 139; and *Kwok Chi Leung Karl v Commissioner of Estate Duty* [1988] 1 WLR 1035. Cf *Power Curber v National Bank of Kuwait* [1981] 1 WLR 1233, where the Court of Appeal held that a debt under a letter of credit is situate in the place where it is payable against documents, even if the debtor is not resident there.

[12] See eg *Royal Trust Co v Attorney-General for Alberta* [1930] AC 144.

[13] See *Re Hoyles*, note 1 above.

[14] See eg *Winans v Attorney-General (No 2)* [1910] AC 27.

[15] See eg *Brassard v Smith* [1925] AC 371.

IMMOVABLE PROPERTY

Jurisdiction

English law has long recognised the general principle that the courts of the country in which immovable property is situated have exclusive jurisdiction to entertain proceedings concerned with title to such property. Accordingly, even before the United Kingdom acceded to the 1968 Convention on civil jurisdiction and judgments in 1987, the English courts lacked jurisdiction (subject to some exceptions) to determine disputes concerning title to, or the right to possession of, foreign land;[16] and foreign judgments determining title to land situated in a country other than that in which the judgment was given were refused recognition in England.[17] Now the matter is largely governed by art 16(1)(a) of the 1968 Convention (as amended), which, in relation to disputes which fall within the material scope of the Convention, confers exclusive jurisdiction over proceedings principally concerned with rights in rem in, or tenancies of, immovable property situated in a contracting state, on the courts of the contracting state in which the property is situated.

This provision (like all those contained in art 16) is overriding in character. It applies regardless of domicile,[18] appearance,[19] or contrary agreement between the parties to the dispute.[20] A court seised contrary to art 16 must decline jurisdiction of its own motion,[21] and a judgment given in contravention of art 16 must be refused recognition in the other contracting states.[22] Similar pro-

---

[16] See *Norris v Chambres* (1861) 29 Beav 246, affirmed (1861) 3 De GF & J 583, and *Deschamps v Miller* [1908] 1 Ch 856, which involved attempts to enforce an estate contract or marriage settlement against a purchaser or donee; and *Re Hawthorne* (1883) 23 ChD 743, which concerned claims to the proceeds of sale of foreign land, sold by an alleged constructive trustee.

One exception under traditional English law enabled the English courts to entertain an action involving foreign land if the defendant was resident in England and the claim was based on a contract or equity between the parties. Thus they would enforce a contract for the sale of foreign land between the original parties to the contract (see *Penn v Baltimore* (1750) 27 ER 1132, and *Richard West & Partners Ltd v Dick* [1969] 2 Ch 424); or enforce the payment of rent under a lease of foreign land against the original lessee and a guarantor (see *St Pierre v South American Stores* [1936] 1 KB 382); or foreclose a mortgage of foreign land (see *Paget v Ede* (1874) LR 18 Eq 118); or declare that a licence was void as a clog on the equity of redemption (see *British South Africa Co v De Beers* [1910] 2 Ch 502; reversed on other grounds, [1912] AC 52); or set aside an unconscionable bargain relating to foreign land (see *Arglasse v Muschamp* (1682) 23 ER 322, 369 and 438); or order redemption after an execution sale abroad (see *Cranstown v Johnson* (1796) 30 ER 952); or act under s 17 of the Married Women's Property Act 1882 in respect of foreign land (see *Razelos v Razelos* [1969] 3 All ER 929). They would even disregard the lex situs so as to enforce mortgages created in accordance with English internal law, but not the lex situs, against creditors of the borrower (see *Re Courtney* [1835–42] All ER Rep 415; *Re Smith* [1916] 2 Ch 206; and *Re Anchor Line* [1937] 1 Ch 483), or against a purchaser who had bought expressly subject to the mortgage and undertaken to pay it off (see *Mercantile Investment Co v River Plate Co* [1892] 2 Ch 303).

[17] See *Duke v Andler* [1932] 4 DLR 529; and the Foreign Judgments (Reciprocal Enforcement) Act 1933, s 4(2)(b) and (3)(a).

[18] See art 16 itself.

[19] See art 18.

[20] See art 17[3], as amended.

[21] See art 19.

[22] See arts 28(1) and 34(2); and Chapter 14 above.

visions are contained in the Lugano Convention; and, in relation to the allocation of jurisdiction between the English, Scottish and Northern Irish courts in relation to land situated in the United Kingdom, in Sched 4 to the 1982 Act. These provisions do not, however, extend to succession on death or matrimonial property, which are excluded from the scope of the Conventions by art 1[2](1),[23] nor do they in terms refer to immovable property situated outside the European Community.

The reference in art 16(1)(a) to 'rights *in rem*' in immovable property is to the ownership of land, and to the existence and ownership of other, more limited, proprietary interests in land. Thus the provision applies to actions seeking determination of the ownership of land, or of the existence or ownership of lesser proprietary interests in land, or of the extent of the rights arising from ownership or a lesser proprietary interest, or seeking the enforcement of any such rights. In *Reichert v Dresdner Bank (No 1)*[24] the European Court of Justice explained that this basis of jurisdiction is confined to 'actions which seek to determine the extent, content, ownership or possession of immovable property or the existence of other rights in rem therein and to provide the holders of those rights with the protection of the powers which attach to their interest'. Accordingly it ruled that art 16(1)(a) does not apply to an action, such as the 'Pauline action' under art 1167 of the French Civil Code, whereby a creditor seeks to have a disposition of land by his debtor set aside as against the creditor on the ground that it was made by the debtor in fraud of the creditor's rights.[25] This decision no doubt applies to the similar English action under ss 423–425 of the Insolvency Act 1986. Similarly in *Lieber v Göbel*,[26] the European Court of Justice ruled that art 16(1)(a) does not apply to a claim for compensation for the use of a dwelling after the annulment of a transfer of its ownership between the parties. For, except in the case of tenancies, art 16(1)(a) is confined to proceedings based on a proprietary right, binding on all persons, rather than a personal right, exercisable only against a particular person.

Despite the Court's adoption of this rather over-simplified distinction between proprietary and personal rights, there can be little doubt that an equitable interest in English land, whether existing under a trust or otherwise (for example, as a restrictive covenant), qualifies as a 'right in rem' for the purpose of art 16(1), since such interests bind all persons other than certain purchasers (protected by lack of notice, non-registration, or overreaching).[27] Thus art 16(1) applies to an action to enforce a trust of or other equitable interest in English land against a third party, such as a subsequent purchaser or donee of the land. On the other hand arts 5(6) and 17[2] indicate that art 16(1) does not

---

[23] See Chapter 7, under 'Subject-matter', pp 121–4 above.

[24] Case 115/88, [1990] 1 ECR 27.

[25] See also Case C-261/90 *Reichert v Dresdner Bank (No 2)*, decided on 26 March 1992, where it was held that such an action does not fall within arts 5(3), 16(5) or 24 of the 1968 Convention.

[26] Case C-292/93, 9 June 1994.

[27] See the Schlosser Report, at paras 166–67, and per Adv-Gen Darmon in Case C-294/92 *Webb v Webb*, note 28 below.

apply to an action concerning an express or statutory trust of land if the parties to the action are confined to the settlor, the initial trustees, and beneficiaries under the trust. Moreover in *Webb v Webb*[28] the European Court of Justice ruled (perhaps surprisingly, though in agreement with Baker J),[29] that art 16(1)(a) did not apply to an action between English domiciliaries, a father and son, in which the father, as beneficiary under a resulting trust of French land arising from its purchase in the son's name with funds supplied by the father, sought to establish the existence of the trust against the son as original trustee, and to require him to transfer the legal title to the land to the father. The court regarded the claim as personal rather than proprietary in character, presumably because of the privity between the parties arising from their consensual participation in the purchase of the land by one of them in the name of the other, and the non-existence under French law, the lex situs, of any consequential rights against third parties.

The rulings in *Lieber v Göbel*[30] and *Webb v Webb*[31] effectively confirm the generally accepted view[32] that art 16(1)(a) does not apply to a dispute between a vendor and a purchaser under a contract for the sale of land, even where specific performance is sought and the adequacy of the vendor's title is in issue; despite the fact that the purposes of art 16(1) include ensuring that questions of title to land, in view of their technical character, should be determined by courts familiar with the relevant system of land law.[33] But there is no doubt that a claim under English law to enforce an estate contract against a third party, such as a purchaser bound by virtue of registration, falls within art 16(1)(a), and not within arts 5(6) or 17(2).[34]

Moreover art 6(4) of the 1968 Convention (added by the 1989 Convention), of the Lugano Convention, and of Sched 4 (as amended by SI 1993/603), permit the joinder, in a court seised under art 16(1)(a) of a claim against a defendant domiciled in a contracting state relating to rights in rem in land, of a contractual claim against the same defendant, if the law of the court seised permits such joinder. Somewhat similarly, art 5(8) of Sched 4 to the 1982 Act, and RSC Ord 11, r 1(1)(i), confer on the English courts non-exclusive jurisdiction over proceedings against a defendant who is domiciled in another part of the United

---

[28] Case C-294/92, 17 May 1994.

[29] [1992] 1 All ER 17, [1991] 1 WLR 1410. The Court of Appeal, on making the reference, were divided; (1992) *Financial Times*, 11 March.

[30] Case C-292/93, 9 June 1994.

[31] Case C-294/92, 17 May 1994.

[32] See the Schlosser Report, at paras 169–72, and dicta of Baker J in *Webb v Webb* [1992] 1 All ER 17, [1991] 1 WLR 1410. This accords partly with an exception under traditional English law, permitting the English courts to determine title to foreign land as between parties resident in England and linked by a direct contractual or other equitable relationship. See *Penn v Lord Baltimore* (1750) 1 VesSen 444; *Richard West and Partners (Inverness) Ltd v Dick* [1969] 2 Ch 424; *Cranstown v Johnston* (1800) 5 Ves 277; *Paget v Ede* (1874) LR 18 Eq 118; and *Mercantile Investment Co v River Plate Co* [1892] 2 Ch 303.

[33] See the Jenard Report at p 35.

[34] See the Schlosser Report at para 117; *Norris v Chambres* (1861) 29 Beav 246, affirmed (1861) 3 De GF & J 583; and *Deschamps v Miller* [1908] 1 Ch 856. Cf *Mercantile Investment Co v River Plate Co* [1892] 2 Ch 303.

Kingdom or is not domiciled within the contracting states, if the proceedings concern a debt secured on immovable property situated in England. In addition RSC Ord 11, r 1(1)(h), creates English jurisdiction over a defendant not domiciled within the contracting states over proceedings for the construction, rectification, setting aside, or enforcement of an act, deed, will, contract, obligation, or liability affecting such land.[35]

It is also clear that art 16(1)(a) does not extend to claims for trespass to or other torts against land, where no serious dispute as to title is involved. Moreover the traditional English rule, which excluded the jurisdiction of the English courts to entertain non-admiralty claims for torts against foreign land, even where title was not involved,[36] has been abrogated by s 30 of the 1982 Act. Even more clearly, art 16(1) does not extend to an action in tort for personal injuries caused by the negligence of an owner or occupier of land; nor even to a claim between a landlord and his tenant for contribution or indemnity in respect of such a liability, if the claim for contribution or indemnity is not based on the terms of the lease.[37]

As regards ownership or other proprietary interests in land at a frontier, the mere fact that an estate straddles a frontier need not give rise to difficulty. Under art 16(1)(a) each part of the estate will be subject to the jurisdiction of the courts of the state in which that part is situated.[38] More difficult, however, is the problem of an easement, such as a right of way or a watercourse, claimed for the benefit of a piece of land in one contracting state over a nearby piece of land in another contracting state. One possible solution would be to regard both states as exclusively competent, in the same way as where a company, in respect of which proceedings falling within art 16(2) are brought, is seated in two different countries, and to give priority to the court first seised in accordance with art 21. But it would probably be better to regard the burden on the servient land as the principal matter, and the benefit to the dominant land as secondary, so that the courts of the state containing the servient land would have exclusive jurisdiction.

What if the action concerns ownership of or other proprietary rights in (or a tenancy of) land situated in a non-contracting state? It is submitted that the proper implication from art 16 is that, in the case of an equivalent connection with a non-contracting state, a contracting state whose courts are otherwise competent, for example by virtue of the defendant's domicile, is free to authorise or even require them to decline jurisdiction in favour of the non-contracting state in which the land is situated.[39] Accordingly, in such a case the traditional

[35] See *Agnew v Usher* (1885) 14 QBD 78; *Kaye v Sutherland* (1887) 20 QBD 147; and *Tassell v Hallen* [1892] 1 QB 321.
[36] See *Doulson v Matthews* (1792) 100 ER 1143; *British South Africa Co v Co de Moçambique* [1893] AC 602; *The Tolten* [1946] P 135; and *Hesperides Hotels v Muftizade* [1979] AC 508.
[37] See *Bell v Exxtor Group*, 23 July 1992, per Sheen J; affirmed by the Court of Appeal, 24 February 1993.
[38] Cf Case 158/87 *Scherrens v Maenhout* [1988] ECR 3791, which left open the possibility of a very limited exception in the case of tenancies.
[39] See Droz, *Compétence Judiciaire et Effets des Jugements dans le Marché Common*, at paras 164–9; and Dicey & Morris, at pp 947–8.

English rule which deprives the English courts of jurisdiction to determine title to foreign land, subject to certain exceptions, will continue to operate.[40]

Article 16(1)(a) refers to 'tenancies of' as well as 'rights *in rem* in' immovable property. Thus in the case of a tenancy the courts of the situs are given exclusive jurisdiction even over disputes between the original parties, between whom there is privity of contract. The rationale, as explained by the European Court of Justice in *Sanders v Van der Putte*,[41] is that tenancies are generally governed by special rules whose complexity makes it desirable that they should be applied only by the courts of the enacting state. Thus, as the court explained in *Sanders v Van der Putte*[42] and *Rösler v Rottwinkel*,[43] art 16(1) applies to disputes between landlords and tenants concerning their respective obligations under a tenancy agreement, and in particular those concerning the existence or interpretation of the agreement, its duration, the delivery-up of possession of the premises to the landlord, compensation for damage caused by the tenant, or the recovery of rent or other charges payable by the tenant (such as for water, gas or electricity).[44]

In *Sanders* the European Court of Justice also ruled that 'tenancy' must be understood in a narrow sense, so that art 16(1) does not apply where the principal aim of the agreement is of a different nature; in particular where it concerns the operation of a business.[45] More recently in *Hacker v Euro-Relais*[46] the European Court of Justice followed *Sanders* and ruled that art 16(1) does not apply to a contract concluded in a contracting state between a travel agent and a customer, both domiciled in that state, whereby the travel agent is to provide for the customer the use for several weeks of a holiday home which is situated in another contracting state and is the property of a third person, and also to arrange transport thereto for the customer. Similarly English courts have held that art 16(1) does not extend to a licence for the use of a ramp attached to a quay, with priority at certain times of the day.[47]

---

[40] See note 16, above, and Dicey & Morris, Rule 116.

[41] Case 73/77, [1977] ECR 2383.

[42] Case 73/77, [1977] ECR 2383.

[43] Case 241/83, [1985] ECR 99.

[44] As regards rent and other charges, the decision in *Rösler* resolved a controversy among the negotiators; see the Jenard Report, at p 35; Droz, *Compétence Judiciaire et Effets des Jugements dans le Marché Common*, at paras 149–53; and the Schlosser Report, at para 164.

[45] The case concerned an alleged agreement between Dutch domiciliaries, whereby the defendant had undertaken to take over from the plaintiff the running of a florist's business in a shop at Wuppertal-Elberfeld in Germany which the plaintiff had leased from a third party. Since the defendant denied the existence of the agreement and refused to take over the business, the plaintiff brought an action in a Dutch court, claiming the rent due under the head lease, rent under the 'usufructuary' lease itself, and payment for the goodwill of the business. The court ultimately ruled that 'tenancies of immovable property', within the meaning of art 16(1), do not include an agreement to rent under a usufructuary lease a retail business carried on in immovable property rented from a third person by the lessor; and added that the fact that there is a dispute as to the existence of the agreement which forms the subject of the action does not affect the applicability of art 16(1).

[46] Case C-280/90, [1992] 1 ECR 1111.

[47] See *Bell v Exxtor Group*, 23 July 1992, Sheen J; affirmed by the Court of Appeal, 24 February 1993.

In *Rösler v Rottwinkel*[48] the European Court of Justice also ruled that in its original version art 16(1) of the 1968 Convention applied even if the letting were of short duration and related to a holiday home. But now art 16(1)(b), added by the 1989 Convention, makes special provision for certain short lettings. Exclusive jurisdiction is shared between the courts of the contracting state in which the land is situated and the courts of the contracting state in which the defendant is domiciled, if the action concerns a tenancy concluded for temporary private use for a maximum period of six consecutive months between individuals domiciled in the same member state. The corresponding provision of the Lugano Convention is slightly wider, since it does not require that the landlord should be an individual and permits him to be domiciled in a third state.[49] Within the United Kingdom, art 16 of Sched 4 has now been amended by SI 1993/603 so as to add an art 16(1)(b) corresponding to the 1989 version of the 1968 Convention, in favour of the courts of the part of the United Kingdom in which both parties are domiciled.

In *Rösler* the European Court of Justice also ruled that art 16(1) does not extend to disputes which only indirectly concern the use of the property let, such as claims by the landlord for lost holiday enjoyment or wasted travelling expenses, even where the liability arises from breach by the tenant of an express term of the tenancy agreement as to how he should use the premises let. In view of the relaxation introduced by the 1989 Convention, this limitation appears to have been superseded. It is noteworthy that it was not repeated by the court in *Hacker v Euro-Relais*.[50]

The problem of a single tenancy agreement relating to land straddling a frontier between, or otherwise partly situated in each of, two member states, was considered in *Scherrens v Maenhout*.[51] The European Court of Justice laid down a general rule that, in the case of an action aimed at determining the possible existence of a contract for the leasing of land situated in two contracting states, the courts of each state have exclusive jurisdiction in relation to the land situated within its own territory. The court admitted, however, the possibility of an exception where there are special features, such as where the lands situated

---

[48] Case 241/83, [1985] ECR 99. The case involved an agreement between German domiciliaries whereby one leased to the other accommodation in his holiday home in Italy for three weeks. During the weeks in question the lessor also spent his holiday in the house, and friction arose between the parties. According to the lessor, the lessee allowed more than the four persons stipulated in the agreement to stay in the accommodation, with the result that the septic tank constantly overflowed and there was also excessive noise, so that the lessor lost the enjoyment of his holiday. Consequently the lessor brought an action against the lessee in a German court, claiming his travelling expenses, wasted as a result of his loss of holiday enjoyment, as damages for breach of the restriction in the agreement to occupation by not more than four persons, and also claiming payment of charges for water, electricity, gas and cleaning, in accordance with the agreement.

[49] See also art Ib of the Protocol annexed to the Lugano Convention, which permits a contracting state to make a reservation that it will not recognise or enforce judgments given in other contracting states under art 16(1)(b) on the basis of the defendant's domicile in respect of tenancies of land situated in the reserving state.

[50] Case C-280/90, [1992] I ECR 1111.

[51] Case 158/87, [1988] ECR 3791.

in the two states are contiguous and almost all of the land is situated in one of the states. In such a case it might be appropriate to treat the estate as a unit, and as if it were wholly situated in one of the states, whose courts would have exclusive jurisdiction over the lease. But there were no such special features in the instant case, which involved an agricultural tenancy allegedly granted to a man by his parents-in-law by means of a single agreement in respect of a farm situated partly in Belgium and partly in the Netherlands; the farmhouse and about one-third of the farmland were situated in Belgium and the remaining two-thirds of the farmland in the Netherlands, and the Belgian and Dutch parts were not actually contiguous, but located about four miles apart. The possible exception may be considered of dubious merit, since a court dealing with the whole estate might still have to sever it according to situs for purposes of choice of law.

The 1968 and Lugano Conventions do not apply to proceedings which are principally concerned with succession on death (including the administration of estates) or matrimonial property.[52] The English courts are competent to determine questions of succession, even to foreign land, whenever they grant administration of the deceased's estate, and such a grant will be made if there is property of the estate in England or if there is some other adequate reason for making a grant.[53] As regards claims based on matrimonial property rights, the English courts are always competent to entertain such a claim to English land, since RSC Ord 11, r 1(1)(g) and (h) permit service abroad if necessary in proceedings whose whole subject-matter is English land, or proceedings for the construction, rectification, setting aside, or enforcement of an act, deed, will, contract, obligation, or liability affecting English land. In the case of a claim based on matrimonial property rights to foreign land, the English courts lack jurisdiction in the absence of a direct contractual or equitable relationship between the parties.[54]

Choice of law

In general proprietary rights over immovables are governed by the lex situs, applied (where the situs is foreign) with total renvoi.[55] Thus it is the lex situs which determines the nature and incidents of a person's interest in land: for example, whether it is in the nature of a fee simple or an entailed interest, and whether he can create successive interests or merely appoint a successor.[56] Similarly the lex situs governs the formal validity of a disposition of land inter vivos;[57] personal capacity to carry out such a disposition of land;[58] and the

---

[52] See art 1[2](1); and Chapter 7, under 'Subject-matter', pp 121–4 above.

[53] See under 'Succession on death: Jurisdiction and administration of estates', pp 368–71 below.

[54] See note 16 above.

[55] See Dicey & Morris, Rule 117. For the use of total renvoi, see *Re Ross* [1930] 1 Ch 377, involving compulsory shares of children in the estate of a deceased parent, and *Re Duke of Wellington* [1948] Ch 118; and Chapter 16 below.

[56] See *Nelson v Bridport* (1846) 50 ER 215; see also *Re Miller* [1914] 1 Ch 511.

[57] See *Adams v Clutterbuck* (1883) 10 QBD 403, upholding a lease of Scottish land although not executed under seal.

[58] See *Bank of Africa v Cohen* [1909] 2 Ch 129.

essential validity of a disposition of land, whether inter vivos or by will, in relation to such factors as mortmain,[59] perpetuity or accumulation.[60] The lex situs also governs the acquisition of title to land by adverse possession or prescription, and the time-limits for enforcing proprietary rights in land.[61] By way of exception, the formal validity of a will is governed, as to immovables as well as movables, by the Wills Act 1963, which upholds a will executed in accordance with the formal requirements of any of a number of internal laws, including (as regards both movables and immovables) that of the testator's domicile, nationality or habitual residence or the place of execution of the will, or (in the case of immovables only) the lex situs.[62]

In contrast to proprietary issues, a contract whose subject-matter is a right in, or a right to use, immovable property, is governed by its proper law. Under arts 3 and 4 of the 1980 Convention on the Law Applicable to Contractual Obligations ('the 1980 Convention'),[63] there is a presumption in favour of the lex situs as the proper law of such a contract, in the absence of an express or implied choice by the parties, and subject to rebuttal where the circumstances as a whole indicate a closer connection with another country. However it is likely that, as under the prior English conflict rules, the common residence of the parties will often prevail over the lex situs.[64] As regards formal validity, art 9(6) of the 1980 Convention derogates from the general rules permitting compliance with either the proper law or the law of the place of contracting, by subjecting such a contract to the mandatory formal requirements of the lex situs, if by that law those requirements are imposed irrespective of the country where the contract is concluded and of its proper law. Probably such mandatory requirements include those now imposed by s 2 of the (English) Law of Property (Miscellaneous Provisions) Act 1989, under which a contract for the sale or other disposition of an interest in land can only be made in writing fulfilling specified requirements.[65]

In *Bank of Africa v Cohen*[66] the Court of Appeal held that personal capacity to contract to dispose of land is governed by the lex situs, and thus refused both specific performance and damages for breach of a contract, concluded in England between a married woman domiciled in England and a bank resident in both England and the Transvaal, whereby she agreed to grant to the bank a mortgage of her land, situated in the Transvaal, as security for her husband's debts, since the contract did not contain, as required by Transvaal law, an

---

[59] See *Duncan v Lawson* (1889) 41 ChD 394, and *Re Hoyles* [1911] 1 Ch 179.
[60] See *Freke v Carbery* (1873) LR 16 Eq 461.
[61] See *Re Peat's Trusts* (1869) LR 7 Eq 302; *Pitt v Dacre* (1876) 3 ChD 295; and the Foreign Limitation Periods Act 1984.
[62] See 'Formal validity of wills', pp 373–6 below.
[63] See Chapter 12 above.
[64] See *Re Courtney* [1835–42] All ER Rep 415; *British South Africa Co v De Beers Consolidated Mines* [1910] 2 Ch 502 (reversed on other grounds, [1912] AC 52); *Mercantile Investment Co v River Plate Co* [1892] 2 Ch 303; *Re Smith* [1916] 2 Ch 206; and *Re Anchor Line (Henderson Brothers) Ltd* [1937] 1 Ch 483.
[65] See Chapter 12, under 'Formal validity', pp 249–50 above.
[66] [1909] 2 Ch 129.

explicit renunciation by her of the benefit of certain protective Transvaal legislation. The decision has been subjected to strong criticism,[67] and the following
objections seem particularly cogent:

(1) In principle there is no reason why, in relation to capacity merely to
     contract to dispose of land (as distinct from capacity actually to dispose), it
     should not be enough that the person is capable under the law of his or her
     domicile or under the proper law of the contract.
(2) In view of the protective purpose of the Transvaal rule, Transvaal law had
     no substantial interest in extending its benefit to a woman not domiciled
     there, and (more specifically) it seems unlikely that a Transvaal court
     would have refused to recognise a disposition by Mrs Cohen of her Trans-
     vaal land, containing a suitable disclaimer, executed in compliance with an
     English decree of specific performance.
(3) Even if it would have so refused, that would only have justified the English
     courts in refusing a decree of specific performance, and should not have
     amounted to a defence against a claim to damages for breach of the contract
     to dispose.

A more attractive decision was given by a New Hampshire court in *Proctor v
Frost*,[68] where it upheld in accordance with Massachusetts law a mortgage of
New Hampshire land granted in Massachusetts by a married woman domiciled
in Massachusetts, despite a New Hampshire rule precluding a married woman
from becoming surety for her husband. As this decision indicates, there is no
reason why an English court should not uphold a disposition of English land
(and a fortiori a contract to dispose thereof) by a foreign domiciliary who is
capable under the law of his domicile, but not under English internal law; for
example, where he is aged 17.

Contrary to principle, the courts have sometimes invoked English law as the
proper law of a contract between English residents, so as to uphold against the
creditors of an insolvent borrower a charge over foreign land which was invalid
under the lex situs for informality, non-registration, or failure to take possession.[69] Indeed in *Mercantile Investment Co v River Plate Co*[70] North J went
even further and enforced a mortgage of Mexican land, which was void in
Mexico for lack of registration, against a subsequent transferee whose transfer
was explicitly subject to the mortgage and who undertook to pay off the loan.
But these decisions disregard the distinction between contractual and proprietary rights and require urgent reconsideration. They are also exceptional:
normally English courts will not enforce against a purchaser with notice, or even
a volunteer, a claim to foreign land which is invalid under the lex situs.[71]

---

[67] See Dicey & Morris, at pp 961–2.
[68] 197 A 813 (1938).
[69] See *Re Courtney* [1835–42] All ER Rep 415; *Re Smith* [1916] 2 Ch 206; and *Re Anchor Line*
     [1937] 1 Ch 483.
[70] [1892] 2 Ch 303.
[71] See *Norris v Chambres* (1861) 54 ER 621, affirmed (1861) 45 ER 1004; *Norton v Florence Land Co*
     (1877) 7 ChD 332; and *Deschamps v Miller* [1908] 1 Ch 856.

PARTICULAR TRANSFERS OF MOVABLE PROPERTY INTER VIVOS

Here we are concerned with the proprietary effects of an individual transaction inter vivos (such as a sale, gift or pledge) in respect of a particular item of movable property (a chattel or an intangible). General transfers of a person's property as a whole (on death, marriage, bankruptcy, or corporate liquidation) are considered elsewhere.[72]

Moreover we are now concerned with the proprietary, rather than the contractual, aspects of such transactions: with the effect on ownership, so as to affect third parties (such as prior owners, subsequent purchasers, or liquidators), rather than with the mutual contractual rights of the parties to the transaction. Such questions as the existence and extent of a seller's obligation to perform such acts as will transfer ownership to the buyer, or his liability to the buyer for defects in his title, are governed by the proper law of the contract of sale, in the same way as a seller's obligation that the goods should answer a description or comply with a standard of quality.[73]

Chattels

It is a well-established rule that the proprietary effects of an individual transaction relating to particular goods are governed by the law of the country in which the goods are situated at the time of the transaction in question.[74] Probably renvoi applies, so that the reference, in the case of a foreign situs, is not to its internal law as such, but to whatever law a court of the situs would apply in view of all the connections involved in the case.[75]

This applies, in particular, to the question whether a sale by a non-owner to an innocent purchaser confers a good title on the purchaser against the original owner, and it is with this type of problem that the leading English cases deal. Thus in *Cammell v Sewell*[76] goods were shipped from Russia to England on a Prussian ship. The ship was wrecked in Norway and the cargo unloaded there and sold there by the master to an innocent purchaser. By Norwegian law the sale was wrongful by the master against the original owner of the goods, but the innocent purchaser obtained a good title. The purchaser proceeded to ship the

---

[72] See Chapter 6 above; and under 'Succession on death', pp 368–78 below.

[73] On the proper law of a contract, see Chapter 12 above.

[74] See Dicey & Morris, Rules 118 and 119, and (in addition to cases discussed below) dicta in *Re Anziani* [1930] 1 Ch 407 at 420, and *Bank voor Handel v Slatford* [1953] 1 QB 248 at 257.

   Dicey & Morris, Rule 118, Exception, suggests that where goods are in transit and the situs is casual or unknown, a transfer will be recognised if it is valid under its proper law (ascertained under contractual principles). But the authority cited, *Northwestern Bank v Poynter* [1895] AC 56, is not very impressive, as there was no difference between the connected laws.

   As regards donatio mortis causa, it seems that it is sufficient to comply with either the lex situs or the law of the donor's domicile. See *Re Korvine's Trust* [1921] 1 Ch 343, and *Re Craven's Estate* (1937) 53 TLR 694. Cf Dicey & Morris, at p 968, favouring the lex situs alone.

[75] See Dicey & Morris, at p 968, and dicta in *Winkworth v Christie, Manson & Woods* [1980] Ch 496. On the doctrine of renvoi generally, see Chapter 16 below.

[76] (1860) 157 ER 1371.

goods to England and sell them. The original owner's insurer sued the purchaser's successor for conversion, but the Exchequer Chamber, per Crompton J, upheld the title acquired by the purchaser under the lex situs and dismissed the action.

Similarly in *City Bank v Barrow*[77] the effect of a pledge made by a possessor against the true owner was referred to the lex situs, and in *Inglis v Robertson*[78] a purported pledge by endorsement and delivery of delivery warrants, effected between English residents in England, in respect of whisky in a Glasgow warehouse was held ineffective against a creditor of the pledgor, since the warehouseman had not been notified of the pledge as required by the Scottish lex situs.

More recently, in *Winkworth v Christie, Manson & Woods*,[79] where works of art had been stolen in England and then taken to Italy and sold there to an innocent purchaser, who then returned the goods to England for resale, Slade J followed *Cammell v Sewell*[80] and *Todd v Armour*[81] and ruled that if under Italian law, as the lex situs at the time of the sale, the innocent purchaser had obtained a title overriding that of the original owner, such title would be recognised in England, despite the fact that the goods had eventually returned here.

The control of the lex situs is not confined to sales by a non-owner, for the passing of title between seller-owner and buyer has important non-contractual consequences, for example upon the insolvency of one of them. As Diplock LJ explained in *Hardwick Game Farm v SAPPA*,[82] although under English internal law a contract for the sale of specific goods will normally transfer title between the parties at the moment of contracting, in the case of a contract governed by English law for the sale of specific goods situated in Germany title will not pass until the goods are delivered, as required by German law. On the other hand, it is submitted that, insofar as the lex situs makes the time of passing of property depend on the intention of the parties to a contract of sale (as, for the most part, does English internal law),[83] their intentions should be ascertained in accordance with the law governing the contract. In any event, a title validly reserved in a credit sale under the law of the then situs will be defeated if the buyer takes the goods to another country and resells them there to an innocent purchaser, and the law of the second situs gives overriding effect to the resale.[84]

Since English law in general refers title to chattels to the lex situs, it also recognises a foreign judgment determining or altering title to chattels which were situated in the country in which the judgment was given at the institution

[77] (1880) 5 App Cas 644, especially at 677.
[78] [1898] AC 616.
[79] [1980] Ch 496.
[80] (1860) 157 ER 1371.
[81] (1882) 9 R (Ct of Sess) 901.
[82] [1966] 1 WLR 287 at 330. The point was not considered on appeal, [1969] 2 AC 31.
[83] See Sale of Goods Act 1979, s 18.
[84] See *Century Credit Corp v Richard* (1962) 34 DLR(2d) 291, where the buyer moved the car from Quebec to Ontario. On the large Canadian case-law in this sphere, see Dicey & Morris, under Rule 119.

of the proceedings there, even if the foreign court lacked personal jurisdiction over persons involved.[85] On the same principle, it recognises a judgment of the situs (usually one given in admiralty) which operates in rem, so as to determine or dispose of a chattel (such as a ship) against all persons interested.[86] Indeed, a foreign admiralty judgment in rem, given by a court of the situs, may be enforced in England at common law by means of an admiralty action in rem,[87] or by means of registration under the Administration of Justice Act 1920,[88] or the Foreign Judgments (Reciprocal Enforcement) Act 1933,[89] or the 1968 or Lugano Conventions.[90]

Negotiable instruments

As regards particular transfers inter vivos, negotiable instruments are governed by the lex situs in the same way as chattels.[91]

Ordinary intangibles

Ordinary intangible property refers to such assets as a simple contract debt, a block of registered shares in a company, an interest in a trust fund, or an item of intellectual property, such as a patent, copyright or trademark. The category does not include claims which are embodied in a document, such as a negotiable instrument. Such an asset has a proper law, which in the cases given below is ascertained as follows:

(1) *a simple contract debt* – the proper law of the asset is the proper law of the contract from which the debt arises;[92]

(2) *a block of registered shares* – the proper law of the asset is the law of the country in which the corporate register, on which ownership of the shares is registered, is kept;[93]

(3) *an interest in a trust fund* – the proper law of the asset is the proper law of the trust, ascertained on contractual principles (that is: the law expressly or impliedly chosen by the settlor in the trust instrument or, in the absence of such a choice, the law with which the trust is most closely connected, usually the residence of the trustee at which the trust is required or expected to be administered);[94]

---

[85] See *Emanuel v Symon* [1908] 1 KB 302, and Stone [1983] 1 LMCLQ 1.

[86] See *Castrique v Imrie* (1870) LR 4 HL 414, and the Foreign Judgments (Reciprocal Enforcement) Act 1933, s 4(2)(b) and 4(3)(a).

[87] See *The City of Mecca* (1879) 5 PD 28, (1881) 6 PD 106, and *The Despina GK* (1982) *The Times*, 13 July.

[88] See ss 9(2)(a) and 12(1).

[89] See ss 1(2)(b) and 4(2)(b).

[90] However art 27(3) and (5), on irreconcilable judgments, being confined to judgments between the same parties, are not aptly worded to deal with judgments in rem.

[91] See *Alcock v Smith* [1892] 1 Ch 238; *Embiricos v Anglo-Austrian Bank* [1905] 1 KB 677; *Koechlin v Kestenbaum* [1927] 1 KB 889; and Dicey & Morris, at pp 1435–8.

[92] See *Le Feuvre v Sullivan* (1855) 14 ER 389.

[93] See *Re Fry* [1946] Ch 312.

[94] See *Kelly v Selwyn* [1905] 2 Ch 117.

(4) *an item of intellectual property* – the proper law of the asset is the law of the country in or for which the monopoly or other exclusive rights in question have been granted or recognised.[95]

Choice of law in respect of a particular and voluntary assignment of an ordinary intangible asset is now governed by art 12 of the 1980 Convention on the Law Applicable to Contractual Obligations, implemented by the Contracts (Applicable Law) Act 1990.[96] An assignment is particular if it relates to a specific asset, as distinct from a general transfer on insolvency, marriage or death. An assignment is voluntary if it is effected by an intentional act of the owner, as distinct from a compulsory legal process (such as the enforcement of a judgment). Article 12 provides that:

(1) The mutual obligations of assignor and assignee under a voluntary assignment of a right against another person ('the debtor') shall be governed by the law which under this Convention applies to the contract between the assignor and assignee.
(2) The law governing the right to which the assignment relates shall determine its assignability, the relationship between the assignee and the debtor, the conditions under which the assignment can be invoked against the debtor and any question whether the debtor's obligations have been discharged.

Article 12(2) undoubtedly accords with the prior English law. Thus in *Re Fry*[97] an instrument executed abroad was held ineffective to assign shares in an English company in the absence of Treasury consent to registration of the transfer, then required by English law, and in *Campbell Connelly v Noble*[98] it was accepted that the assignability of an American copyright was governed by American law, though the actual decision interpreted a contract to assign by reference to English law as the proper law of the contract. Moreover the same rule, referring to the proper law of the asset in question, applies to priorities between competing valid assignments of the same asset.[99]

On the other hand art 12(1), although superficially according with the prior English law as asserted by Dicey & Morris,[100] in reality represents an improvement. For, if due account is taken, where relevant, of the factor of validation, as indicating an implied choice by the parties to an assignment of the law governing the asset assigned, in preference to that of the country where the parties to the assignment resided and the assignment was executed, the courts will no longer reach perverse decisions such as have sometimes been given under the earlier law. For example, in *Lee v Abdy*,[101] an assignment, executed in the Cape

---

[95] See *Campbell Connelly v Noble* [1963] 1 WLR 252.
[96] See Chapter 12 above.
[97] [1946] Ch 312.
[98] [1963] 1 WLR 252.
[99] See *Le Feuvre v Sullivan* (1855) 14 ER 389, applying the proper law of the life insurance policy assigned; and *Kelly v Selwyn* [1905] 2 Ch 117, where priorities between competing assignees to an interest in an English trust fund were determined in accordance with the English rule referring to the order in which the trustees were notified of the assignments.
[100] See 11th ed, Rule 122; 12th ed, Rule 120.
[101] (1886) 17 QBD 309.

between a married couple domiciled there, of an English life insurance policy was held invalid by reference to Cape law, which objected to assignment by an insolvent husband to his wife. Similarly, in *Republica de Guatemala v Nunez*,[102] where the Court of Appeal invalidated an assignment, executed in Guatemala between persons domiciled there, of a sum deposited with an English bank, by reference to Guatemalan law, which required a stamped, notarial contract signed by both parties, and required a judicially appointed representative to accept the gift on behalf of the assignee, a minor. Again, in *Re Anziani*,[103] an assignment, executed in Italy by an Italian assignor, of an interest in an English trust fund, was invalidated by reference to Italian law, which required a notarial instrument, objected to revocability, and required acceptance by the donee. Article 12(1) should encourage better decisions, such as that given in *Lowenstein v Allen*,[104] where the incidents, such as survivorship, of a joint account with an English bank, were referred to English law.

In any event compulsory assignment, such as garnishment in execution of a judgment, is governed by different rules. Until recently it was believed that a debt could be garnished in England if it was situated there[105] but not if it was situated abroad;[106] but now it has been established that it is sufficient that the garnishee is subject to English personal jurisdiction (by domicile, presence or submission).[107] But even if the garnishee is subject to English jurisdiction, the court in its discretion will refuse to order garnishment if there is a real or substantial risk that the garnishee would be made to pay again abroad.[108] On the other hand, whether a foreign garnishment order will be recognised depends on whether the debt was situated in the foreign country in question;[109] and if under the lex situs such a garnishment gives the garnisher priority over voluntary assignees, this effect will be recognised in England.[110]

EXPROPRIATION

The recognition in England of acts of a foreign government expropriating property (that is, compulsorily acquiring property, whether permanently or temporarily, and whether or not the acquisition is accompanied or followed by

---

[102] [1927] 1 KB 669.
[103] [1930] 1 Ch 407.
[104] [1958] CLY 491.
[105] See *Swiss Bank Corp v Boehmische Bank* [1923] 1 KB 673.
[106] See *Martin v Nadel* [1906] 2 KB 26 and *Richardson v Richardson* [1927] P 228.
[107] See *SCF Finance v Masri (No 3)* [1987] 1 QB 1028; *Deutsche Schachtbau- und Tiefbohrgesellschaft mbh v Ras Al Khaimah National Oil Co* [1990] AC 295, CA (reversed by the House of Lords on other grounds); and *Interpool v Galani* [1988] 1 QB 738.
[108] See *Employers' Life v Sedgwick Collins* [1927] AC 95, and *Deutsche Schachtbau- und Tiefbohrgesellschaft mbh v Ras Al Khaimah National Oil Co* [1990] AC 295, HL.
[109] See *Rossano v Manufacturers' Life Insurance Co* [1963] 2 QB 352 at 374–83, and *Power Curber v National Bank of Kuwait* [1981] 1 WLR 1233.
[110] See *Re Queensland Mercantile Agency* [1891] 1 Ch 536 (affirmed on other grounds, [1892] 1 Ch 219), and *Re Maudslay Sons & Field* [1900] 1 Ch 602.

the payment of compensation) depends mainly on where the property in question was situated at the time of the expropriation. If property is situated in England, no act of a foreign governmental body purporting to expropriate it will be recognised in any circumstances; not even a wartime act of an allied government temporarily requisitioning, with compensation, property belonging to its nationals.[111]

If at the time of an expropriating act the property in question is situated in the country by whose authorities the expropriating act is adopted, the act will in general be recognised, in accordance with the general principle referring title to property to the lex situs. Thus in the leading case of *Williams & Humblet Ltd v W & H Trade Marks (Jersey) Ltd*[112] the House of Lords recognised a Spanish act expropriating, with compensation, the shares in a number of Spanish companies. It seems, moreover, that the absence of compensation will not in itself be enough to prevent recognition, even if the prior owners were not nationals of the expropriating state.[113] However public policy will prevent recognition of an expropriation which involves discrimination (for example, on racial grounds) amounting to a gross violation of human rights.[114]

If an expropriating act is in principle recognised, but the property is removed from the expropriating country and brought to England before its authorities have taken possession of it, the English courts will not help them to obtain the property, since this would amount to enforcement (and not merely recognition) of a foreign penal or other public law.[115] On the other hand, after a recognised expropriation of corporate shares situated in the expropriating country, the company under its new management will retain title to its English assets, and will be able to sue in England to vindicate such ownership; thus an expropriation of this type will have indirect extra-territorial effects.[116]

SUCCESSION ON DEATH

Jurisdiction and administration of estates

Under English internal law, with minor exceptions, only a properly constituted personal representative, to whom the High Court has made a grant of probate or administration, is entitled to administer the estate of a deceased individual. Such a grant vests the deceased's property in the personal representative, and

---

[111] See *Bank voor Handel en Scheepvaart v Slatford* [1953] 1 QB 248 (not following *Lorentzen v Lydden* [1942] 2 KB 202); *Government of the Republic of Spain v National Bank of Scotland* 1939 SC 413; and *Williams & Humblet Ltd v W & H Trade Marks (Jersey) Ltd* [1986] AC 368.

[112] [1986] AC 368.

[113] See *Luther v Sagor* [1921] 3 KB 532; *Princess Paley Olga v Weisz* [1929] 1 KB 718; and *Re Heilbert Wagg* [1956] Ch 323 (not following *The Rose Mary* [1953] 1 WLR 246).

[114] See *Oppenheimer v Cattermole* [1976] AC 249; per Lord Cross in *Williams & Humblet Ltd v W & H Trade Marks (Jersey) Ltd* [1986] AC 368.

[115] See *Attorney-General of New Zealand v Ortiz* [1984] AC 1, CA; affirmed by the House of Lords on other grounds.

[116] See *Williams & Humblet Ltd v W & H Trade Marks (Jersey) Ltd* [1986] AC 368.

makes it his duty to collect the assets and pay the debts and taxes of the estate, and then to transfer the remaining assets to the persons beneficially entitled under the deceased's will or intestacy. Anyone else who meddles with a deceased's estate becomes liable, but not entitled, as an executor de son tort.

Since 1932 no connection of the deceased or his property with England has been necessary to enable the English courts to make a grant of probate or administration of his estate. The former requirement that there must have been assets of the estate situated in England was abolished by s 2(1) of the Administration of Justice Act 1932, whose effect is now preserved by s 25 of the Supreme Court Act 1981.[117] But in its discretion the English court will not grant representation where there are no assets in England unless some adequate reason is shown; for example, in order to enable the applicant to obtain a grant in a foreign country in respect of the estate there of an English domiciliary.[118] If the deceased died domiciled abroad, an English grant will usually be made to the person who is entitled to administer the estate under the law of the deceased's domicile.[119]

The jurisdiction of the English courts to grant representation of a deceased's estate, without the need for any connection with England, entails a further jurisdiction to determine questions of beneficial succession to the estate, in the course of or after making such a grant.[120] Both beneficial succession and estate administration are excluded from the scope of the 1968 and Lugano Conventions on civil jurisdiction and judgments by art 1[2](1). Moreover if an English grant is made in respect of an estate which includes property in England and also includes immovable property abroad, the English court's jurisdiction extends to determining the succession to the foreign immovables.[121]

An English grant vests the deceased's English property in the grantee.[122] It is also proper for the English representative to take such steps as are open to him to recover assets situated abroad, and he is then accountable to the English courts for foreign assets which he has received in his capacity as English representative.[123] Where the deceased died domiciled in England, it is hoped that foreign courts will recognise the claim of the English representative to receive a local grant.[124] In any event, an English judicial administration is not in principle confined to English assets.[125]

The administration of assets (as distinct from the beneficial succession to them) is governed by the law of the country from which the personal representa-

---

[117] See also RSC Ord 11, r 1(1)(k) and (l).
[118] See Dicey & Morris, Rule 123, and Re Wayland [1951] 2 All ER 1041.
[119] See Dicey & Morris, Rule 124, and the Non-Contentious Probate Rules 1987, SI 1987/2024, r 30 (as amended by SI 1991/1876).
[120] See Dicey & Morris, Rule 131.
[121] See Nelson v Bridport (1846) 50 ER 215, Re Ross [1930] 1 Ch 377, and Re Duke of Wellington [1948] Ch 118.
[122] See Dicey & Morris, Rule 126.
[123] See Dicey & Morris, Rule 127.
[124] See Blackwood v R (1882) 8 App Cas 82.
[125] See Orr-Ewing v Orr-Ewing (1885) 10 App Cas 453.

tive derives his authority to administer them;[126] normally their lex situs. Questions of administration include the admissibility and mutual priority of debts, and in an English administration there is no discrimination against foreign creditors or debts incurred abroad.[127] It is also a question of administration whether the personal representative has power to postpone the sale of assets during the minority of a beneficiary.[128] But the incidence (or marshalling) of debts against assets destined for different beneficiaries is a matter of beneficial succession.[129]

Where the deceased died domiciled abroad, an English administration is regarded as ancillary to the administration taking place at the deceased's domicile, and once the English administration is completed (by the collection of assets and the payment of debts and taxes), the English representative will normally hand over the surplus assets to the domiciliary administrator for distribution to the persons beneficially entitled. But it is open to the English court to restrain such a transfer, and require a separate distribution by the English representative to the beneficiaries entitled under the English conflict rules, where this would alter the ultimate destination of the English property; for example, because the domiciliary administrator would have had to use them to pay debts which in England were time-barred,[130] or to give effect to a will which was considered in England as validly revoked.[131]

Under s 1 of the Administration of Estates Act 1971, where the deceased died domiciled in Scotland or Northern Ireland, a Scottish or Northern Irish grant noting such domicile is automatically recognised in England, so as to constitute the grantee an English, as well as a Scottish or Northern Irish, representative of the estate; and under the Colonial Probates Act 1892, grants made in many Commonwealth countries (or South Africa) in respect of estates of persons domiciled there will be normally resealed by the English court, so as to constitute the grantee also an English representative of the estate.

Otherwise a personal representative constituted under a foreign grant alone, even one made at the deceased's domicile, has few rights in England:[132]

(1) he may sue here for money payable here under the deceased's life insurance policies;[133]

(2) his title to assets validly acquired abroad under their lex situs will be recognised, even if the assets subsequently come to England, though unappropriated assets which have come to England can be made subject to English judicial administration;

(3) he is not answerable to the English courts for acts of administration

---

[126] See Dicey & Morris, Rule 128.
[127] See *Re Kloebe* (1884) 28 ChD 175.
[128] See *Re Wilks* [1935] Ch 645.
[129] See *Re Hewit* [1891] 3 Ch 568.
[130] See *Re Lorilland* [1922] 2 Ch 638.
[131] See *Re Manifold* [1962] Ch 1.
[132] See Dicey & Morris, Rules 129 and 130.
[133] See the Revenue Act 1884, s 11 (as amended).

performed abroad; but if he interferes with English assets, he may incur liability as an executor de son tort;

(4) if constituted at the deceased's domicile, he may, normally with reasonable hope of success, seek an English grant, or an order that, after completion of the English administration, the English representative should transfer the surplus assets to him.

Beneficial succession

In general the English conflict system refers the beneficial succession to movable property to the law of the deceased owner's domicile at his death, and the beneficial succession to immovable property to the lex situs. In both cases the reference to the law of a foreign domicile or situs is to its conflict rules; in other words, total renvoi is used.[134] For the purposes of beneficial succession, 'domicile' is used in its traditional English sense of origin or permanent residence,[135] and not in the special sense (effectively, of a substantial residence) invented by the Civil Jurisdiction and Judgments Act 1982. These rules reflect the policies of maintaining the unity of the movable estate, regardless of the situs of each individual asset, and respecting the power and interest of the situs of land. They apply, in particular, to intestate succession,[136] and for the most part to the essential validity of wills.[137] For similar reasons the English courts will recognise and follow a judgment determining succession to movable property given by a court of, or given elsewhere and recognised by the law of, the country in which the deceased owner was domiciled at his death, even if the judgment is erroneous as to fact or law (including English law).[138]

Today a claim by a foreign state to the movable property in England of a

---

[134] On renvoi, see Chapter 16 below.

[135] See Chapter 2 above.

[136] On intestacy as to movables, see *Pipon v Pipon* (1744) 27 ER 14 and 507; *Somerville v Somerville* (1801) 31 ER 839; and *Re O'Keefe* [1940] Ch 124 (using renvoi).

On intestacy as to immovables, see *Duncan v Lawson* (1889) 41 ChD 394; *Re Berchtold* [1923] 1 Ch 192; *Re Cutliffe* [1940] Ch 565; *Re Ross* [1930] 1 Ch 377 (using renvoi); and *Re Collens* [1986] 1 Ch 505. Cf Morris (1969) 85 LQR 339.

[137] As to the essential validity of a will in respect of movables, see *Re Groos* [1915] 1 Ch 572 (rejecting a claim by the testatrix's children for a compulsory share under Dutch law, her domicile at the execution of the will, since she had become domiciled in England by her death); *Re Annesley* [1926] Ch 692 (using renvoi); *Re Ross* [1930] 1 Ch 377 (using renvoi); and *Re Priest* [1944] Ch 58. Retroactive changes in the law of the testator's domicile which are made after his death and would invalidate his will are ignored: see *Lynch v Provisional Government of Paraguay* (1871) LR 2 P & D 268; *Re Aganoor* (1895) 64 LJCh 521; and Chapter 16, under 'Retroactive changes in foreign law', pp 401–3 below.

As to the essential validity of a will as regards immovables, see *Nelson v Bridport* (1846) 50 ER 215; *Re Miller* [1914] 1 Ch 511; *Freke v Carbery* (1873) LR 16 Eq 461; *Duncan v Lawson* (1889) 41 ChD 394; *Re Hoyles* [1911] 1 Ch 179; and *Re Ross* [1930] 1 Ch 377 (using renvoi). Changes made in the lex situs after the testator's death are respected; see *Nelson v Bridport* above.

[138] See *Doglioni v Crispin* (1866) LR 1 HL 301, and *Re Trufort* (1887) 36 ChD 600. Dicey & Morris also assert, in Rule 133, that a judgment on succession given at the situs of movable or immovable property would be recognised in respect of such property, regardless of the deceased's domicile.

person who has died intestate, domiciled in that state, without surviving close relatives, is normally characterised as a true right of succession, and thus admitted.[139]

The scission between movable and immovable property on intestacy can have strange results; for example in enabling a widow of a foreign domiciliary to claim out of his English land the full statutory legacy provided for by s 46 of the Administration of Estates Act 1925 as amended, without giving any credit for what she receives from the movable estate under the law of his domicile.[140] English conflict law is unusual in retaining this scission in the case of intestacy, most conflict systems having come to extend the personal law to intestate succession to immovables.[141] Moreover the draft Hague Convention, adopted on 20 October 1988, on the Law Applicable to Succession to the Estates of Deceased Persons[142] contemplates that a single law, normally that of the deceased's habitual residence at death, should usually govern many issues relating both to testate and intestate succession, and to both movables and immovables.

Essential validity of wills covers such questions as whether the testator's spouse or children are entitled to a compulsory share of his estate, despite his will.[143] It also covers the validity of a gift to an attesting witness.[144] However, the Inheritance (Provision for Family and Dependants) Act 1975, which enables the English courts to make orders for financial provision from an estate for certain dependants of the deceased, specifies by s 1(1) that it applies where the deceased was domiciled in England at his death. Thus under the 1975 Act the English courts can override the will of an English domiciliary, even in relation to foreign land; but cannot interfere with the will of a foreign domiciliary, even as regards English land.

In the case of immovables, the lex situs determines what interests can be created and their incidents,[145] as well as the validity of testamentary dispositions in relation to perpetuity or accumulation[146] or mortmain.[147] However a bequest of movables on trusts to be administered in a particular country, other than the testator's domicile, may be upheld against such objections as perpetuity if it complies with the law of the place of the trust administration.[148]

---

[139] See *Re Maldonado's Estate* [1954] P 223; and Chapter 16, under 'Characterisation of issues', pp 386–91 below.

[140] See *Re Collens* [1986] 1 Ch 505, a reluctant decision of Browne-Wilkinson V-C, who shared the dissatisfaction expressed in Dicey & Morris (now under Rule 135).

[141] See Dicey & Morris, p 1025.

[142] See (1989) 28 ILM 150.

[143] See *Re Annesley* [1926] Ch 692 (movables); *Re Ross* [1930] 1 Ch 377 (both movables and immovables); and *Re Groos* [1915] 1 Ch 572 (rejecting such a claim to movables by the testatrix's children under Dutch law, her domicile at execution of the will, since she had become domiciled in England by her death).

[144] See *Re Priest* [1944] Ch 58.

[145] See *Nelson v Bridport* (1846) 50 ER 215, and *Re Miller* [1914] 1 Ch 511.

[146] See *Freke v Carbery* (1873) LR 16 Eq 461.

[147] See *Duncan v Lawson* (1889) 41 ChD 394, and *Re Hoyles* [1911] 1 Ch 179.

The personal capacity of a testator to make a will disposing of movables is governed by the law of his domicile, whether the alleged incapacity relates to lack of age,[149] marital status,[150] or ill-health,[151] but probably the reference is the testator's domicile at the time of execution of the will, rather than at his death.[152] As regards immovables, testamentary capacity is probably governed by the lex situs.[153] However an English personal representative may pay a pecuniary legacy to the legatee on his own receipt as soon as he attains full age either under the law of his domicile or under English law as the law governing administration.[154]

Formal validity, interpretation and revocation of wills require separate examination.

Formal validity of wills

The formal validity of wills, as to both movable and immovable property, is now governed by the Wills Act 1963. The 1963 Act implements the Hague Convention of 1961 on Conflicts of Laws relating to the Form of Testamentary Dispositions[155] and the Fourth Report of the Private International Law

---

[148] See *Fordyce v Bridges* (1848) 41 ER 1035, where Lord Cottenham LC upheld a bequest by an English testator of English movables on trust to sell them, use the proceeds to purchase Scottish land, and settle the land on trusts which were valid under Scottish law but void for perpetuity under English internal law. Cf *Jewish National Fund v Royal Trustee Co* (1965) 53 DLR(2d) 577, where the Canadian Supreme Court applied British Columbian law, that of the testator's domicile, so as to invalidate a bequest on purpose trusts for non-charitability and perpetuity, although it would have been valid under the law of New York, where the trustee was resident. The purpose was to be carried out, at the trustee's option, by purchasing land in Israel, the United States, or any British dominion. Cartwright J emphasised the trustee's option as to the country in which the land was to be purchased, and distinguished *Fordyce v Bridges* as applying the law of the country where the land was to be purchased and managed, rather than the trustee's residence.

See also art 4 of the Hague Convention on the Law Applicable to Trusts and on their Recognition (1986), implemented by the Recognition of Trusts Act 1987, by which the Convention does not apply to preliminary issues relating to the validity of wills or other acts by virtue of which assets are transferred to the trustee.

[149] See *Re Lewal's ST* [1918] 2 Ch 391.

[150] See *Re Maraver* (1828) 162 ER 658.

[151] See *Re Fuld* [1968] P 675, where, however, Scarman J applied the stricter rules of the lex fori on the burden of proof, as a matter of procedure.

[152] See Dicey & Morris, Rule 136.

[153] Cf *Bank of Africa v Cohen* [1909] 2 Ch 129, on capacity to contract to dispose of land inter vivos; and see Dicey & Morris, p 1027.

[154] See *Re Hellman's Will* (1866) LR 2 Eq 363, and *Re Schnapper* [1928] 1 Ch 420. Cf Dicey & Morris, Rule 136, Sub-Rule, which refers to the law of the testator's domicile rather than the law governing administration.

[155] Cmnd 1729. In terms of adoptions, this is one of the most successful of the Hague conventions, with over 30 parties, which include all the EC member states except Italy and Portugal; nine other European countries; and (outside Europe) Australia, South Africa and Japan. See (1990) 29 ILM 1072.

At the substantive level, the Administration of Justice Act 1982, s 27 and Sched 2, which are not yet in force, are designed to give effect to the Washington Convention of 26 October 1973 providing a Uniform Law on the Form of an International Will.

Committee.[156] It replaces the Wills Act 1861 (often referred to as Lord Kingsdown's Act), which is explicitly repealed, and (it is submitted) impliedly abrogates the common law rules on this issue.[157]

The policy of the 1963 Act is to uphold the formal validity of a will which complies with the internal law of any country with which the testator, or the execution of the will, had a substantial connection. Renvoi is excluded by s 6(1), which in effect defines the 'internal law' of a country as the law which would apply there in a case where no question of the law in force in any other country arose. By ss 1 and 2, a will[158] is valid in form if its execution conformed to the internal law of any of the following countries:

(1) a country in which, at the time of its execution or at his death, the testator was either domiciled, or habitually resident, or a state of which, at either of these times, he was a national;[159]

(2) the country in which the will was executed;[160]

(3) where the will was executed on board a vessel or aircraft, the country with which, in view of any registration and of other relevant circumstances, the vessel or aircraft was most closely connected;[161]

(4) insofar as the will disposes of immovable property, the country where the property was situated;[162]

---

[156] Cmnd 491 (1958).

[157] Despite a suggestion to the contrary in Dicey & Morris (at p 1032), it is submitted that the 1963 Act impliedly abolishes the common law rule (recognised in *Collier v Rivaz* (1841) 2 Curt 855) upholding a will, in relation to movables, on the ground that it satisfies the formal requirements of a law referred to by the conflict rules of the testator's domicile at death (and any corresponding common law rule for immovable property, permitting compliance with a law referred to by the conflict rules of the situs). For, while it is true that the 1963 Act is formulated positively rather than negatively, it expresses a clear intention to exclude renvoi, and in view of the wide choice of internal laws which it offers, the further addition of a renvoi-based option is unnecessary to achieve its policy of validation, and would undermine its policy of simplicity and ease of application.

[158] Defined by s 6(1) as including any testamentary instrument or act.

[159] See s 1. The wording of s 1 contemplates that a person can have only one habitual residence, and only one domicile, at a given time, but that he may have several nationalities simultaneously. Thus in cases of dual or multiple nationality, it is enough that the will complies with the internal law of any nationality possessed by the testator at either of the relevant times; see FA Mann (1986) 35 ICLQ 423. Moreover, since domicile and habitual residence are available in any event, it is clear that a stateless person can be accepted as having no national law for the present purpose.

[160] See s 1.

[161] See s 2(1)(a). This applies even where the will is executed on a vessel which is in port or in internal or territorial waters, or an aircraft which is on the ground or in national airspace, and in such a case it is sufficient to comply with either the law of the vessel or the law of the actual location. The cautious wording concerning closest connection is no doubt designed to exclude flags of convenience.

[162] See s 2(1)(b). It must be emphasised that this is merely an additional option capable of validating a will in relation to immovables, and that a will which is formally valid in relation to movables on the basis of the testator's domicile, habitual residence or nationality, or the place of execution, is also formally valid in relation to immovables.

(5) insofar as the will revokes a prior will, any law by reference to which the revoked will would be treated as formally valid under the 1963 Act.[163]

Section 6(2) endeavours to deal with the problem of identifying the relevant internal law where the Act refers to a country or state within which two or more systems of internal law relating to the formal validity of wills are in force. The primary solution offered by s 6(2)(a) is to follow any rule which is in force throughout the country in question indicating which of those systems can properly be applied in the case in question. Such rules will certainly exist in countries where the personal law is dependent on the person's religion. Secondly, if there is no such rule, as may happen where the search is for the national law of a testator who was a national of a state (such as the United Kingdom, the United States, or Canada) which comprises several law districts,[164] s 6(2)(b) requires one to look to the system of internal law with which the testator was most closely connected at the relevant time; apparently meaning the time of the testator's connection with the country in question which served to make its internal law applicable under the Act.[165]

The delightful question thus arises as to the applicable national law of a testator who was, at the execution of his will and at his death, a British citizen, but was domiciled and habitually resident in, and executed his will in, France. One possible solution would be to invoke s 6(2)(a) and follow the analogy of the English rules which would be applicable in a renvoi context, on the assumption that they would be accepted elsewhere in the United Kingdom and islands. These would look first for a domicile of origin within the United Kingdom and islands; failing that, to a domicile therein at some other time; failing that, to the last habitual residence therein before the relevant time; and failing that, finally to English law as that of the national capital.[166] Another possible solution would be to invoke s 6(2)(b) and refer to the law of the territory within the United Kingdom and islands in which he had more property than the other such territories; and if he had no property therein, to treat him as effectively stateless.[167]

By s 6(3) of the 1963 Act, retroactive changes to the formal requirements of an applicable law, made after the execution of a will, are to be recognised where they validate, but not where they invalidate, the will. This seems to include

---

[163] See s 2(1)(c). A further alternative is offered by s 2(1)(d): insofar as the will exercises a power of appointment, it is sufficient that it is formally valid under the law governing the essential validity of the power. In addition, s 2(2) specifies that, insofar as a will exercises a power of appointment, it shall not be treated as improperly executed by reason only that its execution was not in accordance with any formal requirements contained in the instrument creating the power.

[164] By s 6(1), the Act defines 'state' as a territory or group of territories having its own law of nationality; and 'internal law', in relation to any territory or state, as the law which would apply in a case where no question of the law in force in any other territory or state arose.

[165] The actual wording of s 6(2) is: 'for this purpose the relevant time is the time of the testator's death where the matter is to be determined by reference to circumstances prevailing at his death, and the time of execution of the will in any other case'.

[166] See Chapter 16, under 'Renvoi', pp 396–7.

[167] See Dicey & Morris, at pp 1030–31.

changes made after the testator's death, and thus to override any analogy which might have been derived from the decisions in *Lynch v Provisional Government of Paraguay*[168] and *Re Aganoor*[169] on essential validity.

By s 3 of the 1963 Act, any rule of a law of a country outside the United Kingdom requiring that special formalities should be observed by testators answering a particular description, or that witnesses to the execution of a will should possess certain qualifications, must be characterised in England as a formal requirement only. This applies, for example, to the German rule that a testator aged between 16 and 18 can only make a will in notarial form.

Interpretation of wills

It is well settled that the construction or interpretation (as distinct from the validity) of a will, whether in respect of movables or immovables, is governed by the law intended by the testator, and that there is a rebuttable presumption that the testator intended his will to be construed in accordance with the law of his domicile at the time of its execution.[170]

It must be emphasised that construction or interpretation is concerned with imputing an intention in relation to points on which the document is ambiguous or silent; and that after the will has been construed in accordance with the intended law, it is for the law governing essential validity (that of the testator's death, in the case of movables; or the lex situs, for immovables) to determine, by reference to its mandatory rules, how far the provisions of the will, so construed, can be given effect. Essentially, the role of the law governing construction is confined to choosing between possible readings, any of which would have been effective under the law governing essential validity if it had been explicitly specified in the will.

It is a question of construction whether, in the case of a gift to several persons, one of whom predeceases the testator, the testator should be taken to have intended that his share should accrue to the other donees or should fall into a partial intestacy.[171] Another question of construction arises where movables are bequeathed to the next of kin of a specified person whose domicile differs from the testator's: in *Re Fergusson*[172] Byrne J ascertained the next of kin in accordance with the law of the testator's domicile, but Scottish decisions on

---

[168] (1871) LR 2 P & D 268.

[169] (1895) 64 LJCh 521.

[170] As regards movables, see *Bradford v Young* (1885) 29 ChD 617; *Re Fergusson* [1902] 1 Ch 483; *Re Cunnington* [1924] 1 Ch 68; *Re Price* [1900] 1 Ch 442 at 452–3; and *Re Allen* [1945] 2 All ER 264.

    As regards immovables, see *Studd v Cook* (1883) 8 App Cas 577; *Re Miller* [1914] 1 Ch 511; and *Philipson-Stow v IRC* [1961] AC 727 at 761.

    The rule is confirmed by the Wills Act 1963, s 4, which provides that the construction of a will shall not be altered by reason of any change in the testator's domicile after the execution of the will.

[171] See *Re Cunnington* [1924] 1 Ch 68.

[172] [1902] 1 Ch 483.

wills referring to 'heirs' or 'nearest heirs' have referred to the law of the domicile of the person whose heirs have to be ascertained.[173]

Contrary to the views of Dicey & Morris,[174] but in accordance with the decision of Cohen J in *Re Allen*,[175] it is submitted that the applicability of the English doctrine of election is a question of construction, rather than of essential validity, and thus the English doctrine should normally apply where the testator was domiciled in England at the execution of the will, even if he eventually died domiciled abroad (or attempted otherwise ineffectually to dispose of foreign land); but not in the converse case where he was domiciled abroad at the date of the will and in England at the date of his death. Under this strange English doctrine a person to whom a will gives certain property, but from whom it seeks (otherwise ineffectually) to take other property, is in some cases required to elect between the taking under the will and giving up the other property, or retaining the other property but compensating its intended beneficiary out of the property received under the will. For, although the doctrine usually applies in circumstances uncontemplated by the testator, it is based ultimately on his presumed intention, at least in the sense that he was free to exclude the doctrine by unequivocally indicating in his will an intention to do so.[176]

Difficulties in harmonising the testator's intention, as recognised by the law governing construction, with the technicalities of the land law of the lex situs, may occur where a testator, using the legal terminology of the law of his domicile, attempts to dispose in the same way of land situated in his country of domicile and land situated elsewhere. In one such case, *Studd v Cook*,[177] the House of Lords (on appeal from Scotland) managed to give effect to the intention in an English will to create a life interest in Scottish land, despite its saying 'for life', rather than 'for life only', as would have been necessary to make clear this intention under Scottish law. On the other hand, in another such case, *Re Miller*,[178] Warrington J felt unable to reciprocate where a Scottish will attempted to create a Scottish type of entailed interest in English land. He held instead that it operated to create an ordinary English entail, which (before 1926) could not be barred by will. It is worth noting that the opposite result could have been reached by focusing on whether the will impliedly conferred on the entailed owner a power of testamentary appointment.

Revocation of wills

There are essentially three types of act by which a testator may revoke, or attempt to revoke, a will: by the execution of a subsequent will purporting to

---

[173] See *Mitchell's Trustee v Rule* (1908) 16 SLT 189, and *Smith's Trustees v Macpherson* 1926 SC 983. Dicey & Morris, at p 1040, prefers the Scottish approach.

[174] See Rules 142 and 143.

[175] [1945] 2 All ER 264. Cf *Re Mengel* [1962] Ch 791.

[176] See *Cooper v Cooper* (1874) LR 7 HL 53, per Lord Hatherly; and *Re Vardon's Trusts* (1885) 31 ChD 275.

[177] (1883) 8 App Cas 577.

[178] [1914] 1 Ch 511.

revoke, or containing provisions inconsistent with, the prior will; by an act (such as destruction of the will) of a kind which suggests that its sole or primary purpose was to effect its revocation; by an act (such as marriage or divorce) of a kind which does not suggest that its primary purpose was to revoke the will, but which may have that effect under certain laws.

Whether a later will has the effect of revoking an earlier will depends on the validity and construction of the later will.[179] As regards the formal validity of the later will, it is sufficient for this purpose, under the Wills Act 1963, that the later will is formally valid in its own right, or that it complies with the formal requirements of any law under which the earlier will obtained its formal validity.[180]

As regards revocation by marriage, decisions given before the domicile of married women was liberated by the Domicile and Matrimonial Proceedings Act 1973 determined the question whether a marriage revoked the prior wills of both spouses as to movables by reference to the law of the husband's domicile at the time of the marriage,[181] but in the case of a marriage celebrated after 1973 the law of the domicile at the time of the marriage of the spouse whose prior will is in question is likely to be applied.[182] As regards immovable property, the lex situs was applied in *Re Caithness*,[183] but Dicey & Morris[184] and Cheshire & North[185] prefer Commonwealth decisions, such as *Re Micallef's Estate*,[186] applying the law of the domicile as in the case of movables, and this seems clearly more appropriate in relation to English land owned by a foreign domiciliary. No doubt the same rules apply to possible revocation by such acts or events as divorce, becoming a parent, or adopting a child.[187]

As regards revocation by acts such as destruction of the will, there is no English case-law, but Cheshire & North[188] advocate the lex situs as regards immovables,[189] and the testator's domicile at the time of the act in question, as regards movables. It is not inconceivable, however, that the solution eventually adopted may be influenced by s 6(1) of the Wills Act 1963, which defines a 'will' for its purposes as including any testamentary instrument *or act*.[190]

---

[179] See Dicey & Morris, Exception to Rule 144.

[180] See especially s 2(1)(c); and 'Formal validity of wills', pp 373–6 above.

[181] See *Re Reid* (1866) LR 1 P & D 74; *Re Martin* [1900] P 211; and *Re Groos* [1904] P 269.

[182] See Dicey & Morris, at pp 1050–51, and Cheshire & North, at p 850.

[183] (1890) 7 TLR 354.

[184] See at p 1051.

[185] At p 859.

[186] [1977] 2 NSWLR 929.

[187] In English internal law, s 18A of the Wills Act 1837 (added by the Administration of Justice Act 1982) gives a divorce or annulment in respect of a testator's marriage the effect of revoking a disposition in a prior will in favour of his former spouse, unless the will otherwise provides.

[188] At pp 849 and 859. Cf Dicey & Morris, Rule 144, agreeing as to movables, but tentatively preferring the testator's domicile at the time of the revocatory act, rather than the situs, in the case of immovables.

[189] See also *Re Barrie's Estate* 35 NW2d 658 (1949).

[190] Cf Cheshire & North, at p 849, asserting that Parliament has declined to implement a recommendation of the Private International Law Committee (1958) Cmd 491, that the effect of destruction should be treated as if it were a question of the formal validity of a will.

TRUSTS

Choice of law in respect of both inter vivos and testamentary trusts is now governed by the Hague Convention of 10 January 1986 on the Law Applicable to Trusts and on their Recognition, as implemented by the Recognition of Trusts Act 1987.[191]

Article 2 of the Convention defines a trust in a manner consistent with English conceptions: as the legal relationship created – inter vivos or on death – by a person, the settlor, when assets have been placed under the control of a trustee for the benefit of a beneficiary or for a specified purpose; and having the following characteristics: that the assets constitute a separate fund and are not a part of the trustee's own estate; that title to the trust assets stands in the name of the trustee or in the name of another person on behalf of the trustee; and the trustee has the power and the duty, in respect of which he is accountable, to manage, employ or dispose of the assets in accordance with the terms of the trust and the special duties imposed upon him by law. Article 2[3] adds that the reservation by the settlor of certain rights and powers, and the fact that the trustee may himself have rights as a beneficiary, are not necessarily inconsistent with the existence of a trust.

Article 3 confines the Convention to trusts created voluntarily and evidenced in writing, but s 1(2) of the 1987 Act extends the operation in the United Kingdom of the rules laid down by the Convention to cover any other trusts of property arising under the law of any part of the United Kingdom, or by virtue of a judicial decision whether given in the United Kingdom or elsewhere. Thus it seems that the legislation applies to a trust created by oral declaration and not evidenced by any writing, or arising by virtue of a statute, if it would be governed by English law if the legislation applied, but not if it would then be governed by Irish or New York law; a distinction apparently devoid of any intelligible purpose, but probably of small importance, since the common law choice of law rules which apply to the latter case are similar to those laid down by the legislation.[192] Presumably the reference to constructive trusts arising from a foreign judicial decision requires that the decision be recognised in England,[193] though, in view of their remedial or restitutionary nature, the merit of their inclusion seems questionable.

The choice of law rules are laid down by arts 6–10 of the Convention. They are similar to those applicable to contracts, and to the prior English rules on trusts.[194] A trust is governed by what amounts to its proper law, though that

---

[191] The Act entered into force on 1 August 1987. It applies to trusts created earlier, but not so as to affect things done before that date; see art 22 of the Convention and s 1(5) of the Act. The Act applies throughout the United Kingdom, and has been extended to Bermuda, British Antarctic Territory, Falkland Islands, St Helena and Dependencies, South Georgia and the South Sandwich Islands, the British Sovereign Base Areas in Cyprus, and the British Virgin Islands; see s 2 and SI 1989/673.

[192] See Dicey & Morris, at p 1089.

[193] See Dicey & Morris, at p 1089.

[194] See Dicey & Morris, Rule 153; *Duke of Marlborough v Attorney-General* [1945] Ch 78; *Iveagh v IRC* [1954] Ch 364; and *Chellaram v Chellaram* [1985] Ch 409.

phrase is not actually used in the Convention. The primary rule, laid down by art 6(1), is that the proper law of a trust is the law chosen by the settlor, his choice being expressed or implied in the terms of the instrument creating or the writing evidencing the trust, interpreted, if necessary, in the light of the circumstances of the case. Under arts 6(2) and 7, where no such choice has been made, or the chosen law does not provide for trusts, or for the category of trust involved, the proper law of the trust is the law with which it is most closely connected, in the light especially of: the place of administration of the trust designated by the settlor; the situs of the assets of the trust; the place of residence or business of the trustee; and the objects of the trust and the places where they are to be fulfilled.[195] However art 9 permits a severable aspect of the trust, particularly matters of administration, be governed by a different law from its 'overall' proper law. Renvoi is excluded by art 17, but by art 10 it is the law applicable to the validity of a trust which determines whether that law or the law governing a severable aspect of the trust may be replaced at a later date by another law.

The scope of issues governed by the proper law is defined by art 8. It governs, in general, the validity of the trust, its construction, its effects and the administration of the trust; and in particular: the appointment, resignation and removal of trustees, the capacity to act as a trustee, and the devolution of the office of trustee; the rights and duties of trustees among themselves; the right of trustees to delegate in whole or in part the discharge of their duties or the exercise of their powers; the power of trustees to administer or to dispose of trust assets, to create security interests in the trust assets, or to acquire new assets; the powers of investment of trustees; restrictions upon the duration of the trust, and upon the power to accumulate the income of the trust; the relationships between the trustees and the beneficiaries including the personal liability of the trustees to the beneficiaries; the variation or termination of the trust; the distribution of the trust assets; and the duty of trustees to account for their administration. In view of art 8, it seems that the formerly asserted power of the English courts to vary foreign trusts by an order made under the Variation of Trusts Act 1958[196] can only be exercised subject to, and in accordance with any restrictions imposed by, the law governing the trust.[197]

A minimum level of recognition for foreign trusts is provided for by arts 11 and 12; provisions aimed essentially at courts of countries whose laws do not provide for the trust institution.[198] This requires acceptance in general that the trust property constitutes a separate fund, that the trustee may sue and be sued in his capacity as trustee, and that he may appear or act in this capacity before a notary or any person acting in an official capacity; and more specifically, to the extent provided for by the proper law, that: personal creditors of the trustee

[195] Other factors existing at the creation of the trust, such as the settlor's then domicile, may also be taken into account; see Dicey & Morris, at p 1091.
[196] See *Re Ker's Settlement* [1963] Ch 533, and *Re Paget's Settlement* [1965] 1 WLR 1046.
[197] Cf the more cautious formulation by Dicey & Morris, at pp 1094-5.
[198] See Dicey & Morris, at pp 1093-4.

cannot have recourse against the trust assets; the trust assets do not form part of the trustee's estate upon his insolvency or bankruptcy; the trust assets do not form part of the matrimonial property of the trustee or his spouse nor part of the trustee's estate upon his death; and that the trust assets may be recovered when the trustee, in breach of trust, has mingled trust assets with his own property or has alienated trust assets. But the rights and obligations of any third party holder of the assets remain subject to the law determined by the forum's choice of law rules. Further, where the trustee desires to register assets, movable or immovable, or documents of title to them, he must be entitled, insofar as this is not prohibited by or inconsistent with the law of the state where registration is sought, to do so in his capacity as trustee or in such other way that the existence of the trust is disclosed.

Article 4 excludes from the scope of the Convention preliminary issues relating to the validity of wills or of other acts by virtue of which assets are transferred to the trustee, and art 5 excludes cases where the law which would be applicable under the Convention does not provide for trusts, or for the category of trusts involved.[199] By art 15, the Convention can be derogated from in favour of mandatory substantive rules, which are otherwise applicable under the forum's conflict rules, on matters such as: the protection of minors and incapable parties; the personal and proprietary effects of marriage; succession rights, testate and intestate, especially the indefeasible shares of spouses and relatives; the transfer of title property and security interests in property; the protection of creditors in matters of insolvency; and the protection, in other respects, of third parties acting in good faith. But if recognition of a trust is prevented, on this basis the court should try to give effect to the objects of the trust by other means. A further derogation, by art 16, permits the forum to apply any of its own substantive rules which override all conflict rules, and art 18 saves the forum's manifest public policy.

MATRIMONIAL PROPERTY

The concept of 'matrimonial property' appears to refer to the existence and content of any proprietary rights which a spouse (and his or her successors as such) may obtain, in property which would otherwise belong exclusively to the other spouse, as a result of the marriage itself, or of a settlement or contract concluded in connection with the marriage.

Where an explicit settlement of or contract relating to property is concluded between the spouses in connection with their marriage, their matrimonial property rights in respect of property falling within the settlement or contract

---

[199] The 1987 Act does not implement art 13 of the Convention, by which a contracting state may refuse to recognise a trust if, apart from a choice of law by the settlor, the place of administration and the trustee's habitual residence, the significant elements are more closely connected with states which do not have the institution of the trust, or the relevant category of trust.

are governed by the proper law of the settlement or contract, determined under the normal principles applicable to trusts or contracts.[200] In the absence of a choice of law clause, the proper law will usually be that of the husband's domicile at the time of the marriage; but an implied choice of the wife's domicile at the time of the marriage may be indicated by the fact that most of the settled property comes from the wife or her family; and factors such as the residence of the trustees at the time of the settlement, and the place where the settlement indicates that the settled property should be invested, may be of importance.[201] In any event, such a settlement or contract will not be affected by a subsequent change in the domicile of either or both of the spouses, but only by a new settlement or contract, replacing or varying the original one, explicitly concluded by the interested persons, or established by an order of a competent court. It is for the proper law of a settlement or contract to determine, as a matter of construction, whether it extends to immovable property located elsewhere.[202]

As regards the formal validity of an explicit marriage contract or settlement, it is sufficient to comply with the formal requirements of the proper law, or alternatively with those of the law of the place of its conclusion.[203] A spouse's capacity to enter into such a settlement or contract (for example, by reason of minority) is governed by the law of his or her domicile at the time of its conclusion; and if the settlement or contract is initially voidable by a spouse on account of his or her incapacity, his or her capacity to ratify it subsequently is governed by the law of his or her domicile at the time of the alleged ratification.[204]

Where there is no explicit (and valid) marriage settlement or contract, or such a settlement or contract exists but does not extend to the property in question, matrimonial property rights in movables are governed simply by the law of the husband's domicile at the time of the marriage.[205] Although the question is controversial, it is probable that in this case (as in the case where matrimonial property rights are governed by an explicit settlement or contract) the governing law is not affected by a subsequent change of domicile, even by both of the

[200] In the case of a marriage settlement involving trusts, the Hague Convention of 10 January 1986 on the Law Applicable to Trusts and on their Recognition, as implemented by the Recognition of Trusts Act 1987, applies. In the case of a matrimonial property contract not involving trusts, the 1980 Convention on the Law Applicable to Contractual Obligations, implemented by the Contracts (Applicable Law) Act 1990, does not apply, since art 1(2)(b) excludes 'contractual obligations relating to ... rights in property arising out of a matrimonial relationship', but similar common law choice of law rules are applicable.
[201] See *Re Fitzgerald* [1904] 1 Ch 573, and *Duke of Marlborough v Attorney-General* [1945] Ch 78.
[202] See *Callwood v Callwood* [1960] AC 659.
[203] See *Guepratte v Young* (1851) 64 ER 804, and *Van Grutten v Digby* (1862) 54 ER 1256.
[204] See *Re Cooke's Trusts* (1887) 56 LT 737; *Cooper v Cooper* (1888) 13 App Cas 88; and *Viditz v O'Hagan* [1899] 2 Ch 569.
[205] See *Re Martin* [1900] P 211; *De Nicols v Curlier (No 1)* [1900] AC 21; *Re Egerton* [1956] Ch 593. Cf Dicey & Morris, Rule 150, which now refers to the 'matrimonial domicile', meaning: (1) the domicile common to the spouses at the time of the marriage; or if no such common domicile exists, (2) the country with which the spouses and the marriage are most closely connected. Dicey's editors seem unconcerned about the resulting uncertainty.

spouses,[206] but can only be changed by a subsequent explicit settlement or contract concluded between interested and capable parties, or by a court order. It is also less than clear whether the reference to the law of the husband's domicile at the time of the marriage extends to immovable property located elsewhere, but it is thought that an affirmative conclusion is to be preferred.[207]

---

[206] See *De Nicols v Curlier (No 1)* [1900] AC 21, rejecting mutability and not following *Lashley v Hogg* (1804) 2 SRR 182. See also Dicey & Morris, Rule 152.
[207] See *De Nicols v Curlier (No 2)* [1900] 2 Ch 410. Cf *Welch v Tennant* [1891] AC 639.

16

GENERAL CONFLICT PROBLEMS

In this chapter we shall consider certain general problems which may arise in relation to choice of law rules in respect of any sphere of conflict law. One may take as initial examples the rules that a person's capacity to marry is governed by the law of his or her domicile at the time of the marriage, and that the formal validity of a marriage is governed by the law of the place of celebration.[1]

The first problem, characterisation of connecting factors, addresses the meaning of such concepts as 'domicile' and 'place of celebration', and in particular whether any account should be taken of their meaning under a foreign law.

The second problem, characterisation of issues, addresses the meaning of such concepts as 'capacity' and 'formal validity', and the allocation of dispositive rules, for example as to the need for parental consent, to one or other of such issue categories.

The third problem, renvoi, concerns the meaning of 'the law' of a foreign country, and in particular whether, and if so to what extent, the English courts, having determined that the law of a given foreign country governs an issue, should take into account the choice of law rules of that country as to that issue, which might refer the issue back to English law or on to a third law. For example, the law of a person's domicile might refer his capacity to marry to the law of his nationality.

For the fourth problem, the incidental question, to arise a number of conditions must be fulfilled. First, an issue ('the main question') must arise which under the English conflict rules is governed by a foreign law. Then the foreign law which governs the main question must raise another issue of a different nature ('an incidental question'), which could have arisen in other contexts, and for which there is a separate English conflict rule. Finally the foreign law which governs the main question must determine the incidental question in a different way from that in which it would be determined under the English conflict rule which would have applied to it if it had arisen as a main question (or if it had arisen incidentally in relation to a main question governed by English internal law).

For example, let us suppose that Henry, throughout his life a Ruritanian

---

[1] On these rules, see Chapter 3 above.

national domiciled in Ruritania, dies intestate, leaving movable property in England. Under Ruritanian law his widow, if any, would succeed to his movable property. But Ruritanian law does not recognise the validity of his marriage, celebrated in England, to Susan, an English domiciliary. This is because Henry lacked parental consent to marry, as required by Ruritanian law; or because Ruritanian law does not recognise Susan's divorce, obtained in California, from her previous husband, Ronald, a Ruritanian national domiciled in California.

The fifth problem, retroactivity, concerns the extent to which English law will recognise retroactive changes in an otherwise applicable foreign law.

Characterisation of connecting factors

In general the characterisation (definition and interpretation) of connecting factors (such as a person's domicile, or the proper law of a contract) is governed by the lex fori, since the question is essentially that of the meaning of terms used in the forum's conflict rules; and because, until the location of the connecting factor has been established, there is no particular foreign law which merits application. Moreover, any other approach would involve permitting a foreign law to dictate when the forum would apply its rules, and thus would result in the forum losing control of its own conflict system.

The general rule is illustrated by *Re Annesley*,[2] where Russell J, in determining the movable succession of a woman of English origin who had settled permanently in France, proceeded on the basis that she had died domiciled in France and therefore that the succession was governed by French law, even though she had not obtained governmental authorisation to fix her domicile in France, and therefore was not regarded by French law as domiciled there.

There are, however, a number of exceptional cases in which foreign definitions of a connecting factor are taken into account. First, the nature of the concept of nationality requires that, subject only to any stringent English public policy, the question whether a person is a national of a given foreign country must be referred to the law of that country.[3] Secondly, for the purpose of recognition of overseas divorces, separations and annulments, it is a sufficient connecting factor that one of the spouses was domiciled in the country in which the decree was obtained, either in the sense used in family matters by the law of that country, or in the traditional English sense.[4]

Thirdly, in determining for the purposes of the 1968 and Lugano Conven-

---

[2] [1926] Ch 692. See also *Re Martin* [1900] P 211, per Lindley MR at 227..

[3] See Chapter 2, pp 9–12 above, and *Oppenheimer v Cattermole* [1976] AC 249, which involved racist legislation on nationality enacted in Nazi Germany.

[4] See s 46 of the Family Law Act 1986, replacing s 3 of the Recognition of Divorces and Legal Separations Act 1971 and implementing art 3 of the Hague Convention of 1970 on divorce recognition; and Chapter 4 above. See also, as regards the earlier common law, per Lord Pearson in *Indyka v Indyka* [1969] 1 AC 33.

The same alternative reference to domicile in either of the two senses is made by s 46 in the case of a non-procedural divorce, though there both of the spouses must have been domiciled in the relevant country.

tions on civil jurisdiction and judgments, and the Civil Jurisdiction and Judgments Act 1982, whether an individual is domiciled in another contracting state, or the point at which a court of another contracting state has been definitively seised of proceedings, the law of that other contracting state must be taken into account.[5]

Fourthly, in determining the place of performance of a contractual obligation, the contract must be construed in accordance with its proper law.[6] Probably reference should similarly be made to the proper law when determining what was the last act or event necessary to bring a contract into existence, for the purpose of determining where it was technically concluded, where this is relevant; for example, in relation to English jurisdiction under RSC Ord 11, r 1(1)(d)(i), over a defendant not domiciled within the contracting states to the 1968 and Lugano Conventions.

Finally, when applying foreign conflict rules in accordance with the doctrine of renvoi,[7] the foreign interpretation of the connecting factors used in the foreign conflict rules must be respected, in order to achieve the purposes which the admission of renvoi is designed to serve.

Characterisation of issues (or conflicting dispositive rules)[8]

Where there is some difference between the dispositive rules of the various connected laws (for example, as to a person's need for parental consent in order to enter into a valid marriage), it is necessary to identify the issue, among those referred to in the English choice of law rules, to which the difference relates. Thus in the case of parental consent to marry, the issues meriting consideration are the formal validity of marriage, governed mainly by the law of the place of celebration, and a person's capacity to marry, governed mainly by the law of his or her domicile at the time of the marriage.

Essentially this problem (often referred to as characterisation of the issue) requires interpretation of the categories of issue referred to in the English conflict rules, and thus, at least in general, must necessarily be governed by English law, both on account of its nature and in order to avoid the forum losing control of its own conflict system. The sole (but well-established) exception concerns the classification of property as movable or immovable, which is governed by the law of the country in which the property is situated, though such situation is determined in accordance with English conflict rules.[9]

---

[5] See arts 52–53 of the 1968 and Lugano Conventions; ss 41–43 of the 1982 Act; and Case 129/83 *Zelgera v Salinitri (No 2)* [1984] ECR 2397. See further Chapter 8 above, under 'The central role of the defendant's domicile', pp 128–39 and 'Simultaneous actions in different countries', pp 142–9.

[6] See *Horni v Korner* [1951] AC 869, on the traditional English law; and Case 12/76 *Tessili v Dunlop* [1976] ECR 1473, on art 5(1) of the 1968 Convention.

[7] See under 'Renvoi', pp 391–7 below.

[8] See Dicey & Morris, Chapter 2, for an approach to this problem not very different from that adopted here.

[9] See *Freke v Carbery* (1873) LR 16 Eq 461; *Re Hoyles* [1911] 1 Ch 179; *Re Berchtold* [1923] 1 Ch 192; *Macdonald v Macdonald* 1932 SC(HL) 79; *Re Cutliffe* [1940] 1 Ch 565; and Chapter 15, under 'Property: Nature and location', pp 352–3 above.

Moreover it is English conflict law, and not English internal law, which must be followed, even though the terms used in many conflict rules to specify the issues covered (for example, 'contract') are the same, literalistically, as terms used in English internal rules.[10] The literal identity of some of the terms is, of course, misleading, and capable of offering a temptation to fall into the primordial legal error, that the same legal term always has the same meaning, regardless of context. Rather, a term used in a conflict rule to specify an issue must be interpreted in the light of the purpose of the rule. There is no great mystery to this; ordinary principles of purposive interpretation are necessary and sufficient. If they fail to produce ideal results, the fault probably lies in a deeper inadequacy in the existing conflict rules, rather than in a mistaken approach to characterisation. Unfortunately much of the academic discussion of this matter invents a mystery which would be amusing if it were not so unhelpful. The courts, on the other hand, have wisely ignored such discussion, although their decisions in this area, like any other, have been of variable quality.

It is submitted that the problem is to allocate *the difference between the dispositive rules of the connected laws* under a particular category of issue referred to in the English conflict rules. Thus it can never be right to conclude that the dispositive rule of one connected law on a point falls into one category of issue, while the conflicting rule of another connected law on the same point falls into a different category of issue. Moreover, the problem of characterising the issue does not arise at all until some difference between the dispositive rules of the connected laws, relevant to the result of the instant case in view of its factual pattern, has been established; otherwise the court simply applies the dispositive rule which is common to all the connected laws.[11]

The English case-law is rich in examples of characterisation. In the sphere of family law, the formal validity of marriage, rather than capacity to marry, has been held to cover requirements of parental consent,[12] as well as the permissibility of marriage by proxy.[13] The concept of monogamous marriage was defined in *Hyde v Hyde*[14] in terms of exclusivity during subsistence, and clarified in *Lee v Lau*[15] as requiring exclusivity of other legally recognised secondary spouses of lower status.[16] The distinction between void and voidable marriages, as turning on the need for a decree of annulment, was explained in *De Reneville v De Reneville*,[17] and an attempt to define the concept of adoption, as placing

---

[10] This problem does not seem to arise with connecting factors, since they are peculiar to the conflict of laws (and perhaps analogous matters, such as the international scope of the forum's tax net), and lack significance in purely internal law.

[11] For an American aberration, involving requirements of written evidence, see *Marie v Garrison* 13 AbbNC 210 (1883).

[12] See *Simonin v Mallac* (1860) 164 ER 917, *Ogden v Ogden* [1908] P 46, *Bliersbach v MacEwan* 1959 SC 43, and *Lodge v Lodge* (1963) 107 SJ 437.

[13] See *Apt v Apt* [1948] P 83; and Chapter 3, under 'Validity', pp 42–55 above.

[14] (1866) LR 1 P & D 130.

[15] [1967] P 14.

[16] See Chapter 3, under 'Polygamous marriages', pp 55–62 above.

[17] [1948] P 100.

the child in a position substantially equivalent to that of a legitimate child of the adoptive parent, was made in *Re Marshall*.[18]

In the sphere of ordinary obligations, it was established in *Re Bonacina*[19] that a promise unsupported by consideration may be contractually binding in accordance with a foreign proper law, since a requirement of consideration relates not to the contractual nature of a promise, but to its essential validity as a contract. In *Bank of Africa v Cohen*[20] a foreign requirement law that a married woman, before becoming surety for her husband, must clearly and specifically renounce the benefit of certain protective legislation, was characterised as affecting her capacity to contract. In *Batthygany v Walford*[21] the Court of Appeal avoided the rule in *The Halley*,[22] requiring a tort claim to be actionable under the lex fori as well as the lex loci delicti, by characterising a claim under Austrian law by a successor under a settlement of Austrian land, against the executor of the previous owner under the settlement, for deterioration of the land during such ownership, as a matter of implied contract, rather than tort. In the sphere of foreign judgments, the House of Lords in *Nouvion v Freeman*[23] defined the common law requirement of finality by reference to the binding character of the judgment in the foreign court by which it was given.

Interesting questions of characterisation arose in the Greek bank merger litigation. In *National Bank of Greece and Athens v Metliss*,[24] the House of Lords recognised a Greek decree which dissolved two Greek companies, created a third, and transferred the entire assets, rights, obligations and liabilities of the dissolved companies to the new company as their universal successor, by characterising the question as a matter of status or succession. Accordingly the House of Lords held the new company liable on contracts concluded by one of the predecessors which were governed by English law, despite other Greek decrees which purported to suspend these obligations, since these decrees could not affect English contracts. Greece retaliated by amending the amalgamation decree retroactively to exclude the relevant obligations, but in *Adams v National Bank of Greece*[25] the House of Lords held that the new company remained liable, since the amendment amounted in substance to an attempt to discharge obligations governed by English law.

In the sphere of intestate succession, early cases rejected a claim by a foreign state to movables situated in England belonging to a person who had died domiciled in the foreign country without surviving relatives, characterising such a claim, not as a right of succession, but as a regalian claim to seize ownerless property.[26] More recently, however, such a claim has been characterised as a

---

[18] [1957] Ch 507.
[19] [1912] 2 Ch 394.
[20] [1909] 2 Ch 129.
[21] (1887) 36 ChD 269.
[22] (1868) LR 2 PC 193.
[23] (1889) 15 App Cas 1. See Chapter 14 above.
[24] [1958] AC 509.
[25] [1961] AC 255.
[26] See *Re Barnett's Trusts* [1902] 1 Ch 847, and *Re Musurus* [1936] 2 All ER 1666.

true right of succession and accordingly upheld.[27] The change in approach may reflect the introduction by s 46 of the Administration of Estates Act 1925 of the Crown as the last person listed in the table of beneficial successors on intestacy under English internal law.[28] Also in the sphere of succession, *Re Wilks*[29] characterised the power of English administrators to postpone sale of property during the minority of the beneficial successor as a matter of administration, governed by the lex fori, rather than beneficial succession, governed by the law of the deceased's domicile.

Occasionally a statute addresses a question of characterisation. Thus s 3 of the Wills Act 1963, which implements the Hague Convention of 1961 on Conflicts of Laws relating to the Form of Testamentary Dispositions,[30] specifies that any requirement of a foreign law whereby special formalities must be observed by testators answering a particular description, or witnesses to the execution of a will must possess certain qualifications, must be treated as a formal requirement only.

Substance and procedure

English conflict law accords with general international practice in admitting the apparently innocuous, but in reality highly subversive rule that procedure is invariably governed by the lex fori. The rule is uncontroversial in its archetypal applications: it would be absurd to respect foreign rules as the size of the paper on which the pleadings must be typed, or how counsel should be dressed when they address the court. Beyond such issues, however, it is altogether too easy for courts to lose sight of the only legitimate purpose of the rule: as Dicey & Morris put it,[31] 'to obviate the inconvenience of conducting the trial of a case containing foreign elements in a manner with which the court is unfamiliar'. Foreign rules should only be rejected in limine on procedural grounds where they are principally designed to organise the conduct, rather than influence the result, of the proceedings; and only where their attempted application would cause serious practical difficulty to the English court.

Unfortunately courts have all too often used the procedural category as a device for achieving other purposes: sometimes to avoid foreign rules whose content they found less attractive than those of the lex fori, or to circumvent over-generalised choice of law rules which inadequately reflected the appropriate choice-influencing considerations;[32] and sometimes from sheer reluctance to

---

[27] See *Re Maldonado* [1954] P 223.
[28] See *Re Mitchell* [1954] Ch 525, a purely internal case, which indicates that the rights of the Crown under the statute are now successorial rather than regalian.
[29] [1935] Ch 645.
[30] Cmnd 1729. See Chapter 15, under 'Formal validity of wills', pp 373–6 above.
[31] At p 170.
[32] See *Grant v McAuliffe*, 246 P2d 944 (1953), and *Kilberg v Northeast Airlines*, 172 NE2d 526 (1961), where Californian and New York courts relied in part on procedural characterisation to avoid applying to foreign accidents between forum residents rules of the law of the place of the accident, respectively preventing tort actions against a deceased tortfeasor's estate, or imposing an arbitrary monetary limit on the amount awardable for a fatal accident. On the right approach to such situations, see Chapter 13 above.

depart from the internal lex fori, apparently viewed as the epitome of legal perfection, regardless of the considerations (such as the avoidance of unfair disappointment of private expectations) on which the relevant conflict rules are based.[33] It is also worth emphasising that the fact that an English statutory provision is regarded as procedural for internal purposes (such as its retroactive application to facts which occurred before its enactment) is no ground whatever for giving it a procedural characterisation for conflict purposes (so as to prevent its ever giving way to a conflicting foreign rule).[34]

Fortunately in recent years the English courts and legislature have increasingly adopted a more restrictive approach to procedural characterisation for conflict purposes. The clearest illustration relates to time-limits for the bringing of proceedings, which prior to the Foreign Limitation Periods Act 1984 had almost invariably been treated as a procedural matter.[35] Now, however, the 1984 Act (for the most part implementing Law Commission Report No 114 (1982), on the Classification of Limitation in Private International Law)[36] effectively requires, subject to some carefully considered exceptions (relating, for example, to public policy or undue hardship), that such questions should be treated as substantive, and accordingly governed by the law which governs the underlying relationship to which the action relates.[37] The new approach takes proper account of the policy of respecting expectations on which, in contract, the proper law doctrine is based; and avoids unfair surprise to a party who has destroyed his documentation in reliance on the time-limit specified by the proper law.

In *Leroux v Brown*,[38] the requirement of written evidence of certain types of contract, imposed by the Statute of Frauds 1677 (which now applies only to contracts of guarantee), was characterised as procedural for conflict purposes. But this decision has been rendered obsolete by arts 9 and 14(2) of the 1980 Convention on the Law Applicable to Contractual Obligations (implemented by the Contracts (Applicable Law) Act 1990), along with the Law of Property (Miscellaneous Provisions) Act 1989.[39]

At judicial level, an earlier tendency to regard all questions relating to remedies as procedural[40] has since been overcome. It is now recognised that questions of remoteness of damage (in terms of contemplation, foreseeability, or directness), or admissibility of heads of damage (such as pain and suffering, or

---

[33] The English practice, prior to the Foreign Limitation Periods Act 1984, of treating time-limits for commencing proceedings as procedural, illustrates such an attitude.

[34] See Dicey & Morris (less emphatically), at p 170.

[35] See *Huber v Steiner* (1835) 132 ER 80; *Don v Lippmann* (1837) 7 ER 303; *Harris v Quine* (1869) LR 4 QB 653; *De Prayon v Koppel* (1933) 77 SJ 800; and *Black-Clawson v Papierwerke* [1975] AC 591. An exception was recognised for cases involving title to tangible property.

[36] Cmnd 8570 (1982). See also the Law Commission's earlier Working Paper No 75 (1980).

[37] See Chapter 12, under 'Time-limits for bringing actions', pp 254–6 above; and Stone [1985] 4 LMCLQ 497.

[38] (1852) 138 ER 1119. Cf *Bernkrant v Fowler* 360 P2d 906 (1961).

[39] See Chapter 12, under 'Formal validity', pp 249–50 above.

[40] See *Machado v Fontes* [1897] 2 QB 231.

loss of earnings, in personal injury cases), are substantive.[41] But assertions that mere quantification is procedural still lead to avoidable errors, as in *Coupland v Arabian Gulf Oil Co*,[42] where there could have been no possible difficulty or inconvenience in applying a foreign rule that social security benefits received by a personal injury victim should *not* be deducted from his lost earnings. In the contractual sphere, art 10(1)(c) of the 1980 Convention, which specifies that, within the limits of the powers conferred on the court by its procedural law, the proper law governs the consequences of breach, including the assessment of damages insofar as it is governed by rules of law, may lead to a more nuanced approach to quantification, as well as preventing the English courts from granting specific (non-monetary) relief where this is not available under the proper law.[43]

It seems from *Re Cohn*[44] that the applicability of presumptions (in casu, as to survivorship, for succession purposes, where the order of deaths is uncertain) is now regarded as a substantive matter. Somewhat similarly, in the contractual sphere, art 14(1) of the 1980 Convention makes applicable rules of the proper law, contained in its law of contract, which raise presumptions of law or determine the burden of proof.

It is often said that the competence and compellability of witnesses, and their privileges against (for example) self-incrimination, are in all respects procedural and governed by the lex fori.[45] But an invariable adherence to this view could have unjustifiable consequences: for example, if a married couple are domiciled and habitually resident in a foreign country whose law denies any privilege for communications between spouses, to accord them such a privilege in English proceedings, by application of English internal law, would serve merely to deny the court possibly valuable evidence, without effectively promoting frank communication between the spouses, since it is the law of their own country (if any) on which they would have relied in communicating with each other.

Renvoi[46]

The problem of renvoi relates to the meaning of references in English conflict rules to *the law of* a foreign country with which the relevant connection exists. Is the reference simply to the internal law of the country, to the dispositive rules which are applicable in that country to cases involving no foreign element; or is account to be taken of the conflict rules of that country, which may refer the

---

[41] See *D'Almeida v Becker* [1953] 2 QB 329, and *Boys v Chaplin* [1971] AC 356.

[42] [1983] 1 WLR 1136.

[43] According to Dicey & Morris, at pp 171–2, such relief was available prior to the 1980 Convention.

[44] [1945] Ch 5.

[45] See Dicey & Morris, at p 179.

[46] Readers unfamiliar with this problem are advised to have a large whisky and cigar (or equivalent lawful combinations of stimulant and sedative) to hand before proceeding further into its intricacies!

issue back to English law or on to the law of a third country, and if so, to what extent are the foreign conflict rules to be taken into account?

The three logically possible solutions to problems of this kind can be clarified by taking as an example an intestacy as to movable property, situated in England, belonging to a British citizen of English origin who died domiciled in Ruritania. The English conflict rule refers the identification of the beneficial successors under the intestacy to Ruritanian law as that of the deceased's last domicile, and we shall assume that the Ruritanian conflict rule refers the issue to English law as the law of the deceased's nationality. The three solutions will be referred to as the internal law theory, the partial renvoi theory,[47] and the total renvoi theory:[48]

(1) Under the internal law theory, the English court would decide the beneficial succession in accordance with Ruritanian internal law, as if the deceased had been a Ruritanian national, and would disregard the possibility that a Ruritanian court might decide such matters in accordance with English internal law.[49]

(2) Under the partial renvoi theory, the English court would decide the beneficial succession in accordance with English internal law, as if the deceased had died domiciled in England, and would disregard the possibility that a Ruritanian court, noticing that the primary English conflict rule would refer to Ruritanian law as the law of the domicile, might decide such matters in accordance with Ruritanian internal law.[50]

(3) Under the total renvoi theory, the English court would decide the beneficial succession in accordance with whichever internal law, English or Ruritanian, a Ruritanian court would (so far as the English court could tell) in fact apply if this very case of a British citizen domiciled in Ruritania were before it. The result would therefore depend on whether the Ruritanian court would apply an internal law theory (leading it to apply English internal law),[51] or a partial renvoi theory (leading it to apply Ruritanian internal law),[52] or a total renvoi theory (leading it into an inextricable circle, which it would presumably find some, but probably an unforeseeable, way of breaking out of).[53]

---

[47] This is also known as the single renvoi theory.

[48] This is also known as the foreign court theory, or the English doctrine of renvoi.

[49] The internal law theory is systematically adopted by the Italian and, probably, the Spanish conflict systems.

[50] The partial renvoi theory is adopted for most issues by the French, German and Belgian conflict systems.

[51] This would be the case if for Ruritania we substitute Italy or, probably, Spain. See *Re Ross* [1930] 1 Ch 377, *Re O'Keefe* [1940] Ch 124, and *Re Duke of Wellington* [1947] Ch 506.

[52] This would be the case if for Ruritania we substitute Germany. Or if we substitute France, and (since the French conflict rule refers to movable succession to the law of the deceased's domicile in the French sense) we assume further that the deceased had for some reason not acquired a French domicile (in the French sense) but retained an English domicile (in that sense). See *Re Annesley* [1926] Ch 692, and *Re Askew* [1930] 2 Ch 259.

[53] For this situation to arise, Ruritania would have to use nationality as the connecting factor and also adopt total renvoi; probably an unlikely combination. Fortunately no such situation has yet arisen.

The above example deals with a situation of remission. A transmission situation would arise if we substituted Utopian for British nationality of the deceased. Then:

(1) The internal law theory would still lead to Ruritanian internal law.

(2) The partial renvoi theory (at least if the English courts adopted it in its French form) would lead the English court to follow the reference from Ruritanian to Utopian law, and then consider the Utopian conflict rule. If the Utopian conflict rule agreed with the Ruritanian conflict rule in referring to the law of the nationality, the English court would apply Utopian internal law. If the Utopian rule referred to Ruritanian law as that of the domicile, the English court would apply Ruritanian internal law.[54] If the Utopian rule referred to English law as the law of the situs, the English court would apply English internal law. If the Utopian rule referred to Chinese law (presumably out of mere whim), then we would look at the Chinese conflict rule, and apply Chinese internal law if the Chinese conflict rule agreed. Otherwise we would continue our world tour until we reached a country which would accept the reference to its law, or we visited a country for the second time; on such a landing, we would stop, and apply the internal law of the place we had just reached.

(3) The total renvoi theory would lead the English court to apply whatever internal law a Ruritanian court would (insofar as this was discoverable); whether that happened to be Utopian internal law, Ruritanian internal law, English internal law, or the internal law of China, Peru or Somalia.

As regards some issues it is well established that English law adopts the internal law theory, applying the internal law of the country referred to in the English conflict rule, and ignoring the possibility that that country's conflict rules might refer the issue to English law or the law of a third country. This is the case as regards the rule that most contractual issues are governed by the proper law of the contract,[55] and reflects recognition that the adoption of renvoi in contract would undermine the policy of supporting party expectations, which (normally at least) are focused on the choice of an internal law, rather than a conflict system. For similar reasons renvoi is excluded in relation to trusts by art 17 of the Hague Convention of 10 January 1986 on the Law Applicable to Trusts and on their Recognition, which is implemented in the United Kingdom by the Recognition of Trusts Act 1987.

Renvoi is also excluded in respect of the formal validity of wills by s 6(1) of the Wills Act 1963. The Act implements the Hague Convention of 1961 on

---

[54] This type of situation arose in *Re Fuld* [1968] P 675 at 699–703, where English law referred to German law as the law of the domicile, and German law referred to Ontario law as the law of the nationality, but Ontario law referred to German law as the law of the domicile. Applying partial renvoi, a German court would have accepted the reference back from Ontario law and would have applied German internal law. So under total renvoi the English court applied German internal law.

[55] See art 15 of the 1980 Convention; *Re United Railways of Havana* [1960] Ch 52, CA; and *Amin Rasheed v Kuwait Insurance Co* [1984] AC 50.

Conflicts of Laws relating to the Form of Testamentary Dispositions.[56] The Convention and the Act lean in favour of validity by offering a wide choice of connected laws, compliance with any of which is sufficient. Thus the provision of additional choices by means of renvoi would have been an unnecessary complication.

There are no issues for which English law appears to adopt the partial renvoi theory. Nineteenth century decisions which seem to have done so appear to have been superseded by the 20th century decisions applying total renvoi to the relevant issues.

However the case-law indicates strongly that English law adopts the total renvoi theory in relation to the essential validity of wills, whether in respect of movables[57] or immovables;[58] to intestate succession to movables[59] or, no doubt, immovables;[60] and to legitimation by subsequent marriage.[61] It also indicates that the rule referring the formal validity of a marriage to the lex loci celebrationis is a rule of alternative reference, in favour of validity, to the internal law and to the conflict rules of the country of celebration, so that a marriage will be valid as regards formality if it complies with the formal requirements of the internal law of the country of celebration, or with those of any other internal law (for example, that of the spouses' nationality or domicile) which the courts of the country of celebration would apply to the issue.[62] There is also some authority suggesting that a person's capacity to marry should be determined in accordance with the conflict rules of his or her domicile,[63] though capacity to remarry after a divorce or annulment which is effective in England now follows automatically from the effectiveness of the divorce or annulment under s 50 of the Family Law Act 1986.

On issues not specifically mentioned above as governed by either the internal law theory or the total renvoi theory, it remains an open question whether the English courts will adhere to the internal law theory, or adopt the total renvoi theory; it is unlikely that they will adopt the partial renvoi theory. The choice can best be resolved in the light of the purposes of the choice of law rule in question, and of the difficulties involved in total renvoi, which make its extension undesirable in the absence of convincing reasons specific to the issue in question.

The total renvoi doctrine endeavours to harmonise the results to be reached

---

[56] Cmnd 1729. See Chapter 15, under 'Formal validity of wills', pp 373–6 above.

[57] See *Re Annesley* [1926] Ch 692, and *Re Ross* [1930] 1 Ch 377.

[58] See *Re Ross* [1930] 1 Ch 377.

[59] See *Re O'Keefe* [1940] Ch 124.

[60] See also *Re Duke of Wellington* [1947] Ch 506, where the precise issue in connection with succession to immovables is obscure; and *Kotia v Nahas* [1941] AC 403, where a colonial ordinance expressly provided for renvoi in relation to succession.

[61] See *Re Askew* [1930] 2 Ch 259.

[62] See *Taczanowska v Taczanowski* [1957] P 301. Cf *Hooper v Hooper* [1959] 1 WLR 1021.

[63] See *R v Brentwood Registrar ex parte Arias* [1968] 2 QB 956, and *Padolecchia v Padolecchia* [1968] P 314. On their facts these decisions involved capacity to remarry after a divorce, a problem now governed by s 50 of the Family Law Act 1986. But they may still apply to capacity to marry in terms of factors such as consanguinity or age.

by English courts with those which would be reached in the foreign country whose law is referred to by the English conflict rule. Uniformity of results is desirable in all conflict situations, and some English conflict rules have its achievement as their main rationale. Thus rules referring title to land to the lex situs reflect a recognition that ultimately the lex situs is in a position to ensure that its rules prevail, so that, in the context of inter vivos transactions as well as succession on death, such rules are likely to achieve their purposes better through the use of total renvoi than by means of an internal law approach. Similarly, the rules referring most aspects of movable succession to the law of the deceased owner's last domicile are designed to prevent a splintering of the estate according to the, perhaps accidental, location of the assets, and this too can be better achieved through total renvoi than by an internal law approach. It is also arguable that total renvoi is appropriate where the main purpose of the English conflict rule is to respect the interests of the country considered to have the greatest concern with the issue in question; for example, in cases, such as capacity to marry, where personal status remains governed exclusively by the law of the domicile, and in tort, where departure from the lex loci delicti depends on its lacking any substantial interest in the application of its rules in the connectional circumstances of the case. On the other hand, renvoi should be rejected where the conflict rule is designed to respect party expectations, as in the case of the interpretation (as distinct from essential validity) of wills, as well as in relation to the proper law of contracts.

A less respectable argument for renvoi is as a corrective to unduly restrictive English conflict rules, such as the rule insisting that a marriage should comply with the formal requirements of the law of the country of celebration. The ability of renvoi to achieve the desired validation in such contexts is dependent on the foreign law referred to by the English conflict rule happening to have a less restrictive conflict rule; for example, one permitting compliance with the formal requirements of the law of the spouses' nationality or domicile. The real solution to such perceived inadequacies in English conflict rules is surely to reform those English conflict rules themselves.

A final argument for the use of renvoi is that it may avoid the forum finding itself in a position where it appears to be 'more royalist than the king'. In some situations it may be felt irrational to insist on applying a foreign dispositive rule when the courts of the country whose rule is in question would not themselves do so. This sense of irrationality is most justified where the main rationale of the English conflict rule pointing to the foreign law is to respect the interests of the country assumed to be most concerned. On the other hand, it is arguable that where the country assumed to be most concerned effectively disclaims any interest, there is good reason for not applying its internal, dispositive rules; but no particular reason for applying the internal law of another country, merely because the courts of the disclaiming country would do so.

A major disadvantage of total renvoi is the great practical difficulty which may arise in ascertaining what internal law the foreign court would in the end apply. The primary conflict rules of the foreign system will often be reasonably clear, but its attitude to renvoi may be so obscure that the English court can only make a (hopefully inspired) guess as to what attitude the highest court of the foreign country would adopt if presented with the problem. Thus in *Re Duke of Wellington*,[64] Wynn-Parry J said that 'it would be difficult to imagine a harder task than that which faces me, namely, of expounding for the first time either in this country or in Spain the relevant law of Spain [as to whether it adopts renvoi; in particular from the law of the nationality to the lex situs in relation to succession to Spanish land] as it would be expounded by the Supreme Court of Spain which up to the present time has made no pronouncement on the subject, and having to base that exposition on evidence which satisfies me that on this subject there exists a profound cleavage of legal opinion in Spain, and two conflicting decisions of courts of inferior jurisdiction'. He eventually concluded, after finding both the Spanish lower court decisions 'unsatisfactory', that 'it would be against the spirit and intendment of the Spanish Civil Code to hold that, in a case such as this, Spanish law would accept the renvoi which the English law makes to it as the lex situs'. In the result, he therefore applied English internal law. Presumably, if after full consideration of the admissible foreign materials, the attitude of the foreign law to renvoi remains undiscoverable (even on a balance of probabilities), it would be proper, at least in a remission (as distinct from a transmission) context, for the English court to apply the internal law of the country initially referred to by the English conflict rules, on the basis that it has not been established by evidence that the courts of that country would not apply their own internal law.

Another disadvantage is that if the foreign law also adopts total renvoi, there will be an inextricable circle, and some other rule will be needed to break the deadlock. If the foreign law has no discoverable rule for doing so, the English court will be forced to choose between applying the foreign internal law (on the basis that it has not been established that the foreign court would not), or applying English internal law (on the basis that there is no sufficient ground for doing anything else).

A further difficulty with renvoi is that the foreign conflict rule will often refer to the law of a person's nationality, and he may be a national of a state (such as the United Kingdom) which comprises several law districts. Moreover in such situations the referring law will probably expect there to exist, and desire to follow, a rule common to the laws of the territories comprising the state of nationality, identifying one of those territories as the one to which the person belongs, and the law of which is therefore to be treated as his national law.[65] In fact, albeit without full discussion, or freedom from error, the English courts have already to a large extent adopted rules for use in renvoi situations where it is necessary to identify the national law of a British citizen; and there is no

---

[64] [1947] Ch 506. See also *Re Fuld* [1968] P 675.

[65] It seems clear that the national law must be that of a part of the national territory. Thus the decision in *Re O'Keefe* [1940] Ch 124, treating Irish law as the national law of a British subject who was not an Irish citizen, seems quite indefensible.

reason to suppose that these rules would not be followed elsewhere in the United Kingdom and its associated islands.[66] These rules are as follows:

– If, at the time as of which the foreign law refers to the person's nationality ('the relevant time'), he was domiciled within the United Kingdom and islands, his national law is that of the part of the United Kingdom and islands in which he was then domiciled.[67]

– Otherwise one refers to his domicile of origin, if that is within the United Kingdom and islands.[68]

– Otherwise one presumably refers to his domicile, within the United Kingdom and islands, at some intervening time.

– But if he has never been domiciled within the United Kingdom and islands, one refers to his habitual residence therein at the relevant time, or, failing that, to his last habitual residence therein prior to that time.[69]

– Finally, as a last resort, one will no doubt be driven to refer to English law as that of the national capital.

Incidental questions

The problem known as the incidental question (or the preliminary question) involves a certain kind of conflict between two (or more) of the forum's conflict rules. It arises when the following conditions exist:

- The main question before the court is, under the relevant English conflict rule, governed by a foreign law.

  For example, where it concerns succession to the movable property, situated in England, of a deceased man who died, intestate, domiciled in Ruritania. The beneficiaries under such a succession are, under the English conflict rules, determined in accordance with the law of the deceased's domicile at death.[70]

- The foreign law which governs the main question raises (as necessary for its solution) an incidental question relating to a different category of issue.

  For example, the Ruritanian internal rule on succession specifies that in the instant circumstances the deceased's widow, if any, succeeds to his property; so the validity of his marriage becomes crucial.

- The incidental question is one which could arise in an English court as a main question (or incidentally to a main question governed by English internal law), and for which, therefore, there is a separate English conflict rule (or rules).

---

[66] That is: the Channel Islands and the Isle of Man.

[67] Re Duke of Wellington [1947] Ch 506, where Spanish law, as the lex situs of land, referred succession thereto to the law of the deceased owner's nationality at death, and he was then a British subject domiciled in England.

[68] See Re Ross [1930] 1 Ch 377; Re O'Keefe [1940] Ch 124; and Re Johnson [1903] 1 Ch 821.

[69] See Re Fuld [1968] P 675, where the deceased, a German Jew, had gone to Canada just before the Second World War to escape the Nazi persecution, and had acquired Canadian citizenship 'as an escape hatch' during the war. After the war he returned to Europe and 'lived between Germany and England'. Scarman'J held that he remained domiciled in Germany throughout, but treated Ontario law as his national law – as the place where he spent the happiest four years of his life, during which he was a student, obtained a first class Law degree, and fell in love.

[70] See Chapter 15 above.

This is obviously true of the validity of a marriage, which could be the main question in English proceedings for annulment or a matrimonial declaration; and could arise incidentally in relation, for example, to a succession to English land, or to movables of an English domiciliary. The English conflict rules on validity of marriage in general refer formalities to the law of the place of celebration, and a spouse's capacity to the law of his or her domicile at the time of the marriage.[71]

• There is some difference between the conflict rules of the law governing the main question, and the English conflict rules, in relation to the issue which arises as an incidental question, and that difference would lead to a different result in the instant case.

For example, Ruritanian law might regard its internal rule that a Roman Catholic can only validly marry by means of a Roman Catholic ceremony as affecting capacity, and thus invoke it so as to invalidate the deceased's marriage, while domiciled in Ruritania, at an English register office to a woman domiciled in England. The marriage would be valid under the English conflict rules, primarily because the Ruritanian internal requirement would be regarded as a formality, and thus not applicable to a marriage celebrated in England; and alternatively under the rule in *Sottomayor v De Barros (No 2)*,[72] that a marriage celebrated in England between an English domiciliary and a foreign domiciliary is valid despite an incapacity of the foreigner existing under the law of his domicile, but not under English internal law.

Such situations involve a conflict, not only between the English and foreign conflict rules, but, more importantly, between the English conflict rules applicable to the main and the incidental questions respectively. If, in the example, the validity of the marriage were upheld, in accordance with the English conflict rules on marriage (the lex fori solution), and the wife were therefore allowed to succeed to the English movables, then the English movable estate would not be distributed in the same way as the movable property situated in Ruritania (and in other countries which apply the whole Ruritanian law), and this would contradict the purpose of the English conflict rule on succession. It should also be noted that the wife would have had no obvious ground for complaint if Ruritanian law had not given surviving spouses any succession rights at all on intestacy, but had, for example, designated as beneficial successors the members of the trade union to which the deceased had belonged.

If, on the other hand, the marriage were treated as invalid for the purposes of the movable succession (the lex causae solution), an untidy, almost incoherent, situation would emerge, under which a marriage would be valid in England for some purposes but not others. For the marriage would certainly be valid for the purposes of succession to the deceased's English land; and would have been valid for the purpose of the wife's movable succession, if she had been the first to die and had retained her English domicile; and for the purpose of any English matrimonial proceedings which might have been brought. Worse, however,

---

[71] See Chapter 3 above.
[72] (1879) 5 PD 94. See Chapter 3 above.

than such untidiness or incoherence would be the fundamentally oppressive character of an English ruling which denied full effect to a marriage, valid under the English conflict rules on marriage, which an English domiciliary had entered into in England. Such a result seems totally unacceptable, save perhaps if the wife by her subsequent conduct had formally repudiated the marriage (for example, by petitioning a Ruritanian court for an annulment, the proceedings being pending at her husband's death). So, in the example given, it is submitted that English law should have the courage of its convictions in adhering to its conflict rules upholding the marriage, and accept the scission of the movable estate as the lesser evil.

Despite the emergence of the lex fori solution as clearly preferable in the above example, there are a great variety of situations in which an incidental question can emerge, and it is difficult to suggest a general solution. Perhaps the best general approach which can be suggested is that the English court should weigh the relative strength of the policies underlying the English conflict rules on the two questions, especially in their application to the factual pattern of the instant case.

In any event the case-law offers specific answers to some of the most important types of incidental question. As will be seen, situations giving rise to a single incidental question usually involve one of the following scenarios:

(1) both questions are of matrimonial status;
(2) the main question is of filial status, and the incidental question is of matrimonial status;
(3) the main question is of succession (or other proprietary disposition), and the incidental question is of status.

In addition, a situation giving rise to a double (or multiple) incidental question is also possible; as where there is a main question of succession, from which there arises an incidental question of status, from which in turn there arises a further incidental question of status. Various scenarios, and such authority on them as exists, will now be considered.

Where both questions concern marital status

Where both the main and the incidental question concern marital status, English law is now committed to a lex fori approach: the incidental question will be determined as if it had arisen as a main question. Thus, by s 50 of the Family Law Act 1986,[73] a monogamous remarriage will be upheld if the prior divorce or annulment of the earlier marriage of one of the spouses is effective in Eng-

---

[73] This extends a narrower provision formerly made by s 7 of the Recognition of Divorces and Legal Separations Act 1971, and accords with the common law as ultimately developed in *Perrini v Perrini* [1979] 2 All ER 323, and *Lawrence v Lawrence* [1985] Fam 106. Earlier contrary decisions at common law in *R v Brentwood Registrar ex parte Arias* [1968] 2 QB 956, and *Padolecchia v Padolecchia* [1968] P 314, are now discredited. See Chapter 3, under 'Capacity to remarry', pp 53–5 above.

land, even if such divorce or annulment is not recognised by the law of the domicile(s) of the new spouses at the time of the remarriage. The same principle, operating at common law,[74] ensures that a remarriage will similarly be upheld where the prior marriage (although never dissolved or annulled) was void under the English conflict rules, but valid under the conflict rules of the law of the domicile(s) of the new spouses at the time of the remarriage.

In the converse case, where a divorce or annulment from a prior marriage is not recognised under the English conflict rules, but is recognised at the domicile(s) of the new spouses, or where the earlier marriage (which was never dissolved or annulled) was valid under the English conflict rules but void under those of the domicile(s) of the new spouses, the lex fori approach must again apply. For in such circumstances it would be absurd for English law to uphold the monogamous remarriage, since this would involve a person being regarded for English purposes as having two valid monogamous spouses at the same time. Hints to the contrary in *Schwebel v Ungar*[75] and *Padolecchia v Padolecchia*[76] must therefore be rejected.

Where a main question of filial status involves an incidental question of marital status

Here English law adopts what amounts to a rule of alternative reference in favour of validation. A child will be considered legitimate for English purposes if at his birth, conception, or any moment during the pregnancy his parents were validly married to each other according to the English conflict rules on the validity of marriage, or according to the conflict rules of the country in which both his parents or (probably) his father alone were domiciled at the child's birth.[77]

Where a main question of succession involves an incidental question of status

Support for application of the law governing the main question in some cases of this type may be drawn from a dictum in *Baindail v Baindail*[78] in favour of recognising polygamous marriages for the purpose of foreign successions; and from the decision in *Re Johnson*,[79] admitting for the purpose of a foreign succession a child's legitimation by subsequent marriage although the father was domiciled in England. But it remains essentially an open question whether, or in what circumstances, the English court should insist on adhering to its view of the validity or effectiveness of a marriage, divorce or annulment in the context of a succession governed by a foreign law which takes a different view. It is

---

[74] See *Perrini v Perrini* [1979] 2 All ER 323, and *Lawrence v Lawrence* [1985] Fam 106.
[75] (1963) 42 DLR(2d) 622, Ontario CA, and (1964) 48 DLR(2d) 644, Supreme Court of Canada.
[76] [1968] P 314.
[77] See *Re Bischoffsheim* [1948] Ch 79, and *Hashmi v Hashmi* [1971] 3 All ER 1253.
[78] [1946] P 122 at 127–8.
[79] [1903] 1 Ch 821.

thought that, even where s 50 of the Family Law Act applies (so as to make the effectiveness of a divorce or annulment automatically entail the validity of a subsequent remarriage), it does not dictate a solution to the further problem arising from the fact that both the effectiveness of the divorce or annulment and the validity of the remarriage arise incidentally in relation to a main question of succession governed by a foreign law which takes a different view. A possible solution for cases where status is incidental to succession might be as follows:

(1) Where a child's claim under the foreign law governing the succession requires his having legitimate filial status, it should be sufficient if such status exists either under the English conflict rules on filial relationships, or under those of the law governing the succession.

(2) Where the foreign law governing the succession confers rights on a spouse as such, and there is a person who qualifies as a spouse under the English conflict rules on status, the English court should admit the claim of that person, and reject the claim of any other person who qualifies only under the conflict rules of the lex causae. But if there is no spouse under the English conflict rules on status, a claim based on the conflict rules of the lex causae should normally be accepted.

Retroactive changes in foreign law

In general the English courts, when applying foreign law pursuant to an English conflict rule, will apply it as it stands at the date of the English proceedings, so as to include retroactive changes which have been made in the foreign law after the date of the acts or events whose effects are altered thereby. Thus in *Nelson v Bridport*[80] Lord Langdale MR gave effect to a change in Sicilian law which abolished entails of Sicilian land and constituted the existing entailed owner as absolute owner instead. Similarly in *Phillips v Eyre*[81] effect was given to a Jamaican Act of Indemnity, retroactively legalising previous tortious acts. Again in *R v International Trustee*[82] effect was given to American legislation of 1933 abrogating gold-value clauses and thus reducing the amount payable under contracts validly concluded in 1917.

A similar approach was adopted in a later case, *Starkowski v Attorney-General*,[83] which involved the formal validity of a Roman Catholic marriage between Polish domiciliaries celebrated in Austria in May 1945. At that date the marriage was invalid, since Austrian law required a civil ceremony. However in June 1945 an Austrian decree was enacted by which marriages which had been celebrated before ministers of recognised churches would be validated, as from their celebration, as soon as they were registered with the appropriate civil authority. The instant marriage was not so registered until 1949, by which time

---

[80] (1846) 50 ER 215.
[81] (1870) LR 6 QB 1.
[82] [1937] AC 500.
[83] [1954] AC 155.

the couple had become domiciled in England, and in 1950 the wife went through a marriage ceremony in England with another man. The House of Lords nonetheless recognised the Austrian decree and the registration of the first marriage thereunder as effective to validate that marriage, at least as from the date of registration, with the result that the second marriage was void and the child thereof was illegitimate.

In *Starkowski* the House of Lords left open what would have been the result if the second marriage had preceded the registration of the first, and it is submitted that in such a case it would be proper to invoke English public policy so as to prevent recognition of the retroactive validation of the first marriage and the consequent invalidation of the second. This submission gains some support from the decision in *Ambrose v Ambrose*,[84] where a British Columbian court refused to recognise a Californian order, obtained by the wife in 1958, backdating to 1931 her Californian decree absolute of divorce from her first husband, actually granted in 1939, so as to validate her purported remarriage in 1935 to a British Columbian domiciliary.

Apart from public policy, the English case-law has established an exception to the rule in favour of recognition of foreign retroactive legislation, in the case of succession on death to movable property situated in England of a deceased foreign domiciliary. It seems that on this issue, subject to an exception made by the Wills Act 1963 as regards the formal validity of wills, English law looks only to the law of the domicile as it stood at the date of the owner's death, and ignores retroactive changes made in that law after that date. The exception is based on the decision of Lord Penzance in *Lynch v Provisional Government of Paraguay*,[85] refusing to recognise a decree made in Paraguay two months after the death of a Paraguayan domiciliary, purporting to invalidate his will and vest all his property in the Paraguayan state. Although this decision could be explained on grounds of the penal character of the decree or of its obnoxiousness to English public policy, such explanations would not justify the decision of Romer J in *Re Aganoor's Trusts*,[86] where he followed *Lynch* and refused to recognise an Italian decree, made three years after the relevant death, which merely sought to abolish successive trusts and to divide property so held between certain of the beneficiaries. The decision in *Lynch* was approved by the House of Lords in *Adams v National Bank of Greece*,[87] and applied analogistically as one of the grounds for refusing to recognise a Greek decree which purported to amend retroactively an earlier Greek decree, which had merged two Greek companies into a third as their universal successor, by excluding certain contractual obligations from the scope of the succession.[88]

---

[84] (1960) 25 DLR2d 1, on appeal from (1959) 21 DLR2d 722.
[85] (1871) LR 2 P & D 268.
[86] (1895) 64 LJCh 521.
[87] [1961] AC 255.
[88] Another ground for the decision in *Adams* was that the later decree should be characterised as attempting to discharge contractual obligation, and thus refused application because the relevant contracts were governed by English, and not Greek, law.

The rule in *Lynch* appears to be qualified, as regards the formal validity of wills, by s 6(3) of the Wills Act 1963, which requires reference to be made primarily to laws as they exist at the time of execution of the will, but allows subsequent, retroactive alterations of law to be taken into account if they validate the will. It is probable that this extends to alterations enacted after the testator's death.[89]

---

[89] See Chapter 15, under 'Formal validity of wills', pp 373–6 above.

INDEX